Fodor's upCLOSE

LONDON

the complete guide, thoroughly up-to-date

SAVVY TRAVELING: WHERE TO SPEND, HOW TO SAVE

packed with details that will make your trip

CULTURAL TIPS: ESSENTIAL LOCAL DO'S AND TABOOS

must-see sights, on and off the beaten path

INSIDER SECRETS: WHAT'S HIP AND WHAT TO SKIP

the buzz on restaurants, the lowdown on lodgings

FIND YOUR WAY WITH CLEAR AND EASY-TO-USE MAPS

FODOR'S TRAVEL PUBLICATIONS, INC.
NEW YORK • TORONTO • LONDON • SYDNEY • AUCKLAND
www.fodors.com

ISBN 0-679-00382-7

ISSN 1098-996X

FODOR'S UPCLOSE™ LONDON

Editor: Tania Inowlocki, Matthew Lombardi

Editorial Contributors: Robert Andrews, Jennifer Brewer, Boyce Brown, Jacqueline Brown, Jules Brown, David Clee, Pippa Cragg, Sunny Delaney, Paul Duboudin, Gerri Gallagher, Tim Perry, Paula Turnbull

Editorial Production: Nicole Revere

Maps: David Lindroth Inc., Eureka Cartography, *cartographers*; Rebecca Baer, Robert Blake, *map editors*

Design: Fabrizio La Rocca, *creative director*; Allison Saltzman, *cover and text design*; Jolie Novak, *photo editor*

Production/Manufacturing: Judy Emery

Cover Art: ©Pratt-Pries/DIAF

SPECIAL SALES

Fodor's upCLOSE™ Guides and all Fodor's Travel Publications are available at special discounts for bulk purchases for sales promotions or premiums. Special editions, including personalized covers, excerpts of existing guides, and corporate imprints, can be created in large quantities for special needs. For more information, contact your local bookseller or write to Special Markets, Fodor's Travel Publications, 201 East 50th Street, New York, NY 10022. Inquiries from Canada should be directed to your local Canadian bookseller or sent to Random House of Canada, Ltd., Marketing Department, 2775 Matheson Blvd. E, Mississauga, Ontario L4W 4P7. Inquiries from the United Kingdom should be sent to Fodor's Travel Publications, 20 Vauxhall Bridge Road, London SW1V 2SA, England.

IMPORTANT TIP

Although all prices, opening times, and other details in this book are based on information supplied to us at press time, changes occur all the time in the travel world, and Fodor's cannot accept responsibility for facts that become outdated or for inadvertent errors or omissions. **So always confirm information when it matters,** especially if you're making a detour to visit a specific place.

PRINTED IN THE UNITED STATES OF AMERICA

10 9 8 7 6 5 4 3 2 1

CONTENTS

I. BASICS *1*

2. EXPLORING LONDON 33

3. WHERE TO SLEEP 105

4. FOOD 126

5. PUBS AND BARS 151

6. AFTER DARK 162

7. SHOPPING 181

8. OUTDOOR ACTIVITIES 196

9. TRIPS FROM LONDON 207

INDEX 225

TRAVELING UPCLOSE

Shop for a picnic at the Queen's grocers. Commune with Chaucer at Westminster Abbey. Stay at a bargain B&B (and get mothered with a full English breakfast). Take a Beatles' Magical Mystery Walking Tour. Catch a sunset on Waterloo Bridge. Raise a pint at Dickens's favorite pub. Memorize the symphony of the city streets. In other words, if you want to experience the heart and soul of London, whatever you do, don't spend too much money.

The deep and rich experience of London that every true traveler yearns for is one of the things in life that money can't buy. In fact, if you have it, don't use it. Traveling lavishly is the surest way to turn yourself into a sideline traveler. Restaurants with white-glove service are great—sometimes—but they're usually not the best place to find the perfect ploughman's pie. Doormen at plush hotels have their place, but not when your look-alike room could be anywhere from Düsseldorf to Detroit. Better to stay in a more intimate place that truly gives you the atmosphere you traveled so far to experience. Don't just stand and watch—jump into the spirit of what's around you.

If you want to see London up close and savor the essence of the city and its people in all their charming glory, this book is for you. We'll show you the local culture, the offbeat sights, the bars and cafés where tourists rarely tread, and the B&Bs and other hostelries where you'll meet fellow travelers—places where the locals would send their friends. And because you'll probably want to see the famous places if you haven't already been there, we give you tips on losing the crowds, plus the quirky and obscure facts you want as well as the basics everyone needs.

OUR GANG

Who are we? We're artists and poets, slackers and straight arrows, and travel writers and journalists, who in our less hedonistic moments report on local news and spin out an occasional opinion piece. What we share is a certain footloose spirit and a passion for Olde London Towne, which we celebrate in this guidebook. Shamelessly, we've revealed all of our favorite places and our deepest, darkest travel secrets, all so that you can learn from our past mistakes and experience the best part of London to the fullest. If you can't take your best friend on the road, or if your best friend is hopeless with directions, stick with us.

David Clee is, by his own admission, a bit of a London nut. Sometimes he'll even swear the city's streets really are paved with gold. He has spent almost the whole of his life living, working, and dreaming in London and now spends most of his days writing about it as editor of the independent e-zine

LondonNet (www.londonnet.co.uk). Previously David was to be found editing the London evening newspaper *Tonight,* and he has also churned out some quite remarkable stuff for the *Times* and the *Independent.*

When occasional travel writer and full-time spin doctor **Paul Duboudin** took on this assignment, he had to reconcile a demand for relative candidness with a French and Australian heritage notoriously critical of all things British. Fortunately, objectivity and the English bit in his mongrel make-up won the day. Having already visited more than 25 countries in his short life, Paul returned to London—city of his birth—in 1998. Eager to determine what was causing thousands of fellow antipodes to leave their wide brown land for the confines of life in one of the world's biggest and busiest metropolises, he soon established that most Aussies only come to the UK to get their beer in pints (even if it's served lukewarm). That riddle solved, Paul applied years of experience on the backpacker trails of Europe and Asia to his quest for eating and sleeping bargains for Fodor's readers. Paul currently works in the press office of a government department (one of those, "I could tell you, but then I'd have to kill you" affairs, Paul explains).

Since moving to London permanently around six years ago, travel writer **Tim Perry** has become increasingly nocturnal. Although he managed to supply some copy for this book's Exploring (i.e., daytime) section, Tim mainly applied his knowledge of the city to the Pubs and After Dark sections, which include many of the hangouts he visits as a music critic for the *Independent* daily newspaper and various other publications.

A SEND-OFF

Always call ahead. We knock ourselves out to check all the facts, but everything changes all the time, in ways that none of us can ever fully anticipate. Whenever you're making a special trip to a special place, as opposed to merely wandering, always call ahead. Trust us on this.

And then, if something doesn't go quite right, as inevitably happens with even the best-laid plans, stay cool. Missed your train? Stuck in the airport? Use the time to study the people. Strike up a conversation with a stranger. Study the newsstands or flip through the local press. Take a walk. Find the silver lining in the clouds, whatever it is. And do send us a postcard to tell us what went wrong and what went right. You can E-mail us at: editors@fodors.com (specify the name of the book on the subject line) or write the London editor at Fodor's upCLOSE, 201 East 50th Street, New York, NY 10022. We'll put your ideas to good use and let other travelers benefit from your experiences. In the meantime, bon voyage!

INTRODUCTION

London at the threshold of the 21st century is an urban sprawl in transition: although it's riding the coattails of what the *New Musical Express* has called the "carcass" of Cool Britannia (the United Kingdom's popular culture boom that was effectively exploited by Prime Minister Tony Blair in the late '90s), the city is clearly burgeoning with a promise of magnified cultural cachet. Thanks in part to the National Lottery, the investment currently underway in museums, heritage, arts, and sports venues totals into the billions of pounds. The city's metamorphosis is spearheaded by the British Museum Grand Plan, the new Tate Gallery at Bankside, the transformation of tired old Wembley Stadium, and of course the Millennium Dome and the Jubilee tube extension.

Even more exciting than what's new is what's been here for a long time—for the history of London is a rich one, best illustrated by the jumbled layers of its buildings. Low 12th-century fortifications are juxtaposed with soaring 20th-century office blocks, and Victorian churches contrast with Roman city walls. Everywhere you look you'll see a confusion of ages, testaments to the heydays of yesteryear and to the realities of our own age.

Nevertheless, your first impression of the metropolis may not be particularly inspiring. Whether you approach by train from Gatwick or by bus, tube, or the new fast train from Heathrow, you'll thread through the kind of dull and dreary suburbs that clog up most other English townscapes. Once you hit the city pavement, if you're not too familiar with intense urban expanses, you may be shocked by the crowds, the traffic, the down-and-outs and homeless refugees asking for money at the foot of the Underground escalators. Electrically powered trains and staircases may not have been around during the lifetime of Percy Bysshe Shelley, but that didn't prevent the great man from gauging the city's underbelly. Writes the poet: "London, that great sea, whose ebb and flow at once is deaf and loud, and on the shore vomits its wrecks, and still howls for more." You'll find that the city doesn't limit itself to human debris, either. A pile of garbage big enough to fill Trafalgar Square to five times the height of Nelson's Column is swept up every year.

Get your bearings, however, and the magnificent and multiple mysteries of London will readily unfold to your curiosity. During the year 2000, as one of roughly 16 million visitors (more than twice London's population), your only task will be to decide what you want to explore. Keep in mind the words of Samuel Johnson, writer and father of the modern dictionary, who said: "When a man is tired of London, he is tired of life: for there is in London all that life can afford." Whatever you do, try not to let the overwhelming array of choices leave you indecisive. If you're looking for a pub experience, for example, and you can't decide between the pub that serves lovingly hand-pulled traditional ales to gentlemen in tweeds, the one that serves overpriced cocktails to city suits with cellular phones, and the one filled with throbbing techno music and young trendies, just remember that each of these watering holes is a slice of London's life; wherever you decide to go, you'll witness a city with character.

Being picky about what you see and do won't hurt, though, since part of London's appeal lies in discovering the reality behind the preconceptions. Yes, you'll easily find fish-and-chips, though you're not likely to get them served up in newspaper. And unless you go to "Ye Olde Fish and Chip Shoppe" you'll be more likely to find yourself next to a construction worker on lunch break than an American tourist. If you stray from the well-trodden tourist path, you may discover a more rewarding side of London. Wouldn't you agree that meeting new friends over pints at a cricket match on a Saturday afternoon makes for a better memory than fighting the crowds at Madame Tussaud's Wax Museum?

That's not to say that you should miss London's classic sights, for they, too, are the "real" London. A peek at the spoils of empire that are housed within the British Museum reveals more about English imperialism than a stack of history books ever could. By the same token a stroll around Windsor Castle provides a better sense of royal wealth, power, and influence than a thousand stories in the tabloids. Just don't get sucked into the tour-package version of the city that narrowly focuses on traditional and royal London—a Disneyesque montage of Beefeaters, of sentries donning busbies (those full-dress fur hats), and of pomp and circumstance.

Instead, try to appreciate the city for what it is: a thriving cosmopolitan microcosm whose classrooms are abuzz with more than 193 languages, whose myriad restaurant kitchens emit exotic perfumes, and whose residents represent cultures from around the globe—approximately ⅓ of all Londoners were born outside England's borders. You can pick out savories at the Brixton Market or dance to worldbeat tunes in a Covent Garden club. Before you fancy London to be the melting pot you always dreamed of, however, consider the city's recent past. A mere decade and a half after the Brixton riots, racial tensions still seem close to the surface, as evidenced by the indiscriminate bombings of minority groups in Brixton, Brick Lane, and Soho in April 1999. Fortunately these were the actions of a single individual, but as extreme right-wing racist groups deceitfully claimed responsibility for the attacks, Londoners were put on edge about the safety of their communities.

With any luck London's racial, crime, transport, and pollution problems will be tackled in a more coordinated fashion once locals vote in their first Mayor of London since Margaret Thatcher abolished the Greater London Council in the early '80s. This restyling of London's political landscape dovetails the sweeping reforms initiated throughout the nation by Tony Blair's Labour Government, which supplanted the Conservative Party in 1997. While the backlash against the Labour Party during the recent European elections might signal the end of an extraordinary honeymoon for Blair's team, reforms continue to take center stage. Both Scotland and Wales have grasped with both hands the opportunity of self-government and, unimaginable as it may have seemed a year ago, peace may even win out over the troubles in Ireland.

Britain's balkanization might lead you to believe that England's fire sale is the final acknowledgment of the Empire's decline. But the re-invention of the British Isles might just clear the way for England to join the continuing cut-and-thrust of Europe. Most Brits, including most Londoners, are still extremely wary of handing over more fiscal control to the folks across the Channel. But, whereas the rest of country does so out of crude parochialism, worldly Londoners can often be heard arguing that Europe is too small a stage on which to play; they want their city to remain at the center of the whole world, not just the old world. In any event, the days of the euro, Chunnel travel, and lightning-quick global financial transactions are putting an end to the notion that Great Britain can stand alone.

While Britain reconfigures its social, political, and national identity, the royal family—who never featured prominently in Blair's Cool Britannia master plan—is actually enjoying a little bit of an increase in popularity. Over the past few years, the House of Windsor has suffered numerous blows. The sudden and tragic death of Princess Diana in 1997 prompted an unprecedented outpouring of national grief, with the country and London coming to a standstill on the day of and those leading up to her funeral. The intense criticism leveled against Queen Elizabeth and her son Prince Charles in the weeks following Diana's death must have left the Windsors shell-shocked.

Yet Time, perhaps with the help of palace spin doctors, has seen a change in the family's fortunes. Charles has slowly and subtly introduced his mistress, Lady Camilla Parker-Bowles, to the British public, been seen to be a loving and attentive father to his two sons, and smartly aligned himself with middle England on important national issues (most notably his strong stance against genetically modified food). The Queen has also been on the "charm offensive" and recently arranged to spend another rare birthday abroad: she turned 70 in Korea in 1996. If the Queen mother makes it to 100 in the year 2000 and the new marriage of Prince Edward and Sophie Rhys-Jones lasts a little longer than those of either of the Prince's brothers, then the Royals may not be done for yet. For while they may be relatively powerless, they make invaluable contributions to England's tourism earnings. Consider the facts: Most visitors to London are just itching to see the Changing of the Guard, the Tower of London, Buckingham Palace, and Windsor Castle (now you know how to avoid the crowds).

Finally, remember that if you make the mistake of coming to London with generalizations about how bland, uptight, and close-minded the English are, you deserve to have a bland, uptight, close-minded experience. By all means, spend your Saturday doing the sights of classic, once-in-a-lifetime London. But come the wee hours of Sunday morning, why not grab the latest copy of *New Musical Express* and a Thermos full of Earl Grey, and plant yourself on Trafalgar Square to see all the late-night clubbers waiting for the last buses home. This, after all, is the real London, the London that sucks you in and keeps you "howling for more."

CENTRAL LONDON

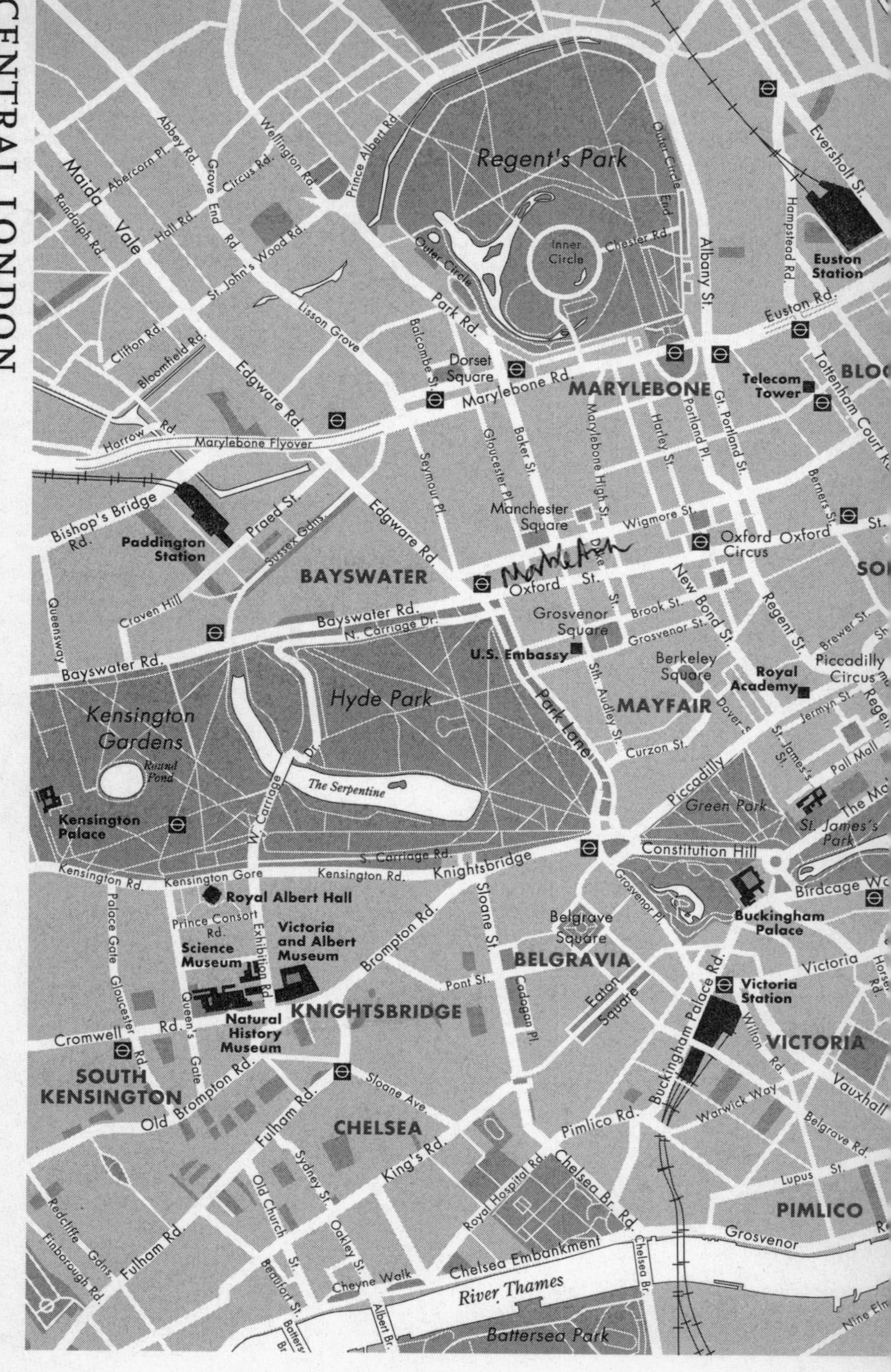

CENTRAL LONDON

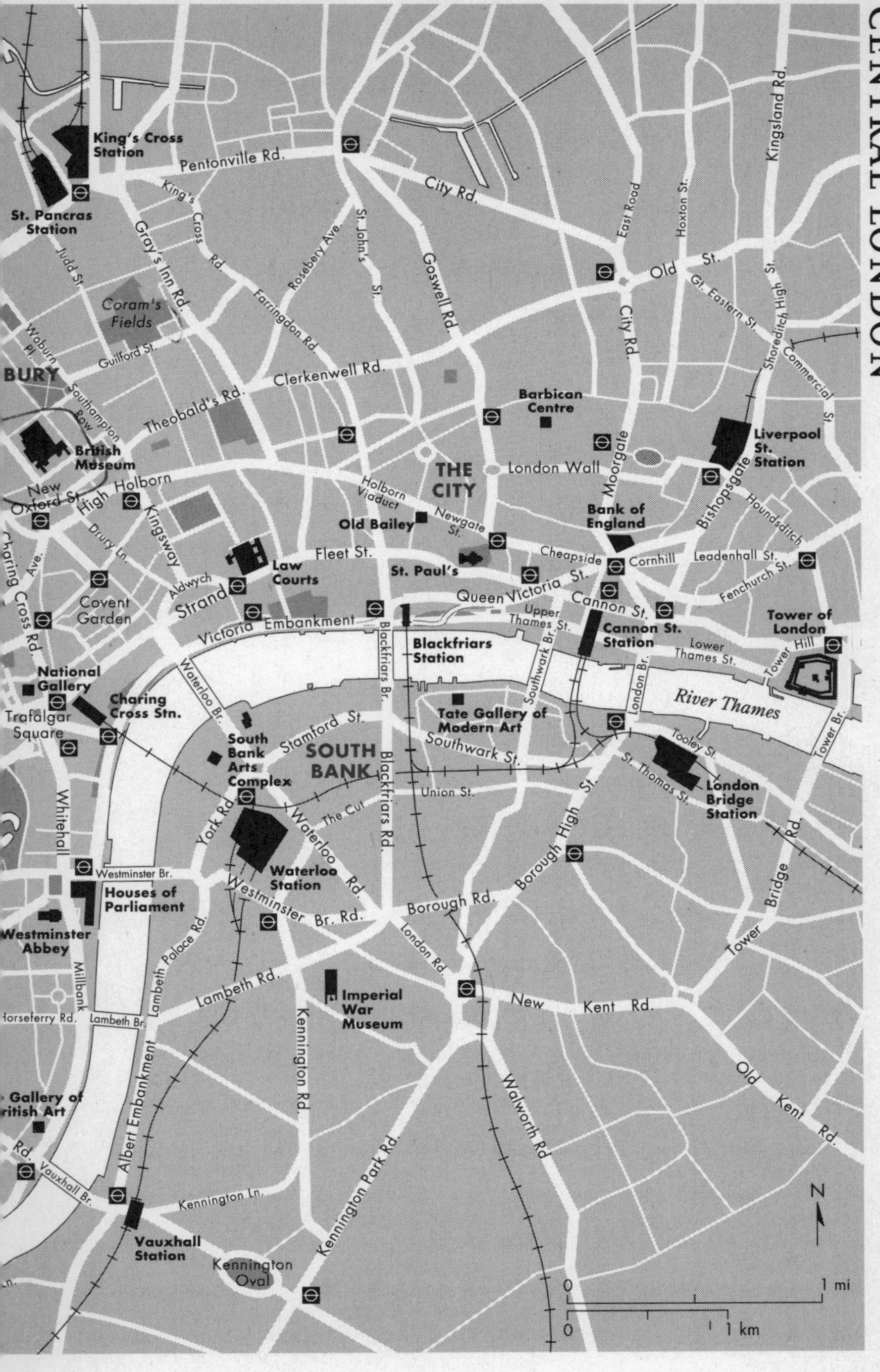

BASICS

I

Basic Information on Traveling in London, Savvy Tips to Make Your Trip a Breeze, and Companies and Organizations to Contact

If you've ever globe-trotted before, you know there are two types of travelers—the planners and the nonplanners. Travel can bring out the worst in both groups. Left to their own devices, the planners will have you charging from attraction to attraction in a cultural onslaught, while the nonplanners will invariably miss the flight, the bus, and maybe even the point. This chapter offers you a middle ground; we hope it provides enough information to help you plan your trip to London without nailing you down. The first step in your vacation will, undoubtedly, be a visit or telephone call to the British Tourist Authority: You'll find the main branches listed below under Visitor Information. Your actual trip will begin once you step off your plane in London—and wonder how to get from the airport to the city center. Don't panic: You'll find all the info under Airports & Transfers, below. Once you arrive in the city center, you'll want the scoop on the London Underground (subway) and bus systems—simply consult the Underground Travel and Bus Travel sections, below. Just remember that the most disconcerting situations turn into the best travel stories back home.

AIR TRAVEL

BOOKING YOUR FLIGHT

When you book **look for nonstop flights** and **remember that "direct" flights stop at least once.** Try to avoid connecting flights, which require a change of plane.

CARRIERS

MAJOR AIRLINES • American Airlines (tel. 800/433–7300; in London, tel. 020/8572– 5555) to Heathrow, Gatwick. **British Airways** (tel. 800/247–9297; in London, tel. 0345/222111) to Heathrow, Gatwick. **Continental** (tel. 800/231–0856; in London, tel. 0800/776464) to Gatwick. **Delta** (tel. 800/241–4141; in London, tel. 0800/414767) to Heathrow, Gatwick. **Northwest Airlines** (tel. 800/447–4747; in London, tel. 0990/561000) to Gatwick. **TWA** (tel. 800/892–4141; in London, tel. 01293/439–0707) to Gatwick. **United** (tel. 800/241–6522; in London, tel. 020/8990–9900) to Heathrow. **Virgin Atlantic** (tel. 800/862–8621; in London, tel. 01293/747747) to Heathrow, Gatwick.

CHECK-IN & BOARDING

Airlines routinely overbook planes on the assumption that not all ticketed passengers will show up for a flight. Whenever too many passengers arrive for a flight, airlines ask for volunteers to give up their seats in return for seats on the next available flight and vouchers for a free flight. If there are not enough volunteers, the airline must choose who will be denied boarding. The first to get bumped are passengers who checked in late and those flying on discounted tickets, so **get to the gate and check in as early as possible,** especially during peak periods.

Always **bring a government-issued photo I.D. to the airport.** You may be asked to show it before you are allowed to check in.

CUTTING COSTS

The least-expensive airfares to London must usually be purchased in advance and are non-refundable. It's smart to **call a number of airlines, and when you are quoted a good price, book it on the spot**—the same fare may not be available the next day. Always **check different routings** and look into using different airports. Travel agents, especially low-fare specialists (*see* Discounts & Deals, *below*), are helpful.

Consolidators can also help you cut costs. They buy tickets for scheduled international flights at reduced rates from the airlines, then sell them at prices that beat the best fare available directly from the airlines, usually without restrictions. Sometimes you can even get your money back if you need to return the ticket. Carefully read the fine print detailing penalties for changes and cancellations, and **confirm your consolidator reservation with the airline.**

When you **fly as a courier** you trade your checked-luggage space for a ticket deeply subsidized by a courier service. There are restrictions on when you can book and how long you can stay.

CONSOLIDATORS • Cheap Tickets (tel. 800/377–1000). **Discount Airline Ticket Service** (tel. 800/576–1600). **Unitravel** (tel. 800/325–2222). **Up & Away Travel** (tel. 212/889–2345). **World Travel Network** (tel. 800/409–6753).

ENJOYING THE FLIGHT

For more legroom **request an emergency-aisle seat.** Don't sit in the row in front of the emergency aisle or in front of a bulkhead, where seats may not recline. If you have dietary concerns, **ask for special meals when booking.** These can be vegetarian, low-cholesterol, or kosher, for example. On long flights, try to maintain a normal routine, to help fight jet lag. At night **get some sleep.** By day **eat light meals, drink water** (not alcohol), and **move around the cabin** to stretch your legs.

FLYING TIMES

Flying time to London is 6½ hours from New York, 7½ hours from Chicago, and 10 hours from Los Angeles.

HOW TO COMPLAIN

If your baggage goes astray or your flight goes awry, complain right away. Most carriers require that you **file a claim immediately.**

AIRLINE COMPLAINTS • U.S. Department of Transportation **Aviation Consumer Protection Division** (C-75, Room 4107, Washington, DC 20590, tel. 202/366–2220). **Federal Aviation Administration Consumer Hotline** (tel. 800/322–7873).

AIRPORTS & TRANSFERS

The major airports are Heathrow and Gatwick; there is also service to Stansted and London City.

Heathrow handles the vast majority of international flights to and from the United Kingdom. Terminals 1 and 2 are reserved for European and domestic flights; Terminal 3 is for most intercontinental and Scandinavian flights; and Terminal 4 handles all long-distance British Airways flights as well as shuttle flights between major British cities. Tourist information counters, accommodations services, and bureaux de change are located in every terminal. Luggage storage, known here as left luggage, is also available at every terminal for £2–£3 per item per day; hours are typically 6 AM–10:30 PM daily—but don't count on left luggage counters being open during terrorist bombing campaigns. Passengers in transit or who have gone through passport control can take showers at Terminals 1, 3, and 4 in designated restroom areas for £2 (including towel and soap).

Gatwick, about 30 mi south of London, accommodates a steady stream of flights from the United States and the Continent. Gatwick has a tourist information booth (tel. 01293/560108), left luggage counter (£2–£3 per item per day; lower rates for long-term storage), accommodation services, and a bureau de change.

Stansted, 35 mi northeast of central London, opened in 1991 to alleviate the overcrowding at Heathrow. It serves mainly European destinations, plus American Airlines flights to Chicago, AirTransit flights to

Toronto and Vancouver, and random charter flights. The airport has a tourist desk (tel. 01279/662520) and a 24-hour bureau de change, but no left luggage service. To reach central London, catch the Stansted Express to Liverpool Street Station: trains run every half hour Monday–Saturday 5 AM–11 PM and Sunday 7 AM–11 PM; the 40-minute trek costs £11 one-way.

The little-known **London City Airport,** about 9 mi southeast of central London in Silvertown, handles mostly European commuter flights. The main terminal has a tourist info desk, a left luggage service (£2 per item per day), and a bureau de change. To reach central London, take London Transport's Bus 473 (90p), which shuttles between the airport and Stratford tube station on the Central Line. Buses depart every 12 minutes Monday–Saturday 5 AM–midnight and every 20 minutes Sunday 6 AM–midnight. Or catch a Blue and White Shuttle bus from the airport to Liverpool Street Station or to the Docklands Light Railway station at Canary Wharf (tel. 020/7918–4000 or 020/7222–1234 for more info).

AIRPORT INFORMATION • Heathrow (tel. 011–44–181/759–4321). **Gatwick** (tel. 011–44–12931/535353). **Stansted** (tel. 01279/680500). **London City Airport** (tel. 020/7474–5555).

DUTY-FREE SHOPPING

Duty-free shopping is no longer available on journeys within the European Union (EU), but you can still purchase duty-free goods (sometimes called tax-free goods or travel value goods) when traveling between an EU country and a country outside the EU.

The new regulation on duty-free shopping went into effect on July 1, 1999, and affects the following countries: Austria, Belgium, Denmark, Ireland, Finland, France, Germany, Greece, Italy, Luxembourg, the Netherlands, Portugal, Spain (but not the Canary Islands), Sweden, and the United Kingdom (but not the Channel Islands or Gibraltar). You may thus purchase duty-free goods when traveling between England and Gibraltar, but not between England and France.

TRANSFERS

The cheapest and quickest way to get from Heathrow to central London is by Underground—to use the most common name for the city's "tube" (or subway) system. Traveling on the Piccadilly Line, the 50- to 60-minute trip costs £5.60. There are two Underground stations at Heathrow: one serving Terminals 1–3 and one at Terminal 4. Hop aboard and you can ride directly to many of London's budget accommodation areas, like Earl's Court, South Kensington, and Russell Square. To reach other cheap lodging neighborhoods, such as around Notting Hill Gate or Victoria Station, change to the District Line at Earl's Court.

The latest and greatest way to get between Heathrow and central London is on the **Heathrow Express** (tel. 0345/484950), which can whisk you from Heathrow to Paddington in just under 15 minutes. Trains service all Heathrow terminals at 15-minute intervals between 5:10 AM and 11:40 PM. This speed and efficiency will set you back £10 each way. If you have a lot of heavy baggage, taking the tube can be a real hassle: It's crowded, and transfer points usually involve lots of walking and stair-climbing. In this case consider taking London Transport's shiny red **Airbuses** (tel. 020/7222–1234 or 020/8897–2688), which make 29 stops in central London. Airbuses run daily 6 AM to around 8 PM, at 15- to 30-minute intervals, and for this 60- to 75-minute voyage to the city center, you pay a reasonable £7. From Heathrow, Airbuses make pickups at all four terminals—just follow the AIRBUS or BUSES TO LONDON signs. Heading to the airport, you can catch Airbus A1 at Victoria Station; Airbus A2 at King's Cross; or Airbus Direct, which stops at the doorstep of many central London hotels. For information, call the Airbus hotline, or grab a brochure at a tourist office or at London Transport's Travel Information Centres (*see* Underground Travel and Bus Travel, *below*).

The train is your best bet for getting from Gatwick into central London. The **Gatwick Express** train (tel. 020/7928–5100 or 0990/301530) to Victoria Station departs Gatwick every 15 minutes daily 5 AM–8 PM, and once or twice an hour at other times. The 35-minute trip costs £8.90 one-way. The **Network South-Central** train (tel. 0345/484950) goes to Victoria Station for £7.50 one-way; departure and travel times are similar. **Flightline 777** (tel. 020/8668–7261) offers hourly bus service between Gatwick and Victoria Coach Station daily from 6 AM to around 11 PM. The 75-minute trip costs £7.50 single.

BOAT & FERRY TRAVEL

If you're not weak of stomach, ferries can be the most amusing way to get around. They are the cheapest way to come from France, Belgium, or the Netherlands. They arrive at Dover and Portsmouth from the French ports of Calais, Boulogne, and Le Havre. The standard round-trip fare is £50, around £25 if you return in fewer than five days, but out of season it can be as low as £5–£15, and in the high season twice the standard rate. Since the opening of the Chunnel, there have been fierce price wars to the traveler's benefit, so watch out for special offers in the national press. The Netherlands, northern Germany, and Scandinavia are best accessed from the East Anglia town of Harwich via ferries bound for Hoek van Holland (Hook of Holland). The Welsh port town of Holyhead is the best place to catch ferries to Dublin (£18–£28 single), though there's also service from the Welsh port of Fishguard to the Irish port of Rosslare, and from Stranraer to Belfast.

FERRY COMPANIES • Hoverspeed and SeaCat (tel. 0990/240241). **P&O Ferries** (tel. 0990/980980). **Stena Line** (tel. 0990/707070).

BUS TRAVEL TO AND FROM LONDON

London's main terminal for all long-distance bus companies is **Victoria Coach Station** (Buckingham Palace Rd., tel. 020/7730–3466), just southwest of Victoria Station. Victoria Coach Station has a bureau de change and luggage storage. Travelers with disabilities, who may need assistance, should contact **Help Point** (tel. 020/7730–3466, ext. 235).

You can save lots of money by taking a bus instead of a train. Economy Return bus tickets, good for travel Sunday through Thursday, can be 30%–50% cheaper than train tickets. Expect to pay about 20% more for Standard Return fares, allowing travel on Friday and Saturday. You can also buy cheap APEX tickets if you book seven days in advance and adhere to exact times and dates for departure and return. Book tickets on **National Express** (tel. 0990/808080) buses at Victoria Coach Station or at one of their branch offices at 52 Grosvenor Gardens or 13 Regent Street. It may be cheaper to buy a bus pass ahead of time in the United States. These are valid for 3 days out of 5 ($85, $65 students); and 5 ($150, $115 students), 8 ($220, $160 students), or 15 ($300, $240 students) days out of 30. Contact **British Travel Associates** (tel. 540/298–2232), which sells tickets over the phone and can quote you the latest price in dollars. In Britain, you can buy a pass at any National Express office and at Heathrow and Gatwick airports.

BUS TRAVEL WITHIN LONDON

Deciphering bus routes can be a bit more complicated than figuring out tube routes. For one, color-coded, comprehensive bus-route maps are only posted at major bus stops; if you really want to master the system, pick up the free "Central London Bus Guide" at an LT Travel Information Centre (*see* Underground Travel, *below*). Bus fares are based on four zones: 1, 2, 3, and Bus Zone 4. (Bus Zone 4 covers approximately the same area as zones 4, 5, and 6 for the Underground and railways.) The more zones you cross through on your trip, the more you pay. With few exceptions, everything you want to see will be within Zone 1 (which covers Westminster, Piccadilly Circus, Soho, Trafalgar Square, Covent Garden, the City, Victoria, Earl's Court, Kensington, and more) and Zone 2 (which includes Camden, Hampstead, the East End, Brixton, and Greenwich Park). Inside Zone 1, the adult one-way fare is 90p, or 60p for a "short hop" of less than ¾ mi; a one-way trip through Zones 1 and 2 is £1.20. But if you're doing a lot of sightseeing, you'll probably want to buy a Travelcard (*see* Underground Travel, *below*).

Out on the street, major bus stops are marked by plain white signs with a red LT symbol; buses stop at these points automatically. At some stops, known as request stops (marked by red signs with a white LT symbol and the word "request"), you'll need to flag the bus down—waving an arm once will do just fine. There are a few busy intersections in London where all buses seem to go, such as Trafalgar Square, Victoria Station, and Piccadilly Circus; for these, you'll need to check a posted bus map to find out exactly where you should be standing for the bus to your destination.

On the newer buses, which you board at the front, you pay the driver as you enter (exact change desired but not required). On older buses, the infamous Routemasters, in which the driver sits in a separate cab, just hop on, take a seat, and the conductor will swing by to check your Travelcard or sell you a ticket from a coffee-grinder-like apparatus. Note that London buses rarely run on time. On most routes they're supposed to swing by every six minutes; in reality it can be a 15- or 30-minute wait. (Please thank the hundreds of pushy BMW owners who drive in the city's bus lanes, rather than cursing the poor bus drivers.) Because of this tarnished service record, Londoners have fled the buses, and tourists like you shouldn't have any trouble getting a seat—sometimes you might even be lucky during rush hour (7 AM–9:30 AM and 4 PM–6:30 PM). To get off a bus, pull the cord running above the windows, or press the button by the exit or on one of the upright support poles.

NIGHT BUSES

From 11 PM to 5 AM, some buses add the prefix "N" to their route numbers and are called Night Buses. They don't run as frequently and don't operate on quite as many routes as day buses, but at least they get you somewhere close to your destination without leaving you pence- and poundless. You'll probably have to transfer at one of the Night Bus nexuses: Victoria, Westminster, and, either Piccadilly Circus or Trafalgar Square (the main transfer points for late-night buses). Note that weekly and monthly Travelcards are good for Night Buses, but One-Day and Weekend Travelcards are not. Night Bus single fares are also a bit more expensive than daytime ones. A final word of advice: Avoid sitting alone on the top deck of a Night Bus unless you're in the mood to be mugged. If you're keen on knowing more about Night Buses, ask at an LT Travel Information Centre for the free, handy "Night Bus Guide," which includes several maps.

BUSINESS HOURS

Standard business hours are Monday–Saturday 9–5:30. Newsagents are open daily. Until recently it was (thanks to the Church) a no-no for stores to remain open Sunday, but plenty of London pharmacies, grocers, department stores, and clothing stores now do.

BANKS & OFFICES

Most banks are open weekdays 9:30–3:30; some have extended hours Thursday evening, and a few are open Saturday morning.

SHOPS

Many major stores stay open later (until 7 or 8) once a week, often Wednesday or Thursday.

CAMERAS & PHOTOGRAPHY

PHOTO HELP • Kodak Information Center (tel. 800/242–2424). ***Kodak Guide to Shooting Great Travel Pictures,*** available in bookstores or from Fodor's Travel Publications (tel. 800/533–6478; $16.50 plus $4 shipping).

EQUIPMENT PRECAUTIONS

Always **keep your film and tape out of the sun.** Carry an extra supply of batteries, and **be prepared to turn on your camera or camcorder** to prove to security personnel that the device is real. Always **ask for hand inspection of film,** which becomes clouded after successive exposures to airport X-ray machines, and **keep videotapes away from metal detectors.**

VIDEOS

Most videos sold in the U.K. do not interface with American video players. Videos geared toward tourists often have versions made for the American market.

CAR RENTAL

When considering a rental car, it's worth noting that unless you will be traveling extensively outside London, a car in the city is often more of a liability than an asset. Remember that Britain drives on the left, and the rest of Europe on the right. Therefore, you may want to leave your rented car in Britain and pick up a left-side drive if you cross the Channel.

Rates in London begin at $39 a day and $136 a week for an economy car with air conditioning, a manual transmission, and unlimited mileage. This does not include tax on car rentals, which is 17.5%.

MAJOR AGENCIES • Alamo (tel. 800/522–9696; 020/8759–6200 in the U.K.). **Avis** (tel. 800/331–1084; 800/879–2847 in Canada; 02/9353–9000 in Australia; 09/525–1982 in New Zealand). **Budget** (tel. 800/527–0700; 0144/227–6266 in the U.K.). **Dollar** (tel. 800/800–6000; 020/8897–0811 in the U.K., where it is known as Eurodollar; 02/9223–1444 in Australia). **Hertz** (tel. 800/654–3001; 800/263–0600 in Canada; 0990/90–60–90 in the U.K.; 02/9669–2444 in Australia; 03/358–6777 in New Zealand). **National InterRent** (tel. 800/227–3876; 0345/222525 in the U.K., where it is known as Europcar InterRent).

CUTTING COSTS

To get the best deal **book through a travel agent who will shop around.** Also **price local car-rental companies,** although the service and maintenance may not be as good as those of a major player. Remember to ask about required deposits, cancellation penalties, and drop-off charges if you're planning to pick up the car in one city and leave it in another. If you're traveling during a holiday period, also make sure that a confirmed reservation guarantees you a car.

Do **look into wholesalers,** companies that do not own fleets but rent in bulk from those that do and often offer better rates than traditional car-rental operations. Payment must be made before you leave home.

WHOLESALERS • Auto Europe (tel. 207/842–2000 or 800/223–5555, fax 800/235–6321). **Europe by Car** (tel. 212/581–3040 or 800/223–1516, fax 212/246–1458). **DER Travel Services** (9501 W. Devon Ave., Rosemont, IL 60018, tel. 800/782–2424, fax 800/282–7474 for information; 800/860–9944 for brochures). **Kemwel Holiday Autos** (tel. 914/825–3000 or 800/678–0678, fax 914/381–8847).

INSURANCE

When driving a rented car you are generally responsible for any damage to or loss of the vehicle. Before you rent see what coverage your personal auto-insurance policy and credit cards already provide.

Collision policies that car-rental companies sell for European rentals usually do not include stolen-vehicle coverage. Before you buy it, check your existing policies—you may already be covered.

REQUIREMENTS & RESTRICTIONS

In London your own driver's license is acceptable. An International Driver's Permit is a good idea; it's available from the American or Canadian automobile association, or, in the United Kingdom, from the Automobile Association or Royal Automobile Club.

SURCHARGES

Before you pick up a car in one city and leave it in another **ask about drop-off charges or one-way service fees,** which can be substantial. Note, too, that some rental agencies charge extra if you return the car before the time specified in your contract. To avoid a hefty refueling fee **fill the tank just before you turn in the car,** but be aware that gas stations near the rental outlet may overcharge.

CAR TRAVEL

EMERGENCIES

For aid if your car breaks down, contact the 24-hour rescue numbers of either the **Automobile Association** (tel. 0800/887766) or the **Royal Automobile Club** (tel. 0800/828282).

GASOLINE

Gasoline is commonly called "petrol" in the U.K. and is sold by the liter, with 4.2 liters to a gallon. Stations can be hard to find in rural areas, and most throughout the nation close on Sunday.

ROAD CONDITIONS

If you plan to travel outside London, you'll be glad to know that Britain has a good network of superhighways (motorways) and divided highways (dual carriageways); note that in remoter parts, especially Wales and Scotland, where unclassified roads join village to village and are little more than glorified agricultural cart tracks, travel is noticeably slower. Motorways (with the prefix *M*), shown in blue on most maps and road signs, are mainly two or three lanes in each direction, without any right-hand turns. Other fast major roads are shown with the prefix *A,* shown on maps as green and red. Sections of fast dual carriageway that have black-edged, thick outlines, have both traffic lights and traffic circles, and right turns are sometimes permitted. Turnoffs are often marked by highway numbers, rather than place names, so it's a good idea to always take note of connecting road numbers.

The vast network of lesser roads, for the most part old coach and turnpike roads, might make your trip take twice the time and show you twice as much. Minor roads drawn in yellow or white, the former prefixed by *B,* the latter unlettered and unnumbered, are the ancient lanes and byways, a superb way of discovering the real Britain. Some of these (the white roads, in the main) are potholed switchbacks, littered with blind corners and cowpats, and barely wide enough for one car, let alone for two to pass. Be prepared to reverse into a passing place if you meet an oncoming car or truck.

Service stations on motorways are located at regular intervals and are usually open 24 hours a day; elsewhere they usually close overnight, and by 6 PM and all day Sunday in remote country areas.

ROAD MAPS

Good planning maps are available from the **Automobile Association** or the **Royal Automobile Club** (see Emergencies, *above*).

RULES OF THE ROAD

Drive on the left! This takes a bit of getting used to, and it's much easier if you're driving a British car where the steering and mirrors are designed for U.K. conditions. You have to strap in in the front seat, and in the back, where seat belts exist. Speed limits are complicated, and traffic police can be hard on speeders, especially in urban areas. In those areas, the limit (shown on circular red signs) is generally 30 mph, but 40 mph on some main roads. In rural areas the limit is 60 mph on ordinary roads and 70 mph on motorways, circulation is clockwise, and entering motorists must yield to cars coming from their right.

THE CHANNEL TUNNEL

Short of flying, the "Chunnel" is the fastest way to cross the English Channel: 35 minutes from Folkestone to Calais, 60 minutes from motorway to motorway, or 3 hours from London's Waterloo Station to Paris's Gare du Nord.

CAR TRANSPORT • Eurotunnel (tel. 0990/353–535 in the U.K.).

PASSENGER SERVICE • In the U.K.: **Eurostar** (tel. 0990/186186), **InterCity Europe** (Victoria Station, London, tel. 0990/848848 for credit-card bookings). In the U.S.: **BritRail Travel** (tel. 800/677–8585), **Rail Europe** (tel. 800/942–4866).

CHILDREN IN LONDON

If you are renting a car don't forget to **arrange for a car seat** when you reserve.

FLYING

If your children are two or older **ask about children's airfares.** As a general rule, infants under two not occupying a seat fly at greatly reduced fares or even for free. When booking **confirm carry-on allowances** if you're traveling with infants. In general, for babies charged 10% of the adult fare, you are allowed one carry-on bag and a collapsible stroller; if the flight is full the stroller may have to be checked or you may be limited to less.

Experts agree that it's a good idea to use safety seats aloft for children weighing less than 40 pounds. Airlines set their own policies: U.S. carriers usually require that the child be ticketed, even if he or she is young enough to ride free, since the seats must be strapped into regular seats. Do **check your airline's policy about using safety seats during takeoff and landing.** And since safety seats are not allowed just everywhere in the plane, get your seat assignments early.

If you need them, **request children's meals or a freestanding bassinet** when you make reservations. Note that bulkhead seats, where you must sit to use the bassinet, may lack an overhead bin or storage space on the floor.

LODGING

Most hotels in London allow children under a certain age to stay in their parents' room at no extra charge, but others charge for them as extra adults; be sure to **find out the cutoff age for children's discounts.**

CONCIERGES

Concierges, found in many hotels, can help you with theater tickets and dinner reservations: a good one with connections may be able to get you seats for a hot show or prime-time dinner reservations at the restaurant of the moment. You can also turn to your hotel's concierge for help with travel arrangements, sightseeing plans, services ranging from aromatherapy to zipper repair, and emergencies. Always, **always tip** a concierge who has been of assistance (*see* Tipping, *below*).

CONSUMER PROTECTION

Whenever shopping or buying travel services in London, **pay with a major credit card** so you can cancel payment or get reimbursed if there's a problem. If you're doing business with a particular company for the first time, **contact your local Better Business Bureau and the attorney general's offices** in your state and the company's home state, as well. Have any complaints been filed? Finally, if you're buying a package or tour, always **consider travel insurance** that includes default coverage (*see* Insurance, *below*).

LOCAL BBBS • Council of Better Business Bureaus (4200 Wilson Blvd., Suite 800, Arlington, VA 22203, tel. 703/276–0100, fax 703/525–8277).

CUSTOMS & DUTIES

When shopping, **keep receipts** for all purchases. Upon reentering the country, **be ready to show customs officials what you've bought.** If you feel a duty is incorrect or object to the way your clearance was handled, note the inspector's badge number and ask to see a supervisor. If the problem isn't resolved, write to the appropriate authorities, beginning with the port director at your point of entry.

IN AUSTRALIA

Australia residents who are 18 or older may bring home $A400 worth of souvenirs and gifts (including jewelry), 250 cigarettes or 250 grams of tobacco, and 1,125 ml of alcohol (including wine, beer, and spirits). Residents under 18 may bring back $A200 worth of goods. Prohibited items include meat products. Seeds, plants, and fruits need to be declared upon arrival.

INFORMATION • Australian Customs Service (Regional Director, Box 8, Sydney, NSW 2001, tel. 02/9213–2000, fax 02/9213–4000).

IN CANADA

Canadian residents who have been out of Canada for at least seven days may bring home C$500 worth of goods duty-free. If you've been away less than seven days but more than 48 hours, the duty-free allowance drops to C$200; if your trip lasts 24–48 hours, the allowance is C$50. You may not pool allowances with family members. Goods claimed under the C$500 exemption may follow you by mail; those claimed under the lesser exemptions must accompany you. Alcohol and tobacco products may be included in the 7-day and 48-hour exemptions but not in the 24-hour exemption. If you meet the age requirements of the province or territory through which you reenter Canada, you may bring in, duty-free, 1.14 liters (40 imperial ounces) of wine or liquor *or* 24 12-ounce cans or bottles of beer or ale. If you are 16 or older you may bring in, duty-free, 200 cigarettes and 50 cigars. Check ahead of time with Revenue Canada or the Department of Agriculture for policies regarding meat products, seeds, plants, and fruits.

You may send an unlimited number of gifts worth up to C$60 each duty-free to Canada. Label the package UNSOLICITED GIFT—VALUE UNDER $60. Alcohol and tobacco are excluded.

INFORMATION • Revenue Canada (2265 St. Laurent Blvd. S, Ottawa, Ontario K1G 4K3, tel. 613/993–0534; 800/461–9999 in Canada).

IN LONDON

There are two levels of duty-free allowance for travelers entering Great Britain: one for goods bought outside the EU, the other for goods bought in the EU (Belgium, Greece, the Netherlands, Denmark, Italy, Portugal, France, the Irish Republic, Spain, Germany, or Luxembourg).

In the first category, you may import duty-free: 200 cigarettes or 100 cigarillos or 50 cigars or 250 grams of tobacco; 2 liters of table wine and, in addition, (a) 1 liter of alcohol over 22% by volume (most spirits), (b) 2 liters of alcohol under 22% by volume (fortified or sparkling wine or liqueurs), or (c) 2 more liters of table wine; 50 milliliters of perfume; ¼ liter of toilet water; and other goods up to a value of £136, but not more than 50 liters of beer or 25 cigarette lighters.

In the second category, the EU has set guidelines for the import of certain goods. Following side trips entirely within the EU, you no longer need to go through customs on your return to the United Kingdom; however, if you exceed the guideline amounts, you may be required to prove that the goods are for your personal use only ("personal use" includes gifts). The guideline levels are: 800 cigarettes, 400 cigarillos, 200 cigars, and 1 kilogram of smoking tobacco, plus 10 liters of spirits, 20 liters of fortified wine, 90 liters of wine, and 110 liters of beer, plus goods to the value of £71. No animals or pets of any kind can be brought into the United Kingdom without a lengthy quarantine. The penalties are severe and are strictly enforced. Similarly, fresh meats, plants and vegetables, controlled drugs, and firearms and ammunition may not be brought into Great Britain.

You will face no customs formalities if you enter Scotland or Wales from any other part of the United Kingdom, though anyone coming from Northern Ireland should expect a security check.

IN NEW ZEALAND

Homeward-bound residents 17 or older may bring back $700 worth of souvenirs and gifts. Your duty-free allowance also includes 4.5 liters of wine or beer; one 1,125-ml bottle of spirits; and either 200 cigarettes, 250 grams of tobacco, 50 cigars, or a combination of the three up to 250 grams. Prohibited items include meat products, seeds, plants, and fruits.

INFORMATION • New Zealand Customs (Custom House, 50 Anzac Ave., Box 29, Auckland, New Zealand, tel. 09/359–6655, fax 09/359–6732).

IN THE U.S.

Non-U.S. residents ages 21 and older may import into the United States 200 cigarettes or 50 cigars or 2 kilograms of tobacco, 1 liter of alcohol, and gifts worth $100. Meat products, seeds, plants, and fruits are prohibited.

U.S. residents who have been out of the country for at least 48 hours (and who have not used the $400 allowance or any part of it in the past 30 days) may bring home $400 worth of foreign goods duty-free.

U.S. residents 21 and older may bring back 1 liter of alcohol duty-free. In addition, regardless of your age, you are allowed 200 cigarettes and 100 non-Cuban cigars. Antiques, which the U.S. Customs Service defines as objects more than 100 years old, enter duty-free, as do original works of art done entirely by hand, including paintings, drawings, and sculptures.

You may also send packages home duty-free: up to $200 worth of goods for personal use, with a limit of one parcel per addressee per day (and no alcohol or tobacco products or perfume worth more than $5); label the package PERSONAL USE and attach a list of its contents and their retail value. Do not label the package UNSOLICITED GIFT or your duty-free exemption will drop to $100. Mailed items do not affect your duty-free allowance on your return.

INFORMATION • U.S. Customs Service (inquiries, 1300 Pennsylvania Ave. NW, Washington, DC 20229, tel. 202/927–6724; complaints, Office of Regulations and Rulings, 1300 Pennsylvania Ave. NW, Washington, DC 20229; registration of equipment, Registration Information, 1300 Pennsylvania Ave. NW, Washington, DC 20229, tel. 202/927–0540).

DINING

In the '90s, London underwent a food revolution—its restaurant scene is Europe's hottest right now. Tasty fusion recipes have been trickling down into many British kitchens, and ethnic cuisines—notably Indian, Chinese, and Thai—continue to play a significant role in the dining world. Old standards such as bangers and mash, fish-and-chips, and meat and veg have been given a nouveau spin, and the traditional Greek, Italian, and French eateries have also become more conscious of decor and style—with prices to prove it. Strike out to London's outlying "villages" such as Barnes, Clerkenwell, Camden, or Hampstead for a lively, less hyped experience with lower prices. Use the dining sections in this guide to hone in on the most dining value for your pound; you can also rely on the good old standby of pub food, which is becoming far more adventurous, and the local Chinese takeout, which often doubles as a fish-and-chippie.

Whatever else ails British cuisine, the country deserves credit for the English breakfast. As Somerset Maugham once pointed out, "If you want to eat well in England, have breakfast three times a day." The morning meal can often be a masterpiece of bacon (usually with the rind still on), egg, grilled tomato, sausage, and fried bread. An English breakfast is often included in a B&B's rates. Pub lunches are another good way to cut down your eating bills, although the fare becomes rather tiring after a while. Staples are bangers and mash, cottage pie, steak-and-kidney pie, Cornish pasties (a type of savory pie), and fish-and-chips. A ploughman's lunch is probably the most appetizing of the lot, consisting of a hunk of fresh bread, English cheese, tomatoes, pickled onions, and Branston pickles or chutney. Some pubs can be a real find, though, as they offer real ham, chicken, or turkey fresh from the bone, smoked mackerel, lasagna, or moussaka, all with the ubiquitous optional chips. Portions are often generous.

The restaurant price categories used in our city listings are loosely based on the assumption that you're going to chow down a main course and a drink. Antacids and dessert are extra.

PUBS

The Brits take their drink very seriously, and pubs (public houses) are where people go to chew over the drama of life or drink themselves into oblivion. Almost every pub has a sign hanging outside, typically bearing a name like The Horse and Plough or The King George. Most pubs are affiliated with a particular brewer (Whitbread, Charringtons, Bass) and sell only that brewery's beer; others are "freehouses," which can sell independent brewers' beers and generally have a better selection of brews.

The beer of choice among Britons is probably **bitter,** a lightly fermented beer with an amber color that gets its bitterness from the fermentation of hops. Names to try are Fuller's, Young's, Tetley's, Watney's Red Barrel, and Samuel Smith's. **Real ale,** served from wooden kegs, is another popular beer. It's flatter than regular bitters and is something else all together. Afficionados claim real ale has as many different characteristics as some vintage wines, and it comes with the most quirky names—Old Growler, Fuggies, and Umbel Magna. **Stouts** like Guinness and Murphy's are thick, dark Irish brews that you'll either love or hate. They're as filling as a small meal. **Lagers** now come in an array of designer names and bottles, and make up half of Britain's beer consumption (try Harp, Carling, Tennent's, Whitbread, and Watney's). The light-colored and heavily carbonated beer is served cold, unlike bitters and ales, which are served only cool. **Cider,** made from apples, is an alcoholic drink in Britain. Most pubs feature at least one dry and one sweet variety; Bulmer's and Strongbow are the names to remember. For a real, rough country taste, without a hint of mass-produced flavor or fizz, try Scrumpy—the true cider of ciders. Another option is a blended drink, like a **shandy,** a mix of lager and lemonade or orange soda; **black and tans,** a blend of lager and stout named for the distinctive uniforms worn by turn-of-the-century British troops. Be warned if you order a drink that would normally be served with ice in the United States—ice cubes are about as common in pubs as they are in Hades.

Unless otherwise noted, pubs are open Monday–Saturday 11–11 and Sunday noon–10:30. Exceptions to the rule are wine bars (which charge handsome prices to subsidize their costly after-hours liquor licenses) and small neighborhood pubs that just don't give a hoot. You'll know you've found one of the latter when, at 11 PM, the barman draws the curtains, locks the door, and asks people to leave at their leisure from a discreet side door. "Lock-ins" are an age-old tradition, and while they're definitely not legal, bobbies tend to overlook them.

DISABILITIES & ACCESSIBILITY

Although the needs of travelers with disabilities are being met in more places, budget opportunities are harder to find. Always ask if discounts are available, either for you or for a companion. London is ahead of the rest of the country in considering the needs of people with disabilities. Many of the big tourist sights and entertainment venues have wheelchair access. Some museums and parks have special attractions, such as touch-tours for the vision-impaired and interpreted events for the hearing-impaired.

LOCAL RESOURCES • Royal Association for Disability and Rehabilitation (RADAR; 12 City Forum, 250 City Rd., EC1 V8AF, tel. 020/7250–3222), open weekdays 9–5, is command central for everything people with disabilities need to know about living and traveling in the United Kingdom. It publishes both travel information and periodicals on political issues. If you're planning an extended stay, check out Greater London Association for Disabled People (GLAD; *see below*), which can put you in touch with folks in your particular neighborhood.

Each London borough also maintains its own information and advice line; two in central London are **Westminster Disability Information Service** (tel. 020/7266–2111) and **Action Disability Kensington and Chelsea** (tel. 020/8960–8888). The **Artsline** (tel. 020/7388–2227), open weekdays 9:30–5:30, can clue you in on accessible goings-on around town. For info about accessible participant sports, call **Disability Sport England** (tel. 020/7490–4919) during normal office hours.

LODGING

When discussing accessibility with an operator or reservations agent **ask hard questions.** Are there any stairs, inside *or* out? Are there grab bars next to the toilet *and* in the shower/tub? How wide is the doorway to the room? To the bathroom? For the most extensive facilities meeting the latest legal specifications **opt for newer accommodations.**

PUBLICATIONS • *Access in London* (£7.95), published by Quiller Press, is the premier travel guide in the genre; it's available in most larger bookstores and at many travel bookshops. Greater London Association for Disabled People (GLAD; 336 Brixton Rd., SW9 7AA, tel. 020/7346–5800) publishes the wonderfully comprehensive "London Disability Guide." It's free if you pick it up in person; otherwise send them a stamped (83p), self-addressed, large envelope. RADAR (*see above*) publishes the useful Accessible Holidays in the British Isles (£7), which lists wheelchair-accessible lodging and attractions all over Britain.

TRANSPORTATION

London Regional Transport publishes a number of helpful pamphlets, one of the best being "Access to the Underground." Wheelchair-accessible **Mobility Bus** services (tel. 020/7918–3312), numbered in the 800 and 900 series, run (albeit infrequently) in many parts of London. **Stationlink** (tel. 020/7918–3312) is a wheelchair-accessible minibus with an hourly circular service that links Waterloo, Victoria, Paddington, Marylebone, Euston, St. Pancras, King's Cross, Liverpool Street, Fenchurch Street, and London Bridge stations; one bus runs clockwise, another counterclockwise. It also connects with the wheelchair-accessible Airbus A1 at Victoria and A2 at Euston for Heathrow Airport.

COMPLAINTS • **Disability Rights Section** (U.S. Department of Justice, Civil Rights Division, Box 66738, Washington, DC 20035-6738, tel. 202/514–0301; 800/514–0301; 202/514–0301 TTY; 800/514–0301 TTY, fax 202/307–1198) for general complaints. **Aviation Consumer Protection Division** (*see* Air Travel, *above*) for airline-related problems. **Civil Rights Office** (U.S. Department of Transportation, Departmental Office of Civil Rights, S-30, 400 7th St. SW, Room 10215, Washington, DC 20590, tel. 202/366–4648, fax 202/366–9371) for problems with surface transportation.

Some feel the cruelest words in the English language are "Drink up, ladies and gents, time to go. Please lads, come now, drink up."

TRAVEL AGENCIES

In the United States, although the Americans with Disabilities Act requires that travel firms serve the needs of all travelers, some agencies specialize in working with people with disabilities.

TRAVELERS WITH MOBILITY PROBLEMS • **Access Adventures** (206 Chestnut Ridge Rd., Rochester, NY 14624, tel. 716/889–9096), run by a former physical-rehabilitation counselor. **Accessible Journeys** (35 W. Sellers Ave., Ridley Park, PA 19078, tel. 610/521–0339 or 800/846–4537, fax 610/521–6959). **Accessible Vans of the Rockies, Activity and Travel Agency** (2040 W. Hamilton Pl., Sheridan, CO 80110, tel. 303/806–5047 or 888/837–0065, fax 303/781–2329). **Accessible Vans of Hawaii, Activity and Travel Agency** (186 Mehani Circle, Kihei, HI 96753, tel. 808/879–5521 or 800/303–3750, fax 808/879–0649). **CareVacations** (5-5110 50th Ave., Leduc, Alberta, Canada T9E 6V4, tel. 780/986–6404 or 877/478–7827, fax 780/986–8332) has group tours and is especially helpful with cruise vacations. **Flying Wheels Travel** (143 W. Bridge St., Box 382, Owatonna, MN 55060, tel. 507/451–5005 or 800/535–6790, fax 507/451–1685). **Hinsdale Travel Service** (201 E. Ogden Ave., Suite 100, Hinsdale, IL 60521, tel. 630/325–1335, fax 630/325–1342).

DISCOUNTS & DEALS

Be a smart shopper and **compare all your options** before making decisions. A plane ticket bought with a promotional coupon from travel clubs, coupon books, and direct-mail offers may not be cheaper than the least expensive fare from a discount ticket agency. And always keep in mind that what you get is just as important as what you save.

DISCOUNT RESERVATIONS

To save money **look into discount-reservations services** with toll-free numbers, which use their buying power to get a better price on hotels, airline tickets, even car rentals. When booking a room, always **call the hotel's local toll-free number** (if one is available) rather than the central reservations number—you'll often get a better price. Always ask about special packages or corporate rates.

When shopping for the best deal on hotels and car rentals **look for guaranteed exchange rates,** which protect you against a falling dollar. With your rate locked in, you won't pay more, even if the price goes up in the local currency.

AIRLINE TICKETS • Tel. **800/FLY-4-LESS.** Tel. **800/FLY-ASAP.**

HOTEL ROOMS • **Hotel Reservations Network** (tel. 800/964-6835). **Steigenberger Reservation Service** (tel. 800/223-5652).**Travel Interlink** (tel. 800/888-5898).

PACKAGE DEALS

Don't confuse packages and guided tours. When you buy a package, you travel on your own, just as though you had planned the trip yourself. Fly/drive packages, which combine airfare and car rental, are often a good deal. In cities, ask the local visitor's bureau about hotel packages that include tickets to major museum exhibits or other special events. If you **buy a rail/drive pass** you may save on train tickets and car rentals. All Eurail- and Europass holders get a discount on Eurostar fares through the Channel Tunnel.

ELECTRICITY

To use your U.S.-purchased electric-powered equipment **bring a converter and adapter.** The electrical current in London is 220 volts, 50 cycles alternating current (AC); wall outlets in London take plugs with two round oversize prongs.

If your appliances are dual-voltage you'll need only an adapter. Don't use 110-volt outlets, marked FOR SHAVERS ONLY, for high-wattage appliances such as blow-dryers. Most laptops operate equally well on 110 and 220 volts and so require only an adapter.

EMBASSIES

AUSTRALIA • **Australian High Commission.** Australia House, The Strand, WC2B 4LA, tel. 020/7379-4334. Tube: Temple. Open weekdays 9:30-3:30.

CANADA • **Canadian High Commission-Consular Section.** McDonald House, 1 Grosvenor Square, W1X 0AB, tel. 020/7258-6600. Tube: Bond St. Open weekdays 9-4 (visas issued weekdays 9-11).

NEW ZEALAND • **New Zealand High Commission.** New Zealand House, 80 Haymarket, SW1Y 4TQ, tel. 020/7930-8422. Tube: Charing Cross or Piccadilly Circus. Open weekdays 9-5.

UNITED STATES • **United States Embassy.** Passports are handled weekdays 8:30-11 (additional hours Monday, Wednesday, and Friday 2-4) around the corner at the Passport Office, 55 Upper Brook Street. Visas are handled by appointment only. Main Embassy Offices: 24 Grosvenor Square, W1A 1AE, tel. 020/7499-9000. Tube: Marble Arch or Bond St. Open weekdays 8:30-5:30.

EMERGENCIES

DENTISTS • **Eastman Dental Hospital** (256 Gray's Inn Rd., WC1, tel. 020/7837-3646. Tube: Chancery La. or King's Cross. Open weekdays 8:30-5:30) for free walk-in emergency dental care. No appointment—it's first come, first served. **Guy's Hospital Dental School** (St. Thomas St., SE1, tel. 020/7955-5000. Tube: London Bridge) provides walk-in emergency dental care, though for nonemergencies you must make an appointment. Open weekdays 9-5, weekends 9:30-4 for emergencies only.

DOCTORS • If you're a visitor from one of the EU or Commonwealth countries, rejoice: You can receive free medical treatment while here in London. If you're from some other country and are seeking nonemergency medical treatment, you should check your insurance policy and call first to inquire about rates. Keep in mind that the ISIC (International Student Identity Card; *see* Students, *below*) comes with hospitalization insurance; read its "Summary of Coverage" card for more info. For serious injuries, the hospitals listed below have 24-hour emergency wards.

EMERGENCY SERVICES • **Police, ambulance,** and **fire** (tel. 999).

HOSPITALS • **Guy's Hospital** (St. Thomas St., SE1, tel. 020/7955-5000. Tube: London Bridge). **Royal Free** (Pond St., Hampstead, NW3, tel. 020/7794-0500. Tube: Belsize Park). **University College London Hospital** (Gower St., WC1, tel. 020/7387-9300. Tube: Euston Sq. or Warren St.).

24-HOUR PHARMACIES • Chemists (equivalent to an American drugstore) are plentiful in London. Those with late hours include **Bliss Chemists** (5 Marble Arch, W1, tel. 020/7723-6116; Tube: Marble Arch), open daily 9 AM-midnight, and Boots (75 Queensway, W2, tel. 020/7229-9266; Tube: Bayswater), open daily until 10 PM. The **Boots** in Victoria Station (tel. 020/7834-0676; Tube: Victoria) is open weekdays 7:30 AM–8 PM and Saturday 9–7, and branches in Oxford Street and Piccadilly Circus are also open late.

HOTLINES • The **Samaritans** (tel. 020/7734–2800) 24-hour help line assists anyone in emotional crisis or feeling suicidal. **National Association of Victims Support Schemes** (Cranmer House, 39 Brixton Rd., SW9, tel. 020/7735–9166) has trained volunteers who can provide advice and emotional support to victims of crime. Hours are weekdays 9–5:30. The **London Rape Crisis Centre** (tel. 020/7837–1600) phone line offers counseling daily 10–10. The nonprofit **Pregnancy Advisory Service** (11–13 Charlotte St., W1, tel. 020/7637–8962) offers a full range of services for women. The toll-free, 24-hour **National AIDS Helpline** (tel. 0800/567123) offers confidential counseling and info.

GAY & LESBIAN TRAVEL

London, with the largest gay community in Britain, has a variety of social venues where alternative sexual orientations can be fully expressed. Of course, Brits can be bigots with the worst of them, but the general atmosphere is one of tolerance—though gay-bashings seem to be on a slight rise. Old Compton Street in Soho, near the Leicester Square tube station, is the heart of London's so-called Gay Village, with lots of gay cafés, nightspots, businesses, and services.

GAY- AND LESBIAN-FRIENDLY TRAVEL AGENCIES • **Different Roads Travel** (8383 Wilshire Blvd., Suite 902, Beverly Hills, CA 90211, tel. 323/651–5557 or 800/429–8747, fax 323/651–3678). **Kennedy Travel** (314 Jericho Turnpike, Floral Park, NY 11001, tel. 516/352–4888 or 800/237–7433, fax 516/354–8849). **Now Voyager** (4406 18th St., San Francisco, CA 94114, tel. 415/626–1169 or 800/255–6951, fax 415/626–8626). **Skylink Travel and Tour** (1006 Mendocino Ave., Santa Rosa, CA 95401, tel. 707/546–9888 or 800/225–5759, fax 707/546–9891), serving lesbian travelers.

LOCAL RESOURCES • **Gay's the Word** (66 Marchmont St., WC1, tel. 020/7278–7654) is a social and intellectual center for London's gay and lesbian community and houses books, magazines, and a bulletin board. Stuff for lesbians to do by and amongst themselves is a bit harder to find, but the **Drill Hall** (16 Chenies St., WC1, tel. 020/7631–1353) is a good start. Aside from hosting women-only Monday nights, it serves as a cultural center and presents theater and music for the rest of the week.

The **Lesbian and Gay Switchboard** (tel. 020/7837–7324) is the main 24-hour info and advice line in the London area. If its lines are busy, you can call **London Friend** (tel. 020/7837–3337), which provides confidential phone counseling for lesbians and gay men daily 7:30 PM–10 PM. It also runs a special **London Friend Women's Line** (tel. 020/7837–2782), open Sunday–Tuesday during the same hours. The Lesbian Line (tel. 020/7253–0924) is there for women Monday and Friday 2 PM–10 PM, Tuesday–Thursday 7 PM–10 PM. There are even more specific hot lines for lesbians and gays who are Jewish, Catholic, in legal trouble, or worried about protecting themselves on the streets; ask any of the folks listed above. The **National AIDS Helpline** (tel. 0800/567123) is a toll-free, 24-hour service offering advice and referrals.

PUBLICATIONS • If you're looking for London-specific information, you're in luck: London has a multitude of publications with info on meetings, cultural events, gay businesses, and entertainment. Many are free—among them the well-written **Pink Paper,** the fluffier **Boyz,** and the impressive glossy **Freedom,** available at cafés and some newsstands around town. The free **Thud** is a good mag for clubbers. Other names to watch for are the lifestyle mags **Diva** (lesbian focus; £2) and **Gay Times** (gay focus; £2.50), and, as always, **Time Out** magazine—they're close to unbeatable when it comes to London's gay club scene.

HOLIDAYS

On the following national holidays, banks and post offices are closed, and public transportation is limited—though some shops, museums, and art galleries may remain open: **New Year's Day** (January 1); **Good Friday** (the Friday before Easter); **Easter Monday** (the Monday after Easter); **May Day** (the first Monday in May); **Spring Bank Holiday** (the last Monday in May); **Summer Bank Holiday** (the last Monday in August); **Christmas Day** (December 25); and **Boxing Day** (December 26).

INSURANCE

The most useful travel insurance plan is a comprehensive policy that includes coverage for trip cancellation and interruption, default, trip delay, and medical expenses (with a waiver for preexisting conditions).

Without insurance you will lose all or most of your money if you cancel your trip, regardless of the reason. Default insurance covers you if your tour operator, airline, or cruise line goes out of business. Trip-delay covers expenses that arise because of bad weather or mechanical delays. Study the fine print when comparing policies.

If you're traveling internationally, a key component of travel insurance is coverage for medical bills incurred if you get sick on the road. Such expenses are not generally covered by Medicare or private policies. U.K. residents can buy a travel-insurance policy valid for most vacations taken during the year in which it's purchased (but check pre-existing-condition coverage). Australian citizens need extra medical coverage when traveling abroad.

Always **buy travel policies directly from the insurance company**; if you buy it from a cruise line, airline, or tour operator that goes out of business you probably will not be covered for the agency or operator's default, a major risk. Before you make any purchase **review your existing health and home-owner's policies** to find what they cover away from home.

TRAVEL INSURERS • In the United States: **Access America** (6600 W. Broad St., Richmond, VA 23230, tel. 804/285–3300 or 800/284–8300), **Travel Guard International** (1145 Clark St., Stevens Point, WI 54481, tel. 715/345–0505 or 800/826–1300). In Canada: **Voyager Insurance** (44 Peel Center Dr., Brampton, Ontario L6T 4M8, tel. 905/791–8700; 800/668–4342 in Canada).

INSURANCE INFORMATION • In the United Kingdom: The **Association of British Insurers** (51–55 Gresham St., London EC2V 7HQ, tel. 020/7600–3333, fax 020/7696–8999). In Australia: The **Insurance Council of Australia** (tel. 03/9614–1077, fax 03/9614–7924).

LAUNDRY

LAUNDROMATS • Launderettes are all over London, but if you find yourself staying near Russell Square in Bloomsbury, do your laundry in style at **Duds 'n Suds** (49–51 Brunswick Shopping Centre, tel. 020/7837–1122). While your clothes circle around, you can play a game of snooker, have a snack at the bar, or watch the large-screen TV.

LODGING

This book lists the total price for a double room, including VAT, when outside the major cities. Within major cities, hotels and other accommodations are instead listed by price category. If not stated otherwise, all accommodations take credit cards. If they do not offer this service, we flag the fact by noting "Cash only."

HOTELS AND BED-AND-BREAKFASTS

When hoping to stretch your pounds, your biggest concern will be choosing your accommodations. Hotel rates are highest, starting around £25 per person and reaching beyond £200.

If you're sick of hostels and campgrounds but can't afford a hotel, bed-and-breakfasts (B&Bs) and guest houses—their slightly snootier cousins—are the perfect, ubiquitous alternatives. A night at a B&B will cost you at least £12–£15, but you'll likely be staying in private homes that owners open to the public. Some B&Bs are grand old houses in the country and some are cramped flats in the suburbs. The quality of B&Bs varies widely—some owners go to great lengths to make their homes as comfortable as possible; others want your money and not a whole lot else. Be aware that some B&B owners discriminate blatantly; and you might be turned away based on your appearance.

Expect to share bathrooms with other guests, although many rooms have their own washbasin. Some B&Bs do offer rooms with private bath, but you'll pay an extra £5–£15 for the privilege. Breakfast is, as the name suggests, almost always included in the rates—and if you're lucky, the breakfast will be solid enough to keep you going until evening. For a small additional fee, many B&Bs also serve dinner upon advance notice. A great plus of staying in a B&B is getting grass-roots information and a better feel of London or other towns from the proprietors. Don't worry if the B&B is outside the center of town; there are almost always buses to ferry you around.

If you plan on traveling outside of London, request a list of local B&Bs at any tourist office; the central tourist organizations produce national lists. Alastair Sawday's valuable guide book *Special Places to Stay in Britain* (ASP, £10.95) highlights the best all-rounders (with less of the UHT milk and sugar sachets). The incisive *Which? Hotel Guide* (Which? Books, £14.99) provides the bottom line on modest hotels and B&Bs under £35 a night. Both are updated annually.

CAMPING

Consider camping if you'll be making excursions from London into the country (*see* Chapter 9, Trips from London). National parks tend to have the most well-equipped sites, while some more primitive campsites offer little more than the ground itself. Some hostels with backyards offer tent sites; resort-style campgrounds offer showers, laundry facilities, bars, and amusement arcades. The latter tend to be overrun by caravanners, the British equivalent of the RV crowd. If you're planning to camp, keep the following in mind: (1) Even in summer, the wind on the northern moors can be bitingly cold and incredibly strong; (2) you're likely to get wet, no matter where you are; (3) campgrounds in rural areas are often poorly served by public transportation; and (4) many campgrounds close outside the summer months.

Nevertheless, Britain has more than 2,000 campsites, and camping is undoubtedly the best way to see the countryside if your interest lies in hiking and nature. Travelers who prefer a comfortable bed at night and a good pub down the road may want to go the B&B route. For more info, contact the **British Tourist Authority** (*see* Visitor Information, *below*) for their free pamphlet, "Self-Catering Holiday Homes." When camping, don't pitch your tent near those plants that look like a fuzzier version of garden weeds—called stinging nettles, they give you a nasty, burning sensation if your skin comes into contact with them.

HOSTELS

If you want to scrimp on lodging, **look into hostels.** In some 5,000 locations in more than 70 countries around the world, **Hostelling International (HI),** the umbrella group for a number of national youth hostel associations, offers single-sex, dorm-style beds, and, at many hostels, "couples" rooms and family accommodations. Membership in any HI national hostel association, open to travelers of all ages, allows you to stay in HI-affiliated hostels at member rates. Members also have priority if the hostel is full; they're eligible for discounts around the world, even on rail and bus travel in some countries.

A Continental breakfast is tea or coffee, orange juice if you're lucky, rolls or toast, and jam and butter. An English breakfast includes the above as well as bacon, eggs, and cereal, perhaps even black pudding, fried toast, and soggy stewed tomatoes.

Hostelling International is the umbrella organization beneath which the Youth Hostel Association of England and Wales (YHA) and the Scotland Youth Hostel Association (SYHA) operate. Purchase a Hostelling International membership card at any hostel for £11 (£5.50 under 18). Non-members must pay an extra £1.55 per night for a guest stamp; after accruing six stamps you're granted full membership. Students between the ages of 18 and 26 and in possession of an ISIC card (*see* Students, *below*) are given a £1 discount on hostel accommodations in England; be sure to ask.

To double check your accommodation plans, we advise you **telephone the hostel in advance—certain hostels close during off-season months.** While we note if any hostel is closed during off-season, it's best to inquire by phone as your arrival date approaches to **get the latest update.**

Most HI hostels have sex-segregated dormitories. They usually have an 11 PM curfew (except in major cities), daytime bedroom lockouts (usually 10–4), check-in times between 8 AM–11 AM and 5 PM–9 PM, and check-out by 10:30 AM. Note that if a hostel keeps different hours, we note those hours separately in the review listing. Some hostels, usually at the lower end of the scale, may wish you to help with a simple chore. In many hostels, you must use a sleep sheet, which is sometimes included at no extra charge. All hostels have basic kitchen facilities and serve their own usually bland meals. If a hostel is full, the desk will have references to nearby places, or might let you sleep in the lounge. Hostels are not allowed to turn anyone away who can't get another place to stay, especially women traveling alone.

There are also a number of independent hostels sprouting up around Britain. These hostels cater to the international cheapo backpacker, with no curfew or lockout and 24-hour reception. Unfortunately, in some cases, the lack of rules often entails lack of cleanliness. Many independent hostels are part of the **Independent Holiday Hostels (IHH)** organization. *The Independent Hostel Guide* (£3.95, Backpackers Press, from most good bookstores, or contact 01629/580427) is a handy book listing their member hostels, though free lists are available at most tourist offices.

ORGANIZATIONS • Australian Youth Hostel Association (10 Mallett St., Camperdown, NSW 2050, tel. 02/9565–1699, fax 02/9565–1325). **Hostelling International—American Youth Hostels** (733 15th St. NW, Suite 840, Washington, DC 20005, tel. 202/783–6161, fax 202/783–6171). **Hostelling International—Canada** (400–205 Catherine St., Ottawa, Ontario K2P 1C3, tel. 613/237–7884, fax 613/237–7868). **Scottish Youth Hostel Association** (SYHA) (7 Glebe Crescent, Stirling FK8 2JA, Scotland, tel.

01786/891333, fax 01786/450198. Office open weekdays 9–12:30 and 1:30–5). **Youth Hostel Association of England and Wales** (Trevelyan House, 8 St. Stephen's Hill, St. Albans, Hertfordshire AL1 2DY, tel. 01727/855215 or 01727/845047, fax 01727/844126). **Youth Hostels Association of New Zealand** (Box 436, Christchurch, New Zealand, tel. 03/379–9970, fax 03/365–4476). Membership in the United States is $25, in Canada C$26.75, in the United Kingdom £9.30, in Australia $44, and in New Zealand $24.

UNIVERSITY HOUSING

During university holidays—usually around Christmas, Easter, and summer—colleges often rent out residence halls to foreign visitors. They're certainly no cheaper than B&Bs unless you pay weekly rates, and finding a room sometimes involves a lot of legwork if you just show up. Many British universities are actually collections of separate colleges; to find a room, you have to contact each individual college. On the plus side, you get your own single, you meet lots of other travelers, and the residence halls are usually within easy walking distance of cheap restaurants and pubs. If you're interested in planning university stays before you arrive, contact the **British Universities Accommodation Consortium** (Box 1735, University Park, Nottingham NG7 2RD, tel. 01159/504571). Before you walk in the door, be sure to **phone ahead to inquire if there are any minimum stay requirements**—some university halls will not accept guests for just one or two nights. And certain university residence halls do not offer rooms to the general public, **inquire if they accommodate nonstudents.**

MAIL & SHIPPING

The Royal Mail service, though fairly reliable, is very slow. Outbound letters to North America take up to four days longer than incoming ones. Well, at least it's easy to buy stamps: Besides the main offices, you'll find mini–post offices in butcher shops, liquor stores ("off-licenses"), and chemists. Just keep your eyes peeled for POST OFFICE signs bearing a red oval with yellow lettering. For post office addresses, check the London Yellow Pages, or call the **Customer Helpline** (tel. 0345/740740), which will furnish post office locations, telephone numbers, and hours. Typically, post offices are open weekdays 9–5:30, Saturday 9–12:30.

POSTAL CODES

Postal codes aren't just for mail: London is divided into postal districts, whose corresponding code is a helpful directional. Postal codes are also used to distinguish between two streets with the same name, so be certain of your destination before jumping in a cab or you may find yourself in NW8 instead of W8. Postal codes are almost always listed on street signs, as is the borough the street falls under. A few handy ones to keep in mind while you're exploring: WC1: Bloomsbury; WC2: Covent Garden, The Strand, Leicester Square; W1: Mayfair, Soho; W8: Kensington; SW1: Westminster, Victoria; SW3: Chelsea, Knightsbridge; SW5: Earl's Court; SW7: South Kensington; N1: Islington, King's Cross; NW1: Camden Town.

POSTAL RATES

Rates from the United Kingdom are from 43p (then more according to the weight) for an international airmail letter, 36p for an international aerogram, and 43p for an international postcard. First-class letters and cards to all EU countries are 26p (up to 20 grams). Be sure to get the free PAR AVION/BY AIR MAIL stickers when you buy your stamps. If you're sending a letter, do it by air mail (a week–10 days) because surface mail can take from four to nine weeks! Surface mail is really for sending home gifts or heavy items you don't want to carry around. Boxes can be bought at office-supply stores like W. H. Smith and at some post offices. You'll need to fill out a small, green customs sticker that states the weight and contents (so much for surprise gifts).

RECEIVING MAIL

If you hold an AmEx card, you can have mail sent to AmEx's Haymarket office (*see* Money, *below*). Otherwise, you can receive letters from loved ones via poste restante at any London post office (check the list in the London Yellow Pages under "Post Offices"). Have your friends write "Hold for 30 days" in the upper left corner of the package/envelope and address it to you, c/o Poste Restante, followed by the post office name, address, and postal code. One option is the mammoth, central **Trafalgar Square Post Office.** Don't forget to bring your passport or photo ID when you go to fetch your mail. Post Office, 24–28 William IV St., WC2N 4DL, tel. 020/7930–8565. Tube: Charing Cross. Open Monday–Saturday 8:30 AM–9 PM.

LONDON POSTAL DISTRICTS

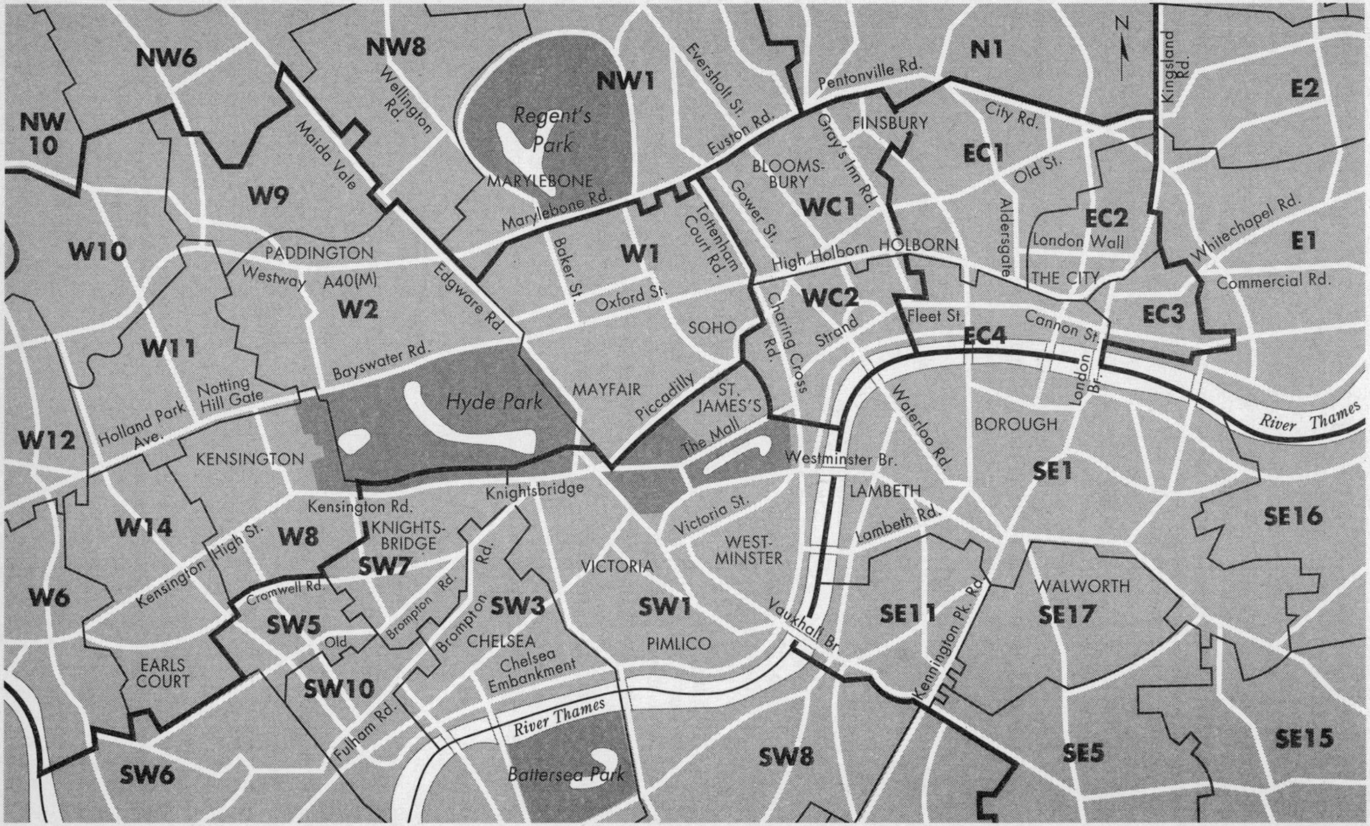

MEDIA

INTERNET ACCESS

Many people are Internet junkies who would shrivel up and die without a regular injection of e-mail and net surfing. Luckily, London has quite a few places where you can check your mail, as well as get your caffeine fix. Visit the amazing **Cyberia** (39 Whitfield St., W1, tel. 020/7681–4200, cyberia@easynet.co.uk; Tube:Goodge St.), which has 10 PCs and one Mac providing Internet access for £3 per half hour (£2.40 for students); a friendly, helpful staff not infected by the "cooler-than-thou" virus; a good range of food; and a varied, lively clientele—not all of whom come for the computers. The Cyberians are also the force behind **Channel Cyberia** (www.channel.cyberiacafe.net), the world's first Internet service with 24-hour programming. The stylish **Café Internet** (22 Buckingham Palace Rd., SW1, tel. 020/7233–5786, cafe@cafeinternet.co.uk; Tube: Victoria) has 10 PCs available for £3 per half hour (£2.50 for students). The 10 PCs at **Global Café** (15 Golden Sq., W1, tel. 020/7287–2242; Tube: Piccadilly Circus) actually seem to clutter up the pristine interior. Internet time costs £5 per hour, £3 per half hour. Good nibbles and some nice art by local artists can distract you as you wait for a terminal. Lurking in the basement of Dillons bookstore, **Cyber.St@tion** (82 Gower St., WC1, tel. 020/7636–1577, cyberstation.dillons.co.uk; Tube: Goodge St.) has eight PCs available for £5 per hour (£4.50 for students), £3 per half hour (£2.50 for students). It's seldom busy and the staff is really helpful, but the environment is rather airless. For more info on on-line resources, *see* Useful Web sites in Visitor Information, *below.*

NEWSPAPERS & MAGAZINES

Rupert Murdoch is a global name, and the Australian-born American has managed to get his hands on several British newspapers including ***The Sun*** (around 30p), which sets the world standard for no-holds-barred pseudo-journalism, with daily features like the topless woman known as the "page three girl." Murdoch also has his moneyed fists on ***The Times*** (35p), a respectable (as far as it goes in journalism these days) newspaper whose Sunday edition (£1) is the perfect accessory for Sunday brunch. The ***Daily Telegraph*** (40p) is Britain's most conservative paper, the liberal ***Guardian*** (45p) argues the other side of the story, and the ***Independent*** (40p) comes down somewhere between the two. The ***Evening Standard*** (30p) also has all-purpose entertainment info, especially in the free supplement "Hot Tickets," which comes out every Friday. Overall, it doesn't hold a candle to ***Time Out,*** but some of its features are quite good.

Time Out (£1.70), fresh off the press every Wednesday, has more event listings than any other magazine in London as well as fine articles on current events, fashion, and entertainment. ***What's On*** (£1.20) has fewer listings, but its reviews are often more detailed. Music fans should check out the weekly newspaper-style ***Melody Maker*** (80p) and ***New Musical Express*** (NME, 85p), or the glossy monthlies ***Vox*** (£2.20), ***Select*** (£2.30), and ***Q*** (£2.60), all of which often have free tapes attached. ***Wax*** (£2.20) focuses on DJ and club culture. And two other goodies among the bookshelves that are bursting with newies are ***The Wire*** (£2.50) and, for clubbing, ***Mixmag*** (£2.20).

Despite murmurs about its decline, the definitive style mag is still ***The Face*** (£2.20). Alongside articles on music and fashion, this monthly also has a comic strip by Jamie Hewlett, creator of Tank Girl. Another style bible is ***I-D*** (£2.20), which wipes out last month's fashion with every new issue. The ***Spectator*** (£2.20) provides news of the enlightened elite and the latest academic debate, while *Private Eye* (£1) dishes out satire so sharp it's sometimes difficult to feel the blade. The ***Economist*** (£2.20) provides comprehensive international news, though with a right-wing bent.

RADIO

London has innumerable pirate radio stations on the FM waveband that disappear as quickly as they appear. Some of the stations seem to serve as training grounds for the legal stations; talented DJs are snapped up, while others remain, singing along (off-key) with their favorite tracks. You'll hear some very obscure titles, and the DJs are sometimes amusing. The following FM mainstays aren't nearly as interesting: BBC Radio 1 (97.6) plays pop and indie music; BBC Radio 2 (88–90.2) plays those forty- or fiftysomething faves; BBC Radio 3 (90.2–92.4) is a sleepy classical station; and BBC Radio 4 (92.4–94.6) is talk, news, and documentary features radio. Jazz FM (102.2) plays jazz and blues, Heart (106.2) features old and new, and Kiss FM (100) plays dance music and often features celebrity DJs mixing live on the air. Capital FM (95.8) and Richard Branson's Virgin 1215 (105.8) offer a wide range of pop music; Gary Crowley's show on part-time talk-radio station GLR (94.9, Mon.–Thurs.10 PM–2 AM) is a great place to hear new British pop. For strictly news there's always London News (97.3).

MONEY MATTERS

For travelers with American dollars, prices in Britain are almost double what they are in the United States. It's more than just a bad exchange rate—the Brits themselves can hardly afford to live in the country. Even if you stay in hostels and eat pub grub, be prepared to drop $50 a day. If you plan to stay in hotels, take cabs, and eat in nice restaurants, that daily bill can easily top $100 per person. To add insult to injury, the British government slaps a whopping 17.5% Value Added Tax (VAT) on almost everything. VAT is usually included in prices, but not always. Lodging will be your greatest expense: Expect to pay around £10–£17 for a dorm bed or £15–£30 per person for a private room. Prices throughout this guide are given for adults. Substantially reduced fees are almost always available for children, students, and senior citizens. For information on taxes, *see* Taxes, *below.*

AMERICAN EXPRESS

American Express has plenty of offices in London that offer the usual array of services, including commission-free currency exchange for cardholders. Only the main office in the Haymarket (6 Haymarket, London SW1Y 4BS, tel. 020/7930–4411. Tube: Charing Cross or Piccadilly Circus. Open weekdays 9–5:30, Sat. 9–4 and until 6 for currency exchange, Sun. 10–6 for currency exchange only) handles client mail. Letter pickup is available during weekday business hours and weekends 9–noon.

Other full-service American Express locations in London include The City (111 Cheapside, tel. 020/7600–5522; Tube: Bank or St. Paul's); Knightsbridge (78 Brompton Rd., tel. 020/7584–6182; Tube: Knightsbridge); Mayfair (89 Mount St., tel. 020/7499–4436; Tube: Bond Street); and Victoria (102–104 Victoria St., tel. 020/7828–7411; Tube: Victoria). There are also a dozen other AmEx branches that only offer bureaux de change; look in the phone book for the location nearest you.

ATMS

To increase your chances of happy encounters with cash machines in London, make sure before leaving home that your card has been programmed for ATM use there—ATMs in London accept PINs of four or fewer digits only; if your PIN is longer, ask about changing it. If you know your PIN as a word, learn the numerical equivalent, since most London ATM keypads show numbers only, no letters. You should also have your credit card programmed for ATM use (note that Discover is accepted mostly in the United States). Local bank cards often do not work overseas or may access only your checking account; ask your bank about a MasterCard/Cirrus or Visa debit card, which works like a bank card but can be used at any ATM displaying a MasterCard/Cirrus or Visa logo. These cards, too, may tap only your checking account; check with your bank about their policy.

ATM LOCATIONS • Cirrus (tel. 800/424–7787). A list of Plus locations is available at your local bank.

BUREAUX DE CHANGE

While bureaux de change are everywhere in London, actually using them is like flushing money down the toilet—their exchange rates are 10%–15% worse than what the banks offer. The only exceptions are Thomas Cook, which has travel offices all over town, and American Express (*see above*); both charge bank rates for their respective checks. Otherwise, if you're desperate for cash after hours, Chequepoint has six 24-hour branches with competitive rates: 37–38 Coventry St. (tel. 020/7839–3772); 222 Earl's Court Rd. (tel. 020/7373–9515); 71 Gloucester Rd. (tel. 020/7379–9682); 548 Oxford St. (tel. 020/7723–1005); 2 Queensway (tel. 020/7229–0093); and Victoria Station (tel. 020/7828–0014). Know that exchange rates go up and down daily and even vary from branch to branch of a particular agency, so it pays to shop around.

CREDIT CARDS

Throughout this guide, the following abbreviations are used: **AE,** American Express; **DC,** Diner's Club; **MC,** Master Card; and **V,** Visa.

CURRENCY

The unit of currency in Great Britain is the pound (£), also known as a quid, broken into 100 pence. Exchange rates change daily, but at press time (1999), £1 was equal to $1.60 and $1 was equal to 70p. In Great Britain, pound notes (nobody calls them "bills") come in denominations of £5, £10, £20, and £50. Coins are available in denominations of 1p, 2p, 5p, 10p, 20p, 50p, £1, and £2. Older coins you may come across include the one-shilling coin (worth 5p) and the two-shilling coin (worth 10p). Remember that coins, no matter how valuable, are not exchangeable outside the borders of the United Kingdom.

CURRENCY EXCHANGE

For the most favorable rates, **change money through banks.** Although ATM transaction fees may be higher abroad than at home, ATM rates are excellent because they are based on wholesale rates offered only by major banks. You won't do as well at exchange booths in airports or rail and bus stations, in hotels, in restaurants, or in stores. To avoid lines at airport exchange booths **get a bit of local currency before you leave home.**

If you are **exchanging a currency from another European Union country** into pounds, do so free of charge at any branch of England's central bank, the **Bank of England** (Threadneedle St., London EC2R 8AH, tel. 020/7601–4444 or 020/7601–4878, fax 020/7601–5460, enquiries£bankofengland.co.uk). You may exchange any EU currency into the currency of the EU country you are in free of charge at any EU central bank. (It doesn't work the other way around, though: You cannot get Italian lire or French francs free of charge at the Bank of England. You can only exchange another currency into pounds free of charge.) To locate another central bank or for information about the European System of Central Banks, go to the web site www.ecb.int.

EXCHANGE SERVICES • International Currency Express (tel. 888/842–0880 on East Coast; 888/ 278–6628 on West Coast). **Thomas Cook Currency Services** (tel. 800/287–7362 for telephone orders and retail locations).

TRAVELER'S CHECKS

Do you need traveler's checks? It depends on where you're headed. If you're going to rural areas and small towns, go with cash; traveler's checks are best used in cities. Lost or stolen checks can usually be replaced within 24 hours. To ensure a speedy refund, buy your own traveler's checks—don't let someone else pay for them: irregularities like this can cause delays. The person who bought the checks should make the call to request a refund.

PACKING

In your carry-on luggage **bring an extra pair of eyeglasses or contact lenses** and **enough of any medication you take** to last the entire trip. You may also want your doctor to write a spare prescription using the drug's generic name, since brand names may vary from country to country. In luggage to be checked, **never pack prescription drugs or valuables.** To avoid customs delays, carry medications in their original packaging. And don't forget to copy down and carry addresses of offices that handle refunds of lost traveler's checks.

CHECKING LUGGAGE

How many carry-on bags you can bring with you is up to the airline. Most allow two, but not always, so make sure that everything you carry aboard will fit under your seat, and get to the gate early. Note that if you have a seat at the back of the plane, you'll probably board first, while the overhead bins are still empty.

If you are flying internationally, note that baggage allowances may be determined not by piece but by weight—generally 88 pounds (40 kg) in first class, 66 pounds (30 kg) in business class, and 44 pounds (20 kg) in economy.

Airline liability for baggage is limited to $1,250 per person on flights within the United States. On international flights it amounts to $9.07 per pound or $20 per kg for checked baggage (roughly $640 per 70-pound bag) and $400 per passenger for unchecked baggage. You can buy additional coverage at check-in for about $10 per $1,000 of coverage, but it excludes a rather extensive list of items, shown on your airline ticket.

Before departure **itemize your bags' contents** and their worth, and label the bags with your name, address, and phone number. (If you use your home address, cover it so that potential thieves can't see it readily.) Inside each bag **pack a copy of your itinerary.** At check-in **make sure that each bag is correctly tagged** with the destination airport's three-letter code. If your bags arrive damaged or fail to arrive at all, file a written report with the airline before leaving the airport.

PASSPORTS & VISAS

When traveling internationally **carry a passport even if you don't need one** (it's always the best form of ID), and **make two photocopies of the data page** (one for someone at home and another for you, carried separately from your passport). If you lose your passport promptly call the nearest embassy or consulate and the local police.

ENTERING THE U.K.

All U.S. citizens, even infants, need only a valid passport to enter Great Britain for stays of up to 90 days.

PASSPORT OFFICES

The best time to apply for a passport or to renew is during the fall and winter. Before any trip, check your passport's expiration date, and, if necessary, renew it as soon as possible.

AUSTRALIAN CITIZENS • Australian Passport Office (tel. 131–232).

CANADIAN CITIZENS • Passport Office (tel. 819/994–3500 or 800/567–6868).

NEW ZEALAND CITIZENS • New Zealand Passport Office (tel. 04/494–0700 for information on how to apply; 04/474–8000 or 0800/225–050 in New Zealand for information on applications already submitted).

U.S. CITIZENS • National Passport Information Center (tel. 900/225–5674; calls are 35¢ per minute for automated service, $1.05 per minute for operator service).

SAFETY

Money belts may be unfashionable and bulky, but it's better to be embarrassed than broke. You'd be wise to carry all cash, traveler's checks, credit cards, and your passport there or in some other inaccessible place: front or inner pocket, or a bag that fits underneath your clothes. Keep a copy of your passport somewhere else. Waist packs are safe if you keep the pack part in front of your body. Keep your bag attached to you if you plan on napping on the train. And never leave your belongings unguarded, even if you're only planning to be gone for a minute.

WOMEN IN LONDON

This being a notoriously polite culture, women can breathe a bit easier in London than, say, in Rome or Paris. Of course, urban precautions are still necessary, and men do still get "friendly" in pubs and clubs—practice snarling "Piss off!" They should catch your drift at that point.

LOCAL RESOURCES • If you're in need of emergency counseling or support, contact REFUGE (tel. 0990 995443 24 hours hotline) weekdays 10–1 and 2–4:45. The London Rape Crisis Centre (020/7837–1600) provides counseling 10–10. Women Welcome Women (WWW) is a nonprofit organization aimed at bringing together women of all nationalities, all ages, and all walks of life. Membership can put you in touch with women around the globe. Call or fax 01494/465441, or write to 88 Easton Street, High Wycombe, Bucks, HP11 1LT for more info.

SENIOR-CITIZEN TRAVEL

To qualify for age-related discounts **mention your senior-citizen status up front** when booking hotel reservations (not when checking out) and before you're seated in restaurants (not when paying the bill). When renting a car ask about promotional car-rental discounts, which can be cheaper than senior-citizen rates.

EDUCATIONAL PROGRAMS • Elderhostel (75 Federal St., 3rd floor, Boston, MA 02110, tel. 877/426–8056, fax 877/426–2166). **Interhostel** (University of New Hampshire, 6 Garrison Ave., Durham, NH 03824, tel. 603/862–1147 or 800/733–9753, fax 603/862–1113).

STUDENTS

To save money, look into deals available through student-oriented travel agencies and the various other organizations involved in helping out student and budget travelers. Typically, you'll find discounted airfares, rail passes, tours, lodgings, or other travel arrangements, and you don't necessarily have to be a student to qualify.

The big names in the field are **STA Travel,** with some 100 offices worldwide and a useful Web site (www.sta-travel.com), and the **Council on International Educational Exchange** (CIEE or "Council" for short), a private, nonprofit organization that administers work, volunteer, academic, and professional programs worldwide and sells travel arrangements through its own specialist travel agency, **Council Travel. Travel CUTS,** strictly a travel agency, sells discounted airline tickets to Canadian students from offices on or near college campuses. The **Educational Travel Center** (ETC) books low-cost flights to destinations within the continental United States and around the world. And **Student Flights, Inc.,** specializes in student and faculty airfares.

Most of these organizations also issue student identity cards, which entitle their bearers to special fares on local transportation and discounts at museums, theaters, sports events, and other attractions, as well as a handful of other benefits, which are listed in the handbook that most provide to their cardholders. Major cards include the International Student Identity Card (ISIC) and Go 25: International Youth Travel Card (GO25), available to nonstudents as well as students age 25 and under; the ISIC, when purchased in the United States, comes with $3,000 in emergency medical coverage and a few related benefits. Both the ISIC and GO25 are issued by Council Travel or STA in the United States, Travel CUTS in Canada, and at student unions and student-travel companies in the United Kingdom. The International Student Exchange Card (ISE), issued by Student Flights, Inc., is available to faculty members as well as students, and the International Teacher Identity Card (ITIC), issued by Travel CUTS, provides similar benefits to teachers in all grade levels, from kindergarten through graduate school. All student ID cards cost between $10 and $20.

STUDENT IDS AND SERVICES • Council on International Educational Exchange (CIEE, 205 E. 42nd St., 14th floor, New York, NY 10017, tel. 212/822–2600 or 888/268–6245, fax 212/822–2699), for mail orders only, in the United States.

Council Travel in the United States: **Arizona** (Tempe, tel. 602/966–3544). **California** (Berkeley, tel. 510/848–8604; Davis, tel. 916/752–2285; La Jolla, tel. 619/452–0630; Long Beach, tel. 310/598–3338; Los Angeles, tel. 310/208–3551; Palo Alto, tel. 415/325–3888; San Diego, tel. 619/270–6401; San Francisco, tel. 415/421–3473 or 415/566–6222; Santa Barbara, tel. 805/562–8080). **Colorado** (Boulder, tel. 303/447–8101; Denver, tel. 303/571–0630). **Connecticut** (New Haven, tel. 203/562–5335). **Florida** (Miami, tel. 305/670–9261). Georgia (Atlanta, tel. 404/377–9997). **Illinois** (Chicago, tel. 312/951–0585; Evanston, tel. 847/475–5070). **Indiana** (Bloomington, tel. 812/330–1600). **Iowa** (Ames, tel. 515/296–2326). **Kansas** (Lawrence, tel. 913/749–3900). **Louisiana** (New Orleans, tel. 504/866–1767). **Maryland** (College Park, tel. 301/779–1172). **Massachusetts** (Amherst, tel. 413/256–1261; Boston, tel. 617/266–1926; Cambridge, tel. 617/497–1497 or 617/225–2555). **Michigan** (Ann Arbor, tel. 313/998–0200). **Minnesota** (Minneapolis, tel. 612/379–2323). **New York** (New York, tel. 212/822–2700, 212/666–4177, or 212/254–2525). **North Carolina** (Chapel Hill, tel. 919/942–2334). **Ohio** (Columbus, tel. 614/294–8696). **Oregon** (Portland, tel. 503/228–1900). **Pennsylvania** (Philadelphia, tel. 215/382–0343; Pittsburgh, tel. 412/683–1881). **Rhode Island** (Providence, tel. 401/331–5810). **Tennessee** (Knoxville, tel. 423/523–9900). Texas (Austin, tel. 512/472–4931; Dallas, tel. 214/363–9941). **Utah** (Salt Lake City, tel. 801/582–5840). **Washington** (Seattle, tel. 206/632–2448 or 206/329–4567). **Washington, D.C.** (tel. 202/337–6464). In **Great Britain**: London (tel. 020/7437–7767).

STA in the U.S.: **California** (Berkeley, tel. 510/642–3000; Los Angeles, tel. 213/934–8722; San Francisco, tel. 415/391–8407; Santa Monica, tel. 310/394–5126; Westwood, tel. 310/824–1574). **Florida** (Miami, tel. 305/461–3444; University of Florida, tel. 352/338–0068). **Illinois** (Chicago, tel. 312/786–9050). **Massachusetts** (Boston, tel. 617/266–6014; Cambridge, tel. 617/576–4623). **New York** (Columbia University, tel. 212/865–2700; West Village, tel. 212/627–3111). **Pennsylvania** (Philadelphia, tel. 215/382–2928). **Washington** (Seattle, tel. 206/633–5000). **Washington, D.C.** (tel. 202/887–0912). In **Great Britain**: London (tel. 020/7361–6123).

Student Flights (5010 E. Shea Blvd., Suite A104, Scottsdale, AZ 85254, tel. 602/951–1177 or 800/255–8000). **Travel Cuts** (187 College St., Toronto, Ontario M5T 1P7, tel. 416/979–2406 or 800/667–2887) in Canada.

STUDYING IN LONDON

Studying in London is the perfect way to shake up your perception of the world and make international friends. You may choose to study through a U.S.-sponsored program, usually through an American university, or to enroll in a program sponsored by a British organization. Do your homework: Programs vary greatly in expense, academic quality, amount of contact with locals, and living conditions. Working through your local university is the easiest way to find out about study-abroad programs in London. Most universities have staff members who distribute information on programs at European universities, and they might be able to put you in touch with program participants. Most programs require that you stay a semester or a year.

RESOURCES • American Institute for Foreign Study (102 Greenwich Ave., Greenwich, CT 06830, tel. 203/869–9090 or 800/727–2437, fax 203/869–9615). **American Council of International Studies** (ACIS; 19 Bay St., Boston, MA 02215, tel. 617/236–2051 or 800/888–2247). **Council on International Educational Exchange** (*see* Students, *above*). **Institute of International Education** (IIE; 809 U.N. Plaza, New York, NY 10017, tel. 212/984–5413). **World Learning** (Kipling Rd., Box 676, Brattleboro, VT 05302, tel. 802/257–7751 or 800/451–4465, fax 802/258–3248).

TAXES

AIRPORT

Travelers departing the United Kingdom must pay a £10 (within EU) or £10 (outside EU) Air Passenger Duty.

VALUE-ADDED TAX (VAT)

The British sales tax (VAT) is 17.5%. The tax is almost always included in quoted prices in shops, hotels, and restaurants.

You can get a VAT refund by either the Retail Export or the more cumbersome Direct Export method. Most large stores provide these services, but only if you request them, and will handle the paperwork. For the Retail Export method, you must ask the store for Form VAT 407 (you must have identification—passports are best), to be given to customs at your last port of departure. (Lines at major airports can be long, so allow plenty of time.) The refund will be forwarded to you in about eight weeks, minus a small service charge, either in the form of a credit to your charge card or as a British check, which American banks usually charge you to convert. With the Direct Export method, the goods go directly to your home; you must have a Form VAT 407 certified by customs, police, or a notary public when you get home and then sent back to the store, which will refund your money. For inquiries, call the local Customs & Excise office listed in the telephone directory.

Global Refund is a V.A.T. refund service that makes getting your money back hassle-free. Global Refund services are offered in more than 130,000 shops worldwide. In participating stores, **ask for a Global Refund Cheque when making a purchase**—this Cheque will clearly state the amount of your refund in local currency, with the service charge already incorporated (the service charge equals approximately 3%–4% of the purchase price of the item). Global Refund can also process other custom forms, though for a higher fee. When leaving the European Union, get your Global Refund Cheque and any customs forms stamped by the customs official. You can take them to the cash refund office at the airport, where your money will be refunded right there in cash, by check, or a refund to your credit card. Alternatively, you can mail your validated Cheque to Global Refund, and your credit card account will automatically be credited within three billing cycles. Global Refund has a fax-back service further clarifying the process.

VAT REFUNDS • Global Refund (707 Summer St., Stamford, CT 06901, tel. 800/566–9828).

TAXIS

Cabs are the most expensive form of transportation in London, but they can be reasonable if you're splitting the cost with a few other people. Traditional "black cabs," which are not always black, are the most reliable. Drivers of these classy carriages have to pass a rigorous test of London streets, known as "The Knowledge," and are required to take passengers on the most direct route possible. That's not a guarantee that every cabbie is 100% honest, which is why all cabs are equipped with a meter and fare table. Weekday fares start at £1.40 and go up 20p per unit of distance/time (every 257 yards or 56 seconds). There are surcharges for each additional person (40p), each piece of luggage (10p), and booking a cab by telephone (£1.20 minimum). If you're traveling on a weekday after 8 PM or on weekends, rates increase 40p–60p. There's a £2 surcharge for rides during the jolly Christmas and New Year's periods. Ho, ho, ho. It's customary to tip the driver 10% of your fare. If you wish to make a complaint, note the cab number and/or the number of the driver's badge; then contact Metropolitan Police's Public Carriage Office (tel. 020/7230–1631 for complaints or 020/7833–0996 for lost property), open weekdays 9–4.

Cabs are easy to hail at all times—except when you really need them, like on weekend nights and when it suddenly begins to pour. To hail a cab on the street, first check that its yellow FOR HIRE sign is switched on, and then flail away. You can also phone ahead for a cab—but keep in mind that companies slap a hefty surcharge on "collections."

TAXI COMPANIES • Radio Taxis (tel. 020/7272–0272) is a 24-hour black-cab company that charges a maximum collection fee of £2.40. **Ladycabs** (tel. 020/7254–3314) is a northeast-London-based minicab service for women who'd rather be driven by women.

MINICABS

An alternative to black cabs are minicabs—their fares can sometimes be cheaper, especially if you're traveling long distances or at night. They are run by private companies or individual drivers, and look just like regular cars. Although it's illegal for minicabs to pick up passengers on the street—you're supposed to call or walk into their office—you can usually find them lurking outside of clubs and on West End corners during the weekend wee hours. Because minicabs aren't licensed or regulated like black cabs, bargaining is possible—but to avoid nasty surprises always confirm the price with the driver before you get in the car. The down side to not being licensed means there is nothing to stop some drivers from taking advantage of "innocents abroad." If you are going to take a mini cab, try to sound like you know the direction (a quick check of the map might help), otherwise you could end up having a rather unpleasant argument at the conclusion of your trip. And a final word: mini cabs are not recommended for women traveling alone late at night.

MINICAB COMPANIES • Abbey Cars (west London, tel. 020/7727–2637). Greater London Hire (north London, tel. 020/8340–2450). London Cabs Limited (east London, tel. 020/8778–3000).

TELEPHONES

COUNTRY & AREA CODES

The country code for Great Britain is 44. When dialing a British number from abroad, drop the initial 0 from the local area code. To give one example: Let's say you're outside Great Britain, calling Buckingham Palace—020/7839–1377—in London to inquire about tours and hours. First, dial 011 (the international access code), then 44 (Great Britain's country code), then 020 (London's city code, dropping the 0), then the remainder of the telephone number. If you come across the outdated 0171 and 0181 codes, replace either with the new 020 code and add either a 7 (from 0171) or an 8 (from 0181) to the front of the local number. For example, 0171/123–4567 would become 020/7123–4567 and 0181/987–6543 will become 020/8987–6543.

The country code is 1 for the United States and Canada, 61 for Australia, 64 for New Zealand, and 44 for the United Kingdom.

LOCAL CALLS

Local calls start at 10p. Modern pay phones display how fast your money is being gobbled up; older phones without displays beep when your money is about to run out. Pay phones will give back any unused coins fed into the slot, but they don't make change, so think twice about using a £1 coin for a local call. If you have credit left and need to make another call, don't hang up. Instead, press the "follow-on call" button—on new phones it's marked, on older phones look for a small, square button away from the keypad—to use the remaining credit. If there's someone waiting when you're on the phone, and you have credit left, it's good karma to press the follow-on button and hand the receiver to the other person.

LONG-DISTANCE CALLS

For long-distance calls within Britain, dial the area code (which usually begins with a 01), followed by the number. To dial overseas direct from England, first dial 00, then dial the country code (1 for the United States and Canada, 353 for the Republic of Ireland, 61 for Australia, and 64 for New Zealand), then the area code and phone number. Calls to Northern Ireland from England, Scotland, or Wales can be dialed without the international code. To dial direct or collect using American carriers, contact AT&T Direct Access℠, MCI, or Sprint—the call to the carrier is free. Direct dialing is considerably more expensive from pay phones than from private ones, but many residential phone bills don't itemize calls, so it's difficult to reimburse your hosts. Have a phone card with lots of credit or a ton of change ready, especially £1 coins. To place an incredibly expensive collect call using BT, dial 155 to be connected with an operator.

LONG-DISTANCE SERVICES

AT&T, MCI, and Sprint access codes make calling long distance relatively convenient, but you may find the local access number blocked in many hotel rooms. First ask the hotel operator to connect you. If the hotel operator balks ask for an international operator, or dial the international operator yourself. One way to improve your odds of getting connected to your long-distance carrier is to travel with more than one company's calling card (a hotel may block Sprint, for example, but not MCI). If all else fails call from a pay phone.

ACCESS CODES • AT&T USADirect (tel. 0800/890011 or 0500/890011). If you're in Great Britain and wish to dial a telephone number in the United States, first dial 0800/013–0011. A USADirect operator will then log on to ask you for the U.S. area code and number plus your private telephone card number for billing. With Touch-Tone phones, this will be done automatically.

MCI Call USA (tel. 0800/890222). Calling from the United Kingdom to the United States, dial 0800/890222. A World Phone operator will then come on the line, request your private telephone card number for billing, and will then access the number you wish to call in the United States. With Touch-Tone phones, this will be done automatically.

Sprint Global One (tel. 0800/890877). From the United Kingdom to the United States dial 0800/890877. A Sprint Global One operator will then come on line to ask you for your card number and the U.S telephone number you wish to access. With Touch-Tone phones, this will be done automatically.

PHONE CARDS

Phone cards are available at newsagents, train and bus stations, tourist-information centers, and numerous other locations. Look for signs saying PHONECARDS SOLD HERE. Phone cards come with a fixed number of units (10, 20, 50, or 100), each valued at 10p.

PUBLIC PHONES

British Telecom (BT) is the major phone company operating in England, Scotland, and Wales although it is fast been caught up by **Cable & Wireless.** BT pay phones are easy to find throughout the United Kingdom. The ones with a red stripe around them accept standard English coins, while phones with a green stripe require the use of a phone card.

TIME

England sets its clocks by Greenwich Mean Time, five hours ahead of U.S. Eastern Standard Time. British summer time (GMT plus one hour) requires an additional adjustment from about the end of March to the end of October.

TIPPING

In the United Kingdom, you only tip generously if the service is excellent. Standard practice is to tip 10%–15% in taxis and restaurants (unless service is included). Bartenders are almost never tipped.

TOURS & PACKAGES

On a prepackaged tour or independent vacation everything is prearranged so you'll spend less time planning—and often get it all at a good price.

BOOKING WITH AN AGENT

Travel agents are excellent resources. But it's a good idea to collect brochures from several agencies because some agents' suggestions may be influenced by relationships with tour and package firms that reward them for volume sales. If you have a special interest **find an agent with expertise in that area**; ASTA (*see* Travel Agencies, *below*) has a database of specialists worldwide.

Make sure your travel agent knows the accommodations and other services of the place they're recommending. Ask about the hotel's location, room size, beds, and whether it has a pool, room service, or programs for children, if you care about these. Has your agent been there in person or sent others whom you can contact?

Do some homework on your own, too: Local tourism boards can provide information about lesser-known and small-niche operators, some of which may sell only direct.

BUYER BEWARE

Each year consumers are stranded or lose their money when tour operators—even large ones with excellent reputations—go out of business. So **check out the operator.** Ask several travel agents about its reputation, and try to **book with a company that has a consumer-protection program.** (Look for information in the company's brochure.) In the United States, members of the National Tour Association and United States Tour Operators Association are required to set aside funds to cover your payments and travel arrangements in case the company defaults. It's also a good idea to choose a company that participates in the American Society of Travel Agent's Tour Operator Program (TOP); ASTA will act as mediator in any disputes between you and your tour operator.

Remember that the more your package or tour includes the better you can predict the ultimate cost of your vacation. Make sure you know exactly what is covered, and **beware of hidden costs.** Are taxes, tips, and transfers included? Entertainment and excursions? These can add up.

TOUR-OPERATOR RECOMMENDATIONS • American Society of Travel Agents (*see* Travel Agencies, *below*). **National Tour Association** (NTA, 546 E. Main St., Lexington, KY 40508, tel. 606/226–4444 or 800/682–8886). **United States Tour Operators Association** (USTOA, 342 Madison Ave., Suite 1522, New York, NY 10173, tel. 212/599–6599 or 800/468–7862, fax 212/599–6744).

PACKAGES

The companies listed below offer vacation packages in a broad price range.

AIR/HOTEL • American Airlines Fly AAway Vacations (tel. 800/321–2121). **British Airways Holidays** (tel. 800/AIRWAYS). **Celtic International Tours** (1860 Western Ave., Albany, NY 12203, tel. 518/463–5511 or 800/833–4373). **Continental Vacations** (tel. 800/634–5555). **Delta Dream Vacations** (tel. 800/872–7786). **DER Tours** (11933 Wilshire Blvd., Los Angeles, CA 90025, tel. 310/479–4140 or 800/937–1235). **United Vacations** (tel. 800/328–6877).

Also contact **Budget WorldClass Drive** (tel. 800/527–0700, 0800/181181 in the U.K.) for self-drive itineraries.

TRAIN TRAVEL

London has eight major train stations (as well as a bunch of smaller ones). Each serves a specific part of the country (or the Continent), so be sure to figure out beforehand where your train leaves from. For nationwide 24-hour train information, call 0345/484950 (accessible from the United Kingdom only). All eight stations have tourist and travel information booths, rip-off bureaux de change, and luggage storage (£2–£5 per day). They are also all served by the London Underground, so it's easy to get around after you arrive in London.The **British Travel Centre** (*see* Visitor Information, *below*) can provide you with train schedules, ticket prices, and other information. The Great Britain Passenger Railway Timetable (£7.50), issued every May and October, contains details of all BritRail services; pick up one at any major train station. If you have questions while still in the United States, the overseas number to call is 020/7928–5151.

Charing Cross serves southeast England, including Canterbury and Dover/Folkestone, and is on the Northern, Bakerloo, and Jubilee tube lines. Strand, WC2.

Euston serves the Midlands, north Wales, northwest England, and western Scotland and is on the Northern and Victoria tube lines. Euston Rd., NW1.

King's Cross marks the end of the Great Northern line, serving northeast England, and Scotland. King's Cross is on the Circle, Metropolitan, Piccadilly, Hammersmith & City, Northern, and Victoria tube lines. York Way, N1.

Liverpool Street serves East Anglia, including Cambridge and Norwich, and is on the Central, Hammersmith & City, Metropolitan, and Circle tube lines. Liverpool St., EC2.

Paddington mainly serves South Wales and the West Country, as well as Reading, Oxford, Worcester, and Bristol. Paddington is on the Circle, Bakerloo, District, and Hammersmith & City tube lines. Praed St., W2.

St. Pancras serves Leicester, Nottingham, and Sheffield and is on the Victoria, Northern, Hammersmith & City, Circle, Piccadilly, and Metropolitan tube lines. Pancras Rd., NW1.

Victoria serves southern England, including Brighton, Dover/Folkestone, and the south coast. Victoria is on the Circle, District, and Victoria tube lines. Terminus Pl., SW1.

Waterloo serves southeastern destinations like Portsmouth and Southampton and is on the Bakerloo and Northern tube lines. York Rd., SE1.

NATIONAL RAIL LINES

The national rail system is a network of above-ground train services that connects outlying districts and suburbs to central London. Recent privatization means its various routes are now handled by a variety of companies; one you're likely to encounter is the North London Line (tel. 0345/484950), running from Richmond to North Woolwich with stops at Kew Gardens, Holburn, Hampstead, Hackney, and Docklands. Prices for overground trains are comparable to prices for the Underground, and you can easily transfer between the Underground and other connecting rail lines at many tube stations (transfer points are marked on tube maps). You can sometimes even use your LT Travelcard (*see* Underground Travel, *below*) instead of buying a separate ticket.

CUTTING COSTS

Compare costs for rail passes and individual tickets. If you plan to cover a lot of ground in a short period, rail passes may be worth your while; they also spare you the time waiting in lines to buy tickets. To price individual tickets of the rail trips you plan, ask a travel agent or call Rail Europe, Railpass Express, or DER Tours. It's cheaper to travel during off-hours. Many lines charge double the amount during the early morning and early evening rush hours, so it's best to travel before or after the frantic business commuter hours. For instance, a round-trip ticket to London from Bath can cost £62 per person at peak, but only £28 at other times. An APEX ticket bought seven days in advance can save even more, and cost only around £14. If you're under 26 on your first day of travel, you're eligible for a youth pass, valid for second-class travel only (like Europass Youth, Eurail Youth Flexipass, or Eurail Youthpass). If you're older, you must buy one of the more expensive regular passes, valid for first-class travel, and it might cost you less to buy individual tickets, especially if your tastes and budget call for second-class travel. Be sure to **buy your rail pass before leaving the United States**; those available elsewhere cost more. Finally, don't assume that your rail pass guarantees you a seat on every train—seat reservations are required on some trains; see your travel agent.

BRITISH PASSES • If you plan on covering a lot of ground, it may be worth investing in a **BritRail Pass,** since full-price tickets (especially one-way) can be very expensive in the United Kingdom. Also remember that most BritRail passes cannot be purchased in the United Kingdom—you must **get them before you leave home.** An adult **Second-Class Pass** costs $265 for eight days, $400 for 15 days, $505 for 22 days, and $600 for one month; all entitle you to free travel on BritRail trains in England, Scotland, Wales, and Northern Ireland. If you're 16–25 years old, consider a **BritRail Youth Pass.** It allows unlimited second-class travel in the following increments: $215 for eight days, $280 for 15 days, $355 for 22 days, and $420 for one month. Another option is the **Brit-Ireland Pass,** valid for travel on trains throughout Great Britain and Ireland and Sealink ferry service between the two, and available in the following increments: 5 out of 30 days ($408) and 10 out of 30 days ($570). All passes are available from most travel agents and from the **BritRail Travel Information Office** (1500 Broadway, New York, NY 10036, tel. 800/677–8585 in the U.S.; 94 Cumberland St., Toronto, Ontario M5R 1A3, tel. 416/482–1777 in Canada).

About the only worthwhile pass available in Britain is the **Young Person's Railcard**; it costs £18 from any main line rail station and is good for ⅓ off most train tickets—an investment that will pay you back immediately. However, you must be under 26 to purchase one; also, you'll need two passport-size photos. Another option is a regional rail pass, which entitles you to free travel within a certain region (e.g., within Wales, Scotland, or Cornwall). These passes must be purchased in the United Kingdom; stop by any main line station for more info or call National Rail (tel. 0345/484950) for details. Prices and schemes will vary according to the issuing rail company (there are now 25 in all).

REGIONAL RAIL PASSES • If you want to explore a specific part of Britain at length, unlimited travel tickets offer excellent value. For price structures and details go to a larger train station, such as Victoria, Paddington, or King's Cross, which is the feeder for that main line out of London, or a national rail travel agent. Tickets are available for Scotland, Wales, and the many different regions of England. A more varied and separate series of tickets covers the Southeast and the London area.

TRAVEL AGENCIES

A good travel agent puts your needs first. Look for an agency that has been in business at least five years, emphasizes customer service, and has someone on staff who specializes in your destination. In addition **make sure the agency belongs to a professional trade organization.** The American Society of Travel Agents (ASTA), with 27,000 agents in some 170 countries, is the largest and most influential in the field. Operating under the motto "Integrity in Travel," it maintains and enforces a strict code of ethics and will step in to help mediate any agent-client disputes if necessary. ASTA also maintains a Web site that includes a directory of agents. (Note that if a travel agency is also acting as your tour operator, *see* Buyer Beware *in* Tours & Packages, *above.*)

LOCAL AGENT REFERRALS • American Society of Travel Agents (ASTA, tel. 800/965–2782 24-hr hot line, fax 703/684–8319, www.astanet.com). **Association of British Travel Agents** (68–271 Newman St., London W1P 4AH, tel. 020/7637–2444, fax 020/7637–0713). **Association of Canadian Travel Agents** (1729 Bank St., Suite 201, Ottawa, Ontario K1V 7Z5, tel. 613/521–0474, fax 613/521–0805). **Australian Federation of Travel Agents** (Level 3, 309 Pitt St., Sydney 2000, tel. 02/9264–3299, fax 02/9264–1085). **Travel Agents' Association of New Zealand** (Box 1888, Wellington 10033, tel. 04/499–0104, fax 04/499–0786).

THE UNDERGROUND

Officially known as the Underground, and nicknamed the "Tube," London's amazing subway system provides comprehensive service throughout central London and more sporadic service to the suburbs. Underground stations are marked by a large red circle overlaid by a blue banner that reads UNDERGROUND. London is served by a dozen Underground lines, each color-coded; it can seem extremely confusing until you get used to it, and you'll find yourself constantly referring to the Underground map.

If you don't plan to use public transport a lot, buy individual tickets for each journey—choose between single and return, the British equivalents of one-way and round-trip. You can also buy a carnet, a packet of 10 single tickets. Otherwise, buy a Travelcard (*see* Fares & Schedules, *below*). Once again, ticket prices are based on zones. Zone 1, the cool zone, is a bit pricier than all the other zones: Scooting around inside it costs £1.30 single (£2.60 for a return ticket). Travel inside any one of the other zones is 90p single (£1.80 return), while a trip through all six zones costs £3.80 single. You can buy tickets at electronic vending machines in most stations or at "Tickets and Assistance" windows. Remember to hold on to your ticket since you'll need it to get through the turnstiles at the exit. And beware: Roving inspectors issue an on-the-spot £10 penalty if you're caught without a ticket valid for the zones you're traveling in.

The Underground gets going around 5 AM and closes between 11:30 PM and 12:30 AM, depending on which station you're in; you'll find the timetable for each station posted near the turnstiles. Generally the Tube is pretty reliable, with trains every 10 minutes—but a multimillion-pound overhaul of new line extensions has recently meant temporary station closures and route changes; listen for announcements in each station. You can roughly calculate how long a particular journey should take by adding three minutes for each station you'll pass through. Because the Tube closes before the rest of London does, it pays to figure out London's Night Buses (*see* Bus Travel, *above*) if you plan to party late.

FARES & SCHEDULES

Fares for the Underground, Docklands Light Railway, and overground rail (*see below*) are based on zones. The Underground, Docklands Light Railway, and BritRail services are divided into zones 1–6. The bus network is divided into four zones: 1, 2, 3, and Bus Zone 4. (Bus Zone 4 covers approximately the same area as zones 4, 5, and 6 for the Underground and railways.) The more zones you cross through on your trip, the more you pay. With few exceptions, everything you want to see will be within Zone 1 (which covers Westminster, Piccadilly Circus, Soho, Trafalgar Square, Covent Garden, the City, Victoria, Earl's Court, Kensington, and more) and Zone 2 (which includes Camden, Hampstead, the East End, Brixton, and Greenwich Park). For more info, pick up LT's free brochures "Buying Your Ticket Made Easier" and "London Transport Fares and Tickets."

The best way to get around London is with a Travelcard available at the "Tickets and Assistance" windows at most Tube and train stations, from some vending machines in Underground ticket halls, from LT's Travel Information Centres, and from any newsstand or tobacconist displaying the LT PASS AGENT sign. The most popular is the Travelcard for zones 1 and 2, which costs £3.80 daily, £17.60 weekly, and

£64.20 monthly. Your Travelcard gets you almost unlimited use of the Underground, London Transport buses (except Airbuses), Docklands Light Railway, and most overground rail services within greater London. (One-Day Travelcards aren't valid on Night Buses, but the rest are.) You need a passport-type photo if you're buying a Travelcard good for a week or more, and a local address—a hostel or hotel address should work fine. LT's Weekend Travelcard works like the One-Day Travelcard but entitles you to two consecutive days' discounted travel on weekends or public holidays; for zones 1 and 2 the cost is £5.20.

DOCKLANDS LIGHT RAILWAY • The Docklands, the massive area east of central London along the Thames River, is served by Docklands Light Railway (DLR), which connects with the Underground at the following stations: Bank, Bow Road, Shadwell, Stratford, and Tower Hill. Dockland's Light Railway trains are overseen by London Transport and use the same system of passes, zones, and fares as the buses and Underground. Its two lines also show up on tube maps. Hours of operation are Monday–Saturday 5:30 AM–midnight and Sunday 7:30 AM–11:30 PM. The **London Travel Information Line** (tel. 020/7918–4000) offers info, including on DLR, 24 hours a day. **DLR Customer Services** (tel. 020/7363–9700) also gives a similar service.

UNDERGROUND INFORMATION • London Transport operates Travel Information Centres at all Heathrow terminals and in the following tube stations: Euston, King's Cross, Liverpool Street, Oxford Circus, Piccadilly Circus, St. James's Park, and Victoria. You'll want to get your hands on two of LT's free maps (available at all tube stations) when you get into town: the pocket-size "Tube Map" and "Travelling in London," which show Underground stops and bus lines for tourist attractions in central London. Travelers with disabilities should get the "Access to the Underground" brochure (70p), which includes info on lifts and ramps, as well as Braille maps.

HELP LINES • **London Transport** (LT; tel. 020/7222–1200 for recorded info or 020/7222–1234 for 24-hour help with routes, schedules, and fares).

VISITOR INFORMATION

IN THE U.S., CANADA, AND U.K. • Contact the **British Tourist Authority (BTA).** In the United States: (551 5th Ave., 7th floor, New York, NY 10176, tel. 212/986–2200 or 800/462–2748; 625 N. Michigan Ave., Suite 1510, Chicago, IL 60611 [walk-in visitors only]; Box 711087, Los Angeles, CA 90071, tel. 213/628–5731); in Canada (111 Avenue Rd., 4th floor, Toronto, Ontario M5R 3J8, tel. 416/925–6326); in the United Kingdom (Thames Tower, Black's Rd., London W6 9EL, tel. 020/8846–9000).

IN LONDON • Go in person to the **London Tourist Information** Centre at Victoria Station Forecourt for general information: in summer, Monday–Saturday 8–7 and Sunday 8–5: in winter, Monday–Saturday 8–6 and Sunday 8:30–4. Or go to the **British Travel Centre** (12 Regent St., SW1Y 4PQ) for travel, hotel, and entertainment information weekdays 9–6:30, weekends 10–4 (Saturday 9–5, May–September). Other information centers are located in Harrods (Brompton Rd.; Tube: Knightsbridge), Selfridges (Oxford St.; Tube: Bond Street or Marble Arch), Liverpool Street Station, Waterloo International Terminal, Heathrow Airport (Terminals 1, 2, and 3), and Gatwick Airport (International Arrivals Concourse).

BY PHONE AND FAX • The London Tourist Board's **Visitorcall** (tel. 0839/123456) phone guide to London gives information about events, theater, museums, transport, shopping, and restaurants. A three-month events calendar (tel. 0839/401279) and an annual version (tel. 0839/401278) are available by fax (set fax machine to polling mode, or press start/receive after the tone). Visitorcall charges are 39p–49p per minute, depending on the time of the call. In addition, the British Tourist Authority offers a 24-hour **Fax Information Line** (tel. 310/820–4770). The deal with this service is that you phone from a fax machine, listen to a menu, make a selection, then receive instant info by fax.

U.S. GOVERNMENT ADVISORIES • **U.S. Department of State** (Overseas Citizens Services Office, Room 4811 N.S., 2201 C St. NW, Washington, DC 20520; tel. 202/647–5225 for interactive hot line; 301/946–4400 for computer bulletin board; fax 202/647–3000 for interactive hot line); enclose a self-addressed, stamped, business-size envelope.

WEB SITES

Do **check out the World Wide Web** when you're planning your trip. You'll find everything from up-to-date weather forecasts to virtual tours of famous cities. Fodor's Web site www.fodors.com, is a great place to start your online travels. Another excellent site is the UK Directory (www.ukdirectory.com), which provides pretty comprehensive listings of all Web sites in the country as well as hundreds of links. Or try

What's New (www.emap.com/whatsnew) for a constantly updated list of the U.K.'s new Internet sites. The on-line version of the Sunday *Times* (www.sunday-times.co.uk) won the "Hottest Site on the Net" Award at the 1996 UK Web Awards; you'll be surprised how much British news is missing from U.S. newspapers. The computer version of *Time Out* (www.timeout.co.uk) doesn't provide you with the week's full listings, but it does have some information and a backfile of stories from previous issues. Like its newspaper equivalent, on-line Loot (www.lootlink.com) is a free ads service selling everything from cars to Caribbean vacations to fish tanks. It's a good place to begin that search for a hotel. For more info on where to find Internet access in London, *see* Media, *above*.

WHEN TO GO

The main tourist season runs from mid-April to mid-October, but hordes really arrive in June, July, and August—consider yourself warned. In summer, prices predictably go up, and many hostels and cheap hotels stop offering weekly rates. Even so, the daffodils and crocuses are in full bloom, and British high society hits its stride with events like Wimbledon and the Royal Ascot. In winter, with all the crowds gone, London refuses to hibernate. In fact, the hardy visitor is more likely to get an honest—albeit a cold and wet—view of the city during the off-season, without the troops of Americans, Australians, French, Japanese, and everyone else who tries to "do" London in two days.

CLIMATE

London is well known for its errant weather. Summer days can be excruciatingly hot and smoggy or cool and overcast. Fall is generally mild. In recent years, winter temperatures have fallen below freezing for short spells. (Beware: The air is damp and the cold seems to go right to your bones.) In spring the weather is incredibly schizophrenic: Sun, rain, and hail can follow one another in rapid succession, and temperatures can fluctuate from the mid-40s to high 60s.

FORECASTS • Weather Channel Connection (tel. 900/932–8437), 95¢ per minute from a Touch-Tone phone.

London's average highs and lows stack up as follows: **January** 37°F/43°F; **April** 42°F/56°F; **July** 56°F/71°F; **October** 45°F/58°F.

FESTIVALS

London has more festivals, street fairs, and royal parades than you can shake a gilded scepter at; what's listed below is merely the tip of the iceberg. For the scoop while you're in town, check the weekly magazine ***Time Out*** (£1.70), available at newsstands. Or, dial London Tourist Board's 24-hour ***VisitorCall*** (tel. 0839/123400 in U.K. only) service, which offers the latest on events throughout the city for 49p per minute. Many of the events listed below are free, though biggies like Wimbledon are not.

JANUARY • The morning after the huge New Year's Eve bash in Trafalgar Square, the fun continues with the splashy, multinational **London Parade** (January 1), which starts at Westminster Bridge and ends at Berkeley Square. On the last Sunday in January, Londoners dressed in 17th-century garb celebrate the **Charles I Commemoration**—held on the anniversary of the monarch's execution—with a march tracing his last walk from St. James's Palace to the Banqueting House in Whitehall.

FEBRUARY • Accession Day Gun Salute (February 6) is a spectacular sight: The Royal Horse Artillery gallops through Hyde Park pulling massive gun carriages, then sets up for a noontime 41-gun salute just across from the Dorchester Hotel. **Chinese New Year** is celebrated on the first Sunday of its new year with lots of firecrackers, lion and dragon dancers, and street performers around Gerrard Street and Newport Place in Chinatown, Soho. Check with Visitorcall (*see above*) for up-to-date details.

MARCH • In early March, the sizzling **Camden Jazz Festival** stirs things up in hip north London; watch for posters around town and check *Time Out* for ticket info. On **St. Patrick's Day** (March 17) raise a celebratory glass of Guinness with resident Irish folk in pubs throughout the city. At the **Head of the River Boat Race,** you can watch 420 eight-man crews from Oxford and Cambridge universities dip their 6,720 oars in the Thames as they race from Mortlake to Putney. The best view is from Surrey Bank above Chiswick Bridge (BritRail: Chiswick); check *Time Out* for the starting time, which depends on the tide.

APRIL • In early April, Londoners don medieval garb and parade from Southwark Cathedral to the Tower of London for the **Chaucer Festival** (tel. 01227/470379). The fete continues at the Tower, with food, jugglers, and strolling minstrels. Battersea Park (Tube: Vauxhall) is the place to watch the festive floats and marching bands of the **Easter Parade** as well as the **London Harness Horse Parade** (Easter Monday), in which trusty steeds are put through their paces to compete for prizes. The **London**

Marathon is one of the great spectacles of the running world with its enthusiastic crowds and more than 25,000 panting participants. Great places to catch the spectacle include Tower Bridge (Tube: Tower Hill) and at the finish line in The Mall (Tube: Green Park); for more info and entry forms, call 020/7620–4117. In this town the **Queen's Birthday** (April 21) still earns a showy 41-gun salute, at Hyde Park, along the lines of Accession Day (*see* February, *above*).

MAY • You may have noticed that Londoners from Prince Charles on down are mad for marigolds and dotty for daisies, but the flora-inspired really bust loose for the ultrahyped, four-day **Chelsea Flower Show** (tel. 020/7834–4333). Tickets must be purchased in advance and usually sell out—check any local newspaper or *Time Out* for details. **Beating the Bounds** is a quaint Ascension Day tradition dating from medieval days when local parishes marked their spiritual and financial territory by beating young boys at the boundaries. These days only the boundaries get beaten, and it's now a coed affair that culminates with a boy or girl beating the "boundary line" down the middle of the Thames with a cane while upended from the Queen's yacht. The procession starts from All Hallows Church at 3 PM and returns in time for evensong (around 4 PM).

JUNE • The **Beating Retreat Ceremony** brings out the best of the Household Division in a floodlit spectacle of marching bands and soldiers on horseback. **Trooping the Colour** (tel. 020/7414–2479), celebrates the official birthday of the Queen and features a contingent of troops accompanied by much pomp and circumstance involving dress uniforms, marching bands, a fly-by by the Royal Air Force, and several gun salutes. The **Royal Meeting at Ascot** brings the horsey set and their enormous hats out in force; *see* Spectator Sports *in* Chapter 8, for more information. The vibrant **City of London Festival** (tel. 020/7377–0540) fills the City with theater, poetry, classical music, and dance performed by a host of internationally known artists. Thespians and their friends flock to London in odd-numbered years for the innovative performances mounted during the **London International Festival of Theatre** (LIFT; tel. 020/7490–3964), held during the month of June. Tickets are allocated by a ballot from August to end of December the previous year for seats at **Wimbledon** (tel. 020/8944–1066), the world's most prestigious tennis competition, but you can still get in if you're prepared to wait in line; *see* Spectator Sports *in* Chapter 8, for details.

JULY • On the first Saturday in July, London's huge **Gay Pride Festival** rallies, parties, and sashays around Clapham Common; check the local gay press or call Pride Trust (tel. 020/7737–6903) for information. From early July until mid-August **The Great Outdoors on the South Bank** (tel. 020/7960–4242) series hosts free weekend entertainment that runs the gamut from ethnic music to French street theater. The **Streets of London Festival** (tel. 01273/821588) brings free music, theater, art, and comedy to public spaces all over London from early July to early September. At the **Royal Tournament** (tel. 020/7373–8141), from late July to early August, a cast of thousands wraps itself in a blow-out of jingoism and glittery pageantry at Earl's Court Exhibition Centre. All branches of the armed forces take part in this Las Vegas/Hollywood/Andrew Lloyd Webber–style spectacle. The four-day **Phoenix Festival** (tel. 020/8963–0940) brings some 350 dance, jazz, folk, rock, and comedy acts to Long Marston near Stratford-upon-Avon on the second or third weekend in July. From mid-July through September the Royal Albert Hall is home to one of the world's premier classical music events, the **BBC Henry Wood Promenade Concerts** (tel. 020/7765–5575)—better known as the "Proms"; *see* Classical Music, Opera, and Dance *in* Chapter 6, for more info.

AUGUST • It's beer heaven at the annual **Great British Beer Festival** (Grand Hall, Olympia, tel. 0172/786–7201), which is organized by the Campaign for Real Ale (CAMRA) and scheduled for early August. On the last Sunday and Monday of the month is **Notting Hill Carnival** (tel. 020/8964–0544), the biggest street festival in Europe. The flavor is strongly Afro-Caribbean with more than 100 costumed bands and floats along the carnival route, as well as food, crafts, and spliffs galore.

SEPTEMBER • The **Chinatown Mid-Autumn Festival,** held on Gerrard Street in Soho, is a smaller but no less colorful version of the Chinese New Year festival (*see* February, *above*). Less glitzy is **Horseman's Sunday** with its Morris Dancers (tel. 020/7262–1732), on the third Sunday of the month, when the good vicar of St. John's Church in Hyde Park Crescent sits on horseback and blesses more than 100 horses, which then proceed to trot through Hyde Park.

OCTOBER • The influential but long-dormant **Soho Jazz Festival** (tel. 020/7437–6437) is trying to make a comeback, and slowly succeeding. It's usually held from the very end of September to the first week of October. The horsey set turns out en masse for the prestigious **Horse of the Year Show** (tel. 0701/070–9901), featuring show jumping and other equestrian hijinks in Wembley Arena. The Pearly Kings and Queens, representatives of costermongers (fruit and vegetable vendors), gather at the Church of St. Martin-in-the-Fields for the **Pearly Harvest Festival Service** on the first Sunday in October.

England expects that every man will do his duty and attend the **Trafalgar Day Parade,** which takes place around—guess where—Trafalgar Square, to commemorate Admiral Nelson's triumph over the French at, ahem, Trafalgar.

NOVEMBER • November 5 marks **Guy Fawkes Night,** a fireworks and bonfire celebration commemorating a foiled attempt to blow up the king and Parliament in 1605. (It all started when James I of Scotland inherited the English throne and began making nasty comments about Catholics. Several plots were hatched against the new king, and just before the 1605 session of Parliament, Guy Fawkes and his accomplices were found in a cellar beneath the House of Lords with enough gunpowder to blow it to bits. The MPs were not amused, and Guy was hanged.) The best place to see fireworks and attend a bonfire is Primrose Hill near Camden Town, but effigies of Guy are burned in various locations around the capital. In mid-November the Queen rides in a coach from Buckingham Palace to the House of Lords to read a speech, followed by a procession and pep talk that mark the **Opening of Parliament.** On the second Saturday in November the **Lord Mayor's Show** (tel. 020/7606–3030) makes a big deal of the person who still has some sort of vestigial sovereignty over the 1-square-mi chunk of land known as the City. A bunch of floats—including the gold-and-scarlet Lord Mayor's Coach—make a ceremonial trek from Westminster to the Law Courts where the Lord Mayor makes a speech, accepts his duties, and so forth. The evening brings fireworks along the Thames. For something a little more modern, make your way to the National Film Theatre at the South Bank Centre for the smashing **London Film Festival** (tel. 020/7928–3232). Get yourself set for the winter holidays with London's **Grand Christmas Parade,** which winds around London from Hyde Park through Oxford and Regent Street on the last Sunday of November.

DECEMBER • The ceremonial heart of London, Trafalgar Square, plays host to an enormous **Christmas tree** (a gift from the people of Norway) from early December until early January. On December 31, Trafalgar Square is also the site of a huge, freezing, drunken slosh through the fountains to celebrate **New Year's Eve.**

WORKING IN LONDON

Getting a job in London or elsewhere in the United Kingdom is no easy matter—prepare for miles of red tape, lengthy booklets of rules and tax regulations, and little respect from British employers who just don't like American and Aussie accents. The most common scenario is perhaps the most bleak: You're in London for a few weeks, decide you love it, and want to stay. Now you need a job. Unless you have a passport from an EU country, however, your only real hope is under-the-table work at pubs and restaurants. These types of thankless positions pay £3–£5 per hour if you're lucky—and don't count on making much in tips. Some people simply walk in the door, ask if the manager needs assistance, and hope he or she doesn't ask for your papers. If you want to go the legal route, contact one of the following organizations long before you arrive in London.

The easiest way to arrange for work in Britain, France, Ireland, and Germany is through Council's Work Abroad Department, which enables U.S. citizens or permanent residents, 18 years or older, to work in Europe at a variety of jobs, for three–six months; you must have been a full-time student for the semester preceding your stay overseas and have a good working knowledge of French. Travel CUTS (*see* Students, *above*) has similar programs for Canadian students. And the Association for International Practical Training sponsors professional internships of 12–18 months in many foreign countries; you must be under 35 and seek a professional internship with a foreign company.

The **Council on International Educational Exchange** (a.k.a. Council, *see* Students, *above*) publishes two excellent resources books with complete details on work/travel opportunities, including the valuable *Work, Study, Travel Abroad: The Whole World Handbook and The High School Student's Guide to Study, Travel, and Adventure Abroad* ($13.95 each, plus $3 first-class postage). The U.K.-based Vacation Work Press publishes the *Directory of Overseas Summer Jobs* ($14.95) and Susan Griffith's *Work Your Way Around the World* ($17.95). The first lists more than 45,000 jobs worldwide; the latter, though with fewer listings, makes a more interesting read.

RESOURCES • Vacation Work Press (c/o Peterson's, 202 Carnegie Center, Princeton, NJ 05843, tel. 609/243–9111). **Association for International Practical Training** (10400 Little Patuxent Pkwy., Suite 250, Columbia, MD 21044–3510, tel. 410/997–2200, fax 410/992–3924).

EXPLORING LONDON 2

UPDATED BY DAVID CLEE AND TIM PERRY

Visitors to London often arrive with more preconceptions than luggage. Like it or not, countless images and symbols of England's capital have become ingrained in the global subconscious, some from contact with Shakespeare, Dickens, and Shaw, others from the Beatles, the Stones, and the Smiths. Even people who've never set foot in London have vivid images of Big Ben, Tower Bridge, red double-decker buses, and ruddy-faced people brandishing raincoats and umbrellas. Newcomers, however, should be prepared to throw most preconceptions out the window. Now that the British empire has come home to roost, large factions of former subjects have relocated to London, and the presence of so many international influences is changing the very essence of what it is to be British. The buses are still here—as are Big Ben and Tower Bridge—but modern London is far more diverse and complex than Dickens could ever have imagined.

With a population of almost 7 million, London is both quintessentially English and an eccentric aberration. For every traditional pub serving bangers (sausages) and chips (french fries), there's a Bengali, Vietnamese, or Caribbean restaurant vying for tourist dollars. For every patriotic Londoner ranting and raving from a Speakers' Corner soapbox about the relative worth of monarchy, there are impassioned activists pressing for socialist reforms. Unlike the traditional picture of England presented by a film like *The Remains of the Day* (adapted, ironically, from the novel by Kazuo Ishiguro, an Englishman of Japanese descent), modern London is perhaps best summed up by nontraditional films like Mike Leigh's *Secrets and Lies.*

Upon arriving in the city proper, you'll find Londoners tend to be very neighborhood-oriented. They spend a lot of time in their particular residential pockets, many of which function as self-contained communities. Indeed, until the industrial revolution of the 19th century, what's now called London was a hodgepodge of villages—suburban satellites of the *original* City of London, the financial heart of London that has existed along the banks of the River Thames since the Romans settled it almost 2,000 years ago. Though the City attracts plenty of visitors, it can't compare with Westminster, London's tourist mecca, home to royal palaces past and present and the government buildings surrounding Parliament Square. This has been Royal London with a capital "R" since the 11th century, when King Edward the Confessor moved his court here, away from the cramped quarters of the City.

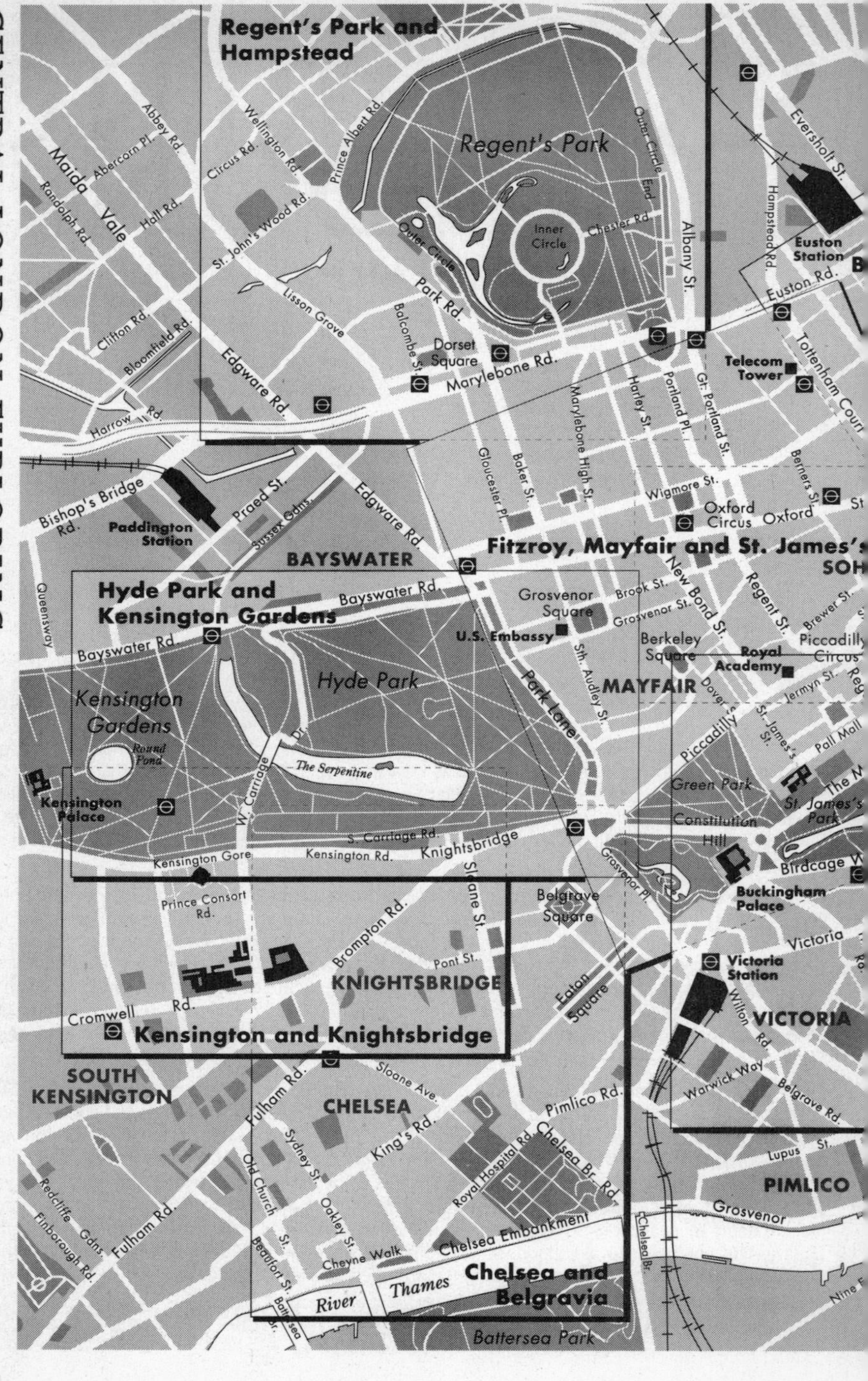
Regent's Park and Hampstead
Regent's Park
Inner Circle
Outer Circle
Chester Rd.
Outer Circle
End
Albany St.
Eversholt St.
Hampstead Rd.
Euston Station
Euston Rd.
Prince Albert Rd.
Wellington Rd.
Circus Rd.
St. John's Wood Rd.
Lisson Grove
Park Rd.
Balcombe St.
Dorset Square
Marylebone Rd.
Edgware Rd.
Abbey Rd.
Abercorn Pl.
Maida Vale
Randolph Rd.
Hall Rd.
Clifton Rd.
Bloomfield Rd.
Harrow Rd.
Bishop's Bridge Rd.
Paddington Station
Praed St.
Sussex Gdns.
Edgware Rd.
BAYSWATER
Telecom Tower
Tottenham Court
Marylebone High St.
Harley St.
Portland Pl.
Gt. Portland St.
Gloucester Pl.
Baker St.
Wigmore St.
Berners St.
Oxford Circus
Oxford
Fitzroy, Mayfair and St. James's
SOHO
Hyde Park and Kensington Gardens
Bayswater Rd.
Bayswater Rd.
Queensway
Grosvenor Square
Brook St.
Grosvenor St.
New Bond St.
Regent St.
Brewer St.
U.S. Embassy
Berkeley Square
Royal Academy
Piccadilly Circus
Hyde Park
Kensington Gardens
Round Pond
The Serpentine
W. Carriage Dr.
Sth. Audley St.
Park Lane
MAYFAIR
Dover St.
Jermyn St.
St. James's St.
Piccadilly
Pall Mall
Green Park
St. James's Park
Constitution Hill
Kensington Palace
S. Carriage Rd.
Kensington Gore
Kensington Rd.
Knightsbridge
Birdcage Walk
Buckingham Palace
Grosvenor Pl.
Sloane St.
Prince Consort Rd.
Brompton Rd.
Belgrave Square
Pont St.
KNIGHTSBRIDGE
Victoria
Victoria Station
Eaton Square
Wilton Rd.
VICTORIA
Cromwell Rd.
Kensington and Knightsbridge
SOUTH KENSINGTON
Fulham Rd.
Sloane Ave.
CHELSEA
Warwick Way
Belgrave Rd.
Pimlico Rd.
King's Rd.
Sydney St.
Royal Hospital Rd.
Chelsea Br. Rd.
Lupus St.
PIMLICO
Redcliffe Gdns.
Finborough Rd.
Fulham Rd.
Old Church St.
Oakley St.
Beaufort St.
Cheyne Walk
Chelsea Embankment
Grosvenor
Chelsea Br.
Chelsea and Belgravia
River Thames
Battersea Br.
Battersea Park
Nine Elms

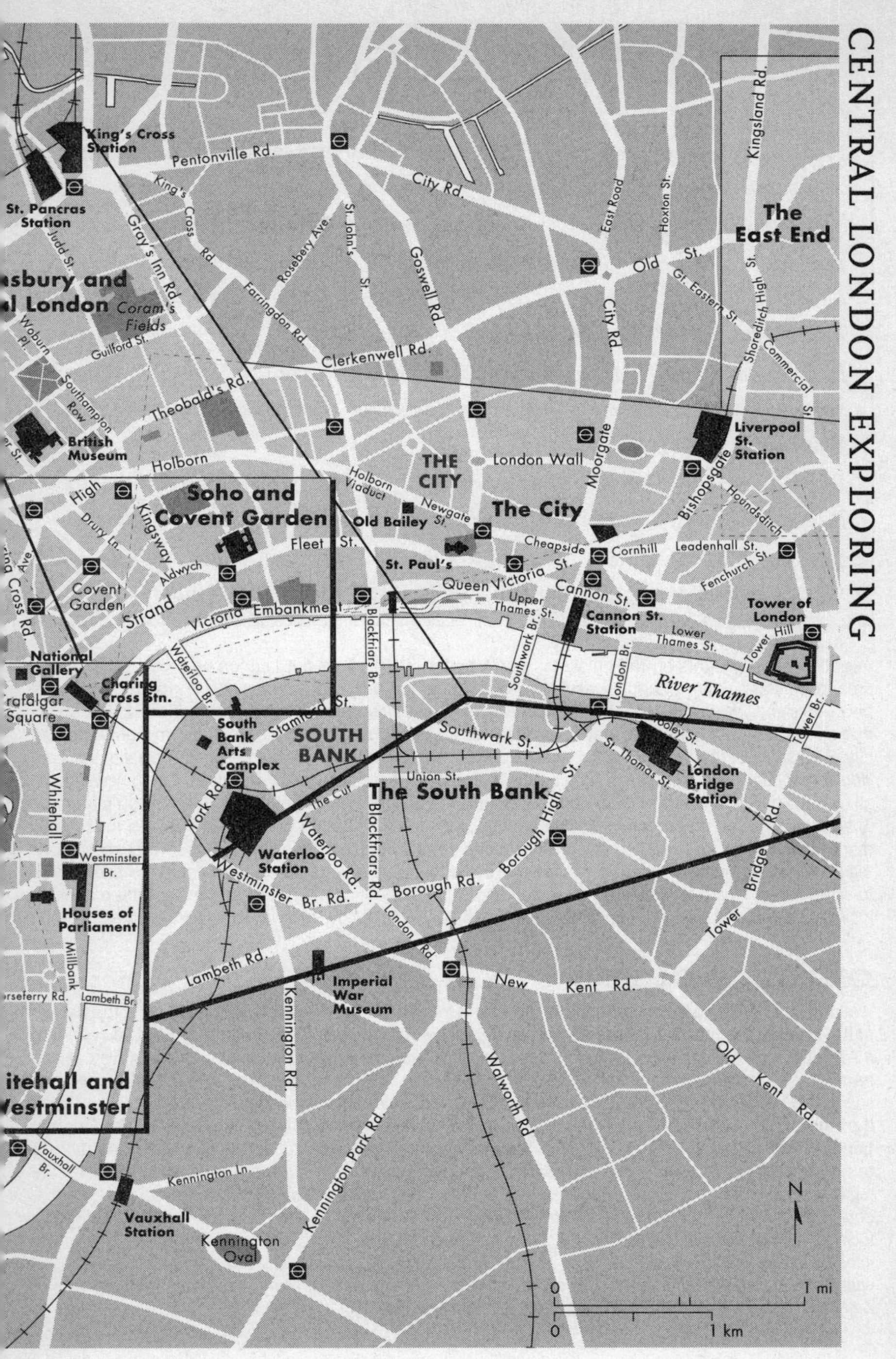

King's Cross Station
Pentonville Rd.
St. Pancras Station
King's Cross Rd.
Judd St.
Gray's Inn Rd.
City Rd.
Rosebery Ave.
St. John's St.
Goswell Rd.
East Road
Hoxton St.
Kingsland Rd.
The East End
Old St.
City Rd.
Gt. Eastern St.
Shoreditch High St.
Commercial St.
Coram's Fields
Woburn Pl.
Guilford St.
Farringdon Rd.
Clerkenwell Rd.
Southampton Row
Theobald's Rd.
British Museum
Holborn
THE CITY
London Wall
Moorgate
Liverpool St. Station
Bishopsgate
Houndsditch
Holborn Viaduct
Newgate St.
Soho and Covent Garden
High
Drury Ln.
Kingsway
Old Bailey
The City
Fleet St.
Cheapside
Cornhill
Leadenhall St.
Fenchurch St.
Aldwych
St. Paul's
Queen Victoria St.
Cannon St.
Covent Garden
Strand
Victoria Embankment
Blackfriars Br.
Upper Thames St.
Cannon St. Station
Tower of London
Lower Thames St.
Tower Hill
National Gallery
Waterloo Br.
Southwark Br.
London Br.
River Thames
Charing Cross Stn.
Trafalgar Square
Stamford St.
Tower Br.
South Bank Arts Complex
SOUTH BANK
Southwark St.
Tooley St.
St. Thomas St.
London Bridge Station
Union St.
Whitehall
York Rd.
The Cut
The South Bank
Borough High St.
Waterloo Rd.
Blackfriars Rd.
Waterloo Station
Westminster Br.
Tower Bridge Rd.
Westminster Br. Rd.
Borough Rd.
London Rd.
Houses of Parliament
Millbank
Lambeth Rd.
Imperial War Museum
New Kent Rd.
Lambeth Br.
Kennington Rd.
Old Kent Rd.
Walworth Rd
Vauxhall Br.
Kennington Ln.
Kennington Park Rd.
Vauxhall Station
Kennington Oval
N
0
1 mi
0
1 km

SIGHTSEEING ON THE CHEAP

If you want a motorized overview of London without the droning commentary, save some cash by joining London's commuters on a standard double-decker bus. You can use your Zones 1 and 2 Travelcard on the following routes:

Bus 11: King's Road, Sloane Square, Victoria Station, Westminster Abbey, Houses of Parliament and Big Ben, Whitehall, Trafalgar Square, The Strand, Fleet Street, and St. Paul's Cathedral.

Bus 12: Bayswater, Marble Arch, Oxford Street, Piccadilly Circus, Trafalgar Square, Horse Guards, Whitehall, Houses of Parliament and Big Ben, Westminster Bridge.

Bus 19: Sloane Square, Knightsbridge, Hyde Park Corner, Green Park, Piccadilly Circus, Shaftsbury Avenue, Oxford Street, Bloomsbury, Islington.

Bus 88: Oxford Circus, Piccadilly Circus, Trafalgar Square, Whitehall, Houses of Parliament and Big Ben, Westminster Abbey, Tate Gallery.

Apart from a few sights on the outskirts, you're better off checking out London on foot. In the central area, tube stations are abundant and fairly close together, but if you *always* hop on the tube to travel between sights, you won't get a decent picture of the city. Note that the tube map is stylized, so stations that appear distant on the map may actually be within blocks of each other. If you're from a grid-oriented city, it's a safe bet that on foot you'll end up hopelessly lost within minutes, so pick up a copy of the ***London A to Z*** street atlas (Brits pronounce it "A to Zed"), sold at newsstands and W. H. Smith newsagents all over town. The mini-London edition (£3.75) is just the right size for your pocket, but if you plan to be in London for a month or more, consider splurging on the wire-bound version (£5.75)—it's much sturdier and you won't be shedding bits of Kensington as you walk down the street. Don't worry about looking like a tourist: locals, including cab drivers, swear by it. Another option is to invest in the pocket-size to-scale tube maps (£2) available in convenience stores and kiosks as well as from vending machines inside underground stations. That way you'll get a better idea of how far away things are from each other.

GUIDED TOURS

Walking tours are favored by London residents and tourists alike. Perennial favorites include the haunts of the Beatles, the trail of Jack the Ripper, and gambols through historic London pubs, but you can find a half-dozen others daily, including tours specializing in arts, architecture, theater, gardens, history, you name it. All are listed in *Time Out* (£1.80), in the "Around Town" section. Tours average £4.50 per person (often less for students), last about two hours, and require no advance reservations (just show up at the starting point and pay the guide). The best and biggest conductor of walking tours is **The Original London Walks** (tel. 020/7624–3978), whose witty, knowledgeable guides offer a wide selection of routes, including the London of Oscar Wilde, Spies' and Spycatchers' London, and London's Secret Village, as well as a bunch of jolly pub crawls (if you plan to go on several walks, ask your guide for a discount walkabout card). **Historical Walks of London** (tel. 020/8668–4019) has a menu of pub walks and tours of literary London, legal London, and royal London. If you're eager to tread in the footsteps of the likes of Mick Jagger, John Lennon, or Johnny Rotten, you can choose any of a number of rock 'n' roll walks of London, which, after all, has served as the launching pad for many a budding rock career. For details, check in *Time Out* or call one of the companies above.

A more flexible (and cost-effective) way to structure your wanderings is to purchase one of the many DIY walking-tour booklets or cassettes available at tourist offices. The **Theatreland Walk** includes many of the historic buildings of central London's theater district as well as some a little more distant. The **Thames Path** is a national trail that extends 180 mi from the river's source in Gloucestershire to the Thames Barrier in London. For those less energetic, however, there are shorter, more central walks along the path, which take you past such areas as leafy Richmond and Kew, through the heart of the city, and past restored warehouses and onto the Docklands.

BY BUS

If you would prefer to remain seated while someone else points out the sights, there is a glut of companies just begging for your tourist dollars. Truth is, these tours can be a real hoot. **The Original London Sightseeing Tour** (tel. 020/8877–1722), **The Big Bus Company** (tel. 020/8944–7810), and **London Pride Sightseeing Company** (tel. 01708/631122) all have open-top, double-decker buses that frequently circumnavigate the major sights of central London. They all charge £12 for a 24-hour ticket and allow you to hop on and off the company's buses at will throughout the day. Additionally, Original London offers £21 combination packages with either Madame Tussaud's Wax Museum or the Tower of London; it saves you a little money and you won't need to wait on line for tickets at either sight. London Pride also offers a route to Greenwich (*see* Near London, *below*) via the Docklands, the developing (and struggling) area along the Thames in east London. For a change of pace, how about dancing and drinking the night away as you watch the sights go by? The **Party Express** (tel. 020/7630–6063) Nightclub Tour offers a "let's party" spin on the bus tour idea: a double-decker hauls a mix of tourists and locals to some of the top clubs in central London every night (£30 including entry to four clubs).

BY BOAT

One of the most pleasant (but least hair-friendly) ways to get a feel for the city is to catch a cruise on the mighty Thames. River-tour companies generally offer live commentary, plus snacks, drinks, and even full bars. **Westminster Passenger Service Association (WPSA) Upriver** (tel. 020/7930–2062) makes the trip from Westminster Pier to **Kew** (90 min; £6 single, £10 return) and **Hampton Court Palace** (3 hrs; £8 single, £12 return) in Richmond (*see below*) five times daily, Easter–October; call for a current schedule. Catch an early boat so you'll have plenty of time to explore the gardens and/or palace. Just as much fun are its 45-min **evening cruises** (£5 return), offered daily May–September at 7:30 and 8:30 PM, between Westminster Pier and the Tower of London. As your boat floats along, lounge on the deck with a glass of wine and watch London transform itself by twilight. **Westminster Greenwich Thames Passenger Boat Services** (tel. 020/7930–4097) runs trips down-river from Westminster Pier to **Greenwich** (50 min; £6 single, £7.30 return) every 30 min from 10:30 to 4, April, May, September, and October; 9:30–5, June, July, and August; and less frequently in winter. Contact **Port of London Authority** (tel. 020/7265–2656) for information on cruises offered by other companies. For information on boat trips along Regent's Canal, *see* Camden Cruising *box*.

MAJOR ATTRACTIONS

When choosing which of London's major sights to visit, listen closely to your internal tour guide. Your budget will also play a role: even though the best and most famous museums are free, many other attractions aren't cheap—though an ISIC card may get you a slight discount. Despite London's size, the major sights are relatively close together, so planning a day can be easy. The best method of all is to admit when you've reached your limit, and head for the pub at the first sign of brain-fade. The great metropolis has more to offer than you could possibly take advantage of in a day, a week, or even a year.

BRITISH LIBRARY

The gigantic British Library, which, by royal decree, is entitled to one copy of everything that is published in the United Kingdom, has found a new home in St. Pancras. At enormous cost, the library's entire holdings were removed from its long-time residence—one it shared with the British Museum—and

MAD DASH THROUGH THE BRITISH MUSEUM

You'd need all the time in the world to fully explore the British Museum, but if you only have a few hours to spare, the following should not be missed.

Room 7: The Nereid Monument

Room 8: Parthenon sculptures (a.k.a. the Elgin Marbles)

Room 12: The Mausoleum at Halicarnassus

Room 17: Lion hunt reliefs from the palace at Nineveh

Room 25: The Rosetta Stone

Room 30: Handwritten prose of Austen, Joyce, and Wordsworth

Room 37: Lindow Bog Man (a.k.a. Pete Marsh)

Room 41: Sutton Hoo Celtic Art Collection

Room 42: Byzantine relics

Rooms 60–61: Mummies

Other must-sees can be found in the Waddesdon Bequest Room, the Persian Landing, the Coptic Corridor, and the Room of the Harpy Tomb.

transferred into what many see as a harsh structure that lacks the historical gravitas peculiar to its ancestor. Nevertheless, the place is much more visitor-friendly, granting everyone who enters access to artifacts like the Magna Carta (1215), one of Britain's founding constitutional documents; hand-written prose by Milton, Joyce, Woolf, and the Brontës; sheet music by Haydn, Bach, and Schubert; letters written by Henry VIII, Elizabeth I, and a host of other monarchs; as well as more recent manuscripts (like records of the Beatles' endeavors). You can catch regular lectures and exhibitions on popular subjects, such as the Poems on the Underground, which adorn many a tube carriage. For £3 (£2 students) you can take a tour (Mon., Wed., Fri., Sat., and Sun. at 3; Sat. also at 10:30) of the library; call 020/7412–7332 to book ahead. St. Pancras Station next door is also well worth a look. The facade (built in 1872) is one of the most extreme examples of Victorian High Gothic, a breathtaking sight made all the more intriguing given that it fronts up a huge 100-ft-high glass-and-iron train shed. *The British Library at St. Pancras, 96 Euston Rd., NW1, tel. 020/7412–7000. Tube: King's Cross. Turn right out of King's Cross station, walk past St. Pancras Station; the library is next door. Admission free. Open weekdays 9:30–6 (Tues. until 8), Sat. 9:30–5, Sun. 11–5.*

BRITISH MUSEUM

Anybody writing about the British Museum in Bloomsbury had better have a large pail of superlatives close at hand: most, biggest, earliest, finest. This is the golden hoard of nearly three centuries of the Empire, the booty bought—and flat-out stolen—from Britain's far-flung colonies. The first major pieces, among them the Rosetta Stone and Parthenon sculptures, were "borrowed" from the French, who "found" them in Egypt and Greece. The museum has since collected countless goodies of worldwide historical significance: the Black Obelisk, some of the Dead Sea Scrolls, the Lindow Bog Man. Heck, that only *begins* the list.

Parliament was inspired to found London's first public museum in 1753, after acquiring the extensive natural history and antiquities collection of Sir Hans Sloane, as well as several smaller collections of books and manuscripts. Soon thereafter, it seemed everyone had something to donate—George II gave the Royal Library, Sir William Hamilton (husband of Nelson's mistress, Emma) gave antique vases, Charles Townley gave sculptures, the Bank of England gave coins—and the museum's holdings quickly outgrew their original space in Montague House. After the addition of such major pieces as the Rosetta Stone and other Egyptian antiquities (spoils of the Napoleonic War), and the Parthenon sculptures (brought from Greece via an Odyssean voyage by Lord Elgin in 1816), Robert Smirke was commissioned to build an appropriately large and monumental building on the same site—though, due to lack of funds, construction work was dragged out more than 20 years and used several architects. The museum has since added millions of other objects, the best of which are exhibited within its vast galleries.

The collection spans the centuries as well as the globe, featuring artifacts from the prehistoric era, ancient Egypt and Assyria, right on through to Renaissance and contemporary works. The sheer magnitude of the collection (and sometimes the crowd) is overwhelming. A good strategy for exploring is to take the 90-min tour (£7). In summer, it's given Monday–Saturday six times a day, three on Sunday; in winter, Monday–Saturday three times a day and twice on Sunday; come back later to whatever intrigued you the most. Another option is to buy the £1 souvenir map and follow one of the recommended tours. The museum also offers gallery talks (10:30), lectures (1:00), and a free 45-min "Eye-Opener" tour that focuses on a small section of the collections; for current listings pick up the "Events" pamphlet at the information desk.

In many ways the **ground floor** is the most impressive in the museum, featuring big name treasures from Greece and Rome (Rooms 1–15). Get up close and personal with the exquisite bas-relief carvings of the Bassae Frieze, from the Temple of Apollo in Room 6. Rooms 16–24 display sculpture and reliefs from western Asia. Don't miss the huge, human-headed, winged bulls from Assyria (Room 16) or the 7th-century BC frieze from Ashurbanipal's palace at Nineveh (Room 17), where a royal lion hunt is depicted in amazing detail. The **basement floor** features more antiquities from Greece and Rome, including huge Ionic capitals from the temple of Artemis (Room 77), Townley's delightful greyhounds and the poorly restored Discus Thrower (Room 84), and a single, very large foot, spoils from a colossal statue of Alexander the Great (Room 83). The **upper floors** house treasures from all over the world, including exhibits from prehistoric and Roman Britain (Rooms 35–40); the Medieval, Renaissance, and Modern Collections (Rooms 41–48); and western Asia (Rooms 52–59). Among the most popular sections of the museum are Rooms 60–65, home to the greater part of the Egyptian collection. Easily the two busiest rooms are numbers 60 and 61, where you'll find the mummies—both human and animal, including gazelles, ibises, crocodiles, kittens (looking for all the world like sock puppets), fish, dogs, falcons, and even a small bull. At the very top of the museum sit some of the Asian collections (Rooms 91–94), where exhibits change very frequently due to the fragility of the items.

The "Great Court" project and other gallery renovations are due to be completed by the end of 2000, but don't hold your breath; a number of galleries may be closed and some objects relocated.

The huge British Library (*see above*), which used to share the building with the British Museum, recently moved lock, stock, and barrel to a new building at St. Pancras. The magnificent domed **Reading Room** (tel. 020/7412–7677), where George Bernard Shaw and Karl Marx (to name only two) warmed their seats while cogitating, is being converted into the museum's own library and will be open to visitors as of November 2000. *Great Russell St., WC1, tel. 020/7636–1555. Tube: Tottenham Court Rd. Walk north on Tottenham Court Rd., turn right on Great Russell St. Admission free; small charge for special exhibits. Open Mon.–Sat. 10–5, Sun. 2:30–6.*

BUCKINGHAM PALACE

One of the most fabled buildings in the world, Buckingham Palace is Her Majesty's London home (the Royal Standard flies above the palace whenever the Queen is in residence, usually on weekdays). Buckingham Palace initially was Buckingham House; never intended as a royal palace, it was originally built for the J. Paul Getty of the 18th century, the Duke of Buckingham. George III—the tea-taxing king who lost a rather important colony—bought the place in 1762. When his eponymous son got the job of monarch in 1820, he decided that the mansion needed complete remodeling to suit his grand tastes.

George IV knew what he wanted and architect John Nash knew how to do it, but the duo hit a snag when they couldn't persuade the government to come up with the necessary funding. A compromise was stitched together when Parliament agreed to pay for repairs and improvements, words which the cheeky

ROYALTY WATCHING

Now that you're in Merrie Olde Englande, just seeing the Queen on a postage stamp doesn't seem to do the trick. Yes, you've toured Buckingham Palace, but forget about spotting the Windsors—you'll never ever see them standing by the palace windows. And the odds are that you won't be bumping into Elizabeth II at the Green Park tube station. But at a surprisingly wide variety of royal events, you can catch a glimpse of her, along with many other Windsor personages. Fairs and fetes, polo matches and horse races, first nights and banquets galore: her date-book is crammed with events (almost 400 a year!) and, on one of them—who knows?—you might even meet her on a royal walkabout.

If you want to know what she and the rest of the RF are doing on any given date, turn to the Court Circular printed in the major London dailies. You might catch Prince Charles launching a ship or Princess Margaret attending a film premiere. The date to note is the second Saturday in June (the palace confirms the actual date several months in advance), when the parade known as Trooping the Colour is held to celebrate the Queen's official birthday. The Queen rides down the Mall in her carriage to arrive at Horse Guards Parade at 11 am exactly for the grand ceremony. (Well, occasionally the clock has been timed to strike as she arrives.) Only 7,000 people are admitted to the 11 viewing stands; if you wish to obtain seats (no more than two per request), enclose a letter and stamped, self-addressed envelope or International Reply Coupon to HQ Household Division, Horse Guards, Whitehall, London SW1X 6AA (send January to mid-March). If you don't get tickets through this ballot system, you can, of course, just line up along the Mall with your binoculars. If you get to meet her—perhaps when she's ribbon-cutting at a hospital or promenading through the Royal Enclosure at Ascot in June—you'll be in for a treat. Contrary to her stodgy persona, she's actually a devilish wit. Just remember: address her as "Your Majesty."

king pushed to the limits of their meaning. Nash went off, stocked up on quarryfuls of Bath stone, took a pickax to the old house, and from the rubble built a three-side palace with an east-facing open court, to be entered via Marble Arch. To Parliament's disgust the final cost was three times the original estimate, but fate gave the money men the last laugh as old George IV died before his beloved project was topped off.

In 1847, just 10 years after the palace was finished, the builders were called back to bestow a new frontage on the building's east side (that's the one with the imposing gates we all peek through nowadays); to compensate, Marble Arch had to be shifted to its present site on the western edge of Hyde Park. For the past two centuries, the palace's great gray bulk has summed up the imperious splendor of so much of London: stately, magnificent, and ponderous. Although the palace contains some 600 rooms, including the State Ballroom and, of course, the Throne Room, Elizabeth II occupies only a dozen rooms on the first floor of the north wing, overlooking Green Park. (She probably likes nothing more than to curl up in front of the telly with her trademark corgi dogs to watch "Coronation Street.")

Several years ago, the Queen opened the palace to the public—for a fee, mind you—to pay for the restorations to Windsor Castle (*see* Windsor, *below*) after the fire in 1992. During summer months, various rooms are open to view—but forget about poking into medicine cabinets: only 17 of the sumptuous (and rather cold) **State Rooms** are on the tour. Here you'll find pomp and circumstance, but little else: these salons are where much of the business of royalty is played out—investitures, state banquets, receptions, lunch parties for the famous, and so on. For many visitors in recent times, the apparent lack of warmth sheds light on Princess Diana's famous complaints about the frosty atmosphere she encountered here—a place she came to see as the enemy camp. Needless to say, these palatial rooms are chockful of treasures—the entire spectacle will leave you either queasy about humankind's acquisitive nature or drooling with envy. Highlights of the tour include the Throne Room; the Picture Gallery featuring masterworks by Van Dyck, Rembrandt, and Vermeer; the Music Room, the place for stunning views across the palace grounds, all 45 acres of them; and, at the foot of the Ministers' Staircase, the sculptures *Fountain Nymph* and *Mars and Venus* by Antonio Canova (1757–1822). The palace opens its doors each August and September. *Queen's Gardens, SW1, tel. 020/7839–1377. Tube: Green Park or St. James's Park. From Green Park, walk ½ mi south on Queen's Walk. From St. James's Park, walk north on Queen Anne's Gate, turn left on Birdcage Walk. Admission £10. Open Aug.–beginning Oct., daily 9:30–4:15. Note that you can prebook your admission ticket over the phone by using credit cards.*

QUEEN'S GALLERY

A short distance down Buckingham Gate, the Queen's Gallery houses rotating exhibits of pieces from her majesty's private art collection. The space will be closed until 2002, when a gallery twice as big as the current showcase will throw open its doors in wild celebration of the Queen's Golden Jubilee. That's also the year some Royal watchers expect HM to abdicate the throne in favor of Charles, but that's by the by. The new gallery will be forced to leave many of its major exhibits in storage due to a severe lack of wall space, but you can still expect to see works by Gainsborough, Rembrandt, Reynolds, and Rubens. For schedule and admissions info, call the Visitor Office, tel. 020/7839–1377. *Buckingham Palace Rd., SW1, tel. 020/7930–4832, ext. 3351. Tube: St. James's Park or Victoria.*

ROYAL MEWS

One of the oldest and finest operating stables around, the Royal Mews houses the monarch's magnificent state carriages (including the Gold State Coach, better known as the Coronation Coach, built in 1762), together with her horses and state liveries. The stunning display of regal equine power carries a certain degree of irony, as Buckingham Palace Road was famous for its highwaymen in the 18th century. If you visit when both the Queen's Gallery and the Royal Mews are open, you can cop a slightly cheaper combined ticket for £7. Otherwise, some might feel it's a lot to pay to look at horses. *Buckingham Palace Rd., SW1, tel. 020/7930–4832, ext. 3351. Tube: St. James's Park or Victoria. Admission £4. Open Apr.–July, Tues.–Thurs. noon–4; Aug.–Sept., Mon.–Thurs. 10:30–3:30; Oct.–Mar., Wed.–Thurs., noon–3:30.*

GUARDS MUSEUM

This museum occupies a set of underground rooms in Wellington Barracks, the regimental headquarters of the palace's Guards Division. Exhibits trace the history of the five Foot Guards regiments—Grenadier, Coldstream, Scots, Irish, and Welsh—from the 1660s through the Gulf War. The massive toy soldier shop is definitely worth a look, even if you're not into that kind of thing. *Wellington Barracks, Birdcage Walk, SW1, tel. 020/7930–4466, ext. 3430. Tube: St. James's Park. Admission £2. Open daily 10–4 (last admission 3:30).*

CHANGING OF THE GUARD

One of the biggest tourist shows in town is the Changing of the Guard ceremony, when the soldiers guarding the Queen hand over their duties to the next watch. Marching to live music, the Queen's Guard proceeds up the Mall from St. James's Palace to Buckingham Palace. Shortly afterward, the new guard approaches from Wellington Barracks via Birdcage Walk. Once the old and new guards are in the forecourt, the old guard symbolically hands over the keys to the palace. The ceremony takes place daily at 11:30 AM, April–July and on alternating days August–March, but the guards sometimes cancel due to bad weather; check the signs posted in the forecourt to find out when and if it will take place. Arrive by

RESURGAM!

A lunette on St. Paul's south door pediment features a carving of a phoenix rising from the ashes, symbolic of the cathedral's fiery history. Samuel Pepys reported in his diary that during the Great Fire of 1666 "the stones of St. Paul's flew like grenados, the melting lead running down the streets in a stream." When Christopher Wren began rebuilding the new St. Paul's a decade later, he asked a workman to bring him a stone to mark the center of the cathedral. The stone happened to be a piece of an old tombstone with the word RESURGAM *(I shall rise again) engraved upon it. Wren took the image of the new cathedral rising from its own ashes to heart, representing it with the aforementioned phoenix.*

The next major catastrophe to befall London was the Blitz, during which Londoners used the Golden Gallery in the dome of St. Paul's to spot fires all over the city. The cathedral was in grave danger, but through the efforts of the volunteer St. Paul's Fire Watch, little damage was incurred. Luck also played a role: a bomb landed on St. Paul's on September 12, 1940, but failed to explode. The cathedral also escaped damage during a German air raid that destroyed most of the city of London on December 29, 1940. A famous (although fabricated) photograph shows the dome standing serenely amid plumes of smoke while the surrounding area is consumed by fire.

10:30 AM for a decent view of all the pomp. Early birds should grab a section of the gate facing the palace, since most of the hoopla takes place inside the fence. For more information, call 089/150–5452.

HOUSES OF PARLIAMENT

The best view of Parliament is probably the most traditional—from halfway across nearby Westminster Bridge or, as immortalized by Monet in *The Thames Below Westminster,* from Albert Embankment on the far side of the Thames. In a recent poll, London cabbies ranked this view above any other of the capital's vantage points. The Empire may be dead, but it's still fascinating to explore the site from which Britain once ruled with imperial impunity. The Houses of Parliament are actually one large building that sprawls along the Thames and are home to the chambers of the House of Commons and the House of Lords, which meet on opposite sides of the octagonal Central Lobby. The complex is officially known as the **Palace of Westminster,** indicative of the strong influence the monarchy held over Parliament for centuries. Parliamentarians rebelled against Charles I during the English Civil War (1642–48), but before then, they were very much at the beck and call of the monarch. In fact, many kings summoned Parliament only when they needed money (it was Parliament's responsibility to levy taxes) and then promptly dismissed it.

A major fire in 1834 destroyed almost all of the original Palace of Westminster except for the massive **Westminster Hall,** built in 1097–99 by William II and rebuilt by Richard II in 1394–99. The only other remnants of the old parliamentary building are the **Crypt of St. Stephen's Chapel,** where the House of Commons met for 300 years, and the medieval **Jewel Tower** (*see below*), used to store Edward III's collections of furs, jewels, gold, and other royal knickknacks. After the blaze, a competition was held for the design of a new Parliament building, and the winners were Charles Barry, a classical architect, and his assistant, Augustus Welby Pugin, a Gothicist. Whereas Barry was responsible for the building's practical plan, the elaborate details are the work of Pugin, a converted Catholic who believed that the Gothic style was the only "true" Christian architecture.

As an overseas visitor, you can request a special "line of route" tour of the Houses of Parliament by writing to the Public Information Office (House of Commons, Westminster, SW1A 2PW) at least a month in advance of your visit. The tour takes you through the Queen's Robing Room, Royal Gallery, House of Lords, Central Hall (where MPs, or Members of Parliament, meet their constituents), House of Commons, and out into the spectacular Westminster Hall. Watch for the "VR" (Victoria Regina) monograms in the carpets and carving belying the "medieval" detailing as 19th-century work. Permits for tours of up to 16 people are available for Friday afternoon while the House is sitting. If you don't arrange for the tour, you can still visit the **Stranger's Galleries** of the House of Commons or the House of Lords. Getting into either gallery is tough, however, so try to get tickets in advance from your embassy, or be prepared to wait in line for several hours (lines are shortest after 5:30). The line for the House of Commons is always longer, especially at Question Time (*see* House of Commons, *below*). *Parliament Sq., SW1, tel. 020/7219–4272. Tube: Westminster. For Strangers' Galleries, line up at St. Stephen's Hall entrance (to the left for the Commons, to the right for the Lords). Admission free. House of Commons open Mon., Tues. 2:30–late, Wed. 9:30–2, 2:30–late, Thurs. 11:30–7:30, Fri. 9:30–3; House of Lords open Mon.–Wed. 2:30–late, Thurs. 3–late, Fri. 11–late.*

HOUSE OF COMMONS

The House of Commons, comprising 659 elected members from around the country, is where the real power lies. Although destroyed by incendiary bombs in 1941, a sympathetic reconstruction by Sir Giles Gilbert Scott, completed in 1950, modernized the chamber to increase the seating capacity—albeit on strictly utilitarian, green benches—while restoring some of the traditional touches. Scott didn't let the increase in capacity go too far, however. The Commons is deliberately designed so that there are fewer seats than Members of Parliament, which helps create a passionate, rowdy atmosphere when it is teeming with mouthy politicos. Even the esteemed Members are not above using brute force to secure their berths. A pair of red lines running the length of the floor date back to more turbulent times, when impassioned debate really raged: the lines are placed exactly two swords'-length apart, and members must still remain behind them. Nowadays, you'll mainly see verbal sparring, making a parliamentary session more exciting than many of the "dramas" playing in West End theaters. The ultimate spectacle is the quick and cutting repartee exchanged during the prime minister's Question Time, held in the House of Commons on Wednesday between 3 and 3:30. This is when the PM defends himself against the slings and arrows of his "right honourable friends." Foreigners are required to secure tickets from their respective embassies, and Brits from their MPs. The next best time to visit is either chamber's regular **Question Time,** held Monday–Thursday between 2:30 and 3:30. It's possible to sit in on other sessions and debates in both houses, but schedules are sketchy since they depend on what crisis the government is currently coping with. Some say the cut and thrust of adversarial debate is threatened by a series of imminent changes that will lead to a more measured, less passionate form of politics. At present the House of Commons is elected on a winner-takes-all system, where the biggest party is all but guaranteed a majority and the losing lot are forced into angry opposition. In future, Britain is likely to switch to the proportional representation system favored by the rest of Europe, where the final outcome usually encourages parties to form alliances. Already the left-leaning Labour government has started on the road to coalition by allowing the center-party Liberals a share of power. Meanwhile, party apparatchiks are taking the heat and individualism out of debates by imposing ever more stringent protocol, and so, as Parliament hands over more of its power to Europe, the memory of its boisterous heyday will get ever dimmer. To witness what's left of the tumult, try to get into the Commons during one of the less-visited evening sessions, starting around 5:30—Parliament is still sitting if the top of Big Ben is illuminated.

Parliament's daily schedule, posted at St. Stephen's Gate, can be amusing. Conflicts with the European Union might get an hour's debate, while the issue of "dog fouling" in London streets gets an entire afternoon's thrashing-out.

HOUSE OF LORDS

The Lords' chamber, masterfully designed by Augustus Welby Northmore Pugin (1812–52), is a sumptuous affair, with lots of carved wood paneling, gilt, and leather. It must have been quite a letdown for the members of Commons to return to their own plain chamber after meeting here while theirs was being rebuilt. The Royal Gallery, adjacent to the Lords' chamber, is decorated with frescoes depicting scenes from British history. The line is always shorter for the House of Lords, but don't come here expecting drama. For many years the Lords were the subject of derision and hilarity, especially since many of their honorable Lordships could be seen snoozing away the afternoon on the chamber's rare live TV appearances; presumably they were full to their aristocratic gills with free food (to which they were entitled from the reputedly excellent Palace of Westminster restaurants). Noble men and women complained of media exaggeration, claiming their heads were rocked backward in order to hear loudspeakers set into the benches, but that hardly explains the closed eyes. Whatever their foibles, catch the Lords while you can, because their days are numbered. Prime Minister Tony Blair has decided to reform the chamber: out will go the iniquitous hereditary principle, to be replaced by a load of worthies (Tony's Cronies) held in esteem by the PM himself. Democracy is promised for Britain's second chamber, but a date has yet to be set.

BIG BEN AND VICTORIA TOWER

The clock tower on the north end of the Palace of Westminster, perhaps the most enduring symbol of both London and Britain, has come to be known as **Big Ben.** It is thought to have been named after Sir Benjamin Hall, the MP who commissioned the works for the clock. Actually, it's only the 13½-ton bell on top that's named Big Ben, although few people are aware of that distinction. Puristic details aside, for the millions of colonials worldwide who hear the Westminster chimes nightly on the BBC World Service, the 16 tones evoke a wide range of emotions: home, security, patriotism, and a sense of belonging. These are feelings unlikely to have been shared with any great enthusiasm by Richard Hannay as he dangled from the clock's minute hand in a famous scene from John Buchan's seminal thriller, *The Thirty-Nine Steps*. Especially when Big Ben is lit up at night, its stature seems to dwarf the other buildings in the Parliament complex, even though it's not the tallest. That distinction belongs to the 323-ft-high **Victoria Tower,** reputedly the largest square tower in the world, which it needs to be, as it holds the 5 million-document parliamentary archives. A Union Jack waves from the top of Victoria Tower whenever Parliament is in session.

JEWEL TOWER

Across the street from Victoria Tower, the stumpy Jewel Tower was built in 1365 to house Edward III's precious gems. It survived the fire of 1834, was severely damaged in the Blitz, and was restored in the 1950s. It is now a very worthwhile museum. Currently on display is the "History of Parliament: Past and Present" exhibition. Don't miss the 1,200-year-old Westminster Sword, found on the river bank alongside Victoria Gardens, or the elaborately embroidered Speakers' Robes. *Abingdon St. (also called Old Palace Yard), south of Parliament Sq., SW1, tel. 020/7222–2219. Tube: Westminster. Admission £1.50. Open Nov.–Mar., daily 10–4; Apr.–Oct., daily 10–6.*

ST. PAUL'S CATHEDRAL

Right in the heart of the city, St. Paul's is instantly recognizable by its huge dome, towering 365 ft above street level and shaming the skyscrapers that surround it with its breathtaking majesty. St. Paul's is also the symbolic heart of the city; unlike Westminster Abbey, which is perceived as a royal and national church, St. Paul's is really viewed as a church for *Londoners*. The present structure, the fourth in a series of cathedrals erected on the site, was built by Christopher Wren between 1675 and 1710. Its predecessors were destroyed by fire (*see box*), Viking raiders, and fire again, but the present structure broke the mold of disaster when it emerged largely unscathed from the bombing blitz unleashed on London by Hitler's air force in World War II. Speculation that the *Luftwaffe* deliberately left St. Paul's untouched to aid nighttime navigation looks wide of the mark, as bombs did hit the north transept and the high altar. Old St. Paul's, the one before this one, was itself one of the great churches of the world, boasting a spire that reached 489 ft skyward. Begun at the tail end of the 11th century, by the time of the Great Fire Old St. Paul's had been ravaged by long years of neglect and mistreatment. At various times it had been used as an army barracks, a traffic shortcut, and a horse market with the font as shop counter. In the absence of Jesus to throw over some tables, Fate intervened in the form of the Great Fire. Before the blaze, Wren was asked to repair the worn-out building and immediately suggested tearing the whole thing down, a request denied by conservative clergymen. Given a surprise clear sheet, Wren came up with some designs and set to work in 1675, and 35 years later the New St. Paul's was up and ready.

The cathedral's interior is every bit as exceptional as its silhouette, containing dozens of memorials and other works of art. The **Wellington Monument** looms more than 80 ft high in an arch between the nave and the north aisle. Wellington's tomb and remains are in the crypt below. **Samuel Johnson's monument,** by the north choir aisle, is as distant from the truth as from his body: Dr. Johnson is actually buried in Westminster Abbey, and his monument, in the view of present-day pundits, transforms the

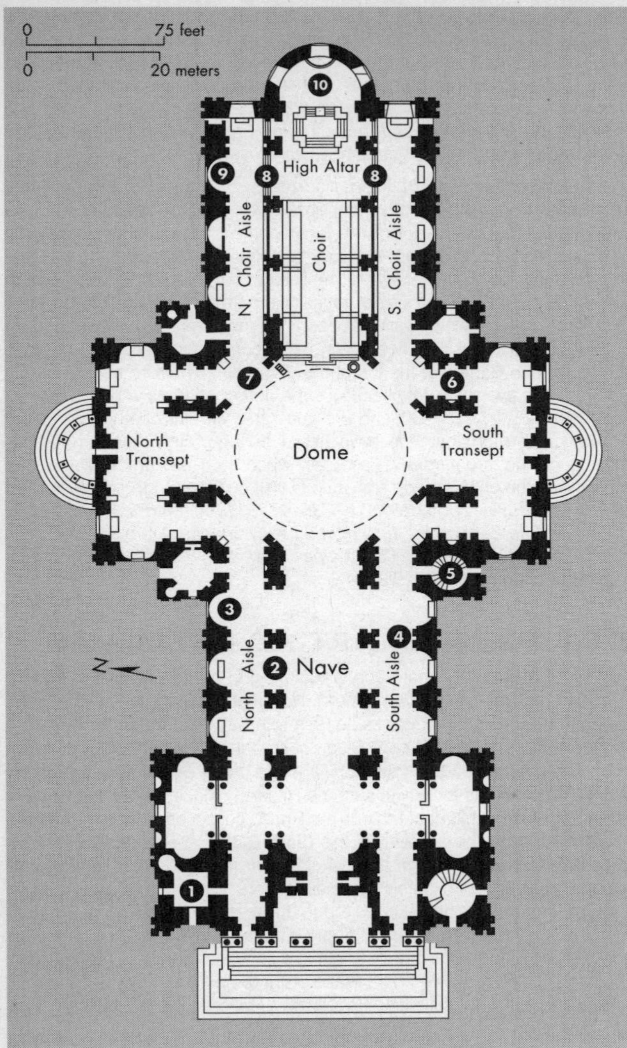

ST. PAUL'S CATHEDRAL

All Souls' Chapel, **1**
American Chapel, **10**
Crypt entrance, **6**
"Light of the World", **4**
"Mother and Child", **9**
Samuel Johnson's Monument, **7**
Staircase to galleries, **5**
Tijou Gates, **8**
Viscounts Melbourne Monument, **3**
Wellington Monument, **2**

obese 18th-century lexicographer into a stately Roman dignitary. Two life-size marble angels adorn the monument to the Viscounts Melbourne located in the north aisle. Also notable is Holman Hunt's famous painting, **The Light of the World,** in the south aisle, depicting Christ knocking at the bramble-covered door of the human soul. The **choir** is the most highly decorated part of the cathedral, with 1890s mosaic ceilings, stalls carved by Dutch artist Grinling Gibbons, and iron screens wrought by the French master Jean Tijou. The **High Altar** baldachin is stunningly gaudy, all carved wood, gold leaf, and twisty columns. Behind the High Altar you'll find the **American Chapel,** dedicated to the 30,000 U.S. servicemen stationed in the United Kingdom during the Second World War. Far below, the **crypt** (the largest in Europe) contains a display on the cathedral's architecture, as well as a small treasury and dozens of tombs of the famous, including military demigods Nelson, Kitchener, and Wellington, and artists William Blake and Joshua Reynolds. The tomb of the great builder himself, Christopher Wren, is adorned by his son's famous epitaph: LECTOR, SI MONUMENTUM REQUIRIS, CIRCUMSPICE (Reader, if you seek his monument, look around you; or, in the words of a contemporary wit, "If you seek his monument, Sir-come-spy-see"). Wren's **Great Model,** an 18-ft, exquisitely detailed model of the way things might have been had Wren been allowed to build St. Paul's on a Greek-cross design, has been removed from the crypt. It has been returned to its earlier home in the Trophy Room (at triforium level), where it's displayed to much better advantage. Wren's classical plan was deemed far too modern and opposed to the clergymen's demand for a traditional, long nave. Ironically, plans for rebuilding the cathedral's neighboring structures have been criticized for being too modern because they aren't classical.

If the cathedral's dome ceiling seems lower than you expected, it's because St. Paul's actually has three domes: a shallow, decorated dome seen from inside; a lofty outer dome seen from the street; and a brick cone between them that provides support. The interior of the inner dome's base is encircled by the **Whispering Gallery**; once you've caught your breath from the 259-step climb, whisper into the wall and you'll be heard 100 ft away on the other side of the gallery—if the listener can discern your voice from the dozens of other whispering tourists. Climb 118 more steps to reach the **Stone Gallery,** just above the eight huge piers that support the dome. Mouth-watering views of London, including a great sweep of the Thames, are on offer here, but this is a mere hors d'oeuvre to the main course. If your legs can stand it, continue 116 more steps up to the **Golden Gallery** at the top of the dome, and you'll be rewarded with unforgettable views of London. If you want every last detail, take a super-informative, slow-paced 90-min **Supertour** (£2.50) Monday–Saturday at 11, 11:30, 1:30, and 2; if you agree with Elizabeth I's comment to one St. Paul's clergyman during a sermon that "we have heard enough," try the 45-min tape-recorded tour (£3). Sauntering through the free gardens, especially when the roses are in bloom, can be most satisfying. Attending services is the only way you'll be able to visit on Sunday; the choir sings at the 11 and 3:15 services. *St. Paul's Churchyard, EC4, tel. 020/7236–4128. Tube: Mansion House or St. Paul's. From Mansion House, walk west on Cannon St., turn right on New Change. From St. Paul's, follow signs. Admission to cathedral and crypt £4, galleries £3.50. Open Mon.–Sat. 8:30–4; crypt and treasury open Mon.–Sat. 8:45–4; galleries open Mon.–Sat. 9:30–4.*

TATE GALLERY OF BRITISH ART AT MILLBANK

The Tate is one of England's principal museums—more contemporary and controversial, but no less impressive, than the National Gallery (*see* Trafalgar Square, *below*). Now that the plans to shift the Tate's modern art collection to a redesigned power station at Bankside (*see* Tate Gallery of Modern Art, *below*) are well underway, the museum at Millbank is nearing completion of its own expansion and redevelopment plans. The new Tate, while still adamant about curating brilliant and thought-provoking temporary exhibits, will expand its displays to house works by artists such as Hogarth, Blake, Constable, Bacon, Spencer, and contemporary artists. A major highlight of the current British collection, which is centered on British painting from the 16th century to the present, is the **Clore Gallery,** dedicated to J. M. W. Turner, hailed as Britain's greatest artist. As with those in the rest of the museum, Clore Gallery exhibits are rotated annually, with selections culled from the Tate's holdings of more than 300 of Turner's paintings, 300 of his personal sketchbooks, and more than 19,000 rough drawings and watercolors. Another feature of the British collection is the work of artist/poet/protohippie **William Blake,** who died in poverty in the 19th century—but is now regularly lauded as one of England's greatest geniuses. Tate curators like to liven things up a bit by hanging works by artists whom Blake inspired next to art by the great man himself. Most unforgettable image in the Tate collection? Probably Sir John Everett Millais's Pre-Raphaelite oil painting *Ophelia*. Don't miss it.

The Tate's modern collection (the bulk of which will open to the public in May 2000 at its new home at Bankside) traces the main currents of Western art in the past century or so from Impressionism and post-Impressionism via cubism, futurism, vorticism, expressionism, and surrealism to abstract expressionism, optical, kinetic, and pop art. Look for works by Van Gogh, Matisse, Picasso, Dalí, Rothko, Léger, Duchamp, and Ernst, to name a few. Contemporary artists are championed in the **Art Now** room, which houses exhibits of recent work by new and established artists. In recent years art has been at the forefront of London's "cool" renaissance, with artists often commanding the kind of media attention usually reserved for rock stars. The undisputed king of the new wave is Damien Hirst, who achieved some notoriety by sticking a sheep in formaldehyde and using lots of urine in his work. Although many see his stuff as little more than rehashed Magritte with extra marketing, the depressingly obvious shock tactics of Hirst and his band have at least secured some space in the headlines for all art. Every now and then, the Tate itself gets into hot water by displaying an exhibit that doesn't please the philistines—probably the most famous brouhaha occurred when the gallery paid a goodly sum for a pile of bricks (in fact, a minimalist masterpiece by Carl Andre). Special exhibitions scheduled in 2000 include a reportedly provocative survey of Modern British Art, Damien Hirst, et al. The special exhibitions are often massively oversubscribed, so it could pay dividends to book in advance by calling the First Call ticket agency (0870/842–2233).

Currently, the gallery offers the following free, guided tours on weekdays: British art from Van Dyck to the Pre-Raphaelites (11); the Turner Collection (11:30); modern art from Impressionism to surrealism (2:30); and late-20th-century art (3:30). On Saturday at 3, the staff will guide you through the highlights of the entire collection. Free lectures, films, and video screenings take place almost daily in the auditorium; pick up a schedule at the info desk. If admiring all the art with your mouth agape makes you want to fill it up, head to the Tate's good restaurant, whose walls were painted by the English illustrator Rex Whistler. *Millbank, SW1, tel. 020/7887–8000 or 020/7887–8008 for recorded info. Tube: Pimlico. Walk north 1 block, turn right on Vauxhall Bridge Rd. (which becomes Bessboro Gardens), left on Millbank. Admission free; £1–£6 for special exhibits. Open daily 10–5:50.*

TOWER OF LONDON

A genuine spine-chiller, the Tower of London is one of the city's leading sights—and it deserves all the attention it gets. With its winding staircases, tunnels, bridges, and narrow passages, the Tower is a great place to get lost in history. It's far more than one tower. In fact, some 20 towers make up the fortress (the largest in medieval Europe), which spreads over 18 acres on the bank of the Thames. Besides serving as the residence of every British sovereign from William the Conqueror (he built the original fortress in 1078) to Henry VIII in the 16th century, the Tower has performed a wide variety of other roles as armory, jewel safe, garrison, and zoo—yes, it's home to Cedric, Gwylum, Hugine II, Munin II, Odin, and Thor, the famed Tower ravens (*see box*). The Tower is most famous, however, for its role as a prison and historic place of execution. Some of England's most notable figures met their death here, including Robert Devereux—the Earl of Essex—when he somersaulted from favor with Elizabeth I, and three queens of England: Lady Jane Grey (crowned in 1553 but deposed and executed after only nine days), Anne Boleyn, and Catherine Howard (Henry VIII's second and fifth wives, respectively). The chapel of **St. Peter ad Vincula,** adjacent to the Tower Green execution site, houses their headless skeletons. Others who met their grisly end in the Tower complex include *Utopia* author Sir Thomas More, pretender to the throne Arabella Stuart, and a German spy who came to grief in 1941. Although the famous names of England's beheaded get the most coverage, it's worth noting that the biggest carnage was visited upon some 300 Jews, imprisoned in the Tower and then slaughtered for the heinous crime of coin clipping in 1279. The death penalty, for high treason, was still on the statute books of Britain until 1999, when the government agreed to abide by Europe's strictly anti–capital punishment laws. Not everyone left the Tower headless or in a wooden box. Two of the prisoners who breathed sweet freedom after an enforced visit behind these walls are the famous diarist Samuel Pepys and another World War II German, Rudolph Hess, who would spend the rest of his life in Berlin's Spandau jail.

In the eyes of many Brits, a janitor couldn't leave a mop leaning against the wall at the Tate without museum patrons evaluating it with a critical eye.

A good way to get a sense of the layout of the Tower grounds is to take the free, hour-long tour led by the witty Yeoman Warders—better known as Beefeaters—dressed to the gills in Tudor-style costume. Tours leave from just inside the main entrance every half hour until 3:30 (2:30 in winter), except in bad weather. Every night at 10 the Tower is locked during the **Ceremony of the Keys.** Those who have planned ahead—and have sent a self-addressed, stamped envelope at least two months in advance to Ceremony of the Keys, Queen's House, HM Tower of London, EC3N 4AB, for tickets—are treated to low-key pomp and circumstance and a bugler who sounds the all-clear as the chief Yeoman Warder bolts the front gate. If you fancy yourself as a dashing figure in that costume, you'll have a long wait: warders must have 22 years of honorable service in the Army, Royal Marines, or Royal Air Force before they can even apply for the job.

The most impressive and oldest of the towers is the **White Tower.** It was one of a number of fortified structures erected in London by the justifiably nervous William the Conqueror (angry Saxon kings craved Will's hide after he tanned theirs in 1066). The White Tower is currently under renovation, with new displays from the **Royal Armouries** collection being installed. These will tell the story of this medieval building as well as the history of its arms and immaculately polished, beautifully crafted suits of armor. Look for four suits of Henry VIII's armor marking his transmogrification from a "very fair" and "admirably proportioned" young king to the bloated tyrant he became in middle age. The tranquil **Chapel of St. John,** on the tower's first floor, is a haven amid all the military paraphernalia. The curved arches of its Norman

RAVEN MAD

Perhaps the most important man in the Tower is the Yeoman Ravenmaster, responsible for tending the Tower's ravens. In the 17th century, King Charles II decreed that six ravens should be kept at all times at the Tower, fearing the legend that should the ravens leave the grounds, the Tower would crumble and the monarchy would fall. In recent times, three "reserve" ravens have been added for good measure. Although the ravens are captive (their wings are clipped), they are well cared for and even buried within the tower when they die. The cast of characters does change with the years—but the last time we looked in, the feathered residents were Cedric, Gwylum, Hugine II, Munin II, Odin, and Thor. Ravens used to share the Tower with plenty of other animals—and we don't mean the long succession of bloodthirsty kings and queens. Way back in 1235, the Holy Roman Emperor gave Henry III three leopards to start an early trend for exotic beasts at the Tower; later arrivals included a polar bear (1252), who fished in the nearby Thames, and elephants (1255), a gift from Louis IX of France. During the following centuries jackals and wild cats became established favorites at court, until an attack on a guard by one fed-up lion in 1835 signaled the end of the Tower's zoological pretensions.

architecture are stunning in their simplicity and grace. Recently refurbished, the chapel features curved Norman arches that are stunning in their simplicity and grace.

The Crown Jewels, housed in the **Jewel House,** just north of the White Tower, are the star attraction. The Sovereign Sceptre boasts the largest cut diamond in the world, a 530-carat monster from the Cullinan diamond. The Imperial State Crown, made for the coronation of George VI in 1937 and altered for Her Majesty Queen Elizabeth II in 1953, is studded with more than 2,800 precious stones, including the second-largest diamond in the world, also cut from the Cullinan stone. This crown is due to be worn at the coronation of England's next monarch, whoever he or she may be. Although the design of the new Jewel House speeds things up a bit, shiny objects tend to attract huge crowds, so it's best to visit immediately after the Tower opens or just before it closes. Make the mistake of going at midday, especially on weekends, and the wait could last hours. And remember, the NO PHOTOGRAPHY ALLOWED signs are very strictly enforced. A new permanent exhibition, "Crowns and Diamonds," is on display at nearby **Martin Tower** (the original Jewel House—the only successful attempt by Colonel Blood to steal the Crown Jewels took place here in 1671). This exhibition traces the development of English royal crowns and tells the story of some of the most famous stones set in them. A number of royal crown frames are displayed for the first time.

Other points of interest include **Beauchamp Tower**—which has more than 400 eerie notes and doodles carved over centuries into the stone by prisoners—and **Lanthorn Tower,** which contains small but excellent exhibits on life in medieval England. Another tower, the famed **Bloody Tower,** may be where the so-called Little Princes, Edward V and his brother, were murdered in the 15th century, probably by henchmen of either Richard III or Henry VII. It is also where Sir Walter Raleigh spent 13 years of imprisonment, during which he wrote the immodestly titled *History of the World.* Raleigh's incarceration wasn't all that harsh: he had three servants, enjoyed the company of his wife and son, and even fathered a second son while imprisoned. The newly opened **Medieval Palace** is the site of Edward's Magna Camera (Great Chamber), from which he ruled the country, and **Wakefield Tower** has an impressive Throne Room with 13th-century replicas showing the opulence of Edward's court. The **Wall Walk,** linking the Wakefield and Lanthorn towers, offers great views of Tower Bridge. You'll notice the so-called moat around the Tower is in fact a dry old

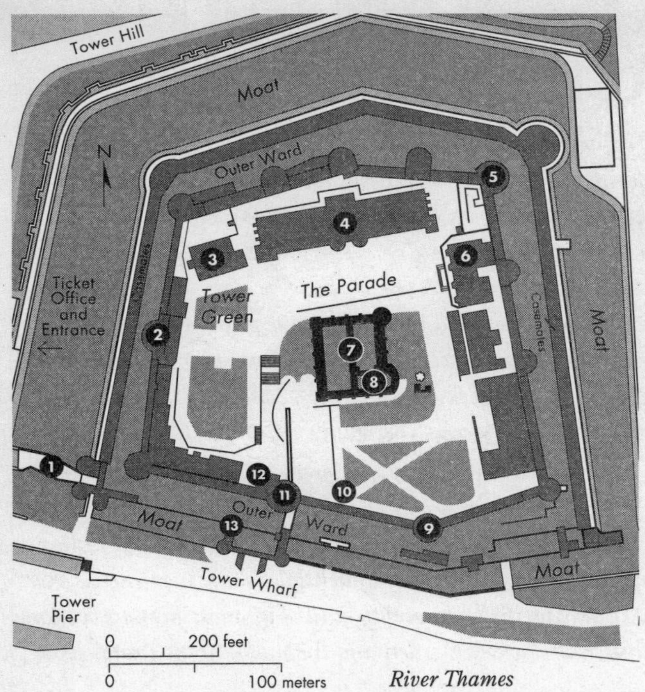

TOWER OF LONDON

Beauchamp Tower, **2**
Bloody Tower, **12**
Chapel of St. John, **3**
Chapel of St. Peter ad Vincula, **8**
Jewel House, **4**
Lanthorn Tower, **9**
Martin Tower, **5**
Medieval Palace, **13**
Ravens' Lodgings, **10**
Royal Fuseliers' Museum, **6**
Wakefield Tower, **11**
White Tower, **7**
Yeoman Warder Tour meeting point, **1**

ditch. It was drained in 1840 but could once again host the wet stuff if tentative plans by local authorities for a refill come through. *Tower Hill, EC3, tel. 020/7709–0765. Tube: Tower Hill. Walk south following signs. Admission £10.50. Open Mar.–Oct., Mon.–Sat. 9–5, Sun. 10–5; Nov.–Feb., Tues.–Sat. 9–4, Sun. and Mon. 10–4 (last admission 1 hr before closing; last entry to exhibits 30 min before closing).*

TOWER BRIDGE

A three-minute walk along the Thames from the Tower of London brings you to Tower Bridge, a Gothic fancy built in 1894. Inside the bridge's hard-to-miss twin towers, you will find the Tower Bridge Experience, a multimedia attraction recounting more than 100 years of the bridge's fascinating history. Highlights of the visit include the storytelling animatronic characters, interactive computers, and other hands-on activities; the original Victorian steam engine rooms; and, of course, the magnificent views of London from the 140-ft-high walkways above the Thames. The bridge itself still opens approximately 500 times a year; if you're lucky you'll catch the spectacle (call 020/7378–7700 for a current schedule). *Tel. 020/7403–3761. Tube: Tower Hill. Admission £5.95. Open Apr.–Oct., daily 10–6:30 (last admission 5:15); Nov.–Mar., daily 9:30–6 (last admission 4:45).*

TRAFALGAR SQUARE

To you, Trafalgar Square might seem no more than a huge traffic circle or a place to spend an afternoon poking through some unforgettable museums (*see below*). Many Londoners, however, consider it the heart of their town, and its notable landmark, **Nelson's Column,** probably makes it the city's most famous square. In 1829, Trafalgar Square was transformed from royal stables to public square in honor of nationally revered naval honcho Lord Horatio Nelson, who died in battle after decimating the French fleet at Cape Trafalgar (on the southwest coast of Spain) in 1805. In 1840, architect E. H. Baily began work on the 185-ft-tall column, Trafalgar Square's most obvious landmark (and a heroic overstatement, considering wee "Baron Nelson of the Nile" measured only 5′4″ in life). Four gigantic **bronze lions** were added by sculptor Sir Edward Landseer in 1858.

LONDON ARCHITECTURE

Great architectural achievements in London have often been motivated by extreme disaster or misfortune. After the Great Fire of 1666 destroyed four-fifths of a city still reeling from the onslaught of the plague the previous year, London required almost complete restoration. Three centuries later, much of central and suburban London was flattened by the German air raids of the early 1940s; postwar rebuilding allowed modern architecture to creep into the city. As a result of these intense civic reconstructions, a few individuals had the opportunity to leave significant marks on the city. Following are architects whose work will literally surround you as you wander through London.

Inigo Jones (1573–1652), one of England's first great architects, was almost single-handedly responsible for the resurgence of classical styles of architecture in the early 17th century. Often directly modeling his work after that of Italian architect Andrea Palladio, Jones was highly influential during his time, as the Palladian style quickly spread throughout England. His most famous works include St. Paul's Church at Covent Garden and the magnificent Banqueting House in Whitehall.

Sir Christopher Wren (1632–1723) was given the daunting task of overseeing the rebuilding of London following the Great Fire. His ambitious plans for a complete redesign of the formerly medieval city, drawn up within a week after the fire, were shot down by landowners, businesspeople, and private citizens intent on a quicker reconstruction. It remains a mystery what effect Wren's membership in the secretive Masonic Lodge had on his efforts. Nevertheless, Wren was responsible for 51 new churches (all in the city) and the amazing St. Paul's Cathedral. Only 23 still survive, the finest of which are St. Bride's (Fleet Street), St. Mary Abchurch (Abchurch Yard), and St. Stephen Walbrook (Walbrook Street).

John Nash (1752–1835) completely redesigned a large section of the city stretching from the Mall northward to Regent's Park and also remodeled Buckingham Palace. He is largely responsible for the look of much of central London; it was his idea to clear Trafalgar Square of its royal stables to make room for the public space as it exists today.

The square is also a fine place for people-watching. It's a spot where Londoners can be seen at their artiest, nuttiest, most passionate, and most political, not to mention their plain, hick, drunkest. Long after sunset, its role as the main stopping point for late-night buses makes the square one of the trippiest places in London. Packs of clubbers and tourists mill around boozily, making nocturnal hot-dog vendors rich and happy. On New Year's Eve, you can multiply the nightlife factor at Trafalgar Square by about 100: it's the most popular place in the city to ring in the new year, possibly because the large clocks around the square are perpetually out of sync; loopy crowds get a chance to celebrate the coming of midnight two or three times.

Political demonstrations are frequently held on Trafalgar Square, which has occasionally been the site of outright rioting since the 19th century. In 1990 hundreds of thousands of people gathered here before attacking police and ransacking nearby shops in response to one particularly severe tax hike. Not that you'll get too much of all that on an average visit.

NATIONAL GALLERY

If you can get past the legions of pigeons guarding the front doors of this magnificent museum, you'll find one of the world's most impressive collections of Western European art. Want a very small Whitman's Sampler of what you'll find here? How about Jan van Eyck's *Arnolfini Marriage,* Leonardo's *Madonna of the Rocks* and *Burlington Virgin and Child,* Uccello's *Battle of San Romano,* Giovanni Bellini's *The Doge Leonardo Loredan,* Caravaggio's *Supper at Emmaus,* Velázquez's *Rokeby Venus,* and that icon of golden age rural England, Constable's *Hay Wain.* There are plenty of other treasures by Tintoretto, della Francesca, Michelangelo, Monet, Titian, Rubens, Van Dyck, Goya, Rembrandt, Turner, Gainsborough, Seurat, et cetera, et cetera. Prepare yourself for a staggering variety of Virgins and Childs. This incredible collection was begun in the 19th century, when Great Britain got rich and began feeling compelled to start amassing a little (well, a lot of, actually) accredited culture to prove it wasn't arriviste. To accommodate the growing collection of masterpieces, Parliament bought a plot of land on the edge of Trafalgar Square in 1828 and began to build the present building, a chilly, classical structure best known for its tall, sandy-brown columns.

For its 150th birthday, the statue atop Nelson's Column received a present: a good scrubbing and a coat of pigeon-proof gel.

Inside, all is splendor and color—and we're not even talking about the art. Thanks to government patronage and public lottery moneys, salons here gleam with expensive brocades and silks. On them hang the painting collections, which continue to be enriched year by year with important works of art. The collections are displayed chronologically in the building's four wings. The **Sainsbury Wing** (paid for by the Sainsbury supermarket family) displays medieval and early Renaissance works (1260–1510). The **West Wing** is devoted to the High Renaissance (1510–1600), the **North Wing** to the Dutch Masters (1600–1700), and the **East Wing** to English portraiture and some of the better-known Impressionists, spanning the centuries from 1700 to 1900. Free, one-hour guided tours begin in the Sainsbury Wing weekdays at 11:30 and 2:30, and on Saturday at 2 and 3:30. If you decide to walk about on your own, pick up a floor plan at the entrance, or stop by the museum's free, technophobe-friendly **Micro Gallery,** where you can use a computer to look at your favorite paintings and then print out your own "grand tour." The Gallery Guide Soundtrack, which allows you to select the paintings you want to hear about, is also available. Free lectures on a variety of topics take place at 1 on weekdays and noon on Saturday; check at an information desk for more details. *Trafalgar Sq., WC2, tel. 020/7747–2885. Tube: Charing Cross or Leicester Sq. Admission free. Open Mon.–Sat. 10–6 (Wed. until 6:30), Sun. noon–6.*

NATIONAL PORTRAIT GALLERY

Painted faces, sculpted faces, drawn faces, photographed faces—the National Portrait Gallery, next door to the National Gallery, is as much about the act and the art of portraiture as it is about the men and women (mostly men) who made Britannia great. The pieces are arranged chronologically from the top floor to the bottom; take the elevator up and wind your way down through the ages. The final leg of the display brings you right up to the present, and walking out onto the streets of London afterward provides a fitting sense of closure. Special upcoming exhibitions include major retrospectives on Sir Henry Raeburn (1756–1823)—the best known of all Scottish painters—and Bruce Weber, the American photographer. The gallery is well-known for its impressive free lectures; pick up a calendar at the information desk. *St. Martin's Pl., WC2, tel. 020/7306–0055. Tube: Charing Cross or Leicester Square. Admission free; small fee for some special exhibitions. Open Mon.–Sat. 10–6, Sun. noon–6.*

ST. MARTIN-IN-THE-FIELDS

In the northeast corner of Trafalgar Square stands the plain, white-stone church of St. Martin-in-the-Fields. This is a beloved landmark in the music world. Handel played on the church's first organ, Mozart is reputed to have given a concert here on one of his—for his day—mega-world tours, and the prestigious Academy of St. Martin-in-the-Fields was founded here in 1958. These days, free music recitals take place Monday, Tuesday, and Friday at 1:05—and are probably the best way to take in the church's grim memo-

PIGEONS—PEST, PIE, OR PETS?

Trafalgar Square is dominated by a vast swarm of pigeons, encouraged to make this part of the world their home by the generosity of cooing humans who scatter birdseed bought (for just 20p) from canny vendors. They might be good fun, but health watchdogs often accuse the pigeons of spreading disease and pestilence, and most Londoners usually leave the birds and tourists to get along together.

Health scares are not the only regular rumors to do the rounds on the subject of the square's pigeons. Every so often the London media gets itself into a frenzy over the possibility of a mysterious pigeon thief who, urban legend has it, emerges in the small hours to entrap the pigeons with a giant net before selling them to West End restaurants the next morning. The moral here is not to turn your nose up at London's restaurant food, but to take everything you read in the city's papers, especially the gossipy Evening Standard, *with a bucket full of salt.*

There has even been a Tidy Britain *campaign to stop feeding the pigeons so that their numbers gradually fall off. Previous half-baked schemes include shooting the overfed birds in an annual cull, netting them, and even feeding the highly reproductive beasts with contraceptive pills.*

The pigeons have definitely made some powerful enemies. One time a policeman guarding Prime Minister Tony Blair fired shots at the poor birds, believing them to be intruders after they set off a security alarm. If only they had been born as birds of prey in an earlier, more forgiving, age. From around 1300, hawks, the feathered playthings of monarchs including Edward I, made their homes in the King's Mews, sited where Trafalgar Square is today.

rials to the British war dead. Evening concerts (£6–£16, Thurs.–Sat. 7:30) usually feature big-name ensembles performing by candlelight. Like most other churches, St. Martin's possesses a **crypt,** but this isn't your typical musty repository of old bones. Instead, the **Café-in-the-Crypt** (tel. 020/7839–4342) is one of the coolest, most atmospheric places for latte in all of London. With roughhewn stone pillars, low vault ceilings, and floors tiled with worn grave markers, it's the perfect place to pen moody, intense postcards to the folks back home. Additionally, the crypt houses a modest art gallery and bookstore, and the **London Brass Rubbing Centre** (tel. 020/7930–9306), where for £2.50–£15 (depending on size) you can make rubbings from historic brasses using gold, bronze, or silver wax. *East side of Trafalgar Sq., WC2, tel. 020/7930–0089 or 020/7839–8362 for box office. Open Mon.–Sat. 10–8, Sun. noon–8.*

WESTMINSTER ABBEY

So popular has Westminster Abbey become as a tourist attraction—during the day, announcements over the nave loudspeakers actually have to request moments of silence from the milling throngs—that it's easy to forget the enormous religious and cultural importance of this magisterially beautiful house of worship. Legend has it that the first church on this site was built in the 7th century at the say-so of St. Peter. Founded for certain in 1065 by Edward the Confessor, who was both king and saint, Westminster

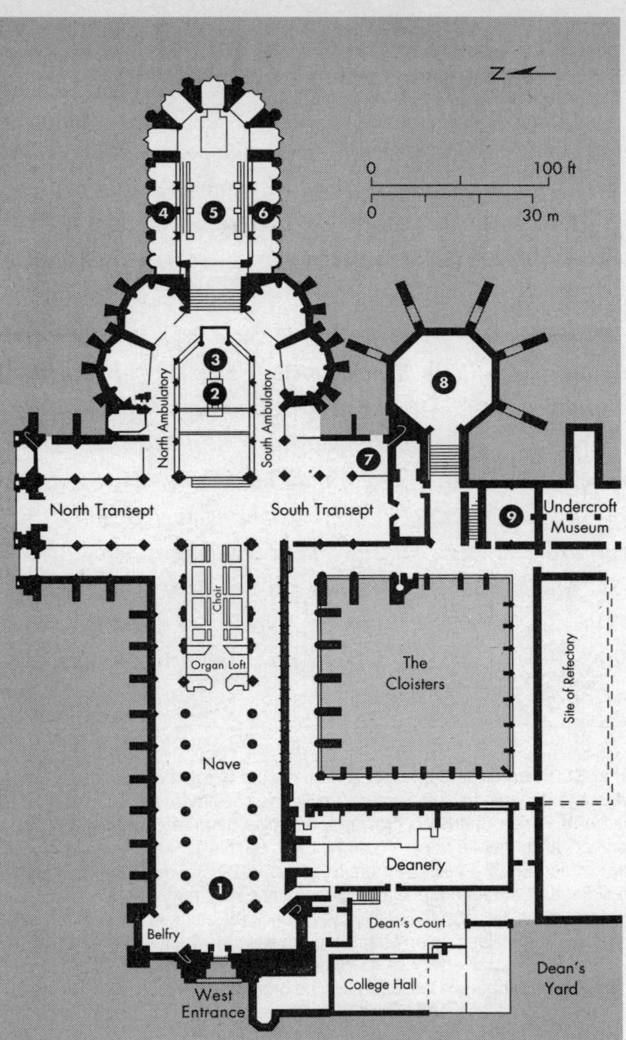

WESTMINSTER ABBEY

Chapel of Edward the Confessor, **3**

Chapter House, **8**

Coronation Chair, **2**

Henry VII's Chapel, **5**

Poets' Corner, **7**

Pyx Chamber, **9**

Tomb of Mary, Queen of Scots, **6**

Tomb of Queen Elizabeth I, **4**

Tomb of the Unknown Warrior and Memorial to Sir Winston Churchill, **1**

Abbey reflects the close relationship of church and state in Britain. The country's monarchs have been crowned and buried here since William the Conqueror assumed the English throne on Christmas Day, AD 1066. Burial in Westminster is one of the highest honors the country can bestow and, accordingly, a walk through this vast, ornate abbey is like perusing a *Who's Who* of British history. Among the deceased sovereigns buried here are Elizabeth I, Mary Queen of Scots, Richard II, and Henry VII. Two of the most famous statesmen, at least to modern sensibilities, commemorated in the Abbey are wartime leaders Winston Churchill and Franklin D. Roosevelt, whose stone tributes are near the tomb of the Unknown Warrior, a nameless soldier brought back from the French killing fields after the First World War. You'll now pay £5 just to get your size nines through the front door, a new charge that raised a storm of protest among Londoners and tourist organizations, unfortunately to no avail. The good side of the new fee is that crowd figures are slightly lower and there are now no separate charges for all the other bits of the building, like the popular Poets' Corner and the Royal Chapels.

BLUE PLAQUE ATTACK!

As you wander around London, you'll see lots of small, blue, oval-shape plaques on the sides and facades of buildings, describing which famous, semifamous, or obscure but brilliant person once lived there. Unfortunately, the handy little guides that index such plaques are out of print indefinitely, so we've listed a few highlights below.

Elizabeth Barrett Browning (50 Wimpole St., Bloomsbury); Sir Winston Churchill (28 Hyde Park Gate, South Kensington); T. S. Eliot (3 Kensington Ct., Kensington); Mahatma Gandhi (20 Baron's Court Rd., West Kensington); George Frideric Handel (25 Brook St., Mayfair); Karl Marx (28 Dean St., Soho); Piet Cornelis Mondrian (60 Parkhill Rd., Camden); Sir Isaac Newton (87 Jermyn St., St. James's); Florence Nightingale (10 South St., Mayfair); George Bernard Shaw (29 Fitzroy Sq., Marylebone); Percy Bysshe Shelley (15 Poland St., Mayfair); Dylan Thomas (54 Delancey St., Camden); Oscar Wilde (34 Tite St., Chelsea); Virginia Woolf (52 Tavistock Sq., Bloomsbury); William Butler Yeats (23 Fitzroy Rd., Camden); Émile Zola (Queen's Hotel, 122 Church Rd., Croydon).

Behind the altar, the **Chapel of St. Edward the Confessor** is home to the Coronation Chair, still used for the crowning of Britain's kings and queens. In recent years, hooligans have managed to etch graffiti all over the wooden chair; when or if Prince Charles is crowned, his royal derriere could rest on incisive comments like "C loves S forever" and "smoke dope." The chair was built in 1300 to enclose the Stone of Scone (pronounced skoon), which Edward I swiped from Scotland in 1296. The Stone of Destiny, as it is also known, is a symbol of Scottish independence and its residence here had naturally given rise to some friction between the two countries. Scottish nationalists stole back the stone in 1950, but Scotland Yard (a misnomer) recovered it six months later. In an attempt to appease the Scottish nationalists, John Major announced in 1996—the 700th anniversary of its removal—that the stone should indeed be returned to Scotland: today, it rests in Edinburgh Castle (but will be brought back to London for the coronation of future monarchs). Farther back you'll find **Henry VII's Chapel,** one of Britain's most beautiful examples of the rich Gothic style. The tomb of Henry VII and his wife, Elizabeth, was created by Italian artist Torrigiano, best known for popping Michelangelo on the nose during an argument.

Nearly all the deceased greats of English literature are featured in Westminster's **Poets' Corner,** in the south transept. Geoffrey Chaucer was the first to be buried here, in 1400. Memorial plaques pay homage to other luminaries, such as Shakespeare, T. S. Eliot, Byron, Tennyson, and, more recently, Oscar Wilde. Ye olde monks once pontificated and wandered through the **Cloisters** on the south side of the nave. Open to the air, the cloisters retain a tranquility that the main portion of the abbey loses after the early morning hours. At the end of a passage leading from the Cloisters is the octagonal, spacious **Chapter House,** once a meeting place of England's Parliament. If you want all the details, 90-min **Supertours** of the abbey (£3) are given four times a day on weekdays, and twice on Saturday morning if demand warrants; book ahead by calling 020/7222–7110, or ask at the inquiry desk. *Dean's Yard, SW1, tel. 020/7222–5152. Tube: St. James's Park. Walk south on Broadway, turn left on Victoria St. Admission £5. Nave and Cloisters open daily 8–6. Royal Chapels open weekdays 9–4:45 (last admission 3:45), Sat. 9–2:45 (last admission 2), and 3:45–5:45 (last admission 2:45). Closed Sun.*

LONDON NEIGHBORHOODS

London is best approached as a series of highly distinct, diverse neighborhoods, many of which were once towns or villages in their own right. Regardless of who you are or what you're after, London has a neighborhood to fulfill your every whim. If it's government buildings and famous monuments, Whitehall has more than enough for the hardiest tourist. If you prefer a little boho culture, head for the likes of Camden, Notting Hill, or Hampstead. For a vicarious taste of the good (or at least expensive) life, sashay over to ritzy Mayfair, St. James's, or Chelsea. If you're interested in London's legal and financial institutions, make your way to Holborn and the City, respectively. There's great people-watching at Covent Garden, as well as in the various central squares. And for a taste of authentic, workaday London (and an earful of Cockney accents), check out the East End, once the horrific haunt of Jack the Ripper.

Below we first navigate the city's neighborhoods West End to East End, then venture into South and North London. We begin with the posh West End (Chelsea, Notting Hill, Kensington, Knightsbridge, Mayfair), move over to Central London (St. James's, Whitehall, Westminster, Soho, Covent Garden, Bloomsbury, Strand and Embankment, the City), then head over to East London (the East End), take a turn south of the Thames (the South Bank, Brixton, Richmond), then head up to North London (Marylebone, Regent's Park, Camden Town, Islington, Hampstead, Highgate), and finally head out of the city for two easy day trips (Greenwich, Windsor). Within each neighborhood, **leading sights are discussed sequentially, making up the route of a pleasant walk.**

Famous faces in the National Portrait Gallery include Shakespeare, the Brontë sisters (minus their brother—look for the smudge), and Virginia Woolf. The ones that draw the crowds, however, are the royal portraits of Diana and Charles.

Most first-time travelers pick Piccadilly Circus as their starting point in Central London. The Circus is a swirl of traffic, rather fetchingly surrounded by grand Edwardian-era buildings; from here, walk toward the area of central London you want to explore. To the north runs Regent Street, a shopper's mecca that curves up one side of mostly residential Mayfair. To the south is Lower Regent Street, leading toward Whitehall, the parks, and the palaces. To the east are Shaftesbury Avenue and Leicester Square, for theater and Soho; to the west is Piccadilly itself, heading out to Hyde Park and Knightsbridge. Piccadilly Circus is also a great place to board a double-decker sightseeing bus to get a roaring overview of the "flower of cities all." Just remember to bring something to keep you warm—atop these buses it's *always* windy.

WEST LONDON

CHELSEA AND BELGRAVIA

Chelsea is where Henry James died, T. S. Eliot lived, James McNeill Whistler painted his "nocturnes," and the King's Road scene gave birth to the Swinging '60s and Punk '70s. Today, however, the artists have moved out and the Gettys have moved in. Located just south of Knightsbridge, it's a mostly quiet and residential district—except for its famous **King's Road** (*see below*), which is a swell place for a stroll if you like to shop. South of King's Road, running along the Thames between Battersea and Albert bridges, is one of London's ritziest pieces of real estate: **Cheyne Walk** (pronounced chainy), which once boasted such heavyweight residents as George Eliot (No. 4), Dante Gabriel Rossetti (No. 16), and Mick Jagger (No. 48). Certainly no artists or literary masters roam the streets now, but if you're lucky you might clap eyes on the likes of Jagger, Bob Geldof, or Phil Collins as this salubrious part of the world is the favored semi-retirement home for members of the aging rock fraternity. Apart from rockers who are well past their sell-by date, all you'll find are privileged Chelseans walking their privileged Labradors along the privileged streets. You can, however, get a glimpse into the life of one long-gone literary giant. **Thomas Carlyle's House** (24 Cheyne Row, SW3, tel. 020/7352–7087) is just as the Carlyles left it more than 150 years ago—Thomas's hat is still where he put it before he died, and all the furniture, books, and possessions remain intact. It's open April–October, Wednesday–Sunday 11–5, and admission is £3.30. The

CHELSEA AND BELGRAVIA

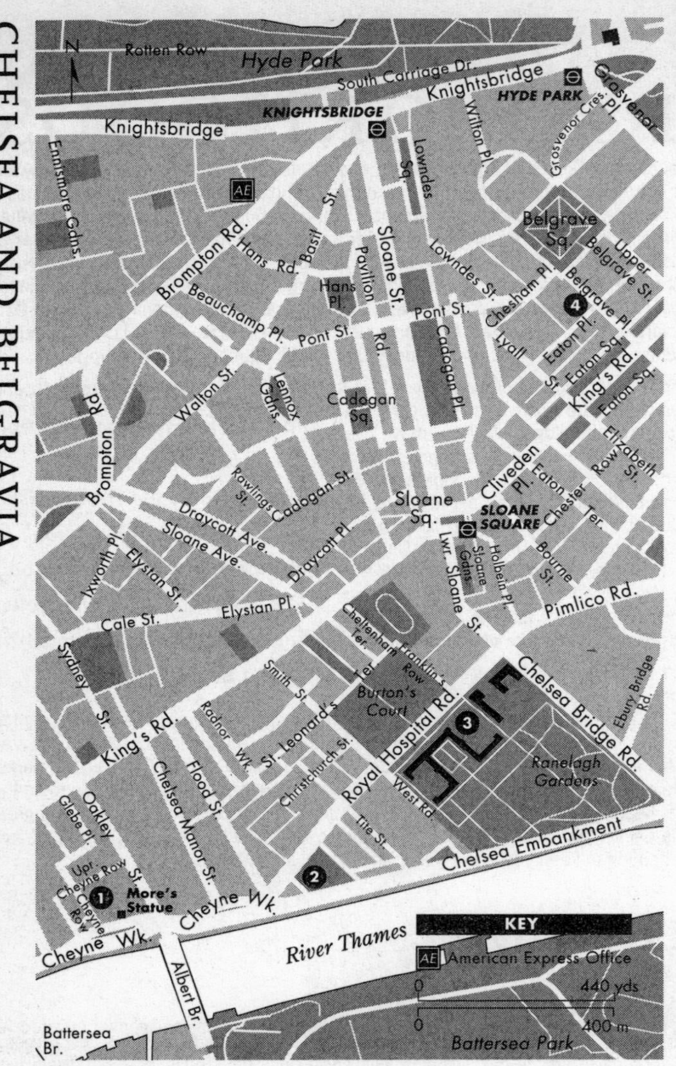

Belgrave Place, **4**
Chelsea Physic Garden, **2**
Royal Hospital, **3**
Thomas Carlyle's House, **1**

romantic **Ranelagh Gardens,** off the Chelsea Embankment (that's what they call Cheyne Walk east of Albert Bridge), is a fine place to visit, especially on warm summer nights. Mozart gave a concert here in 1764 at the age of eight, and it's easy to imagine the London elite of past centuries putting on airs while meandering along the footpaths. The famous Chelsea Flower Show is held here in May (*see* Festivals *in* Chapter 1).

CHELSEA PHYSIC GARDEN

Established in 1676 by the Society of Apothecaries, this garden was used to teach about medicinal properties of herbs and other plants. Cottonseed sent from here in 1732 helped establish the cotton industry in the Americas, starting in the depths of Georgia. The Physic Garden is now an important botanical research and education center. The high walls surrounding the garden serve to create a Mediterranean ambience. Afternoon tea is served between 2:30 and 4:45—it's a double treat to munch on cakes while feasting your eyes on the floral blossoms all about. *66 Royal Hospital Rd. (entrance on Swan Walk), SW3, tel. 020/7352–5646. Tube: Sloane Sq. Walk south on Lower Sloane St., turn right on Royal Hospital Rd. Admission £4. Open Apr.–Oct., Wed. Noon–5, Sun. 2–6.*

SLOANE SQUARE

Most visitors planning to promenade among the fashionable folks of the King's Road start their journey at Sloane Square after emerging from the tube station. But wait, that underground cavern has its own fascinating bits of history to impart. Look up as you detrain; on its mysterious way down to Old Father Thames, one of London's many hidden rivers, the Westboure, gushes through the huge iron pipe you'll see running across the ceiling. Parts of the river are still used as the basis for a sewer, like its East London counterpart, the Fleet. During the Second World War, a time during which a number of tube stations in central London doubled as bomb shelters, many Londoners were killed when Sloane Square took a direct hit from the Luftwaffe in 1940. Sloane Square itself was first built in 1771 by Sir Hans Sloane, the doctor whose donations helped start the British Museum. On the west side stands the Royal Court Theatre, home of the English Stage Company; on the west is department store Peter Jones, a kind of stress-free Harrods. *Tube: Sloane Sq.*

KING'S ROAD

King's Road has gone yuppie in the last decade or so, but this was where rebel chicks bought the world's first miniskirts (invented by designer Mary Quant, who had a boutique here) in the '60s, and where punk rock was born in the 1970s. Legend goes that the whole punk thing started when the Sex Pistols popped into fashion designer Vivienne Westwood's little King's Road boutique, named Sex, for a few pairs of bondage trousers. Within a few years the whole boulevard was crammed with counterculture clothing shops, record stores, and disaffected youth. The aggressively weird among today's offspring still assemble on weekends at the northeast end of King's Road, around **Sloane Square.** Famous former residents of the King's Road in previous ages include legendary stage actress Ellen Terry, who was stationed at No. 215 from 1904 until 1920, and toilet pioneer Thomas Crapper who established offices at No. 120 in the 19th century. *Tube: Sloane Sq.*

ROYAL HOSPITAL

More commonly known by its unofficial name, Chelsea Hospital, the Royal was commissioned by Charles II in 1682 to house veteran soldiers. Wren's Royal Hospital is still home to around 400 "Chelsea Pensioners"—retired servicemen "of good character," who proudly wear their distinctive uniforms: the everyday dark blue overcoat and the more ceremonial scarlet frock coat. The pensioners take part in all the ceremonial and traditional happenings attached to Royal Hospital life—attending church, marching in parades—and are given food, lodging, clothing, and a daily ration of beer and tobacco. You're welcome to enter the grounds and pay a visit to Verrio's famous painting of Charles II on horseback and Van Dyck's portrait of Charles I and his family. The Royal's history is illustrated in a museum on the hospital grounds, and the fairly dull **National Army Museum** is just to the south. *Royal Hospital Rd., SW3, tel. 020/7730–0717. Tube: Sloane Sq. Walk south on Lower Sloane Square St., turn right on Royal Hospital Rd. Admission free. Open Mon.–Sat. 10–noon and 2–4, Sun. 2–4.*

BELGRAVIA

Just to the north of Chelsea is Belgravia—London's most princely and pricey residential quarter. No sights here, but a promenade along its infinitely graceful streets will reveal London at its *Upstairs, Downstairs* best (the Bellamys, you may recall, lived on Belgravia's Eaton Square). Head for **Belgrave Place** and check out the imposing embassies and incredibly picturesque mews. Comparisons to a stage set designed by Cecil Beaton after visiting Ascot would not be amiss: most of the neighborhood houses are stuccoed Wedgwood-china white—to indicate they are the property of the Dukes of Westminster, England's biggest real estate family.

Kensington is museum central: in one large block you'll find three major museums—the Victoria and Albert Museum, the Natural History Museum, and the Science Museum. The neighborhoods of **South Kensington** and **Earl's Court** are riddled with budget lodgings and hordes of travelers—Londoners themselves can be a bit thin on the ground around here. As you move northeast toward Knightsbridge, however, the streetscape gets more ritzy and prices go through the roof—only Mayfair and St. James's carry more snob value. Though prices are prohibitive, you can always window-shop on the long east–west thoroughfare of **Knightsbridge** and **Kensington High Street** (different names, same street). Just north of Knightsbridge lie two of London's best parks, Hyde Park and Kensington Gardens (*see below*).

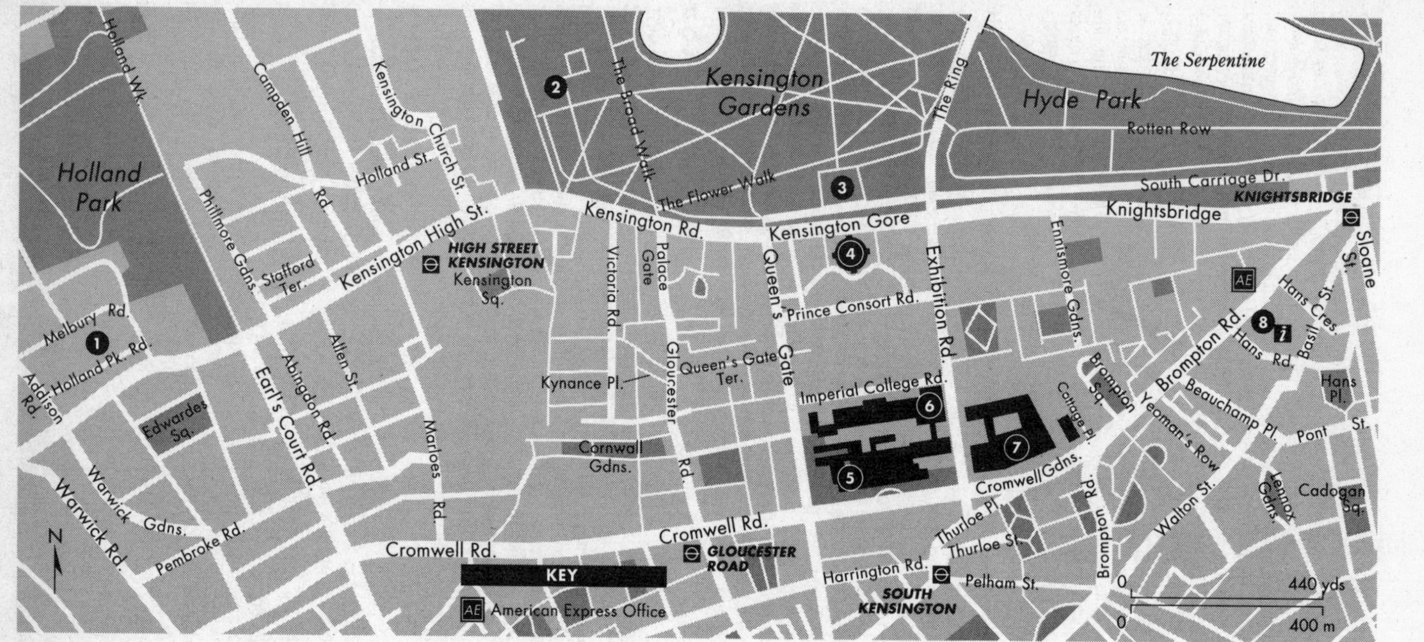

Albert Memorial, **3**
Harrods, **8**
Kensington Palace, **2**
Leighton House, **1**
Natural History Museum, **5**
Royal Albert Hall, **4**
Science Museum, **6**
Victoria and Albert Museum, **7**

KENSINGTON AND KNIGHTSBRIDGE

KENSINGTON AND KNIGHTSBRIDGE

HOLLAND PARK

Beautiful Holland Park inhabits a sizable chunk of posh Kensington, just north of the intersection of Kensington High Street and Earl's Court Road. The whole 52 acres were originally the private grounds of the stately Jacobean **Holland House,** now a youth hostel (*see* Chapter 3), and have only been open to the public since 1952. Thanks to progressive aristocrat Lady Holland, a charming and witty hostess, Holland House became a kind of drop-in center for liberal politicians in the late 18th century. Unlike most of her countrymen, Lady Holland was a big fan of Napoléon and sent him plum jam, books, and a refrigerator during his enforced stay on Elba. To the north you'll find stunning gardens and woodlands where wild peacocks roam. At the park's center is the formal **Dutch Garden** (first planted by Lady Holland in the 1790s) and a glass-wall art gallery, the **Orangery.** *Tube: High St. Kensington.*

NOTTING HILL GATE

Ultrahip and sizzling with activity, this district, centered around the Portobello antiques market and Westbourne Grove, is home to many of London's style-setting elite (dubbed Notting Hillbillies by the media) and several of the city's best gastro-pubs. Notting Hill has few sights—but go on a pavement crawl and you might just wind up seeing Mick Jagger chowing down on Caribbean grub, supermodels like Kate Moss (a resident) shopping for '60s-vintage shoes, and noted natives like fashion designer Rifat Ozbek and author Lady Antonia Fraser out for a Sunday afternoon stroll. With Rastafarians rubbing elbows with wealthy young Brits (a.k.a. "Trustafarians"), Notting Hill is—at least for now—one of the city's leading scene-arenas. If you're here in late summer and in the mood for music and lots of company, Notting Hill is the place to be. The **Notting Hill Carnival** is the biggest in Europe with well in excess of a million people strutting their stuff each year on the last weekend of August. Now more than 40 years old, the Carnival has gone through several stages of evolution to arrive at its present fun-for-all format. In the '60s it was essentially a chance for west London's Caribbean community to display its pride; although the '70s saw mass battles with police, creeping commercialism threatened the Carnival's spirit in the '80s. Now the still-dominant Caribbean flavor (steel bands, reggae, Jamaican goat patties) is peppered with influences from South America and Asia, and white folks are turning up in ever greater numbers. Nighttime can still be a bit edgy but, given the huge crowds involved, crime is really on the low side.

LEIGHTON HOUSE

Once one of London's most exotic abodes, Leighton House is the former home and studio of Lord Frederic Leighton (1830–96), a classical painter and avid collector of Islamic art and Asian treasures. Today, it is a beautifully decorated museum, highlighted by the breathtaking **Arab Hall,** constructed with intricately detailed tiles and mosaic friezes. Leighton and pals were not bad painters either, as evidenced by the many Victorian oils in the other rooms. *12 Holland Park Rd., W14, tel. 020/7602–3316. Tube: High St. Kensington. Walk west on Kensington High St., turn right on Melbury Rd., left on Holland Park Rd. Admission free. Open Mon.–Sat. 11–5:30.*

NATURAL HISTORY MUSEUM

Out of all the museums, this one and the Science Museum next door are the best if you've got the kids in tow. So when you can feel that all too common London rain emerging from the clouds, whip yourself and your kin in here and disappear into a strange world of dead animals housed in this magnificent monument to Victorian confidence. A thorough collection of plants and animals is housed in the impressive Earth and Life galleries. There are fossils, dinosaur skeletons, stuffed animals (in the literal, taxidermic sense) from every corner of the earth, and amazing interactive exhibits such as a simulated earthquake—the whole shebang. Perhaps more impressive than the contents is the building itself. Designed by Alfred Waterhouse in 1862, the museum was built as a cathedral to science, decorated throughout with images of living and extinct animals and fossils. The modern extension on the east flank of the museum has caused much undeserved controversy. Prince Charles, no friend to the modern architect, called it a "carbuncle on the face of a much-loved friend." Stop in during the free hours just to take a peek. *Cromwell Rd., SW7, tel. 020/7938–9123. Tube: South Kensington. Walk north on Exhibition Rd., turn left on Cromwell Rd. Admission £6; free weekdays after 4:30, weekends after 5. Open Mon.–Sat. 10–5:50, Sun. 11–5:50.*

SCIENCE MUSEUM

The Science Museum's six floors are chockful of groovy, user-friendly exhibits about science, technology, industry, and medicine. Exhibits at the science museum include early examples of the machines that drove Britain's industrial revolution, such as Puffing Billy, Stephenson's Rocket, and Arkwright's spinning machine. More modern technological achievements get a look in, too, with a recent, kid-friendly emphasis on space. Check at the front desk for info on free daily workshops and guided tours. *Exhibition Rd., SW7, tel. 020/7938–8111 (recorded info) 020/7938–8000 (info desk). Tube: South Kensington. Walk north on Exhibition Rd. Admission £6.50; free after 4:30. Open daily 10–6.*

VICTORIA AND ALBERT MUSEUM

The best way to take in the enormous collection of this stellar and chic museum, affectionately called the V&A, is to allow yourself a whole day to get lost in its 7 mi of gallery space, then try to find your way out. The place is packed with a vast and eclectic collection of fine and decorative arts, crossing all disciplines, all periods, all nationalities, and all tastes. Prince Albert, Victoria's adored consort, was the man with the V&A plan back in the 19th century: it was to be a permanent version of the enormously popular 1851 Great Exhibition, also his creation. Now, a century and a half later, the V&A has stirred up enormous controversy with announcements of a financially taxing addition, a building that is likely to be set wackily at a 45° angle to the ground. Called the **Boilerhouse Project,** it will house a state-of-the-art multimedia gallery with computers and virtual reality gizmos, and galleries for contemporary exhibits.

Sauntering through the galleries, you'll pass treasures weird and wonderful, like the snuffbox believed to have been a gift to Nell Gwyn from Charles II, the great Mogul emperor Shah Jahan's jade cup, or the 12-ft-square, solid-oak, four-poster **Great Bed of Ware,** immortalized by Shakespeare in *Twelfth Night.* The **Art and Design Galleries** exhibit everything from Indian art to Italian Renaissance sculpture. Another top-flight section is the **Dress Collection** (Room 40), with, you guessed it, dresses, some from as far back as 1600. Stairs from the Dress Collection lead to an exhibit of finely crafted musical instruments. The **Raphael Gallery** displays seven priceless cartoons by the great Renaissance master Raphael, and the **Frank Lloyd Wright Gallery** houses the only re-created Wright interior in Europe. In the more recent **Silver Galleries,** you'll find some 1,500 silver objects dating from 1300 to 1800—including royal flatware and booty from sunken galleons. Other galleries include the Tsui Gallery of Chinese Art, Nehru Gallery of Indian Art, 20th Century Gallery, Glass Gallery, and Iron Gallery, and that's just a fraction of what this unique museum has to offer.

One of the most impressive sections of this multifaceted museum is the **Medieval Treasury,** which is especially strong on religious artifacts. With its ancient religious pieces set in a dim room lit only by the shafts of light that seep through the stained glass, the Treasury helps set a tone of serenity for the rest of the museum.

The V&A offers two varieties of free guided tours daily: introductory tours leave from the info desk at 10:30, 11, noon, 1, 2, and 3 daily; gallery talks (daily at 2 PM, 45 min–1 hr) focus on special displays. During summer months the V&A stays open from 6:30 to 9:30 on Wednesday evening, when it offers live music, a garden wine bar, free gallery talks, and lectures. *Cromwell Rd., SW7, tel. 020/7938–8500 (for recorded info, 020/7938–8349). Tube: South Kensington. Walk north on Exhibition Rd., turn right on Cromwell Rd. Admission £5; free entry 4:30–5:30. Open daily 10–5:45.*

HARRODS

This granddaddy of all London department stores is a magnet for every tourist on the planet. Don't come here to shop—it's expensive—but rather to browse. Many of the upper floors are just like any other department store, so you're much better off moseying down to the lavish **food halls,** where you can pick and choose from an enticing array of food. Mouth-watering meats and cheeses hang from the ceiling, smoked salmon is sliced ever-so-thin, and skilled butchers and fishmongers in white aprons make it all look even better. If you don't mind carnage, visit the meat hall, where skilled butchers bustle under ceiling tiles illustrating *The Hunt,* painted by W. J. Neatby in 1902. Throughout the store, however, are other yummy sights, such as the new Egyptian-theme central escalators. If you're here around Christmas, ogle the decorations and displays—they really do it up grand. In the future there could be one sight to beat all the sumptuous goodies that adorn the inside of the store, as Harrods' Egyptian owner Mohamed Al Fayed has earmarked the store's roof as the site of his tomb. The father of Dodi, the doomed lover of Princess Diana, has had an ax to grind with the British establishment ever since being refused citizenship many years ago. Not a man to slough off personal slights, Al Fayed caused a political scandal in the early '90s by admitting he had bribed Members of Parliament; after his son's death, he was one of the first to back outlandish conspiracy theories concerning the fateful Paris road smash. Given Al Fayed's antiestablishment attitude, it's a mite surprising that Harrods should operate one of the stuffiest door policies in the history of world shopping. Tales are legion of would-be customers getting the thumbs down from overzealous staff. Those offending have included men wearing shorts, young women exposing too much flesh, and one poor unfortunate American soul deemed too fat to be clothed in leggings. *87135 Brompton Rd., SW1, tel. 020/7730–1234. Tube: Knightsbridge. Walk south on Brompton Rd. Open Mon.–Tues. and Sat. 10–6, Wed.–Fri. 10–7.*

ROYAL ALBERT HALL

This prestigious venue (named after Queen Victoria's hubby) is currently undergoing a massive development program, funded in part by the National Lottery. Home to the acclaimed **Royal Philharmonic Orchestra** and the enormously popular **Promenade Concerts** (*see* Classical Music, Opera, and Dance *in* Chapter 6), the vast interior, done up in wine-red and gold, is the height of Victorian imperial architecture and is graced with the largest pipe organ in Great Britain. Unfortunately, tours of these splendors aren't available during the renovations. To see the splendors, you'll have to buy a concert ticket. Barring that, pop by for a look at the exterior, if only because it's mentioned in the Beatles song "A Day in the Life." *Kensington Gore, near Exhibition Rd., W8, tel. 020/7589–3203 (box office 020/7589–8212). Tube: Knightsbridge. Walk west on Knightsbridge (which becomes Kensington Rd. and Kensington Gore).*

HYDE PARK AND KENSINGTON GARDENS

Hyde Park and Kensington Gardens blend together to form one large, 634-acre park, the biggest in London. Although these days it's difficult to tell where one ends and the other begins, each has a unique origin: Hyde Park began as the hunting grounds of Henry VIII (who swiped the land from the monks at Westminster), whereas Kensington Gardens was first laid out as the grounds for William and Mary's Kensington Palace (*see below*). In summer this is a great place to lounge in one of hundreds of conveniently placed deck chairs available for hire (£0.80), or just kick back in the tall grass under a huge shady tree. Small boats cruise on the **Serpentine,** a long, thin lake that arcs through the middle of the two parks. You can rent a rowboat or a pedal boat at the boathouse (tel. 020/7262–3751) for £7.00 an hour (*see* Participant Sports *in* Chapter 8).

You're also duty-bound not to miss **Speakers' Corner** on the northeast edge of Hyde Park (tube: Marble Arch). Since 1873, this has been hallowed ground for amateur orators burning to make a point—in the early days, speakers used soapboxes; now they climb aboard aluminum stepladders. Speakers' Corner represents only a small slice of the park's role as site for great political events. Hundreds of thousands of reformists massed here at various times during the 19th century, and the Park has been the end point of many a march in the modern era, from student protests in the '60s, to antinuclear demos in the '80s. Indeed, the original reason for creating Speaker's Corner was as a kind of safety valve following serious disorder in the 1800s. The oratorical fireworks hit full swing by about 2 or 3 on weekends, as the spielers spiel, the hecklers heckle, and free speech dovetails into street theater. There could be as many as a dozen speakers declaiming to individual crowds of more than 100 people, on subjects as diverse as justice and democracy, the evils of meat-eating, or invaders from Mars. In 1996 Speakers' Corner became a sparring ground for Islamic extremists and Christian evangelists (who both still make appearances on a regular basis).

Kensington Gardens contains a cute statue of Peter Pan, the park being a particular favorite of J. M. Barrie, the lost boy's creator who once donated a set of kiddie swings. You can catch sight of plenty of Wendys to this day, as these beautiful open spaces are still used by pristine nannies out walking the offspring of wealthy west London denizens. Of course joggers (including Madonna on her visits to London) and rollerbladers are just as likely to zoom past people-watchers, a pacific group in comparison to the duel fighters and highwaymen who frequented Hyde Park during the 17th and 18th centuries. Finally, Hyde Park and Kensington Gardens are the places to crash after haggling at the splendid **Portobello Road Market** (*see* Street Markets *in* Chapter 7), although rest might not so easily be obtained when at least one chunk of the Gardens become part of a planned shrine to Diana, the size of which is still to be determined. *Tel. 020/7298–2100 for park info.*

APSLEY HOUSE • At the southeast corner of Hyde Park stands Apsley House, also known as the Wellington Museum, once home to the "Iron Duke" Wellington. Inside you will find the great man's collection of paintings, silver, porcelain, furniture, and sculpture, including Canova's massive nude-but-for-a-fig-leaf statue of his archenemy, Napoléon Bonaparte. The glitzy highlight is the Waterloo Gallery, one of the grandest salons in Europe. *149 Piccadilly, tel. 020/7499–5676. Tube: Hyde Park Corner. Admission £4.50. Open Tues.–Sun. 11–5.*

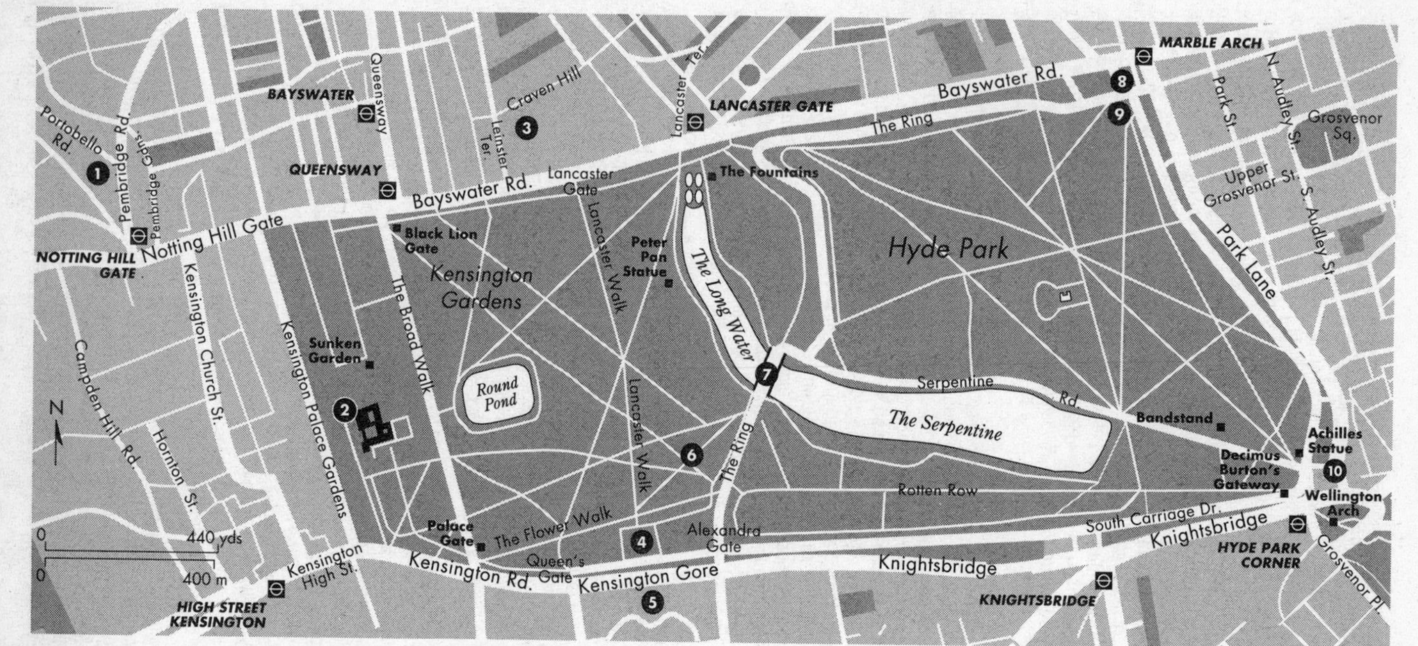

Albert Memorial, **4**
Apsley House/ Wellington Museum, **10**
Kensington Palace, **2**
London Toy and Model Museum, **3**
Marble Arch, **8**
Portobello Road Market, **1**
Royal Albert Hall, **5**
Serpentine Bridge, **7**
Serpentine Gallery, **6**
Speakers' Corner, **9**

HYDE PARK AND KENSINGTON GARDENS

KENSINGTON PALACE • Kensington Palace has seen a lot of history since it was converted from a plain old mansion to a royal homestead by Christopher Wren in 1689. As the London residence of Prince Charles and Princess Diana, the palace saw some of the couple's lowest moments, including Diana's infamous suicide attempt, when she threw herself down the sweeping palace staircase. It was also here that Diana is reckoned to have conducted a number of her extramarital affairs, such as the cloak and dagger assignation with England's rugby star Will Carling. The palace is still home to other royals, including the Prince and Princess of Kent. Happily, the State Apartments are open to the public. They include the **Cupola Room,** where Queen Victoria was baptized; the **King's Gallery,** filled with fine 17th-century paintings, and the **King's Drawing Room,** once used by Mary II. The noted **Royal Ceremonial Dress Collection** has greatly benefited from recent remodeling; here you can inspect Queen Mary's wedding dress and ogle fine embroidery, glittering thread, and feathered hats. Part of the complex, and just a few steps from the palace, is the Orangery—a delightful place for an expensive cuppa. *Kensington Gardens, W8, tel. 020/7937–9561. Tube: High St. Kensington or Queensway. Admission £8.50. Open May–Sept., daily 10–5.*

ALBERT MEMORIAL • Across from the Royal Albert Hall is the grandiose Albert Memorial, commissioned by Queen Victoria as an expression of her obsessive reverence for her dead husband. Here a 25-ft-tall, gold-plated Albert sits under an ornate canopy, clutching a catalog of the Great International Exhibition of 1851 (his brainchild). The base is decorated with 169 life-size figures of poets, composers, architects, and sculptors. The Albert Memorial has recently been the subject of a costly restoration, its almost garish new appearance causing a small sensation when revealed. *Kensington Gardens, SW7. Tube: High St. Kensington or Knightsbridge.*

MARBLE ARCH • Originally this Nash-designed edifice fronted up Buckingham Palace, but it was shifted to the present site in 1851. Despite its apparent demotion in rank, the arch, modeled on the Arch of Constantine in Rome, still retains considerable regal connections; only top-flight members of the Royal family and the King's Troop Royal Horse Artillery are allowed to mosey on through it. In 1996 the whole shebang was completely renovated (and pigeon-proofed): to help defray costs, the Department of National Heritage installed tenants in two tiny rooms built into the sides of the monument. *Tube: Marble Arch (surprise!).*

MAYFAIR

Mayfair, sandwiched between hip and happening Soho and Hyde Park/Kensington Gardens, is an ultra-ritzy residential neighborhood lined with beautiful 18th-century apartment towers faced with deep red brick. In the London version of Monopoly, Mayfair is the priciest asset, although at £400 you probably wouldn't get more than a designer doormat nowadays. Many national embassies, and some of London's wealthiest citizens, call Mayfair home, and the area is the address of many of London's most haute stores. Unless you have a ton of money, however, window-shopping could be your only option. The sheer number of Rolls Royces, Bentleys, and Jaguars rolling around Mayfair is staggering; even the delivery vans seem to bear some royal coat of arms, proclaiming them to be purveyors of fine goodies for as long as anyone can remember. The one exception is noisy, rollicking Oxford Street (*see below*). To reach Mayfair, take the tube to Bond Street or Green Park.

WALLACE COLLECTION

Hertford House makes a suitably impressive gallery for this incredible art collection, including 18th- and 19th-century French paintings and furniture; Dutch, Italian, English, and Spanish paintings; medieval, Renaissance, and Baroque works of art; and even arms and armor. Titian, Rembrandt, and Poussin are among the bigger names here, but the collection is very strong on Greuze's doe-eyed, soft-focused maidens, and Franz Hals's *Laughing Dutchman* hangs in an upstairs gallery. Look for Thomas Sully's *Queen Victoria* hanging in a blushingly pink salon that must be one of the prettiest rooms in England. Try to be in Room 5 at the top of an hour; the musical clock chimes one of 14 tunes. The Wallace Collection is a perfect place to contemplate the art, since the place is relatively quiet and not crammed with tourists. *Hertford House, Manchester Sq., W1, tel. 020/7935–0687. Tube: Bond St. Walk west on Oxford St., turn right on James St., left on Manchester Sq. Admission free. Open Mon.–Sat. 10–5, Sun. noon–5.*

ST. CHRISTOPHER PLACE

Just north of the shopping chaos of Oxford Street, tucked away behind the Bond Street tube station, lies one of the many hidden spots of town that help give London its often secretive character. St. Christopher's Place is a pretty little street filled with cutesy shops and classy eateries. Pubs here haven't been

FITZROY, MAYFAIR, AND ST. JAMES'S

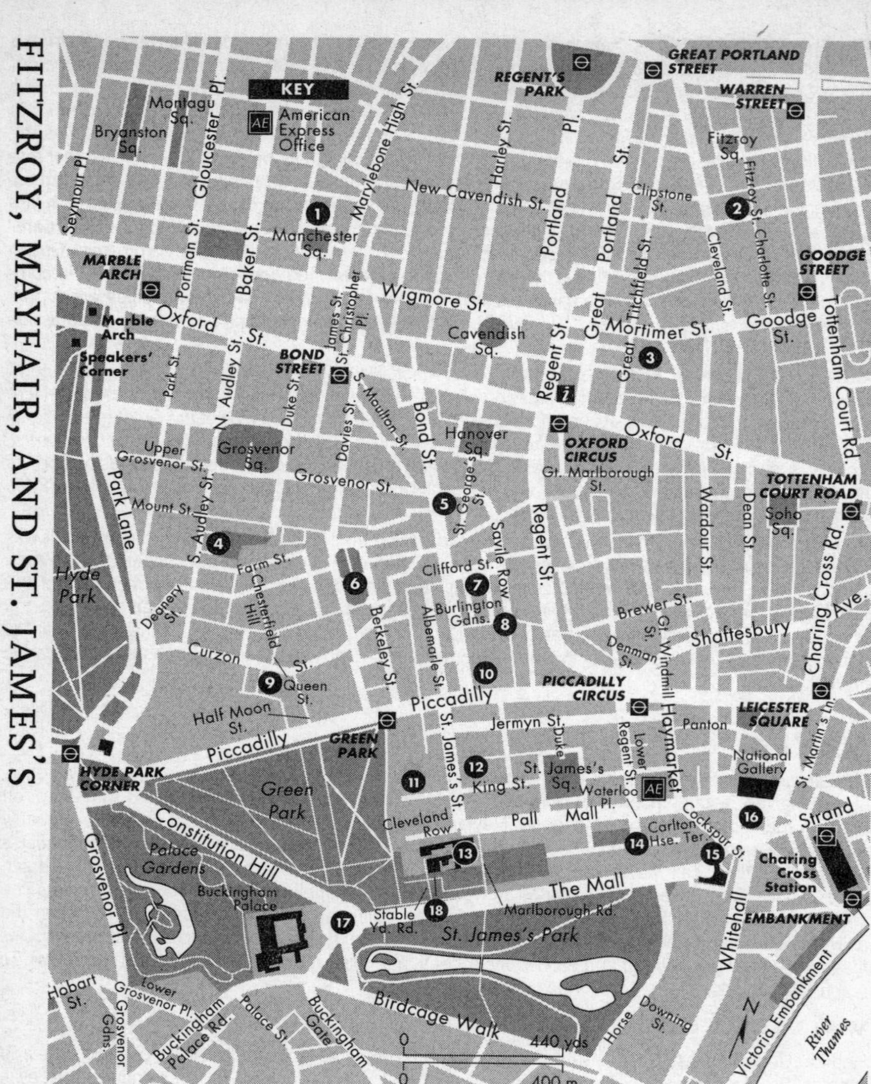

Admiralty Arch, **15**
All Saints, **3**
Berkeley Square, **6**
British Telecom Tower, **2**
Christie's, **12**
Clarence House, **18**
Cork Street, **7**
Institute of Contemporary Arts, **14**
Mount Street Gardens, **4**
Museum of Mankind, **8**
Queen Victoria Memorial, **17**
Royal Academy of Arts, **10**
St. James's Palace, **13**
Shepherd's Market, **9**
Sotheby's, **5**
Spencer House, **11**
Trafalgar Square, **16**
Wallace Collection, **1**

thrown over to the whims of the makeover menace that has seen so many of the city's watering holes lose their traditional homey feel in favor of a more businesslike, ship-'em-in-ship-'em-out approach. *Tube: Bond St. Next to and opposite entrances to the tube station.*

PARK LANE

Alongside the eastern edge of Hyde Park runs Park Lane, a road now mainly famous for the exclusive hotels stationed here, but at one time one of the prime residential sites for extremely well-to-do Londoners, including one of Britain's most famous leaders, late 19th-century Prime Minister Benjamin Disraeli. One of the drawbacks of this grand old street, for those on foot at least, is the constant traffic that plies its way up and down, morning, noon, and night. Once plans for a partial pedestrianization are realized, it will be easier to ignore the cars and concentrate on splendid park-side establishments such as the Dorchester, the Grosvenor, the London Hilton, and the Inn on the Park. Consider feasting your eyes by taking a quick refreshment at the Windows Piano Bar, right at the top of the Hilton, whose view across large swathes of west London are simply spectacular. Another option is to indulge your taste buds in that set-piece spectacular of upper-class English living—the afternoon tea. Served in the late afternoon, "tea" in this case refers to sandwiches (usually with the crusts helpfully cut off), buns, and cakes, as well as the esteemed beverage itself. Expect to pay around £15 for this quintessential experience of aristocracy, and console yourself with the thought that if your stomach can take the punishment, you won't have to bother with an evening meal later. Want to rate the high teas at Park Lane's establishments against those turned out by other Mayfair hotels? Then head on over to the Ritz (Piccadilly), Brown's (Albermarle Street), Claridge's (Brook Street), or the Park Lane Hotel (Piccadilly). *Tube: Marble Arch or Hyde Park Corner. Walk south from Marble Arch; north from Hyde Park Corner.*

GROSVENOR SQUARE

Apart from Lincoln's Inn, (*see* Bloomsbury and Legal London, *below*) Grosvenor Square is the largest square in London. Many consider the huge, fortresslike American embassy building, which dominates the west side of Grosvenor Square, to be a hopeless ugly duckling, but that's wide of the mark. Although its modernism is perhaps not fully realized, the building's simple lines offer a welcome rest for eyes overfed on the opulent surroundings of much of Mayfair. But it wasn't the controversial architecture that provoked thousands of protesters to gather here during the Vietnam War, when the U.S. Embassy became the focal point for often-violent antiwar demonstrators in 1967–68. The American global presence was felt even more poignantly during World War II, when many of the buildings here were occupied by U.S. military authorities; the square quickly earned the nickname Eisenhower Platz. The good general himself holed up at No. 20 during the war and is now commemorated by a statue that fronts up the embassy. There is also a rather plain statue of Franklin D. Roosevelt, erected in the center of the square in 1948. Nearby, look for the plaque commemorating John Adams, the first American ambassador to Britain and second president of the United States; he lived at the corner of Brook and Duke streets. *Tube: Bond St. Walk west on Oxford St., turn left on Duke St.*

BERKELEY SQUARE

Shaded by tall trees and populated by cheeky squirrels, Berkeley Square (pronounced *bark*lee) is a great place to get the feel of Mayfair. The park is ringed with a high iron fence, and on one side you'll find a Rolls Royce dealership that stays open late during the annual Berkeley Square Ball—in the hope that some wealthy reveler will spring for a new £60,000 roadster. Although the square suffered from a poor redevelopment plan in the 1930s, a line of fine Georgian houses (circa 1737) remains on the west side. Number 44, built in 1740 for one Lady Isabella Finch, has been called London's finest terraced house. Clive of India overdosed on laudanum next door at No. 45 in 1774. Look also for the 30 huge plane trees, reckoned to have been planted back in 1789, the year of the French Revolution, and a marble statue of a nymph pouring water from a vase, by Pre-Raphaelite Alexander Munro. The nightingale who sang on Berkeley Square may be long gone, but that doesn't stop the occasional amateur crooner from breaking the stillness of the night. Just west of Berkeley Square, **Mount Street Gardens** (also called St. George's Gardens) is a fine place for a picnic. Want to take a chic promenade? Head a bit north to the area around the famed Connaught Hotel—elegant Mount Street, Carlos Place, and Mount Row. *Tube: Green Park. Walk northwest 1 block on Piccadilly, turn left on Berkeley St.*

SHEPHERD'S MARKET

The May Fair, the market that gave its name to the neighborhood, moved here in 1686 from the Haymarket and was famed for its ribald entertainment; later, the area became a popular haunt of prostitutes. Today, Shepherd's Market is a charming nest of pedestrian-only alleys teeming with cafés and wine bars. It's a tiny, quiet, and exceedingly pleasant place to while away an hour over a cappuccino. Best to avoid lunchtime, however, unless you want to share your coffee with the elbows of one of the many office sophisticates who pour into the area for a fuel stop at midday. At one end, the market opens onto **Curzon Street,** where the British secret service (of 007 fame) had its unmarked headquarters before moving to Gothamesque **Vauxhall Cross** (*see* London's Modern Architecture *box*). *Tube: Green Park. Walk west on Piccadilly, turn right on Half Moon St., left on Curzon St.*

OXFORD STREET

Oxford Street—which runs from Marble Arch to Tottenham Court Road—is also known as London's Golden Mile. Cramming both sides of the street are some 300 clothing stores, lots of steak houses, a few mammoth department stores (*see* Chapter 7), scads of souvenir shops, and four major music and video stores. The shops nearest Hyde Park are the swankiest, but the whole of Oxford Street is loud and crowded with wild-eyed shoppers sucking up £10 Lycra outfits. Such is the crush on the pavements that planners are considering a scheme to pedestrianize Oxford Street and install a tram line running up and down its middle. Don't whisper that one too loudly inside a taxi, mind you. Cabbies, along with bus drivers, currently enjoy free reign over the street and might blow a fuse if reminded of their impending doom. A worthwhile detour is **South Molton Street,** a pedestrian arcade at the corner of Oxford and Davies streets. If you ferret around in the little alleys and passageways, you'll find some nice sandwich shops and pubs. *Tube: Bond St., Marble Arch, Oxford Circus, or Tottenham Court Rd.*

BOND STREET

Bond Street may be the most exclusive shopping street in London. Perpendicular to Oxford Street, it is divided into **New Bond** and **Old Bond,** but prices are very, very modern wherever you go. Jewelers, antiques stores, and art galleries predominate, and many of them won't give you a second look unless you're dressed to buy. If you want to play well-to-do for a day, attend an auction at **Sotheby's** (3435 New Bond St., W1, tel. 020/7493–8080). They usually have morning lots at least three days a week from 10 to 11 (call to make sure), and sometimes an afternoon run at 2:30. You may also want to browse through the goods for sale weekdays 9–4:30 and Sunday noon–4. East of Bond Street is **Savile Row,** famous for its many accomplished tailors and the site of the Beatles' last public appearance: an impromptu performance on the roof of the Apple Records building (at No. 3, now a private business office) in 1969. *Tube: Bond St., Green Park, or Piccadilly Circus.*

CORK STREET

Parallel to Bond Street is Cork Street, the center of the established commercial art scene in London, with more than a dozen private galleries between **Burlington Gardens** and **Clifford Street.** They're close together, so it's easy to hit them all within a few hours. Although they sometimes look intimidating, all are open to the public free of charge. You'll find that Cork Street galleries tend to fixate on contemporary Western art, although a handful emphasize material ranging from 20th-century canonical "avant garde" to Australian aboriginal art and contemporary Russian realism. On Burlington Gardens you'll also find the Museum of Mankind, which displays artifacts of indigenous peoples from around the world (*see* Museums and Galleries, *below*). *Tube: Green Park or Piccadilly Circus. From Green Park, walk east on Piccadilly, turn left on Old Bond St., right on Burlington Gardens. From Piccadilly Circus, walk northwest 1 long block on Regent St., turn left on Vigo St. (which becomes Burlington Gardens).*

FITZROVIA

Take just a few northward steps off busy, brassy Oxford Street (between Oxford Circus and Tottenham Court Road) into **Fitzrovia** and you're in a different, altogether more elegant world. Nowadays overshadowed by happening Soho directly to the south, Fitzrovia is still a fascinating area of urbane sophistication, even if its reputation does rest on glamorous figures from yesteryear. Ford Madox Brown, William Morris, George Bernard Shaw, James Abbott McNeill Whistler, and various members of the Pre-Raphaelite and Bloomsbury groups were regulars on this patch. They handed Fitzrovia an artistic image that it has retained, thanks in part to the plethora of laid-back restaurants, wine bars, and pubs that serve growing numbers of ad agency execs. On Fitzroy Street, you can't fail to see the **British Telecom Tower,** the third tallest building in town, which was sadly closed to tourists after an IRA bomb in 1971.

ALL SAINTS CHURCH

Pre-Raphaelites had a hand in some of the startling tile and marble decorations that make All Saints Church on **Margaret Street** worthy of visitor respect. To get to All Saints, you have to nip under an archway before entering a wonderfully peaceful courtyard off which the church itself lies. Also off the courtyard is a well-respected choir school, which numbers a young Laurence Olivier, reckoned to be England's greatest actor, among its former pupils. *Tube: Oxford Circus. Walk east from Oxford Circus, turn left onto Great Titchfield St. until you reach Margaret St., then turn right.*

CHARLOTTE STREET

A few hundred yards around the corner from All Saints Church is Charlotte Street, not the one made famous by '80s singer Lloyd Cole—that's in Edinburgh—but the social hub of Fitzrovia. Choose from a wide variety of cuisines at any price—"take away" from el cheapo kebab shop or take a cushioned seat in a chichi nouvelle cuisine eatery. Charlotte Street makes a fine resting spot for weary tourists and office workers alike. *Tube: Goodge St. Walk east on Goodge St.; Charlotte St. runs north–south across Goodge St.*

FITZROY SQUARE

Fitzroy Square is at the top end of Charlotte Street, which is by then named Fitzroy Street. Developed by the first Baron Southampton with the able assistance of the brothers Adam, the square was built from 1790 to 1829 and by the end of the last century had become a full-fledged artistic enclave. Politics got a look in, too, with the likes of radical playwright George Bernard Shaw and socialist designer William Morris strutting their antiestablishment stuff. At the tail end of the 19th century, the International Anarchist School caused a storm when bombs were found on its Fitzroy Square premises and it was summarily closed down. These days things are pretty quiet, with pedestrianization adding to the general, and not unwelcome, air of calm stillness. Sit down for a while and prepare yourself for a cheap treat; in the southeast corner of the square you'll happen upon the **YMCA Indian Students Union,** where tasty curries are served for well under £10. *Tube: Great Portland St. Walk south on Cleveland St., then left onto Grafton St.*

POLLOCK'S TOY MUSEUM

Kids of all ages will be entranced at Pollock's Toy Museum, which features the intricately engineered toys of the Victorian era. Benjamin Pollock was famous in the 19th century primarily for his superbly crafted toy theaters, but there are plenty of other goodies here, including toy soldiers and wax dolls. "If you love art, folly, or the bright eyes of children," said *Treasure Island* author R. L. Stevenson, "speed to Pollock's." The museum has an adjoining shop. Prices are high for the real things, but reproductions are available at a fraction of the cost. *1 Scala St. 020/7636–3452. Tube: Goodge Street. Walk west down Goodge St., take a right onto Whitfield St., then a left onto Scala St. Admission £2. Open Mon.–Sat. 10–5.*

CENTRAL LONDON

ST. JAMES'S

After Henry VIII's lovely **Whitehall Palace** burned down in 1698, all of London turned its attention to St. James's Palace (*see below*), the new royal residence. During the 18th and 19th centuries, the area around the palace became *the* fashionable place to live, and many of the local estates disappeared in the ensuing frenzy as mansions were built, streets laid out, and expensive shops established. Today, St. James's—along with Mayfair, Belgravia, and Sloane Square in Chelsea—remains London's most elegant and fashionable address. (*See* the Mayfair and St. James's map, *above*).

PICCADILLY

Step out of Green Park tube station, head east down Piccadilly and you'll get a good grasp of the fascinating contrast between old and new London. Piccadilly became one of the smartest residential streets in the 19th century, and, despite a takeover by corporate money, it still retains the air concomitant with that legendary figure, the English gent. You'll trot past the Ritz on the south side and the Royal Academy on the north—temples to extravagant leisure and high culture respectively. The gent theme continues in the snobby arcades located here—Burlington, Piccadilly, and Prince's—as well as in such names as Fortnum and Mason. But as Piccadilly Circus (*see* Soho, *below*) comes into view, things change; olde worlde class is hit by the kind of improvised response to modern times that gave London its cool image in the 1990s. The turning point, strangely enough, is a church. St. James's Church has a foot in both camps. Built by Wren (it was his personal favorite), St. James's still boasts an up-market congregation, but nevertheless straddles the social divide in its extensive work for the homeless and via its trendy vegetarian food, sold at lunchtime to office workers and tourists. *Tube: Green Park or Piccadilly Circus.*

JERMYN STREET

Some visitors are disappointed to learn that London is no longer populated by gentlemen who don bowler hats. If you fall into this camp, take a wander down Jermyn Street, where you'll find plenty of evidence that the days of the English gent are not quite over yet. Bowlers, toppers, and other hats are up for grabs at Bates (No. 21A), whose only serious rivals in this market niche is Lock's on nearby St. James's Street. Classic English shirts can be found at, among others, Harvie and Hudson (No. 97) and Turnbull and Asser (Nos. 70–72), where Ronald Reagan once shopped, and to bottom off one's outfit there's the original shop of specialist boot and shoe retailers Russell and Bromley. To complete the picture of a true gent, cigar and pipe fiends are catered to at Davidoff and Dunhill, respectively. *Tube: Green Park. Walk east down Piccadilly, turn right onto St. James's St.; the first left is Jermyn St.*

PALL MALL

Pall Mall (pronounced pal mal) is a haven of quiet and refinement that has managed to survive from more regal days. The street gets its name from *paille maille,* a French version of croquet that was popular during the reigns of both Charles I and Charles II. A number of gentlemen's clubs, those quintessentially snobby English institutions, line Pall Mall, including the Athenaeum, United Oxford and Cambridge University Club, Travellers' Club, and the Reform Club. Many clubs went under after World War II, although several made comebacks in the conservative, free-market '80s. **Christie's** (8 King St., SW1, tel. 020/7839–9060), the premier art auctioneers of the Western world, resides north of Pall Mall. The auctions are open to the public and are free, but loitering is discouraged—unless, of course, you look like you can wield a platinum card. *Pall Mall runs almost parallel to the Mall from Trafalgar Sq. and dead-ends at St. James's Palace. Tube: Charing Cross, Green Park, or Piccadilly Circus.*

GREEN PARK

Although nearby St. James's Park is the perfect place for a genteel evening stroll or a quiet afternoon snooze, Green Park is much more upbeat. Unencumbered by lavish lakes or spectacular flower displays, it is just the job for a wide range of impromptu sports and games. Especially in summer, you'll find groups of Londoners throwing off their work shackles and clothes to play soccer and softball, while visitors put their own sports on show. Australian Rules football is a common sight, as are its Gaelic and American cousins, and even the ancient Indian sport Kabadi has been spotted on occasion. Present-day athletes can count themselves lucky. The games of choice in Green Park in previous centuries included dueling and highway robbery, whereas in the Victorian era, stray fireworks from the frequent displays often maimed hapless passersby. One of the most used routes through the park is along Queen's Walk on the east side, which is ideal for spying Lancaster House, a neoclassical structure used for exclusive government functions that is almost next door to Spencer House. *Tube: Green Park.*

SPENCER HOUSE

The London house to end all London houses, this spectacular 18th-century mansion was built in 1766, after it was commissioned by the first Earl Spencer, heir to the incredibly wealthy first Duchess of Marlborough. A Doric facade, complete with pediment adorned with classical statues, announces at once Earl Spencer's passion for the Grand Tour and for classical antiquities. As the ancestral digs of Diana, Princess of Wales, the house was recently and superlatively restored by Lord Rothschild. Inside, James "Athenian" Stuart decorated the State Rooms, including the Painted Room, the first completely neoclassic room in Europe. The most ostentatious part of the house (and of the Spencer family—witness the £40,000 diamond-studded shoe buckles the first countess proudly wore) is the florid bow-window of the Drawing Room: covered with stucco palm trees, it conjures up both ancient Palmyra and modern Miami Beach. *27 St. James's Pl., SW1, tel. 020/7499–8620. Tube: Green Park. Admission £6. Open Sun. 10:45–4:45 (guided tours only; tickets go on sale each Sun. at 10:30). Closed Aug., Jan.*

ST. JAMES'S PALACE

This elegant redbrick palace lies at the end of Pall Mall, on the former site of a hospital for women lepers. The ever-so-sensitive Henry VIII bought the hospital in 1532 and erected a royal manor in its stead. Only the **Chapel Royal** and four-story **Gatehouse** remain of Henry's original manor—most of the palace was rebuilt after a fire in 1809. For much of its existence, the palace has played second fiddle to the now-gone Whitehall Palace and to Buckingham Palace, although all foreign ambassadors to Britain are still officially accredited to "The Court of St. James." Although the palace is shared by Prince Charles and a number of minor royals, such as the Duke and Duchess of Kent, the cohabitation could soon end in tears. Future king Charles is known to favor a thorough modernization of the monarchy, which is likely to include the withdrawal of privileges such as occupying royal palaces rent free (as is the case with the Kents). On the road from St James's Palace you'll happen upon the **Queen's Chapel,** designed by Inigo Jones for Charles I and French wife Henrietta Maria. *Pall Mall, at St. James's St., SW1. Tube: Green Park. Walk east on Piccadilly and turn right on St. James's St.*

THE MALL

The red-paved Mall cuts a wide swath from Trafalgar Square all the way to Buckingham Palace. It was laid out in 1904, largely to provide the British monarchy with a processional route in keeping with its imperial status. After all, the French had their Champs-Elysées, and they didn't even have a sovereign anymore. The 115-ft-wide Mall is no Champs-Elysées, however; without a royal procession dressing it up, the Mall seems soulless. **Admiralty Arch,** a triumphal arch bordering Trafalgar Square, marks the start of the Mall. Built in 1911, the central gate is now opened only for royal processions. From here, the Mall sweeps past St. James's Park and **Carlton House Terrace,** a stately 1,000-ft-long facade of white stucco arches that is the home of the ICA (*see* Museums and Galleries, *below*), a first-rate contemporary gallery. Farther down on the right is **Clarence House,** raised by genius John Nash between 1812 and 1830, and now home of the Queen Mother. Nowadays, the best time to explore the Mall is Sunday, when it is closed to traffic. The moving scenes of mass grieving along the Mall at the time of Princess Diana's funeral prompted calls for it to become traffic-free every day, and city planners are now seriously considering this option.

ST. JAMES'S PARK

Sitting amid London's grandest monuments, this 93-acre park is remarkably peaceful—it enjoys an almost librarylike hush. It is a stroller's park, a place to wander among the flowers, feed the ducks, or sit and read. The focal point is an ornamental lake, added by Charles II and redesigned by George IV, dotted with geese and weeping willows. Watch out for the huge, admittedly beautiful, pelicans, which have an irksome habit of sneaking up behind you and making a strange throaty noise. For the better part of the 17th and 18th centuries, the park was the playground for England's elite, who would gather here to stare down their noses at one another before heading off to be idle elsewhere. At night—when the fountains, Westminster Abbey, and the Houses of Parliament are illuminated—the scene is breathtaking. *Tube: Charing Cross, St. James's Park, or Westminster.*

WHITEHALL AND WESTMINSTER

Whitehall is the name of both a street and a vast, faceless bureaucracy. Whitehall the street runs from Trafalgar Square to Parliament Square through the heart of official London—which means it's a major tourist stomping ground. Whitehall the bureaucracy can't be so easily demarcated. Essentially, the term applies to the central British government, whose ministries fill many of the buildings off Whitehall and around Richmond Terrace. Adjacent Westminster is a small section of London most noted for its abbey, bridge, and palace, each named Westminster—although the palace is more commonly known as the **Houses of Parliament** (*see* Major Attractions, *above*). Southern Westminster is a sleepy residential area with charming old homes—worth wandering through if you're on your way to the splendid **Tate Gallery** (*see* Major Attractions, *above*).

HORSE GUARDS AND PARADE GROUND

As you walk down Whitehall toward **Parliament Square,** you will pass Horse Guards on the right. This stone building was constructed between 1745 and 1755 and was once the headquarters of the British Army. It's the traditional entrance to **St. James's Palace,** which is why mounted troopers of the Household Cavalry Regiment can be seen during daylight hours in the sentry boxes facing across Whitehall. Each day at 11 AM (10 AM Sunday) you can witness the **change of the Queen's Life Guard** on Horse Guards Parade, the open area behind Horse Guards (adjacent to St. James's Park). On occasions such as the State Opening of Parliament or a State Visit, the whole thing is usually postponed until the afternoon. The New Guard on horseback makes his way from Hyde Park Barracks, past **Buckingham Palace,** and along the Mall to Horse Guards Parade where the Old Guard is waiting to meet him. If you don't feel like battling the crowds at Buckingham Palace, this is the next-best ceremonial relic. The site of a jousting arena in Henry VIII's time, the area in front of the building is still known as the Tilt Yard. It was also used for less noble pursuits, such as bear baiting, cock fighting, and tennis. During the year

WHITEHALL AND WESTMINSTER

Admiralty Arch, **5**
Banqueting House, **8**
Buckingham Palace, **18**
Cabinet War Rooms, **11**
Cenotaph, **10**
Clarence House, **20**
Downing Street, **9**
Horse Guards and Parade Ground, **7**
Houses of Parliament, **13**
Institute of Contemporary Arts, **6**
National Gallery, **1**
National Portrait Gallery, **2**
Nelson's Column, **4**
Parliament Square, **12**
Queen Victoria Memorial, **19**
Queen's Gallery and Royal Mews, **17**
St. James's Palace, **21**
St. Martin-in-the-Fields, **3**
Tate Gallery, **15**
Wellington Barracks (Guards Museum), **16**
Westminster Abbey, **14**

this parade ground comes alive when it hosts some of London's most important State occasions, including the Queen's Birthday Parade, better known as **Trooping the Colour,** and **Beating Retreat** (both in June), and royal receptions for state visits. To the west of the parade ground lies St. James's Park, and to the north looms **Admiralty Arch** (look for all the incongruous high-tech antenna equipment on top), an interesting combination of pomp and practicality.

BANQUETING HOUSE

Designed by Inigo Jones and built between 1619 and 1622, Banqueting House is one of the earliest examples of Renaissance architecture in England. It's also the only surviving building from the original Whitehall Palace, the one-time home of Henry VIII, which went up in flames in 1698. The House's main room was originally used as a venue for the court entertainments of Charles I and, in 1649, was the backdrop for his beheading. These days, it's a popular spot for state banquets. The chief attractions are Rubens's ceiling paintings, commissioned by Charles I, which portray him and his father, James I, in a favorable, even divine, light. After the Restoration, Charles II used the place to indulge his pleasures, installing wife, mistresses, and occasional prostitutes in the handily located palace. *Whitehall, across from Horse Guards Arch, SW1, tel. 020/7930–4179. Tube: Charing Cross or Westminster. Admission £3.25. Open Mon.–Sat. 10–5 (last admission 4:30). Closed occasionally for government functions.*

DOWNING STREET

If it weren't for the massive security measures and the ogling tourists, you would never suspect the importance of the rather ordinary homes on this street. The mammoth iron gate gives the first hint, but the guys checking under every car for bombs are a dead giveaway. The gates were installed by Margaret Thatcher in 1990, mainly to deter any demonstrators attempting to storm up the little street, but they weren't much use a year later, when the IRA's mortar bomb attack nearly succeeded in blowing No. 10 and the whole cabinet to kingdom come. Until now, Britain's prime minister has lived at **10 Downing Street,** guarded by the famous black door and more than one policeman. In fact the house, which is much bigger inside than it looks from the street, was handed to Britain's first Prime Minister, Sir Robert Walpole, in 1732. Tony Blair, who won a landslide Labour Party victory in the May 1997 elections, has moved into No. 11 instead; the bigger living quarters house Blair's lawyer wife Cherrie (pronounced SheREE) and three teenage kids. Number 11 is traditionally the home of Britain's finance minister or Chancellor of the Exchequer. The present incumbent, Gordon Brown, was kind enough to let Blair and his brood move in, but is reckoned to be seething with jealousy at his boss's popularity.

CABINET WAR ROOMS

Winston Churchill, the Cabinet, and the Chiefs of Staff coordinated Britain's war effort from this fortified basement in a civil-service building—definitely worth a few hours' exploration. The War Rooms were converted from civil-service basements and by the end of the war had extended to 3 acres, enough space to squeeze in more than 500 top political and military brass. A free audio tour guides you through rooms that have been reconstructed to look as they did at the close of World War II. Especially interesting is a map covered with pushpins representing advancing Allied armies in the final weeks of the war. Old American vets and young German tourists roaming the war rooms together make for their own curious spectacle. Nearby is the **Cenotaph** monument—the annual Remembrance Day ceremonies (equivalent to the American Veterans' Day) take place here at 11 AM on the Sunday closest to the 11th day of the 11th month, when the Queen and other dignitaries lay wreaths of poppies on the Cenotaph. *Clive Steps, at end of King Charles St., SW1, tel. 020/7930–6961. Tube: Westminster. Walk west on Bridge St., turn right on Parliament St., left on King Charles St. Admission £4.80. Open Apr.–Sept., daily 9:15–6; Oct.–Mar., daily 10–6 (last admission 5:15).*

SOHO

Soho began its tenure as one of the leading bohemian neighborhoods of London during the 1950s, when it emerged as a beatnik stomping ground and the heart of the London jazz scene. In the 1960s, rock took over and the area became home to a new counterculture, with clubs featuring headliners like the Rolling Stones, the Who, and the Kinks, in their respective heydays. With the coming of punk and seminal bands like the Sex Pistols, Generation X, the Clash, and X-Ray Spex, King's Road (*see* Chelsea, *above*) replaced Soho as the home of London's pop culture, leading to a resurgence of jazz here. Today, much of Soho has suffered from the yuppification and commercialization that are, ironically, so common in former bastions of urban hipness. Its streets are lined with an odd amalgam of fashionable clothing

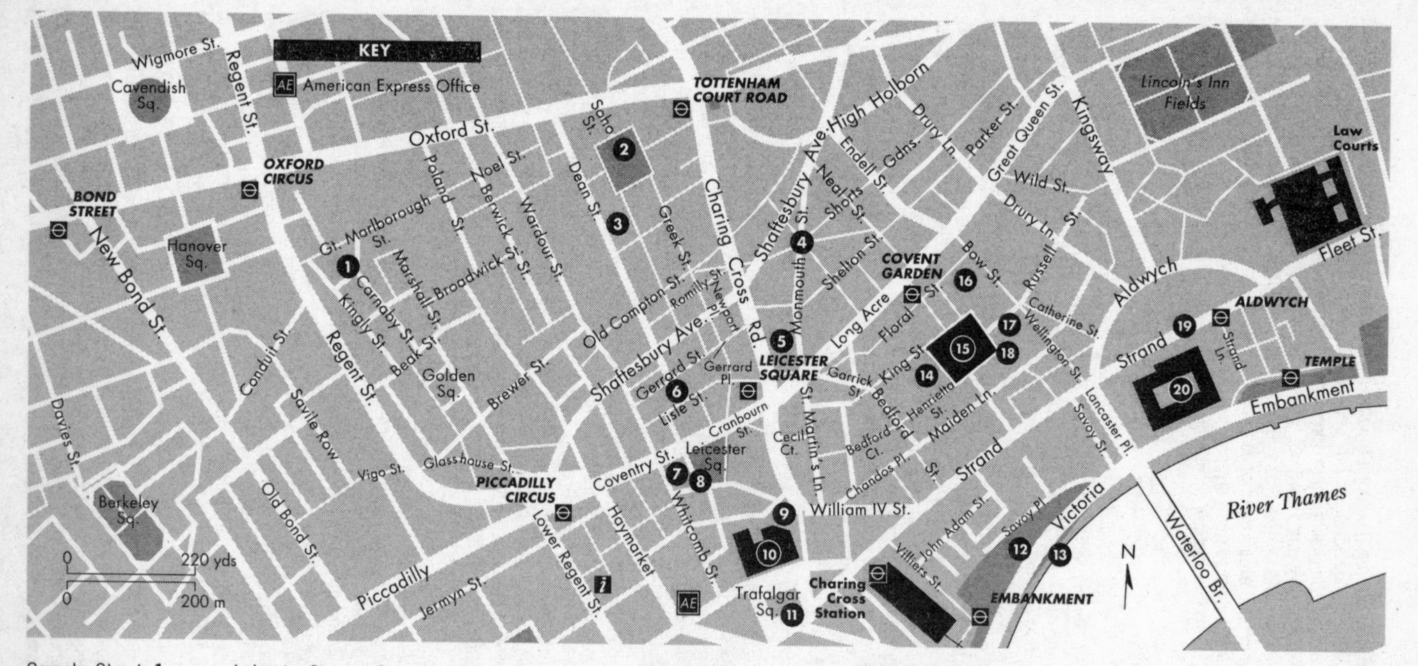

Carnaby Street, **1**
Central Market Building, **15**
Chinatown, **6**
Cleopatra's Needle, **13**
Karl Marx House, **3**
Leicester Square, **8**
London Transport Museum, **18**
National Gallery, **10**
National Portrait Gallery, **9**
Nelson's Column, **11**
Notre Dame de France, **7**
Photographer's Gallery, **5**
Royal Opera House, **16**
St. Mary-le-Strand, **19**
St. Paul's Church, **14**
Seven Dials, **4**
Soho Square, **2**
Somerset House, **20**
Theatre Museum, **17**
Victoria Embankment Gardens, **12**

SOHO AND COVENT GARDEN

stores, gourmet restaurants, high-power hair salons, trendy cafés, theaters, and nightclubs, plus a smattering of XXX-rated sex shops (remnants of the 'hood's long-ago incarnation as the red-light district of London). Additionally, a huge number of Hollywood studios have their postproduction facilities here, so you'll also see names like TriStar, Warner Bros., and Lucasfilm etched over dozens of Soho doors.

Soho has an international flavor that many of central London's neighborhoods lack; generally, you'd have to go to the city outskirts to find such a polyglot community. French Huguenots arriving in the 1680s were the first foreigners to settle the area en masse, followed by Germans, Russians, Poles, and Greeks—although Soho today displays more Chinese and Italian influences. The Chinese community is crowded around **Gerrard Street** (*see* Chinatown, *below*). If you're looking for traditional Italian restaurants and cafés, head for **Old Compton Street,** which is also a major center for gay life in the city. **Berwick Street** is home to a market popular with tourists and locals alike (*see* Street Markets *in* Chapter 7). If you catch the tube to Leicester Square, Oxford Circus, Piccadilly Circus, or Tottenham Court Road, you'll find yourself right on the edge of Soho.

LEICESTER SQUARE

Leicester Square is often compared with New York's Times Square, but it isn't as big or as bright. Just like any other major entertainment district, Leicester (pronounced lester) has some shady characters and an off-and-on drug scene. Huge movie houses, many converted from grand old theaters, surround the square, showing the latest releases. The biggest cinema of the lot, the Empire, hosts lively premier nights, which are best avoided unless you are star-struck enough to take part in the mass brawls that ensue when big names exit their limos. The crowds on premier nights have slackened off a bit since the death of Princess Diana, who was a genuine movie lover, as the ill-fated royal was often the real fan-magnet.

When Soho used to be royal parklands, huntsmen filled the air with their cries of "Soho! Soho!" Though nobody knows for sure, the direct translation in modern English is probably "Hey, guys, let's quit hunting foxes and go grab some beers."

Sandwich munchers and statues (Charlie Chaplin and Sir Isaac Newton, among others) share the central part of the square, a welcome break from its previous role as a site for drug users. Tacky tourist attractions line some of the side streets, and weird street theater is often staged on the pedestrian mall at the western edge of the square (although you may get tired of that punker playing the same six notes over and over on his sax). Most of the year, the square is also home to several fun-fair rides, including an old-time Wurlitzer, whose tunes can add an air of romance if you're in the right mood. Near the east entrance, around the corner from the tube station, tired feet are offered relief in the form of a series of alfresco cafés. Nowadays these stay open until the wee hours and are a boon for people-watchers or those who need to stave off that looming hangover with a late-night cappuccino. Over in the northwest corner, on the short trek to Piccadilly Circus, you can't fail to notice the incongruous **Swiss Centre,** whose main claim to fame is the elaborate cuckoo clock that puts on a show on the hour every hour. On the west side is the **Society of London Theatres (SOLT)** ticket kiosk (*see* Theater *in* Chapter 6), where you can buy half-price, same-day tickets for many London shows. Just off Leicester Square on Leicester Place stands the oasislike **Notre Dame de France,** a modern French Catholic church worth visiting if only to see an impressive Jean Cocteau mural in a chapel dedicated to the Virgin. *Tube: Leicester Sq.*

PICCADILLY CIRCUS

Only the most gullible of tourists (surely not you) still believe Ringling Brothers tigers and acrobats perform at Piccadilly Circus. Rather, the weird name comes out of the dark days of the 17th century, when men wore picadils (ruffled collars) and one smart young tailor grew rich enough on the proceeds to build a fine house. Snobs sneeringly labeled it Piccadilly Hall, and when the mansion was later ripped down to build a circular junction for five major roads, the name morphed into Piccadilly Circus. Despite the lack of rainbow-hair clowns, the circle offers plenty of fine people-watching, especially on the steps of the famous **Eros** statue (which gained this nickname from its reputation as a meeting place for lovers) or on the wall of the fountain beneath the bronze **Horse of Helios** sculpture. On the western edge, Tower Records is probably the most popular music store in town, and the northern side is dominated by a Burger King branch that should not be overlooked. If you can bag a window seat on the second floor, you'll have a rewarding view of the massed throng below.

Before it became known as one of the primary meeting points for visitors, Piccadilly Circus was best known for its huge neon ads, which were among the first, and biggest, in Britain. One vital tip is not to look up at the blinding neon as you traverse one of the roads that zip through this major traffic junction. The experience of tackling one of the pedestrian crossings here must be akin to that of a wildebeest herd heading over river rapids in the rainy season. Note to rockers, kitsch-seekers, and lovers of the Pop Life: Piccadilly Circus is also home to such treasures as an animatronic Janis Joplin, a 100% wax Artist-Formerly-Known-as-Prince, lots of laser lights, and plenty of taped guitar solos, all at **Madame Tussaud's Rock Circus** (The London Pavilion, 1 Piccadilly Circus, tel. 020/7734–7203). They call it the "No. 1 Rock Attraction in Britain," but you'd have to overdose on postmodern irony to get any genuine enjoyment from these singing stiffs, although a recent refurbishment has improved matters somewhat. Admission is £8.25, and it is open daily summer 10–8, winter 10–5:30 (Tuesday from 11). *Tube: Piccadilly Circus.*

CHINATOWN

Known as **Tong Yan Kai** (Chinese Streets) by residents, Chinatown has some pure tourist trappings—telephone booths topped by pagodas, for example. But before you work yourself into a tizzy thinking you've rediscovered Shanghai in Greenwich Mean Time, understand that London's Chinatown is very small—only two short streets, **Gerrard** and **Lisle,** which run between Leicester Square and Shaftesbury Avenue. That said, it remains a real, not just Disneyesque, center for London's Chinese community. The restaurants are used predominately by the Chinese themselves, there are plenty of minimarkets stuffed full of produce unfathomable to Westerners, and you can even hear the sound of old women throwing down mahjong tiles if you cock your ear at enough doorways. Most of all the little area smells different from the rest of the West End, with the aromas of stir-fry cooking wafting through the air and assorted traffic fumes. Feast on a meal of dim sum in one of the many restaurants (*see* Chapter 4), or stop by for February's New Year's celebration and September's Mid-Autumn Festival (*see* Festivals *in* Chapter 1). *Tube: Leicester Sq. Walk north on Charing Cross Rd., turn left on Lisle St.*

SHAFTESBURY AVENUE

Cutting through the center of Soho, Shaftesbury Avenue is one of London's three principal theater streets (along with the Haymarket and Coventry Street). Built side by side in the early 1900s, many of the theaters survived the war and retain the grand look espoused by Edwardian theater. Sir Noël Coward, Sir John Gielgud, and Sir Laurence Olivier all made it big in Shaftesbury Avenue theaters like the Apollo, the Lyric, the Globe, and the Queen's. Today, you're likely to find these same theaters hosting the works of such playwrights as Tom Stoppard and Peter Shaffer. For more info, *see* West End Theaters *in* Chapter 6. *Tube: Leicester Sq. or Piccadilly Circus.*

CARNABY STREET

During the '60s and '70s, this pedestrian area was a groovy place to hang out, buy flowery fashions, and pick up the latest tunes. Although times have changed, Carnaby Street and the surrounding area still deserve a look. In fact, some clued-in London experts are predicting a full-blown renaissance for the area. Among its established advantages is the complete lack of traffic, which provides breathing space after the packed sidewalks of nearby Regent and Oxford streets. The mix of shops is set to change back in favor of boutiques, more in keeping with the original Carnaby Street myth. The top end of the street is where things have already changed, most for the better, with a branch of Muji's proving a big draw and a variety of coffee bars adding an almost mainland European touch. Elsewhere on the street, you can find everything from classic shoes to original '70s wigs, from hot new makeup to ultracool designer jewelry. Come early or in the late afternoon to miss the worst of the crowds, but don't spend too much time on Carnaby Street itself—it's still mostly cheap leather-pocketbook stores and tourist shops. Instead, explore the small alleys and streets to the east, which have some hip clothing stores (Yesterday's Bread sells original unused clothing from the '60s and '70s) and tiny crafts shops (try Foubert's Place and Newburgh Street). Above the hubbub of Carnaby Street is a bank of 14 tailors (who have even made suits for the likes of Brad Pitt and Tom Cruise). *Tube: Oxford Circus. Walk south on Regent St., turn left on Great Marlborough St., right on Carnaby St.*

SOHO SQUARE

Built in the 1670s to honor Charles II, Soho Square is one of the oldest public squares in London. Nowadays this pleasant village green acts as a welcome open space in the middle of hectic Soho. It's shared in perfect harmony by businesspeople on lunch break, pram-pushing nannies, tourists, elderly folks, and the homeless—all under the watchful gaze of a dilapidated 19th-century statue of King Charles. The statue once towered over the square, but its present position, almost at eye level, seems to fit in more closely with the egalitarian spirit of the neighborhood. At the center of this sylvan stretch of green is a storybook timber-and-thatch cottage—a great sight when you're enjoying a take-out munch in the park during summer. Just off Soho Square are two streets that boast some of the most interesting spots in the area. **Greek Street** is famous for the Coach and Horses pub, which was home to a heavy-drinking arty bunch, including the likes of painter Francis Bacon and jazz singer George Melly; **Frith Street** counts leading jazz venue Ronnie Scott's and legendary Greek restaurant Jimmy's among its number. In recent times Frith Street's coffee and small eats spot Bar Italia has become famous, especially as a wind-down venue for late-night ravers. *Tube: Tottenham Court Rd. Walk west on Oxford St., turn left into Soho Sq.*

COVENT GARDEN

Just east of Soho lies Covent Garden, London's first public square. These days the name also applies to the nest of narrow streets, arcades, and pedestrian malls surrounding the square. For penny-counting travelers, this is one of the best places in London for free entertainment: musicians, buskers, jugglers, and comics all perform in the streets and squares; look at the daily schedule of events posted in the management office (41 The Market, Covent Garden, WC2).

THE MARKET AND PIAZZA

Historically speaking, the original Covent Garden was just that—a plot of land used to grow fruit and vegetables for the 13th-century Abbey of St. Peter at Westminster. With the 16th-century dissolution of the monasteries, the land passed into the hands of the Earls of Bedford. Covent Garden then evolved into London's principal produce market, a bustling maze of stalls and shops. In 1830 the **Central Market Building** was built, but increasing traffic congestion forced produce sellers to relocate south of the Thames in 1974. The original market building has been completely renovated and is now filled with boutiques, health-food shops, and trendy restaurants. (*See* the Soho and Covent Garden map, *above*).

London's 1851 census lists a "Charles Mark, Doctor (Philosophical Author)" living at 28 Dean Street, southwest of Soho Square. Today, a blue plaque commemorates this site as Karl Marx's residence from 1851 to 1856.

Facing away from the market, **St. Paul's Church** (Bedford St., WC2, tel. 020/7836–5221) is often called the "actor's church" because of the walls lined with memorials to well-known British thespians such as Ellen Terry, Charlie Chaplin, and Noël Coward. The rest of the church, built by Inigo Jones in 1631 and rebuilt in 1795 after a fire, is rather stark. The rear portico, site of the opening scene with Eliza Doolittle and Professor Higgins in *My Fair Lady,* serves as a great stage for the daily program of free entertainment—everything from mimes to fire-eaters. On the southeast corner of the square are the **London Transport Museum,** housed in the former flower market building, and the **Theatre Museum** (*see* Museums and Galleries, *below*). East of the market is Bow Street, famous for the **Royal Opera House,** home to the Royal Ballet and the Royal Opera Company. It has been closed for major renovations since 1997 and won't reopen again until sometime in 2000, if all goes well. The resident troupes will be appearing at other venues during this time (*see* Classical Music, Opera, and Dance *in* Chapter 6).

FLORAL STREET

Although Covent Garden market itself has ossified into a fairly mundane shopping experience, the surrounding area has kept up the traditions of designer glam and kooky charm that drew the crowds in the first place. Immediately north of the piazza, Floral Street begins on its path west toward Leicester Square. It has now emerged as one of the top streets in town for the fashion conscious, hosting names such as Paul Smith, Nicole Farhi, and Agnes B. Even chains like Jigsaw, which have been quick to muscle in on the atmosphere, have made efforts at assimilation by investing in well-designed stores. Parallel to Floral Street, **Long Acre** isn't as stylish but offers more of a big-city bustle flavor. The Dôme café bar located here is a favorite early evening meeting place for working Londoners.

SEVEN DIALS

The number refers to the seven roads that meet at this tiny intersection between Long Acre and Shaftesbury Avenue, which wouldn't look out of place in the land of the seven dwarfs. Keep out of the way of cabbies who use the narrow streets that radiate from here as shortcuts, and you'll find one of the most intriguing zones of new-look London. Each of the seven has its own character, from the grumpy market traders on Earlham Street to the dozy hippies behind the counters of the wacky shops on Mercer Street. Nearby, at the bottom of Earlham Street, the **Neal Street** pedestrian mall sports a young, laid-back, bohemian crowd. Join the happy shoppers in tiny **Neal's Yard,** a courtyard full of funky world and natural-food cafés. Have a pint in front of one of the many pubs and take a gander at the folks who walk by.

BLOOMSBURY AND LEGAL LONDON

The **British Museum** (*see* Major Attractions, *above*) and the **University of London** (*see below*) impart something of an intellectual atmosphere to the residential neighborhood of Bloomsbury, located just to the north of the Soho and Covent Garden districts. Yet apart from some blue plaques on **Gordon Square,** you're far more likely to find a schmaltzy B&B than any reminders of Virginia Woolf, Vanessa Bell, Lytton Strachey, J. M. Keynes, E. M. Forster, or G. E. Moore—the core of the so-called Bloomsbury Group, which would assemble in the 1920s and 1930s on most Thursday nights to drink and discuss the Victorian era's resistance to sexual, religious, and artistic enlightenment. Few traces remain of the personalities that brought Bloomsbury renown as the cradle of British philosophical and aesthetic modernism, yet it still has an active café and pub scene fortified by the students who liven up the area after classes. Plan your day sitting in one of the many charming coffeehouses or wine bars on **Lamb's Conduit Street** or, if weather permits, enjoy the outdoor cafés on **Russell Square. Sir John Soane's Museum** makes a nice, eclectic visit, and hard-core fans will enjoy poking about **Dickens House** (*see below*). If you're wandering around Euston Street, near King's Cross Station, definitely check out the fairy-tale exterior of the edifice (once a famed hotel) atop the St. Pancras train station—a Victorian extravaganza that is Sir George Gilbert Scott's most stunning feat of architecture. Russell Square tube station puts you right in the belly of the beast; otherwise, it's just a short walk north from the Tottenham Court Road or Holborn tube stations to Russell Square.

When you hear the word "lawyer," the immediate tendency is to yawn, grimace, or check your wallet. It's surprising, then, just how pleasant it can be to wander around the **Inns of Court** in Holborn, the heart of legal London. In the 15th and 16th centuries, the Inns of Court were exactly what they sound like—crash pads for lawyers who had business at the city's courts. Eventually, the lawyers took over the hotels and added offices and dining halls. Over time, the various inns were consolidated into just four—Lincoln's, Gray's, Middle Temple, and Inner Temple—and became the focal point of legal work in the city. Today, London barristers (trial lawyers) are still required to maintain an association with one of the inns, such as having an office there or dining in the hall a certain number of times each year. Law students must take their examinations at an inn and dine in one of the halls 24 times before they are admitted to the bar. Similar in style to the courtyards of Cambridge and Oxford, the inns still retain a dignified academic air. Hang out on **Chancery Lane** and watch all the bewigged and gowned lawyers heading for court. The legal attire is just one indicator of how differently British and Americans approach the question of law: it's tough to imagine these guys coming on TV and saying, "Have you or a loved one been injured lately?"

UNIVERSITY OF LONDON

University College, the oldest of several colleges and schools that make up the University of London, was once accused of being that "godless college in Gower Street." Today, the college and the university as a whole continue to be places where you can act in ways that the vicar would never condone. Its students have access to probably the best nightlife in the nation—pubs, cafés, and cheap restaurants dot the residential streets around the university, and the lively clubs and action of Soho are nearby. University College was founded in 1827 by educators who objected to the fact that Oxford and Cambridge would accept only students indoctrinated by the Church of England. With a curriculum modeled after those of German universities, University College was the first English school to accept Jews, Catholics, and Quakers. In 1878, the university became the first in England to also accept women.

One of several collections administered by the university, the **Percival David Foundation of Chinese Art** (53 Gordon Sq., WC1, tel. 020/7387–3909), open weekdays 10:30–5, has a magnificent collection of 10th- to 18th-century Chinese ceramics. The top floor features some jewellike colored pottery—sort of like 17th- and 18th-century Fiestaware. Inside the D. M. S. Watson Library, the small **Petrie Museum of Egyptian Archaeology** (tel. 020/7387–7050) houses a deservedly famous collection of Roman-era mummy portraits and an amazing array of objects relating to Egyptian everyday life. The museum is open Tuesday–Friday 1:15–5, Saturday 10–1, but closes frequently in August and September, so call ahead. Both museums are free but accept donations. The college's main courtyard and portico are on Gower Street, opposite the redbrick University College Hospital. *Gower St., WC1E, tel. 020/7387–7050. Tube: Euston Sq. Walk south on Gower St.*

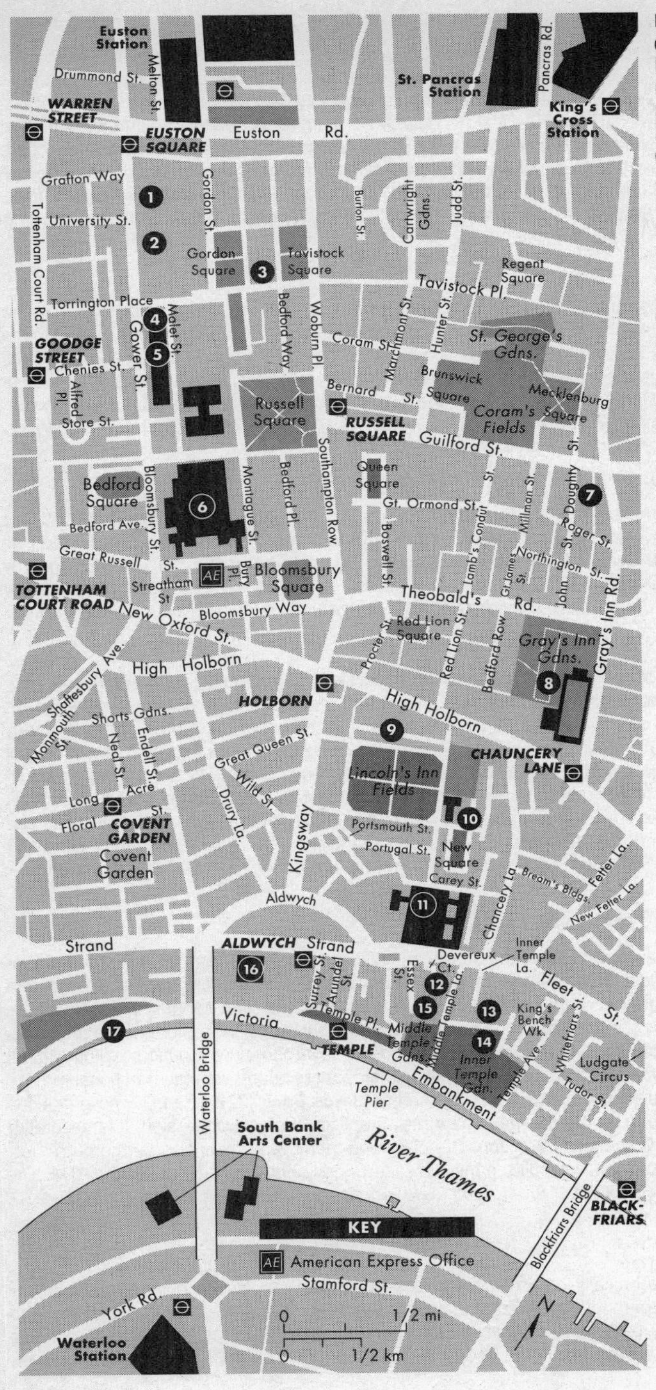

British Museum, **6**
Cleopatra's Needle, **17**
Dickens House, **7**
Dillon's Bookstore, **4**
Gray's Inn, **8**
Inner Temple, **14**
Lincoln's Inn, **10**
Lloyds Bank, **12**
Middle Temple, **15**
Percival David Foundation of Chinese Art, **3**
Petrie Museum of Egyptian Archaeology, **2**
Royal Courts of Justice, **11**
Sir John Soane's Museum, **9**
Somerset House, **16**
Temple Church, **13**
University College, **1**
University of London Union, **5**

DICKENS HOUSE

One of the first fruits of Charles Dickens' literary and financial success was this house in a thoroughly bourgeois district of town. During the three years (1837–39) he lived at 48 Doughty Street, Dickens churned out *Oliver Twist* and *Nicholas Nickleby* and finished up *Pickwick Papers.* One visitor remembers Dickens scribbling away at *Oliver Twist* at his desk while a dinner party went on around him, "the feather of his pen still moving rapidly from side to side," as he made the occasional witty interjection. The house is now an interesting museum and library, containing a large collection of Dickens's household goods, his desk, and the ubiquitous lock of hair. *48 Doughty St., WC1, tel. 020/7405–2127. Tube: Russell Sq. Walk east on Bernard St., turn right at Coram's Fields, left on Guilford St., right on Doughty St. Admission £3.50. Open Tues.–Fri. 9:45–5:30, Sat. 10–5.*

GRAY'S INN

Gray's Inn, on the other side of High Holborn from Lincoln's Inn, was blown to bits during the Blitz, and the entire roof had to be rebuilt in the 1950s. Before he was caught taking bribes and imprisoned in the Tower of London, Francis Bacon (1561–1626), whose statue is on the grounds, kept chambers here and is thought to have designed the impressive gardens. Charles Dickens, who spent time as a clerk here, looked "upon Gray's Inn generally as one of the most depressing institutions of brick and mortar, known to the children of men." *8 South Sq., Gray's Inn Rd., WC1, tel. 020/7458–7800. Tube: Chancery La. or Holborn. Grounds open weekdays early morning–midnight.*

LINCOLN'S INN

Beautiful gardens and immaculate lawns surround Lincoln's Inn, the only inn unaffected by World War II bombings. The impressive architectural features of Lincoln's Inn range from the 15th-century Old Hall to New Square, the only surviving 17th-century square in London. Don't miss the chapel, redesigned by Inigo Jones between 1619 and 1623. *Chancery La., WC2, tel. 020/7405–1393. Tube: Chancery La. or Holborn. Admission free. Chapel open weekdays noon–2:30, grounds open weekdays 9–6.*

SIR JOHN SOANE'S MUSEUM

This fascinating ex-abode of one of Britain's greatest architects is full of antiquities, gargoyle heads, pediments, and a plethora of other chunks of buildings. Soane had so much stuff that special walls—which open on hinges to reveal other walls—were constructed so that he could hang three times as many paintings in his small Picture Room. Fortunately, Soane liked Hogarth's *Rake's Progress* enough to put it on the outside. The Sepulchral Chamber holds the alabaster sarcophagus of Seti I; Soane was so pleased with his purchase that he held a three-day party to celebrate its installation in 1825. As you walk around the museum, make sure you peep out the windows and over the railings—Soane left bits and pieces everywhere. Call for details of the program of architectural exhibits. *13 Lincoln's Inn Fields, WC2, tel. 020/7405–2107. Tube: Holborn. Walk south on Kingsway, turn left on Remnant St. Admission free. Open Tues.–Sat. 10–5.*

ROYAL COURTS OF JUSTICE

G. E. Street's impressive Law Courts lie on the Strand, a block away from the Temple. To watch the proceedings, walk (quietly) into a public gallery at the rear of any of the 58 courts. Don't come expecting to be regaled with tales of horror and gore, however: the murder trials you read about in the tabloids are held at the Old Bailey (*see* the City, *below*), whereas the Law Courts deal with more mundane cases involving fraud and swindle. It's still fun to wander around the cavernous, neo-Gothic building with all the judges and lawyers in their wigs and gowns, carrying their papers bound with the traditional red ribbon. Directly across the street is the Law Courts branch of **Lloyds Bank** (222 Strand), whose glorious Victorian interior is well worth a visit. Designed as a restaurant for the legal profession, it is decorated with Doulton tile panels with scenes of Ben Jonson's plays and many varieties of chrysanthemum. Outside of normal banking hours, you can still see the glazed terra-cotta entryway—it houses the ATM. *The Strand, WC2, tel. 020/7936–6000.**Tube: Temple.đđ Admission free. Open weekdays 9:30–4:30. Closed Aug.–Sept.*

THE TEMPLE

South of Fleet Street and technically in the City, the Middle and Inner Temples (collectively known as the Temple) got their name from the Knights Templar, an 11th-century chivalric order that owned the land here. Sadly, about the only part of the complex that is open to the public is the gardens of the Middle Temple. If you can sneak a peek inside the Middle Temple Hall, look for the 29-ft-long Bench Table, donated by Elizabeth I. A smaller table, the "Cupboard," is reputedly made from wood taken from Sir Francis Drake's ship, the *Golden Hind.* Although little of the original church survives, nearby **Temple Church** (open Wednesday–Saturday 10–4), built by the Knights Templar in the 12th century, is one of only three round churches in England and one of Britain's finest examples of early English Gothic. *The Temple, EC4, tel. 020/7797–8250. Tube: Temple. Grounds open Mon.–Sat. 10–4, Sun. 1–4.*

STRAND AND EMBANKMENT

Strand, which turns into Fleet Street about ½ mi from Charing Cross, is smelly, noisy, and dirty. And not in an interesting way either—just a lot of cars in a boring concrete canyon that's crowded by sidewalks and mediocre restaurants. Tea-totalers may be interested in the oldest tea shop in London, **Twinings** (216 Strand, tel. 020/7353–3511), but unless you're a very methodical sightseer or really into carbon monoxide, you could forgo this particular area with no adverse effect. The Embankment, on the other hand, is a bit more intriguing. Constructed between 1868 and 1874 by Sir Joseph Bazalgette (the same man who designed London's sewers), the Embankment, which runs all the way from Westminster to the City, was designed to protect the city from flooding (a job now handled by the Thames Barrier, out east near Charlton). **Victoria Gardens,** in the shade of the swank **Savoy Hotel**—whose celebrity guests have ranged from Monet to Bob Dylan (who shot the video for *Subterranean Homesick Blues* 'round the back)—and near the Hungerford and Waterloo bridges, is a quiet chill-out zone among the bustle of traffic. Stroll along Waterloo Bridge and you'll have one of the best views of London. Eastward there's St. Paul's, to the west the Houses of Parliament, and over the river, with the Millennium Big Wheel in front of it, the South Bank arts complex (eyesore to some, modernist masterpiece to others). The Kinks's *Waterloo Sunset,* voted best-ever London track by a local radio station, refers to this sublime view, perhaps one of the most evocative anywhere in the urban world. As the minstrel says: "As long as I gaze on Waterloo sunset/I am in paradise." (*See* the Soho and Covent Garden map, *above.*)

CHARING CROSS

"Charing" is an Old English word derived from the French for "dear queen" (*chère reine*). The story goes that Edward I erected 13 crosses in 1290 to mark the funeral route of his beloved queen, Eleanor of Castile, entombed in Westminster Abbey. Londoners cast copies of the crosses in the 19th century and sunk one in front of Charing Cross station, hence the name. These days, few people notice the somber memorial in what's essentially a tube station parking lot. *Tube: Charing Cross.*

CLEOPATRA'S NEEDLE

Across the road from Victoria Embankment Gardens, right by Old Father Thames, lies Cleopatra's Needle, the oldest monument in town. Nearly 60 ft high, weighing in at 186 tons, and one of a pair—its twin is in New York's Central Park—the needle dates back to 1475 BC, to the time of Pharaoh Tethmosis III. (It had the name Cleopatra added later.) One legend has it that Julius Caesar had the obelisk moved to Alexandria from Heliopolis in honor of a son the Roman Emperor is said to have had by Cleo. By the time the British got their mitts on the thing—as a gift from the Turkish ruler of Egypt in 1819—it had toppled over. Leading engineers were called in to work out how to transport the huge spike to England, but it wasn't until 1878 that it eventually made the journey, and even then six sailors lost their lives in the voyage. Cleopatra's Needle was to have been put outside the Houses of Parliament, but subsidence caused a rethink and here it stands instead. Should it once again take a dive, there would be reason enough to unearth a number of items reportedly buried beneath the needle for posterity: newspapers, bibles, a Railway Guide, and photos of the 12 most attractive Englishwomen of the time. *Tube: Embankment. Follow the river eastward.*

SOMERSET HOUSE

Constructed between 1776 and 1786 by William Chambers, Somerset House replaced a Renaissance palace used by members of the royal family. Until 1973, Somerset House was the home of the Registrar General of Births, Deaths, and Marriages, as well as a number of other government offices. Today, the building houses Inland Revenue (the British equivalent of the IRS) and the **Courtauld Institute Galleries,** affiliated with the University of London. The gallery has a collection of oils from the 15th to the 20th centuries, of which the Impressionist and post-Impressionist movements (displayed in Rooms 8 and 10) are the best represented. The Cézanne collection is considered the finest in London, as is the collection of Manet's works, including *A Bar at the Folies-Bergère* (you know, the one with the bored-looking waitress). Modigliani's wonderful *Female Nude* coyly looks away from poor van Gogh's *Self-Por-*

trait with Bandaged Ear, and Degas's dancers stand *en pointe.* Classic works by such artists as Lely, Giovanni Bellini, and Rubens are also exhibited in the newly refurbished gallery. Special exhibitions for 2000 include *Art Made Modern,* a spiky look at present artistic trends. *The Strand, WC2, tel. 020/7873–2526. Tube: Temple. Walk west on Temple Pl., turn right on Surrey St., left on the Strand. Admission £4; free after 5 PM. Open Mon. 10–2, Tues.–Sat. 10–6, Sun. noon–6.*

ST. MARY-LE-STRAND

Constructed between 1714 and 1717, St. Mary-le-Strand was the first of 50 churches that devout Queen Anne ordered built to lure London's growing population back to religion and away from wantonness following the twin whammies of the plague (1665) and the Great Fire (1666). Twelve churches were about all that anyone could take, however. The architect was Scotsman James Gibbs, who melded elements of Italian Baroque with Christopher Wren's distinctive style. Gibbs probably never intended to surround his church with an unceasing flow of traffic, but those are the breaks. *The Strand, across from Somerset House, WC2, tel. 020/7836–3126. Tube: Temple or Charing Cross. Open weekdays and Sun. 11–4.*

THE CITY

The "City" is to London what Wall Street is to New York. It smells of money and deals. And like all other good capitalist animals, the City answers to the markets and nothing else, not even the rest of London—it's an administrative and legal entity in itself. Taking up just over a square mile in east London, the City is home to the stock exchange, the Bank of England, Lloyd's, and a host of large banking and trading firms. The traditional view of the City has always been that of upper- and upper-middle-class gentlemen in bowler hats carrying brollies and briefcases. That all changed in the headlong rush for money during the Thatcher '80s, when once-staid companies began hiring employees who may not have attended the right schools, but who could produce the goods. Of course, the old-boy network hasn't dried up and blown away—the snobbery has just grown a little more subtle. In fact, the City's newly made millionaires are still referred to by their upper-class brethren as "barrow boys." The '90s have brought recession to the area, and competition from lower-rent areas like Docklands has resulted in a lot of vacant buildings. Still, on weekdays the City vibrates with tension, cellular phones, and power ties, and it makes for some interesting people-watching and eavesdropping.

Although there has been a recovery since the '90s, there is some trepidation among traders as to the future. With Britain semidetached from the fabled Eurozone, there are fears that rival financial centers like Frankfurt and Paris will snatch chunks of the City's business. Meanwhile, the development of Docklands continues apace with more huge new projects planned. Then there's the looming threat of a take-off in share trading via the Internet, which will, reckon a number of doom-mongers, result in catastrophe for the financial establishment. City elders have been slow to recognize the dangers, but recent plans to build a huge new tower block to rival Canary Wharf imply a change of tack.

Although the City lies to the east of central London, it actually rests on the original Celtic settlement that the Romans conquered and built up into Londinium. Vestiges of this ancient heritage pop up all over the City, even though the Great Fire of London, which started in a baker's shop on Pudding Lane in September 1666, destroyed almost every building in the area. In the years that followed, architect Christopher Wren redesigned the entire district, building 51 new churches, including **St. Paul's Cathedral** (*see* Major Attractions, *above*), which stood as the focal point of a new city of spires. German bombers wrecked most of Wren's work, however (fewer than half remain), and postwar London architects managed to brutalize much of the rest. Unfortunately, the once-dramatic views of St. Paul's have slowly disappeared behind concrete behemoths. For a calendar of events and recommended walks in the area, contact the **City Information Centre** (tel. 020/7332–1456) at the south side of St. Paul's Cathedral.

ST. BRIDE'S FLEET STREET

Known as the printers' church, St. Bride's is surrounded by now predominantly empty offices that once made up the Fleet Street newspaper empire. The first St. Bride's was destroyed in the Great Fire. Rebuilt by Wren, St. Bride's spire is the tallest he ever built; its distinctive shape is said to have inspired the first tiered wedding cake. Although gutted in the Blitz, with only the steeple and outer walls surviving, the church has been nicely restored and provides a welcome haven from the anxiety of city life. The **crypt** contains an excellent exhibition about the history of the church, revealing its Roman and medieval foundations, and a history of Fleet Street itself. Free lunchtime recitals are held Tuesday, Wednesday, and Friday at 1:15, and evensong is held Sunday at 6:30. *Bride La., EC4, tel. 020/7583–0239. Tube: Blackfriars. Walk north on New Bridge St., turn left on Fleet St., left on Bride La. Open weekdays 8–4:45, Sat. 9–4:30.*

THE CITY

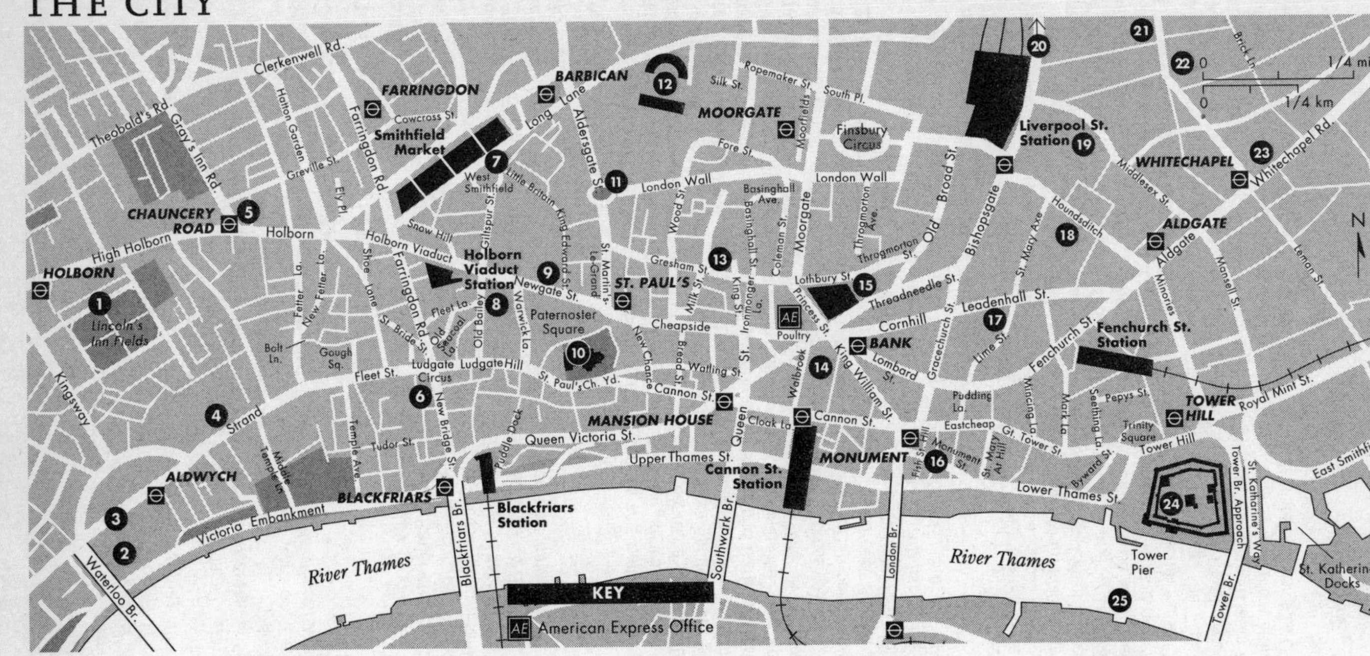

Bank of England Museum, **15**
Barbican Centre, **12**
Bevis Marks Synagogue, **18**
Christ Church, **22**
Geffrye Museum, **20**
Guildhall, **13**
H.M.S. *Belfast*, **25**
Lloyd's Building, **17**
Monument, **16**
Museum of London, **11**
National Postal Museum, **9**
Old Bailey, **8**
Petticoat Lane Market, **19**
Royal Courts of Justice, **4**
St. Bartholomew-the-Great, **7**
St. Bride's Fleet Street, **6**
St. Mary-le-Strand, **3**
St. Paul's Cathedral, **10**
St. Stephen Walbrook, **14**
Sir John Soane's Museum, **1**
Somerset House, **2**
Spitalfields Market, **21**
Tower of London, **24**
Waterhouse Square, **5**
Whitechapel Gallery, **23**

OLD BAILEY

If you can't afford theater tickets or you're a fan of "Rumpole of the Bailey," go watch a trial at the Old Bailey, officially known as the Central Criminal Court. You can't beat the drama (it's all for real) or the price (it's free). Just line up outside and scan the offering of trials—they're posted on a sort of legal menu du jour at the Newgate Street entrance. It lists the cases only by name of defendant; you'll have to ask a regular voyeur where exactly the accusations of murder and mayhem are going down. Generally, the juiciest trials are heard in Courts 1–3, the old courts. In the modern Courts 4–19, it's difficult to see unless you're in the front row, or actually on trial yourself. No bags or cameras are allowed in the building, and there's nowhere to safely store them nearby, so come empty-handed. While you're waiting for the show to begin, check out Pomeroy's famous bronze statue of Justice atop the building, overlooking the spot where prisoners of notorious Newgate Prison were once executed. Rough justice indeed. *Newgate St., EC4, tel. 020/7248–3277. Tube: St. Paul's. Walk northwest on Newgate St. Public Gallery open weekdays 10:30–1 and 2–4.*

ST. BARTHOLOMEW-THE-GREAT

Behind a 13th-century stone gateway topped with a 16th-century Tudor gatehouse hides beautiful St. Bartholomew-the-Great. Built in 1123 by Henry I's court jester, Rahere (whose tomb is to the left of the altar), St. Bart's is the oldest standing parish church in London, and its pealing bells are the oldest in the city. The quaint Lady's Chapel was once a printing shop where Benjamin Franklin was employed as a youngster. If the church looks familiar, it may be because it was featured in *Four Weddings and a Funeral* as the site of the fourth wedding. *W. Smithfield, EC1, tel. 020/7606–5171. Tube: Farringdon. Walk south on Farringdon, turn left on W. Smithfield. Open weekdays 8:30–4, Sat. 10:30–1:30, Sun. 8:30–1 and 2–8.*

BARBICAN CENTRE

This large complex of residential towers and cultural venues was built between 1959 and 1981 in an attempt to resurrect the city environs as a living city instead of merely a place of work. Although the complex's modern concrete blocks are inordinately ugly and look more like something you would find in Eastern Europe, the recent creation of a grand entrance portal softens the blow a little. After three decades, the seemingly ill-conceived Barbican Centre has managed to evolve into one of the city's principal cultural institutions. Varied musical performances are held in **Barbican Hall** (*see* Classical Music, Opera, and Dance *in* Chapter 6), **Barbican Theatre** is the London home of the Royal Shakespeare Company, which also stages smaller performances in the **Pit** (*see* Theater *in* Chapter 6), and the **Barbican Cinema** shows mostly mainstream films. There are also some impressive visual arts displays at the **Barbican Art Gallery.** Free music and art exhibitions are usually held in one of the many foyers, and the huge, glass-encased conservatory, filled with exotic plants and trees, is open to the public (80p) on weekends noon–5:30. *Silk St., EC2, tel. 020/7638–4141 or 020/7638–8891 for box office. Tube: Barbican or Moorgate. Barbican Art Gallery, tel. 020/7588–9023. Admission £5; £3 weekdays after 5. Gallery open Mon.–Sat. 10–6:45 (Tues. until 5:45, Wed. until 7:45), Sun. noon–6:45.*

MARX MEMORIAL LIBRARY

To the west of the Barbican, **Clerkenwell** was an early suburb of the city and is the traditional heart of Islington's Italian community. Off **Clerkenwell Green**—the centuries-old hangout of London's political radicals, including John Stuart Mill and Vladimir Lenin—is Marx Memorial Library, commonly known as Marx House, housed in a beautiful Georgian building with a long history of radicalism. Marx and his fellow council members met here to plan the 1864 International, and in 1886 and early 1887 Marx's daughter Eleanor was involved in the London Patriotic Club, which was headquartered here. The upstairs reading room is decorated with a 1935 fresco called *The Worker of the Future Clearing Away the Chaos of Capitalism*; a banner made by William Morris for the Hammersmith Socialist Society hangs downstairs. You can also see the office from which Lenin published the Russian Social Democratic newspaper *Iskra* and fomented ideas leading to the 1917 Bolshevik Revolution. Other important 20th-century collections are devoted to the Spanish Civil War and the American labor movement. The library itself has one of the world's premier collections of radical books and written artifacts of Marxist history. In spring and fall they offer a lecture series featuring top Marxist scholars. *37A Clerkenwell Green, EC1, tel. 020/7923–2994. Tube: Farringdon. Walk north on Farringdon Rd., turn right on Clerkenwell Rd. Admission free. Open Mon. 1–6, Tues.–Thurs. 1–8, Sat. 10–1. Closed in Aug.*

GUILDHALL

The Guildhall was built between 1411 and 1440 as a central meeting place for craftsmen of various trades, and although the original building was damaged by the Great Fire of 1666 and again by the Blitz in 1940, it has been carefully reconstructed to its original splendor. The stained-glass windows display the name of every Lord Mayor since 1189, and the hall is adorned with the elaborate banners of the 12 major livery companies as well as the arms of all 101 of the livery companies of the city of London. Adjacent to the Guildhall is the **Clock Museum,** run by the Worshipful Company of Clockmakers, which contains more than 700 exhibits about the history of timekeeping, including a silver, skull-shape watch that probably belonged to Mary Queen of Scots. *Guildhall Yard, EC2, tel. 020/7606–3030. Tube: Bank. Walk north on Prince's St., turn left on Lothbury, right on Aldermanbury. Admission free. Open daily 10–5; closed Sun. Nov.–Apr.*

ST. STEPHEN WALBROOK

Considered by many to be Wren's most perfect church, St. Stephen Walbrook has a high dome ceiling supported by 16 Corinthian columns. The dark wood of the organ and pulpit contrasts wildly with the church's most controversial feature: a gray, marshmallowy, marble altar sculpted by Henry Moore from Roman travertine marble and dedicated in 1987. The Samaritans organization was founded here in 1953; the original help-line telephone sits on a pedestal in the southwest corner of the church. *Walbrook, EC4, tel. 020/7283–4444. Tube: Bank. Open Mon.–Thurs. 10–4, Fri. 10–3.*

Famous defendants tried at the Old Bailey include Oscar Wilde, convicted of homosexuality in 1895; William "Lord Haw Haw" Joyce, who did pro-Nazi radio shows from Berlin during World War II; and Peter "Yorkshire Ripper" Sutcliffe, a serial killer convicted in 1981.

LLOYD'S BUILDING

Like it or not, the Lloyd's building is the most aggressively "modern" building in the City and certainly one of the most architecturally important structures built in the '80s. The duo that put it up, celebrity architect Richard Rogers and structural engineer Peter Rice (engineer of the Sydney Opera House), also worked together on the equally revolutionary Centre Georges Pompidou in Paris. The Lloyd's building makes no effort to hide its "builtness," a key element in Rice's project of "humanizing" architecture by reintroducing evidence of human participation in construction. Actually, you might mistake Lloyd's for a building still under construction. But now that the initial furor over its architecture has died down, Londoners have warmed to the building, one of the very few modern structures to be taken into the city's bosom. Try to visit at sundown, and approach from the north. That way, Lloyds's lights are at their most magical and the whole thing has the appearance of a futuristic ship that has somehow floated into town. Lloyd's hit hard times in the early '90s, resulting in a number of its investors, the so-called Names, going bankrupt. There used to be an observation deck that was open to the public, but for security reasons, it's now kept closed. *1 Lime St., EC3, tel. 020/7327–1000. Tube: Monument. Walk north on Gracechurch St., turn right on Fenchurch St., right on Lime St.*

BANK OF ENGLAND

Established by William III to finance one of Britain's periodic wars with France, the Bank of England was built in 1734. A few versions have come and gone since then but whatever its guise, its austere walls have always conveyed the idea of financial probity. The Old Lady of Threadneedle Street, as the bank is known, was only recently cut loose from Government apron strings and given the kind of independence enjoyed by the U.S. Federal Reserve. The snag for proud bank chiefs is that their moment in the sun is set to be overshadowed when, as most experts assume, Britain hands over most of its financial policy making to European institutions. In the Bank's museum previous versions of the building are on view in model form, there's a stock market game to try, and some old and new bank notes to examine. *Museum on Bartholomew La., EC3, tel. 020/7601–5545. Admission free. Open weekdays 10–5.*

MONUMENT

The Monument, designed by Christopher Wren, is now rather dwarfed by the city's office buildings, although it used to loom majestically as one of the world's tallest columns. Completed in 1677 to commemorate the Great Fire, the column is 202 ft high—the exact distance westward from the fire's Pudding Lane origin. For breathtaking views of the city, climb the spiraling 311 steps to the platform at the top. The platform was enclosed in 1847, following several shocking suicides. *Monument St., EC3, tel. 020/7626–2717. Tube: Monument. Admission £1.50. Open daily Apr.–Sept., 10–6. Last admission is 20 min before closing.*

EAST LONDON

THE EAST END

No one denies that the East End is not the "Queen's London" (and they certainly don't speak the Queen's English here), but that's because it is the *people's* London—an ethnically diverse, hardened, very much alive district that is actually one of the city's most fascinating experiences. If you're a fan of the 19th century, you'll know the East End well—some of Dickens's novels made the area famous; the mystery case of Jack the Ripper then made it infamous. Historically, it has always been one of London's poorest areas, home to successive waves of immigrants, many of whom came to avoid religious persecution. A building on the corner of Brick Lane and Fournier Street in Spitalfields is the perfect illustration of the area's changing character: built in 1743 as a Protestant church for French Huguenots, the building became a Methodist chapel in 1809, then a synagogue serving the Orthodox Machzikei Hadath sect in 1897, and more recently a mosque serving the large Muslim community. As a new mosque is being built a few blocks north, one wonders what incarnation the building will take on next—perhaps housing for artists, the most recent wave of "immigrants" to the East End, who have come to take advantage of the large studio/living spaces in the many dilapidated warehouses.

Like the rest of London, the East End is a jumble of grown-together villages. Much of the area is well served by public transit. **Spitalfields,** the district that encompasses Brick Lane and a couple of amazing markets, fans out eastward from the front door of Liverpool Street Station. To the south and southeast of Spitalfields, **Whitechapel** is home to Whitechapel Art Gallery (*see* Museums and Galleries, *below*) and best served by the Aldgate and Aldgate East tube stations. **Bethnal Green,** northeast of Spitalfields, has its own tube station on the Central Line. The massive **Docklands** area, far to the east along the Thames, is served by the **Docklands Light Railway,** which makes connections at Bank, Tower Hill, Shadwell, Stratford, and Bow Road tube stations. Stop by the **Tower Hamlets Environment Trust** (150 Brick La., tel. 020/7377–0481), weekdays 9–5, to pick up info on the sights, sounds, tastes, and history of the East End.

SPITALFIELDS

As you read this, Spitalfields is becoming a new London frontier for chic restaurants, intriguing boutiques, and home base for leading London artists (such as Gilbert and George). This future-forward district, however, is one of the city's oldest.

Spitalfields area takes its name from St. Mary Spital, a hospital founded in 1197. The area has a long history of involvement with the clothing trade; Huguenots fleeing Catholic France after the revocation of the Edict of Nantes settled in the area in the 1680s, bringing with them their silk-weaving skills. Many of the silk-weaving workshops survive, although the workers shifted from French Protestants to Jewish refugees to Bangladeshis, and the textiles from silk to cotton, Lycra, and leather. At Bishopsgate, the thoroughfare in front of Liverpool Street station, flamboyant office buildings and construction projects that reflect city-style gentrification meet the western border of the East End. To the east is one of Spitalfields's main commercial avenues, the ugly and appropriately named **Commercial Street,** with the sprawling **Old Spitalfields Market** building to the left (*see* Street Markets *in* Chapter 7). At the intersection of Commercial and Fournier streets is Hawksmoor's definitively steepled **Christ Church,** begun in 1714, when the area was populated mostly with French immigrants; check out the old French gravestones in the churchyard. Christ Church is also the venue for a quality lineup of classical concerts that are part of the annual **Spitalfields Festival** (tel. 020/7377–1362), held over three weeks in June each year. Mid-December brings similar programs with the smaller Winter Festival. Get information about the district's history and sights at the small **Tower Hamlets Information Service** at 18 Lamb Street near the Old Spitalfields Market (tel. 020/7375–2549), open Monday, Tuesday, Thursday, and Friday 9:30–1:30 and 2:30–4:30, Wednesday 9:30–1, and Sunday noon–2:30.

Head east on Fournier Street to reach **Brick Lane**; a visit to one or more of the ethnic restaurants lining the street is almost obligatory for food lovers. As evidenced by its name, the area was once a brick-making center. Although it went on to become a thoroughly blue-collar Jewish community, today's Brick Lane is known for leather shops and the fulsome smells that emanate from its curry restaurants—evi-

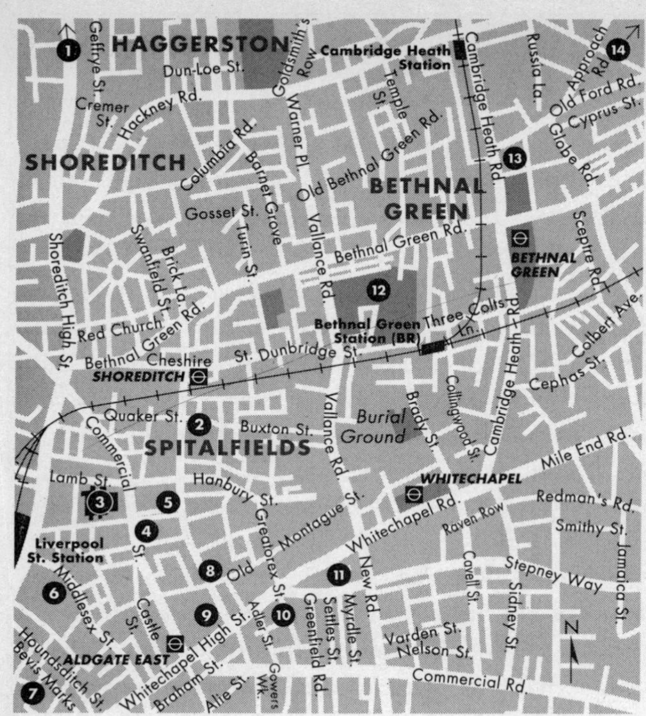

Bethnal Green Museum of Childhood, **13**
Bevis Marks Synagogue, **7**
Brick Lane, **8**
Christ Church, **4**
East London Mosque, **11**
Geffrye Museum, **1**
Petticoat Lane Market, **6**
Spitalfields Heritage Centre, **5**
Spitalfields Market, **3**
Tower Hamlets Environmental Trust, **2**
Victoria Park, **14**
Weavers Fields, **12**
Whitechapel Art Gallery, **9**
Whitechapel Bell Foundry, **10**

dence of its sizable Bengali community. The conversion of old Truman's Brewery into a shopping and arts complex indicates that a yuppie and artist presence is already at hand. Continue north on Brick Lane, past the Shoreditch tube station—be warned that it only operates during peak hours on weekdays and Sunday morning—to reach the large, flavorful **Brick Lane Market** (*see* Street Markets *in* Chapter 7), which roars to life on Sunday morning.

WHITECHAPEL

In the Victorian era, Whitechapel was the site of some of the most terrible slums in London. The area was already notorious when, in August 1888, the mutilated body of Polly Nicholls was found. The Whitechapel Murders, perpetrated by the mysterious Jack the Ripper, had begun. Nowadays, there's little evidence of these grisly crimes, apart from the clusters of tourists being led on "Jack the Ripper" tours every evening (*see* Guided Tours, *above*). Along **Whitechapel High Street** and its continuance, **Whitechapel Road** (which runs in front of the Aldgate and Aldgate East tube stations), you will, however, find evidence of the area's changing demographic makeup. Whitechapel was the heart of London's Jewish community until the 1950s; prior to World War II the district had about 90,000 Jews, compared with today's 6,000. Those interested in East End Jewish culture shouldn't miss the **Bevis Marks Synagogue** (Bevis Marks, off Duke's Pl., EC3, tel. 020/7626–1274), Britain's oldest. In 1699, Oliver Cromwell, who believed that there should be a Jewish presence in the community, invited a dozen Jewish families from Amsterdam, whose families had previously fled persecution in Spain and Portugal, to start a synagogue. Joseph Avis, a Quaker, was commissioned to build this beautiful structure, which was completed in 1701.

An example of the changing face of East London is the renowned **Whitechapel Art Gallery.** This large, well-designed venue with lots of natural light was built in the 1890s to bring culture to the East End (these days, cheap studio spaces are responsible for attracting more than 7,000 artists to the area). Besides regular exhibits, the gallery has a great lineup of art talks and other special events; call for details or check listings in *Time Out. 80 Whitechapel High St., E1, tel. 020/7522–7888 or 020/7522–7878 for recorded info. Tube: Aldgate East. Admission free; small charge for some exhibits. Open Tues.–Sun. 11–5 (Wed. until 8).*

LONDON'S MODERN ARCHITECTURE

Although contemporary architects are not allotted the enormous spaces of their predecessors, their work is often just as noticeable—for better or worse. One good example is Vauxhall Cross at the Albert Embankment, the new home of MI6, otherwise known as the British Secret Service. Despite its theme-park appearance, this center of espionage is absolutely inaccessible. Terry Farrell designed the moated, cream-and-green building in a style vaguely reminiscent of the background settings of 1960s comic books. Of the rash of skyscrapers that went up in the mid-1980s boom, Minster Court on Mark Lane stands out garishly. Best described as "notionally Gothic," the home of the London Underwriting Centre is really just a boring office block with "Gothic" pretensions. Not surprisingly, no individual will take responsibility for this architectural anomaly—a plaque reads GMW Partnership. A better compromise of old and new is Waterhouse Square, on Holborn near the Chancery Lane tube station. Formerly known as the Prudential Assurance building, Alfred Waterhouse's bright-red terra-cotta structure was built between 1879 and 1906 and has recently been remodeled. The amazing Gothic exterior hides a sunny courtyard, so don't be afraid to go inside. The Docklands area (see below) is another good place to scout out interesting new buildings.

Hasidim still walk the streets of Whitechapel in their somber black attire, but the area's blocky flats are slowly being filled by immigrants from Asia. Hundreds of Bangladeshi residents congregate at the tremendous **East London Mosque** (82–92 Whitechapel Rd., tel. 020/7247–1357), the first building in London built specifically for use as an Islamic place of worship. Just west of the mosque is **Whitechapel Bell Foundry** (34 Whitechapel Rd., tel. 020/7247–2599), established in 1570. One of the most famous bells to be cast here is Philadelphia's Liberty Bell—but don't let that make you think they do bad work. Big Ben, the 13-ton bell in the famous clocktower at Westminster, was cast here in 1858 and is still perfectly sound. Find out more trivia in the small museum in the front store, but the foundry itself is closed to the public.

Just south of the intersection of Whitechapel and New roads, the free **Royal London Hospital Archives and Museum** (Newark St., tel. 020/7377–7608, open weekdays 10–4:30) is small but filled with wonderful oddities and memorabilia, including small sections on dentistry (look for the false teeth of one George Washington, president of the United States), x-rays, and frightening 18th- and 19th-century medical tools. The museum also honors figures such as Florence Nightingale, who was a governor of the hospital, and Dr. Barnardo, who left the profession to run a string of homes for kids in the East End in the late 19th century (his charity, now a national concern, still bears his name). After a man called Joseph Merrick was discovered on display at an East End freak show in the mid-1880s, he was admitted to the hospital, where he was treated until his death in 1890. He's of course better known as the Elephant Man. Although the hospital still owns his bones, they are not on display; a small section illustrates Merrick's sad life.

On Sunday morning, the colorful and value-packed **Petticoat Lane Market** (*see* Street Markets *in* Chapter 7) on Middlesex Street is a favorite destination for thousands of Londoners. Those with a taste for East

End gore and gangsterism may want to combine a visit with a pint in the **Blind Beggar,** where Ronnie Kray (of *The Krays* movie fame) shot rival thug George Cornell dead in 1966 (*see* Pubs *in* Chapter 6).

BETHNAL GREEN

Northeast of Whitechapel lies Bethnal Green, a downtrodden area dotted with pretty green parks. Sprawling **Victoria Park** was the first park in London created specifically for public use (1842); social reformers felt that the poor needed space, fresh air, and light—none of which they had in their tiny, grim tenements. To get here head north on Cambridge Heath Road, turn right on Old Ford Road and follow it east about ½ mi. On the way you'll pass the free **Bethnal Green Museum of Childhood** (Cambridge Heath Rd., E2, tel. 020/8983–5200), open Saturday–Thursday 10–5:45, an offshoot of the Victoria and Albert Museum. A huge collection of toys, games, puppets, dolls, and dollhouses, some dating as far back as 1760, is housed in this free museum. Look for the box containing the musical wooden sheep, just up the right stairs to the lower galleries; playing "Mary Had a Little Lamb" may be the best 20p you spend all day. Another monstrous, grassy expanse (Frisbee heaven) is **Weavers Fields,** accessible by heading south on Cambridge Heath Road and continuing right on Three Colts Lane, past the garages where London taxicabs come to die.

DOCKLANDS

Sprawling eastward along the Thames from Tower Bridge, Docklands is a marvelous and sad ode to "progress." Despite being hard hit in the Blitz, the London docks remained very busy up until the 1960s, carrying more than 60 million tons of cargo as late as 1964. Abrupt dock closures in the '70s sank the area into economic decline, but by the '80s the wide-open spaces (read "cheap land") of the Docklands seemed like a possible solution to inner-city decline. The London Docklands Development Company took over, and money was lavished on several developments, most notably **Canary Wharf.** One Canada Square, the complex's 800-ft tower (the tallest building in Britain), still has plenty of floor space to rent, even though it's home to several newspapers that used to line Fleet Street. Conspicuous contrast to the modern wharf is provided by **West India Quay** (just north of Canary Wharf, across a floating footbridge), which retains its 19th-century warehouses. One of these has been converted into a five-floor **Docklands Museum,** due to open in early 2001; its exhibit will detail the history of the area's commerce and communities through oral testimonies, photographs, and other exhibits.

The Docklands is a great place to see modern and postmodern architecture. Some interesting buildings to look out for are the red-front, oddly shaped **China Wharf** (29 Mill St., Bermondsey), John Outram's Legos-meets-ancient-Egypt **Storm Water Pumping Station** (Stewart St., Isle of Dogs), and the parabolic roof of the Canary Wharf Docklands Light Railway station. **Docklands Light Railway** (tel. 020/7363–9700) glides through much of the area, offering stunning views as well as efficient service. Travel on DLR is included in the normal London Transport Travelcards, although DLR also offers a special one-day combo ticket (£7.60) that includes unlimited travel on the railway and a single journey by river between Greenwich and Westminster. An extension to the DLR will be completed sometime in 2000; it will run from Island Gardens to unlovely Lewisham via Greenwich.

The wise traveler will take the DLR immediately to the Crossharbour/London Arena stop and visit **London Docklands Visitor's Centre** (3 Limeharbour, E14, tel. 020/7512–1111) on the Isle of Dogs. The center, open weekdays 8:30–6, between 9 and 3 on Saturday, and at variable times on Sunday, has loads of information, an interesting exhibit on the area's history, and free pamphlets on walks in the area that take you past some of the more obscure architectural gems and points of interest. Another converted warehouse area is **St. Katherine's Dock,** just east of the Tower of London, now a peaceful stomping ground for tourists, yachting enthusiasts, and city professionals.

SOUTH OF THE THAMES

THE SOUTH BANK

The Thames weaves and winds a watery curtain that divides the city in half. North Londoners often claim they never venture south across the river and, until recently, the area was rarely troubled by tourists unless they were departing from Waterloo Station or going to a performance at the **South Bank Centre** (*see* Chapter 6). Much of the area was bombed flat during the war, so no one was likely to bandy about clichés like "quaint" to describe it. During the '80s, hundreds of homeless people roughed it in

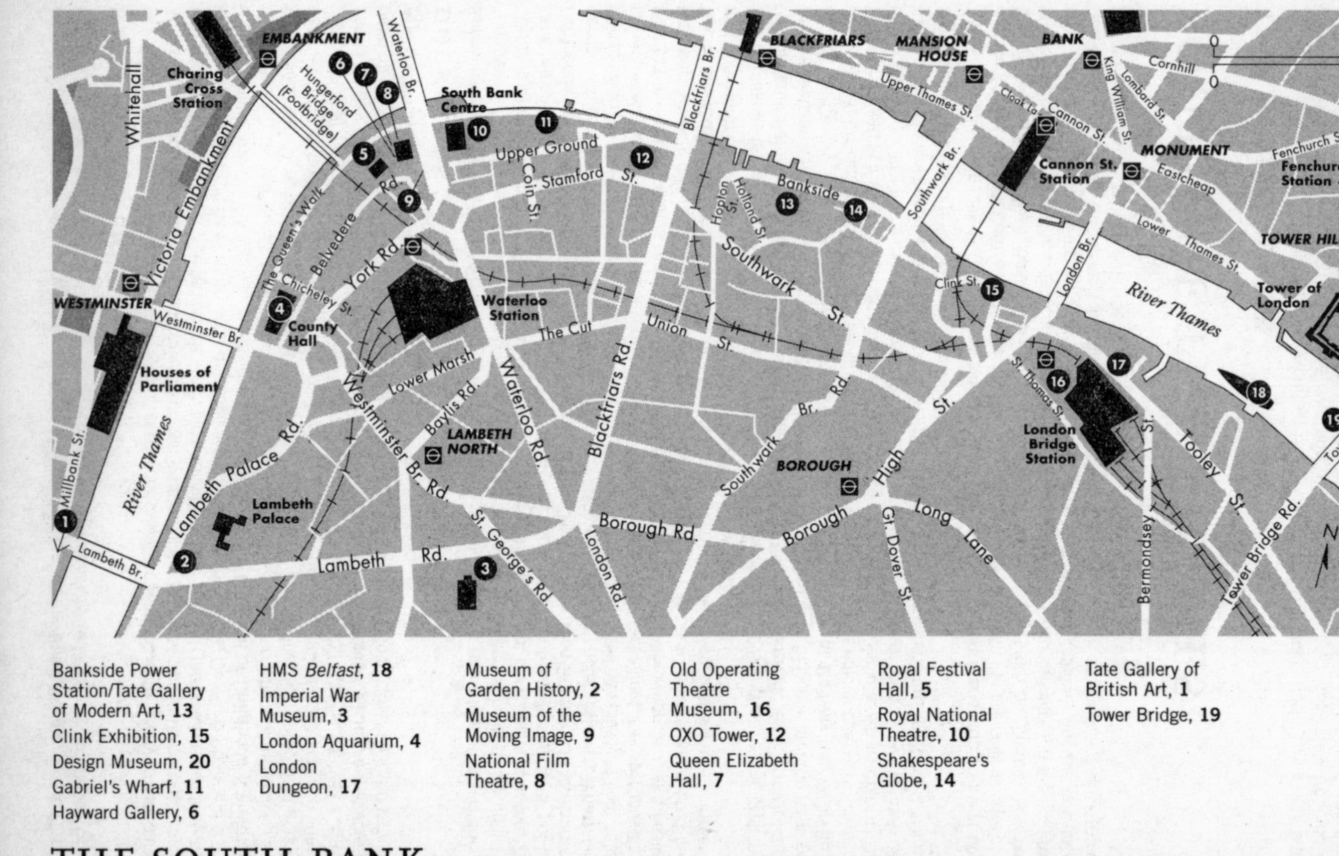

THE SOUTH BANK

cardboard boxes around South Bank's subway and railroad arches. Even though a new IMAX theater recently appropriated much of the space occupied by the "Cardboard Cities," poverty and panhandling are still commonplace in the area. Since the late '90s, the South Bank has been exploding with life—all sorts of headline-making attractions are opening or being planned, the most exciting of which is the spectacular new reconstruction of **Shakespeare's Globe Theatre,** which officially opened in 1997, just 200 yards from where the first "wooden O"—the most famous theater in the world—originally stood.

Right next to Westminster, the bulky colossus of County Hall is being converted into various ventures, including the **London Aquarium** (*see below*), the **FA Premier League Hall of Fame** (*see* Museums and Galleries, *below*), a couple of hotels, apartments, and various chichi restaurants. The adjacent Jubilee Gardens have been torn up in favor of the 450-ft-high **British Airways London Eye** (*see below*), the largest Ferris wheel in the world. The stunning new **Eurostar Terminal** at Waterloo Station is located between here and the South Bank Centre. Designed by Nicholas Grimshaw, the terminal boasts an intricate roof composed of huge overlapping glass panels. Walking farther east, just beyond the South Bank Centre, the **Gabriel's Wharf** area provides fancy places to eat, none more so than the swank top-floor restaurant at **OXO Tower,** a glitzy, neon-bedecked Art Deco showpiece that's now apartments and malls.

On the east side of Blackfriars Bridge looms the forbidding brick **Bankside Power Station,** currently being transformed into the Tate Gallery's modern art branch (due to open in May 2000). The Globe Theatre and **HMS Belfast** (*see below*) follow before the tourist magnet of **Tower Bridge** (*see* Main Attractions, *above*) appears. Next to the bridge is **Butler's Wharf,** a gaggle of tumbledown warehouses that have been recently spruced up and interspersed with ultramodern architecture. The wharf is home to trendy bistros, delicatessens, and offices, along with the excellent **Design Museum** (*see* Museums and Galleries, *below*).

In the Middle Ages, Southwark was London's equivalent of Las Vegas, where everybody would go to drink and party.

THE BRITISH AIRWAYS LONDON EYE

London's millennium fever adds a new lookout point for the city's skyline in the form of this 450-ft-high observation Ferris wheel. As one of 770 passengers, you'll need 30 min to complete a full rotation inside one of the 32 fully enclosed capsules. There is river access via the new Waterloo Millennium Pier. *Jubilee Gardens, SE1. 020/7229–9907. Tube: Waterloo. Admission £6.95. Open Apr.–Oct., daily 10–9; Nov.–Mar. 10–6.*

LONDON AQUARIUM

London's only attraction of its kind stands just across the river from the Houses of Parliament. The 40-plus display tanks—including two massive ones containing sharks and stingrays—are arranged along darkened corridors that try to conjure up a *Jaws* vibe but, in the end, just seem claustrophobic and dimly lit. It's no bargain, but kids will probably love it. *County Hall, Riverside Bldg., Westminster Bridge Rd., SE1, tel. 020/7967–8000. Tube: Westminster or Waterloo. Admission £7. Open June–Aug., daily 9:30–7:30; Sept.–May, daily 10–6.*

SOUTH BANK CENTRE

This sprawling, multi-tier monument to modernist poured concrete is home to the **Royal National Theatre,** the **National Film Theatre,** and the **Royal Festival Hall** (*see* Chapter 6), as well as the **Hayward Gallery** and the **Museum of the Moving Image** (*see* Museums and Galleries, *below*). This progressive institution hosts a number of free foyer events; pick up a thick monthly brochure listing these and other attractions at the various buildings of the complex. The complex is awkward and fragmented, a product of its piecemeal growth; more than a "center," it's a collection of buildings. Efforts to make this prestigious gaggle of institutions a little more aesthetically pleasing may call for a bit of expansion here, a bit of demolition there, but nothing much is likely to happen before 2004. *South Bank, Belvedere Rd., SE1, tel. 020/7960–4242. Tube: Embankment or Waterloo.*

SOUTHWARK

It is difficult to tell that Southwark (pronounced *suth*-uk), directly opposite the Tower of London, is London's oldest suburb, dating back to Roman times. Most of the buildings today are post–World War II, with a few notable exceptions. The site of London's entertainment district in Tudor times, Southwark is again set to become a popular area through projects like the rebuilt **Globe Theatre** (*see below*), and the Tate Gallery's new Modern Art Museum, which is slated to open in the **Bankside Power Station** (past

Blackfriars Bridge) in May 2000. Clink Street, east of Southwark Bridge, was the site of the notorious prison that gave its name—the Clink—to jails everywhere. Inmates were those who ran afoul of the Bishops of Winchester, who controlled this part of Southwark and licensed prostitutes ("Winchester Geese") and brothels, among other entertainments—taxing the profits heavily. **The Clink** exhibition (1 Clink St., SE1, tel. 020/7403–6515) seeks to tell the story of the prison and its inmates but looks a bit run-down for the £4.50 admission. If you like your gore a little more graphic, don't miss **The London Dungeon** (28–34 Tooley St., tel. 020/7403–7221), open daily 10:30–5. It's a total hoot of a place—tacky, expensive at £9.50, and packed with waxwork tortures, executions, and disembowelments—the place is like a lower-brow Madame Tussaud's with more blood. An enormous hit with kiddies and medievalists, it's "a perfectly horrible experience" (as the posters proudly proclaim).

SHAKESPEARE'S GLOBE • That long-missing Exhibit A of Elizabethan-era England—the **Globe Theatre**—has finally (re)appeared thanks to this grand reconstruction of the arena in which Shakespeare premiered many of his peerless dramas. The Bard of Bards staged numerous plays in Southwark at the old Globe Playhouse, which burned down in 1613 when a spark from a cannon used in *Henry IV* ignited the thatch roof. Although the theater was rebuilt immediately after the fire, the brimstone of the Puritans proved too much, and the Globe was closed in 1642. In those days, people didn't pay £20 a ticket for a theater seat, and they didn't look for neo-Marxist-feminist symbolism in Shakespeare's works. Going to the theater, it seems, was more like going to a baseball game, with people in the cheap seats acting oafish. Instead of peanuts, the playgoers cracked hazelnuts (whose hulls will again be scattered on the floor of the new Globe). The *New York Times* reports that Mark Rylance, the artistic director of the Globe, would be "delighted" if the audience shouted during performances or even threw fruit at the actors, as they did in Shakespeare's time—so come prepared to hiss at Iago.

Indeed, a performance at the new Globe is not at all like your usual evening of theater—literally. Most performances begin in the afternoon and, although flood lighting will be used to illuminate the theater at dusk, there are no spotlights to focus on the action onstage. The audience, on view at all times, becomes as much a part of the theatrical proceedings as the actors onstage. There is no scenery per se—rather, the magnificent twin-gabled stage canopy, framed by *trompe l'oeil* marble columns and a "lords' gallery" is the one setting—but, to quote Master Will, "the play's the thing." Then again, the entire theater is one amazing stage set: a soaring 45-ft-high arena picturesquely encircled by three half-timbered galleries. In the center of it all is the "pit," or orchestra level, with room for 500 standees. If you're planning to be one of these "groundlings"—at £5, the ultimate London theater bargain—be sure to bring an umbie if the London skies look threatening. If not, you might wind up enjoying an authentic Shakespearian drenching!

The reconstruction of the Globe Theatre is the work of the late American filmmaker Sam Wanamaker, who slaved for two decades to raise funds for the project, which even uses the same construction materials and techniques as 16th-century craftsmen did. A second indoor theater, the **Inigo Jones Theatre,** based on the venerable architect's 17th-century designs, is also planned, although no completion date has been set. Both theaters will be used for performances of old and new plays in 16th- or 17th-century style. Note that the Globe will be open May through September only; performances are Tuesday–Saturday at 2 and 7:30, and Sunday at 1, 4, or 6:30. Tickets run from £5 to £25. Happily, the theater can be seen all year long if you purchase a ticket to the accompanying **Shakespeare's Globe Exhibition,** a fascinating look at the archaeological research on this reconstruction. *Bear Gardens, SE1, tel. 020/7401–9919 (box office), 020/7902–1500 (exhibition). Tube: London Bridge. Walk south on Borough High St., quick right on Southwark St., right on Southwark Bridge Rd. Exhibition admission £6. Exhibition open May–Sept., daily 9–noon, times can vary according to performances, so phone to check; Oct.–Apr., daily 10–5.*

OLD OPERATING THEATRE MUSEUM • Don't come to this museum if you are facing surgery anytime soon. The display of a 19th-century operating room, complete with sawdust to soak up the blood, is enough to convert any visitor to Christian Science. The operating room, glimpsed in the film *The Madness of King George III,* is all that remains of the original St. Thomas's Hospital, which occupied the site from the 13th to the mid-19th century, before moving to Lambeth. It's been restored to its original, gruesome, and doubtlessly unsterile state. *9A St. Thomas St., SE1, tel. 020/7955–4791. Tube: London Bridge. Follow signs from the station. Admission £2.50. Open Tues.–Sun. 10–4 (and most Mon.).*

HMS *BELFAST* • Part of the Imperial War Museum, HMS *Belfast* was the pride of the Royal Navy during the mid-20th century. It remains the largest cruiser ever built for the British and is the only warship of the British fleet still afloat. It helped shell the Normandy beaches on D-day and later served in the Far East. Roam around the decks, which feature dioramas reconstructing life on the ship; climb in the "A" turret near the fo'c'sle (the ship's front to you, landlubber) and aim the big, empty gun; or sit in the captain's chair and bark orders at wax dummies or other tourists. A nice way to arrive (or leave) is to ferry across from Tower Pier (75p each way). Ferries leave daily, April–October, every 15 min from 11 to 5. *Morgan's La. off Tooley St., SE1, tel. 020/7407–6434. Admission £4.90. Open daily 10–6 (Nov.–Feb. until 5); last admission 45 min before closing.*

TATE GALLERY OF MODERN ART AT BANKSIDE • Most of the Tate's renowned collection of 20th-century art (*see* Tate Gallery of British Art, *above*) will be shown off to the public in this renovated power station, whose doors will swing open in May 2000. The huge brick building dominates this reach of the Thames with its severe outline and a lofty central chimney. It was designed by Sir Giles Gilbert Scott, who drew up the plans for the beautiful Battersea Power Station just east of Chelsea Bridge as well as those adorable red phone boxes they used to have all over Britain. Built just after World War II, the station ceased generating in 1980, after which a Swiss team of architects was recruited to give the plant a £130 million facelift and refit. They've spent a lot of that money adding two extra floors and splashing glass over the building's exterior. The purpose of the glass work is twofold: it provides natural lighting for the artwork and also allows great views out onto the capital's skyline. Some of the Tate's collection of 20th-century British art will still be on display at its Gallery of British Art at Millbank. For information before the opening, contact the Visitor Center at Bankside Power Station (25 Summer St., tel. 020/7401–7302, fax 020/7401–7272; open weekdays 10–5). *Queen's Walk by Blackfriars Bridge. Tube: Blackfriars.*

BRIXTON

Brixton, in south central London at the end of the Victoria line, looks pretty funky and is rarely visited by the casual tourist. Another of the city's multiethnic areas, Brixton is where many young Londoners venture for raves and to dance to world-beat sounds in the district's innumerable clubs. Another draw is the excellent **Brixton Market** (*see* Street Markets *in* Chapter 7), an open-air affair that grooves Monday to Saturday on Electric Avenue (that's right, the one in the Eddy Grant song), right around the corner from the tube station. Brixton's population is mostly of West Indian and African descent, and primarily working class. One of the best places to get in touch with Brixton's African and West Indian community is at the free **Black Cultural Archives** (378 Coldharbour La., SW9, tel. 020/7738–4591), open Monday–Saturday 10–6. It houses a small collection of photographs, letters, storyboards, artwork, and other cool stuff chronicling the plight and achievements of black immigrants from Roman times until today. You'll also find changing displays of works by locally and widely known black artists. To get to the Archives, take the tube to Brixton, make a left onto Brixton Road and turn left onto Coldharbour Lane.

In the recent past, Brixton's dealt with more than its share of urban blight: in 1981 and 1985 it was rocked by a series of riots that—although they were dubbed "race riots"—were sparked by worsening socioeconomic conditions and police insensitivity. The area was treated to another round of arson in late 1995, when a protest against the death of a local black man while in police custody spilled over into the main drag. Brixton has had plenty of money thrown at it, but a current joint private and public sector plan—the Brixton Challenge—seems intent on yuppifying the place. Although some of the new bars and restaurants are popular, most locals fear that the neighborhood's gritty yet likable character is at stake.

A half-mile south, uphill on Effra Road, is the reasonably pleasant Brockwell Park (open daily 8 AM–dusk), most notable for its fine lido (*see* Swimming *in* Chapter 8), to which locals flock in summer.

RICHMOND

The borough of Richmond-upon-Thames, southwest of central London, is filled with culture and money. The startlingly lavish Victorian mansions you'll see around Richmond have belonged to the families of various countesses and earls for generations; the rest house a sprinkling of rock stars and TV celebrities. One of the highlights of any visit here is a climb up **Richmond Hill** for sweeping views over the river. From Richmond Hill it's an easy walk to **Richmond Park,** one of the largest parks in Europe, with about 2,500 acres of heathland still roamed by herds of wild deer. Richmond's **Tourist Information Centre** (Old Town Hall, Whitaker Ave., tel. 020/8940–9125) is open weekdays 10–6 and Saturday 10–5; between April and October it's also open Sunday 10:15–4:15. In late June–early July the **Richmond Festival** kicks in for a few weeks of music and street theater on and around the Richmond Green and Richmond Bridge. *Tube or BritRail: Richmond.*

KEW GARDENS

Founded in 1759 by Princess Augusta (wife of Frederick, Prince of Wales), 300-acre Kew Gardens (also known as the Royal Botanic Gardens) is the mother of all botanical gardens. Wild thickets, manicured flower beds, lakes, ponds, and paths abound. Seven **glasshouses**—many huge and architecturally magnificent—house some of Kew's 60,000 species of plants, from arctic to tropical vegetation, and from huge trees to humble ground cover. Although it's hard to choose favorites, the **Princess of Wales's Conservatory** is especially charming. Here, in a modernist structure, a tropical jungle has been re-created in lush detail: mist blows out of pipes every 45 seconds, birdcalls resound from hidden speakers, and the atmosphere is hot and sultry. Another wonder is **Kew Palace,** a 1631 Jacobean mansion that was home to George II and Queen Caroline in the 1720s and a vacation residence of George III in the late 18th century. It's open April–September, daily 9:30–5:30, and worth the £1 admission (50p if you pay at the entrance to the gardens) to poke around the small museum of items from the Georgian era and relax in its peaceful café. The grounds also hold two art galleries; the Kew Gardens Gallery offers temporary exhibits on mostly horticultural themes whereas the other, smaller gallery is devoted to the paintings of Marianne North. Finally, be sure to check out special garden displays such as the popular Orchid Festival in early spring. *Kew Rd. at Lichfield Rd., tel. 020/8332–5000 or 020/8940–1171 for recorded info. Tube: Kew Gardens. Follow the signs to Victoria Gate on Kew Rd. Admission £5. Open daily 9:30–7 (Oct.–Mar. until 6); greenhouses and galleries close 1 hr 15 min before the gardens.*

MARBLE HILL HOUSE

Marble Hill House was the former home of Henrietta Howard, the mistress of King George II. Later occupants of this riverside abode included another royal concubine—Mrs. Fitzherbert, who was secretly wedded to King George IV. The house has been recently restored, and the details—from the furnishings to the moldings—are exquisite. Concerts are held in the small park in back July–August. *Richmond Rd., Twickenham, tel. 020/8892–5115. Tube: Richmond. Walk southwest on Kew Rd. (which becomes George St.), cross Richmond Bridge to Richmond Rd., follow path on Beaufort Rd. Admission £3. Open Apr.–Sept., daily 10–6; Oct., daily 10–5; Nov.–Mar., Wed.–Sun. 10–4.*

HAMPTON COURT PALACE

Up the Thames west from Richmond is Hampton Court Palace, party house of English royalty since the early 16th century. The palace was built in 1514 for Cardinal Wolsey, Henry VIII's primary adviser. The jealous king compelled Wolsey to give him the palace, and added the great hall in 1532. Henry is said to have rushed construction of the hall by having laborers toil 24 hours a day in shifts, working by candlelight at night. Centuries later, William III and Mary II toyed with tearing the whole thing down and building an imitation British Versailles; they contented themselves instead with adding the graceful South Wing, designed by Wren. The shameless extravagance of the palace is evident in its size, but the ornate interior and exterior decoration puts its value far beyond comprehension. Within the grounds are the world's first indoor tennis court, massive state bedrooms, kitchens capable of feeding a thousand a day, plus gardens, canals, and the oldest known grapevine in the world (it's more than 220 years old). The big deal is the giant maze of hedges, even better than the one in *The Shining,* that was planted in 1690. Most people can negotiate their way to the center in less than half an hour, but gardeners often have to dive in to rescue lost souls. *Hampton Court Bridge, tel. 020/8781–9500. Take London Transport Bus R68 from central Richmond, BritRail to Hampton Court, or the ferry from Westminster Pier. Admission £10; maze only £2.50; gardens £2.50. Open Mon. 10:15–6, Tues.–Sun. 9:30–6 (Oct.–Mar. until 4:30). The gardens are open until dusk or 9 PM, whichever is earlier.*

NORTH LONDON

MARYLEBONE AND REGENT'S PARK

There are those who say Marylebone—home base to many budget hotels—is one of London's more ho-hum neighborhoods. It can't be *too* ho-hum: after all, Madame Tussaud and Sherlock Holmes are two of its "residents." For reasons unknown—to each his own?—people have been flocking to **Madame Tussaud's Wax Museum** (Marylebone Rd., tel. 020/7935–6861), open weekdays 10–5, weekends 9–5, for eons. Madame Tussaud's is full of dummies: both the waxy sort and the sort who are willing to pay the £10 admission. Still, what kid could resist the famous Chamber of Horrors? The **London Planetarium,** in the same building as Tussaud's, is less hokey, and the virtual-reality effects of space and motion are quite good, but did you really come to London to see a simulation of the night sky? In case you did, shows start every 40 min (weekdays noon–5; weekends 10–5), and tickets are £6.50 (£13 for combined ticket with wax museum). Don't be taken in by the official-looking blue plaque mounted at 221B Baker Street (tel. 020/7935–8866), purportedly the home of the (fictional) detective **Sherlock Holmes,** open daily 9:30–6. The "museum" here strives to make Holmes real by scattering a few "artifacts" throughout the four-story Victorian. Although some may feel it's not interesting enough to warrant the £5 admission, you may well ponder why the address receives letters almost every day for Holmes—up to 50 per week.

REGENT'S PARK

Once yet another one of Henry VIII's hunting grounds, Regent's Park was developed in the early 19th century by architect John Nash for his pal the Prince Regent as an elite residential development for "the wealthy and the good." Today it is one of London's biggest parks, with a small lake and an even tinier pond, both of which can be traversed by rented rowboats, pedal boats, and canoes (*see* Participant Sports *in* Chapter 8). The **Inner Circle,** a perfectly round lane, encloses the beautiful **Queen Mary Gardens.** The presence of the **London Central Mosque,** on the western edge of the park, ensures that on weekends large numbers of Muslims from the ex-dominions are out promenading in their finest. For a relaxing (some would say blissfully boring) day out, catch a match at nearby Lord's Cricket Grounds (*see* Spectator Sports *in* Chapter 8). *Tube: Baker St., Great Portland St., or Regent's Park.*

LONDON ZOO

The northern end of Regent's Park is the site of the London Zoo, opened in 1828 as the world's first institution dedicated to the display and study of animals. The zoo fell on hard times at the start of the '90s, but a successful "Save Our Zoo" campaign raised sufficient funds to keep the zoo open and modernize its facilities. The zoo has since turned its focus to wildlife conservation and breeding programs. Every day at 2:30 it's feeding time at the **Penguin Pool.** The abstract building by Bernard Lubetkin makes an interesting backdrop for the playful birds. The reptile house is extensive, as is the aquarium. Pick up a schedule of daily events at the entrance; one of the best is "Duck!" (4 PM), during which birds of prey swoop over the audience. Newest attraction: the **Web Of Life** exhibit, which demonstrates the variety of life on earth and how it is conserved. This biodiversity center is mostly populated by invertebrates such as dung beetles and robber crabs, but you'll also find beautiful mammals like the golden-headed lion tamarins. The most direct way to get here is Bus 274, heading west from the Camden Town tube station (get off the bus at Ormonde Terrace); or take a canal boat from Little Venice or Camden Lock. It's also a nice walk from Camden Town along the canal—just walk up the dirt path after you've passed the looming aviary and cross the bridge. Regent's Park, NW1, tel. 020/7722–3333. Tube: Baker St. or Camden Town. Admission £9. Open daily 10–5:30.

BBC EXPERIENCE

The British Broadcasting Corporation, the world's best-known television and radio company, celebrated its 75th anniversary by opening its first permanent exhibition center in October 1997. There's a strong bias toward radio, but among many other things, there's an audiovisual show that traces the BBC's history, an interactive section—where you can try your hand at commentating on a sports game, presenting a weather forecast, or making your own director's cut of a segment of the *Eastenders* soap opera—and, of course, a massive gift shop. Admission works on a prebooked and timed system. *Broadcasting House, Portland Pl., W1, tel. 0870/603–0304; outside U.K., 01222/57771. Tube: Oxford Circus. Walk north on Regent St., which becomes Portland Pl.; the center is on the right. Admission £6.50. Open Mon. 1–4:30; Tues.–Sun. 10–4:30.*

HAMPSTEAD AND HIGHGATE

Four miles north of central London, the posh and stylish village of Hampstead—and it is still recognizably a village—has always had the reputation of being a place apart from the rest of the capital. The reasons for its semi-independence are partly geographical, of course, but the almost countrified atmosphere of the neighborhood has exerted a special attraction over the years for literati, artists, radical politicians, and thinkers, as well as for anyone wanting to combine the pleasures of country life with the excitement of being close to the center of things. Cool cafés, chic restaurants, trendy boutiques, and a growing number of chain stores line the two main drags, **Hampstead High Street** and **Heath Street,** both right by the Hampstead tube station. Hampstead is well-known for its grand houses, winding

REGENT'S PARK AND HAMPSTEAD

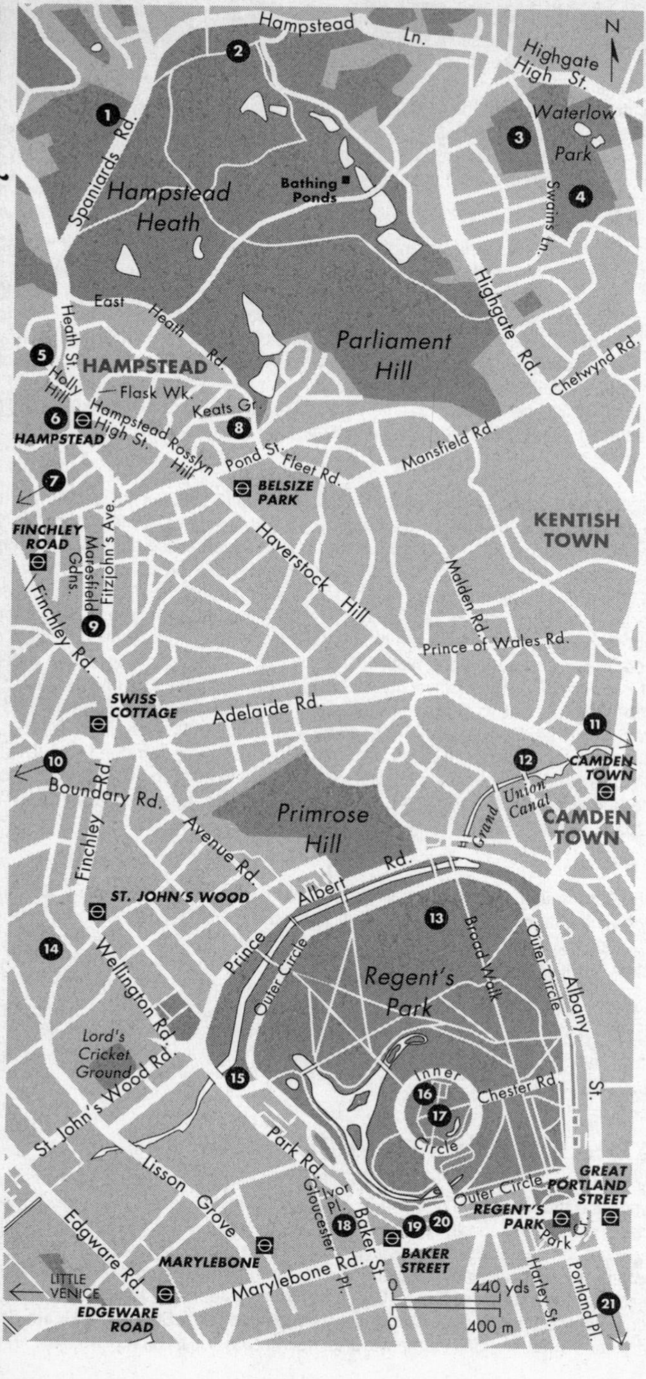

Abbey Road Studios, **14**
BBC Experience, **21**
Camden Arts Centre, **7**
Camden Lock, **12**
Church Row, **6**
Fenton House, **5**
Freud Museum, **9**
Highgate Cemetery East, **4**
Highgate Cemetery West, **3**
Keats House, **8**
Kenwood House, **2**
London Canal Museum, **11**
London Central Mosque, **15**
London Planetarium, **19**
London Zoo, **13**
Madame Tussaud's Wax Museum, **20**
Open-Air Theatre, **16**
Queen Mary Gardens, **17**
Saatchi Collection, **10**
Sherlock Holmes Museum, **18**
Spaniard's Inn, **1**

streets, country lanes, and the beautiful **Hampstead Heath** (*see below*). On **Church Row** just off the bottom end of Heath Street, you'll find some of the finest 18th-century houses in London. Besides the houses of Freud and Keats (*see below*), the more famous Hampstead abodes include **Fenton House** (Hampstead Grove, tel. 020/7435–3471), a National Trust building that houses the Benton Fletcher collection of early keyboard instruments and is open in summer, Wednesday–Friday 2–5, weekends 11–5; in winter, weekends only. Hampstead also has some cool little pubs, including the **Holly Bush** and **Spaniard's Inn** (*see* Bars *in* Chapter 5) where Keats, Shelley, and Byron tipped pints, as did highwayman Dick Turpin. Northeast of Hampstead across the Heath, **Highgate** is another tony residential area. **Highgate High Street** is lined with boutiques and a few cafés that give it a bohemian flair. If you want to avoid paying the extra 80p it costs to get off at Highgate station (it's in Zone 3), get off at Archway and hike up Highgate Hill past Waterlow Park. On your way you'll pass **Dick Whittington's Stone,** supposedly placed at the point where young Dick Whittington heard the bells pealing, telling him to "turn round" and return to London.

ABBEY ROAD

All you need is Beatles! Here, outside the legendary Abbey Road Studios, is the most famous zebra crossing in the world. Immortalized on the Beatles's *Abbey Road* album of 1969, this footpath is a spot beloved to countless Beatlemaniacs and baby boomers, many of whom venture here to leave their signature on the white stucco fence that fronts the adjacent studio facility at No. 3 Abbey Road ("Strawberry Beatles Forever," "Imagine—John coming back!" and "Why don't you do it in the road?" are a few of the flourishes left; note that these are whitewashed out every three months, by agreement with the neighborhood community, to make room for new graffiti). Studio 2 is where the Beatles recorded their entire output, from "Love Me Do" on, including, most momentously, *Sgt. Pepper's Lonely Hearts Club Band* (early 1967). It was on August 8, 1969 that John, Paul, George, and Ringo posed for photographer Iain Macmillan (walking symbolically *away* from the recording facility, incidentally) for the famous album shot. Today, tourists like to Beatle-ize themselves by taking the same sort of photo, but be careful: rushing cars make Abbey Road a dangerous intersection. Currently, there are few places in London that commemorate the mop tops, so the best way Beatle-lovers can enjoy the history of the group is to take one of the smashing walking tours offered by Original London Walks, including "The Beatles In-My-Life Walk" (11 AM at the Baker Street Underground on Saturday and Tuesday) and "The Beatles Magical Mystery Tour" (11 AM Sunday and Thursday, 2 PM Wednesday, outside Tottenham Court Road tube station at the Dominion Theatre exit; tel. 020/7624–3978). Abbey Road is in the elegant neighborhood of St. John's Wood, a 10-min ride on the tube from central London. Take the Jubilee subway line to the St. John's Wood tube stop, head southwest three blocks down Grove End Road—and be prepared for a heart-stopping vista right out of memory lane.

FREUD MUSEUM

The pad of the father of psychoanalysis still feels eerily lived in. Freud spent the last year of his life here, having fled Vienna in 1938 to escape Nazi persecution. After he died, his daughter Anna—a pioneer in the field of child psychology—maintained the house as a shrine to him, and after her death it was turned into a museum. Take a peek into Freud's life and try to analyze *his* psyche by inspecting the strange toys, art, and curious knickknacks. You can also check out his library and study—complete with the (in)famous couch—where he spent his final year on some of his most important theorizing. On the landing there is a remarkable drawing of Freud by Dalí, who sketched Freud secretly and later completed this portrait. Ask about the schedule of special exhibits, lectures, and showings of archival films. *20 Maresfield Gardens, NW3, tel. 020/7435–2002. Tube: Finchley Rd. Walk south on Finchley Rd., turn left on Trinity Walk, left on Maresfield Gardens. Admission £4. Open Wed.–Sun. noon–5.*

KEATS HOUSE

The great romantic poet John Keats (1795–1821) wrote many of his masterpieces during his two-year stay at this Hampstead home—in fact, it is said the house's garden provided the inspiration for "Ode to a Nightingale." It was also here that he met and fell in love with the girl next door, Fanny Brawne, for whom he pined for years. Though they became engaged in 1819, Keats's declining health prevented the marriage from taking place. He sailed to Italy in 1820 hoping to recuperate, but instead his condition worsened and he died in Rome at the young age of 25. Their two houses have since been combined to form an all-encompassing Keats museum, furnished just as it was during the poet's lifetime. Be sure to check out the full-scale plaster "lifemask" of Keats's head, created by a painter friend, and other goodies like the engagement ring Keats gave to Fanny, his letters, and first editions of *Poems* (1817) and *Endymion* (1819). The adjacent **Keats Memorial Library** (open by appointment only; tel. 020/7794–

6829) contains all the poet's compositions, as well as scholarly studies dedicated to him. *Keats Grove, NW3, tel. 020/7435–2062. Tube: Hampstead. Walk southeast on Hampstead High St., turn left on Downshire Hill, veer right on Keats Grove. Or take BritRail to Hampstead Heath, walk north on South End Rd., turn left on Keats Grove. Or take Bus 24 from Victoria via Trafalgar Sq. Admission free. Open Apr.–Oct., weekdays 10–1 and 2–6, Sat. 10–1 and 2–5, Sun. 2–5; Nov.–Mar., weekdays 1–5, Sat. 10–1 and 2–5, Sun. 2–5.*

HAMPSTEAD HEATH

If you dig traipsing through hill and dale, following narrow paths to nowhere, and crashing through bushes, the 800-acre Hampstead Heath is the place for you. For a big-city park, Hampstead Heath has a surprisingly rural air—despite the omnipresent litter. There are some fine views of central London from Parliament Hill, but beware the deadly stunt kites flown by well-meaning novices. Swimming, tennis, cricket, and even the occasional softball game are some participant or spectator sports (*see* Chapter 8). Otherwise, the principal sight is **Kenwood House** (Hampstead La., tel. 020/8348–1286), a 17th-century, Robert Adam–designed mansion with landscaped gardens; there are only one or two period rooms, but the real reason to visit the house—and what a reason—is to enjoy the **Iveagh Bequest,** a spectacular collection of paintings, including works by Gainsborough, Van Dyck, Rembrandt, and Turner. The high point is *Lady Playing a Lute*—London's most beautiful Vermeer. The house is open daily 10–6 (October until 5, November–March until 4), and admission is free. *Tube: Hampstead. Walk ½ mi north on Heath St. Or take BritRail to Hampstead Heath or Gospel Oak.*

HIGHGATE CEMETERY

A light drizzle (not unlikely in London) creates a wonderful gloom in Highgate Cemetery, where a maze of narrow footpaths cuts through a forest of vine-covered Victorian tombstones. The cemetery is divided into two parts: the **Eastern Cemetery** is still in use and contains the somber tombs of George Eliot (a.k.a. Mary Ann Evans) and Karl Marx, the German philosopher with whom political theorists all over the world would like to have a chat. Coincidence makes strange bedfellows: just a few feet away, across the gravel path, lies Marx's dialectical opposite (and one of George Eliot's lovers), social Darwinist Herbert Spencer, who once wrote that "socialism is slavery." The **Western Cemetery,** open only for tours (£3), has a spectacular Egyptian Avenue, incredible landscaping, and eerie catacombs. Buried here are Radclyffe Hall, author of *The Well of Loneliness;* the poet Christina Rossetti; and bare-knuckle prizefighter Tom Sayers, whose tomb is guarded by a sculpture of Lion, his devoted dog. **Waterlow Park,** at the northern border of the cemetery, is one of the only parks in London where you'll encounter some formidable hills, which run down to rush-bordered ponds inhabited by waterfowl. *Swains La., N6, tel. 020/8340–1834. Tube: Archway. Walk north on Highgate Rd., turn left on Bisham Gardens, left on Swains La. Admission to Eastern Cemetery £1. Open weekdays 10–5 (Oct.–Mar. until 4). Tours of Western Cemetery offered weekends, hourly 11–4 (also Mar.–Nov., weekdays at noon, 2, and 4).*

CAMDEN TOWN

One of the most bohemian and diverse neighborhoods in London, Camden Town developed around Regent's Canal during the industrial revolution. In this former working-class neighborhood, successive waves of immigrants helped shape a cosmopolitan atmosphere—although it's becoming increasingly gentrified. It becomes a serious mob scene on weekends, when tens of thousands of people flock here to shop the Camden markets, particularly **Camden Lock** (*see* Street Markets *in* Chapter 7). The crowds don't thin much at night, either, since Camden has some great bars and clubs, and many live music venues. The interesting **Jewish Museum** (*see* Museums and Galleries, *below*) usually provides a good respite from the crowds.

The Camden Town tube station is on **Camden High Street,** which runs north–south through the heart of the district. Take a right from the station to reach Camden Lock. If crowds give you claustrophobia, visit during the week when you can snooze on the banks of Regent's Canal or enjoy the village's many cool cafés, restaurants, and pubs in relative peace; the spectacle of the crowd is absent, as are many of the vendors, but it's still a great place to spend a sunny day in London. Another quick getaway is a cruise down the canal past Regent's Park and on to Little Venice, near Paddington Station (*see* Camden Cruising *box*).

PRIMROSE HILL

Like Regent's Park, Primrose Hill was once part of Henry VIII's hunting grounds. A tall hill commands a fine view of central London—check out the plaque identifying the buildings on the skyline. A young, cool crowd, many from nearby Camden Town, hangs out here, as do plenty of dogs. There are also lots of local "characters," one of whom inspired Paul McCartney to write "Fool On the Hill." Every November 5, the park is the focus of huge Guy Fawkes Night celebrations (*see* Festivals *in* Chapter 1), complete with fireworks and a huge bonfire. *Tube: Chalk Farm. Walk south on Regent's Rd.*

ISLINGTON

The Borough of Islington is an increasingly stylish area occupying about 6 square mi east of Camden and north of the city. Before the great amalgamation of London, the village of Islington was a popular stopover for travelers on their way to the budding metropolis, and lots of inns and watering holes cropped up to serve the transients. During Tudor times, the lush, low hills in the wilderness around the village were prime royal romping and hunting grounds, supposedly the favorite of Henry VIII. As London grew and modernity arrived with a bang, Islington was not what you'd call a preferred address. Ugly industrialization consumed a great deal of the countryside, especially along Regent's Canal, which runs through the borough. The excellent **London Canal Museum** (*see* Museums and Galleries, *below*), not far from the center of Islington, has displays showing the way "canal people" have lived their lives on and along Regent's Canal.

*Quintessential Camden: an early morning poke around the markets, followed by a walk down the canal to Little Venice, a canal-boat trip back to Camden Lock in the afternoon, and dinner at the Lansdowne (*see *Camden* in *Chapter 4).*

Ascending from the depths of the Angel tube station—on what is allegedly the longest escalator in Europe—you stumble upon the main drag, **Islington High Street,** in the heart of the old village. Just north, **Upper Street** is a busy thoroughfare lined with art galleries, antiques stores, and swank shops and eateries, as well as some great pubs and fringe theaters—easily Islington at its trendiest. Islington is trying to promote itself as a cultural attraction, especially on the basis of its artistic bent. The extremely friendly and helpful staff at the **Discover Islington Visitor Information Centre** (44 Duncan St., off Upper St., tel. 020/7278–8787), open Monday 2–5 and Tuesday–Saturday 10–5 (closed 1:30–2:30 on Saturday), can provide info on all sorts of things going on around the borough. **Angel Walks** (tel. 020/7226–8333) also offers interesting tours (£4), such as "George Orwell and Islington" (Tues. 11, Sun. 11:30) and "Village Islington" (Wed. and Sat. 11), both of which leave from Highbury and Islington tube station, plus "Charles Dickens' Islington" (Thurs. 11, Sat. 2), which departs from the Angel tube station.

CANDID ARTS TRUST

Set in an alley behind the Angel tube station, Candid Arts Trust wants to revitalize the area through the arts. It is home to three galleries with changing exhibits, a theater, and **Candid Café** (tel. 020/7278–9368), where savories are served in a warm, funky atmosphere. Book ahead for one of its increasingly popular four-course meals (£13.50)—even Björk has been sighted dining here. On weekends, an art market is held in the alley. *3 Torrens St., EC1, tel. 020/7837–4237. Tube: Angel. Walk left on Islington High St., turn left on City Rd., left on Torrens St. Gallery hrs vary but are generally Tues.–Sun. 10–6; café open Tues.–Sat. noon–10, Sun. noon–6.*

CRAFTS COUNCIL

This is the primary national organization for promoting contemporary crafts in Britain. Though they celebrate "the mark of the hand," the council members are willing to go against the popular grain in their rotating displays of different craft mediums: in 1996, while the rest of England swooned, quivered, and displayed their Strawberry Thief wallpaper in celebration of the William Morris centenary, they held an exhibition entitled "William Morris Revisited: Questioning the Legacy." They also have an art reference library, a small café, and the scoop on the best artisans' shops in the city. *44A Pentonville Rd., N1, tel. 020/7278–7700. Tube: Angel. Walk left out of the station, turn right on Pentonville Rd. Admission free. Open Tues.–Sat. 11–6, Sun. 2–6.*

CAMDEN CRUISING

Spend a sunny afternoon drifting along in one of the narrow boats traditionally used on Regent's Canal. The following companies offer trips between Little Venice and Camden Lock.

Jason's Trip (tel. 020/7286–3428) has three to four boats departing daily. Live commentary directs your attention to sights along the way and informs you about the history of the canal. A full bar keeps the 45-min (each way) journey all too brief. Tickets are £4.95 single, £5.95 return. Trips are run between Easter and the end of October.

Cruise with the London Waterbus Company (tel. 020/7482–2660 for recorded info) from Little Venice to the London Zoo (30 min). The £10.30 price includes zoo admission. Alternatively, stay on board to Camden Lock (45 min, £3.80 or £5 for a return trip). You can also make the short 15-min trip from Camden Town to the zoo for £8.50, which again includes admission. The peace is unbroken by commentary, although the gung-ho can peruse the free information leaflets available on board. Boats leave Little Venice daily from 10 to 5 on the hour between April and October, and every 90 min on weekends from November through March.

If you're heading toward Camden, be sure to allot time for the fab and fun Camden Lock market—great shopping and even better people-watching.

NEAR LONDON

GREENWICH

It used to be that if you were nearing saturation point with the traffic and crowds of London, you could go to Greenwich (pronounced *gren*-itch). Although it's only a few miles from the city, it used to feel worlds apart. The millennium year, however, has changed all that: Greenwich could well be the most touristed little town on the planet. To join the hordes, you can take the slow and scenic way, by river (*see* Guided Tours, By Boat, *above*), or a quick 25-min ride on Docklands Light Railway (from Tower Hill or Bank station to the Island Gardens station, on the Isle of Dogs). Check out the view from the park before crossing the Thames, and then head for the squat, circular brick building with a glass roof—this marks the entrance to the Greenwich Foot Tunnel, a passage with tiled curved walls and magnificent echoes that is the final leg of your journey. You'll emerge at Greenwich Pier, very near where the ***Cutty Sark*** (tel. 020/8858–3445), open daily 10–5, sits in dry dock. Now more familiar as the symbol of a brand of rum, this 19th-century, tea-trading clipper was once the fastest ship in the world: in 1871 it completed the journey from China to London in only 107 days. For £3.50 you can climb aboard the decks, ogle the world's largest collection of figureheads, or grab hold of the wheel and play captain. For landlubbers, there's **Greenwich Royal Park** (tel. 020/8858–2608), the oldest of London's Royal parks, containing incredible flower gardens, a Victorian tea pavilion, a boating lake, the Royal Greenwich Observatory (*see below*), and a stunning view of London from Greenwich Hill.

Greenwich's markets command reasonable popularity, although the trail of cutesy tea shops in the area can sometimes feel like tourism industry overload. The small, covered **Bosun's Yard Market** (59 Greenwich Church St., tel. 020/8293–4804) is packed with stalls selling arts and crafts, books, and other small items; it's open daily in summer (weekends only in winter). **Greenwich Market** (College Approach, Stockwell St., High Rd., and surrounding alleys) is held weekends 9–6 and features a wide range of antiques, old books and records, and odd bits of bric-a-brac. Fewer tourists means better deals; still, you should bargain hard. For information on guided walks and the like, stop by the **Greenwich Tourist Office** (46 Greenwich Church St., tel. 020/8858–6376); it's open daily 10:15–4:45 (shorter hours in winter).

Given its connections with time, Greenwich has understandably been chosen as the site for the United Kingdom's main millennium celebrations. The centerpiece is the Millennium Dome on a 300-acre site at Greenwich Peninsula, northeast of the town center. It is served by the new Jubilee tube line extension and the nearby Docklands Light Railway extension to Cutty Sark Gardens, at the south end of the Greenwich Foot Tunnel. Closer to the town center at Greenwich Reach, new hotels have sprung up and there are plans to build a cruise liner terminal. Alas, this trendy little backwater has become incorrigibly accessible—and a lot more crowded.

MILLENNIUM DOME

Although many Londoners expected the Millennium Dome to be late to its own party, the spiky, futuristic structure managed to fling open its doors on January 1, 2000. A total of £758 million–truly a severe amount of quids—was sunk into the Home of Time, but the project could well be seen as a financial flop. Almost ¾ mi in circumference, the dome is supported by 43 mi of cables that buttress its 160-ft-high translucent roof. Fourteen interactive exhibition zones enclose a central theater that hosts three daily performances of the **Millennium Show,** a display of stunning visuals, special effects, and futuristic circus-type performances. Exhibition areas that surround the arena celebrate British thought and technology and focus on themes such as health (with a walk-through body), work, education, travel, and communications, always with an eye to the future. The Dome **opensďď daily at 10 AM; tickets cost £20 (£16.50 under 16) and are available from the Web site (www.dome2000.co.uk) and wherever National Lottery tickets are on sale. As of January 1, 2001, the millennium displays will give way to another, undetermined at press time, set of exhibits.

> *The line in the Royal Greenwich Observatory's courtyard divides the world into halves, the Eastern and Western hemispheres. Straddle it and you're standing in both hemispheres simultaneously.*

Although London's transport planners envisage the dome and environs as a car-free zone, the recently extended Jubilee underground can zip you from Waterloo to the new North Greenwich tube station in a mere 12 min. The Docklands Light Railway will link up with the Jubilee extension at Canary Wharf. The rail option is to go to nearby Charlton and hop on shuttle buses; you can also take a riverboat from Waterloo (stopping at Blackfriars) and from the new Millennium Pier close to Westminster Bridge.

NATIONAL MARITIME MUSEUM

When King Charles II ordered Christopher Wren to build "a small observatory within our part of Greenwich" in 1675, few realized the impact this unassuming building would have on the future of world navigation. Although the **Royal Greenwich Observatory** is no longer used for astronomical observations (London's bright lights obscure the view), this is the place the BBC is talking about when it announces **"Greenwich Mean Time (GMT)"**; it's also the point from which sailors around the globe determine their bearings, using Greenwich as the prime meridian (0° longitude). The building holds a remarkable collection of beautiful antique timepieces and several antique telescopes. The observatory is now part of the nearby **National Maritime Museum,** which boasts the world's largest collection of maritime artifacts, including paintings, medallions, and reclaimed wreckage from England's mighty days of thalassocracy (that's maritime supremacy, mate). It recently opened 14 new galleries, increasing the scope of its displays significantly. The £9.50 admission gets you into the observatory, the museum, and the Queen's House (*see below*). Admission to the museum alone is £7.50, the observatory £5. *Romney Rd., SE10, tel. 020/8858–4422. Open daily 10–5 (last admission at 4:30).*

QUEEN'S HOUSE

Designed by Inigo Jones in 1616, the Queen's House was Britain's first classical building. The royal apartments have been restored to their 1660 state and feature a surprisingly vibrant color scheme. The highlight of the building is the **Great Hall,** a perfect cube, 40 ft in all three directions, decorated with

ISLINGTON MARKETS

Islington High Street (tube: Angel) is the beginning of the serious antiques-selling area that eventually funnels into the pedestrian-only Camden Passage, one of the hottest markets around for antiques and plain old junk. With more than 300 dealers, Camden Passage is in full swing on Saturday and Wednesday (with a curtailed version on Thursday). If a £45 teaspoon is out of your price range, follow Liverpool Road to Chapel Market, home of a daily street market featuring everything from stationery and clothes to flowers, produce, and sweets; come in the morning to see it at its boisterous best.

paintings of the Muses, the Virtues, and the Liberal Arts. For admission prices, *see* National Maritime Museum, *above. Romney Rd., SE10, tel. 020/8858–4422. Open daily 10–5 (last admission at 4:30).*

ROYAL NAVAL COLLEGE

Founded by William III as the naval equivalent to Chelsea Royal Hospital (*see* Chelsea, *above*), these Wren buildings were converted into a college for aspiring sailors in 1873. The symmetrical blocks were designed to preserve the view from the Queen's House to the river, and wandering around the grounds and the two buildings open to visitors makes a nice diversion. Students dine in the **Painted Hall,** decorated with Baroque murals (1707–17) of William and Mary by Sir James Thornhill, who also painted the interior of the dome of St. Paul's. The **College Chapel** was rebuilt after a fire in 1779 in a neo-Grecian style. Nelson's body lay in state here after his death at the battle of Trafalgar in 1805. *West Gate, King William Walk, tel. 020/8858–2154. Admission free. Open daily 2:30–4:45.*

WINDSOR

Windsor, about 20 mi west of central London along the Thames, is the sort of place where rowboats glide gently upriver, where swans along the riverbank noisily hustle for crumbs, and where families stroll with ice cream. Of all the day trips you could make from London, this is one of the nicest; Windsor Castle and the royal pomp are simply bonuses. That said, the royal presence draws throngs of foreign and English visitors, packing the narrow, cobble streets of what would otherwise be a charming village. Trains make the trip from London's Waterloo to **Windsor and Eton Riverside Station** (Datchet Rd., tel. 0345/484950) and from London's Paddington to **Windsor and Eton Central Station,** changing at Slough (Thames St., tel. 0345/484950). Both trips leave about every half hour, last 50 min, arrive near the center of town, and cost £6 return. **Green Line** (tel. 020/8668–7261) Buses 700 and 702 also travel from the Colonnade near Victoria Station, to Windsor (one hr, £7 return). Windsor is an easy day trip from London, but if you want to spend the night, there's a **YHA hostel** (Mill La., tel. 01753/861710) 1 mi west of the castle. It's open year-round except for the last week of December, and beds cost £10.25. The **Tourist Information Centre** (24 High St., tel. 01753/743900), open weekdays 10–4, Saturday 10–5, and Sunday 10–4:30, is just around the corner from the castle, and if you need information you'll probably have to visit as it's nigh on impossible to get through by phone.

Across from the tourist office is Christopher Wren's **Guildhall,** begun in 1687. Look carefully at the pillars in the center of the forecourt—Wren added them later when townsfolk expressed their concern that the slender outer pillars weren't strong enough to support the upper story. Note that they don't rise all the way to the ceiling, proving Wren's original design to be sound. In pleasant contrast, nearby **Market Cross House** slants sharply to one side and now houses the Sophie Grace Tea Rooms (51 High St., tel. 01753/857534), where you can buy tasty lunches and afternoon teas for under a fiver. Running the length of the Market Cross House is **Queen Charlotte Street,** recognized as the shortest street in Britain, at 51 ft, 10 inches long.

WINDSOR CASTLE

What William the Conqueror originally built out of dirt and wood (and what Henry II rebuilt in stone) has survived countless alterations over the centuries to become today's Windsor Castle. The process of restoration continues: a 1992 fire heavily damaged several rooms in the State Apartments, most of which were for the private use of the Queen, who spends most of her weekends here (the castle remains open even when she's in residence). Whenever the Queen is at Windsor, the Union Jack that usually flies from the Round Tower is replaced with the royal coat of arms.

The castle is divided into the Lower, Middle, and Upper Wards. Many of England's kings and queens are buried in the 15th-century **St. George's Chapel,** the principal structure of the Lower Ward. The tomb of Henry VIII—located in the choir—is a simple slab that he shares with Charles I, and a remarkably meager monument to such a megalomaniac it is. The Gothic chapel is the shrine of the Order of the Garter, a chivalric order founded in 1438 by Edward III. The **State Apartments** are in the Upper Ward and feature an amazing collection of royal portraiture and other paintings, including works by Dürer, Rubens, and Van Dyck. Check out the Gobelin tapestries, too, and the Louis XVI bed. The **Gallery** hosts changing exhibitions taken from the Royal Collection, one of the finest art collections in the world. For an additional £1 fee you can visit **Queen Mary's Dolls' House,** a masterpiece by the architect Edwin Lutyens. The Dolls' House, measuring 8 ft by 5 ft, is a fully functional marvel of miniature engineering with electric lights, running faucets, and elevators. Prominent authors and artists of the day contributed miniature paintings and handwritten books to the house's library, and seamstresses invested some 1,500 hours stitching monograms on the tiny little linens. Be aware that the State Apartments are occasionally closed when the Queen is in residence; call ahead before making the trek to avoid disappointment. The Gallery closes in January and reopens in May; St. George's Chapel and the Albert Memorial Chapel are closed every Sunday. The **Changing of the Guard** takes place Monday–Saturday at 11 AM between April and June. During the rest of the year it takes place only on odd-numbered days of the month, except Sunday. *Castle Hill, tel. 01753/831118. Admission £10, £8.50 when State Apartments are closed. Open Mar.–Oct., daily 10–5:30 (last admission 4); Nov.–Feb., daily 10–4 (last admission 3).*

ETON

Just across the Thames from Windsor, Eton is home to one of England's most exclusive public (read: private) schools. Don't be too impressed: academic standards are no higher here than at other public schools, although the old-boy network is, indeed, intimidating. Since the school was founded by Henry VI in 1440 for the expenses-paid education of "poor scholars," many Eton graduates have gone on to Oxford or Cambridge and fame in public life. Eighteen prime ministers, the King of Siam, Henry Fielding, Percy Bysshe Shelley, Aldous Huxley, George Orwell, and Ian Fleming have all studied at Eton, but who's counting? Eton's 15th-century **chapel** is a highlight, with its famous gold-inlaid pipe organ, although the modern stained glass near the altar is a bit disturbing. The **Museum of Eton Life** provides a brief glimpse into a day in the life of an Eton brat; the **Brewhouse Gallery** displays changing exhibitions. *Brewhouse Yard, tel. 01753/863593. Admission to grounds and museums: £2.60. Open daily 2–4:30, from 10:30 during school holidays.*

MUSEUMS AND GALLERIES

In addition to the museums reviewed below, the following museums are discussed above: Barbican Art Gallery (*see* the City); BBC Experience (*see* Marylebone and Regent's Park); Bethnal Green Museum of Childhood (*see* The East End); Black Cultural Archives (*see* Brixton); British Museum (*see* Major Attractions); Cabinet War Rooms (*see* Whitehall and Westminster); Candid Arts Trust (*see* Islington); Courtauld Institute Galleries (*see* Somerset House *in* Strand and Embankment); Crafts Council (*see* Islington); Dickens House (*see* Bloomsbury); Fenton House (*see* Hampstead and Highgate); Freud Museum (*see* Hampstead and Highgate); Guards Museum (*see* Buckingham Palace *in* Major Attractions); HMS *Belfast* (*see* The South Bank); International Shakespeare Globe Centre (*see* The South Bank); Jewel Tower (*see* Houses of Parliament *in* Major Attractions); Keats House (*see* Hampstead and Highgate); Kensington Palace (*see* Hyde Park and Kensington Gardens *in* Kensington and Knightsbridge); Kenwood House (*see* Hampstead and Highgate); Leighton House (*see* Kensington and Knightsbridge); London Aquarium (*see*

The South Bank); London Dungeon (*see* The South Bank); Madame Tussaud's Wax Museum (*see* Marylebone and Regent's Park); National Gallery (*see* Trafalgar Square *in* Major Attractions); Natural History Museum (*see* Kensington and Knightsbridge); National Maritime Museum (*see* Greenwich); National Portrait Gallery (*see* Trafalgar Square *in* Major Attractions); Old Operating Theatre Museum (*see* The South Bank); Percival David Foundation of Chinese Art (*see* University of London *in* Bloomsbury); Queen's Gallery (*see* Buckingham Palace *in* Major Attractions); Science Museum (*see* Kensington and Knightsbridge); Sir John Soane's Museum (*see* Bloomsbury); Spencer House (*see* St. James's); Tate Gallery (*see* Major Attractions); Thomas Carlyle's House (*see* Chelsea); Victoria and Albert Museum (*see* Kensington and Knightsbridge); the Wallace Collection (*see* Mayfair); Whitechapel Art Gallery (*see* Whitechapel).

Bank of England Museum. Housed in the Bank of England Building, this multimedia museum has some cool historic artifacts, early photographs, collections of old coins and banknotes, original artwork from Britain's currency, and interactive videos about the history of banknotes. *Bartholomew La., EC2, tel. 020/7601–5545. Tube: Bank. Walk east on Threadneedle St., turn left on Bartholomew La. Admission free. Open weekdays 10–5.*

Camden Arts Centre. This is one of the best places in London to see contemporary international art by the likes of Sophie Calle, Richard Wentworth, and Anna Best, who have all recently shown work. Exhibits rotate frequently through the center's three galleries, and on-site projects provide the opportunity to meet and discuss works in progress with rotating resident artists (usually on Saturday afternoon). Call ahead to see what's on. *Arkwright Rd., NW3, tel. 020/7435–2643 or 020/7435–5224. Tube: Finchley Rd. Walk north (uphill) on Finchley Rd., turn right on Arkwright Rd. Admission free. Open Tues.–Thurs. 11–7, Fri.–Sun. 11–5:30.*

Design Museum. This elegantly laid-out museum houses two floors of 20th-century international design, with an emphasis on mass-produced consumer goods. The hypermodern Review Gallery displays a constantly changing survey of contemporary design, whereas the Collection Gallery has a more historical emphasis; there's even a computer database connecting objects with the historical circumstances in which they were produced. Major exhibits include "Design Process Progress Practice" (until February 2000), which looks at 100 different 20th-century designs, "Luis Barragan" (June–October 2000), and I. K. Brunel (October 2000–February 2001). *Butler's Wharf, 28 Shad Thames, SE1, tel. 020/7403–6933 or 020/7378–6055 for recorded info. Tube: Tower Hill. Cross Tower Bridge and head east along the Thames. Admission £5.50. Open daily 11:30–6 (last admission at 5:30).*

Dulwich Picture Gallery. Britain's oldest public art gallery (opened in 1817) is from a grand design by the neoclassic architect Sir John Soane. Housed within is a breathtaking display of old masters, including works by Rembrandt, Rubens, Canaletto, and Van Dyck, still hung as tightly together as they would have been in the 19th century. The gallery alters its exhibition from time to time with visiting collections; note that it will be closed for refurbishment and rehangings through the beginning of May 2000. *College Rd., SE21, tel. 020/8693–5254. Rail: West Dulwich, from Victoria. Or take Bus 3 from Oxford Circus, Trafalgar Sq., or Westminster. Admission £3. Open Tues.–Fri. 10–5, weekends 11–5.*

FA Premier League Hall of Fame. Opened in spring of 1999, this is the country's main soccer museum, spread over two floors and tracing the "beautiful game" from medieval times right up to the present. A flashy collection, in vogue with the game's current status and high profile, it celebrates today's superstars and the heroes of yesteryear in educational, informative, and interactive exhibits. Don't miss the "Hall of Fans" for a look at what drives celebrities and ordinary Joes to be so passionate about their favorite clubs. *County Hall, Westminster Bridge Rd., SE1, tel. 020/7928–1800. Tube: Westminster or Waterloo. Admission £9.95. Open daily 10–6.*

Geffrye Museum. This wonderful museum features excellent displays of 11 complete period rooms, dating from the 16th century to the 1950s. Sir Robert Geffrye, a merchant and once Mayor of London, left part of his fortune to the Ironmongers' Company to build almshouses for the elderly poor. When the buildings were sold in 1911 (to build healthier homes in outer London), they became a museum to educate local craftsmen in interior fashions. There's also a beautiful herb garden and what they term "period room" gardens (open April–October) fashioned to reflect some of the interior designs. *Kingsland Rd., E2, tel. 020/7739–9893. Tube: Liverpool St. From the station, walk east to Bishopsgate and take Bus 242 or 149. Admission free. Open Tues.–Sat. 10–5, Sun. noon–5.*

Hayward Gallery. This flagship art gallery of the South Bank Centre often hosts major retrospectives of modern artists—recent shows have been devoted to Magritte, Jasper Johns, Dalí, Toulouse-Lautrec, Francis Bacon, and the Harlem Renaissance. *South Bank, Belvedere Rd., SE1, tel. 020/7261–0127. Tube: Embankment or Waterloo. Admission £6, or £12 for a multivisit ticket. Open daily 10–6 (Tues. and Wed. until 8).*

Imperial War Museum. Housed in the former home of the Royal Bethlehem for the Care of the Insane, or "Bedlam," this museum in Geraldine Mary Harmsworth Park outlines the history of Britain's 20th-century wars using weaponry, mementos, and reconstructions. Despite a bristling array of planes, field guns, and other war toys in the entrance hall, the museum's exhibits focus on the horror, rather than the "glory," of war. Two galleries upstairs house large collections of art from the two world wars. Downstairs you can visit "The Trench Experience," re-created from the Great War, and "The Blitz Experience," an excellent eight-min trip through London's Blitz. The "Secret War" exhibit details the world of espionage, especially the work of MI5 and MI6, Britain's intelligence forces. Until May 2000 there is a major special exhibit called "From The Bomb to the Beatles," which looks at all aspects of British life from 1945 to the present. A new permanent exhibit on the Holocaust entitled "The Total Age of War" is also planned for 2000. *Lambeth Rd., SE1, tel. 020/7416–5000. Tube: Lambeth North. Walk south on Kennington Rd. and turn left onto Lambeth Rd. Admission £5.20, free after 4:30. Open daily 10–6.*

Institute of Contemporary Arts (ICA). Lectures, avant-garde films, contemporary music concerts, and rotating exhibits of photography, painting, sculpture, and architectural drawings by international and homegrown talent make ICA the headquarters for lusty cultural bolshevism. Its café and bar are hangouts for black-clad, hip intellectuals, who love to smoke, drink, and discuss German Expressionist films or vernacular architecture. There's also a video library, where you can watch films, and a bookshop (offering choice bargains). *Nash House, The Mall, SW1, tel. 020/7930–6393 for recorded info or 020/7930–3647 for the box office. Tube: Charing Cross or Piccadilly Circus. From Charing Cross, walk southwest on The Mall. From Piccadilly Circus, walk south on Regent St., turn right on The Mall. Admission for exhibits: weekdays £1.50, weekends £2.50. Gallery open daily noon–7:30 (Fri. until 9); café open Mon.–Sat. noon–3 and 5:30–9; bar open Mon. noon–11, Tues.–Sat. noon–1 AM, Sun. noon–10:30.*

Jewish Museum, Camden Town. This collection of art and artifacts illustrates Jewish rituals and culture and the history of Jews in Britain. The items are beautifully displayed and carefully labeled. The upstairs gallery contains many precious antiques, including manuscripts, embroidery, silver, a 16th-century ceremonial synagogue ark, and the oldest English-made "Hanucah" lamp. *129–131 Albert St., NW1, tel. 020/7284–1997. Tube: Camden Town. Head southwest on Parkway, turn left on Albert St. Admission £3. Open Sun.–Thurs. 10–4 (last admission 3:15). Closed national and Jewish holidays.*

Jewish Museum, Finchley. London's East End was the gateway for most Jewish immigrants arriving in Britain over the centuries, but a larger Jewish community now exists here in Golders Green. This wing of the Jewish Museum features social history collections, which use photographs, storyboards, and historical artifacts to trace the immigration, settlement, and lifestyles of local Jews. A recent addition has been reconstructions of the working environments of early immigrant tailors, bakers, and cabinet-makers. The upstairs gallery is devoted to Holocaust education; one section tells the story of Leon Greenman, a British Jew who survived Auschwitz. *80 East End Rd., N3, tel. 020/8349–1143. Tube: Finchley Central. Turn right on Station Rd., left on Regent's Park Rd., left on East End Rd. Admission £2. Open Mon.–Thurs. 10:30–5, Sun. 10:30–4:30. Closed national and Jewish holidays.*

London Canal Museum. Located in a former ice storage house, this museum concentrates on the growth and decline of London's canal network. These waterways were once important venues for trade and transportation, and a distinct way of life evolved for the "canal people" who lived and worked on them. Make sure to look at the trippy narrow boats of modern canal-dwellers on nearby Regent's Canal. *12–13 New Wharf Rd., N1, tel. 020/7713–0836. Tube: King's Cross. Walk north on York Way, turn right on Wharfdale Rd., left on New Wharf Rd. Admission £2.50. Open Tues.–Sun. 10–4:30 (last entry 3:45).*

London Transport Museum. After an expensive overhaul in 1993, the London Transport Museum is more fascinating than ever. Dozens of buses, trams, and trains from the early 1800s to the present are on display (including an improbable-looking double-decker tram once pulled by a single, obviously overworked horse). The accompanying info tells the story of mass transportation's impact on both the growth of London and the class stratification within it. If that sounds dry, you can gambol with costumed actors, watch multilingual videos, or "test-drive" your own bus or tube train. The interactive "Kidszone" is a big hit; some excellent recent exhibits have looked at nighttime transport in the capital and the role of immigrant workers in the system. *39 Wellington St. (entrance on The Piazza), WC2, tel. 020/7836–8557. Tube: Covent Garden. Admission £4.95. Open daily 10–6 (Fri. from 11), last admission at 5:15.*

Museum of Garden History. This peaceful little spot of green is hidden away from the smoggy, concrete world. Housed in the former St. Mary-at-Lambeth Church—an interesting sight in itself—the churchyard contains a replica of a 17th-century garden, built to honor Charles I's royal gardeners, the Tradescants, who are buried here, as is William Bligh, captain of the *Bounty. Lambeth Palace Rd., SE1, tel.*

020/7261–1891. Tube: Lambeth North. Walk southwest on Hercules Rd., turn right on Lambeth Rd. Admission free. Open Mar.–Dec., weekdays 10:30–4, Sun. 10:30–5.

Museum of London. Come here for an extremely thorough look at the history of the city, from the Stone Age to the present. A lot of the older material on display was dredged from the Thames or found at modern building sites. Be sure to see the sculptures from the Temple of Mithras, god of heavenly light. Worshippers of Mithras buried the sculptures so they wouldn't be destroyed by their rival cult, the Christians. Other don't-miss items include the amazing Cheapside Hoard of jewelry, a beautiful Art Deco elevator from Selfridges, and the glitzy Lord Mayor's Coach. The ticket is good for an entire year from date of purchase, so you can visit over and over. Temporary exhibits take a diverse look at London life and historical figures. *150 London Wall, EC2, tel. 020/7600–3699. Tube: Barbican or St. Paul's. From Barbican, walk south on Aldersgate St. From St. Paul's, walk north on St. Martin's-Le-Grand. Admission £5; free after 4:30. Open Tues.–Sat. 10–5:50, Sun. noon–5:50.*

Museum of the Moving Image (MOMI). This impressive television and film museum traces the history of man's manipulation of light and shadow. Tons of interactive exhibits—plus snippets from groundbreaking flicks—make this a definitively cool museum. The museum also has a wide collection of movie memorabilia, like Charlie Chaplin's costume from *Modern Times.* Mildly embarrassed and embarrassing actors employed by the museum float around, trying to add period flavor—a few of them succeed. *South Bank, Belvedere Rd., SE1, tel. 020/7401–2636. Tube: Embankment or Waterloo. Admission £6.25. Open daily 10–6 (last admission 5).*

Photographer's Gallery. This is the leading locale in London for contemporary British and international photography. Exhibitions change several times a year, and symposia on various topics are occasionally held. Just as fascinating is the gallery store, with an excellent selection of prints for sale. *5 Great Newport St., WC2, tel. 020/7831–1772. Tube: Leicester Sq. Walk north on Charing Cross Rd., turn right on Great Newport St. Admission free. Open Mon.–Sat. 11–6.*

Royal Academy of Arts. The venerable Royal Academy, an art school founded in 1768, is the oldest institution in London devoted to the fine arts. It houses a permanent collection of works by Royal Academicians and stages impressive special exhibitions throughout the year. The millennium kicks off with "The Year 1900: Art at the Crossroads," a retrospective of the 20th century though 250 paintings and sculptures curated in conjunction with the Guggenheim Museum in New York. The Academy's annual Summer Exhibition of contemporary art is a noted event that usually takes place between early June and mid-August—anyone can submit work, although only 1,200 are chosen from an average of 12,000 applicants. The Academy's postgraduate students show off their final exam projects to the public every June and July. *Burlington House, Piccadilly, W1, tel. 020/7439–7438. Tube: Green Park or Piccadilly Circus. From Green Park, walk northeast on Piccadilly. From Piccadilly Circus, walk west on Piccadilly. Admission varies; average £7. Open daily 10–6 (last admission 5:30).*

Saatchi Gallery. The megabucks of adman Charles Saatchi fuel this huge gallery, one of the most coveted venues for contemporary art in the land. As one of the most influential private collectors, Saatchi has made the careers of a number of artists and has spent the '90s focusing on British artists like Damien Hirst (the dead-animals-in-formaldehyde guy) and Rachel Whiteread (the plaster-casts-of-rooms-and-buildings woman). Exhibits change frequently; the annual Young British Artists show is always thought provoking. *98A Boundary Rd., NW8, tel. 020/7624–8299. Tube: Swiss Cottage. Walk ½ mi south on Finchley Rd., turn right on Boundary Rd. Admission £4; free Thurs. Open Thurs.–Sun. noon–6.*

Serpentine Gallery. Search for this tea-pavilion-turned-art-gallery just north of the Albert Memorial in Kensington Gardens. Consult *Time Out* to see what's new here (usually some sort of cool modern multimedia work) because the gallery closes sporadically throughout the year. Free gallery talks are offered Sunday at 3 during exhibitions. *Kensington Gardens, W2, tel. 020/7402–6075. Tube: Lancaster Gate or South Kensington. Admission free. Open daily 10–6; closed occasionally for 2- to 3-wk periods.*

Theatre Museum. With fascinating goodies galore, the Theatre Museum illustrates life on the British stage from Shakespeare's time through the present. On exhibit are theatrical memorabilia of every kind, including prints and paintings of the earliest London theaters, early scripts, costumes, and props. It's not all highbrow drama stuff either—the galleries include art and artifacts of the circus, modern musicals, and puppetry. For the price of admission you can also join guided tours and attend stage-makeup demos and costume workshops. The box office sells tickets for West End theatrical events. *1E Tavistock St. (entrance on Russell St.), WC2, tel. 020/7836–7891. Tube: Covent Garden. Admission £4. Open Tues.–Sun. 11–7.*

3 WHERE TO SLEEP

UPDATED BY PAUL DUBOUDIN

Dream about London hotels and what comes to mind? Visions of pastel chintzes, rich mahogany furnishings, beckoning Chesterfield sofas, and extra-solicitous staff stuck in the pampering mode (the Queen should have it so good) dance in your head. On this trip, however, those visions will have to remain dreams, for the most part. On this London go-round, at least, you're planning to be budget-conscious, and that means a willingness to settle for plain rather than paisley decor. In fact, because London can be *so* expensive, even affordable lodging options can fall significantly short of your expectations. You'll find that instead of cozy bed-and-breakfasts (B&Bs) with plump matrons stuffing you with scones and cream, you're more likely to find damp, dim, and dingy rooms and breakfasts of rolls and tea. Clearly, a B&B in London does not mean the same as it does in the United States. In old Londontown, they're mostly small, converted row houses, with standards of decor like a budget motel—not at all like home. So, if you're lucky enough to find yourself in a snug room with a lumpy mattress, pipes that gurgle in the night, a defective heating system, and a family of pigeons in the tree by the window that coo dolefully all night long, just tell yourself that it's *atmosphere*! Of course, there are lodgings on pleasantly leafy side streets, promising peace and quiet. Other London home-away-from-homes are set in 19th-century town houses, with an air of elegance just slightly gone to seed, and with large windows that catch the elusive London sun.

As for price, the listings below encompass places that range from dirt cheap to a dash ritzy. One piece of good advice is to "mix and match." Alternate guest houses with one-star hotels: your wallet can remain fat, and you can remain contented. And because living on bread and butter most of the time should entitle you to enjoy a little caviar every so often, we also include several splurge-worthy places.

Basically, however, finding a tolerable double room in pricey London for less than £40 a night will be a coup; your best bet is to look around **Bloomsbury,** the streets around **Victoria** and **King's Cross** stations, **Earl's Court,** and **Notting Hill Gate.** Even many of the hostels charge up to £20 for a dorm bed in a room crammed with nine other people. Winner of the "too good to be true—there must be a catch" category, **Tonbridge School Club** (120 Cromer St., WC1, tel. 020/7837–4406, fax 020/7278–7738), near King's Cross Station, provides safe, spartan, dormitory accommodation, along with showers, luggage storage, and use of a kitchen for a mere £7 per night. The catches: you must show a foreign passport, check in between 10 PM and midnight, abide by the midnight curfew, and check out by 9:30 AM. Understandably, the club's 50 beds are in high demand, especially during the summer months, so call ahead.

The only other bargains are the city's two campgrounds (*see* Camping, *below*), where hard-core penny-pinchers can camp for £5–£6 a night in London's outskirts.

Some places may be prepared to drop their rates during the off-season, so try your luck at haggling. Your cheapest options are a B&B or a dorm bed in a hostel; you could stay a week at either for as little as £70–£100 per week. During summer, most places stop offering a weekly rate and charge a straight £15–£25 per night for a dorm bed. Reserve as far in advance as possible for hotels and hostels from June to August—March is not too early. Reservations usually require a credit card number or a deposit for the first night. If you do arrive without reservations, the **Tourist Information Centre** on Victoria Station forecourt (look up and follow the signs) offers an accommodation booking service (tel. 020/7824–8844) and sells the handy guide *Where to Stay in London* (£2.95), which lists hundreds of B&Bs and hotels throughout the city. They can book a bed in the £15–£25 range for a £5 fee and, rest assured, all accommodations are inspected before they go on their books. They have other locations at Heathrow Airport in the tube station that serves Terminals 1, 2, and 3 and at the Liverpool Street station. There are also lodgings hustlers in Victoria Station hoping to whisk you from the station to a local hotel via their free van service, but it's best to avoid these shady vultures altogether. University residence halls (*see* Student Housing, *below*) offer a clean, cheap alternative to dodgy hotels and noisy hostels.

What follows is the peak of the pick when it comes to affordable lodgings in London. Where you stay—pound-wise or pricey—depends on one decision: do you want to pay a fair amount of money for a night's oblivion in chintz-adorned, antiques-bedecked surroundings, or would you rather spend your money while *conscious?*

HOTELS AND B&BS

The ever-growing demands of the tourist market have caused a revolution in London lodging. In the past, most rooms had very basic facilities, but nowadays, most have sinks and TVS, quite a few provide tea- and coffeemaking supplies, and many hoteliers are installing showers or bathrooms en-suite. Breakfasts vary widely, from dry toast and tea, with butter and jam if you're lucky ("Continental breakfast"), to toast with butter and jam, eggs, cereal, tea or coffee, and maybe bacon, sausage, fried tomatoes, beans, or the dreaded blood pudding ("English breakfast"). We've listed the type of breakfast provided (if any) at the end of each review. The price categories below refer to a double room, including the VAT.

AROUND VICTORIA STATION

The area around Victoria Station—including the neighborhoods of **Belgravia, Pimlico,** and **Westminster**—has a billion cheapish hotels, all of which make their living off this mammoth, sprawling BritRail terminal–bus depot–tube station. Most hotels are less than a 10-min walk from the station along residential streets, and the farther from the station you go, the cheaper rooms become. The good news is that B&B owners here compete fiercely for customers. If you are willing to bargain, you might get cheaper rates, especially during the off-season or if you agree to stay more than a few nights. If you're brave or brazen enough, you might even amble down one of the main budget hotel drags, like **Belgrave Road, Ebury Street,** or **Warwick Way** and see who makes the best counteroffer (of course, it's always best to be booked in advance at some hotel). The tiny **Windsor Guest House** (36 Alderney St., SW1, tel. 020/7828–7922, no fax) has shared-bath and shower doubles for £35 (cash only).

UNDER £40 • Georgian House Hotel. The reception area of this hotel may seem a little tacky, but the rooms recently received fresh wallpaper and new furnishings. There are five bargain "student rooms" on offer: singles (£20), doubles (£35), triples (£50), and quads (£60). You don't have to be a student to qualify, but you do have to be fit enough to make it to the third and fourth floors. Less demanding are their regular singles (£40), doubles (£58), triples (£75), and quads (£80), all with bath or shower rooms en-suite. All rooms have TVS and tea- and coffeemaking facilities; some have phones. *35 St. George's Dr., at Warwick Way, SW1, tel. 020/7834–1438, fax 020/7976–6085. Tube: Victoria. Walk south on Buckingham Palace Rd., turn left on Elizabeth St. (which becomes St. George's Dr.). 34 rooms, 29 with bath or shower rooms en-suite. English breakfast.*

Limegrove Hotel. Although this minuscule guest house can't offer much in the way of beauty or luxury, it compensates with friendly, caring management. Some rooms have been renovated, whereas others are a bit run-down; all come with a TV. Singles are £20–£26, doubles £30–£36 (£40–£45 with shower en-suite), triples £39–£45 (£54–£60 with shower en-suite). *101 Warwick Way, SW1, tel. 020/7828–0458, no fax. Tube: Victoria. Walk southeast on Wilton Rd., turn right on Warwick Way. 9 rooms, 2 with shower rooms en-suite. Cash only. English breakfast.*

UNDER £50 • Elizabeth House (YWCA). Definitely one of the nicest places to bed down near Victoria Station, Elizabeth House is run by the Young Women's Christian Association (YWCA), but don't let that scare you away: it's coed and nondenominational. The whole place is clean and cheery, has TV lounges, provides excellent 24-hour security and an on-site safe, and even features a heavenly garden patio. If you're watching your pounds or tired of eating out, they'll gladly let you use their microwave oven. Handsome singles cost £22, doubles £44 (£48 with private bath or shower room). Dorms (£15 per person) sleep three or four to a room. Weekly rates are available. *118 Warwick Way, SW1, tel. 020/7630–0741, fax 020/7630–0740. Tube: Victoria. Walk south on Buckingham Palace Rd., turn left on St. George's Dr., right on Warwick Way. 31 rooms, 9 with private bath or shower rooms. Laundry. Continental breakfast.*

Luna & Simone Hotel. This family-run hotel looks just like the others on Belgrave Road, but it's probably one of the best (plus, it's only 300 yards from Victoria Station). The immaculate, comfortable rooms all have TVS, phones, and hair dryers. Singles are £30–£35 (£40–£50 with shower room en-suite), doubles £45–£50 (£55–£65 with shower room en-suite), and triples with shower room en-suite £65–£80. *47–49 Belgrave Rd., SW1, tel. 020/7834–5897, fax 020/7828–2474. Tube: Victoria. Walk southeast on Wilton Rd., turn right on Bridge Pl., left on Belgrave Rd. 36 rooms, 28 with shower rooms en-suite. English breakfast.*

If you find yourself without a place to stay in London, sleeping in the open is highly discouraged. Shelter Londonline (tel. 0800/446441) can provide advice for stranded visitors.

Melita House Hotel. This comfortable, family-run hotel is on a quiet, residential street. The small rooms—all with TV, phone, and hair dryer—are fairly clean, though the furniture is strictly garage-sale. Singles are £36–£45, doubles £50, twins £45–£50, triples £60–£65, quads £80, and quints £90. *33– 35 Charlwood St., SW1, tel. 020/7828–0471, fax 020/7932–0988. Tube: Victoria. Walk southeast on Wilton Rd., turn right on Bridge Pl., left on Belgrave Rd., right on Charlwood St. 20 rooms, 16 with shower or shower/toilet cubicles. English breakfast.*

UNDER £60 • Caswell Hotel. In its quiet cul-de-sac, the Caswell does a good job of avoiding the hustle and bustle of the busy Victoria area. Apparently Mozart lived nearby while composing his first symphony; the buildings in this prized district will help you imagine what it might have been like back then. Although the chintz-laden front lobby is a bit hard to take, the attentive staff and well-furnished yet simple double room are worth the £54 (£75 with bathroom). *25 Gloucester St., London SW1, tel. 020/7834–6345, no fax. Tube: Victoria. Walk south on Belgrave Rd., turn right on Gloucester St. 18 rooms, 7 with showers. English breakfast.*

Collin House. The Thomases, the friendly owners of this spotless Victorian B&B, maintain a quiet, nicely conservative atmosphere (no late-night revelers here, please). Each room comes with a sink, a handsome wood-frame bed, and framed photos of Wales taken by the proprietor. There is one room with a balcony, which you can request. Singles cost £38 (£42 with shower room en-suite), doubles £52 (£65 with shower room en-suite), and triples £80 (£85 with shower room en-suite). *104 Ebury St., SW1, tel. and fax 020/7730–8031. Tube: Victoria. Walk south on Buckingham Palace Rd., turn right on Eccleston St., left on Ebury St. 13 rooms, 8 with shower rooms en-suite. Cash only. English breakfast.*

Ebury House Hotel. At this small, pleasant place you can relax and make yourself at home—rooms aren't palatial, but they're clean and tastefully decorated in pastel florals. Singles (£45), doubles (£60), and triples (£80) all have TVS, sinks, and hair dryers, but none has en-suite bathroom facilities. *102 Ebury St., SW1, tel. 020/7730–1350, fax 020/7259–0400. Tube: Victoria. Walk south on Buckingham Palace Rd., turn right on Eccleston St., left on Ebury St. 13 rooms. English breakfast.*

Lynton House Hotel. For more than 40 years, the friendly Batey family has welcomed travelers to its cozy B&B. Comfy singles (£30–£40) and doubles (£50–£55) come equipped with TVS and wash basins. If they have a few vacancies, you might be able to wrangle a cheaper rate—so ask! There's a small common terrace and excellent security. *113 Ebury St., SW1, tel. 020/7730–4032, fax 020/7730–9848. Tube: Victoria. Walk south on Buckingham Palace Rd., turn right on Eccleston St., left on Ebury St. 12 rooms, 2 with shower cubicles. Cash only. English breakfast.*

UNDER £80 • Elizabeth Hotel. This elegant hotel once served as the private home of aristocrats (including relatives of Edward VII). These days it offers luxuriously appointed rooms overlooking an attrac-

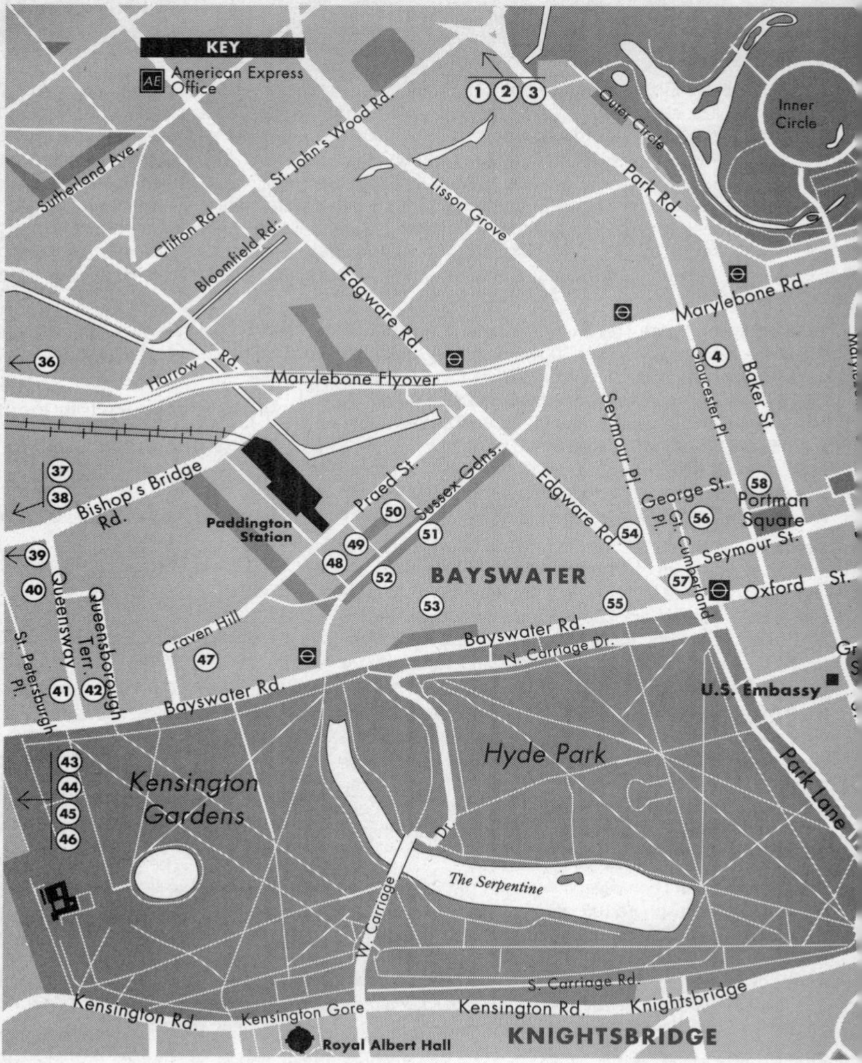

Abbey House Hotel, **43**

Adare House, **51**

The Alhambra Hotel, **21**

Arosfa Hotel, **25**

Avalon Private Hotel, **15**

Boston Court Hotel, **54**

Campbell House, **9**

Central University of Iowa Hostel, **34**

City of London Hostel (YHA), **61**

College Hall, **29**

Commodore Hotel, **47**

Connaught Hall, **14**

Continental Hotel, **48**

County Hotel, **11**

Crescent Hotel, **12**

Edward Lear Hotel, **57**

Euro Hotel, **13**

Europa House Hotel, **53**

Fairways Hotel, **52**

Five Kings Guest House, **1**

Garth Hotel, **27**

The Gate Hotel, **37**

The Generator, **18**

Glynne Court Hotel, **56**

Hallam Hotel, **8**

Hampstead Heath (YHA), **2**

Hart House Hotel, **58**

Highgate Village (YHA), **3**

Holland House Youth Hostel (YHA), **46**

Hotel Cavendish, **26**

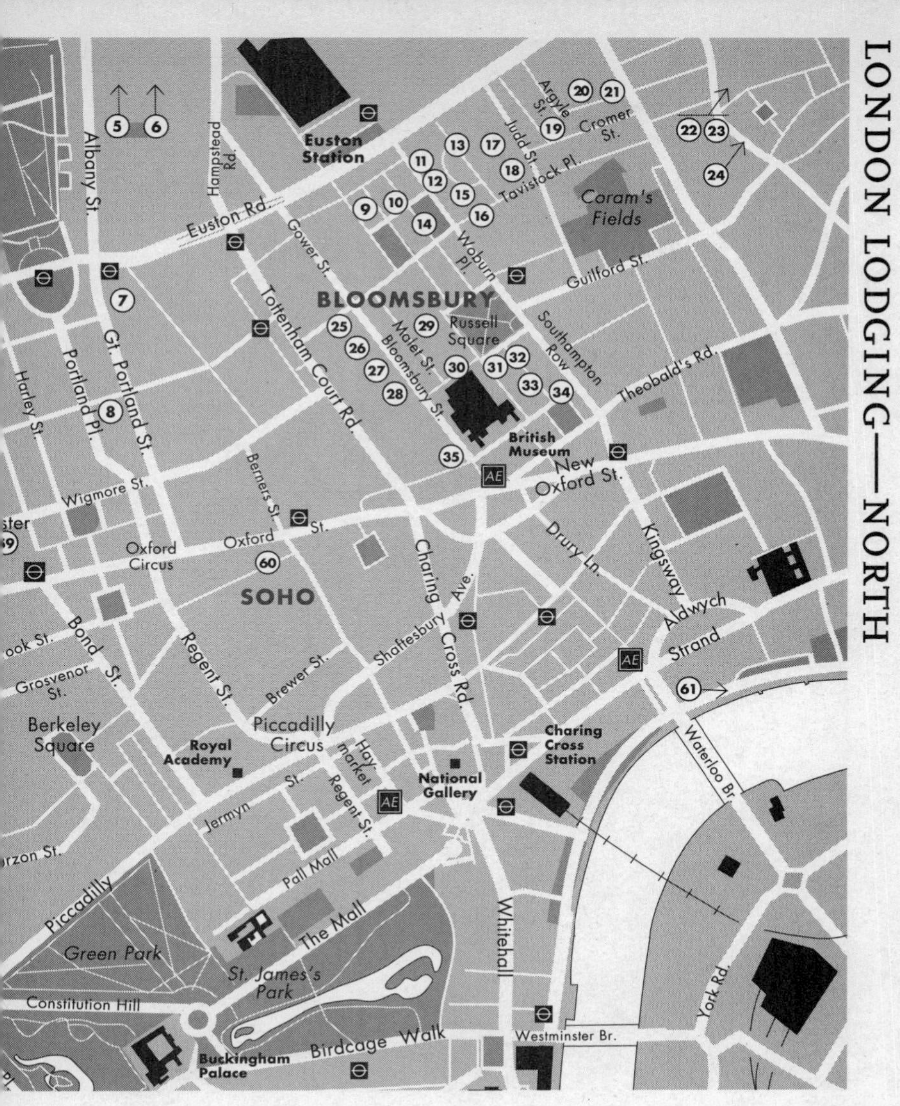

Hyde Park House, **41**

International Student House, **7**

Ivanhoe Suite Hotel, **59**

Jenkins Hotel, **17**

Jesmond Dene Hotel, **20**

John Adams Hall, **10**

Kandara Guest House, **23**

Kenwood House Hotel, **4**

The Kingsway Hotel, **49**

Lion Court Hotel, **40**

Lords Hotel, **38**

The Morgan, **35**

Norfolk Court and St. David's Hotel, **50**

The Oxford Arms, **22**

Oxford Street (YHA), **60**

Palace Hotel, **45**

Parkland Walk Guest House, **6**

Parkwood Hotel, **55**

The Phoenix Hotel, **39**

Primrose Hill Agency, **5**

Repton Hotel, **32**

The Ridgemount Private Hotel, **28**

Ruskin Hotel, **31**

St. Athans Hotel, **16**

St. Charles Hotel, **42**

St. Margaret's Hotel, **33**

Tent City Acton, **36**

Tent City Hackney, **24**

Tonbridge School Club, **19**

University of London Accommodations Office, **30**

Vicarage, **44**

LONDON LODGING—SOUTH

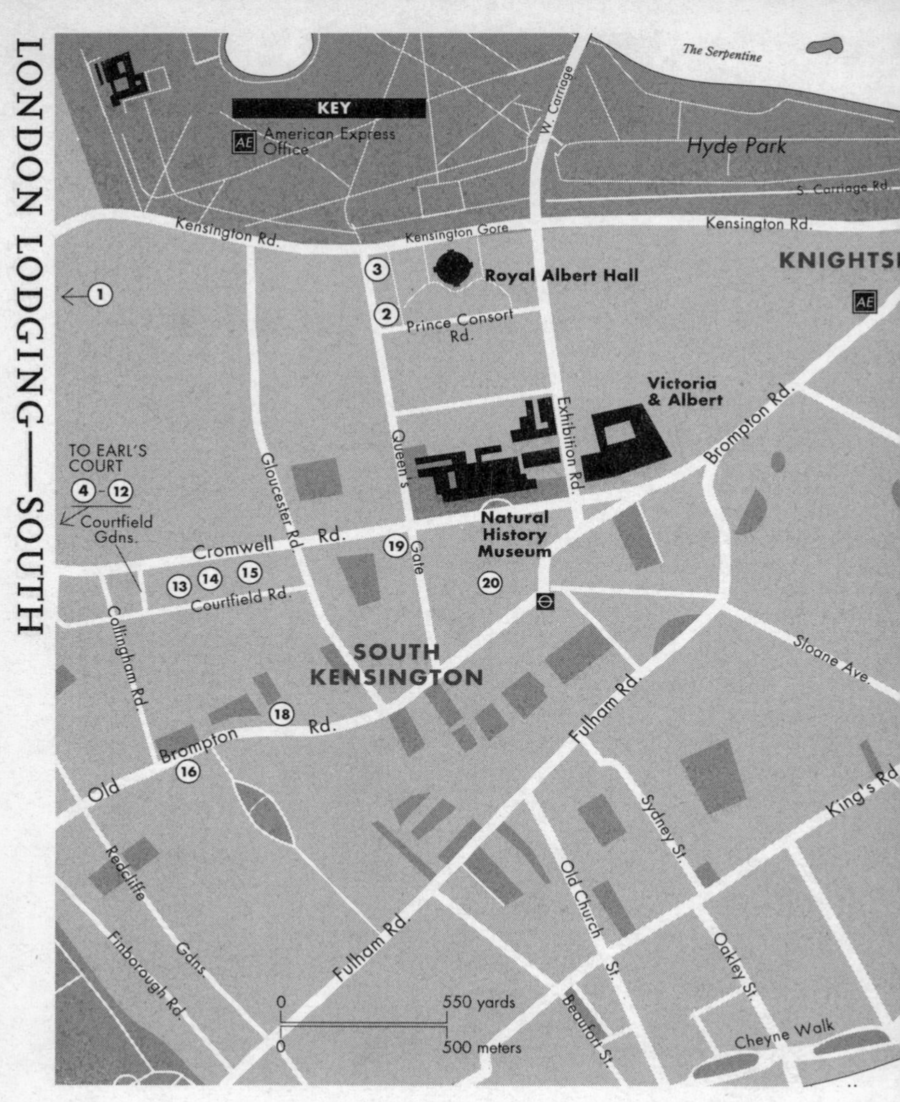

Aaron House, **13**
The Albert Hotel, **3**
Aston's Budget Studios & Aston's Designer Studios and Suites, **18**
Beaver Hotel, **4**
Caswell Hotel, **33**
Chelsea Hotel, **5**
Collin House, **24**
The Court Hotel, **10**
The Curzon House Hotel, **15**
Earl's Court (YHA), **6**
Ebury House Hotel, **25**
Eden Plaza, **19**
Elizabeth House (YWCA), **22**
Elizabeth Hotel, **28**
Fieldcourt House, **14**
Georgian House Hotel, **31**
The Gore, **2**
Green Court Hotel, **7**
Henly House, **12**
Hunter's Lodge Hotel, **8**
James House/ Cartref House, **26**
Limegrove Hotel, **27**
Luna & Simone Hotel, **29**
Lynton House Hotel, **23**

LONDON LODGING—SOUTH

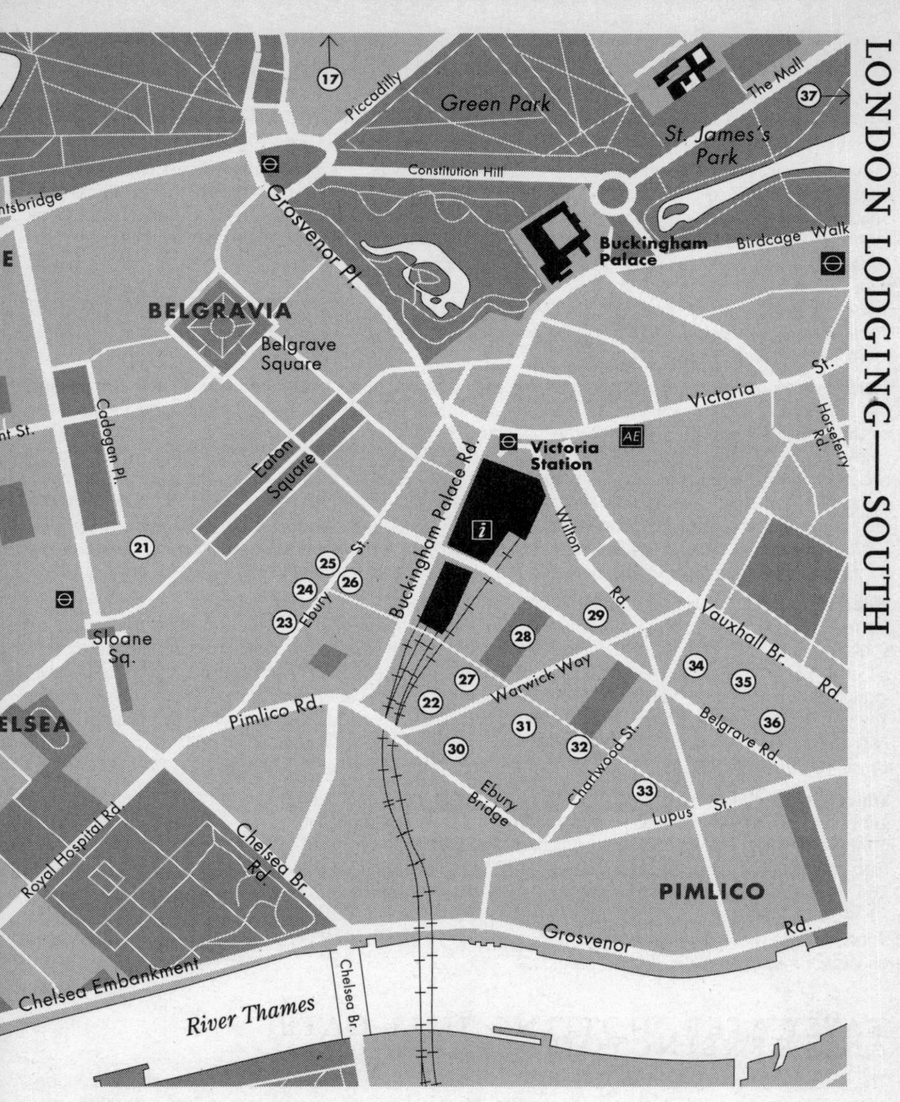

Melbourne House Hotel, **36**

Melita House Hotel, **35**

The Pelham Hotel, **20**

Philbeach Hotel, **9**

Regency Hotel, **17**

Rotherhithe (YHA), **37**

Rushmore Hotel, **1**

The Swiss House, **16**

Table Mountain Hotel, **11**

Victoria Hotel (Astor), **34**

Wilbraham Hotel, **21**

Windermere Hotel, **30**

Windsor Guest House, **32**

tive garden square. Singles (£60), doubles (£70–£80), triples (£100), and quads (£110) come with a bath or shower room en-suite, a TV, and a knockout English breakfast. A less luxurious, shared-bath single (£36–£40) and double (£62) are also available. *37 Eccleston Sq., at Warwick Way, SW1, tel. 020/7828–6812, fax 020/7828–6814. Tube: Victoria. Walk southeast on Wilton Rd., turn right on Bridge Pl., left on Belgrave Rd., right on Eccleston Sq. 40 rooms, 35 with bath or shower rooms en-suite. Cash only.*

James House/Cartref House. Hailed by those in the know as one of the area's finest B&B establishments, James House and Cartref House owe their exalted status to their tireless hosts, James and Sharon James. The place is constantly being refurbished, and all singles, doubles, and family bunk rooms have been individually designed. The breakfast is so generous you could consider skipping lunch altogether. Don't worry too much about which house you're assigned to, either is great. You'll pay £65 for a double (£75 with bathroom) and £105 for a quad with bathroom. *108 and 129 Ebury St., SW1. James House tel. and fax 020/7730–7338, Cartref House tel. 020/7730–6176, fax 020/7730–7338. Tube: Victoria. Walk south on Buckingham Palace Rd., turn right on Eccleston St., left on Ebury St. 21 rooms, 9 with bath. English breakfast.*

Melbourne House Hotel. Besides the attributes of a recent coat of paint and new, simple furnishings, this family-run hotel has a warm and welcoming atmosphere. Rooms are kept in immaculate condition by the caring owners who also offer free luggage storage if you're traveling abroad. Most rooms are no-smoking, so check before you book. Singles cost £40–£48, doubles £60–£70, triples £75–£85, and the two-room family suite £90–£100. The rooms generally have either shower rooms or bathrooms en-suite, except for two single rooms that share a bathroom (£25–£30). All rooms have TVS, tea- and coffeemaking facilities, and telephones. *79 Belgrave Rd., Victoria, SW1, tel. 020/7828–3516, fax 020/7828–7120. Tube: Victoria. Walk southeast on Wilton Rd., turn right on Bridge Pl., left on Belgrave Rd. 17 rooms, 14 with shower rooms en-suite, and 1 with bathroom en-suite. English breakfast.*

Wilbraham Hotel. A lovely grandmother of a hotel, this place is as British as tea and crumpets. It's set not far from swanky Sloane Square, comprises three 19th-century row houses, and is decorated in best shabby-genteel Brit fashion, right down to floral wallpapers (some of those roses *do* look like they need a bit of watering) and Victorian bric-a-brac. Guest rooms don't have many frills, but there's a pleasant lounge and restaurant, The Bar and Buttery, which is a nice place to greet friends over a glass of sherry. You're just a few blocks from the heart of Belgravia, London's ritziest neighborhood. Doubles run about £80–£85. *1–5 Wilbraham Pl., Victoria, SW1, tel. 020/7730–8296, fax 020/7730–6815. Tube: Sloane Sq. Cross the square to Sloane St., walk up to the second turn on the right. 53 rooms, 40 with bath en-suite.*

Windermere Hotel. Housed in a pair of Victorian-era buildings at the far end of the Warwick Way budget-hotel strip, the Windermere offers friendly, professional service with a reasonably priced restaurant on the premises. The impeccably furnished rooms (the top room is the best) have TVS, phones, and high ceilings. The basic single is £51 (£65–£84 with bathroom or shower room en-suite), doubles are £64 (£78–£92 with bathroom or shower room en-suite), triples with en-suite facilities are £99, quads £104. *142–144 Warwick Way, SW1, tel. 020/7834–5163 or 020/7834–5480, fax 020/7630–8831. Tube: Victoria. Walk southeast on Wilton Rd., turn right on Warwick Way. 23 rooms, 19 with bathrooms or shower rooms en-suite. English breakfast.*

BAYSWATER, NOTTING HILL GATE, AND KENSINGTON

The selections here range from Bayswater—a budgeteer's heaven—to Kensington, one of London's poshest neighborhoods. Bars and cheap eateries on Bayswater cater to the budget and middlebrow travelers who pack the neighborhood's innumerable hotels. Notting Hill, as we speak, is one of London's hottest neighborhoods, a fave for London's hip youth. **Queensway,** perpendicular to Notting Hill Gate and Bayswater, is a party-hearty tourist strip lined with pubs blaring "You Shook Me All Night Long" and other sing-along favorites. Luckily, the more sedate environments of Hyde Park and Kensington Gardens are just across Bayswater Road. Kensington is loaded with great shops, restaurants, pretty streets, and truly wonderful splurge hotels.

UNDER £40 • Continental Hotel. This is both a good value and a top choice for the younger traveler—the hotel caters largely to groups of foreign students (although there is a separate part of the hotel for nongroup bookings). The rooms are fairly spacious and clean, if a little worn around the edges. All rooms have TVS and refrigerators. Singles are £20 (£25 with shower/toilet cubicle), £120–£150 weekly; doubles are £28 (£33 with shower/toilet cubicle), £168–£228 weekly; triples are £36 (£41 with shower/toilet cubicle), £216–£306 weekly; quad £48 (£53 with shower/toilet cubicle), £288–£408 weekly. *40 Norfolk Sq., W2, tel. 020/7723–3926, fax 020/7262–0238. Tube: Paddington. Walk north on Praed St., turn right on London St., left on Norfolk Sq. 84 rooms, 21 with shower/toilet cubicles. Continental breakfast.*

Lion Court Hotel. If you are on a budget and long for the '70s grunge experience, the Lion Court is for you. Set in what was once a very elegant house, the hotel is reasonably clean. Most rooms have shower facilities, and there is a kitchen that guests can use. Singles are £25 (£30 with shower cubicle), £120 per week; doubles are £35 or £160 per week; triples are £40 with shower/toilet en-suite or £150 per week. *26 Prince's Sq., W2, tel. 020/7229–2621 or 020/7221–1536. 15 rooms, 13 with shower/toilet cubicle. Cash only. Continental breakfast.*

Lords Hotel. The rooms are an improvement on the shabby, unwelcoming hallways, reception area, and dining room. Most of them have a tiny shower/toilet cubicle, and all have color TVS, hair dryers, and beds that tend to be on the small side. The staff isn't particularly friendly, but if you're backpacking on a budget and want to meet lots of people, then this hotel may suit you. It is located on the edge of a lovely tree-dotted square and the Heathrow Airbus passes along Bayswater Road. The best rooms have wide windows and balconies. Singles are £30 (£40 with shower cubicle and toilet), doubles £40 (£55 with shower cubicle and toilet), triples £50 (£66 with shower cubicle and toilet), and quads are £60 (£75 with shower cubicle and toilet). *20–22 Leinster Sq., W2, tel. 020/7229–8877, fax 020/7229–8377. Tube: Bayswater. Walk north on Queensway, turn left on Moscow Rd., right on Chester Gardens. 67 rooms, 54 with shower cubicle and toilet. Continental breakfast.*

Don't be afraid to haggle for reduced rates on multinight stays; you shouldn't be forced to pay the daily rate if you're staying somewhere for a week or more.

UNDER £50 • Boston Court Hotel. Not too far away from a pleasant morning's walk in Hyde Park, this unpretentious place is set amid a collection of little B&Bs. Housed in a pretty Victorian terrace, each room at the Boston offers a private shower, central heating, hair dryers, coffeemakers, and small refrigerators. A double with shower costs £49 (£65 with bath), a triple with bath runs £75. Not too bad when you consider that the place has been recently refurbished (and when you compute the probable cost of the local real estate!). *26 Upper Berkley St., at Marble Arch, W1, tel. 020/7723–1445, fax 020/7262–8823. Tube: Marble Arch. Walk north on Edgeware Rd., turn right onto Upper Berkley St. 13 rooms, 5 with showers only. Continental breakfast.*

Europa House Hotel. If you don't mind being lumped in with a group to save a few pennies, then this place might sound too good to be true. Like most along the Sussex Gardens strip, the rooms are a little on the cramped side, but they are well maintained. All the doubles (£48–£60) have TVS and private bathrooms. Defying the notion of gloomy London, the breakfast room can be a bit on the bright side if you've had a few too many the night before. One of 10 beds in the dorm-style family room costs £18–£20. *151 Sussex Gardens, W2, tel. 020/7402–1923, fax 020/7224–9331. Tube: Paddington. Walk south on Spring St., turn left onto Sussex Gardens. 18 rooms. English breakfast.*

Hyde Park House. The Hyde is one of the nicer hotels in the area, despite somewhat dated decor; it's on a quiet side street close to the Bayswater and Queensway tube stations and a short walk from Hyde Park. The management is friendly (perhaps a little too much so—they still have a dog left by one of their guests). Until recently, prices had been stabilized at 1984 rates, but then the proprietors reviewed the situation and made nominal adjustments. Simple singles now run £30, doubles £42. *48 St. Petersburgh Pl., W2, tel. 020/7 229-9652 or 020/7229–1687. Tube: Queensway. Walk west on Bayswater Rd., turn right on St. Petersburgh Pl. 14 rooms, 1 with bath. Continental breakfast.*

Kenwood House Hotel. The British Army once owned this place and used it to billet officers during the Second World War. Today, the small Kenwood Hotel occupies this 18th-century building, which retains many period features, both inside and out. The rooms here are basically furnished, but were updated in 1993. If you opt for a room without bathroom, you'll find the facilities on each floor modern and spic-and-span. Your wallet will suffer a £44 blow for a double without bathroom, £56 for a double with bathroom, £64 for a triple without bathroom, and £70 for a family room with bathroom. *114 Gloucester Pl., W1, tel. 020/7935–7323, fax 020/7224–0582. Tube: Baker St. Walk west on Marylebone Rd., turn left onto Gloucester Pl. 16 rooms, 9 with bath. English breakfast.*

The Kingsway Hotel. The Kingsway Hotel was recently refurbished to a very good standard with excellent facilities in the rooms (phone, TV, tea- and coffeemaking supplies, hair dryer, and iron). Many of the rooms have proper bathrooms rather than shower units, and there is an elevator. Singles are £35 (£52 with bath/shower en-suite), doubles are £48 (£72 with bath/shower en-suite), triple £90, quad £96. *27 Norfolk Sq., W2, tel. 020/7723–5569 or 020/7723–7784, fax 020/7723–7317. Tube: Paddington. Walk north on Praed St., turn right on London St., left on Norfolk Sq. English breakfast.*

Norfolk Court and St. David's Hotel. The Regency-style Norfolk Court joined the neighboring tacky art deco–style St. David's Hotel a few years ago, resulting in a simple, comfortable guest house. The Norfolk Court section is the place to book—don't get down by the reception area in the shabby part of the hotel. Some second-floor rooms have French windows and balconies that overlook Norfolk Square (a B&B mecca). Singles are £30 (£40 with shower/bath en-suite), doubles £44 (£55 with shower/bath en-suite). *16–20 Norfolk Sq., W2, tel. 020/7723–4963, fax 020/7402–9061. Tube: Paddington. Walk north on Praed St., turn right on London St., left on Norfolk Sq. 70 rooms, 25 with bath/shower en-suite. English breakfast.*

UNDER £60 • Adare House. Run by the same hospitable owner for the last 25 years, Adare house is a gem among some rather lifeless spots that inhabit this B&B strip. The property is well maintained and has been gradually improved during the past few years. The Regency-era wallpaper and red carpeting give the place a strange touch of class, and although some of the rooms might seem a little cramped, they are always comfortable and particularly tidy. You can grab a double with shower for £58. *153 Sussex Gardens, W2, tel. 020/7262–0633, fax 020/7706–1859. Tube: Paddington. Walk south on Spring St., turn left onto Sussex Gardens. 16 rooms. English breakfast.*

Edward Lear Hotel. Occupying two adjoining 18th-century terraces, the Edward Lear was once the home of . . . well, it was once Edward Lear's place. Unless you're a student of 18th-century English verse, this trivia tidbit might not register. Nonetheless, there's nothing trivial about this cute little hotel. Full of refined English touches, like freshly cut flowers in every common room, this hotel has a number of small, but well-appointed rooms upstairs. Ask for the one toward the rear of the hotel to avoid the street-side noise. You'll fork over £60 for a double (£79 with bath) and £85 or more for a suite. *28–30 Seymour St., W1, tel. 020/7402–5401, fax 020/7706–3766. Tube: Marble Arch. Walk north on Old Quebec, turn right onto Seymour St. 35 rooms, 12 with bath. English breakfast.*

Fairways Hotel. At the Fairways, modernity is scorned in favor of things "traditional," so you'll be in for a quasi-bucolic B&B experience. Right near Hyde Park, the Fairways is easily distinguished by its colonnaded front entrance and wrought-iron balustrade stretching across the front second-floor window. The homey breakfast room is adorned with family photos and plenty of blue china depicting rural scenes. Attractively decorated rooms (£60 for a double, £66 with bath) come with TV, tea- and coffeemakers, and intercom. *186 Sussex Garden, W2, tel. 020/7723–4871, fax 020/7723–4871. Tube: Paddington. Walk south on Spring St., turn left onto Sussex Garden. 17 rooms, 10 with bath. English breakfast.*

Glynne Court Hotel. The Glynne Court is actually in the Marble Arch area adjacent to Bayswater, right off Oxford Street (London's main shopping drag)—but despite the location, it is on a quiet street. For late-night runs to Virgin Records, this is the place to stay. Although it's not the Ritz, it is a very clean, quiet, and pleasant hotel. The rooms are spacious and all have hair dryers, phones, TVS, sinks, and tea- and coffeemaking facilities. The management is friendly yet unobtrusive. This hotel is pricey considering you don't get an English breakfast, but if you want to be in this area, it's your best bet. Singles are £50 with bath/shower en-suite, doubles £60 with bath/shower en-suite, triples are £70. Discounts are offered for longer stays. *41 Great Cumberland Pl., W1, tel. 020/7262–4344, fax 020/7724–2071. Tube: Marble Arch. Walk west on Bayswater Rd., quick right on Great Cumberland Pl. 14 rooms, 11 with bath/shower en-suite. Continental breakfast.*

Parkwood Hotel. Parkwood occupies a great location for a good value hotel in London: it's near Oxford Street and Marble Arch and just 50 yards from Hyde Park, in an area known as Connaught Village. The hotel prides itself on an excellent breakfast; in fact it's one of those "let's skip lunch" deals, with the menu stating that if you're still hungry, you can have another meal—for free. The well-maintained, simple bedrooms have coffeemakers and radios. A double runs £59 (£85 with bath), a triple £74 (£97 with bath), and a quad £100 (with bath). *4 Stanhope Pl., W2, tel 020/7402–2241, fax 020/7402–1574. Tube: Marble Arch. Walk west along Bayswater Rd. and then turn right onto Stanhope Pl. 18 rooms, 12 with bath. English breakfasts.*

St. Charles Hotel. This place is lovingly kept and offers an old-world ambience, complete with sumptuous wood-paneled accents and molded ceilings. The five single rooms are £50, the nine double rooms go for £57. All rooms have showers and washbasins; only half have bathrooms en-suite. *66 Queensborough Terr., W2, tel. 020/7221–0022. Tube: Queensway. Walk toward Kensington Gardens, turn left on Queensborough Terr. 14 rooms, 7 with bath en-suite. English breakfast.*

UNDER £70 • Abbey House Hotel. Next door to the Vicarage (*see below*), Abbey House has been voted "Best Value, Best Quality B&B in London" in many surveys, so you'll have to book well in advance. The place occupies a pretty, white-stucco 1860 Victorian town house—once home to a bishop and an MP before World War II—and overlooks a leafy garden square. Rooms are spacious and have color TVS and washbasins. The management is very helpful and professional, providing a very "English" experience at a most attractive value. Singles are £40, doubles £63, triple £78, and quad £90, with winter discounts available. *11 Vicarage Gate, W8, tel. 020/7727–2594. Tube: High St. Kensington. Walk right on Kensington High St., turn left on Kensington Church St., veer right at fork onto Vicarage Gate. 16 rooms, none with bath. Cash only. English breakfast.*

Aston's Budget Studios & Aston's Designer Studios and Suites. This place offers London's best-valued studio and apartment-style accommodation in a carefully restored row of Victorian terrace town houses. Everything is done with a touch of style, right down to the heavy oak doors at the entrance and the Victoriana-style wall hangings. If you go for the budget studio option, you'll have to share a full-service bathroom; the designer studios and suites offer full marble bathrooms. All rooms have compact kitchenettes. Budget studios run £68 for a double, £95 for a triple, and £115 for a quad. A designer studio will cost you £105 for a double. (Weekly rentals are preferred, although daily bookings are accepted.) *39 Rosary Gardens, SW7, tel. 020/7370–0737, fax 020/7835–1419. Tube: Gloucester Rd. Walk south on Gloucester Pl., turn right onto Erby Pl., then left onto Rosary Gardens. 76 studios and apartments, 54 with bath.*

Commodore Hotel. This peaceful hotel of three converted Victorian houses is ensconced in the big, verdant square known as Lancaster Gate. It's a find of a very different stripe, as you'll notice on entering the cozy, carpeted lounge. There are some wonderful split-level rooms, with sleeping gallery—all large, all individually decorated with, for example, a walk-in closet with its own stained-glass window. It's getting very popular, so book ahead. Singles go for £60, doubles for £70. *50 Lancaster Gate, W2, tel. 020/7402–5291, fax 020/7262–1088. Tube: Lancaster Gate. Turn right from the tube station, walk west along Bayswater Rd., turn right on Lancaster Gate. 90 rooms with bath.*

The Gate Hotel. Hanging baskets filled with colorful flowers adorn the outside of this tiny hotel at the top of Portobello Road—the only hotel to boast this rather stylish address. The nicely decorated rooms are clean and equipped with refrigerators, TVS, phones, ceiling fans, and radio/alarm clocks. Singles are £58, doubles from £65, triples are £90 (third bed is a fold-out). Breakfast is served in the rooms, as there is no dining room. *6 Portobello Rd., W11, tel. 020/7221–2403, fax 020/7221–9128. Tube: Notting Hill Gate. Walk north on Pembridge Rd., turn left on Portobello Rd. 6 rooms, 5 with shower room en-suite.*

Vicarage. A stunning hotel run by the same family for nearly 30 years, the Vicarage is in a posh residential square. It's beautifully decorated (although it is fraying a little at the seams), quiet, and overlooks a lovely garden square near Kensington's main shopping streets. Rooms are individually and tastefully decorated, and the building is full of original features. There is a cozy sitting room and dining room, and hot drinks and ice are available at all times. This is a very popular place, so book well in advance. Expect to pay £43 for a single and £65 for a double. *10 Vicarage Gate, W8, tel. 020/7229–4030, fax 020/7792–5989. Tube: High St. Kensington. Walk right on Kensington High St., turn left on Kensington Church St., veer right at fork onto Vicarage Gate. 18 rooms, none with bath. Cash only. English breakfast.*

UNDER £80 • Eden Plaza. When a hotel calls its own rooms "compact," you should imagine a double bed, then add a foot all around, and, yes, that is about the size of a room here. As in a cruise ship's stateroom, however, all you need is creatively secreted—there's a closet, mirror, satellite TV, tea- and coffeemaker, and hair dryer. Windows are double-glazed against noisy Cromwell Road; the real noise in the room will come from the painfully loud color scheme produced by this small chain's tropical parrot logo. The kids can share free, or they can get their own room at half price. The Natural History Museum is just across the street. Singles are £63, doubles £74. *68–69 Queen's Gate, SW7, tel. 020/7370–6111, fax 020/7370–0932. Tube: Gloucester Rd. Turn left from tube station, walk north along Gloucester Rd., turn right on Cromwell Rd., left on Queen's Gate. 61 rooms with bath.*

Hart House Hotel. In the heart of the West End, this well-preserved historic building (one of a group of Georgian mansions occupied by exiled French nobles during the French Revolution) lies within easy walking distance of many theaters, as well as some of the most sought-after shopping areas and parks in London. Each cozy, tidy room in this topnotch Marylebone B&B sports its own combination of furnishings, ranging from Portobello antiques to modern touches. Guest services include baby-sitting, dry cleaning, laundry service, and a massage service; a double runs £75 (£93 with bath), a triple is £98

(£110 with bath), and a quad will cost you £130 (with bath). *51 Gloucester Pl., Portman Sq., W1, tel. 020/7935–8516, fax 020/7935–8515. Tube: Marble Arch. Walk east onto Oxford St., turn left onto Gloucester Pl. 16 rooms, 10 with bath. English breakfast.*

Ivanhoe Suite Hotel. Right in the heart of the Oxford Street shopping district, this little place may not leave you with that much money to blow on Armani et al, but the locale and services make it worth that extra shell-out (£74 per double). Rooms are stylish and secure and each room comes complete with a little sitting area (useful after elbowing your way through frantic shoppers on the street below). Ivanhoe services include videotape rental, laundry, and room service. There's no shortage of restaurants or comfy corner pubs in the neighborhood. *1 St. Christopher Pl., Barrerr St. Piazza, W1, tel. 020/7935–1047, fax 020/7224–0563. Tube: Bond St. Walk west on Oxford St., right onto James St., right onto Wigmore St., then a quick right onto St. Christopher Pl. 8 rooms. Continental breakfast.*

UNDER £90 • Hallam Hotel. An easy 10-min stroll from Oxford Street, the Hallam is a shopaholic's ideal pied-à-terre. The hotel occupies a heavily ornamented stone and brick Victorian and was one of the area's few fortunate buildings to escape the Blitz. Rooms, revamped in 1991, are comfortable but can be small—some singles are so tiny, they're called cabinettes. In addition to 24-hour room service, there's a bar in which residents gather to exchange tales, and a bright breakfast room overlooking a pleasant patio. Ready? It's £90–£97 for a double. *12 Hallam St., Portland Pl., W1, tel. 020/7580–1166, fax 020/7323–4527. Tube: Oxford Circus. Walk north on Great Portland St., left onto Langham St., right onto Hallam St. 25 rooms. English breakfast.*

The Phoenix Hotel. In what is now an ethnically mixed neighborhood, the Phoenix rose out of a series of town houses and now occupies the entire south side of one of Europe's most famous garden squares. The atmosphere is welcoming and gracious throughout, with a decor of muted tones and fabrics The well-furnished bedrooms keep to the smart international standard. Everything is designed for comfort and ease, including the luggage racks. The bar is a good place to unwind, and moderately priced meals are served in the downstairs café. The only downside to this place is the fact that the public area is way too small for a hotel this size. A double costs £82 , a family room £110, and a suite £145. *1–8 Kensington Garden Sq., W2, tel. 020/7229–2494, fax 020/7727–1419 Tube: Bayswater. Walk north on Queensway, left onto Porchester Gardens, right onto Kensington Garden Sq. 128 rooms with bath.*

Regency Hotel. Like most of its neighbors in the protected historic city center, the Regency was built in the late 1800s. Although it has functioned as some kind of hotel since the 1940s, in 1991 it was gutted and tastefully renovated; today it offers four floors of simple, conservatively decorated modern bedrooms and a breakfast room set in what used to be the cellar. Each room has a radio, hair dryer, and ironing board. Marble Arch, Regent's Park, and Baker Street all lie within a 12- to 15-min stroll. Doubles are £85, family rooms are £99 and sleep four. *19 Nottingham Pl., W1, tel. 020/7486–5347, fax 020/7224–6057. Tube: Bakers St. Head east along Marylebone Rd., turn right onto Nottingham Pl. 20 rooms with bath.*

SPLURGE • The Gore. Just down the road from Albert Hall, this small, very friendly hotel features an eclectic selection of prints, etchings, and antiques. Here, though, are spectacular follylike rooms—Room 101 is a Tudor fantasy with a minstrel gallery, stained glass, and four-poster bed. Despite all that, the Gore manages to remain most elegant. On premises are two high-style brasseries. Singles run £128, doubles £178. *189 Queen's Gate, SW7, tel. 020/7584–6601, fax 020/7589–8127. Tube: Gloucester Rd. Take a left at the station, walk 5 min, then right at Queen's Gate. 54 rooms with bath.*

The Pelham Hotel. The second of Tim and Kit Kemp's gorgeous hotels opened in 1989 and is run along the same lines as their others, except that this one looks less town than country. There's 18th-century pine paneling in the drawing room—one of the most magnificently handsome hotel salons in the city—flowers galore, quite a bit of glazed chintz, and the odd four-poster and bedroom fireplace. The Pelham stands opposite the South Kensington tube stop, by the big museums, and close to the shops of Knightsbridge, with the Kemps supplying an on-site trendy menu. Singles run £140, doubles £170. *15 Cromwell Pl., SW7, tel. 020/7589–8288, fax 020/7584–8444. Tube: South Kensington. The hotel is to the left of the NatWest building directly across from the station. 37 rooms with bath.*

BLOOMSBURY AND KING'S CROSS

The former stomping ground of the Bloomsbury Group—the famed literary clique that included Virginia Woolf, E. M. Forster, Lytton Strachey, and John Maynard Keynes—is today the stomping ground of thousands of students from the nearby University of London and an equal number of tourists marching toward the British Museum. It is also prime lodging territory, with student dorms, hostels, and dozens of

Finally, a travel companion that doesn't snore on the plane or eat all your peanuts.

When traveling, your MCI WorldCom Card is the best way to keep in touch. Our operators speak your language, so they'll be able to connect you back home—no matter where your travels take you. Plus, your MCI WorldCom Card is easy to use, and even earns you frequent flyer miles every time you use it. When you add in our great rates, you get something even more valuable: peace-of-mind. So go ahead. Travel the world. MCI WorldCom just brought it a whole lot closer.

You can even sign up today at www.mci.com/worldphone or ask your operator to make a collect call to 1-410-314-2938.

MCI WORLDCOM

EASY TO CALL WORLDWIDE

1. **Just dial the WorldPhone access number of the country you're calling from.**
2. **Dial or give the operator your MCI WorldCom Card number.**
3. **Dial or give the number you're calling.**

France ◆	**0-800-99-0019**
Germany	**0800-888-8000**
Ireland	**1-800-55-1001**
Italy ◆	**172-1022**
Spain	**900-99-0014**
Sweden ◆	**020-795-922**
Switzerland ◆	**0800-89-0222**
United Kingdom	
To call using BT	**0800-89-0222**
To call using CWC	**0500-89-0222**

For your complete WorldPhone calling guide, dial the WorldPhone access number for the country you're in and ask the operator for Customer Service. In the U.S. call 1-800-431-5402.

◆ Public phones may require deposit of coin or phone card for dial tone.

EARN FREQUENT FLYER MILES

AmericanAirlines®
AAdvantage®

Delta Air Lines
SkyMiles®

MILEAGE PLUS®
United Airlines

U·S AIRWAYS
DIVIDEND MILES

B&Bs lining the streets all the way up to King's Cross station. Try Cartright Gardens, Tavistock Place, or Gower Street if you're having trouble finding a bed for the night. Whereas Bloomsbury has a quiet, academic atmosphere, King's Cross is busier, noisier, and a touch seedier. Argyle Street, across from King's Cross Station, is a good place to look for clean budget accommodations. **The Generator** (*see* Hostels, *below*), just down the street, is a clean, large, and funky bet.

UNDER £40 • The Alhambra Hotel. This is definitely the best bargain in Bloomsbury. After all the interminable London B&B rooms done up in cream and rose, these spotless rooms, hued in either blue or red, will come as a welcome change. The singles (£30–£50), doubles (£36–£50), and triples (£48–£65) have either shared facilities, shower cubicles, or shower rooms en-suite. The quads are £85 and come with a shower room en-suite. All rooms have TVS. An added plus is Mrs. Valoti, the friendly and gracious host. *17–19 Argyle St., WC1, tel. 020/7837–9575, fax 020/7916–2476. Tube: King's Cross. Head west on Euston Rd., turn left on Argyle St. 52 rooms, 15 with shower cubicles or shower rooms en-suite. English breakfast.*

Hotel Cavendish. This is a clean, simple, family-run B&B just down the road from Dillon's bookstore. Singles cost £30–£40 and doubles are £40–£50, depending on the size of the room and whether it faces the street or the lovely garden. The friendly owners will make a full vegetarian breakfast on request. *75 Gower St., WC1, tel. 020/7636–9079, fax 020/7580–3609. Tube: Goodge St. Turn right on Tottenham Court Rd., quick left on Chenies St., left on Gower St. 22 rooms, none with en-suite facilities. English breakfast.*

Jesmond Dene Hotel. The Jesmond Dene has possibly the smartest decor in London for any budget accommodation—many rooms feature stylish combinations of pale blues or black and white, and even the hallway carpeting is chic. It's a real gem, and well priced: singles cost £25 (£40 with shower room en-suite), doubles £36 (£50 with shower room en-suite), triples £48 (£65 with shower room en-suite), and quads £70 (£85 with shower room en-suite). Shower rooms are small, and every room has a sink and TV. *27 Argyle St., WC1, tel. 020/7837–4654, fax 020/7833–1633. Tube: King's Cross. Head west on Euston Rd., turn left on Argyle St. 24 rooms, 7 with shower rooms en-suite. English breakfast.*

UNDER £50 • Arosfa Hotel. Mr. and Mrs. Dorta, the friendly owners, are what make this B&B a cut above the others on Gower Street—that, and the fact that the house was originally the home of Sir John Everett Millais, the famed Pre-Raphaelite painter. The rooms are simple yet spotless; ask for one facing away from the street. Bibliophiles will be happy to know that Dillon's is directly across the road. Singles cost £37, doubles £50 (£62 with shower room en-suite), triples £68 (£75 with shower room en-suite), and quads £78 (£85 with shower room en-suite). Every room is equipped with a TV and a sink. *83 Gower St., WC1, tel. and fax 020/7636–2115. Tube: Goodge St. Turn left on Tottenham Court Rd., right on Torrington Pl., right on Gower St. 15 rooms, 2 with shower rooms en-suite. Cash only. English breakfast.*

County Hotel. The County is huge by budget standards, with 175 rooms. Smallish singles (£37) and more spacious doubles (£50) are clean but bleakly decorated in '60s-institutional style. The lobby is quite nice (revolving wooden door!), but the clientele at the downstairs pub are mainly foreign businessmen—you may want to tipple elsewhere. *Upper Woburn Pl., WC1, tel. 020/7387–5544 or 020/7278–7871, fax 020/7837–4653. Tube: Euston. Walk south on Ersholt St., cross Euston Rd. to Upper Woburn Pl. 175 rooms, none with en-suite facilities. English breakfast.*

Crescent Hotel. With the University of London's student halls just across the road, the Crescent is set right smack in the middle of academic London. Not to mention the fact that the private garden across the road is owned by the City Guild of Skinners and guarded by the University of London. But don't let this trick you into thinking that you are entering some secret society; the hosts are great and as a guest you have access to the garden. The Crescent has a lot of repeat business, perhaps because the place (and rooms) are comfortable and are set in a glorious Georgian building. Hit the double-room hay for £50 (£68 with bath). *49–50 Cartright Gardens, WC1, tel. 020/7387–1511, fax 020/7382–2054. Tube: Russell Sq. Walk north on Marchmont St., left onto Cartright Gardens. 24 rooms, 15 with bath. English breakfast.*

Garth Hotel. The simple rooms are softened by a very friendly staff. Potter William de Morgan was born in this building—it's a pity none of his glorious tile work graces the showers here. Singles go for £34 (£37 with shower cubicle and £39.50 with shower room en-suite), doubles £47 (£55 with shower cubicle). All rooms have washbasins and TVS. Because the hotel caters to many Asian guests, it also offers a traditional Japanese breakfast on request. *69 Gower St., WC1, tel. 020/7636–5761, fax 020/7637–4854. Tube: Goodge St. Turn right on Tottenham Court Rd., quick left on Chenies St., left on Gower St. 17 rooms, 9 with shower rooms or cubicles en-suite. English breakfast.*

The Ridgemount Private Hotel. The kindly owners, Mr. and Mrs. Rees, add that personal touch to make you feel right at home, and the public areas—especially the family-style breakfast room—have a friendly, cluttered Victorian feel. Ask for a room that overlooks the garden. Singles are £32 (£43 with shower room en-suite), doubles £48 (£58 with shower room en-suite), triples £60 (£75 with shower room en-suite), and quads £75 (£85 with shower room en-suite). *65–67 Gower St., WC1, tel. 020/7636–1141, fax 020/7636–2558. Tube: Goodge St. Turn right on Tottenham Court Rd., quick left on Chenies St., left on Gower St. 34 rooms, 5 with shower rooms en-suite. English breakfast.*

St. Athans Hotel. This simple but appealing Edwardian guest house is close to Russell Square. The sloping walls and sagging staircases have a certain charm, and your hosts, Hans and Lucia Geyer, are delightful. Singles are £36 (£46 with shower rooms en-suite), doubles £46 (£56 with shower rooms en-suite), triples £60 (£72 with shower rooms en-suite), and quads £76 (£84 with shower rooms en-suite). *20 Tavistock Pl., WC1, tel. 020/7837–9140, fax 020/7833– 8352. Tube: Russell Sq. Exit station to the left, turn right on Herbrand St., right on Tavistock Pl. 50 rooms, 8 with shower rooms en-suite. English breakfast.*

UNDER £60 • Avalon Private Hotel. Resident Victorian-era bohemians won't be part of the picture, but something about the Avalon's tired lounge, mixed decorations, and top-floor student chatter make things seem like someone's trying (though it's unlikely to be the decorator). You can leave the top floors to the students, unless you like lugging your pack up impossibly steep stairs. You're better off staying in one of the pleasant lower-level rooms, from where it's easier to get to the lovely little residential garden just across the road. Doubles run £52 (£65 with shower), triples go for £70 (£80 with shower), and quads are £80 (£90 with shower). *46–47 Cartright Gardens, WC1, tel. 020/7387–2366, fax 020/7387–5810. Tube: Russell Sq. Walk north on Marchmont St., left onto Cartright Gardens. 28 rooms, 4 with shower. English breakfast.*

Euro Hotel. If you've stayed at any of the dingier budget hotels in London, this large, spacious hotel will come as a welcome relief. It is set in one of the prettier, quieter parts of the city and overlooks the Cartright Gardens' lawns and tennis courts. The big, bright rooms of the Euro complement the airy bistro atmosphere of the breakfast room. All rooms have TVS, telephones, radios, and tea- and coffeemaking facilities. Singles cost £43.50 (£60 with bath or shower rooms en-suite), doubles £59 (£75 with bath or shower rooms en-suite). *53 Cartright Gardens, WC1, tel. 020/7387–4321, fax 020/7383–5044. Tube: Russell Sq. Walk north on Marchmont St., turn left on Cartright Gardens. 35 rooms, 7 with bath or shower rooms en-suite. English breakfast.*

Jenkins Hotel. If you're afraid of or allergic to dogs, move on to the next review. The Jenkins is home to two big, friendly Labradors, Charlie and Georgie, and two friendly humans, Felicity and Sam. Rooms are nicely furnished and all have a TV, phone, hair dryer, refrigerator, and tea- and coffeemaking facilities. Singles cost £45 (£55 with shower room en-suite), doubles £55 (£65 with shower room en-suite), and triples with shower room en-suite are £76. If the entrance looks familiar, it's because it was featured in the Agatha Christie television series, *Poirot. 45 Cartright Gardens, WC1, tel. 020/7387–2067, fax 020/7383–3139. Tube: Russell Sq. Walk north on Marchmont St., turn left on Cartright Gardens. 14 rooms, 8 with bathroom or shower rooms en-suite. English breakfast.*

Repton Hotel. The Repton, on a breezy road between Bloomsbury and Russell squares, has small but well-equipped rooms—note the TVS, phones, and tea- and coffeemaking facilities. If you want the Georgian terrace-house experience in central London, this is your best and cheapest bet. It's in high demand, so call ahead. Singles cost £45, doubles £55–£60, triples £70, quads £79 (all with shower rooms en-suite), and dorm beds £15 per person. Weekly rates are available. *31 Bedford Pl., WC1, tel. 020/7436–4922, tel. and fax 020/7636–7045. Tube: Russell Sq. Exit station to the left, turn left on Herbrand St., quick right on Guilford St., left on Southampton Row, right on Russell Sq., left on Bedford Pl. 29 rooms, all with shower rooms en-suite. Continental breakfast.*

Ruskin Hotel. Named after author John Ruskin, this hotel is set right beside the British Museum and has a private garden and chambers to the rear, which makes up for the tiny rooms. Like many other hotels in the area, the Ruskin has a good repeat clientele, probably thanks to the owners, who keep the place as tidy as a button. A solid double glazing at the front of the hotel keeps the noise down, and both shared and private bathrooms are kept clean. A snooze in a double will cost you £60 (£74 with bath), in a triple £75 (£85 with bath). *23–24 Montague St., WC1, tel. 020/7636–7388, fax 020/7323–1662. Tube: Russell Sq. Walk south onto Southampton Row, right onto Russell Sq., left onto Montague St. 32 rooms, 6 with showers. English breakfast.*

St. Margaret's Hotel. Another hotel with a view: this time, the Duke of Bedford's private garden, viewed from the back of this Georgian building. With the exception of a few single rooms, most in the St. Margaret are well proportioned and the furnishings are endurable, if a little tired. All rooms retain original fireplaces. Bathroom facilities are located on each floor and guests have use of one of two lounge areas. For £54–£66 you can take possession of a double (make that £70–£72 if you want a shower). *26 Bedford Pl., WC1, tel. 020/7636–4277, fax 020/7323–3066. Tube: Holborn. Walk north along Southampton Row, turn left onto Omsbury, and then right onto Bedford Pl. 63 rooms, 6 with shower. English breakfast.*

UNDER £80 • The Morgan. One of the more spotless hotels in the area, the Morgan is part of an 18th-century Georgian-terraced row, which has been run by the same family for more than 20 years. The rooms are small, but all have TVS and hair dryers. The day begins with a smile in the wood-paneled breakfast room—cozy and cluttered with paintings. Singles go for £55, doubles £75, triples £110, and suites £100. 24 Bloomsbury St., WC1, tel. 020/7636–3735, no fax. Tube: Tottenham Court Rd. Walk east on New Oxford St., left on Bloomsbury St. 21 rooms, all with shower rooms en-suite. Cash only. English breakfast.

EARL'S COURT

The area around Earl's Court and Gloucester Road tube stations has the highest concentration of inexpensive lodgings in London. Unfortunately, the rooms are also some of the skankiest, though we've tried to pick some winners for you. If you want to troll the neighborhood for bargains, try Hogarth Road, Earl's Court Gardens, Penywern Road, and Eardley Crescent; all are chock-full of budget sleeping options. Once you're settled you can explore the area's fast-food restaurants and pubs and laugh with glee at how close you are to the museums in neighboring South Kensington.

UNDER £40 • The Albert Hotel. Just down the street from Kensington Gardens, this old house serves as an inviting, inexpensive haven. Rooms come in many shapes and sizes: singles cost £35 and doubles £40 (£45 with shower en-suite); there are also four- to six-person rooms (£13–£14 per person), and 9- to 11-bed dorm rooms (£10 per person). Beds are given on a first-come, first-served basis. *191 Queen's Gate, SW7, tel. 020/7584–3019, fax 020/7823–8520. Tube: Gloucester Rd. Walk east 1 block on Cromwell Rd., turn left on Queen's Gate. 30 rooms, 22 with shower rooms en-suite; 39 dorm beds. Continental breakfast.*

The Court Hotel. This is a backpacker-style accommodation that features a self-catering kitchen, a dining area, and friendly management. The guest rooms are spacious but shabby and have TVS. Singles are £26 (£154 weekly), doubles £30–£35 (£175–£189 weekly), shared £13 (£77 weekly); further reductions for extended stays. *194–196 Earl's Court Rd., SW5, tel. 020/7373–0027, fax 020/7912–9500. Tube: Earl's Court. Turn left onto Earl's Court Rd. 13 private rooms, none with en-suite facilities, 29 dorm beds.*

The Curzon House Hotel. If you book at this hotel, try to get a room with a view—the Curzon overlooks Courtfield Gardens, a lovely, leafy square centered around an old church. The hotel is friendly, clean, and a good value (good winter discounts, too), despite being a bit frayed. There is a kitchen for guests' use and a few studio apartments. None of the rooms have bath or shower rooms en-suite. Singles cost £35, doubles £40–£55, triples £60, quads £80, quints £105. *58 Courtfield Gardens, SW5, tel. 020/7581–2116, fax 020/7835–1319. Tube: Earl's Court. Walk south 2 blocks on Earl's Court Rd., turn left on Barkston Gardens (which becomes Courtfield Gardens). 19 rooms, 10 with shower/bath en-suite. Continental breakfast.*

Fieldcourt House. The Fieldcourt is a grand old Victorian place with clean, pleasant rooms and—to quote one guest—"befuddled" French management. Add a number of permanent residents (who have their tab picked up by the dole), and you'll agree that all it's missing is Barton Fink. Rooms have their own hot plates and refrigerators; there's a microwave, too. As the hotel is located just two min from a supermarket, this place can be a great choice if you want to save and cater for yourself. Singles cost £20 (£120 weekly), doubles £35 (£200 weekly), triples £47, and quads £57. *32 Courtfield Gardens, SW5, tel. 020/7373–0153. Tube: Earl's Court. Walk south 2 blocks on Earl's Court Rd., turn left on Barkston Gardens (which becomes Courtfield Gardens). 40 rooms, none with bath. Cash only.*

Green Court Hotel. The "green" in Green Court is the management's fondness for plastic potted flowers. Rooms here are extremely worn, and each is furnished with TV, phone, and clashing floral fabrics. For the price, it's the best of the crew of bargain-basement digs on Hogarth Road. Singles run £30–£40, doubles £40–£50, and triples £50–£60. *52 Hogarth Rd., SW5, tel. 020/7370–0853, fax 020/7370–3998. Tube: Earl's Court. Cross Earl's Court Rd., turn right on Hogarth Rd. 25 rooms, all with shower room en-suite. Continental breakfast.*

Hunter's Lodge Hotel. There's absolutely nothing fancy or luxurious about this low-key hotel, but the bathrooms are clean and the staff is friendly. Singles cost £20 (£30 with shower cubicle en-suite), doubles £28 (£45 with shower cubicle en-suite), and triples £36 (£55 with shower cubicle en-suite). They also offer dorm beds for £10 per night (£60 weekly). *38 Trebovir Rd., SW5, tel. 020/7373–7331. Tube: Earl's Court. Walk north 1 block on Earl's Court Rd., turn left on Trebovir Rd. 25 rooms, 3 with shower cubicles en-suite. English breakfast.*

Table Mountain Hotel. This is a basic but comfortable hotel/hostel with a friendly atmosphere. There's a lounge with cable TV, kitchen facilities, and postings for temp work. Dorm beds are £15–£18, doubles are £35–£45. There are cheaper winter rates and weekly discounts. *109 Warwick Rd., SW5, tel. 020/7370–4474, fax 020/7370–2623. Tube: Earl's Court. Take the Warwick Rd. exit and head 2 blocks on right. 19 rooms, 50 beds, 4 rooms with en-suite shower/toilet cubicles. Cash only. Continental breakfast.*

UNDER £50 • Aaron House. On a tranquil Victorian square, this place features some lovely accents—etched glass, carved moldings, antique cornices—along with your basic accommodations. Rooms are large and some are pleasantly adorned with stylish mantels, gilded mirrors, and parquet floors. All front rooms come with baths en-suite and tea- and coffeemaking facilities. Rates range from £44–£60. *17 Courtfield Gardens, SW5, tel. and fax 020/7373–2303. Tube: Earl's Court. Walk 3 blocks east of tube station to the west side of the square. 23 rooms, 15 with bath. Continental breakfast.*

UNDER £60 • Philbeach Hotel. This 19th-century Victorian building houses London's best and largest gay hotel, as well as a bar and a restaurant called **Wilde About Oscar.** And it occasionally hosts diversions such as cabaret shows and garden parties. Singles are £45 (£50 with bath), doubles £55 (£60 with bath). *30–31 Philbeach Gardens, SW5, tel. 020/7373–1244 or 020/7373–4544, fax 020/7244–0149. Tube: Earl's Court. Exit on Warwick Rd., walk north 1 block, turn left on Philbeach Gardens. 35 rooms, 18 with bath. Continental breakfast.*

UNDER £80 • Beaver Hotel. If you're looking to splash out in Earl's Court, book at the Beaver. It's on a charming, tree-lined street of late-Victorian town houses. Rooms, all with TV and phone, are spiffy and modern, and you get access to lounges with cable TV, a self-serve bar, and a pool table. Private-bath singles are £55, doubles £77; a few shared-bath singles are £34, and twins are £50 per person. *57–59 Philbeach Gardens, SW5, tel. 020/7373–4553, fax 020/7373–4555. Tube: Earl's Court. Exit on Warwick Rd., walk north 1 block, turn left on Philbeach Gardens. 37 rooms, 24 with either bath or shower rooms en-suite. English breakfast.*

Henly House. At breakfast time Henly House engenders a really communal atmosphere, but the management is only too keen on offering advice to the newly arrived throughout the day—a big bonus for culture-shocked antipodes. Set in a pleasant row of Victorian terraces, all rooms are clean and well appointed; a great ground floor sitting room overlooks a rear courtyard, where you can compare notes with fellow visitors. If the outside world is simply too wound-up for you, curl up with a book from the hotel's ever-expanding collection of left-behind/forgotten paperbacks. You'll pay £80 for a double. *30 Barkston Gardens, SW5, tel. 020/7370–4111, fax 020/7370–0026. Tube: Earl's Court. Walk south on Earl's Court Rd., left onto Barkston Gardens. 20 rooms. Continental breakfast.*

Rushmore Hotel. The Rushmore stands on the site of the old Manor House of Earl's Court Farm, and the Victorian building that houses it emerged from a complete refurbishment in the late 1980s. Each room is individually decorated and the breakfast room is full of delightful touches—note the French limestone floors, a glass wall, floor lighting, and antique terra-cotta urns. The attentive staff is truly multilingual. Doubles run £79–£85, triples go for £89–£95, the family room is yours for £99–£110 (ideal for a group of 4–5). *11 Trebovir Rd., SW5, tel. 020/7370–3839, fax 020/7370–0274. Tube: Earl's Court. Head north on Earl's Court Rd., make the first right onto Trebovir Rd. 22 rooms. Buffet breakfast.*

The Swiss House. Trailing ivy and hanging baskets decorate the exterior of the Swiss House. The staff is friendly and helpful, and the rooms are clean and decorated with decent pine furniture; some of them overlook a pretty garden. All rooms have TVS and phones. Singles are £45–£60 with shower cubicles en-suite, doubles are £80 with shower/toilet cubicles en-suite. There is a £15 charge for an extra bed. *171 Old Brompton Rd., SW5, tel. 020/7373–2769 or 020/7370–6364, fax 020/7373–4983. Tube: South Kensington. Follow Old Brompton Rd. south, 500 yards on the left. Continental breakfast or £4.50 supplement for English breakfast.*

NORTH LONDON

For a taste of bohemian suburbia (i.e., nice neighborhoods with cool cafés) and a homier and less touristy atmosphere than Earl's Court or Bayswater, try the neighborhoods north of central London, which roughly encompass the massive expanse of trees, ponds, and rolling hills known as the Heath. You may have to sit on the tube an extra few stops or even catch a bus to central London, but that's the price you pay for a quieter, more residential quarter for your London home-away-from-home. Hotel rates are about the same in north London as in most other areas, but you're more likely to get what you pay for here.

If you want a taste of English country–style living while still being near central London, definitely contact the **Primrose Hill Agency.** This small B&B association believes that "travel shouldn't be a rip-off"; to prove it, they book guests into beautiful family homes at reasonable rates—£25–£45 per person in single or double rooms. All houses are in or around leafy Primrose Hill and Hampstead, where you'll find London's best parks. Expect cozy rooms, your own latchkey, and scrumptious breakfasts. There's a three-night minimum, and you should book ahead to be safe. *Contact Gail O'Farrell, 14 Edis St., London, NW1, tel. 020/7722–6869, fax 020/7916–2240. 20 rooms in various locations and a suite at £65 for 2 people.*

UNDER £40 • Five Kings Guest House. Although the surrounding neighborhood is quintessentially residential, you're only 15 min by foot from both Camden and the Heath. The friendly proprietors run a tight ship and offer nothing fancy, but good value for the traveler in search of peace and quiet. Singles are £20 (£27 with bath), doubles £32 (£38 with bath). *59 Anson Rd., Kentish Town, N7, tel. 020/7607–3996 or 020/7607–6466. Tube: Tufnell Park. Turn left on Brecknock Rd., left on Anson Rd. 16 rooms, 7 with shower/toilet en-suite. English breakfast.*

UNDER £50 • Kandara Guest House. The main reason to stay here is location—just a short bus ride from the heart of lively Islington. The guest house is small and tidy, with recently remodeled singles (£34), doubles (£45), and triples (£57) that have TVS, sinks, tea- and coffeemaking facilities, and shaving sockets. *68 Ockendon Rd., Islington, N1, tel. 020/7226–5721 or 020/7226–3379. Tube: Angel. From station, take Bus 38, 56, 73, or 171A northeast on Essex Rd. to Ockendon Rd. 10 rooms, none with bath or shower rooms en-suite. English breakfast.*

The Oxford Arms. This traditional pub and inn is the place to stay if you want a neighborhood atmosphere and easy access to local brew. The double rooms (£48) are equipped with showers and toilets, and the lone single (£35) has a shower and a toilet down the hall. All rooms feature TVS and tea- and coffeemakers. Depending on your cholesterol level, the lack of a cooked breakfast may be a blessing or a curse—but they do offer self-service cold cereal. *21 Halliford St., Islington, N1, tel. 020/7226–6629, fax 020/7226–5302. Tube: Angel. From the station, take Bus 38, 56, 73, or 171A northeast up Essex Rd. to Halliford St. 5 rooms.*

UNDER £60 • Parkland Walk Guest House. The luxurious Parkland Walk is near Crouch End, a change from the hustle and bustle of the West End. The welcoming owners will make you feel right at home in the comfortable sitting and breakfast rooms. The house is decorated in Victorian style and retains many of its original features; the top bathroom is a must-see. Parkland is a no-smoking guest house and the rooms are equipped with TVS, radios, tea- and coffeemaking facilities, hair dryers, and lots of creature comforts like hot water bottles and heaps of books. Modern renovations haven't sanitized the style and character of the Parkland, nor have they obstructed the great views of London. The fresh, delicious food is yet another reason to come. Singles are £34, doubles £55 (£67 with en-suite shower/bathroom), a bit less if you stay more than two nights. If you want to book here, plan to make reservations well in advance. *12 Hornsey Rise Gardens, N19, tel. 020/7263–3228, fax 020/7263–3965. Tube: Archway or Finsbury Park. From Archway, take Bus 41 to Crouch End. From Finsbury Park, take Bus 210 to Crouch End. Or take Bus 91 from King's Cross or Euston to Hornsey Rise. 5 rooms, 2 with bath. English breakfast.*

HOSTELS

England's **Youth Hostel Association** (YHA) (tel. 020/7248–6547, fax 020/7236–7681 for reservations) operates seven hostels in central London (some are more central than others). These Formica-and-linoleum wonders tend to be clean to the point of sterility: even if the outside looks cool, it's a safe bet that the rooms are basic and bland and packed to the rafters with space-age bunk beds. None of the seven YHA hostels listed below have a lockout, and the reception desks are usually open daily 7 AM–11 PM, with all providing 24-hour access. Purchase a YHA membership card at any hostel for £12.50, or pay an extra

£2 per night for a guest stamp; after accruing six stamps you're granted full membership. **Astor Hostels** (tel. 020/7229–7866, fax 020/7727–8106), a private hostel firm, runs four places in London that cater to international cheapo travelers. Astor also provides free Continental breakfasts of cereal, bread, rolls, and tea or coffee. Wherever you stay, reservations are imperative from June through August, particularly if you want a single or double room in one of the few hostels that offer such options (don't let this scare you, but many are booked solid for summer by the end of May). Unless otherwise noted, the non-YHA hostels listed below do not have curfews or lockouts and are open 24 hours for check-in.

Some London B&Bs also offer dorm-style accommodations in addition to their more expensive singles and doubles. B&Bs can be a welcome respite from snoring bunkmates, noisy school groups, and 8 AM wake-up calls. The following B&Bs charge £15–£20 for dorm beds and are reviewed above: the **Albert Hotel** (*see* Earl's Court, *above*), **Elizabeth House** (YWCA; *see* Around Victoria Station, *above*), **Hunter's Lodge Hotel** (*see* Earl's Court, *above*), and **Repton Hotel** (*see* Bloomsbury and King's Cross, *above*).

Chelsea Hotel. This huge Earl's Court hostel is incredibly popular with backpackers, and for good reason: rooms (though worn) are clean and cheap, from the dorm rooms (beds £10) to singles (£18), doubles (£28, £30 with bathroom en-suite), triples (£36), and quads (£44). You may even be lucky enough to get one of the upgraded rooms. But wait, there's more, including a common room with video games, a pool table, CD jukebox, and special party nights. They'll even collect you from Victoria Station by minibus (at no extra charge). If you're after a cheap bite to eat, the restaurant on the premises offers meals for £2–£4. *33–41 Earl's Court Sq., SW5, tel. 020/7244–6892 or 020/7244–7395, fax 020/7244–6891. Tube: Earl's Court. Walk south 3 blocks on Earl's Court Rd., turn right on Earl's Court Sq. 180 beds. Continental breakfast.*

City of London Hostel (YHA). Formerly the home of the St. Paul's Cathedral boys' choir, this hostel has a great location in the middle of town and spotless rooms. Note, however, the beds here are not well suited to taller folk. Although there are no age restrictions, a mature attitude is preferred. Dorm beds cost £18.50–£23.50 per person, depending on the number of beds in the room; doubles for families are £42, triples £59, and quads £76.50. *36–38 Carter La., EC4, tel. 020/7236–4965, fax 020/7236–7681. Tube: Blackfriars or St. Paul's. From Blackfriars, walk east on Queen Victoria St., turn left on St. Andrew's Hill, right on Carter La. From St. Paul's, follow signs to cathedral, cross in front of cathedral entrance to Dean's Ct., turn right on Carter La. 191 beds. Laundry. English breakfast.*

Earl's Court (YHA). From the outside, this Victorian town house turned hostel looks deceptively small and cozy. Inside you'll find institutional-looking dorm rooms, each packed with 10 beds. You won't get sparkly clean bathrooms, but you will get convenience to the tube, a large common room, and an in-house tourist info center where you can make travel arrangements and onward accommodation bookings with other YHA establishments. Beds cost £22. *38 Bolton Gardens, SW5, tel. 020/7373–7083, fax 020/7835–2034. Tube: Earl's Court. Walk south on Earl's Court Rd., turn left on Bolton Gardens. 155 beds. Kitchen, laundry. English breakfast.*

The Generator. This two-year-old hostel is easily the grooviest in town, with a friendly, funky vibe, lots of young people, and vibrant decor—blue neon and brushed-steel downstairs, and upstairs dorm rooms painted in bright blue and orange. The Generator Bar has cheap drinks, and the Fuel Stop cafeteria provides inexpensive meals. Rooms are simple but clean; singles are £38, twins £23.50 per person, dorm beds £18.50–£20 depending on the number of beds in the room. Prices do drop by a few pounds October–March. *MacNaghten House, Compton Pl., WC1, tel. 020/7388–7666, fax 020/7388–7644. Tube: Russell Sq. Turn right on Bernard St., left on Marchmont St., right on Tavistock Pl., left on Compton Pl. 800 beds. Continental breakfast.*

Hampstead Heath (YHA). This great hostel is well out of the hustle and bustle of central London, yet convenient to the tube. The grounds are beautiful, and on sunny days you can play in nearby Hampstead Heath. There's a bureau de change and a TV lounge on site. Doubles are £40, dorm beds £18, with a supplement of £3 for breakfast. *4 Wellgarth Rd., NW11, tel. 020/8458–9054, fax 020/8209–0546. Tube: Golders Green. Walk southeast on North End Rd., turn left on Wellgarth Rd. 200 beds. Kitchen, laundry. Buffet breakfast.*

Highgate Village (YHA). If you're not bothered by a midnight curfew, this hostel will reward you with lodgings in an attractive Georgian house in a quiet neighborhood. It's also just a hop, skip, and jump away from Highgate Cemetery, Hampstead Heath, and the Flask (a cool pub just up the road). Dorm beds cost a mere £15, so reservations are a good idea. It's a long uphill trek from the Archway tube station, or you can take Bus 143, 210, or 271 to the top of Highgate Hill. *84 Highgate West Hill, N6, tel.*

020/8340–1831, fax 020/8341–0376. Tube: Archway. Walk north on Highgate Hill, turn left on South Grove. 70 beds. Midnight curfew. Reception open 7 AM–11:30 PM. Kitchen.

Holland House Youth Hostel (YHA). This hostel is one of the most famous in the world: it incorporates part of a fabled Jacobean mansion, and it's set right in the middle of woodsy Holland Park. Unfortunately, it's also a hike from the nearest tube station. For £22 per person you can take a spot in the 10- to 20-bed dorm rooms, or scrap for the single, double, triple, or quad rooms (there's one of each). *Holland Walk, Kensington, W8, tel. 020/7937–0748, fax 020/7376–0667. Tube: High St. Kensington or Holland Park. From High Street Kensington, walk west on Kensington High St., turn right on Holland Walk; or take Bus 9, 9A, 10, 27, 28, or 49 west to Commonwealth Institute, then walk north on Holland Walk. From Holland Park, walk east on Holland Park Ave., turn right on Holland Walk. 201 beds. Kitchen, laundry. English breakfast.*

Oxford Street (YHA). The big draw at this hostel is its location: smack in the center of hip Soho. It's so convenient (imagine staggering home from the pubs instead of dealing with the tube), you'll overlook the cramped rooms. You'll also battle hordes of other backpackers who want to stay here, so make reservations. There's a bureau de change and TV lounge on site. Beds go for £18, except the doubles, which go for £19.50 per person regardless of age. Most rooms are doubles, triples, or quads. *14 Noel St., W1, tel. 020/7734–1618, fax 020/7734–1657. Tube: Oxford Circus. Walk east on Oxford St., turn right on Poland St., left on Noel St. 76 beds. Kitchen.*

You do not need a YHA hostel card if you already have a Hostelling International (HI) card. In England the two cards are essentially interchangeable.

Palace Hotel. This tidy, cheerful Bayswater hostel has recently renovated its kitchen and bathrooms. It's situated just north of Kensington Gardens on a pleasant street lined with redbrick buildings. There is a café on the premises serving a small selection of evening meals. Beds in the six- to eight-bed dorms are £12. If there is space they may offer a weekly rate of £60. Reservations are strongly recommended, especially June–August. *31 Palace Ct., W2, tel. 020/7221–5628, fax 020/7243–8157. Tube: Notting Hill Gate. Walk east on Notting Hill Gate (which becomes Bayswater Rd.), turn left on Palace Ct. 74 beds. Continental breakfast.*

Rotherhithe (YHA). Although this hostel is really cool architecturally, it's tucked away near the Docklands, quite a trek from central London. Fortunately, the neighborhood is interesting in its own right, and the rooms, although pretty shrimpy, all have shower rooms en-suite. There's a bureau de change and restaurant on site. Twin rooms are £25.50 per person, and dorm beds are £22.75 (in a four-person room) and £22.15 (in a six-person room); all rates include breakfast. *Island Yard, Salter Rd., SE16, tel. 020/7232–2114, fax 020/7237–2919. Tube: Rotherhithe. Walk northeast on Brunel Rd., which becomes Salter Rd. 320 beds. Laundry.*

Victoria Hotel (Astor). The Victoria, less than 500 yards from Victoria Station, is terrific if you just want to collapse at the end of a long journey. Dorm beds cost £15–£20 daily, about £75 weekly. This place may not be spotless, but it's brightly painted, cheerful, and a great place to meet fellow travelers—the common room is crowded, smoky, loud, and congenial, like a cool pub without the beer. *71 Belgrave Rd., SW1, tel. 020/7834–3077, fax 020/7932–0693. Tube: Victoria. Walk south on Buckingham Palace Rd., turn left on Eccleston Bridge, which becomes Belgrave Rd. 70 beds. Kitchen.*

STUDENT HOUSING

Many university residence halls earn some extra pounds by throwing their doors open to backpackers and the great unwashed during school vacations. Life in college dorms will give you the pleasure of rubbing shoulders with like-minded young expatriates, but the most significant advantage is location: student housing is often in northwest Bloomsbury, an easy 10-min walk from London's West End. Although the dorms are often spartan, they are usually much cleaner than those in cheap hotels, and you get access to such amenities as saunas, tennis courts, laundry rooms, kitchens, gyms, and cheap eats at university pubs and cafeterias. These places fill up fast in summer, and reservations are a must. Student identification, however, is not: nonstudents usually pay a small supplement to stay in the dorms. Other than the individual residence halls listed below, the main resource for student housing is the **University of London Accommodations Office** (Room B, Senate House, Malet St., WC1, tel. 020/7636–2818). London's largest university offers rooms during the summer vacation—from mid-June to mid-August—and also during Easter and Christmas holidays. Intercollege Hall rooms, usually two or more beds to a room, run about £20 per room; rooms in Halls of Residence, which offer single or twin beds, run about £30–£45. If you're having trouble finding space in one of the following student dorms, contact the **Vacation Bureau** at King's College (127 Stamford St., SE1, tel. 020/7928–3777). It offers bed and breakfast in six halls around central London, available April and June–September in 2000. The student rate for a single room is £14; nonstudents pay £17–£23. There's no minimum stay, and you'll get a 10% discount if you stay a week. Unless otherwise specified, the following dorms rent available space year-round.

Campbell House. This is definitely one of London's nicer residence halls. The rooms are large (especially the doubles), some have (faux) fireplaces, and those in the back overlook a private terrace and garden. Excellent kitchen facilities make this a great place to settle in for a while. Singles cost £20 nightly, £120 weekly; doubles are £33 nightly, £220 weekly. *5–10 Taviton St., WC1, tel. 020/7391–1479, fax 020/7388–0060. Tube: Euston Sq. Walk east on Euston Rd., turn right on Gordon St., left on Endsleigh Gardens, right on Taviton St. 100 rooms, none with bath or shower rooms en-suite. Kitchen, laundry. Cash only.*

Central University of Iowa Hostel. Nestled amongst the B&Bs on Bedford Place, this spot has an excellent location and simple, clean rooms. Dorm beds are £20 in a three- or four-person room, £25 in a two-person room. All rooms have wash basins. There is a single room for £20. *7 Bedford Pl., WC1, tel. 020/7580–1121, fax 020/7580–5638. Tube: Russell Sq. Exit station to the left, turn left on Herbrand St., quick right on Guilford St., left on Southampton Row, right on Russell Sq., left on Bedford Pl. 31 beds. Reception open 8–8 (usually closed 1–3). Check-in 11 AM. Kitchen, laundry. Open mid-May–mid-Aug. Continental breakfast.*

College Hall. This hall in the center of London's student ghetto gives you easy access to university pubs and facilities—it's across the street from the student union and just down the block from Dillon's bookstore. Students can stay in singles for £18 with breakfast, £23 with breakfast and dinner. Nonstudents pay £22 with breakfast, £28 with breakfast and dinner. *Malet St., WC1, tel. 020/7580–9131, fax 020/7636–6591. Tube: Goodge St. or Russell Sq. From Goodge St., turn left on Tottenham Court Rd., right on Torrington Pl., right on Malet St. From Russell Sq., walk southwest across the square to Montague Pl., turn right on Malet St. 200 rooms, none with bath or shower rooms en-suite. Laundry. Cash only. Open mid-June–mid-Aug. English breakfast.*

Connaught Hall. This residence hall overlooks pleasant Tavistock Square. Singles cost £25 with breakfast, £30 with breakfast and dinner. *36–45 Tavistock Sq., WC1, tel. 020/7387–4120 (front desk) or 020/7387–6181 (reservations), fax 020/7383–4109. Tube: Euston or Russell Sq. From Euston, walk southwest on Eversholt St. From Russell Sq., walk northwest on Woburn Pl. 206 rooms, none with bath or shower rooms en-suite. Kitchen, laundry. Open July–mid-Sept.*

International Student House. This fun, monstrously huge establishment sits at the southeast corner of Regent's Park, right across from Great Portland Street tube station. Popular with international students, this place fills up fast despite its size, and reservations are almost obligatory. A bar, restaurant, and fitness center are all on site. A dorm bed in a clean three- or four-bunk room costs £20; a bed in an "economy" dorm with six or more beds is £12. Singles are £30, twins £22 per person. All prices include breakfast, except the "economy" dorm. The best deal, however, is for stays of three months or longer: if you pay in advance for an entire month, a dorm bed costs a mere £47 a week without breakfast. *229 Great Portland St., W1, tel. 020/7631–8300, fax 020/7631– 8315. Tube: Great Portland St. Walk straight across the road. 800 beds. Laundry. Continental breakfast.*

John Adams Hall. This group of Georgian houses has been converted into student lodging, and rooms are available at bargain rates during school vacations. Although there's nothing luxurious about the complex or the small and dim (but clean) rooms, the residence is only a short walk from the British Museum and Euston Station. Singles are £25, doubles £40, less if you stay a week or more. *15–23 Endsleigh St., WC1, tel. 020/7387–4086 or 020/7387–4796 (ask for booking office), fax 020/7383–0164. Tube: Euston Sq. Walk west on Euston Rd., turn right on Gordon St., left on Endsleigh Gardens, right on Endsleigh St. 151 rooms, 2 with bathrooms en-suite. Laundry. Open July–mid-Sept. English breakfast.*

CAMPING

Camping in London is a weird enough idea to be interesting, and if you don't mind a longish commute, it's practical, too. God knows, it's cheap enough. Both Tent City locations are actually inside Zones 1 and 2, which is great for Travelcard holders (*see* Getting Around, By Underground and Bus, *in* Chapter 1).

Halfway there, the Underground trip turns into a pleasant train ride through the country. The campgrounds do fill up in the summer months, so call ahead.

Tent City Acton. Have you ever wanted to live the M*A*S*H experience? This west London institution has 450 cots in 14 large tents spread across Wormwood Scrubs. You can choose between men's, women's, and mixed tents, or else pitch your own tent for the same daily price of £8. A fun and friendly crowd comes here, and all profits go to Tree of Life, a charity that works to revitalize the community. *Old Oak Common La., W3, tel. 020/8743–5708, fax 020/8749–9074. Tube: East Acton. Walk northeast on Erconwald St., turn left on Wulfstan St., which merges with Old Oak Common La. 450 beds. Fire grates, toilets, showers. Open June–Aug.*

Tent City Hackney. This small enclosed grove in a huge park on the outskirts of London is ideal for cheap sleeping. As with Tent City Acton, they donate all their profits to charity. BYOT (bring your own tent) and camp for a mere £7 per person, or call ahead and try to get one of the 30 dorm beds. *Millfields Rd., E5, tel. 020/8985–7656. Tube: Liverpool St. From the station, take Bus 22A to Millfields and Mandeville Sts., cross the bridge, and follow signs. 200 sites, 30 dorm beds. Toilets, showers. Open June–Aug.*

FOOD

UPDATED BY PAUL DUBOUDIN

Once upon a time, eating in London was an experience to be endured rather than enjoyed. Visitors would invariably finish a meal, pay the check, and shake their heads. Then again, they agreed, had the British cooked better food, they would never have bothered to found an Empire. Today, however, the great news is that the days of green meat and two soggy vegetables are long gone. British cuisine is no longer a contradiction in terms. In fact, London is now on the cutting edge of food fashion—its leading chefs are cult heroes, its dining scene is the most talked about in Europe, and everyone (even Andrew Lloyd Webber, composer of *Phantom* and *Cats,* who has become a newspaper food critic) is talking turkey—literally. The hotter-than-hot cuisine scene has even filtered down to the simple local pub. Toad-in-the-hole and bangers and mash (respectively, cooked link sausages baked in Yorkshire pudding batter, sausages, and mashed potatoes) are still available at many of London's 1,000 or so public houses, but now the fashionable new gastro-pubs are offering modern Brit fare—roast chicken with saffron mash, lamb shank with caper berries, and rum-chocolate tart. More and more, pubs are installing char grills in kitchens out back, and faded wallpaper is being replaced with abstract canvases up front. Even the notorious "greasy spoons" (an English spin on the corner diner, where the smell of chip oil prevails and baked beans come in umpteen different flavors) are on the way out.

Still, now that you're in London, you'll want to check out some of those legendary options in British budget land. Everyone has to try fish-and-chips—battered and deep-fried whitefish with thick fries shaken with salt and vinegar (when well prepared, sinfully delicious). Egg-and-chips, sausage-and-chips, or chips and ketchup are some other old-time faves. Then there's always a ploughman's lunch (cheddar cheese and crusty bread, with pickled onion or sweet pickles) or steak and kidney pud. And of course there are those desserts—jam roly-poly and custard, rhubarb crumble, or treacle tart. Even this diet is changing, as health consciousness replaces the Church of England. The old traditional stodgy pies and puddings have given way to basket meals—fried chicken or fish pieces with the ubiquitous chips—and in some places, quite adventurous meals and vegetarian options. Pub Sunday roast dinners can often be the cheapest and the best in town. By now, indeed, good sandwich bars are more ubiquitous in central London than the old greasy spoons, many of which have taken to opening evenings, wearing tablecloths, and serving nouveau pub food. Modern Continental-style cafés are also sprouting up throughout the capital, providing a source of deli sandwiches on all kinds of exotic bread as well as delectable cakes and—surprise, surprise—good-quality coffee.

Then there are always the city's fabulous ethnic eateries—there's an endless array, one of the benefits of London's having been an imperial capital with far-flung dominions. (Britain probably conquered half the world for no other reason than to get some decent food.) When starving and not rich, a Londoner with *nouse*—British for savvy—invariably heads for Indian restaurants. Tandoori dishes have gone beyond a cliché into national-dish territory, and Southern Indian food, known as *balti,* has become almost as popular. Italian, Continental, and Middle Eastern restaurants are ubiquitous; other regional feathers flock together in particular parts of London. In Soho, wander along **Gerrard Street,** and enter a Hong Kong–like street, with crates of fresh produce, skinned ducks hanging in shop windows, and the omnipresent stench of yesterday's fish. You'll find Bengali on the East End's **Brick Lane** (Tube: Aldgate East), Indian on Bloomsbury's **Drummond Street** (Tube: Euston Sq.), and Vietnamese on **Lisle Street** (Tube: Piccadilly Circus).

As London remains one of the priciest places in the world, needless to say, your purse will not always be as happy as your stomach. The cheapest sit-down meals cost at least £4, more likely £6–£9, and if you want any sort of ambience you'll pay £8–£14. Usually the 17.5% VAT (value-added tax) is already included in the prices, but you may want to check the menu just to be sure. Some restaurants also include a mandatory service charge; inspect the bill to avoid paying twice. Otherwise, the standard tip is 10%.

In the end, any lengthy stay in London requires a strategy for eating on the cheap—like making lunch the biggest meal of the day to take advantage of discounted lunch specials. Even the hautest of haute restaurants offer luncheon menus, which makes dining in some of the very fanciest places within the budget of almost any visitor. Hot spots like Soho and Covent Garden, where lunchtime competition is at its stiffest, are your best bets for value meals. The typical city pub—more popular for its drink than its food—usually serves soups and sandwiches for less than £5, and fish-and-chips or steak and peas for £4–£7 (for these pubs, *see* Chapter 5; gastro-pubs are reviewed below). If you can't afford to eat out all the time, acquaint yourself with the department store **Marks & Spencer** (*see* Clothing *in* Chapter 7), which sells surprisingly yummy and diverse prepared meals at decent prices. A good and relatively inexpensive grocery chain is **Tesco,** with convenient locations at 21 Bedford Street in Covent Garden and 224 Portobello Road in Notting Hill. You'll also find chains like **Safeway** and **Sainsbury's** all over town. If you're on a really tight budget, avoid the over-priced **Cullens** minimarket chain. Most of London's neighborhoods also have regular fruit and vegetable markets with great deals on fresh produce (*see* Street Markets *in* Chapter 7). Then again, if you've been a good egg and saved your pounds and pence by going to a lot of bargain places, you're entitled to some blow-outs where you can really splurge. This chapter includes a few top options where the pleasures are, well, all-consuming.

So here you are, sitting in your hotel room, watching the rain streaming down the Georgian sash windowpane, surrounded by history, and hungry as a horse. What do you do? Just check the reference listings at the end of this chapter—restaurants are listed by type of cuisine, price range, and their neighborhood locations are also provided. Hopefully, most of our options will allow you to fill your stomach—and excite your taste buds—without emptying your wallet.

RESTAURANTS

BAYSWATER AND NOTTING HILL GATE

Bayswater is crowded with kebab joints, chippies, and delis—good restaurants are a bit thin on the ground here, and people in the know join British trendsetters in Notting Hill Gate, which is a cut above Bayswater when it comes to food. If you're poking around Portobello Road, avoid the scary beef-burger vans and stop in at **The Grain Shop** (269B Portobello Rd., W11, tel. 020/7229–5571) for an ever-changing menu of stews, pasta dishes (£2–£4.30), and yummy spinach pie (£1.30). Make room for a cheese croissant (£1).

UNDER £5 • Costas Fish Restaurant. Set in a back room behind a take-out operation facade, this place sees a surprising number of Notting Hill celebs walk through its doors. It's a fair bet that they, like you, have come to sample some very reasonably priced fish fare. You'll find a great range of Greek-influenced starters (£1.50–£3) and mains (try the haddock in batter for £5). This place really gives its more famous neighbor, **Geales** (*see below*), a run for its money. *18 Hillgate St., W8, tel. 020/7727–4310 Tube: Nottinghill Gate. Walk west on Nottinghill Gate and turn right onto Hillgate St. Closed 2:30–5:30 and Sun.–Mon.*

Manzara. This place doubles as a pâtisserie in the early hours, but come noon, the kitchen kicks into high gear and starts serving good-size portions of tasty Turkish food like grilled lamb with pine nuts on hummus and grilled chicken skewers with rice. After 7 PM, splurge on their buffet (£6), where you pick what you want from an array of ingredients and the chef cooks it in front of you. *24 Pembridge Rd., W11, tel. 020/7727–3062. Tube: Notting Hill Gate. Walk north on Pembridge Rd.*

UNDER £10 • Agadir. For a bit of authentic Moroccan food you could do a lot worse than Agadir, where the generous helpings and fair prices more than compensate for the rather drab interior. Try the famous spicy Moroccan soup *harira* (£2.90) and follow up with the juicy chicken *tagine* (£6.75). If you're up for a third course, you'll find that most desserts are priced around the £2.50 mark. *84 Westbourne Grove, W2, tel. 020/7792–2207. Tube: Bayswater. Walk north on Queensway and west onto Westbourne Grove. No lunch.*

Calzone. Sporting crisp modern decor and great views of the busy street, Calzone will tempt you to chow down on some of their marvelous pizzas with great combinations of toppings. Most pies cost around £6. *2A Kensington Park Rd., W11, tel. 020/7243–2003. Tube: Notting Hill Gate. Walk west on Notting Hill Gate and turn right onto Pembridge Rd.*

Geales. Wildly popular Geales has been serving some of the best fish-and-chips in London—to clerks and truck drivers as well as to the rich and famous—for more than 50 years. The homemade fish soup (£2.50) makes an excellent appetizer; follow it with a small fillet of haddock, plaice, or cod costing between £6 and £8 depending on weight and market price. An order of chips is £1.20 and peas are £1. It's not hypergreasy either, despite the fact that Geales fries fish in beef drippings. *2 Farmer's St., W8, tel. 020/7727–7969. Tube: Notting Hill Gate. Walk west on Notting Hill Gate, turn left on Farmer St. Closed 3–6 and Sun.–Mon.*

Paradise By Way Of Kensal Green. A converted Victorian pub, this spot is a bit off the main drag but is worth hunting out—it's got superb-value modern Brit dishes, and a lively clientele of music-industry mavens to boot. Roast cod with green salsa and saffron mash or rack of organic lamb with an herb and garlic crust are two tops *and* everything comes in generous portions. Vegetarian dishes are also highly rated. *19 Kilburn La., W10, tel. 020/8969–0098. Tube: Kensal. Then take Bus 52 and get off at the stop after Sainsbury's supermarket. No lunch Mon.–Sat., closed Sun. 3:30–7.*

Rodizio Rico. Although you may be pushing it to scrape in under the £10 mark, meat lovers would curse us if Rodizio Rico were to miss inclusion in this book. This South American–style steakhouse is the place to chew on perfectly pink and butter-textured steak, which is sometimes hard to find in Olde London Towne. For a fixed price (£9 for a two-course lunch and £15 for a three-course dinner), you'll get to choose from a buffet of side dishes and salads, plus as much meat as you can get your mouth around. Don't bother with the desserts unless crème caramel is your thing; you've come here for the meat, after all. *111 Westbourne Grove, W2, tel. 020/7792–4035. Tube: Bayswater. Walk north on Queensway and west onto Westbourne Grove. Closed 3–6.*

UNDER £20 • The Cow. Sir Terrence Conran's son, Tom, opened this tiny and chic gastro-pub several years ago, and it quickly attracted hordes of the local fabulous people. A faux-Dublin back-room bar serves up oysters, crab salad, and pasta with wine; upstairs, a serious chef whips up Tuscan–British specialties—skate poached in minestrone is one temptation. *89 Westbourne Park Rd., W2, tel. 020/7221–5400. Tube: Westbourne Park. Turn right, take first left on Westbourne Park Rd. and walk 2 blocks. No lunch Mon.–Sat., no dinner Sun.*

Prince Bonaparte. This gastro-pub draws in the crowds (and why not—food is great but prices are gentle, since there's no restaurant-scale overhead). Forget bangers and mash: here you'll get blackened salmon with refried beans, a yummy toffee pudding, and a wide range of interesting beers. Singles take over during the week, young families take up residence on the weekends. As the night wears on, the place—accented with large windows, church pews, and farmhouse tables—becomes a lively preclub stop (complete with thumping music on weekends). *80 Chepstow Rd., W2, tel. 020/7229–5912. Tube: Westbourne Park. Turn right out of the station, head down Great Western Rd., then left on Chepstow Rd. Cash only. No lunch Tues.*

BLOOMSBURY

Once London's literary slum, Bloomsbury is now better known for its thriving Asian and Indian communities. Bloomsbury's cramped lanes and alleyways harbor the highest concentration of Indian restaurants in the United Kingdom. Near Euston station, **Drummond Street** is lined with East Indian curry houses and southern Indian vegetarian restaurants. A variety of cuisine is available on Lamb's Conduit Street and Goodge Street. Bloomsbury is also home to the original **Wagamama** (*see* Soho, *below*), if you need your ramen fix.

UNDER £5 • Anwars. Super-low prices make this simple canteen especially popular with students from nearby colleges. Although the interior has seen better days (the 1970s, by the looks of things), the prices are right: you can get a bowl of chicken or meat curry or a yummy mutton *biryani. 64 Grafton Way, W1, tel. 020/7387–6664. Tube: Warren St. Walk south on Tottenham Court Rd., turn right on Grafton Way.*

Diwana Bhel Poori House. They serve up fresh southern Indian (read: vegetarian) cuisine on big plates at Diwana. Try the *thali*, a set meal with rice, dal, vegetables, chapatis, and *pooris* (£3.80–£6.50), or come between noon and 2:30 daily for their all-you-can-eat buffet (£4). BYOB. *121–123 Drummond St., NW1, tel. 020/7387–5556. Tube: Euston. Walk right on Melton St., turn left on Drummond St.*

Goodfellas. Not happy with serving up some of the most inspired sandwich fillings seen in these parts for a while, the Brazilian owners of this popular delicatessen have got locals and tourists lining up to get into the downstairs buffet. So if you're not content with a minty lamb or tarragon chicken sandwich, try your luck downstairs. The buffet menu varies from day to day, but the price (£3.50) and quality don't. Expect wholesome meals like leek and ham pie, Spanish omelet, or bacon and carrot bake. *50 Lamp's Conduit St., WC1, tel. 020/7405–7088. Tube: Russell Sq. Walk west on Guilford St. and south on Lamb's Conduit St. Closed Sun.*

British food used to be described as cold, fattening, unhealthy, expensive, life-threatening, tear-provoking, and gut-wrenching—literally. Some restaurants seemed to be in cahoots with the pharmaceutical companies.

Greenhouse. This subterranean veggie heaven is located beneath the Drill Hall, a gay and lesbian theater and cultural center, and gets quite crowded just before performances. Main courses like lentil stew with rice or a pasta bake with veggies change daily; salads range from £1.80 to £4. Greenhouse is "womyn only" on Monday night, and always no-smoking. *16 Chenies St., WC1, tel. 020/7637–8038. Tube: Goodge St. Walk south on Tottenham Court Rd., quick left on Chenies St.*

October Gallery Café. You'd be forgiven for expecting your Sunday Holy Communion in this place. Set in an anteroom off the hallway of an ex-chapel, this art gallery-cum-café certainly has the feel of a rectory. Step into the café to ponder the wonders of modern art over lunch. Generous portions and high quality more than compensate for the humble variety. *24 Old Gloucester St., WC1, tel. 020/7242–7367. Tube: Holborn. Walk north on Southampton Row, east onto Theobalds Rd. and immediately left onto Old Gloucester Rd. No dinner, closed Sun.–Mon.*

UNDER £10 • Chutney's. It's on everybody's short list for London's best vegetarian Indian restaurant. The £5 buffet is one of the city's few culinary steals. If you come for dinner, start with the vegetable kebab (£2.20) and continue with spicy mixed vegetables or *muttar panir* (tofu and peas in a hot sauce; £2.80) over a plate of rice. Add a glass of passion fruit, mango, or pineapple juice or the cool yogurty lassi drink, available with either salt or sugar. *124 Drummond St., NW1, tel. 020/7388–0604. Tube: Euston. Walk right on Melton St., turn left on Drummond St. Closed Mon.–Sat. 2:45–6.*

La Bardigiana. It's simple, it's small, and the staff is sometimes curt, but the price is right—especially if you can't face another biryani. A wide selection of toothsome pizzas and pastas runs £4.60–£5.20. *77 Marchmont St., tel. 020/7837–5983. Tube: Russell Sq. Turn right on Bernard St., left on Marchmont St. Closed Sun.*

Malabar Junction. This bright, spacious establishment is where you'll get your Southern Indian spice fix. Rooted in the cuisine from the Kerala region of southwestern India, the food here is the real thing—especially the fish. Try the marinated deep-fried Malabar fish (£7.50) or the intensely flavored peppery *rasam* (£2.50). The pace is relaxed and unhurried, which is fortunate because the tamarind rice dish (a meal in itself) takes some time to consume. *107 Great Russell St., WC1, tel. 020/7580–5230. Tube: Tottenham Court Rd. Walk north on Tottenham Court Rd., then west onto Great Russell St.*

Mandeer. Has London started to take its toll on your general well-being? Then a quick bite at Mandeer might just be in order. Cooks here adhere to principles of the ancient Indian holistic system known as *Ayurveda* ("knowledge of life"). Restore balance to your body by treating yourself to any of a variety of vegetarian, vegan, and *Jainist* (free of onions, garlic, and root vegetables) dishes. The organic vegetable curry (£4.25) and *kadhi* (yoghurt and chickpea sauce, £2.75) are the standouts. *8 Bloomsbury Way, WC1, tel. 020/7242–6202. Tube: Holborn. Walk north onto Southampton Row, then west on Bloomsbury Way. Closed Mon.–Sat. 3–5 and all day Sun.*

Museum Tavern. Before or after a trip to the British Museum, why not pop directly over the street to this big, ornate, Victorian pub, agleam with mirrors? Karl Marx quenched his thirst here while writing *Das Kapital,* and today it hosts a mix of scholars, tourists, and locals. It opens for breakfast at 9:30 (10:30 on Sun.), but alcohol is only served during regular pub licensing hours. *49 Great Russell St., WC1, tel. 020/7242–8987. Tube: Tottenham Court Rd. Walk north on Tottenham Court Rd., turn right on Russell St.*

BRIXTON

Brixton is brimming with Afro-Caribbean joints. Most are within several blocks of the Brixton tube station and cater to the crowds who swarm Brixton Market (*see* Street Markets *in* Chapter 7). If you're in the mood for a quick nosh, try **Miss Nid's Good Food** (397 Coldharbour La., tel. 020/7274–5605), which serves cheap West Indian–style snacks. Tucked away between market stalls, tiny **Bushman Kitchen** (36 Brixton Station Rd., tel. 020/7737–0015) serves West African snack foods and "natural medicinal herbs and root drinks."

UNDER £5 • Café Goya. Are you ready to venture down this stretch of uneven road between Brixton and Clapham to discover what the twentysomething trendies south of the Thames are up to? Colorful and lively is not just a way to describe the interior here. The food may not thrill you either—polenta with tomato and coriander salsa (£3.45) is a fair example. But at £6.50 the deluxe breakfast complete with black pudding and bubble and squeak (leftover potatoes, cabbage or other greens, and meat fried together) is worth the extra splurge. *85 Acre La., SW2, tel. 020/7274–3500. Tube: Clapham North. Walk south on Bedford Rd., then east on Acre La. No dinner on weekends.*

Café Pushka. Named after the hashish-friendly hippy stronghold in Rajasthan, Café Pushka is a very traveler-oriented place, not unlike the cafés you'd find between Goa and Kathmandu. The Indian-inspired dishes tend to be rather basic, but a relaxed atmosphere ensures you'll feel right about lingering and swapping travel tales with other wayfarers. Go for the pumpkin and spinach bake with red wine sauce (£4.50). *16C Market Row, Brixton Market, Coldharbour La., SW9, tel. 020/7738–6161. Tube: Brixton. Walk south on Brixton Rd., east on Coldharbour La. Closed Wed. and Sun.*

Jacaranda Café. Despite the presence of fresh flowers on the tables, the Jacaranda is a spare and mellow café, where Brixtonians come for their world-food fix: Jamaican-style rice and peas with salad, focaccia sandwiches, quiche, and vegetarian gumbo. And if you want to linger a few hours over coffee, penning poetry or reading a few chapters from *Heart Sutra,* hey, that's OK. *11–13 Brixton Station Rd., SW9, tel. 020/7274–8383. Tube: Brixton. Walk north on Brixton Rd., turn right on Brixton Station Rd. Closed Sun.*

Noodle House. It may just be aping the minimal-decor Japanese places in the West End, but this little joint serves up big plates of food for just under £4. The best bets are not the noodle dishes but the marinated salmon or tofu dishes that are accompanied by a generous helping of rice—a bit stodgy and certainly not authentic Japanese, but extremely good value. *426 Coldharbour La., SW9, tel. 020/7274–1492. Tube: Brixton. Walk left out of the station and turn left on Coldharbour La.*

UNDER £10 • Bah Humbug. Set in a church crypt, this cozy restaurant has not only a cool ambience but also some high-quality food—and it won't break the bank. The menu is exclusively vegetarian and fish. Starters (e.g., baked goat's cheese) hover around the £4 mark and entrées start at £6.10 and go up to £7.80, which gets you a terrific teriyaki tuna. Reservations are highly advisable; you might want to linger in the adjacent **Bug Bar** to make a night of it. *The Crypt, St. Matthew's Peace Garden, Brixton Hill, SW2, tel. 020/7738–3184. Tube: Brixton. Walk south on Brixton Rd. and look for the big building where the road forks.*

Helter Skelter. This vegetarian joint, set in what can only be described as a designer canteen, has the same smart young following found at Bah Humbug (*see above*), but offers higher quality food for a slightly higher price. Appetizers range from £3–£5, while most mains do not exceed £10. Asparagus and fresh broad bean risotto with baby red chard (£8.50) is a meal in itself. *50 Atlantic Rd., SW9, tel. 020/7274–8600. Tube: Brixton. Walk south on Brixton Rd., turn right onto Atlantic Rd. immediately before the railway bridge. Closed Sun.*

Zed. In many ways this place typifies the transformation that is occurring in and around Brixton. Galvanized metal bars and purple and orange walls—normally associated with trendy areas like Chelsea and the West End—go a long way to help Zed break some new ground in Brixton. The service may be variable, but perhaps this too has been borrowed from the très chic. Some of the bizarre pizza toppings are certainly worth the risk (Pizza Zed with pancetta, sweet onion, herbs, béchamel, mozzarella, and an egg works wonderfully at £6.50). Try to save a bit of room for puds like amaretto bread pudding and chocolate fudge nut brownie with a Jack Daniels sauce. *30 Acre La., SW2, tel. 020/7501–9001. Tube: Brixton. Walk south on Brixton Rd. and west on Acre La. Closed Mon.*

CAMDEN TOWN

There's no shortage of food in Camden, with dozens of stalls in the markets selling all kinds of cheap grub. **Camden High Street** is the main drag, interspersed with stands selling kebabs, pizza, and sausage, and the odd café. **Inverness Street, Parkway,** and **Bayham Street** have eateries that are slightly less clogged with Camden shoppers.

UNDER £5 • The Bagel Bar. This is the perfect place to grab a filling, cheap breakfast before hitting the markets. Full English breakfasts are a mere £2–£3 and freshly made sandwiches are a bargain at 90p–£2. Hot salt-beef (that's "corned beef" to you) bagels (£1.90) make a mighty good snack. *12 Inverness St., NW1, tel. 020/7284–0974. Tube: Camden Town. Walk north on Camden High St., turn left on Inverness St. Cash only.*

Cactus. Halfway between Camden Town and Hampstead, this funkily decorated basement restaurant serves up the best-value all-you-can-eat deal in the city. For just £4.88 there's a massive spread of 15 freshly cooked hot dishes plus loads and loads of salads and dips. Enjoy the upbeat atmosphere of this joint as you dig into a good chili, mussels, burritos, and other Southwestern American foods. Drinks prices are on a par with pubs and, due to its popularity, reservations are essential. *83 Haverstock Hill, NW3, tel. 020/7722–4112. Tube: Chalk Farm or Belsize Park. From Chalk Farm, walk up Haverstock Hill; from Belsize Park, walk downhill. Closed Mon.*

UNDER £10 • Cotton's Rhum Shop. "A taste of Jamaica in London" is how the owners describe their restaurant. Settle into the Caribbean atmosphere and choose from among a slew of generous starters (like chicken wings blackened with molasses) and popular entrées (like curry goat or mango chicken). Don't forget to sample the golden rums. *55 Chalk Farm Rd., NW1, tel. 020/7482–1096. Tube: Chalk Farm. Closed 4–6:30.*

Daphne's. Daphne's has fast, friendly service and excellent appetizers—try the grilled sausages or deep-fried calamari—and main dishes like moussaka, *tavvas* (cubes of lamb baked with herbs), and *ortikia* (quail with lemon and oregano). If the weather is even remotely pleasant, sit in the rooftop garden. *83 Bayham St., NW1, tel. 020/7267–7322. Tube: Camden Town. Walk southeast on Camden High St., turn left on Greenland St., right on Bayham St. Closed 2:30–6 and all day Sun.*

Luna. Luna is a welcome respite from the bustle of Camden Stables market. Sandwiches like grilled chicken and arugula or sausage on focaccia bread come with a small salad; or try the large portions of pasta, or monkfish on a bed of risotto. Weekends, they serve brunches like eggs Benedict or scrambled eggs with smoked salmon for £7.20, including orange juice and coffee. *48 Chalk Farm Rd., NW1, tel. 020/7482–4667. Tube: Chalk Farm. Walk southeast on Chalk Farm Rd. Cash only.*

Mango Room. Francis Bacon–style prints do their best to adorn the walls of this Caribbean joint, where the kitchen marries big flavors with attention to detail—the results of which are something to behold. Authentic seafood dishes include green-lipped mussels in a ginger, garlic, and coconut broth (£4.50); the jerk chicken is cooked perfectly: pepper-drenched but with a full meat flavor intact. *10 Kentish Town Rd., NW1, tel. 020/7483–1896. Tube: Camden Town. Walk north on Kentish Town Rd.*

Thanh Binh. Just north of Camden Lock, Thanh Binh is deservedly a long-time *Fodor's* favorite. Sit down and enjoy the delicate Vietnamese prawns or finger-licking-good Mongolian lamb, or order a chicken with lemongrass and rice lunch box to take away and eat by the lock. On weekends, they sell lunch boxes with curried chicken or beef and rice or noodles from the front of their restaurant all day. *14 Chalk Farm Rd., NW1, tel. 020/7267–9820. Tube: Chalk Farm. Walk southeast on Chalk Farm Rd. Closed Tues.–Sat. 3–6.*

Trojka. The obligatory babushka dolls are never far away at this Russian throwback, where '50s-style furnishings sit atop bare floorboards and the walls are laden with gaudily framed paintings. Come here for a good mix of Eastern European and Jewish favorites, but be prepared to do battle with a mix of Eastern Europeans, well-healed locals, and bohemian types for the waitstaff's attention. When you get it, ask for the marinated herring filets with dill and caper sauce (£3.70) or a filling beef Stroganoff (£7). *101*

Regent's Park Rd., NW1, tel. 020/7483–3765. Tube: Chalk Farm. Walk south on Chalk Farm Rd. and turn left on Regents Park Rd.

UNDER £20 • Engineer. One of the better new gastro-pubs, the Engineer is owned by the daughter of noted aristocrat Lord Oliver, Tamsin, and makes a wonderful place to hang out after a walk along the canal. The cosmopolitan menu changes biweekly, but you can expect inventive salads for around £5.50, such as arugula, pecan, and poached pear. Staples include eggs Benedict or eggs Florentine and salmon fishcakes. A steak will cost around £12.50—but the meat is organic. Reserve ahead if you're coming for dinner; try for an outside table if the weather's warm. *65 Gloucester Ave., NW1, tel. 020/7722–0950. Tube: Camden Town or Chalk Farm (recommended after dark). From Camden Town, walk north on Camden High St., at the bridge turn left on the Canal and watch for signs. From Chalk Farm, walk south across Adelaide Rd., veer left on Gloucester Ave. Closed Mon.–Sat. 3–7, Sun. 3:30–7.*

The Lansdowne. The NO MOBILE PHONES sign over the entrance sets the tone for this mellow, upscale pub on the fringe of Camden Town. Sit next to north London's young affluents at huge wooden tables and sample food from a menu that changes daily. The linguine with pine nuts, chili, garlic, and Parmesan and the grilled lamb with ratatouille and rice are both excellent with glasses of house wine. *90 Gloucester Ave., NW1, tel. 020/7483–0409. Tube: Chalk Farm. Walk southeast on Chalk Farm Rd., turn right on Regent's Park Rd., cross the bridge, veer left on Gloucester Ave. Bar closed Sun. 3–7; restaurant closed daily 2:30–7.*

CHELSEA

Trendy Chelsea is loaded with good places to graze, but many of the restaurants price their entrées as though they're major investments. If you're looking to dine on a budget, stick to the restaurants at the top of **King's Road,** between the Sloane Square tube station and Beaufort Street. Or try **Fulham Road,** where the pace is less frenetic and the prices more reasonable.

UNDER £5 • Chelsea Bun Diner. The oddly named Bun Diner is always jam-packed with locals, and here's why: damn good breakfasts. They serve breakfast the whole day long, but if you show up before 10:30 AM you can get the "Early Bird Breakfast" for £2.50. PS: Lunch and dinner are terrific here, too. BYOB. *9A Limerston St., SW10, tel. 020/7352–3635. Tube: Earl's Court or Sloane Sq. From either tube station, take Bus 11, 19, 22, or 31. Cash only.*

UNDER £10 • Ambrosiana Crêperie. This hip, attractive Chelsea restaurant dishes out a variety of both sweet and savory crepes. Start with a savory one like salami, ratatouille, and cheese, or chicken, spinach, tomato, and cheese. Or hey, why not skip straight to a dessert crepe, like pears and cinnamon? Serious crepeophiles dine on Monday and Thursday, when all crepes are half price. *194 Fulham Rd., SW10, tel. 020/7351–0070. Tube: South Kensington. Walk southwest on Old Brompton Rd., turn left on Sumner Pl., right on Fulham Rd. Closed weekdays 3–6.*

Buona Sera at the Jam. The Jam is a classy little '70s-era restaurant with a surprise: there appear to be only six tables at first, but then the host will direct you to climb above those already seated into a little cubby that makes a romantic, cozy setting for tucking into the special pastas and new-British dishes. The effect is like dining in a double-decker bus, and, best of all, you can do it until 1 AM. *289A King's Rd., SW3, tel. 020/7352–8827. Tube: Sloane Sq. Walk southwest on King's Rd. Closed weekdays 3–7.*

Delizia. People-watching is as important as the food at this little Farmers Market pizza place. Pies are reasonably priced for Chelsea, and the alfresco seating can be very pleasant in the warmer months. Delizia is not licensed, so a quick trip to the off license (liquor shop) before arrival is advised. And one last tip: watch out for the hot salami on the four seasons—it burns! *Chelsea Farmers Market, Sydney St., SW3, tel. 020/7351–6701. Tube: Sloane Sq. Walk southwest on Kings Rd., then right onto Sydney St.*

Market Place. On warm days, it's worth wandering into the über-touristy Chelsea Farmers Market for a decent breakfast or lunch at one of this café's peaceful, outdoor tables. During summer evenings it's home to a popular à la carte barbecue feast-o-rama (£8.50). *Chelsea Farmers Market, 215 Sydney St., SW3, tel. 020/7352–5600. Tube: South Kensington. Walk south on Onslow Sq., turn right on Fulham Rd., left on Sydney St. Cash only.*

UNDER £20 • Montana. Very trendy but extremely casual, Montana might be a bit off the beaten track and not for shoestring travelers, but it's one of Britain's very best for top-class Southwestern American food—and prices are a snip compared with West End prices. Although the menu changes regularly, you can expect dishes such as freshwater trout in a blue corn crust with crab and green chili stuffing (£11.25). The massively popular brunch (Friday–Sunday noon–3:30) is the best time to sample the fare on a budget: a big Southwestern breakfast costs £6.50. *125–129 Dawes Rd., SW6, tel. 020/7385–9500. Tube: Fulham Broadway. Walk right from the tube station along Fulham Broadway; cross North End Rd. and veer left onto Dawes Rd.*

THE CITY AND ISLINGTON

Restaurants in the City mainly cater to suited office folk; after all, this is the financial heart of London. Predictably, the area is busiest on weekdays from dawn until early evening, and it slows to a crawl on weekends. There's no lack of sandwich shops, delis, pubs, and restaurants, but if you're not desperately hungry as you explore the City, consider a short tube ride to nearby Islington. Once the center for '70s dropouts, Islington is now a community on the rise, with a surfeit of happening places to dine, especially along **Islington High Street.**

UNDER £5 • Alfredo's. Virtually unchanged since the 1920s, Alfredo's is more than your average neighborhood café. Join the crowd of regulars for hearty English breakfasts, sandwiches, and homemade pies with two veggies, served in a homey interior. *4–6 Essex Rd., N1, tel. 020/7226–3496. Tube: Angel. Walk north on Islington High St., veer right on Essex Rd. No dinner, closed Sun.*

Ravi Shankar. Filling, cheap food is served in this airy space with pale yellow walls. If you're especially hungry order Mysore thali, with dal, *bhaji* (deep-fried veggies), rice, and chapati. Partake of the 22-item, all-you-can-eat lunch buffet, served noon–2:30 (Sunday until 5), or take out lunch packs with veggie curry, rice, *samosa* (a stuffed deep-fried savory pastry), and salad. *422 St. John St., EC1, tel. 020/7833–5849. Tube: Angel. Walk south on St. John St. Closed Mon.–Sat. 2:30–6, Sun. 5–6.*

No chippie worth its salt is open on Monday; with most fishermen sitting at home on Sunday, Monday's fish would be more than a day old.

UNDER £10 • Afghan Kitchen. It's possible to eat at this functional but friendly place for under a fiver, but why only snack when you can put down a feast for less than £10? Great stuff includes various types of meatballs, baked eggplants, and lamb stews, all in delicious spiced sauces. Do sample some of the sesame-topped flat bread. BYOB. *35 Islington Green, N1, tel. 020/7359–8019. Tube: Angel. Walk north on Upper St. Cash only. Closed Sun.–Mon.*

Arkansas Café. This glorified stall with tables in Spitalfields Market is the *only* place to eat brilliant barbecue in London. You can get a pork rib plate with salad or veg, a USDA Texas beef brisket platter, or probably the best handmade half-pound burger in the capital. Pecan and other pies are £1.20, and beer is reasonable. With an American owner who insists on being called Bubba, it's a fun place to eat, but more important, it's totally authentic. *Unit 12, Old Spitalfields Market, E1, tel. 020/7377–6999. Tube: Liverpool St. Cash only. Dinner by appointment only.*

The Place Below. It takes some gumption to bill yourself as "London's best vegetarian restaurant," but The Place Below—set in the crypt beneath St. Mary-le-Bow church—may be justified in doing so. The changing menu features large portions of salads, hot dishes like ratatouille, and quiche with salad. For a light meal consider a bowl of soup with bread. *St. Mary-le-Bow, Cheapside, EC2, tel. 020/7329–0789. Tube: Mansion House. Walk north on Bow La., left on Cheapside. No dinner, closed weekends.*

The Quality Chop House. Once a quiet little chop house, The Quality Chop House went upscale a few years ago and never looked back. Although it still serves large portions of hearty British grub like eggs, bacon, and chips, some of what it offers is almost a parody of the traditional: bangers and mash becomes Toulouse sausages with mash and onion gravy. Try to ignore the sounds of the city folk and imagine what it would have looked like when it was, indeed, a "progressive working-class caterer"—same wood and cast-iron booths and black-and-white tile floor, but the suits would have been shabbier. *94 Farringdon Rd., EC1, tel. 020/7837–5093. Tube: Farringdon. Walk right on Cowcross St., turn right on Farringdon Rd. Closed Sun.–Fri. 3–6:30, no lunch Sat.*

UNDER £20 • The Eagle. Originator of the "good food in a pub" genre, The Eagle is one of the top gastro-pubs and has the requisite open kitchen, young city folk, and changing menu of Mediterranean edibles. Spanish ham with bruschetta and tomato salad, and home-salted cod with mash are both good bets. They also serve a tasty homemade soup du jour, almost a meal in itself. *159 Farringdon Rd., EC1, tel. 020/7837–1353. Tube: Farringdon. Walk right on Cowcross St., turn right on Farringdon Rd. Closed weekdays 2:30–6:30, Sat. 3:30–6:30, all day Sun.*

COVENT GARDEN

There's no "garden" at Covent Garden, and the lively open-air market that once captivated visitors (and fed Londoners) is long, long gone. Alas, this is now the land of pricey crafts shops and a boggling array of almost identical yuppie bistros. Your strategy? Check out the places below or get your food from produce and snack sellers on Endell or Neal streets, then picnic on the Covent Garden piazza—filled with street performers vying for your pocket change on weekday evenings and Sunday afternoons. Otherwise, Neal's Yard (a tiny courtyard sandwiched between Monmouth and Endell streets, just north of Shorts Gardens) is a cool, peace-love-and-granola kind of place, packed with juice bars, natural-foods shops, and idyllic outdoor tables.

UNDER £5 • Food for Thought. Food for Thought serves large portions of fresh, inventive vegetarian and vegan food like roast pepper and almond soup and pasta with mushrooms and sage. Everything on the menu is under £3.50—which explains why this snug basement café is never empty. They charge no extra for corkage (BYOB) and it's a no-smoking joint. *31 Neal St., WC2, tel. 020/7836–9072. Tube: Covent Garden. Walk right on Long Acre, turn left on Neal St. Cash only. No dinner on Sun.*

The Rock & Sole Plaice. This family-run diner—a cross between your basic fish-and-chips bar and a pretheater bistro—has no aspirations to be anything other than traditionally British, with options like cod and chips and chicken mushroom pie. Expect small crowds after the pubs close. *47 Endell St., WC2, tel. 020/7836–3785. Tube: Covent Garden. Walk right on Long Acre, turn left on Endell St. Cash only.*

UNDER £10 • Belgo Centraal. Step onto the industrial elevator and descend into deep, deep trendiness. Don't ask why the waiters are dressed like Trappist monks in this Belgian restaurant—it's just one of those things, much like the exposed brick arches, brushed copper walls, and stylish furniture. Belgo's specialty is mussels, prepared in a variety of ways on platters (£9) or in pots (£11). At lunchtime try their wild-boar sausage with mash and a beer. Weekdays, come early for dinner and play Beat the Clock: order one of three set meals (chicken, sausages, or mussels and a beer) and pay a price corresponding to the time you order—if it's 6:10 PM, you pay £6.10. Wash it down with a selection from their 101 Belgian beers. *50 Earlham St., WC2, tel. 020/7813–2233. Tube: Covent Garden. Cross Long Acre to Neal St., turn left on Earlham St. Closed 3–5:30.*

Calabash. Re-creating Kenya in a London basement isn't easy, but this excellent African restaurant does the job with bright woven tablecloths, colorful paintings, and lots of leafy plants. Go for *yassa* (onion stew with pepper and lemon juice), veggie or lamb couscous, or hearty groundnut (peanut) stew. *38 King St., Africa Centre, WC2, tel. 020/7836–1976. Tube: Covent Garden. Walk south on James St., turn right on King St. Cash only. Closed weekdays 3–6, no lunch Sat., closed Sun.*

Cranks. The Covent Garden outpost of this no-meat-allowed chain trumpets itself as "the largest vegetarian restaurant in Europe." The menu changes weekly and usually includes a vegan soup and enterprising but occasionally disappointing entrées. Never less than heavenly are the desserts (£1–£3). If you're looking to conserve cash, get your grub from the self-service counter upstairs. *1 The Market, WC2, tel. 020/7379–6508. Tube: Covent Garden. Head right and walk 1 block to the extreme right-hand corner of the old market buildings. Cash only.*

Mars. Mars is definitely on a planet of its own: it's got funky blue and orange walls, broken-china mosaics, and strangely named, vaguely French food. The ever-changing menu features specialty soups and an entrée list that always has some interesting veggie options as well as meat and fish. *59 Endell St., WC2, tel. 020/7240–8077. Tube: Covent Garden. Walk right on Long Acre, turn left on Endell St. Cash only. No lunch Mon., closed Sun.*

Navajo Joe's. Although this spot unabashedly caters to tourists, you could do a lot worse in some of Covent Garden's overhyped (and priced) eateries. The decor's a bit "done before," with lots of bare brick walls and metal, but the lovely long bar invites you to sip margaritas among a crowd of suited twentysomethings. The innovative appetizers and main courses pack a spicy punch, but the real treat here is the white chocolate cheesecake with raspberry coulis (not very Mexican, but delectable nonetheless). *34 King St., WC2, tel. 020/7240 4008. Tube: Covent Garden. Walk west on Long Acre, left on Garrick St., then left on King St. Closed Sun.*

Neal's Yard Dining Room. Let the drifting sounds of mellow world-beat music lead you upstairs from Neal's Yard to this "world food" café. On the changing menu you'll find a choice of light meals (soup, mixed salad, Indian thali, oat pancake) for £5 and larger plates such as groundnut stew, Turkish *meze,* more thali, and a Mexican platter for £7. After 3 PM, £2.45 buys you an afternoon special of tea and a cake. *14 Neal's Yard, WC2, tel. 020/7379–0298. Tube: Covent Garden. Walk right on Long Acre, turn* *left on Neal St., left on Shorts Gardens, right on Neal's Yard, and look for the stairway on the right. Cash only. Closed Sun. BYOB.*

Plummers. The simple yet elegant decor (cream walls and simply framed pictures), fast and efficient service, and great food are only surpassed by Plummers' fantastic location; smack in the heart of it, just off Covent Garden piazza. If your stomach's up for it, mix and match items from the "United Nations" menu. You could have apple and Stilton soup followed by Thai crab cakes or pimento roulade with feta cheese followed by lamb with rosemary and Madeira. With either of these you'd end up with change out of a £10 note. *33 King St., WC2 tel. 020/7240–2534. Tube: Covent Garden. Walk west on Long Acre, left on Garrick St., left on King St. Closed Mon.–Sat. 2:30–5:30, Sun. 2:30–6.*

Texas Embassy Cantina. This big Texan-owned eating house is a safe bet if your craving for a burrito won't go away. The best bets are the combo plates that are filling enough for you to forgo the starters. The honky-tonk style bar upstairs can also be a good laugh at times. *1 Cockspur St., SW1, tel. 020/7925–0077. Tube: Leicester Sq. Walk south down Charing Cross Rd., turn right onto Trafalgar Sq. and walk past the National Gallery.*

SPLURGE • Rules. Come, escape from the 20th century. Almost 200 years old, this gorgeous London institution has welcomed everyone from Dickens to Charlie Chaplin to the Prince of Wales. The menu is historic and good, even if some food critics feel it's "theme-parky"; try the noted steak and kidney and mushroom pudding, and finish with homemade whiskey-and-ginger ice cream. Happily, the decor is even more delicious: with plush red banquettes and lacquered Regency-yellow walls (which are festively adorned with 19th-century oil paintings and dozens of framed engravings), the ground floor salon remains unchallenged in London for its splendid period atmosphere (note there are three floors to this place). If you're an ambience freak and want to have one truly grand London splurge, do it here. Of course, reservations are essential and this is jacket-and-tie territory. Dinners range around £40–£50. *35 Maiden La., WC2, tel. 020/7836–5314. Tube: Covent Garden. Turn right to head south through Covent Garden's Piazza area, passing Henrietta St. to Maiden La.*

EARL'S COURT AND SOUTH KENSINGTON

Although the situation has improved of late, Earl's Court is known for loads of cut-rate kebab shops, greasy chippies, and generic sandwich shops—no wonder many refer to this neighborhood as a "culinary black hole." If you're really hankering for fish-and-chips, grease and all, get thee to ancient **Maxwell's** (263 Old Brompton Rd., SW5, tel. 020/7373–5130). If you're at all concerned about healthy eating, your choices are better in neighboring South Kensington, particularly in the blocks surrounding the museums and South Kensington tube station, and along **Pelham Street** and **Brompton Road.**

UNDER £5 • Admiral Cordington. You'll find an upscale crowd chatting on the outdoor patio of this handsome Victorian relic; note the gas lamps and antique mirrors. Come for a satisfying pub-grub lunch. *17 Mossop St., off Draycott Ave., SW3, tel. 020/7581–0005. Tube: South Kensington. From Fulham Rd., walk to Sloane Ave., turn left after a block, take the next right, then head for the second street on the left—better ask some passersby! Cash only.*

Al Rawshi. Quick and greasy satisfaction is guaranteed from the chicken or lamb shwarma and falafel at this tiny Lebanese snack bar. Wash it all down with a variety of fresh fruit juices. *3 Kenway Rd., SW5, no phone. Tube: Earl's Court. Walk north on Earl's Court Rd., turn right on Kenway Rd. Cash only.*

Benjy's. The deal at divey Benjy's is breakfast: it's big, it's cheap, and it's served all day. If you're ravenous, you'll covet the Builder's Breakfast, a freight-load of baked beans, two sausages, two pieces of toast, a heap of fries, bacon, one egg, and as much tea and coffee as you can put down. Would you like extra sausage with that? *157 Earl's Court Rd., SW5, tel. 020/7373–0245. Tube: Earl's Court. Cash only.*

Francofill. In South Kensington it sometimes becomes a bit hard to escape the pretentious crowds—thank goodness for Francofill. OK, so the furnishings are straight from IKEA, but the happy staff and the low-frills and low-cost menu more than compensate. A mixture of appetizers includes toasted goat cheese or garlic mushrooms (£3.50); main courses can involve a slab of meat on fresh-baked bread, fries or salad, and one of four sauces. *1 Old Brompton Rd, SW7, tel. 020/7584–0087 Tube: South Kensington. Walk west on Old Brompton Rd.*

Troubadour. This is the place where you'll find your frustrated latter-day Keats or Shelley. The wooden floors, low lights, and collection of old mandolins, drums, and fiddles help create this place's moody and timeless feel. The food is good, but the coffee is better. You can get a reasonable omelet, pasta, or filling soup for under £5, but you'll have as much fun sipping coffee while you imagine what it might have

BEYOND MICKEY D'S

If the thought of dining in a chain restaurant makes you break out in a rash, relax—we're not suggesting McDonald's. The places listed below all have great food, decent prices, attractive decor, and, hey, they just happen to have more than one location. Maybe there's one near you.

AROMA. This bright, vibrant string of cafés was recently voted best in a Time Out *reader poll. Its specialty coffee is a hit, perhaps because it's served with a little piece of chocolate. Pastries and snacks are £1–£3. 273 Regent St., W1, tel. 020/7495–4911; 120 Charing Cross Rd., WC2, tel. 020/7240–4030; 1B Dean St., W1, tel. 020/7287–1633; 381 Oxford St., W1, tel. 020/7495–6945; 168 Piccadilly, W1, tel. 020/7495–6995; 36A St. Martin's La., WC2, tel. 020/7836–5110.*

DÔME. One of the best deals in town is the £5 three-course meal available all day long at this string of hip, French bistros. The selection changes daily, with possibilities like ginger-carrot soup, onion tart, liver pâté, roast chicken, and many delicious desserts. 32 Long Acre, Covent Garden, WC2, tel. 020/7379–8650; 35A Kensington High St., W8, tel. 020/7937–6655; 289–291 Regent St., W1, tel. 020/7636–7006; 354 King's Rd., SW3, tel. 020/7352–2828; 57–59 Charterhouse St., EC1, tel. 020/7336–6484.

NANDO'S. This South African chain looks like a fast-food joint, but the chicken, basted in either lemon and herb or mild and hot chili, is cooked to order and is served on proper plates. Half a chicken and fries costs £5.20. The most central locations are at 57 Chalk Farm Rd., NW1, tel. 020/7424–9040 and 204 Earl's Court Rd., SW5, tel. 020/7259–2544.

PIZZA EXPRESS. For a pizza chain, this place ain't bad: pies arrive at your table hot and tasty, and the prices (£3.40 and up) are pretty cheap. Some of the branches even host live jazz. Approximately 25 locations throughout London.

PRET A MANGER. For quick sandwiches (£1.20–£2.50), salads (£1.50–£2.80), and even sushi (£5–£5.85), Pret A Manger can't be beat. Everything is prepared hourly on the premises, with the emphasis on fresh, natural ingredients (no grease, no preservatives). There are approximately 40 locations.

THE STOCKPOT. Count on these old-time café-diners for inexpensive English and Continental fare like soups (80p), omelets (£2.50), and casseroles (£2.75). 6 Basil St., SW3, tel. 020/7589–8627; 273 King's Rd., SW3, tel. 020/7823–3175; 40 Panton St., SW1, tel. 020/7839–5142; 18 Old Compton St., W1, tel. 020/7287–1066; 50 James St., W1, tel. 020/7486–1086.

been like when Jagger, Dylan, and Clapton used to pop in for a jam. *265 Old Brompton Rd., SW5, tel. 020/7370–1434. Tube: Earl's Court. Walk south on Warwick Rd., left on Old Brompton Rd.*

UNDER £10 • Spago. This enthusiastically Italian restaurant has a delightful array of pasta dishes, including penne with Gorgonzola and spinach, and baked rigatoni. *6 Glendower Pl., SW7, tel. 020/ 7225–2407. Tube: South Kensington. Walk west on Old Brompton Rd., turn right on Glendower Pl.*

Thai Taste. Thai Taste is an elegant oasis in a wasteland of fluorescent-lit chip shops. On the menu you'll find expertly prepared traditional dishes like pad thai, red curry chicken, and beef with black beans, ginger, and mushrooms. Note: the entrance is easy to miss, so keep a sharp eye out. *130 Cromwell Rd., SW7, tel. 020/7373–1647. Tube: Gloucester Rd. Walk north on Gloucester Rd., turn left on Cromwell Rd. Closed 2:30–6.*

THE EAST END

Spitalfields, in the heart of the East End, was once the center of London's Jewish community, but as the Jews left, so did **Bloom's,** a much beloved kosher restaurant that recently moved north to Golders Green (130 Golders Green Rd., NW11, tel. 020/8450–1338). The area is now better known for Asian shops, restaurants, and markets; **Brick Lane** and surrounding streets are where you'll find the best choices. There are a number of reasonable sandwich shops and cafés in the Docklands, but it's very much a lunch venue, as the place empties after 6.

UNDER £5 • Brick Lane Beigal Bake. This East End institution churns out freshly baked bagels (10p each) 24 hours a day. Add smoked salmon and cream cheese to your bagel for 90p, or go for succulent slices of salted beef and mustard (£1.70). This place gets packed with clubbers coming down after a long night, and on Sunday during the Brick Lane market. On New Year's Day the queue stretches down the block. *159 Brick La., E1, tel. 020/7729–0616. Tube: Aldgate East. Walk east on Whitechapel High St., turn left on Osborn St. (which becomes Brick La.). Cash only.*

Clifton. It's one of the more stylish Pakistani eateries on Brick Lane, but still cheaper than most; chicken vindaloo or lamb *phal* (hotter than hell) will set you back £3.30. The late open hours attract a zany clientele. *126 Brick La., E1, tel. 020/7377–9402. Tube: Aldgate East. Walk east on Whitechapel High St., turn left on Osborn St. (which becomes Brick La.).*

Dino's Grill. Who knew Formica came in so many faux wood grains? City suits and folks from nearby garment factories come for surprisingly tasty lasagna, cod or plaice and big, fat chips, and spaghetti Dino. Go ahead and have a Budvar with your lunch—you're on vacation, right? The same food is served downstairs in a more stylish setting, but you'll miss Dino's singing and banter. *76 Commercial St., E1, tel. 020/7247–6097. Tube: Aldgate East. Walk north on Commercial St. No dinner, closed Sat.*

Lahore Kebab House. Lahore serves excellent tandoori dishes in purely functional surroundings. There's a bare sink to wash your hands in before eating, and the staff makes no bones about hurrying customers in and out. Well-spiced lamb *karahi* (a pound of seared meat served on a sizzling plate) costs £5, vegetable curry £3, and lamb shish kebabs are a steal at 50p a skewer. *2 Umberston St., E1, tel. 020/7488–2551. Tube: Aldgate East. Walk northeast on Whitechapel High St., turn right on Commercial Rd., right on Umberston St.*

Le Taj. Standard curries aside, this little place has a great range of Bangladeshi specialties. In contrast to the slightly grim surroundings, the decor here is bright and fresh, although the service can be a little aloof. If you're adventurous, try the tangy pumpkin and prawn concoction called *lau gootha.* It's a touch outside the £5 range at £6.30, but definitely worth the extra outlay. *134 Brick La., E1, tel. 020/7247–4210. Tube: Aldgate East. Walk east on Aldgate High St. (which turns into Whitechapel Rd.), left onto Brick La. Closed Mon.–Sat. 2–5:30 and all day Sun.*

Sweet and Spicy. Bizarre is about the only way to describe the interior of this Pakistani restaurant. The Formica tables, metal beakers of water, and strip lights on high Victorian ceilings seem standard enough. But the 1950s pictures of the Lahore intercollege wrestling championship and lurid posters of strapping young lads stripping down to their underwear are a little harder to understand. Nevertheless, the cheap food's what you came for, not a history lesson in postwar Pakistani wrestling photography. Try the chicken liver curry (£3) or the excellent thick dahl (£2.20). *40 Brick La., E1, tel. 020/7247–1081. Tube: Aldgate East. Walk east on Aldgate High St. (which turns into Whitechapel Rd.), left onto Brick La.*

UNDER £10 • Mesón Los Barriles. Smack in the middle of Spitalfields Market, this busy spot serves up some excellent fresh seafood dishes, most of which are prepared with a Spanish touch. Try the langoustines, poached in oil and garlic (£8.50) or the clams in wine and garlic (£6). As you're bound to have trouble reading the bill, it is worthwhile pointing out that service is included in the total. *8A Lamb St., E1, tel. 020/7375–3136. Tube: Liverpool St. Walk north on Bishops Gate, right onto Lamb St. No dinner Sun., closed Sat.*

HAMPSTEAD AND HIGHGATE

The wealthy, genteel surroundings—Hampstead Heath is but a step away—ensure that Hampstead is littered with overpriced bistros and trendy cafés. Don't restrict yourself to **Hampstead High Street**; explore the side streets for tearooms and a smattering of mellow cafés. On busy **Heath Street,** fill up on delicious Hungarian poppy-seed cake at **Louis Patisserie** (32 Heath St., NW3, tel. 020/7435–9908). Highgate is much of the same, with little beyond the usual faux French or Italian chain cafés on Highgate High Street. If **Café Vert** (*see below*) is closed, you'd be better off catching a bus to Hampstead, or even Camden Town.

UNDER £5 • Café Vert. Tucked away in a community center inside a converted church, Café Vert serves up delicious vegetarian food. Try a huge portion of spinach and mushroom lasagna served with a tasty salad, quiche and salad, or a big veggie breakfast. *Jackson's Lane Centre, 269A Archway Rd., N6, tel. 020/8348–7666. Tube: Highgate. From the station turn left onto Archway, walk 100 m (328 ft), the café is on your right. Cash only. No dinner Sat.–Mon.*

Viva Zapata. The £5 all-you-can-eat Tex-Mex buffet is a long trek from the Hampstead tube, but there's a decent selection of cocktails and food—mussels, shrimp, fish, and vegetables, in addition to the usual tacos, chili, rice, sour cream, and guacamole. The staff can be offhand, but they fit in with the laid-back atmosphere. *7 Pond St., NW3, tel. 020/7431–9134. Tube: Hampstead. Walk southeast on Hampstead High St., turn left on Pond St. Cash only.*

UNDER £10 • Café des Arts. This place has an excellent prix-fixe lunch, featuring a choice of three appetizers (like soup, pan-fried whitebait with garlic mayonnaise, and vegetable omelet), three entrées (cod with spinach and garlic mash, steak and chips, and vegetable couscous), and two desserts (bread and butter pudding or sorbet) for £7.95. The decor's pleasant and service is snappy. *82 Hampstead High St., NW3, tel. 020/7435–3608. Tube: Hampstead. Walk south on Hampstead High St. Closed Mon.–Sat. 4–5:30 and all day Sun.*

Jin Kichi. This rather scruffy and occasionally hot place remains one of the best places in London for the Japanese specialty *yakimono* (literally, "fried things"). You can keep your costs down by ordering a set combination for £7.10 or £8.90—seven skewers of bite-size bliss, such as shiitake, prawns, or quail eggs and various chicken parts. Try the sashimi as well. *78 Heath St., NW3, tel. 020/7794–6158. Tube: Hampstead. Walk north on Heath St. No dinner Tues. and Sun., no lunch Mon. and Wed.–Fri.*

Zamoyski's. Start off your meal by sampling some of the 30 different vodkas (£1.60 a shot)—those with a sweet tooth should try the honey vodka. Then get to work on the Polish *mezze,* nine dishes for a bargain £5.50, or the amazing *pieczeń po husarsku* (marinated lamb roasted with wild mushroom sauce). Portions are on the small side, but the food is rich and perfectly seasoned. This is a very popular spot, so phone ahead on weekend nights or expect a long wait. *85 Fleet Rd., NW3, tel. 020/7794–4792. Tube: Hampstead. Walk south on Hampstead High St., turn left on Pond St., veer right on Fleet Rd. No lunch Mon.–Sat.*

KENSINGTON AND KNIGHTSBRIDGE

Kensington and Knightsbridge are posh neighborhoods, full of lavish designer boutiques and "my god, you're joking"–priced restaurants. Best bets for cheap noshes in Knightsbridge are the pubs and sandwich shops on **Beauchamp Place** (off Brompton Road), and in Kensington, the fast-food joints scattered along **Kensington High Street.** Just for thrills, you might also want to stalk the food halls at Harrods and Harvey Nichols, the area's two tony department stores (*see* Markets and Specialty Stores, *below*).

UNDER £5 • Cuba. Best known to the locals for its wicked cocktails, this prototype of London's Cuban craze makes up for its hackneyed decor with a generous range of tapas. Main courses are roughly divided into tortillas, salads, grills, and Cuban specialties. If you don't want the cocktails and food to go straight to your waist line, pop downstairs for a spot of energetic salsa. *11–13 Kensington High St., W8, tel. 020/7938–4137. Tube: High St. Kensington. Walk east on Kensington High St.*

La Barraca. The menu at this mellow, attractive place features tons of tapas like calamari with white beans, garlic chicken, and steamed mussels. Weekends, La Barraca is popular with young Londoners as a late-night watering hole. *215 Kensington Church St., W8, tel. 020/7229–9359. Tube: Notting Hill Gate. Walk east on Notting Hill Gate, turn right on Kensington Church St.*

UNDER £10 • Caravela. This Portuguese basement bistro, done up like an old fishing village, is a great place if you can stomach the outrageous £1.25 cover charge and mandatory 12.5% service charge. Your choices include traditional dishes like *sardinhas assadas* (charcoal-grilled sardines), lulas á *marinheira* (squid simmered in tomatoes and onions), and the ultradelicious *cataplana* (thick seafood stew served in a giant copper bowl). Most nights you'll be serenaded by Portuguese folk guitarists. *39 Beauchamp Pl., SW3, tel. 020/7584–2163. Tube: Knightsbridge. Walk southwest on Brompton Rd., turn left on Beauchamp Pl. Closed 3–7.*

Curry Inn. In a city packed with Indian restaurants vying for the title of "best," it's easy to overlook this tiny, tastefully decorated contender. The dishes here, like biryani and curries, are generous and expertly prepared, and the staff will cheerfully make suggestions or explain ingredients. *41 Earl's Court Rd., W8, tel. 020/7937–2985. Tube: High St. Kensington. Walk west on Kensington High St., turn left on Earl's Court Rd. Closed Mon.–Sat. 2:30–5:45, no lunch Sun.*

Maggie Jones. This candlelit spot serves traditional English fare amid dried flower arrangements, pine benches and pews, and agricultural artifacts. You'll spot black mackerel with gooseberries and wild boar sausages with mash on the menu. *6 Old Court Pl., Kensington Church St., W8, tel. 020/7376–0510. Tube: High St. Kensington. Walk east on Kensington High St., north on Church St., right onto Old Court Pl. Closed 2:30–6:30.*

A sign outside the Clifton reads "ALL THE SPICES OUR CHEF USES ARE APHRODISIAC." Perhaps that explains the lascivious murals.

Scandies. You may want to kneel and kiss the ground before entering this tidy eatery, because if you're hungry and you're in Knightsbridge, it's going to save your derrière. The fairly standard pan-European menu changes daily, but regular items include salad of the day, salmon fishcakes, and bangers and mash. *4 Kynance Pl., SW7, tel. 020/7589–3659. Tube: Gloucester Rd. Walk north on Gloucester Rd., turn left on Kynance Pl. Closed weekdays 2:30–5:30, no lunch weekends.*

SPLURGE • Bibendum. When it opened a decade ago, this converted Michelin showroom, adorned with Brit Art Deco stained glass and tile work, became one of London's dining showplaces and scene-arenas; today it's still a major lure. You can come here for the Conran Shop, or Oyster Bar, but most arrive to enjoy the kitchen's superlative creations. Nighttime is very pricey (£30–£50) but the £27 set-price menu at lunchtime is money very well spent. Reservations are essential. *Michelin House, 81 Fulham Rd., SW3, tel. 020/7581–5817. Tube: South Kensington. Walk east on Pelham St. and turn right onto Fulham Rd. Closed Sun.*

SOHO AND MAYFAIR

Soho, the heart of tourist London, is a happy hunting ground when it comes to restaurants, cafés, trattorias, and food stands—in fact, it's tops for just about every type of eatery imaginable. In London's small Chinatown, on **Lisle Street** (pronounced Lyle) and **Gerrard Street** between Leicester Square and Shaftesbury Avenue, you'll find the city's best Asian restaurants, as well as plenty of stores selling bulk herbs, produce, fresh fish, meats, Asian teas, and miracle cures. **Wardour Street** has an amazing array of international cuisine: Asian, American, French, Italian, you name it. **Old Compton Street** is the place to go for a traditional (though often expensive) Italian meal. Mayfair, on the other hand, is mainly a ritzy residential neighborhood, with a sprinkling of sandwich shops along **Piccadilly** and around the **Marble Arch** tube station, and fast-food stands of all types along **Oxford Street**; while you're there, stop in Selfridges (*see* Markets and Specialty Stores, *below*) to gape at its splendid food halls.

UNDER £5 • Café Emm. Unlike some of its stuffy neighbors on Frith Street, Café Emm has a vibrant air about its food and atmosphere. On the weekends you'll have to do battle with the party people who create a hum of shouted conversations over loud dance music. But don't let this put you off, as the food is just as loud and colorful. For £4.99 you can get dishes like Cajun chicken and a folded crepe with salmon and cheese, while £6.50 will get you smoked salmon salad with rice and potato mayonnaise. The waitstaff here must be the hardest working bunch in the West End. *17 Frith St., W1, tel. 020/7437–0723. Tube: Leicester Sq. Walk north on Charing Cross Rd., west onto Old Compton St., right onto Frith St. No lunch weekends, closed weekdays 3–5:30.*

Café Sofra. If you're looking to escape the fast-food frenzy of Piccadilly, duck down windy, historic Shepherd Street and start hunting for this cozy café. On the menu are Middle Eastern–type snacks and light meals, like mixed mezze or lentil casserole, plus standard sandwiches and desserts. *10 Shepherd St., W1, tel. 020/7495–3434. Tube: Green Park. Walk southwest on Piccadilly, turn right on White Horse St., left on Shepherd St. Cash only.*

Carlton Coffee House. What looks like your average sandwich bar from the outside in fact hides a quality pasta and fry-up house known only to Soho media types. If you're in for breakfast and are positively famished, you shouldn't miss the "full English fry-up" (£3.60), which comes with an alarming amount of bacon and sausage. Otherwise you can take your pick of the imaginative pastas (£4.30–£4.60). *41 Broadwick St., W1, tel. 020/7437–3808. Tube: Piccadilly Circus. Walk north on Regent St., right onto Beak St., left onto Lexington St., and left again onto Broadwick. Closed Sun.*

Centrale. No pretentiousness here, just gargantuan dishes of basic food at low prices. Meals are so big that, unless you just finished Ramadan, you're best off avoiding the appetizers and skipping dessert. A mixed clientele of down-and-out suits and students adds to the place's low-life Soho feel. Try the risotto tonno (£ 3.75) on for size. *16 Moor St.,W1, tel. 020/7437–5513. Tube: Leicester Sq. Walk north on Charing Cross Rd., then left onto Moor St. (after Shaftesbury).*

Govinda's. There's no proselytizing at this friendly Hare Krishna restaurant, just tasty vegetarian grub at rock-bottom prices. On the regular menu are basics like baked potato with cheese, spinach lasagna with salad, and a small vegetable curry. A full meal of rice, soup, two veggies, salad, and bread goes for £6. Every night from 7:30, it's all-you-can-eat for £4, and if that isn't good enough, on Sunday evening at around 4 or 5, the Krishnas serve a free—yes, free—feast. No alcohol is allowed. *9–10 Soho St., W1, tel. 020/7437–4928. Tube: Tottenham Court Rd. Walk west on Oxford St., turn left on Soho St. No lunch Sun. (open only at free food time).*

Malaysia Hall Dining Hall. It's no big secret among hungry Londoners that Malaysia Hall's student cafeteria serves excellent food at dirt-cheap prices. Fortunately, the public is welcome, and you can't do better for so little money. The set meal (£2) is rice, vegetables, and a main dish, like sweet-and-sour fish or spicy noodles. Breakfast includes tasty traditional *roti canai* (deep-fried bread with curry dipping sauce). As you can imagine, lines are long. *46 Bryanston Sq., W1, tel. 020/7723–9484. Tube: Marble Arch. Walk west on Oxford St., turn right on Great Cumberland Pl. Cash only. Closed 10–noon and 3–5.*

Mildred's. This eatery offers above-average, 100% organic veggie food, a genial staff, and a boho hipster clientele. The menu changes daily, but generally you'll find entrées like stir-fried vegetables, frittatas, or a chili bean burrito. For dessert, spoon into a bowl of yogurt, honey, and nuts. *58 Greek St., W1, tel. 020/7494–1634. Tube: Leicester Sq. Walk north on Charing Cross Rd., turn left on Shaftesbury Ave., right on Greek St. Cash only.*

The New Piccadilly. The decor in this hole-in-the-wall is so weird it's interesting: red and yellow Formica furniture, an old unfinished floor, and a curious collection of "art." It serves simple, no-frills, British–Italian food like omelets, pizzas, casseroles, steaks, and pastas. *8 Denman St., W1, tel. 020/7437–8530. Tube: Piccadilly Circus. Walk northeast on Shaftesbury Ave., turn left on Denman St. Cash only.*

New World. It's a world unto itself at this huge Chinese dim sum-o-rama with paper tablecloths, schlocky Chinese lanterns, and tacky Muzak. Choose from a variety of dumplings, noodle dishes, and steamed buns—each costs around £1.50. It's a great bargain, and if you're not stuffed to the gills for £5, you'd better have that tapeworm checked out. *1 Gerrard Pl., W1, tel. 020/7734–0677. Tube: Leicester Sq. Walk north on Charing Cross Rd., turn left on Little Newport St., and continue 1 block to the alley.*

Pollo. At this Soho institution, you can pick from an extensive menu of incredibly cheap pastas: basic spaghetti runs £3.30; with chicken, £4.65. The atmosphere is jovial, noisy, and crowded—you may have to share a table. *20 Old Compton St., W1, tel. 020/7734–5917. Tube: Leicester Sq. Walk north on Charing Cross Rd., turn left on Moor St. (which becomes Old Compton St.). Cash only.*

Poons. Once a hole-in-the-wall, now a smart restaurant, Poons offers more than just stir-fry. Try the special "wind-dried" duck with rice, hotpot (soup with stuffed bean curd), or deep-fried oysters. The staff is friendly, and they'd like you to be so, too—when the place gets busy, waiters don't ask before seating people at your table. *27 Lisle St., WC2, tel. 020/7437–4549. Tube: Leicester Sq. Walk north on Charing Cross Rd., turn left on Newport St., left on Newport Pl., right on Lisle St. Cash only.*

Star Café. Housed inside an old pub and sporting a mish-mash decor of old shop signs, a radio, and vases of fresh flowers, this café routinely draws a Soho crowd at lunchtime. The lunch menu can be a tad predictable, but the breakfast is worth getting up for early. For vegetarians the fried breakfast comes with diced roast potatoes, mushrooms, tomatoes, two eggs garnished with parsley, and fried onions with green, red, and yellow peppers. *22 Great Chapel St., W1, tel. 020/7437–8778. Tube: Tottenham Court Rd. Walk west on Oxford St., left onto Great Chapel St. Closed weekends.*

Taffgoods Sandwich Bar. Here you'll find London's cheapest noshes: bagels with lox and cream cheese cost £1, salt-beef bagels £1.70. It's possible to eat in, but most order to go. *128 Wardour St., W1, tel. 020/7437–3286. Tube: Piccadilly Circus. Walk northeast on Shaftesbury Ave., turn left on Wardour St. Cash only. Closed weekends.*

West End Kitchen. Run by the same genius who brought you the Stockpot chain (*see* Beyond Mickey D's *box*), West End Kitchen offers hearty, cheap food such as lentil soup, fish-and-chips, and omelets. Their three-course lunch special goes for £3.10 (£3.60 on weekends), and there's a similar deal for £4.90 in the evening. Gourmets may think this joint totally lacking, but less finicky folk will find its comfort and simplicity charming. *5 Panton St., SW1, tel. 020/7839–4241. Tube: Piccadilly Circus. Walk south on Haymarket, turn left on Panton St. Cash only.*

UNDER £10 • Aurora. This cozy little spot may not have a liquor license, but it has the feel of a private club—and it comes highly recommended. Sink into one of the saggy upholstered chairs while you peruse the menu, or just gaze out onto the cute courtyard garden and let the modern classical music wash over you. The innovative menu here is seasonal; look for dishes like guinea fowl on a potato pancake or borlotti bean, watercress, and roast pepper lasagna (each just under £10). Drop by for brunch on Saturday (12:30–3). *49 Lexington St., W1, tel. 020/7494–0514. Tube: Oxford Circus. Walk south on Regent St., left onto Beak St., then left onto Lexington St. Closed weekdays 11–12:30 and 4–6:30, and all day Sun.*

TIP FOR MASOCHISTS: The staff at Wong Kei's *(41–43 Wardour St., W1, tel. 020/7437–6833) is legendary for its rudeness. They ignore you, then they yell insults, and still people line up around the block. Could the noodle dishes really be worth it? Go find out.*

Bar Sol Ona. You walk through a vibrantly painted hallway and descend into the basement to enter this Spanish tapas joint. Choose from a large variety of tapas in three sizes, priced £3.50 and up. Don't miss happy hour (Mon.–Thurs. 6–10, Fri.–Sun. 6–8), with Estrellas beer for £1.20. *17 Old Compton St., W1, tel. 020/7287–9932. Tube: Leicester Sq. Walk north on Charing Cross Rd., turn left on Moor St. (which becomes Old Compton St.). No lunch.*

Gaby's Continental Bar. Gaby's menu features cuisine from all over the Continent (and other parts of the planet as well). There's schnitzel, falafel, and lamb couscous, plus tons of salads and vegetarian dishes. The restaurant itself has been newly repainted a cheery all-white. *30 Charing Cross Rd., WC2, tel. 020/7836–4233. Tube: Leicester Sq. From the station turn right and head south on Charing Cross Rd.*

Hamine. Patrons of this slick noodle shop run the gamut from homesick Japanese businessmen to local cognoscenti. And most are here for one thing: huge, steaming bowls of ramen with meat or vegetables, guaranteed to leave you stuffed. Note to the uninitiated: place your order and pay at the counter first, then take a seat. *84 Brewer St., W1, tel. 020/7287–1318. Tube: Piccadilly Circus. Walk north on Sherwood St., turn left on Brewer St. Cash only.*

Harry's Bar. The happy, happy, happy world of Harry's Bar can be confusing at first: it's a bar, yes, but by day it also serves Thai food. Then from 11 PM to 6 AM it morphs into one of Soho's only late-night nosh spots, serving full English breakfasts and the even fuller Harry's Breakfast Blowout. *19 Kingly St., W1, tel. 020/7434–0309. Tube: Piccadilly Circus. Walk north on Regent St., turn right on Beak St., left on Kingly St. Closed Sun.*

Italian Graffiti. This fun joint makes inexpensive gourmet pizzas; a large prosciutto-and-mushroom runs £5.90. Graffiti also does a good job with calzones and pasta, particularly spaghetti puttanesca, with tomatoes, olives, and onions. If it's even vaguely warm enough, sit at one of their sidewalk tables. *163–165 Wardour St., W1, tel. 020/7439–4668. Tube: Oxford Circus. Walk east on Oxford St., turn right on Wardour St. Closed weekdays 3–6 and all day Sun.*

Red. Although it may be argued that the Russian-inspired food plays second fiddle to the vodka, this colorful restaurant is still worth a visit, if only to watch the comings and goings of Soho's "in" crowd. Red has more than 50 vodkas on the books from places as distant and varied as Croatia, Iceland, and Estonia. If you don't mind breaking the budget a little, you'll find that Russian vodka tastes even better with a little ossetra caviar (£10.95 for 25 grams or £18.50 for 50 grams). *4 Greek St., W1, tel. 020/7287–4448. Tube Tottenham Court Rd. Walk north on Charing Cross Rd., left onto Manette St., right onto Greek St. No lunch, closed Sun.*

Tokyo Diner. Inside Tokyo Diner you'll find decently priced, well-prepared Japanese food, such as sushi (from £6; a box loaded with goodies is £9.50) and *donburi* (sticky rice flavored with soya, egg, onion, and the meat of your choice). The trick is finding the doorway, hidden Japanese-style behind flapping fabric (city council boors would like to see this replaced with a proper British facade). *2 Newport Pl., WC2, tel. 020/7287–8777. Tube: Leicester Sq. Walk north on Charing Cross Rd., turn left on Little Newport St., right on Newport Pl. Cash only.*

Wagamama. A Japanese word meaning "selfishness," Wagamama is the home of positive eating and the first of the trendy noodle houses in the capital. Don't let the long lines put you off; rest assured that the turnover rate of customers is high at this ramen bar. The menu features a staggering variety of noodles, including *yaki udon* (pan-fried noodles with shiitake mushrooms, eggs, prawns, and chicken) and the spicy chili chicken ramen. The menu is nearly as entertaining as the waitstaff, who are clad in Paul Smith gear. Slurping is encouraged; apparently the extra oxygen enhances the flavor. *10A Lexington St., W1, tel. 020/7292–0990. Tube: Oxford Circus. Walk south on Regent St., turn left on Beak St., right on Lexington St. Other location: 4a Streatham St., WC1, tel. 020/7323–9223. Tube: Tottenham Court Rd. From the station walk east on New Oxford St., left onto Bloomsbury St., right onto Streatham St.*

SPLURGE • Alastair Little. Don't be put off by the sparse interior—it's intentional, darling. Chef Little has made quite a name for himself with delicious Asian- and Mediterranean-influenced food, the ultimate in modern British cooking. On a given day you might tuck into sea bass with roast vegetables, basil, and olives, or lamb with rosemary gravy. Set lunches are £15 for two courses, or £25 for a decadent three. Dinner gets very pricey. *49 Frith St., W1, tel. 020/7734–5183. Tube: Tottenham Court Rd. Head down Oxford St., take a left to Soho Sq. and look for Frith St. leading off the square. Closed weekdays 3–6, no lunch Sat., closed Sun.*

SOUTH BANK AND WATERLOO

For a bit of river culture, grab a sandwich in Gabriel's Wharf and chill out in South Bank, London's answer to Paris's Left Bank. A number of expensive restaurants have sprung up along the river, but for better value you'll need to wander farther afield into the urban sprawl of Waterloo. **Lower Marsh,** behind Waterloo Station, is dotted with anonymous little cafés.

UNDER £5 • Côte à Côte. If it's rich French food you're craving, look no farther. The restaurant is a bit dark, but the food is guaranteed to satisfy both wallet and palate. Generous starters are a steal at £1.85; try the mussels in wine and garlic or the avocado, mozzarella, tomato, and basil salad. Delicious entrées like chicken marinated in chili and coconut milk served over pasta or baked eggplant stuffed with tofu and vegetables cost a mere £4.45. *74–76 Battersea Bridge Rd., SW11, tel. 020/7738–0198. Tube: Sloane Sq. From the station, take Bus 19 or 249 to Battersea Bridge Rd. Closed weekdays 3–6.*

M. Manze. Eels aren't for everyone, especially not the squeamish, but M. Manze has been serving steaming plates of them to happy, daring customers since 1892—making it the oldest remaining eel, pie, and mash shop in the world. The traditional meat pie and mash, eels and mash, and (ulp!) jellied eels are all served with a ladleful of "liquor," a spring green, parsley-based sauce. *87 Tower Bridge Rd., SE1, tel. 020/7407–2985. Tube: London Bridge. Walk southeast on St. Thomas St., turn right on Bermondsey St. (which joins Tower Bridge Rd. just before M. Manze). Cash only. No dinner, closed Sun.*

UNDER £10 • Master Super Fish. A known haunt among Waterloo Station's ever-growing army of cabbies, this comfortable place buzzes with the sound of large men discussing fares and football. To start, go for the lobster tails in garlic or the tiger prawns in batter. By now you'll be wondering why this place has the audacity to call itself "Super Fish." Once your main course arrives, you'll be wondering no longer. "I thought I ordered haddock, not whale," you'll be muttering to yourself. Yep, it's fresh, it's nicely battered, the chips are good, and the fish is huge. *191 Waterloo Rd., SE1, tel. 020/7928–6924. Tube: Waterloo. Walk north on York Rd., right onto Waterloo Rd. No lunch Mon., closed Sun.*

Waterloo Dumpling Inn. The informal nature and cheap, fast, and good food have helped make this place a handy little drop-in for the locals. Stranded somewhere behind Waterloo station, the Dumpling Inn serves up hearty portions of Chinese noodles and dumplings. Try the mixed seafood soup noodles or the boiled noodles with roast duck, both presented in charming little blue bowls (£5). Note that the namesake dumplings have a tendency to be a bit too floury. *57 Baylis Rd., SE1, tel. 020/7928–9972. Tube: Lambeth North. Walk north on Baylis Rd. Closed Sun.*

Waterloo Fire Station. This huge establishment occupies a converted fire station: the old tiles and metal supports remain, but the red engines have been replaced by a huge bar, an open kitchen, and rows of wooden tables. The Italian-Continental menu changes twice daily, and it's always good. In the restaurant, happy diners chow down on goodies like braised lamb with broccoli and butter-bean mash, or pasta with oyster mushrooms, garlic, and truffles served by a friendly staff. There's a limited bar menu (of equally tasty food) when the full restaurant is closed. Get in early on Friday, as this place is jam-packed with the TGIF crowd. *150 Waterloo Rd., SE1, tel. 020/7620–2226. Tube: Waterloo. Walk south on Waterloo Rd. Restaurant closed Mon.–Sat. 2:30–6:30, no dinner Sun.*

SPLURGE • OXO Tower Brasserie and Restaurant. How delightful it is for London finally to get a room with a view, and *such* a view. On the eighth floor of the beautifully revived OXO Tower Wharf building near the South Bank Centre is this elegant space, run by the same people who put the chic Fifth Floor at Harvey Nichols on the map, and featuring Euro food with the requisite trendy ingredients (acorn-fed black pig charcuterie with tomato and pear chutney; calves' kidneys with persillade and beetroot jus; Dover sole with sea urchin butter). The ceiling slats turn and change from white to midnight blue, but who on earth notices, with St. Paul's dazzling you across the water? Book at the Brasserie for dinners around £30; the restaurant proper is more expensive, but both share great food-with-a-view vistas. *Bankside, SE1, tel. 020/7803–3888. Tube: Blackfriars. Head over Blackfriars Bridge to the Southwark side, walk to Stamford St., and aim for the tower. Closed 3–6.*

CAFES, PATISSERIES, AND TEAS

Let's be honest: London is not Paris or Rome, and cafés don't crowd the squares and line the boulevards here. Although the Italians and French may swear by their lattes and cappuccinos and gâteaux, Brits prefer to relax over pints at the corner pub. That said, you'll find Euro- and Seattle-style cafés on the rise in London—perhaps they're just trying to keep up with the influx of caffeine-craving foreigners. At any rate, the city recently received its first Starbucks and has grown a few coffee chains of its own: you'll find branches of **Aroma** (*see* Beyond Mickey D's *box*), which makes a mean cuppa joe, just about everywhere. Of course, some may feel a London visit must have at least one grand afternoon high tea—check out the Ritz or Fortnum and Mason.

Al's Café Bar. This city café features half a dozen styles of chairs and flatware, city folk in suits, and a funky staff. Fortify yourself with a "super big breakfast," or go decadent with a muffin and custard and a serious cappuccino. Hearty soups like lobster bisque, scotch vegetable, or carrot and butter-bean come with a hefty hunk of bread—the perfect lunch on a chilly day. *11–13 Exmouth Market, EC1, tel. 020/7837–4821. Tube: Farringdon. Walk right on Cowcross St., turn right on Farringdon Rd., right on Exmouth Market. Cash only.*

Amato. Even though the hodgepodge decor won't make you want to linger that long, it's easy to get carried away and spend lots when you see what's on offer at this great spot. Focaccia sandwiches such as olive pâté are £4.75, scrumptious creamy cakes average £2.20, and top cappuccinos cost £1.30. *14 Old Compton St., W1, tel. 020/7734–5733. Tube: Leicester Sq. Walk north on Charing Cross Rd., turn left on Old Compton St. Cash only.*

Bar Italia. In Soho's primo coffee bar, ineffably cool Italian waiters serve what's generally considered one of the best cappuccinos in town, though the food is fairly average. If you're looking for quiet contemplation, head elsewhere—but if you want hip crowds, blaring MTV on a giant-screen television, funky surroundings, and 24-hour access to caffeine, then baby, this is your café. *22 Frith St., W1, tel. 020/7437–4520. Tube: Leicester Sq. Walk north on Charing Cross Rd., turn left on Old Compton St., right on Frith St. Open 24 hrs (closed some weekdays 6 AM–7 AM). Cash only.*

Bliss. Let the tricolor awning decorated with a large chicken lead you to Bliss, just south of the Angel tube station in Islington. Munch on a delicious array of baked goods such as fruit tarts, phyllo pastries, and ham or basil and tomato quiche in a brightly painted room peopled with Islingtonians in the know. Surprisingly good coffees (11 varieties) and teas round out the menu. *428 St. John St., EC1, tel. 020/7837–3720. Tube: Angel. Cash only.*

Bunjie's Folk Cellar. Opened in 1954 this is the only remaining coffee bar from London's folk-music scene, and the little basement joint still has that old-time atmosphere. More important, this period treasure is a great alternative to bustling Soho cafés, and you can linger over an espresso and vegetarian food (mega slices of pizza, £2) or cakes for as long as you like. Their beer prices are refreshingly good for the West End, and at day's end they host acoustic evenings and spoken word sessions. A blast from the past, and a real find. *27 Litchfield St., WC2, tel. 020/7240–1796. Tube: Leicester Sq. Walk north on Charing Cross Rd. and turn right onto Litchfield St. Cash only.*

Café Internet. The best 'net joint in the city, this is a spacious, friendly place that serves up freshly made food, savory pies, and generous salads (a bargain at £1.80), as well as coffees and cakes. It also has a full bar. Internet access is £3 per 30-min session. *22 Buckingham Palace Rd., SW1, tel. 020/7233–5786. Tube: Victoria. Walk out of Victoria station and turn right onto Buckingham Palace Rd. Cash only.*

Café Mezzo. One of the big hitters in the London foodie scene is Sir Terence Conran, who made his fortune with the chichi Habitat furniture stores and now runs several acclaimed restaurants in the city. Most of them are too damn upscale, leaving the Café Mezzo the only place to sample his style on a budget. Line up at the service counter and help yourself to such goodies as their splendid sausage rolls; Brie, plum tomato and oak leaf sandwiches; or pavlova with fresh berries. Their tremendous range of breads are baked daily on the premises. *100 Wardour St., W1, tel. 020/7314–4060. Tube: Leicester Sq. Head for the big Häagen-Dazs store, then take the first right turn onto Wardour St.*

Café Panini. This tiny little café is tucked away in the elegantly restored Northampton Lodge, which houses the Estorick Collection of modern Italian art. Once you've done your art gazing, duck in here, rest your craned neck, and enjoy the authentic Italian cuisine and charming service. The insalata selection makes for good value and the dishes are particularly fresh. Try the feta cheese and aubergine cakes with yogurt and mint sauce (£4.95) or the goat's cheese, tomato, and leek tart with salad (£4.75). In good weather the Panini opens onto its own pleasant garden space. *Northampton Lodge, 39a Canonbury Sq., N1, tel. 020/7704–6545. Tube: Highbury and Islington. Walk south on Upper St., left onto Canonbury La. Canonbury Sq. is at the end of Canonbury La.; the café is on the north side of the square. Closed Sun.–Mon.*

Caffè Mobile. Is there anything worse than being stuck in the middle of nowhere and hankering for a caffeine fix, only to realize you're in some instant coffee wasteland? Until recently, this might have been just about anywhere in London, but as local tastes have become more and more Continental, well-run chains and independent operations have popped up all over the place. Wherever they haven't, you'll be very thankful for the sight of one of the little Caffé Mobile vans. These nifty Italian vans, with espresso machines cleverly fitted into the back, can be found in strategic locations throughout London—and all serve fantastic coffee. *At press time Caffè Mobiles could be found at Islington High St., N1, Tube: Angel; Camden Stable Market, Chalk Farm Rd., NW1, Tube: Chalk Farm; The Courtyard, Columbia Road Market, E1, Tube: Highbury and Islington; Fenchurch Pl., Fenchurch St., EC3, Rail: Fenchurch St. Station.*

Coffee Gallery. This homely café is conveniently close to the British Museum and is a great stop for breakfast or an afternoon cream tea with two scones (a bargain at £2.90). Get here right around noon if you want to sample the homemade Italian lunch specials or get a big ciabatta-bread sandwich. The totally chocolate cakes average £2.50. *23 Museum St., WC1, tel. 020/7436–0455. Holborn Tube. Walk north on Southampton Row, turn left onto Vernon Pl., which becomes Bloomsbury Way, and turn right on Museum St. Cash only. Closed Sun.*

Coins Coffee Store. The delicious coffee and a buzzing atmosphere make Coins a great backdrop from which to watch Notting Hill life go by. Cast in the mold of New York's designer-diners, Coins is bright and spotlessly clean, with red lamps, large fans, and various art installations hanging from the ceilings. Start the day with a mean English breakfast for £6 (or if you prefer, a decent veggie version, too), or come for some of the best, hefty, golden chips in town. This would explain the slightly unpleasant chip oil smell, but that's a minor grumble. Of greater concern is the quasi-intolerable amount of smoking that goes on here. *105–107 Talbot Rd., W11, tel. 020/7221–8099. Tube: Ladbroke Grove. Walk south on Ladbroke Grove, left onto Westbourne Park Rd., right onto Powis Terr., left onto Talbot Rd.*

Crowbar. This minimal little joint serves java in paper cups but has become so popular it could break out into a franchise. In summer there's a little patch of garden where you can enjoy sandwiches (chorizo, Parma ham), savories (spinach and feta tart), and muffins. In all, relaxing, chilled out, and worth a call. *406 St. John St., EC1, tel. 020/7713–1463. Tube: Angel. Walk left out of station, cross Pentonville Rd. onto St. John St. Other location: 55 Exmouth Market, EC1, tel. 020/7833–4725. Tube: Farringdon. Walk north on Farringdon Rd., turn right onto Exmouth Market. Cash only.*

Cyberia. More than just a cybercafé, Cyberia is a way of life. There are 10 PCs with Internet access (£3 per half hour); a good range of hot and cold food like filled baguettes; a friendly staff not infected by the "cooler-than-thou" virus; and a varied and lively clientele—not all of whom come for the computers. The Cyberians are also the force behind *Cyberia* magazine (£2.20) and Channel Cyberia, the world's first free 24-hour Internet service (channel.cyberiacafe.net). *39 Whitfield St., W1, tel. 020/7209–0982, cyberia@easynet.co.uk. Tube: Goodge St. Turn left on Tottenham St., left on Whitfield St. Cash only.*

Fortnum & Mason. Upstairs at the queen's grocers, three set teas are ceremoniously offered in the St. James's Restaurant: standard Afternoon Tea (sandwiches, scone, cakes; £10.50), old-fashioned High Tea (the traditional nursery meal, adding something more robust and savory; £12.25), and Champagne Tea (£15.75). Tea is served Monday through Saturday, 3–5:20. Downstairs, at the back, is the Fountain, an old-fashioned restaurant that's as frumpy and as popular as a boarding-school matron. During the day, try the Welsh rarebit; in the evening, the no-frills fillet steak. This is just the place for a bite after the Royal Academy or Bond Street shopping. *St. James's Restaurant, 4th floor, 181 Piccadilly, W1, tel. 020/7734–8040. Tube: Green Park or Piccadilly Circus. From Green Park, walk northeast on Piccadilly. From Piccadilly Circus, walk southwest on Piccadilly. Closed Sun.*

It's hard to believe such a thing could be true, but Tokyo Diner has a "no tips accepted" policy.

The Living Room. There's no better place in Soho to chill for a few hours than this newish café, which offers comfy chairs, sofas, and stacks of old books for your lounging pleasure. Cappuccino is £1.20, and tasty sandwiches (there are also some wonderfully weird ones, including a great PBJ-and-marshmallow-fluff number) run from £3.20 to £4.30. *3 Bateman St., W1, tel. 020/7437–4827. Tube: Leicester Sq. Walk north on Charing Cross Rd., turn left on Old Compton St., right on Greek St., left on Bateman St. Cash only.*

Maison Bertaux. It's not much to look at, but this decades-old shop is one of Soho's best-loved pâtisseries. Settle at one of the Formica tables and enjoy an éclair, strawberry tart, or gooey, flaky almond croissant—all baked fresh daily on the premises. *28 Greek St., W1, tel. 020/7437–6007. Tube: Leicester Sq. Walk north on Charing Cross Rd., turn left on Old Compton St., right on Greek St. Cash only. Closed Sun. 1–3.*

Marnie's. This airy, friendly place in Notting Hill Gate is regularly packed to the hilt. Fill up on bacon and eggs and fresh coffee before an arduous day of bargain hunting. Or settle in with a slice of one of their rich, delicious cakes. *9 Portobello Rd., W10, tel. 020/7229–8352. Tube: Notting Hill Gate. Walk north on Penbridge Rd., turn left on Portobello Rd. Cash only. Closed Sun.–Mon.*

The Muffin Man. Just off Kensington's tony High Street is this snug little shop—which hasn't changed an iota since opening its doors more than 60 years ago. Regulars drop by afternoons for full tea and delicious baked goodies. Best of all, lingering is encouraged. *12 Wright's La., W8, tel. 020/7937–6652. Tube: High St. Kensington. Walk west on Kensington High St., turn left on Wright's La. Cash only. Closed Sun.*

Pâtisserie Valerie. Valerie is a cool, dark Soho café that's been around since 1926. Most recently it's become a hangout for artsy types, and it's packed day and night. For snacking, there are sandwiches, luscious desserts like éclairs, berry tarts, and white-chocolate truffle cake, and a stellar selection of handmade chocolates. *44 Old Compton St., W1, tel. 020/7437–3466. Tube: Leicester Sq. Walk north on Charing Cross Rd., turn left on Old Compton St. Other locations: 215 Brompton Rd., SW3, tel. 020/7589–4993; tube: Knightsbridge. Walk south on Brompton Rd.; 66 Portland Pl., W1, tel. 020/7631–0467; tube: Regents Park. Walk south on Park Crescent and immediately onto Portland Pl. Cash only.*

Photographers' Gallery Café. If you like to consume your coffee among a bit of art, then this is the place for you. The owners here are dedicated to the art of photography and it shows. We suggest you get your mouth around the fantastic £1 banana cake as you gaze at the vast array of photographic artwork that adorns these walls. Or sample any of the very pleasant snacks, such as mixed salad for £3.50 or a mozzarella and sun-dried tomato ciabatta for £1.50. Be aware that this place does have some rather confronting pics on the walls, so you might find yourself staring down the barrel of a gun or munching on your banana cake before 2-m-long genitals. *5 Great Newport St., WC2, tel. 020/7831–1772. Tube: Leicester Sq. Walk north on Charing Cross Rd., right onto Great Newport St.*

Primrose Pâtisserie. This Polish café is popular with locals, in part because it's far from the madding crowds on Camden High Street. Sit in the cozy dining room, or take your food away to eat at nearby Primrose Hill. Sandwiches, small salads, and cakes all go for £1.50, about 50p less if you take them out. There are also six daily hot specials (goulash, stuffed pepper, spinach pancakes, etc.) for a commendable £3.10. Cappuccino is a mere 90p. *136 Regent's Park Rd., NW1, tel. 020/7722–7848. Tube: Chalk Farm. Head south on Chalk Farm Rd., take the first right onto Adelaide Rd., then the first left onto the rail bridge, which turns into Regent's Park Rd. Cash only.*

The Ritz. The Ritz's new owners have put the once-peerless Palm Court tea back on the map, with proper, tiered, cake stands and silver pots, a harpist, and Louis XVI chaises, plus a leisurely four-hour time slot, all for £18.50. Drinking in the palatial decor—which would surely bring a tear to Marie-Antoinette's eye—is a good excuse for a glass of champagne. Reservations are taken only to 50% capacity. Note that jacket and tie are mandatory. Tea is served daily 2–6. *Piccadilly, W1, tel. 020/7493–8181. Tube: Green Park. Head to the south side of Piccadilly and walk 1 block.*

Tea House at College Farm. Prepare to step into a time warp when you head to the Tea House at College Farm. Housed in an old dairy with an original '20s interior, the tea rooms come complete with bentwood chairs and round tables laid with lacy cloths and willow-pattern china. Don't expect an extensive menu, though. This is more your tea and scones place, but they do it very well and even insist on having their clotted cream delivered weekly from Devon. Try to visit on the first Sunday of the month, as the College Farm comes alive to the sights and sounds of the fair. That's right, Punch and Judy shows, donkey rides, raffles, the whole lot. *45 Fitzalan Rd., N3, tel. 020/8349–0690. Tube: Finchley Central. Walk south on Regents Park Rd., right onto Fitzalan Rd. Only open Sun. 2:30–5:15.*

MARKETS AND SPECIALTY STORES

For excellent deals, especially on produce, you can't beat London's street markets; once you hear a barrow boy bellowing out the bargains of the day, you'll know you've arrived in Londontown. Street markets are described in detail in Chapter 7, but briefly, here are a few of the best for food. In the East End, the **Old Fruit and Vegetable Market** (Brushfields Street), held Sunday 9–3, is known for its selection of organic produce, as is **Spitalfields Market,** held Friday and Saturday. **Berwick Street Market** is one of the best-loved food fairs in London's West End. **Brixton Market** on Electric Avenue features Afro-Caribbean and Latin foods like yams, papayas, and pig trotters. In the vast **Camden Markets,** look for cheese stalls on Inverness Street and organic produce at the Stables (Chalk Farm Road).

Much more upscale, although equally frenzied, are the **food halls** in various department stores. All the big ones have 'em: **Harvey Nichols** (*see* Department Stores *in* Chapter 7); **Harrods** (*see* Kensington and Knightsbridge *in* Chapter 2); **Fortnum & Mason** (*see below*); and **Selfridges** (*see below*). With their elaborate (bordering on grotesque) displays of abundance, they're just as much tourist spectacle as they are source of sustenance.

Carluccio's. At this traditional Italian shop, mouthwatering pasta sauces and ready-to-eat dishes like pizzas, calzones, and marinated chicken are prepared fresh daily. You can also pick up the essentials to make your own affordable Italian feast: dried pasta, mushrooms, fresh veggies, cured meats, and all sorts of herbs. *28A Neal St., WC2, tel. 020/7240–1487. Tube: Covent Garden. Turn right on Long Acre, left on Neal St. Open Mon.–Thurs. 11–7, Fri. 10–7, Sat. 10–6.*

Fortnum & Mason. Wealthy Londoners have flocked to Fortnum & Mason since 1707, shopping for everything from caviar and truffles to Swiss cheese and bacon in an environment of crystal chandeliers and royal red carpets. For decades it has also held the title of "supplier to the royal household," but mum's the word on whether the queen is a cornflakes girl. For exotic splurges, this is indeed the place.

Don't leave without a peek at the tea shop. *181 Piccadilly, W1, tel. 020/7734–8040. Tube: Green Park or Piccadilly Circus. From Green Park, walk northeast on Piccadilly. From Piccadilly Circus, walk southwest on Piccadilly. Open Mon.–Sat. 9:30–6.*

Neal's Yard Wholefood Warehouse. London's original health-food emporium has all sorts of seeds, nuts, fruits, and cakes. There's also an impressive selection of British and Irish cheeses at nearby **Neal's Yard Dairy** (17 Shorts Gardens, tel. 020/7379–7646), and fresh loaves of bread at **Neal's Yard Bakery** (6 Neal's Yard, tel. 020/7836–5199). *21–23 Shorts Gardens, WC2, tel. 020/7836–5151. Tube: Covent Garden. Walk right on Long Acre, turn left on Neal St., left on Shorts Gardens. Open weekdays 9–7, Sat. 9–6:30, Sun. 11–5:30.*

Selfridges. The food hall at Selfridges is a very modern, chrome and white-tile Aladdin's cave piled with food. It's particularly strong in ethnic and international stuff, including beers, cheeses, and ready-to-eat snacks. It's also a good stop for perishable gifts, and a fine place to shop for groceries if you live nearby. *400 Oxford St., W1, tel. 020/7629–1234. Tube: Bond St. Open Mon.–Sat. 10–7 (Thurs. and Fri. until 8), Sun. noon–6.*

Steve Hatt. If you're a fish fiend then this is the place to come—even if only to admire the array of absolutely fresh creatures in scales and shells. *88 Essex Rd., N1, tel. 020/7226–3963. Tube: Angel. Walk north on Upper St., veer right on Essex Rd. Open Tues.–Sat. 7–5.*

The Tea House. This store takes the traditional British beverage—tea—and stands it on its ear. Of course you can get Earl Grey, but you can also buy funky blends like "Lovers' Tea" (flavored with passion fruit), "Campfire Tea" (flavored with cinnamon and almonds), and strawberry-kiwi tea. They also stock a hundred fancy teapots and kettles. *15A Neal St., WC2, tel. 020/7240–7539. Tube: Covent Garden. Open Mon.–Sat. 10–7, Sun. noon–6.*

Villandry. The food hall here is even larger than the one at Harrods! French pâtés, Continental cheeses, fruit tarts, biscuits, and breads galore, and if you must indulge but can't wait, there's a tearoom café and dining room that both serve exquisite lunches. Twice a month, dinners are offered, but they are among the hardest reservations to book in London. *170 Great Portland St., W1, tel. 020/7631–3131. Tube: Great Portland St. Walk south 2 blocks on left. Mon.–Sat. 7:30 AM–10:30 PM, Sun. 11–5.*

REFERENCE LISTINGS

BY CUISINE

AFRO-CARIBBEAN AND AFRICAN

under £5

Jacaranda Café *(Brixton)*

under £10

Asmara *(Brixton)*

Calabash *(Covent Garden)*

Mango Room *(Camden Town)*

AMERICAN AND TEX-MEX

under £5

Cactus *(Camden Town)*

under £10

Arkansas Café *(The City and Islington)*

Cuba *(Hampstead and Highgate)*

Navajo Joe's *(Covent Garden)*

Rodizio Rico *(Bayswater and Notting Hill Gate)*

Texas Embassy Cantina *(Covent Garden)*

Viva Zapata *(Hampstead and Highgate)*

under £20

Montana *(Chelsea)*

BRITISH

under £5

Alfredo's *(The City and Islington)*

Benjys *(Earl's Court and South Kensington)*

Chelsea Bun Diner *(Chelsea)*

Dino's Grill *(The East End)*

M. Manze *(Southbank and Waterloo)*

The New Piccadilly *(Soho and Mayfair)*

The Rock & Sole Plaice *(Covent Garden)*

West End Kitchen *(Soho and Mayfair)*

under £10

Geales *(Bayswater and Notting Hill Gate)*

Harry's Bar *(Soho and Mayfair)*

Maggie Jones *(Hampstead and Highgate)*

Master Super Fish *(Southbank and Waterloo)*

Paradise by Way of Kensal Green *(Bayswater and Notting Hill Gate)*

The Quality Chop House *(The City and Islington)*

under £20

The Cow *(Notting Hill Gate)*

The Eagle *(The City and Islington)*

The Engineer *(Camden Town)*

The Lansdowne *(Camden Town)*

Prince Bonaparte *(Notting Hill Gate)*

splurge

Alastair Little *(Soho and Mayfair)*

Bibendum *(Kensington)*

OXO Tower *(South Bank)*

Rules *(Covent Garden)*

CHINESE AND VIETNAMESE

under £5

New World *(Soho and Mayfair)*

Noodle House *(Brixton)*

Poons *(Soho and Mayfair)*

under £10

Thanh Binh *(Camden Town)*

Waterloo Dumpling Inn *(South Bank and Waterloo)*

CONTINENTAL

under £5

Café Emm *(Soho and Mayfair)*

Centrale *(Soho and Mayfair)*

Star Café *(Soho and Mayfair)*

under £10

Ambrosiana Crêperie *(Chelsea)*

Belgo Centraal *(Covent Garden)*

Côte à Côte *(South Bank and Waterloo)*

Francofill *(Earl's Court and South Kensington)*

Gaby's Continental Bar *(Soho and Mayfair)*

Goodfellas *(Bloomsbury)*

Luna *(Camden Town)*

Mars *(Covent Garden)*

Mesón Los Barriles *(East End)*

Scandies *(Kensington and Knightsbridge)*

Waterloo Fire Station *(South Bank and Waterloo)*

ECLECTIC

under £10

Aurora *(Soho and Mayfair)*

Café des Arts *(Hampstead and Highgate)*

Plummers *(Covent Garden)*

Zed *(Brixton)*

GREEK AND MIDDLE EASTERN

under £5

Al Rawshi *(Earl's Court and South Kensington)*

Café Sofra *(Soho and Mayfair)*

Costas Fish Restaurant *(Bayswater and Notting Hill Gate)*

Lahore Kebab House *(The East End)*

Manzara *(Bayswater and Notting Hill Gate)*

under £10

Afghan Kitchen *(The City and Islington)*

Agadir *(Bayswater and Notting Hill Gate)*

Daphne's *(Camden Town)*

Neal's Yard Dining Room *(Covent Garden)*

INDIAN AND BENGALI

under £5

Anwars *(Bloomsbury)*

Clifton *(The East End)*

Diwana Bhel Poori House *(Bloomsbury)*

Govinda's *(Soho and Mayfair)*

Lahore Kebab House *(The East End)*

Le Taj *(East End)*

Ravi Shankar *(The City and Islington)*

Sweet and Spicy *(East End)*

under £10

Chutney's *(Bloomsbury)*

Curry Inn *(Kensington and Knightsbridge)*

Malabar Junction *(Bloomsbury)*

Mandeer *(Bloomsbury)*

ITALIAN

under £5

Coffee Gallery *(Cafés)*

The New Piccadilly *(Soho and Mayfair)*

Pollo *(Soho and Mayfair)*

under £10

Buona Sera at the Jam *(Chelsea)*

Calzone *(Bayswater and Notting Hill Gate)*

Italian Graffiti *(Soho and Mayfair)*

La Bardigiana *(Bloomsbury)*

Spago *(Earl's Court and South Kensington)*

Troubadour *(Earl's Court and South Kensington)*

Waterloo Fire Station *(South Bank and Waterloo)*

JAPANESE

under £10

Hamine *(Soho and Mayfair)*

Jin Kichi *(Hampstead and Highgate)*

Tokyo Diner *(Soho and Mayfair)*

Wagamama *(Soho and Mayfair)*

JEWISH AND EAST EUROPEAN

under £5

The Bagel Bar *(Camden Town)*

Brick Lane Beigal Bake *(The East End)*

Taffgoods Sandwich Bar *(Soho and Mayfair)*

under £10

Bloom's *(Golders Green)*

Red *(Soho and Mayfair)*

Trojka *(Camden Town)*

Zamoyski's *(Hampstead and Highgate)*

SPANISH AND PORTUGUESE

under £5

La Barraca *(Kensington and Knightsbridge)*

under £10

Bar Sol Ona *(Soho and Mayfair)*

Caravela *(Kensington and Knightsbridge)*

THAI, MALAYSIAN, AND INDONESIAN

under £5

Malaysia Hall Dining Hall *(Soho and Mayfair)*

under £10

Harry's Bar *(Soho and Mayfair)*

Thai Taste *(Earl's Court and South Kensington)*

VEGETARIAN

under £5

Bunjie's Folk Cellar *(Cafés)*

Café Pushka *(Brixton)*

Café Vert *(Hampstead and Highgate)*

Diwana Bhel Poori House *(Bloomsbury)*

Food for Thought *(Covent Garden)*

Govinda's *(Soho and Mayfair)*

Greenhouse *(Bloomsbury)*

Mildred's *(Soho and Mayfair)*

under £10

Bah Humbug *(Brixton)*

Chutney's *(Bloomsbury)*

Cranks *(Covent Garden)*

Helter Skelter *(Brixton)*

Neal's Yard Dining Room *(Covent Garden)*

October Gallery Café *(Bloomsbury)*

The Place Below *(The City and Islington)*

SPECIAL FEATURES

ARTSY DINING

under £10

Café Panini *(Soho and Mayfair)*

Photographers' Gallery Café *(The City and Islington)*

BREAKFAST PLACES

under £5

Alfredo's *(The City and Islington)*

The Bagel Bar *(Camden Town)*

Benjy's *(Earl's Court and South Kensington)*

Brick Lane Beigal Bake *(The East End)*

Café Vert *(Hampstead and Highgate)*

Carlton Coffee House *(Soho and Mayfair)*

Chelsea Bun Diner *(Chelsea)*

Coins Coffee Store *(Cafés)*

Coffee Gallery (*Cafés*)

Food for Thought *(Covent Garden)*

Market Place *(Chelsea)*

Norman's *(Bayswater and Notting Hill Gate)*

Taffgoods Sandwich Bar *(Soho and Mayfair)*

under £10

Café Goya (Brixton)

Harry's Bar *(Soho and Mayfair)*

OUTDOOR DINING

under £5

Market Place *(Chelsea)*

Pizzeria Franco *(Brixton)*

Portobello Café *(Bayswater and Notting Hill Gate)*

under £10

Arkansas Café *(The City and Islington)*

Churchill Thai Kitchen *(Bayswater and Notting Hill Gate)*

Cranks *(Covent Garden)*

Daphne's *(Camden Town)*

Delizia *(Chelsea)*

Engineer *(Camden Town)*

Italian Graffiti *(Soho and Mayfair)*

Scandies *(Kensington and Knightsbridge)*

LATE-NIGHT DINING

under £5

Brick Lane Beigal Bake *(The East End)*

Clifton *(The East End)*

La Barraca *(Kensington and Knightsbridge)*

under £10

Bar Sol Ona *(Soho and Mayfair)*

Buona Sera at the Jam *(Chelsea)*

Caravela *(Kensington and Knightsbridge)*

Hamine *(Soho and Mayfair)*

Harry's Bar *(Soho and Mayfair)*

Pucci Pizza *(Chelsea)*

Red *(Soho and Mayfair)*

Spago *(Earl's Court and South Kensington)*

HIGH TEAS

under £10

Tea House at College Farm *(Hampstead and Highgate)*

under £20

Fortnum & Mason *(Mayfair)*

The Ritz *(Mayfair)*

5 PUBS AND BARS

UPDATED BY TIM PERRY

The English take their drink very seriously, and pubs are where Londoners go to hang out, to see and be seen, to act out the drama of life, and occasionally to drink themselves into varying degrees of oblivion. Today, London is in the middle of a full-swing pub renaissance, with more and more stylish places opening, not just in central London but in most of the city's neighborhoods. Some of these take the form of café bars, serving light meals, a good range of quality wines, and sometimes even cocktails. Two trends in particular have been getting much attention. One is the "gastro-pub"—chic places that offer the likes of salsify and truffle risotto instead of the usual ploughman's special (some of these luxe pubs are reviewed in Chapter 4, Food). The other is the late-opening club-bar where DJs spin tunes—sometimes ambient background noise, sometimes full-on rave sounds; these have become a strong rival to proper nightclubs, thanks to low or even no cover charges and fewer security hassles. A less interesting trend involves a number of Irish-theme pubs, often decorated with rural memorabilia from a bygone age. They might look interesting at first, but they're not cheap and not Irish—most of them, such as the O'Neill's chain, are owned by big breweries like Bass. Whatever your tastes, don't deny yourself the pleasure of a pub crawl. The best places are spectacular Victorian-era mini–theme parks, with etched glass, chandeliers, gleaming wood paneling, and art nouveau sculptures. Sit at a table if you want privacy; better, help prop up the bar, where no introductions are needed, and new acquaintances are quickly made. Locals congregate in vast numbers at lunch and in the evening—either right after work for a sundowner pint, or right after dinner.

Once you decide where to drink, the big decision is *what* to drink. The traditional beer of choice among Britons is **bitter,** a lightly fermented, amber-color beer that gets its bitterness from hops. Over the past two decades, however, bitters have been surpassed in popularity by lager, and small breweries, such as Shepherd Neame and Fuggles, have begun to resurface as part of a new specialty beer fad. Many of these specialty beers fall into the **real ale** category: They're served from wooden kegs (or sometimes they're "bottle-conditioned") and made without chilling, filtering, or pasteurization. Real ale is flatter than regular bitters, in which the yeast is still alive. **Stouts** from Ireland, like Guinness, Murphy's, and Beamish, are a meal in themselves and something of an acquired taste—they have a burnt flavor and look like thickened flat Coke with a frothy top. **Lagers,** most familiar to American drinkers, are light-colored and carbonated and come from all corners of the world (there's no definitive British product). Although you'll find many designer beers and popular American brands, most English pubs are still affiliated with particular breweries and are beholden to sell only beers produced by that brewery. Some of the larger chains, identified on the pub's sign, include Bass, Chef and Brewer, Courage, Samuel Smith, and Whitbread. In contrast, "free houses" can serve whatever they wish and tend to offer a more extensive selection; however, most free houses are themselves major chains (Weatherspoon's and Firkin, for example) and there are very, very few genuinely independent pubs across the capital.

Besides beers, all pubs stock a range of bottled drinks from the alcoholic lemonade family; look for brand names like Hooch and Two Dogs, which taste like fizzy soda even though their alcohol contents hover around 5%. Other junk booze to watch out for includes Schott's line of alcoholic seltzers, bottled mixed drinks like Moscow Mule (vodka, ginger ale, and lime), Ginzing (gin, ginseng, and lemon-lime soda), and even alcohol-laced sparkling water.

Two reminders: Britons drink their bitter *warm* (that is, at roughly room temperature). Even though you pay a handsome price for bottled lagers, they are rarely served cold enough to suit Americans—the city's pubs need to invest in bigger and better refrigerators. Also, if you're out for some feed, remember you have to amble over to the food bar—don't expect waiter service, except in the new breed of luxe pub.

Unless otherwise noted, all pubs listed below—as well as most pubs throughout the city—are open Monday–Saturday 11–11, Sunday noon–10:30. For late-night drinking, try wine bars (which charge exorbitant prices to subsidize their costly after-hours liquor licenses), club-bars (which charge a cover on weekends but are always less expensive than nightclubs), pubs that feature music or theater, or a small neighborhood pub that just doesn't give a damn. People also head to restaurants for after-hours drinking since some serve alcohol as late as 2 AM. Of course, the pints there are more expensive, and sometimes you must also order food. Finally, if you're a student (or not too old to pretend), most colleges have on-campus pubs for socializing between lectures. Although the atmosphere is rarely inspiring, the clientele certainly is, and you won't find cheaper alcohol unless you buy discount cans at an "off-licence" (the British equivalent of a liquor store).

BLOOMSBURY

With its myriad tourist attractions, Bloomsbury might seem a more likely locale for afternoon tea than a nighttime pub crawl. On the other hand, after blitzing the British Museum, you'll be parched. Besides, all those University of London students have to drink *somewhere.* Many choose to drink in their own college bars. **University of London Union** (Malet St., WC1, tel. 020/7580–9551) opens daily at noon and stays open "until at least 11." Unfortunately, after 7 PM you'll probably need to show a University of London ID—so go early or go elsewhere. Less rigid "security" can be found two blocks north, at **University College London Union** (25 Gordon St., WC1, tel. 020/7387–3611), which has a number of bars, though most close during the summer break.

A.K.A. If you don't feel like standing on the outrageously long line to get into the superb End Club (*see* Chapter 6, After Dark), step into this big new club-bar right next door. You'll get in free to dance and hear rather celebrated DJs spin (weekends only) house and techno, but be prepared to pay a pretty penny for cocktails that are more sloppily mixed as the night progresses. *18 W. Central St., WC1, tel. 020/7836–0110. Tube: Tottenham Court Rd. or Holborn. Open Mon. 6 PM–1 AM, Tues.–Thurs. noon–4 PM and 6 PM–3 AM, Fri. noon–3 AM, Sat. 6 PM–3 AM, Sun. 4 PM–10:30 PM.*

The Lamb. Lamb's Conduit Street is peppered with bars and cafés, but The Lamb is the best of the bunch. Bask in the sun (if applicable) at an outdoor table with the relaxed crowd of locals and students. *Lamb's Conduit St., WC1, near Guilford St., tel. 020/7405–0713. Tube: Russell Sq. Open Mon.–Sat. 11–11, Sun. noon–4 and 7–10:30.*

Museum Tavern. Before or after a trip to the British Museum why not pop directly across the street to this big, ornate Victorian pub, stuffed to the gills with etched mirrors and gilded carvings. Karl Marx quenched his thirst here while writing *Das Kapital*; today the tavern hosts a mix of scholars, tourists, and locals. *49 Great Russell St., WC1, tel. 020/7242–8987. Tube: Tottenham Court Rd.*

Old Crown. Despite its name this joint is an airy, pastel-color place with huge storefront windows; looking out at the packed traffic on the street will make you glad you've got your nose in a glass of relaxing booze. The crowd is usually young and unpretentious. *33 New Oxford St., WC1, tel. 020/7836–9121. Tube: Tottenham Court Rd. or Holborn. Open Mon.–Sat. noon–11.*

Point 101. Loud funk, soul, and jazz resound in this new club-bar on this busy block—its full-length windows face the Oxford Street and Tottenham Court Road intersection. Join a clubby well-dressed crowd in the evening or hang out in the daytime to watch the world go by over a plate or two of designer nibbles. *101 New Oxford St., WC1, tel. 020/7379–3112. Tube: Tottenham Court Rd. Open Mon.–Thurs. 11 AM–2 AM, Fri.–Sat. 11 AM–2:30 AM, Sun. 5 PM–11:30 PM.*

Princess Louise. This fine, popular pub has an over-the-top Victorian interior—glazed terra-cotta, stained and frosted glass, and a glorious painted ceiling. It's not all show, either: the food is a cut above normal pub, and there's a good selection of real ales. *208 High Holborn, WC1, tel. 020/7405–8816. Tube: Holborn. Open weekdays 11–11, Sat. noon–11.*

BRIXTON

If you had told people you were going out for a night in Brixton just a few years ago, they would have thought you were mad. Thanks to a number of clubs, the district (*see* Chapter 2) is now popular, but it still has a bit of an edge to it, which is kinda part of its charm. A night out here is considerably cheaper than in some of the more-established nightlife neighborhoods, and it's also easier to grab a late drink. The **Dog Star,** the **Junction** (*see* Clubs, *in* Chapter 6), and the **Fridge Bar** (*see* Gay and Lesbian Pubs, *below*) moonlight as clubs and stay open during the week until 2 AM; they only charge a cover on weekends.

Bartenders don't get tipped in the vast majority of ordinary pubs. If you want to show appreciation for exceptional service, buy the bartender a drink: After placing an order say, "And one for yourself." In up-market café bars and club-bars, where your change arrives on a little saucer or tray, a 10% tip is customary.

Duke of Edinburgh. The walk past a scrap yard could be more pleasant, but Duke's gigantic garden makes the trek worthwhile. In summer it's *the* place to nurse your hoppy companion. Drop by on a weekend, when the place vibrates with dynamic sounds—expect anything from folk to DJ-spun techno. *204 Ferndale Rd., SW9, tel. 020/7738–3299. Tube: Brixton. Walk south on Brixton Rd., turn right on Ferndale Rd. and at the railroad bridge continue to veer left.*

Prince Albert. Despite a refit that makes it look like a bar in the States trying to look like a bar in Britain, the Albert is the most central and busiest of the Brixton pubs. Come here to find out what raves and club events are on later, or just relax in the courtyard out back. *418 Coldharbour La., SW9, tel. 020/7274–3771. Tube: Brixton. Turn left out of station, left onto Coldharbour La.*

Sun and Doves. This airy, bright bar attracts a lively, young clientele for reasonably priced wine, cocktails, and food. Check out the art on the walls, then go relax in the cool patio. (You're right, this place is technically in the Camberwell neighborhood; a walk from Brixton entails passing through dodgy Loughborough Junction.) *61–63 Coldharbour La., SE5, tel. 020/7733–1525. Tube: Brixton and then Bus 35 or 45.*

SW9. At the end of a quiet pedestrianized street more or less opposite the tube station, this tiny bar above a restaurant packs in a trendy but friendly crowd. Join them for (mostly rum-based) cocktails and funky, cutting-edge sounds. In summer, when tables are sprawled outside, it's a great place for a late-night drink or three. *11 Dorrell Pl., SW9, tel. 020/7738–3116. Tube: Brixton. Open Sun.–Wed. 10 AM–11 PM, Thurs.–Sat. 10 AM–1 AM.*

Trinity Arms. It's only 100 yards from the bustle of Brixton's main drag, but this pub has an almost rustic air. It squats on a nice Victorian square, onto which drinkers spill out on warm summer nights. *Trinity Gardens, SW2, tel. 020/7274–4544. Tube: Brixton. Cross Brixton Rd., walk south, turn right onto Trinity Brighton Terr.*

CAMDEN TOWN

Camden's pubs reflect the trendy, boho character of the neighborhood. Unwind with a pint after haggling at the markets or strolling along the canal. Some two or three years ago, the place was buzzing with almost everyone who was anyone in the Britpop world. The place still boasts great venues (*see* Clubs *in* Chapter 6) that also act as quiet daytime boozers, but these days the pubs are far from where it's at in London—although try telling that to the young tourists who still come in droves.

Bar Hawley. Even though it's in the middle of the busy market area, the recently refurbished Hawley offers a great range of liquor, wine, and import beers in a truly relaxing setting. The food is up to gastro-pub level; the Mediterranean and traditional English dishes bear a fresh twist. *2 Castlehaven Rd., tel. 020/7267–7106. Tube: Camden Town. Walk northwest on Camden High St. and turn right on Castlehaven Rd.*

Crown & Goose. One of several clean modern pubs in the area that serves up good food. Fill up on excellent, inventive pastas and salads for around a fiver in a relaxed, cosmopolitan atmosphere. *100 Arlington Rd., off Parkway, NW1, tel. 020/7485–8008. Tube: Camden Town.*

The Good Mixer. Don't be surprised if you spot a mid-level Britpop celeb or two hanging out after a recording session at a nearby studio. There's a pool table and lots of smoke, but not much space, and it gets crammed on the weekend. *30 Inverness St., off Camden High St., NW1, tel. 020/7916–7929. Tube: Camden Town.*

Queens. There's a rural feel to this pub on the swank main drag of Primrose Hill. A mixed crowd comes here to sit in comfy environs of pastel shades and green trim with wooden floorboards. Art and mirrors take up much of the wall space. *49 Regents Park Rd., NW1, tel. 020/7586–0408. Tube: Chalk Farm.*

Quinn's. Ostensibly an Irish bar, Quinns has a relaxed cosmopolitan feel with a hint of Bourbon Street jazz, lots of strong Belgian beers and real ales, plus a good selection of Irish coffees that are the best in the area. *65 Kentish Town Rd., NW1, tel. 020/7267–8240. Tube: Camden Town. Open Mon.–Sat. 11 AM–midnight, Sun. noon–10:30.*

Spread Eagle. Since the Good Mixer has been commandeered by star seekers, this comfier pub is where many of the music business people in the area have repaired to. *141 Albert St., NW1, tel. 020/7267–1410. Tube: Camden Town. Walk west on Parkway and turn left on Albert St.*

WKD. One of Camden's trendiest club-bars, WKD has a wide range of clientele and music. Truly brave souls may want to try "Cool Runnin's" (£4), a vicious, opaque mix of rum, blue curaçao, and fruit juices—tasty, but deadly! During happy hour (weekdays 4–8) jugs of cocktails are £7.50; beers, £1.50. After 9, there's live music and a £3–£7 cover; check *Time Out* for live music listings. *18 Kentish Town Rd., NW1, tel. 020/7267–1869. Tube: Camden Town. Open Mon.–Tues. noon–2 AM, Wed.–Fri. noon–2:30 AM, Sat. noon–3 AM, Sun. noon–1 AM.*

CHELSEA AND KENSINGTON

Chelsea's resident wealthy young things love to drink almost as much as they love to shop, and you'll find tons of pubs that strike a careful balance between street hip and yuppie chic. Typically, the farther you get from King's Road, the more mellow the pub.

Ferret & Firkin. The full name is "The Ferret & Firkin in the Balloon up the Creek," and it's a trek south from King's Road. Your reward is cool indie tunes on the jukebox and an alternative crowd at the bar. Have a pint of Dogbolter (£2.15) and watch the world blur. *114 Lots Rd., SW10, tel. 020/7352–6645. Tube: Fulham Broadway. Open Mon.–Sat. noon–11, Sun. noon–10.*

Front Page. This classy, intimate pub is currently the in spot for Chelsea's in crowd. By day, it's more mellow, and perfect for lingering. The menu features delicious "new British"–style dishes (£3–£9). *35 Old Church St., just south of King's Rd., SW3, tel. 020/7352–2908. Tube: Sloane Sq.*

Man in the Moon. Let the rich Georgian splendor of this theater pub dazzle you—then join the arty crowd in the back room for a show (Tues.–Sun., £4–£8). *392 King's Rd., at Park Walk, SW3, tel. 020/7352–5075. Tube: Sloane Sq.*

Orange Brewery. Many champion the solid, clubby, Victorian-era Orange as the "best pub in London." It makes its own brews: try SW1 (a bitter) or Pimlico Porter (a dark ale) for £1.85–£2.10 per pint. Brewery tours are £2. *37 Pimlico Rd., off Lower Sloane St., SW1, tel. 020/7730–5984. Tube: Sloane Sq.*

The Scarsdale Tavern. This discreet pub—it looks more like a terraced house—takes some finding, but it's worth it if you want to get away from the chic and the bustle of Kensington. Six well-kept real ales are always on tap. *23a Edwardes Sq., W8. tel. 020/7937–1811. Tube: High St. Kensington.*

Surprise. Escape from the King's Road into this quiet and jovial local pub with pretty lanterns, traditional bar games, and outside tables. It's a music-free zone, so if it's a quiet pint you're after, this is the place. *6 Christchurch Terr., SW3, tel. 020/7349–1821. Tube: Sloane Sq.*

The Water Rat. Don't come to this standard-looking pub for the pounding music (house to opera) or outdoor tables with prime views of King's Road. Come for exotic shots (£1.30) of Absolut vodka, flavored with red-hot chili peppers, passion fruit, mint, marshmallow, and even Mars Bars. *1–3 Milman's St., at King's Rd., SW10, tel. 020/7351–4732. Tube: Sloane Sq.*

THE CITY AND SHOREDITCH

The City is mainly a daytime drinking area: When the suits leave at the end of the business day, so does the life, such as it is. Regardless, the pubs here are some of the oldest in London—once frequented by the likes of Dr. Samuel Johnson and Charles Dickens. The Shoreditch neighborhood is within easy walking distance of Old Street and even Liverpool Street tube stations. At the start of the '90s this was a rundown inner-city mess, but it has waxed up-market since then, particularly around Hoxton Square. Shoreditch is where you'll find the preclubbing crowd having a drink in designer surrounds.

Black Friar. This City pub is one of London's most amazing—it's an art nouveau–arts and crafts orgy of mosaic work, burnished wood, and gilt trim. Let the wealthy brokers from the nearby City hang out on the large outdoor terrace—you have to check out the back stone-wall room whose barrel-vault ceiling is decorated with maxims like "Industry is all" and "Wisdom is rare." *174 Queen Victoria St., EC4, tel. 020/7236–5650. Tube: Blackfriars. Open weekdays noon–11, Sat. noon–5.*

Cantaloupe. Just a short walk from—and a big contrast to—the stuffy City, this friendly, trendy bar fills up with a hip but unpretentious clientele of preclubbers and residents of increasingly young and upscale Hoxton Square. DJs take care of the background sounds. *35 Charlotte Rd., EC2, tel. 020/7613–4411. Tube: Old St. Open weeekdays 11 AM–midnight, Sat. 6 PM–midnight.*

Cittie of Yorke. Order a pint at what's reputedly the largest bar in London and retire to one of the dozen or so wooden "snugs" that line the walls. The clientele leans toward the white-collar set at lunchtime, but it's the young urban professionals who flock here after work. The Cellar Bar is cozier and quieter. *22 High Holborn, WC1, tel. 020/7242–7670. Tube: Chancery La. Open weekdays 11:30–11, Sat. noon–11.*

Counting House. With its blue and gold ceiling and ornate dome skylight, this converted bank offers beautiful space in which to sip pricey wine (from £10 a bottle). Beer, thankfully, is in line with pub standards. With few tables, you may wind up standing next to the ubiquitous City suits. *50 Cornhill, EC3, tel. 020/7283–7123. Tube: Bank. Open weekdays 11–11.*

Fox & Anchor. Big breakfasts and the early opening time mean that this otherwise ordinary pub gets a weird morning mix of workers from the neighboring meat market and clubbers who don't want to go home just yet. *115 Charterhouse St., EC1, tel. 020/7253–4838. Open weekdays 7 AM–11 PM.*

The Old King Lud. A young, friendly crowd gathers in this woodsy pub on the east end of Fleet Street. They serve 20 cask-conditioned real ales, and host frequently changing guest kegs. *78 Ludgate Circus, EC4, tel. 020/7329–8517. Tube: Blackfriars. Walk north on New Bridge St. Open weekdays 11:30–11.*

Terry Neill's Sports Bar & Brasserie. Well-established and confident about its friendly, homey feel, this joint is run by a famous ex-soccer player. Watch soccer, rugby, cricket, or racing on the TV screens and peruse the great memorabilia; keep an eye out for celebrities as many stars of British sport drop in for a casual drink. Food ranges from pub grub to a bistro fare in the downstairs brasserie. The bar often opens on weekends when there are big sporting events; phone to check. *Bath House, Holborn Viaduct, EC1, tel. 020/7329–6653. Tube: Chancery La. Open weekdays 11–11.*

Ye Olde Cheshire Cheese. One of the oldest pubs in London (rebuilt after the Great Fire of 1666), YOCC has long been a famous haunt of Fleet Street journalists. Charles Dickens and lexicographer Samuel Johnson also both drank here. Although it's an institution, you're still more likely to see suits than tourists. *Wine Office Ct., 145 Fleet St., EC4, tel. 020/7353–6170. Tube: Blackfriars. Open weekdays 11:30–11, Sat. noon–11, Sun. noon–3.*

COVENT GARDEN AND STRAND

Covent Garden may be one of the most popular hangouts in the West End, but the uniformly expensive pubs are not its strong point. This is the land of theme bars and restaurants, most of them filled with loud, boozed-up office workers out celebrating someone's promotion or birthday. Most of them are to be avoided, but there are some quirky, kitschy, and unusual places around.

American Bar (Savoy Hotel). For a touch of class try this real institution at London's most famous hotel. These people know how to mix cocktails—and a drink will set you back eight quid. It's worth it, though, and the toilets are a must-see. The traditional dress code of jacket and tie for men is still observed, rather strictly. *Strand at Savoy Ct., WC2, tel. 020/7836–4343. Tube: Charing Cross Rd. Open Mon.–Sat. 11–11, Sun. noon–2:30 PM and 7 PM–10:30 PM.*

Detroit. The decor looks like it's been borrowed from a Flintstones set rather than a Diego Rivera mural, and although Motor City connections are tenuous, Detroit is a fun place that plays decent beats and has great (but rather pricey) cocktails. The food is inventive and prices are on par with other Covent Garden bars. *35 Earlham St., WC2, tel. 020/7240–2662. Tube: Covent Garden. Open Mon.–Sat. 5 PM–midnight.*

Freud. Hidden in a cellar bar whose walls are lined with art, Freud has been attracting a fairly hip crowd for pretty potent cocktails. Come to linger and tap your fingers to the beat of jazzy tunes. *198 Shaftesbury Ave., WC2, tel. 020/7240–9933. Tube: Covent Garden or Tottenham Court Rd.*

Gordon's. Both indoor and outside, Gordon's looks like it's still in Dickensian times. This shabby, time-warp of a cellar attracts suits and street life who come to the smoky interior for a range of reasonably priced wines, ports, and sherries (they don't serve beer). It's a rarity and an undersung institution. *47 Villiers St., WC2, tel. 020/7930–1408. Tube: Embankment or Charing Cross. Open weekdays 11–11, Sat. 5–11.*

Lamb & Flag. "The oldest tavern in Covent Garden" sits in an alley just off Floral Street. With the cobblestone courtyard and the wee, fluffy lamb on the sign outside, you'd never guess people once boxed bare-knuckle upstairs, prompting the pub's nickname, "Bucket of Blood." *33 Rose St., between Long Acre and Flora St., WC2, tel. 020/7497–9504. Tube: Covent Garden.*

La Perla. A laid-back and authentic Mexican bar (in a city where things Tex and Mex are almost uniformly inauthentic), the friendly and efficient staff serves up a great selection of snacks and full meals, a wide range of Mexican beers, and a slew of tequila-based drinks (they stock more than 80 types of tequila, including Cuervo 1800 Collección at £100 a shot). *28 Maiden La., WC2, tel. 020/7240–7400. Tube: Covent Garden. Open Mon.–Sat. noon–midnight, Sun. 5–10:30.*

Maple Leaf. Probably the only West End bar serving Molson on tap (£2.70), this spacious bar is Canada's cultural ambassador in London. As such it attracts mostly sports fans and Canucks for hockey games, a wide range of beers, and decent burgers. *41 Maiden La., WC2, tel. 020/7240–2843. Tube: Covent Garden.*

EARL'S COURT AND SOUTH KENSINGTON

Earl's Court and South Kensington may be popular budget-lodging areas, but that's about it. When night falls, the streets are pretty empty—except for wandering bands of jet-lagged tourists looking for a nearby, no-hassle drink.

Blackbird. Housed in a converted bank building, this no-nonsense pub stands out as a likable oasis compared with the other places on Earl's Court main drag. The pub grub is reasonable, and they pull a good pint of Fuller's ESB (£2.15). *209 Earl's Court Rd., SW5, tel. 020/7835–1855. Tube: Earl's Court.*

Drayton Arms. This grand Victorian pub on the edge of the Earl's Court neighborhood flaunts a real fire, lanterns, and terra-cotta trims—a classic example of old-time London. On weekends, it fills up and turns up the volume for live music. *153 Old Brompton Rd., SW5, tel. 020/7997–6562. Tube: Gloucester Rd.*

Hoop and Toy. From the gaslights outside to the beef-and-ale pie on the menu, everything about the Hoop and Toy says "Edwardian!" It's a free house, with more beer to choose from than usual, and they're open for breakfast from 8 to 11 on weekdays. *34 Thurloe Pl., off Cromwell Pl., SW7, tel. 020/7589–8360. Tube: South Kensington.*

The Prince of Teck. Come here to tip cans of Victoria Bitter ("VB") with Aussie, Kiwi, and South African crowds. Authentic touches include a stuffed male kangaroo, Kevin "Bloody" Wilson on the jukebox, and toilets marked SHEILAS and BRUCES. It can get deafeningly loud at times, but an upstairs bar is quieter and more relaxed. *161 Earl's Court Rd., SW5, tel. 020/7373–3107. Tube: Earl's Court.*

THE EAST END AND DOCKLANDS

London's least-touristed and most stereotypically blue-collar quadrant is home to most local pubs, where, urban legend has it, you'll get the "are you looking at me" or thousand-yard stare greeting from regulars. Although this isn't (quite) true, we'll recommend a few spots that reflect the process of gentrification that has given a face lift to a few pockets of the East End.

Approach Tavern. This traditional pub with a stark black frontage has undergone conversion into a kind of new art–theme bar, attracting the boho loft residents and the young artists of the area. An upstairs gallery has changing exhibits. *47 Approach Rd., E2, tel. 020/8980–2321. Tube: Bethnal Green.*

Bar Risa. Owned by the people who run the Jongleurs comedy club next door, this fresh airy space is adorned with comic murals and is a decent place to linger for a while. *221 Grove Rd., E3, tel. 020/8980–7874. Tube: Mile End.*

Blind Beggar. What's basically an ordinary pub with a big rear garden in a dull, downbeat neighborhood gets its fair share of shock-tourists—they come to see where legendary East End gangster Ronnie Kray (of *The Krays* movie fame) shot George Cornell dead in 1966. Locals never seem impressed when the subject is broached—they've heard it all before. *337 Whitechapel Rd., E1, tel. 020/7247–6195. Tube: Whitechapel.*

Ferry House. If you're in the Docklands area, ride the Docklands Light Railway (DLR) a few stops for a cheery drink at this boozer near the north mouth of the Greenwich Foot Tunnel. You can expect a small, no-nonsense pub, with an agreeably dated feel. *26 Ferry St., E14, tel. 020/7987–5141. Tube: Island Gardens DLR.*

291. A magnificently restored old church now houses east London's one true drinking destination. The nave is a video art gallery, and the smaller bar has DJs spinning tunes every evening. A good but pricey restaurant serves modern takes on British food. *291 Hackney Rd., E2, tel. 020/7613–5676. Tube: Bethnal Green or Old St. Open Tues.–Thurs. noon–midnight, Fri. and Sat. noon–2 AM.*

GREENWICH

There are plenty of pubs in Greenwich, but most of them are made to look old, often carry too much kitschy nautical decor, and attract tourists who pop in for a quick thirst-quencher and then move promptly on. The neighborhood pubs listed below have authentic character and will give you a better sense of how the locals enjoy their brew.

Ashburnham Arms. Take a 10-min walk off the beaten path from the bustle of Greenwich center (or half of that time from the railway station) and you'll find this plain, satisfying local boozer on an unassuming residential street. Few if any tourists make it out here, so you'll have easy access to excellent Shepherd Neame bitters on tap, along with a good range of lager. *25 Ashburnham Grove, SE10, tel. 020/8692–2007. Rail: Greenwich. Open Mon.–Sat. noon–3 and 6–11, Sun. noon–3 and 6–9.*

Cutty Sark. Half a mile east from the famous old tea clipper (*see* Near London *in* Exploring London, Chapter 2) after which it was named, this very likable pub right on the Thames is worth the riverside walk. Have a drink in its old-fashioned interior marked by huge wooden beams, or take it outside. A mix of locals and tourists enjoy the beers and the good homemade traditional pub food. *Ballast Quay, off Lassall St., SE10, tel. 020/8858–3146. Rail: Maze Hill.*

Gipsy Moth. Probably the pick of the pubs in the center of Greenwich, the Gipsy Moth carries on with the area's nautical theme (it's named after the tiny boat in which Sir Francis Chichester sailed around the world); a youngish crowd flocks here to drink and chat. *60 Greenwich Church St., SE10, tel. 020/8858–0786. Rail: Greenwich.*

Trafalgar Tavern. This huge elegant pub regularly picks up awards from the capital's media, which makes it a busy joint. But don't let that put you off: it's rich in atmosphere, promotes jazz sessions, and has excellent food. *Park Row, SE10, tel. 020/8858–2437. Rail: Greenwich.*

HAMPSTEAD

Upmarket Hampstead holds some of the most atmospheric old-world pubs in the city. Main-street bars are crammed with shoppers, but some of the outlying hostelries are perfect for a pint after a walk on Hampstead Heath.

Bar Room Bar. A hopelessly trendy haunt where the art and sculpture on display is for sale, Bar Room Bar attracts some of the richer young denizens of the district (and they *are* rich!). The rear garden is a pleasant place in the summer. *48 Rosslyn Hill, NW3, tel. 020/7435–0808. Tube: Belsize Park or Hampstead.*

Freemasons Arms. On the lower end of Hampstead Heath, this huge pub (with a massive terrace and garden) manages to retain a cozy air thanks to partitions and the great big bench seats and tables. Take a look downstairs at the skittles alley—one of the few remaining reminders of what was once a popular bar game throughout London. *32 Downshire Hill, NW3, tel. 020/7433–6811. Tube: Hampstead.*

Hollybush. Up a steep hill from the tube station in a hard-to-find cul-de-sac, this delightful pub is a real "find." With tiny rooms, wooden boards and furniture, gas lamps, and all-round coziness, this is as close as you can get to reliving Dickensian times. *22 Holly Mount, NW3, tel. 020/7435–2892. Tube: Hampstead. Open weekdays noon–2:30 and 5:30–11, Sat. noon–11, Sun. noon–10:30.*

King William IV. Central Hampstead's swanky dress stores coexist with King William's four separate drinking areas (some corners of which are candlelit), all of which seem dominated by long-standing regulars, many of them gay. It's a friendly place that's always hopping, and there's a good selection of bottled lagers and wine. *75 Hampstead High St., NW3, tel. 020/7435–5747. Tube: Hampstead.*

Spaniard's Inn. Formerly the regular boozing call of famed highwayman Dick Turpin, this oak-panel pub is as good an excuse as any for walking on Hampstead Heath. A big hearth fire warms you up in the winter, and in summer there's a sizable beer garden in which to stretch the limbs. *Spaniard's La., NW3, tel. 020/8731–6571. Tube: Hampstead, then Bus 210.*

ISLINGTON

Upper Street, running for more than a mile between the Angel and the Highbury and Islington tube stations, is awash with designer bars, revamped pubs, flashy restaurants, and anything else that can tempt the young local residents to part with their money. The area has become so popular that a second drag along Essex Road (a sleazy downtrodden place as recently as the early '90s) now boasts some of the coolest designer bars in the city.

Compton Arms. Situated on a quiet alley, the Compton feels like a country pub, yet it's a two-minute walk from all the traffic chaos around Highbury and Islington tube. It boasts a range of well-kept beers, cheap homemade food (sausages and mash, pie, and chips) for around £4 and has a very mixed bunch of regulars. A cathartic experience—if you want to get out of the crowds quickly. *4 Compton Ave., N1, tel. 020/7359–6883. Tube: Highbury and Islington. Walk south on Upper St., turn left on Canonbury La. and left on Compton Ave.*

Filthy McNasty's. Don't think Filthy's is another Irish theme bar. It preceded the flood of fake bars and has a genuine arty–bohemian–heavy-drinking feel. Big plates of country-style food cost between £4 and £7, and two evenings a week there's the Vox 'n' Roll nights with spoken word interspersed with musical interludes. They also manage to cram some indie and Irish bands into the smoky back room on weekends; cover charges are very rare. *68 Amwell St., EC1, tel. 020/7837–6067. Tube: Angel.*

Lark In The Park. Another Irish bar that's free from chain affiliations, the Lark has become known for its brand of left-field poetry, acoustic music, and general arty entertainment. Don't worry about the hulking figure in a long overcoat who never moves from his hunched-up position by the bar—he's a statue. *60 Copenhagen St., N1, tel. 020/7837–3784. Tube: Angel. Open Mon.–Thurs. 11–11, Fri. and Sat. 11 AM–2 AM, Sun. noon–10:30.*

Medicine Bar. In essence it's just a revamped pub with boho decor, but it's probably the best place along the hectic Upper Street drag of bars and cafés. Expect a trendy local crowd, loud music, and a good choice of beers. Arrive early on the weekend if you want to get in. Due to its popularity, Friday and Saturday evenings are members-only, but you can usually get enrolled for free during the week. *181 Upper St., N1, tel. 020/7704–9536. Tube: Highbury and Islington. Open Mon.–Thurs. 5 PM–midnight, Fri. 7 PM–1 AM, Sat. 2 PM–1 AM, Sun. 2–10:30.*

The Purple Turtle. More than 130 beers from around the world are served up in this purple heaven. Try a bottle of Samiclaus (£4.50), which is in the *Guinness Book of Records* as the strongest ale on the planet. One barman warns that "it tastes disgusting, like treacle, and few people can stand up after two of them." A fun, funky crowd and a well-stocked CD jukebox make it all the better. *108 Essex Rd., off Upper St., N1, tel. 020/7704–9020. Tube: Angel. Open daily noon–11.*

NOTTING HILL GATE

If you want to avoid the tourist crowd in Bayswater, wander just a little way west to style-conscious Notting Hill Gate, where London's fashionable crowd dines in ever-so-trendy restaurants before winding things up with a refined pint.

Elbow Room. At last! A chic, postindustrial pool hall that's miles away from the smoky, macho image of the country's snooker clubs. The seven full-size American tables are rented by the hour (generally £6–

£9, depending on the time of day). While you're waiting for your turn, try your luck at the pinball tables or join the cool crowd in sampling any of a range of imported premium lagers. *103 Westbourne Grove, W2, tel. 020/7221–5211. Tube: Notting Hill Gate or Bayswater. Open Mon.–Sat. noon–11, Sun. noon–10:30.*

The Market Bar. Weird, drippy candles and heavy velvet curtains give this very busy Notting Hill locale an almost clubby feel. A mix of urban trendies, rastas, trustafarians, and punks haunt the bar, which has a selection of cocktails in addition to your basic beer. *240A Portobello Rd., at Lancaster Rd., W11, tel. 020/7229–6472. Tube: Ladbroke Grove. Open Mon.–Thurs. 11–11, Fri.–Sat. 11–midnight, Sun. noon–10:30.*

Pharmacy. Designed by the semicontroversial, youngish British artist, Damian Hirst, this restaurant and bar is where the pretty people come and have a titter at the pharmaceutical theme. Glass cabinets on the walls are stuffed with medicines and pill bottles, the decor is lab-white, and the staff wears mock surgical clothing. It's trés trendy and rather smug with it. *150 Notting Hill Gate, W11, tel. 020/7221–2442. Tube: Notting Hill Gate. Open Mon.–Thurs. noon–3 PM and 6 PM–1 AM, Fri. and Sat. 11:30 AM–3 PM and 6 PM–2 AM, Sun. 11:30 AM–3 PM and 6 PM–midnight.*

Prince Bonaparte. A lively preclub stop with thumping music on weekends, the Bonaparte—a minimalist place with wooden tables, big windows, and a range of interesting beers—also serves great inventive pub cuisine. *80 Chepstow Rd., W2, tel. 020/7229–5912. Tube: Notting Hill Gate or Westbourne Park.*

The Westbourne. Dressed-up media and movie types throng here and spill out onto the street in summer. You might have to wait some time to get served by the bar staff, who seem more concerned with looking good than with pouring a drink. The food, mostly Anglo-Mediterranean items, is up to gastro-pub standards. *101 Westbourne Park Villas, W2, tel. 020/7221–1332. Tube: Westbourne Park. Open Mon.–Sat. noon–11, Sun. noon–12:30 AM.*

Windsor Castle. Drinkers of every ilk are welcome at this cozy pub with sloping, wooden floors. On warm summer nights the large garden out back (which sports heaters in the winter) is packed with students from King's College and denizens of the nearby Holland Park hostel. *114 Campden Hill Rd., off Notting Hill Gate, W8, tel. 020/7243–9551. Tube: Notting Hill Gate.*

SOHO

Thousands of revelers, both tourists and Brits, crowd the pubs of Soho every night of the week. You'll find cigar and martini bars, trendy club-bars, and even biker pubs, where you might run into faded locals (yes, there is a residential population in these cramped and brightly lighted city streets). Most nights of the week, even in winter, folks spill out into the streets with pints in hand—bring your mates and join the fun. One caveat: if you're allergic to crowds and noise, go elsewhere. And know that some local pubs levy a cover charge of a pound or so on weekends. Old Compton Street is the nucleus of the gay district within Soho (*see* Gay and Lesbian Pubs, *below*).

Bradley's Spanish Bar. Bradley's is a real idiosyncratic joint, whose gaudy decor is heavy on red velvet and paintings of bullfights. Although it's cramped and very popular, there's a guy here who will always try to find you a table. Food comes in the shape of a limited but tasty tapas selection, and on weekends there's a flamenco guitarist on hand to build up the atmosphere. *42 Hamway St., off Oxford St., W1, tel. 020/7636–0359. Tube: Tottenham Court Rd. Open Mon.–Sat. 11–11.*

Coach & Horses. Bright orange lights and lots of Naugahyde make this place look like a new Denny's franchise, but the crowds aren't here for the decor. It's a historic hard-drinking place—local character Jeffrey Barnard (a British Bukowski) spent the 1950s piss drunk at this bar, observing Soho's "Low Life" for *Spectator* magazine. The manager delights in the title of "The Rudest Landlord in London" and even has that legend inscribed on the matchboxes. *29 Greek St., off Shaftesbury Ave., W1, tel. 020/7437–5920. Tube: Leicester Sq.*

De Hems. Although it's just steps away from Chinatown, De Hems's theme, if you can't guess, is Dutch; hence the gins and Orangeboom beers in the hands of the youngish, mixed crowd. Suits overrun the pub between 5 and 7. *11 Macclesfield St., off Shaftesbury Ave., W1, tel. 020/7437–2494. Tube: Piccadilly Circus.*

Dog & Duck. Perhaps the most beautiful pub in Soho, this tiny joint, boasting lots of tile-work and mirrors, gets cramped in the evenings—not just for the pleasant vibe, but for a good range of bitter. *18 Bateman St., W1, tel. 020/7437–4447. Tube: Tottenham Court Rd. or Piccadilly Circus. Open weekdays noon–11, Sat. 6–11, Sun. 7–10:30.*

The Dog House. The Dog House has the hippest divey scene in Soho. It's belowground, with weird little rooms, funky furniture, and bright, spacey murals on the walls. The music kicks, it's smoky, and it's loud. *187 Wardour St., W1, tel. 020/7434–2118. Tube: Tottenham Court Rd. Open weekdays 5–11, Sat. 6–11.*

French House. The unofficial Resistance headquarters during World War II, this tiny pub offers a bohemian atmosphere. Look for yellowing photographs of some of its boozy clientele (actors, writers, and the like) placed in cabinets on the walls. Predictably, given its French associations, there's a good wine selection. *49 Dean St., at Shaftesbury Ave., W1, tel. 020/7437–2799. Tube: Leicester Sq.*

The Intrepid Fox. If you're into hard-core punk–thrash–metal, hey, yeah, this is your place. Join the raucous, pierced, tightly packed crowd boozin' on Carlsberg's extrapotent Elephant Ale beneath posters of gods like Metallica. *99 Wardour St., W1, tel. 020/7287–8359. Tube: Piccadilly Circus. Open Mon.–Sat. noon–11, Sun. 3–10:30.*

Moon Under Water. As part of the very reliable Wetherspoon's chain, this spacious conversion of the much-missed Marquee rock club offers a light, airy atmosphere and bargain beer prices. Promotional pints and bottles of lager cost around £1.30. Hurray! *105–107 Charing Cross Rd., W1, tel. 020/7287–6039. Tube: Leicester Sq. or Tottenham Court Rd.*

O Bar. The extremely popular O Bar, with its gaggle of bouncers wearing headsets outside, promotes itself as more of a club, but no club would remain open for long if it played the bland thumping house music that supposed DJs spin here. O's probably packed because it's one of the most accessible late-night joints in the district. It'll set you back £3–£5 for a cover after 11 PM. *83 Wardour St., W1, tel. 020/7437–3490. Tube: Tottenham Court Rd. or Piccadilly Circus. Open Mon.–Sat. 3 PM–3 AM, Sun. 4–10:30.*

Sun & Thirteen Cantons. There's been a pub on this site since the 17th century; the modern incarnation very successfully attracts Soho's young preclubbers, who meet here for a few drinks before going dancing. Be aware that loud music in both the ground floor and basement bars tends to stifle conversation. *21 Great Pulteney St., W1, tel. 020/7734–0934. Tube: Piccadilly Circus or Oxford Circus. Open weekdays noon–11, Sat. 5–11.*

GAY AND LESBIAN PUBS

London has a great gay scene, but pubs are a bit hard to find, especially if you're looking for something that caters exclusively to lesbians. Browse through free magazines that you'll find all over Soho for current details on pubs that nurture London's sizable community. *Time Out* also lists some pubs in its "Gay" section. A wander around London's Gay Village in Soho (the area around Old Compton Street) will lead you to any number of gay-owned or gay-friendly nightspots.

Angel Café Bar. A relaxed atmosphere and friendly staff make this a wonderful place to hang out. Older couples lounge on the comfy sofas and nibble on delicious vegetarian food like lasagna (£3) or quiche (£2), as well as lots of cakes. Tuesday is women's night, but the crowd is always mixed. Every Friday there's a DJ and dancing. *65 Graham St., between Vincent Terr. and City Rd., N1, tel. 020/7608–2656. Tube: Angel. Open Mon.–Sat. noon–midnight, Sun. noon–11:30.*

The Box. This supertrendy, girl-friendly Covent Garden spot does duty as café by day and bar by night. The crowd is always mixed. *32–34 Monmouth St., WC2, tel. 020/7240–5828. Tube: Leicester Sq. Open Mon.–Sat. 11–11, Sun. noon–6 and 7–10:30.*

Candy Bar. Spread over three swish Soho floors, this is the country's first every-night-of-the-week lesbian club-bar. Men are always welcome as "guests." *4 Carlisle St., W1, tel. 020/7494–4041. Tube: Tottenham Court Rd. Open Mon.–Thurs. 5–midnight, Fri. 5–2 AM, Sat. noon–2 AM, Sun. 5–11.*

Drill Hall. This gay cultural center and meeting place also has a cozy, popular bar. The folks are friendly, the music is sociable, and the drinks are decently priced. On Monday night it's women only. Come for the generous happy hour between 5:30 and 7:30. *16 Chenies St., WC1, tel. 020/7631–1353. Tube: Goodge St. Open daily 6 PM–11 PM (Mon. from 5:30).*

Freedom. During the day the predominantly gay Freedom is a relaxed designer café with a huge choice of cutesy sandwiches and flavored coffees. In the evenings the music gets pumped up and it's a popular hangout for both gay men and women, with club nights downstairs (usually with a small cover charge, around £3–£5). *60–66 Wardour St., off Oxford St., W1, tel. 020/7734–0071. Tube: Oxford Circus or Tottenham Court Rd. Open Mon.–Sat. 11 AM–3 AM, Sun. noon–midnight.*

Fridge Bar. Adjacent to the storied Fridge Club, this long, slender bar serves premium beers and spirits, plus coffees and cakes, to a mixed, relaxed crowd. At night the sweaty basement resembles a club (sometimes graced with the presence of noted DJs); a small cover of around £3 is charged on weekends. *Town Hall Parade, Brixton Hill, SW2, tel. 020/7326–5100. Tube: Brixton. Open Mon.–Thurs. 10 AM–2 AM, Fri.–Sat. 10 AM–4 AM.*

The Yard. Here we have a gorgeous, almost idyllic mixed gay bar and restaurant that, thanks to its courtyard at the end of a short alley, seems miles from the noise of Soho. There's all the fancy import beers and alcoholic sodas that you could care to try and the food is also excellent. A club sandwich (£4.95) is deliciously overstuffed, but keep an eye out for the daily two-course special for £5.95 (including coffee). *57 Rupert St., off Shaftesbury Ave., W1, tel. 020/7437–2652. Tube: Piccadilly Circus. Open Mon.–Sat. noon–11.*

6 AFTER DARK

UPDATED BY TIM PERRY

London has a raging after-hours scene that's been setting global trends for decades—and when you include Shakespearian theater and Handel oratorios, for centuries. Rock music, jazz, raves, fringe theater, classical chorales, you name it, London probably did it first and often does it best. If London is a wonderful place to party, it can also be a pricey one: a pint in most venues will cost you £2.50, movie tickets are £4–£9, tickets to the Royal Opera can soar heavenward, and clubs usually charge covers of £6 and up-up-up, with a bottle of beer in these places leaving your pocket £3 lighter. Student and rush tickets often soften the blow for theater and classical music, and many dance and live-music clubs distribute half-price flyers on street corners. Even so, London is an expensive place to play.

First-run movie theaters, jazz joints, dance clubs, and Theatreland—the district that's home to more than 40 big West End theaters—are concentrated around Soho and Covent Garden, but you'll find hip alternative clubs and theaters all over London. A number of publications give detailed rundowns of what's on where and are great resources if you plan to stay in London for more than a few days. The best of the lot by far is the weekly magazine ***Time Out*** (£1.80), which is absolutely invaluable to travelers and locals for listing and reviewing the barrage of options that make up the ever-evolving night scene in London. ***What's On*** (£1.30) is a cheaper but less comprehensive version of the same information. Alternatives to these relatively mainstream rags include *New Music Express* (*NME*; £1.10) and *Melody Maker* (95p). *The Evening Standard* (35p), available at all newsstands, also has all-purpose entertainment info, especially in the free supplement "Hot Tickets," which comes out every Thursday. The Saturday editions of the *Independent*, the *Times*, and the *Guardian* newspapers also have free booklets giving London-wide listings. Be sure to check out the weekly listings somewhere: today's cool spot is often tomorrow's forgotten or closed venue.

Pubs (*see* Chapter 5) generally close at 11 PM, which can put a major damper on your evening if you just wanted to enjoy a quiet pint; however, the growing number of club-bars (*also see* Chapter 5) stay open later, and although most play banging music at that time of night, some do have a quiet corner or room. The tube also closes early (about 12:30 AM), so for late-night fun you'd better figure out London's extensive night bus system (*see* Getting Around London *in* Chapter 1), or budget in taxi fare. Night Buses operate on fewer routes and less often than daytime buses, but you still won't wait much more than 30 min for your double-decker. Remember: NEVER sit alone on the upper deck of a Night Bus (these cold and lonely spots attract unsavory characters). Rides with minicab drivers who chirp "Taxi? Taxi?" outside nightclubs should also be avoided, especially by women traveling alone. They are often illegal and uninsured, and they sometimes overcharge for late-night trips, especially if they hear a foreign accent. For more details on the taxi scene, *see* Getting Around London *in* Chapter 1.

THEATER

London is the theater capital of a country that truly loves the stuff, training would-be actors with a devotion often reserved for bankers and academics. The theater sections in *Time Out* and *What's On* run for pages and pages, with everything from Shakespeare to Mike Leigh to Brecht. Theater in London falls into two basic categories: West End and Fringe. The **West End** is London's equivalent of Broadway, featuring big-budget productions and musicals like *Cats, Les Misérables,* and *Sunset Boulevard.* It's a dubious distinction, but London has even overtaken New York as the launching ground for new Andrew Lloyd Webber–ish "vehicles," so if you must see the latest round of dancing cats, orphans, or silver-screen divas, do it here. **Fringe** theaters present everything from small productions by prominent playwrights—folks like Samuel Beckett, Harold Pinter, Caryl Churchill, David Mamet, and Tom Stoppard—to experimental offerings by young local talent. Fringe performances are sometimes pretentious and obscure, but rarely boring.

It shouldn't come as a surprise that this theater-mad city hosts some extravagant summer whoop-de-dos. The **London International Festival of Theatre (LIFT)** (tel. 020/7490–3964), with performances from all genres, is held every other year June–July, with the next scheduled for 2001. Events are staged in theaters around London and even in the great outdoors. British Telecom recently began sponsoring the **BT Streets of London Festival,** also every other year, with free performances by international casts held in locations throughout London; look for it in summer 2000.

As Frank Sinatra said, "London by night is a wondrous sight," but not from the often deserted and cold upper deck of a Night Bus. Stay on the lower level.

MAJOR VENUES

The Barbican and the Royal National Theatre are major-league houses, but the productions they stage are often fringe in style—partly because they're both state-subsidized and housed within larger arts centers.

Barbican Centre. This giant arts complex has two venues for drama: its **Barbican Theatre** is home to the Royal Shakespeare Company, which stages productions of the Bard's great works on a regular basis. Its smaller, more intimate theater, **The Pit,** is the place for avant-garde and whimsical stuff. Student standby tickets (£6) are sometimes available for performances to either theater; call to check. *Silk St., EC2, tel. 020/7638–8891. Tube: Barbican. Barbican Theatre tickets £7–£25; The Pit tickets £6–£17.*

National Theatre. The National Theater (home of the Royal National Theatre Company) offers three performance venues: the **Olivier Theatre,** the **Lyttleton Theatre,** and the **Cottesloe Theatre.** The Cottesloe is the smallest and usually puts on new works by up-and-coming playwrights. The range at the other two spans everything from cutting-edge stuff to imaginative interpretations of old standbys. "Platforms" (admission £3.50, £2.50 students), a series of talks and lectures by playwrights, directors, and other theater personnel, is also presented here. Student standby tickets (£7) are available for select performances; call to inquire. *South Bank, Belvedere Rd., SE1, tel. 020/7928–2252 (box office) or 020/7633–0880 (for recorded info). Tube: Waterloo. Tickets £10–£24.*

WEST END THEATERS

The principal West End theaters are on **Shaftesbury Avenue** in Soho, **Haymarket** in St. James's, and around **Covent Garden.** Tickets can run anywhere from £10 to £40, depending on the performance and available seating; book way in advance if you're planning to see a hit show. You can reserve tickets directly through the theater, either in person at the box office or over the phone using a credit card. Or you can use a 24-hour ticket agency such as **First Call** (tel. 020/7240–7200) or **Ticketmaster** (tel. 020/7379–4444), which will levy a hefty 10%–20% service charge. You'll also see ticket outlets in tube stations and in the West End—they may be convenient, but the commissions are a rip-off.

Poetry readings and workshops featured heavily in the first **London Festival of Literature,** which was held in 1999 and is due to continue each year from mid- to late March throughout the city.

If your day of drama is starting to sound like an enormous, expensive hassle, relax. Many theaters also offer cheap preview performances or matinees—although you're more likely to see understudies at these instead of big stars. You can get half-price, same-day tickets from the phoneless **Society of Lon-**

POETS' CORNER

London does not lack for poets, and a look at the "Books and Poetry" section in Time Out *will clue you in to a variety of readings, workshops, poetry-slams, happenings, and benefits held in bookstores, university halls, and sometimes pubs. One of the city's premier spots to catch a notable performance by artists, authors, and poets is Voice Box (tel. 020/7921–0906), a small space on Level 5 of the South Bank Centre (*see below*). Tickets cost £2.50–£7. The well-established "Vox 'n' Roll" nights in the smoky environs of Filthy McNasty's pub in Islington (*see *Chapter 5) features spoken word interspersed with musical selections.*

don Theatres (SOLT) kiosk on Leicester Square. Show up to stand on line Monday–Saturday noon–6:30 and Sunday noon–3; you'll pay a £2 service charge and usually get one of the best-priced seats.

If you have a student ID, you can also score cheap same-day tickets directly from individual theaters' box offices; call or visit to inquire about availability. Call the Society of London Theatres' **Student Theatreline** (tel. 020/7379–8900) for limited recorded info on where to find student tickets on a given night; or surf over to www.officiallondontheatre.co.uk for general info. Some prominent long-in-the-tooth West End shows that are booking into 2000 are listed below.

Aldwych. Andrew Lloyd Webber wrote the music, Jim Steinman supplied the words, but the city's theater critics generally label *Whistle Down the Wind* a dull show. *The Aldwych, WC2, tel. 020/7416–6000. Tube: Covent Garden.*

Dominion Theatre. This theater next to the tube station is a big pink beast of a place, an appropriate host of *Disney's Beauty and the Beast. Tottenham Court Rd., W1, tel. 020/7656–1857. Tube: Tottenham Court Rd.*

Her Majesty's Theatre. *The Phantom of the Opera,* which has played here for more than a decade, has really taken root at HMT. *Haymarket, SW1, tel. 020/7494–5400. Tube: Piccadilly Circus.*

New London Theatre. Now and forever, New London is home to *Cats. Drury La., WC2, tel. 020/7405–0072. Tube: Covent Garden.*

Palace Theatre. Here's *Les Misérables,* the world's most popular musical; wouldn't Victor Hugo be proud? *Shaftesbury Ave., W1, tel. 020/7434–0909. Tube: Leicester Sq.*

St. Martin's Theatre. Home to that Agatha Christie thriller *The Mousetrap* for five decades and counting. *West St., WC2, tel. 020/7836–1443. Tube: Leicester Sq.*

Shaftesbury Theatre. The musical production of *Rent* brings a rare glimpse of contemporary political consciousness to the West End, and there's no sign of it closing. *Shaftesbury Ave., WC2, tel. 07000/211221. Tube: Holborn.*

Theatre Royal, Drury Lane. Home indefinitely to *Miss Saigon. Catherine St., WC2, tel. 020/7494–5062. Tube: Covent Garden.*

FRINGE THEATERS

For the price of one West End blowout you can afford to see three fringe plays—shoestring affairs staged in basements, pubs, or anywhere else they can squeeze in a small stage and an audience. Tickets are usually in the £4–£10 range, and most offer discounts to students. Fringe theaters generally sell cheap student standbys and standing-room tickets just before show time. In addition to the venues listed below, **Man in the Moon** pub in Chelsea (*see* Chapter 5) stages various theater productions.

The Almeida. This old, successful theater maintains high standards for its contemporary and classical offerings. *Almeida St., N1, tel. 020/7359–4404. Tube: Highbury and Islington.*

BAC (Battersea Arts Centre). Three stages offer new plays and reworked classics by some of Britain's best touring companies. The £1 BAC membership fee is included in the ticket price (usually £9, students £6). *Lavender Hill, SW11, tel. 020/7223–2223. Rail: Clapham Junction.*

The Bush. This small room above the Fringe & Firkin pub promotes plays by young British writers, many of which have gone on to tour successfully, such as *Beautiful Thing* (later adapted to the silver screen) and the first London staging of *Trainspotting. Shepherds Bush Green, W12, tel. 020/8743–3388. Tube: Goldhawk Rd. or Shepherds Bush.*

Donmar Warehouse. Boasting a cutting-edge program and circular stage, the Donmar—which recently made an international name for itself by getting Nicole Kidman to play here before Broadway—is a bit more pricey than other small theaters. *Thomas Neal's Yard, Earlham St., WC2, tel. 020/7369–1732. Tube: Covent Garden.*

Drill Hall Arts Centre. All sorts of cool plays are here for the watching. Its forte? Excellent gay and lesbian productions. *16 Chenies St., WC1, tel. 020/7637–8270. Tube: Goodge St.*

Etcetera Theatre. Esoteric one-night productions make appearances at this quaint 50-seater. *Oxford Arms, 265 Camden High St., NW1, tel. 020/7482–4857. Tube: Camden Town.*

The Gate. Reworkings of European classics are the specialty at the Gate, a highly regarded pub theater. *The Prince Albert, 11 Pembridge Rd., W11, tel. 020/7229–5387 or 020/7229–0706. Tube: Notting Hill Gate.*

London has always been passionate about its theater. When the Puritans tried to ban performances in the 16th century, underground productions simply moved to the hot-chocolate houses that were the new vogue in town.

Greenwich Theatre. This 400-seat theater hosts everything from comedies to classics to the experimental. *Crooms Hill, SE10, tel. 020/8858–7755. BritRail: Greenwich. Or take DLR to Island Gardens, then walk under the river via Greenwich Foot Tunnel.*

Hampstead Theatre. Plays that impress the discerning patrons at this prestigious local theater-bar often go on to the West End. They lured John Malkovich here for a run in 1998. *Swiss Cottage Centre, Avenue Rd., NW3, tel. 020/7722–9301. Tube: Swiss Cottage.*

ICA (Institute of Contemporary Arts). A mixed art space known for innovative and often ahead-of-our-time productions, ICA is sometimes criticized for putting on stuff that's so way out, it has already left the building. *The Mall, SW1, tel. 020/7930–3647. Tube: Charing Cross.*

King's Head Theatre. This is one of the oldest, best known, and most respected venues for pub-theater in London. The ancient, high-ceiling pub (no cover) is an experience in itself. *115 Upper St., N1, tel. 020/7226–1916. Tube: Highbury and Islington.*

Lyric Studio. Bookworms love this place, which offers up mainly contemporary works, with plenty of literary adaptations. *Lyric Theatre, King's St., W6, tel. 020/8741–2311. Tube: Hammersmith.*

PLACE PULL QUOTE HERE

New End Theatre. This intimate theater in Hampstead is known for presenting period works rarely staged in London's bigger venues. The New End also tackles modern politics, both left- and right-wing. *27 New End, NW3, tel. 020/7794–0022. Tube: Hampstead.*

Tricycle Theatre. Up north in the Irish neighborhood of Kilburn, this small theater puts on innovative Irish plays as well as other cosmopolitan themes. *269 Kilburn High Rd., NW6, tel. 020/7328–1000. Tube: Kilburn.*

The Young Vic. The nominal offspring of the nearby Old Vic (which still puts on the best quality programs of the major theaters), this venue showcases cutting-edge productions and actors. *66 The Cut, SE1, tel. 020/7928–6363. Tube: Waterloo.*

OUTDOOR THEATER

Outdoor theater in London is not a completely ridiculous, hideous, and cruel idea; believe it or not, summers can be warm. Really. The big news on this front is that the spectacular reconstruction of the most famous playhouse in the world, Shakespeare's own "wooden O" has finally opened on the banks of the Thames, a mere 200 yards from where the original once stood. **Shakespeare's Globe** (*see* The South Bank, Southwark *in* Chapter 2) now presents a season that runs from May to September, with most performances offered in the late afternoon. You can sit under the eaves or, for a mere £5, be one of the "groundlings" and stand directly in front of the magnificently Elizabethan stage.

The biennial **London International Festival of Theatre** (*see above*) always includes offerings in the great outdoors. From May through September, **Regent's Park Open-Air Theatre** (Regent's Park Inner Circle, tel. 020/7486–2431; Tube: Baker St.) offers performances ranging from Shakespeare to contemporary works, but the emphasis is on Shakespeare. Tickets cost from £6 to £18.50; check *Time Out* for details.

COMEDY

London had a pitifully weak live comedy scene until The Comedy Store (*see below*) opened its doors in 1979. Although many London comedians are still understated, dry, and cerebral, today there's also plenty of cussing, physical comedy, and other comic vulgarity that goes over fine with British audiences. Be warned that many stand-ups pad their show out by picking on the audience. A favorite trick is to ask members of the crowd where they come from, so if you're from Iowa and don't like to have the almighty piss taken out of your home state, it might be best to avoid front-row seats.

Nowadays several purpose-built comedy clubs are sprinkled throughout the city, and dozens of pubs, bars, and clubs host weekly comedy nights. Shows can involve big names playing cozy little rooms or no-hopers ranting away at people for standing at the bar and talking among themselves. *Time Out* has several pages of comedy listings each week; look for highlighted shows.

August is a poor month for comedy in the capital as most of the big names and many aspirants are up in Scotland doing the rounds at the Edinburgh Festival. Once September rolls around, however, virtually all the award-winning shows are back in London and you'll have to pick among a number of top events each night.

BAC (Battersea Arts Centre). You might pay a bit more than you expected to see cutting-edge comic plays and stand-up routines at this innovative mixed arts venue. September and October is when the best Edinburgh Festival shows are unveiled for the London audience. *Hill, SW11, tel. 020/7223–2223. Rail: Clapham Junction.*

Canal Café Theatre. The witty and long-running "Newsrevue" team takes the rip out of current events Thursday through Sunday at this canalside venue in Little Venice. The rest of the week has an ever-changing program of comic theater, improv, and various other brands of laughter. The cover'll set you back £5– £7. *The Bridge House, Delamere Terr., W2, tel. 020/7289–6054. Tube: Warwick Ave.*

Comedy at Soho Ho. This intimate room brims with atmosphere and has a reputation for original comics and impressionists. The show's on every Wednesday for just £4. *Crown & Two Chairmen, 31 Dean St., W1, tel. 0956/996690. Tube: Piccadilly Circus or Tottenham Court Rd.*

Comedy Café. Big-hitters often reign on weekends in this well-established club. The new talent night on Wednesday is free, the show on Thursday costs just a few quid, and then it's a tenner on weekends, when the joint is open until 2 AM. *66 Rivington St., EC2, tel. 020/7739–5706. Tube: Old St.*

Comedy Store. Monday nights vary from week to week and include a monthly black comedy review. Tuesday is "Cutting Edge" night, based on topical events; Wednesday and Sunday boast the improvisational skills of the resident Comedy Store Players; the country's leading stand-ups take the stage Thursday through Saturday. Shows usually start at 8 PM and finish around 10:30, although Friday and Saturday midnight shows carry on till 2 AM. Tickets average around £12. *1A Oxenden St., SW1, tel. 020/7344–4444. Tube: Piccadilly Circus.*

Comedy Theatre. Comic plays are the name of the game at this Theatreland venue, where big recent productions have lured the likes of Ewan McGregor. *Panton St., W1, tel. 020/7369–1731. Tube: Piccadilly Circus.*

Embassy Rooms. Your feet get treated to a plush carpeted entrance at this welcome new addition to the central London scene. Join about 600 people inside for comedy on the weekends or a wide range of bands during the week—you'll find it an easy-going spot, free from the hassle of heavy-handed security. *161 Tottenham Court Rd., W1, tel. 020/7387–2414. Tube: Warren St. or Tottenham Court Rd.*

Hackney Empire. Black comics and adherents of political radicalism do their thing at this great old community theater in a dog-eared part of town. *291 Mare St., E8, tel. 020/8985–2424. Rail: Hackney Central or Hackney Downs.*

Jongleurs Battersea. Jongleurs is the first chain of comedy clubs in the country, an empire built on providing strong big-name bills. You'll pay around £12, £8 if you're a student. *The Cornet, 49 Lavender Gardens, SW11, tel. 020/7564–2500. Rail: Clapham Junction.*

Jongleurs Bow Wharf. The Jongleurs chain's East End option encompasses the friendly Bar Risa (*see* Pubs and Bars, Chapter 5). *221 Grove Rd., E3, tel. 020/7564–2500. Tube: Mile End.*

Jongleurs Camden Lock. Possibly the most popular Jongleurs joint in the city (maybe because the bar is open to 3 AM on Friday and Saturday), this well-designed space hosts rock concerts during the week. *Dingwalls Bldg., Middle Yard, Chalk Farm Rd., Camden Lock, NW1, tel. 020/7564–2500. Tube: Camden Town.*

Lee Hurst's Backyard Comedy Club. Owned by comic and regular TV performer Lee Hurst (who is the regular MC here), this purpose-built 400-seat club offers stand-up shows from 8:30 to 11:30 on Friday and Saturday, with a view to opening during the week sometime soon. After the gags have been spent, a "disco" runs until 2 AM, as does the bar. Cover is £10, with a £7 student concession on Friday. *231 Cambridge Heath Rd., E2, tel. 020/7739–3122. Tube: Bethnal Green.*

CLASSICAL MUSIC, OPERA, AND DANCE

The last night of the Proms at Royal Albert Hall is the capper, a madly jingoistic display of singing, Union Jack waving, and general merriment. Demand for tickets is so high that you must enter a lottery.

The arts scene in London is unbelievably rich and varied. A bounty of internationally respected orchestras, opera companies, and ballet troupes make their homes here, including the **London Symphony Orchestra** (the most-recorded symphony orchestra in the world), the **London Philharmonic Orchestra,** and the world-famous **Royal Ballet** and **Royal Opera** troupes. Although it's true that ticket prices to any of these groups' performances can easily reach right into the stratosphere, that's no reason to retreat to your hotel room with an armload of Hobnob cookies (although do try these most excellent munchies at sometime during a stay in the United Kingdom). With some careful planning or a bit of luck, you can fill your evenings with song and dance, rub shoulders with the rich, and still have a few quid left over for a late-night snack. First of all, reserve early. If a program interests you, it has probably also captivated hundreds of others, and performances do sell out; check *Time Out* and *What's On* for schedules. Tickets for classical concerts, ballet, and opera range anywhere from £2.50 to more than £100 for special performances. Most venues offer **standby tickets** to students with valid ID, available an hour or so before curtain (call first to check on availability). In some cases this means whichever seats are left go for the lowest-cost ticket price—so you can get a £45 front-row seat for, say, £6.

In summer your arts options expand exponentially, as gala festivals fill theaters, concert halls, and even parks and squares. Probably the biggest—and most affordable—spectacle for lovers of classical music are the **Proms,** more formally known as the BBC Henry Wood Promenade Concerts, held at the gorgeous Royal Albert Hall (*see* Major Venues, *below*). The series runs for eight weeks from mid-July to mid-September and features a smorgasbord of well-known pieces, as well as a smattering of new works. Tickets are £5–£30; call 020/7589–8212 for more info. The **City of London Festival** (*see* Festivals *in* Chapter 1), held the first three weeks in July, features classical performances in venues and squares throughout the city; many are free. The **BOC Covent Garden Festival** (tel. 020/7312–1997), in May and June, showcases opera and the musical arts. The **South Bank Centre** (*see* Major Venues, *below*) hosts the summertime dance festival **Ballroom Blitz** and **Meltdown,** a showcase for contemporary music. The **Greenwich Festival** (tel. 020/8317–8687) features some classical music in the neighborhood's old maritime buildings. During summer you can also enjoy alfresco opera and ballet performances at **Holland Park Theatre** (Kensington High St., W8, tel. 020/7602–7856), a graceful open-air pavilion, and classical concerts at **Kenwood House** (Hampstead La., NW3, tel. 020/7973–3427). Many churches offer free (or low-cost) **lunchtime concerts** throughout the year; several are listed below.

MAJOR VENUES

Barbican Centre. Barbican Hall, the music hall at this giant arts center (*see* The City *in* Chapter 2) is home to the famous **London Symphony Orchestra** and the **English Chamber Orchestra.** Frequent guests include the Royal Philharmonic, City of London Symphonia, and the Philharmonia Orchestra. And if that's not music to your ears, perhaps its eclectic menu of everything from brass bands to smoky jazz acts is. Student standby tickets (£6.50 or £8.50) are available for select performances beginning 1½ hours before curtain. *Silk St., EC2, tel. 020/7638–8891. Tube: Barbican or Moorgate. Signposted from tube stations. Admission £5–£45.*

BMIC (British Music Information Centre). Recitals, mostly of new British music, take place on Tuesday and Thursday evenings at 7:30; tickets cost roughly £5. *10 Stratford Pl., W1, tel. 020/7499–8567. Tube: Bond St. From the tube, walk a few yards east on Oxford St., turn left into Stratford Pl.*

The London Coliseum. For opera and ballet, the Coliseum is a good bet. In 1997 it became the permanent home of the **English National Ballet** troupe, formerly in residence at the South Bank Centre. It also attracts talented dance companies from around the world. Sharing the stage, so to speak, is the **English National Opera (ENO) Company.** It's well known for English-language operas and offers lower prices (and less stodgy renditions) than the Royal Opera Company. One drawback: the Coliseum is huge. The cheapest upper balcony seats are known jokingly as "the gods"—consider renting a pair of opera glasses (20p) unless you like your art served up with severe eye strain. One hundred balcony seats go on sale the day of the performance at 10 AM for £5. *St. Martin's La., WC2, tel. 020/7632–8300. Tube: Leicester Sq. Walk northeast on Long Acre, turn right on St. Martin's La. Admission £5–£50.*

Royal Academy of Music. Three lunchtime recitals and one evening concert are held each week during term in the Duke's Hall. *Marylebone Rd., NW1, tel. 020/7873–7373. Tube: Regent's Park or Baker St. From Regent's Park walk west on Marylebone Rd., the building is on the right; from Baker St. walk east on Marylebone Rd., the building is on the left. Admission free–£5.*

Royal Albert Hall. This beautiful major-league concert venue really comes into its own during summer, when it hosts the **Proms** (*see above*). Otherwise, it's home to the acclaimed **Royal Philharmonic Orchestra.** Looming in the near future for the Royal Albert Hall is a £40 million-plus refurbishment that will, with luck, sort out the cramped bar areas. *Kensington Gore, SW7, tel. 020/7589–8212 or 020/7589–3203. Tube: Knightsbridge. Walk west on Kensington Rd. Admission £5–£40.*

Royal Opera House. This fabled theater—the classiest and most expensive in Britain, home to both the world-renowned Royal Ballet and the Royal Opera—closed its doors between summer and November of 1997 for a grand-scale renovation. During this time, the managers also rethought their admission policies—largely in response to rabid accusations of elitism from the media and the public. In the past most shows sold out even though prices were hideously high because corporate bodies gulped up all the tickets; now, the ROH is reducing most ticket prices and promises to sell around 20% of all tickets to the public. You can now mill around the newly accessible ROH during the day and attend recitals, workshops, and small-scale performances in the new Studio Theatre and the Studio Upstairs. Anticipated productions planned for early 2000 include *Otello* and *Romeo and Juliet* (with internationally renowned vocalists); the Royal Ballet also has star-studded presentations of new works by Matthew Bourne and Siobhan Davies. *Bow St., Covent Garden, WC2, tel. 020/7304–4000. Tube: Covent Garden. Turn right onto Long Acre and right onto Bow St. Admission £6–£150.*

Sadler's Wells. After two years of extensive reconstruction, the city's primary venue for dance flung open its doors once again. Both traditional and innovative dance from around the world take to the stage of this state-of-the-art space. *Rosebery Ave., EC1, tel. 020/7713–6060. Tube: Angel. Walk south down St. John St. and right onto Rosebery Ave. Admission £5–£35.*

St. James's Church. This 17th-century church was the last of Sir Christopher Wren's London churches and his favorite. What better place to enjoy a free lunchtime concert? Performances are at 1:10 PM Wednesday–Friday, year-round. The church hosts frequent evening recitals and, in summer, the world-renowned **Lufthansa Festival of Baroque Music.** *Piccadilly, W1, tel. 020/7734–4511 or 020/7437–5053 for box office. Tube: Piccadilly Circus. Admission £5–£15.*

St. John's Smith Square. This beautiful Baroque-era church, blessed with excellent acoustics, has rapidly become one of London's leading venues for classical music. Programs vary widely, but renowned chamber orchestras and soloists are frequently featured. The BBC hosts lunchtime concerts (£6) Monday at 1. *Smith Sq., SW1, tel. 020/7222–1061. Tube: Westminster. Walk south on St. Margaret St., which becomes Old Palace Yard, Abingdon St., and Millbank; turn right on Dean Stanley St. Admission £5–£20.*

St. Martin-in-the-Fields. This attractive church (*see* Trafalgar Square, Major Attractions, *in* Chapter 2) is a cool venue for classical recitals, both acoustically and atmospherically. Free concerts, which often feature noted solo performances, take place Monday, Tuesday, and Friday at 1:05 PM. On Wednesday, at the same time, there is a choral Eucharist. Evening candlelight gigs (£6–£15) often feature big-name ensembles, although the acclaimed Academy of St. Martin-in-the-Fields Orchestra only plays here once or twice a year. *St. Martin's Pl., Trafalgar Sq., WC2, tel. 020/7839–8362 box office or 020/7930–0089 for recorded info. Tube: Charing Cross or Leicester Sq.*

South Bank Centre. This mammoth arts complex (*see* South Bank *in* Chapter 2) is a haven for fans of music, opera, and dance, with three venues to choose from: the largest is the **Royal Festival Hall,** which reigns as one of the finest concert halls in Europe. It's home to the **London Philharmonic Orchestra** (March–July and September–December) and the **Philharmonia Orchestra** (May–July and September–March), which recently appointed Christoph von Dohnányi (of Cleveland Orchestra fame) as principal conductor. Additionally, it usually hosts the **Opera Factory** two times per year and is the site of numerous literary events (*see* Poets' Corner *box*). A bit smaller in size is **Queen Elizabeth Hall,** which features visiting modern-dance companies, chamber orchestras, and performances of lesser-known symphonies by the Philharmonic. Finally, the tiny **Purcell Room** hosts performances by up-and-coming chamber groups and soloists, plus the occasional visiting tap-dancing troupe. For many performances, student standbys are available two hours before curtain. The South Bank Centre is also home to two major annual festivals: **Ballroom Blitz,** with free performances and classes in everything from belly dancing to the waltz, as well as **Meltdown,** featuring contemporary music. *South Bank, Belvedere Rd., SE1, tel. 020/7960–4242. Tube: Waterloo. Admission £5–£30.*

Wigmore Hall. The Wigmore's Sunday "Coffee Concerts" (11:30 AM), held year-round, are enormously popular with musically inclined Londoners; tickets are £8, including program and a coffee, sherry, or juice, and breakfast is available from the Wigmore Hall café. Otherwise, chamber music, period music, and all sorts of other soothing melodies fill the air of this pleasant, acoustically stellar forum most evenings. *36 Wigmore St., W1, tel. 020/7935–2141. Tube: Bond St. Walk north on James St., turn right on Wigmore St. Admission £4–£35.*

DANCE CLUBS

Every night of the week, scores of clubs spin contemporary dance music (jungle, drum 'n' bass, breakbeat, *every* variety of house and techno), old R&B hits, '70s funk and disco, and the occasional indie/alternative platter. One-nighters (theme nights that take place at particular clubs on the same night every week, or move around from club to club) are very popular but tend to confuse matters with erratic opening and closing times—always check the daily listings in *Time Out* for current info. Some live-music venues bring out DJs after the bands have finished.

The dress code at most of London's clubs is casual; jeans are often okay, although some places will specify "no trainers" (athletic shoes) or "smart dress" (no blue jeans). Throughout London, clubs typically open by 10 PM and close around 3 AM (when many liquor licenses expire). Although you might have to pay handsomely for the privilege of partying into the wee hours, some "after-hours clubs" *open* at 3 AM and run until after sunrise—perfect for those who can't face the prospect of returning to their schoolkid-infested hostel. Even a few daytime clubs, where the fashionably idle can while away those empty hours until the sun sets, appear from time to time. The current trend is going back to small, sweaty clubs, such as the Blue Note, and away from the super-size joints like the Ministry of Sound. The standard cover charge for dance clubs on weekday nights is £5–£7, although you may get a break for arriving early—usually before 11 PM—or for showing a student ID. On weekends, prices can skyrocket up to £15, but some clubs still offer cheaper fun.

There are plenty of trendy, expensive discos spread throughout Soho and Covent Garden. Many are around Leicester Square, and all charge covers of £10–£15. If you're looking for nothing more than flashing lights, chart-friendly dance music, and meat-market crowds, try upscale **Stringfellows** (16 Upper St. Martin's La., WC2, tel. 020/7240–5534), or the showy **Hippodrome** (Leicester Sq., WC2, tel. 020/7437–4311)—just look for the neon horses over the entrance. If a bouncer refuses you admission into one of these trendy clubs because you're "not a member," it most likely means your 501s and hiking boots just don't cut it. But don't worry, you'll definitely fit in somewhere else.

Aquarium. Yes, it's got a pool, so dress accordingly. Aquarium is on anthemic house and garage, but it can get a bit cheesy. On some nights, like CCCP Thursdays, you'll pay an extra cover. Try to come on "Absolute Sunday," when a smart crowd extends the weekend into Monday. *256 Old St., EC1, tel. 020/7251–6136. Tube: Old St. Cover: £5–£12.*

The Astoria. Although normally a live-music venue, the Astoria also hosts a variety of one-nighters like the *verrrry* popular "G.A.Y." on Friday and Saturday nights. A mixed crowd comes for dated disco tunes, live acts, and cabaret. The Astoria's huge balcony is a good place to chill out and peer down on the dancing masses. Also *see* the listing for its little sibling neighbor, LA2. *157 Charing Cross Rd., WC2, tel. 020/7434–0403. Tube: Tottenham Court Rd. Cover: £3–£6.*

BEYOND BALLET

There's a whole world beyond the saccharine ballets of "Swan Lake" and "The Nutcracker Suite"—the world of modern dance. Performances are often highly charged and attuned to the audience (possibly because many modern dance performance spaces are so darn small). If this piques your interest, London is a great place to broaden your horizons: Michael Clark, Yolanda Snaith, and the Cholmondeleys troupe are all examples of hot homegrown talent. Tickets to modern-dance performances run £3–£10; check Time Out *for current listings. If you're in town during autumn, don't miss the five-week, citywide festival "Dance Umbrella" (tel. 020/8741–4040). Some of London's top spots for modern dance are as follows:*

CHISENHALE DANCE SPACE. For avant-garde dance by promising new dancers from around the globe, this is the spot. Sadly they only stage around 10 performances a year nowadays, usually in late spring and fall. 64–84 Chisenhale Rd., E3, tel. 020/8981–6617. Tube: Mile End. Admission free–£7.

INSTITUTE OF CONTEMPORARY ARTS (ICA). Often the site of unconventional dance performances. The Mall, SW1, tel. 020/7930–3647. Tube: Piccadilly Circus. Admission £5–£15.

THE PLACE. A dance school by day, a small, cheap, cutting-edge performance space by night. 17 Duke's Rd., WC1, tel. 020/7387–0031. Tube: Euston. Admission £3–£12.

Bagley's Studio. Possibly the largest club in town, Bagley's is notable for getting in the big DJs for one-night blitzes. It doesn't come cheap, though. *King's Cross Freight Depot, off York Way, N1, tel. 020/7278–2777. Tube: King's Cross. Walk north on York Way, turn left on Goods Way. Cover: £10–£15.*

Bar Rumba. This underground hot spot hosts a variety of wildly popular one-nighters every night of the week. Check out the well established but still immensely popular and pioneering "Movement" (Thursday) for edge drum 'n' bass, "Bubblin Over" (Sunday) for R&B, and "Space" (Wednesday) and the "Disco Spectrum" (Friday) for eclectic house. Saturdays are regularly packed to the rafters for garage and disco house, so come early or prepare to queue; good hip-hop defines Monday, lively salsa Tuesday. Drinks can be pricey. *36 Shaftesbury Ave., W1, tel. 020/7287–2715. Tube: Piccadilly Circus. Cover: £3–£10.*

Café de Paris. This recently refurbished old ballroom adds a touch of class to the London scene. The music is the usual garage, house, funk mixture, but the dress code is pretty smart. *3 Coventry St., W1, tel. 020/7734–7700. Tube: Leicester Sq. or Piccadilly Circus. Cover: £5–£12.*

Camden Palace. A wide mix of nights draws large dancing crowds throughout the week. Tuesday's "Feet First" features a fun mix of indie, guitar, and rock music, along with a live band that might just be the next big thing. The lively "Peach" rears its garage-and-house-music head Friday until 6 AM. Look for flyers near the Camden Town tube station for discounted admission. *1A Camden High St., NW1, tel. 020/7387–0428. Tube: Camden Town. Walk south on Camden High St. Cover: £5–£12.*

Chunnel Club. The Club's old-school recipe of trance and banging house with an up-for-it atmosphere recalls the early days of acid house. *101 Tinworth St., SE1, tel. 020/7820–1702. Tube: Vauxhall.*

Cloud 9. Although it's comparable to the Chunnel Club, Cloud 9 pumps out old-school repetitive techno. Thankfully they have a big chill-out area as well. *67–68 Albert Embankment, SE1, tel. 020/7735–5590. Tube: Vauxhall.*

The Complex. Owned by the Mean Fiddler organization, this big postindustrial club gets in all the top names from Detroit, Chicago, and every other music hot spot that you would expect with such connections. The big nights are "Voyager" (Friday) and "Camouflage" (Saturday) with techno, hard-driven house, and eclectic sounds spread over the three floors. *1–5 Parkfield St., N1, tel. 020/7428–1986 or 020/7428–9797. Tube: Angel. Cross the street to Liverpool Rd., then take a sharp right on Parkfield St. Cover: £10–£15.*

The Cross. Inside a set of converted railway arches that also offer a patio space, the Cross draws an up-for-it crowd for mad house and garage. It attracts a fair amount of the beautiful people, so dress *way* up or stay home. *Goods Way Depot, off York Way, N1, tel. 020/7837–0828. Tube: King's Cross. Walk north on York Way, turn left on Goods Way. Cover: £5–£15.*

Crossbar. The Crossbar, open from 5:30 PM each day, has grown from its roots as a club-pub into a serious nighttime contender. Friday is usually breakbeat and progressive house, and the rest of the weekend has a more indie music feel. One to watch for is Scratch, the capital's most acclaimed hip-hop night, held on the first Thursday of every month. *257 Pentonville Rd., N1, tel. 020/7837–3218. Tube: King's Cross. Cover: £2–£7; free before 10 PM.*

Dog Star. Basically the first of London's club-bars to make it big, the Dog is a large, restyled pub that's packed all week with dancers who appreciate the very eclectic DJ sounds. The popular weekends command a £5 cover and sizable lines outside, although Sunday currently offers a cheesy school disco feel. It costs nothing extra to get to the more exclusive rooms upstairs, but you'll have to get an invite flyer or look like you belong. Drink prices are good compared with the West End. *389 Coldharbour La., SW9, tel. 020/7733–7515. Tube: Brixton. Turn left out of the station and left onto Coldharbour La. Cover: free–£5.*

The End. The Shamen's Mr. C set up The End to be a club for clubbers run by clubbers. And he's done a pretty good job—air-conditioning means you won't sweat to death without really trying. Mr. C takes over the decks himself a couple of nights a week along with big name U.S. techno DJs and the best homegrown drum 'n' bass names. Wednesday is a good night to sample this stylish club; there are often promotions by the best underground breakbeat labels, and admission is as low as £3. The first Friday of each month is the Skint records night, where Fatboy Slim has played on several occasions. *16A W. Central St., WC1, tel. 020/7419–9199. Tube: Tottenham Court Rd. Walk west on New Oxford St., turn right on W. Central St. Cover: £3–£15.*

The Fridge. Brixton's major dance venue is like a three-ring circus, often with multimedia displays, live performances, and go-go dancers. Friday night sees monthly clubs such as "Escape to Samsara" plying psychedelic trance and hippie visuals to a fluorescent-painted crowd. The "Hard Muscle" gay night fills the place every Saturday. The adjacent **Fridge Bar** (*see* Gay and Lesbian Pubs *in* Chapter 5) usually charges no cover; the small downstairs room gets overly sweaty on weekends for some top rootsy DJs—it reopens at 6 AM on Sunday morning for those who still haven't had enough. *Town Hall Parade, Brixton Hill, SW2, tel. 020/7326–5100. Tube: Brixton. Walk south on Brixton Rd. Cover: £7–£15.*

Gardening Club. All sorts of stylish one-nighters—such as the funky underground garage-flavored "Dolly Mixture" on Friday—are held in this upbeat, easygoing club. As it's part of the Rock Garden story, it does tend to be a bit over-touristed. *4 The Piazza, Covent Garden, WC2, tel. 020/7497–3154. Tube: Covent Garden. Cover: £3–£12.*

Hanover Grand. A swank and opulent big West End club, the Hanover attracts TV stars and soccer players whose exploits here you can later read about in the tabloids. Nights to watch for are the R&B grooves of "Fresh 'N' Funky" (Wednesday), the anthemic house of "The Next Big Thing" (Thursday), and "Haute Couture" (Friday); Saturday's glam disco "Malibu Stacey" pulls in all those who want to be seen. The lines outside get long, so dress up to impress the bouncers. *6 Hanover St., W1, tel. 020/7499–7977. Tube: Oxford Circus. Walk south on Regent St. and sharp left on Hanover St. Cover: £5–£15.*

Heaven. This massive club turns into London's largest lesbian and gay party spot several nights a week. The partied-up "Fruit Machine" (Thursday) night has been going for more than six years, and the big blast of "Heaven" (Saturday) brings in a throbbing gay crowd. Monday night's "Popcorn" session will ease you into the new week. Heaven's maze of rooms is great for getting lost. *Under The Arches, Villiers St., WC2, tel. 020/7930–2020. Tube: Charing Cross or Embankment. From Charing Cross, walk northwest on the Strand, turn left on Villiers St. From Embankment, walk northwest on Villiers St. Cover: £3–£12.*

THE '70S AND '80S ARE ALIVE AND WELL AND LIVING IN LONDON

You want a blast from the past? Try some of these long-running club nights that hark back to the past for their kicks:

Club Fantastic: One of the best of the '80s revival throng, Fantastic draws late-twentysomethings who danced with their friends in high school cafeterias under balloons and streamers. Go for the £2 drinks. It's currently at Samantha's Disco, 2 New Burlington St., off Regent St., W1, but has hopped around a bit. Their info line is 020/8455–3741; the Web site is clubfantastic.co.uk.

Good Times: This club has taken over at the venue that Club Fantastic vacated a year or so ago, but still does that '70s and '80s thing. Cairo Jack's, 10 Beak St., W1, tel. 020/8906–9921.

Saturday Night Fever: Camden's entry into the tacky-taste league comes in the form of this not-so-originally-named night at the Electric Ballroom, 184 Camden High St., tel. 020/7485–9006. With rooms called "Sylvester's Sanctuary," "Penelope's Pitstop," and "Huggie's Joint," you kind of know what to expect. Cover is £8; £5 if you wear '70's garb.

Starsky & Hutch: Not to be missed if you have a '70s-friendly bone in your body. Funk, soul, jazz, and disco keep it smokin' at the Leisure Lounge, 121 Holborn, EC1, on Friday; a smaller midweek affair shakes the house on Wednesday and Thursday at Ronnie Scott's, 47 Frith St., W1. For S&H information, tel. 020/8654–0523.

Voulez Vous: This club bills itself as the city's most authentic '70s night, and they'll take £4 off the £10 cover fee if you don the flares and stuff. It's at the Volcanic Nightclub, 1 Marylebone La., W1, near Bond Street tube, tel. 020/8455–3741.

HQs. A canalside club with outdoor decks in chichi Camden Yard, HQs is worth a visit on Wednesday for the friendly house and garage vibes of "The Loft." On Saturday there's a big salsa blow-out with free lessons before 10 PM. *West Yard, Camden Lock, NW1, tel. 020/7485–6044. Tube: Camden Town. Cover: £5–£8.*

Iceni. This slick, well-decorated Mayfair venue pulls in a well-dressed and well-to-do crowd that's a little older than some of the more ravey joints. With three separate rooms it offers choice, and Saturday's "Spoilt For Choice" mixes up sexy soul, funk, and house. *11 White Horse St., off Curzon St., W1, tel. 020/7495–5333. Tube: Green Park. Cover: £5–£10.*

Junction. A half-mile further along nonsalubrious Coldharbour Lane from the Dog Star is this more down-home pub conversion. Specialties of the house are heavy drum 'n' bass and breakbeat, but the overall policy is very eclectic. There's music every night of the week and a small cover only on weekends. *242 Coldharbour La., SW9, tel. 020/7738–4000. Tube: Brixton. Cover: free–£5.*

LA2. Adjacent to the Astoria, the LA2 (it stands for London Astoria 2) attracts droves after the rock crowd has gone for the amazingly popular "G.A.Y. Pink Pounder" on Monday and Thursday nights. They're popular for a few simple reasons: it's a whole English pound to enter (with flyer or ad), then the first drink is free, and from there on it's two for the price of one. Friday brings the busy indie/alternative rock "Popscene" night. *157 Charing Cross Rd., WC2, tel. 020/7434–0403. Tube: Tottenham Court Rd. Cover: free–£8.*

Leisure Lounge. The club that hosted the ultrainnovative "Metalheadz" nights now has the retro-cheese of "Starsky & Hutch" filling the floorboards on Friday night. Saturday sees a popular garage session called "Cookies & Cream"; this cavern gets pretty hot inside and is always one to watch. *121 Holborn, EC1, tel. 020/7242–1345. Tube: Chancery La. Cover: £5–£12.*

Madame Jo Jo's. This fun and kitschy club was set up in the '80s as a place for top drag acts to perform; although that's what packs the house every Friday and Saturday, it also has top club nights. Tuesday's ever-popular "Indigo"—playing Bacharach, Gainsbourg, et al.—started the easy-listening boom in the city. "Deep Funk" spins rarities from the '70s every Sunday, and "Deep Disco" on Wednesday night deals with soul from the '70s. *8–10 Brewer St., W1, tel. 020/7734–2473. Tube: Piccadilly Circus. Walk north on Regent St., and turn right on Glasshouse, which forks left onto Brewer St. Cover: £5–£8.*

Mass. Opened by the Dog Star people in fall '98, this was supposed to be the ultimate Brixton clubbing experience, but it hasn't quite taken off. Nevertheless, with its concentration on quality drum 'n' bass and breakbeat with a regularly rotating roster of nights, there's always something of extreme quality happening on several nights of the month—try to catch the live electronica acts who prefer to play here rather than at traditional venues. *St. Matthew's Church, Brixton Hill, SW2, tel. 020/7738–5255. Tube: Brixton. Walk left out of the station, it's in the triangular garden at the end of the road. Cover: £5–£10.*

Ministry of Sound. Yes, it's global, yes, there are now record and clothing labels and even a monthly magazine available on the news stands, but the Ministry of Sound has (just about) stopped short of becoming a mere tourist attraction. The cavernous club retains a decent atmosphere and good grooves, probably because it can regularly attract such big names as Paul Oakenfold and Armand van Helden. Expect huge lines (although you'll be glad to have people around in this neighborhood late at night), a snobby staff, and scads of Italian tourists with cell phones. *103 Gaunt St., SE1, tel. 020/7378–6528. Tube: Elephant & Castle. Walk north on Newington Causeway, turn left on Gaunt St. Cover: £12–£15.*

The Office. This neat and cozy Soho haunt is more of a club-bar, but it does have regular nights—come for Wednesday's "Double Six Club," which lopes along on a hilarious "easy-listening" vibe, with every board game you played in your elementary-school years spread out on tables. The rest of the week features eclectic one-nighters covering the pop, rock, disco, and northern soul bases. *3–5 Rathbone Pl., W1, tel. 020/7636–1598. Tube: Tottenham Court Rd. Walk west on Tottenham Court Rd., turn right on Rathbone Pl. Cover: free–£6.*

The Rocket. Cheap and cheerful, this student-run venue and home of the "Dub Club" (Wednesday) is known for its old-school reggae. Other nights shift between roots sounds and Britpop, and there's usually a live electronic-oriented band each week. Drinks are a bargain compared with other clubs, and students with ID get £1 off the cover. *166–220 Holloway Rd., N7, tel. 020/7753–3200. Tube: Holloway Rd. Turn right out of the station and it's there. Cover: £3–£5.*

St Moritz. At possibly the weirdest and longest-running Soho club you'll find a decor that makes you feel you're in an après-ski session in a Swiss chalet. Nevertheless, it's the perfect atmosphere for the hot and sweaty "Gaz's Rockin' Blues" on Thursday—a mix of rock, ska, and blues, with a live band. Share the floor with heavy drinkers and rockabilly tourists from Japan. Other nights of the week the club deals mostly in indie sounds. *159 Wardour St,. W1, tel. 020/7437–0525. Tube: Leicester Sq. Walk west on Shaftsbury Ave. and turn right on Wardour St. Cover: £3–£7.*

Smithfields. Now incorporating the **Jazz Bistro** venue, this dark warren presents cutting-edge underground sounds that rival the best of the city. Friday sees big one-off events, and the wide-ranging but up-to-the-second "Happiness Stan's" (Saturday) mixes soul, psychedelia, and jazz. There's no dress code (imposed either by management or style fascists), but remember it gets real sweaty. *334–338 Farringdon St, EC1, tel. 020/7236–8112. Tube: Farringdon. Cover: £5–£8.*

Spitz. A good-looking modern space in the likably offbeat Old Spitalfields market area, the Spitz specializes in avant-garde and experimental electronic nights, ambient sessions, and even rootsy nights with live laid-back bands. Trés arty. *Old Spitalfields Market, 109 Commercial St., E1, tel. 020/7247–9747. Cover: £3–£7.*

Subterrania. Dance all night long at this small but outrageous and funkily decorated club, which showcases live rap, hip-hop, funk, and R&B acts during the week. On Friday, "Rotation" whoops up a party atmosphere for funky hip-hop grooves, and "SoulSonic" on Saturday explores every corner of house. Both nights get big-name DJs, and the balcony makes a great chill zone. Wednesday adds a reggae vibe to the joint. *12 Acklam Rd., W10, tel. 020/8960–4590. Tube: Ladbroke Grove. Walk north on Ladbroke Grove, turn right on Cambridge Gardens, right on Acklam Rd. Cover: £8–£10.*

333. This innovative space paved the way for anything-goes nights—it's not unusual to hear the best new drum 'n' bass in one room while tacky American rock classics blast away in the upstairs room. Occupying three floors of a rambling old pub, 333 is one of the best experimental clubs in London, strong on breakbeats and all sorts of twisted dance sounds. *333 Old St., EC1, tel. 020/7630–5949. Tube: Old St. Cover: £4–£10.*

Turnmills. Although the legendary "Heavenly Jukebox" night has now shut down, Turnmills still thrills with all sorts of one-nighters, including Saturday's "Headstart," with big-name guest DJs and a diverse policy that takes in breakbeat, hip-hop, and ambient. It's followed by the hugely popular gay rave "Trade" from 4 AM until 1 PM. Friday's long-running "the Gallery" plays a tough brand of house to a smartly-dressed crowd. *63B Clerkenwell Rd., EC1, tel. 020/7250–3409. Tube: Farringdon. Walk north on Farringdon Rd., turn right on Clerkenwell Rd. Cover: £6–£10.*

Velvet Room. This intimate venue with velvet couches and bubble pillars regularly gets revamped, but it's the current home of the ever-popular funky techno "Ultimate BASE" night (Thursday). Also good are "Swerve," serving up massive breakbeats on Wednesday, and the pumping house of "Whoop It Up" on Friday. *143 Charing Cross Rd., WC2, tel. 020/7439–4655. Tube: Tottenham Court Rd. Cover: £4–£10.*

Wag Club. This Soho club keeps shedding its skin and renewing itself. The one-nighters nowadays lean toward the guitar side of things: Thursday's unimaginatively named "Cigarettes & Alcohol" plays guitar rock from the '60s to the '90s, and yes, yes, some Oasis. "Planet Earth's Big Night Out" (Friday) packs the Wag for an '80s revival, and "Blow Up" (Saturday) features a jarring mix of Britpop, R&B, and easy listening. *35 Wardour St., W1, tel. 020/7437–5534. Tube: Leicester Sq. Walk west on Shaftesbury Ave., turn left on Wardour St. Cover: £3–£8.*

LIVE MUSIC

On any given night London hosts a stupefying number of music sets and concerts, but nothing comes cheap: Covers and tickets cost anywhere from £3 to £20, with most falling in the £5–£8 range. On the upside, you generally get what you pay for: London's jazz clubs are first-rate, as are its rock and indie venues. There is also a thriving international music scene, with Caribbean, African, and Latin bands playing to enthusiastic crowds. Britpop continues to crest, with acts like Blur, Pulp, and Gene drawing ever-larger crowds. But for how long? London audiences are, notoriously, a "show me" lot; they've seen it (or pretend that they have) all before. It is, however, a friendly scene and embraces all ages—if you're 50 years old and want to attend an Ash or Silverchair concert, most teens will think that's cool. Oasis, international chart-toppers that they are, are still huge, but the standard two-guitars-bass-and-drums-indie-band lineup is no longer flavor-of-the-month. London's best small venues—including the bars of Camden Town that fortified Britpop for so many years—these days present a challenging and eclectic roster of bands offering all types of dance and rock crossover potential. Pick up *Time Out, What's On, Melody Maker,* or *New Music Express (NME)* and face the music.

More established (some might say "over the hill") bands like the Rolling Stones and U2 are usually booked at **Wembley Stadium** (Empire Way, Wembley, Middlesex, tel. 020/8900–1234), an easy walk from the Wembley Park tube station. Next door is **Wembley Arena,** which has some big rock bands but mostly specializes in "middle of the road" (MOR) crooners. Another huge hangar space is **Earl's Court** (Warwick Rd., SW5, tel. 020/7835–1200), where recent visitors have included Oasis, Pink Floyd, and REM. The **London Arena** (Limeharbour, Isle of Dogs, E14, tel. 020/7538–1212), near the Crossharbour/London Arena Docklands Light Railway station, is attracting a growing number of not-quite-mega acts. Some of pop music's royalty also graces the stage of the **Royal Albert Hall** (*see* Classical Music,

Opera, and Dance, *above*). Smaller gigs are also held at pubs and colleges around town; check bulletin boards or *Time Out, NME,* or *Melody Maker* for the latest. Free live music can also be found in pubs (*see* Chapter 5) and at local record stores like HMV, Tower, and Virgin Megastore (*see* Music *in* Chapter 7), which often host in-store performances.

MAJOR VENUES

The Astoria/LA2. All sorts of good bands play at this 2,000-capacity venue—lots of rock, some indie, a splash of reggae, and crossover dance acts. Come early and snag a seat in the upstairs bar; it overlooks the stage. Under the Astoria's roof is its half-size sibling LA2 (London Astoria 2), which also hosts bands and one-night clubs, so make sure you're in the proper line. Make sure you arrive on time—bands are made to stick firmly to schedule so that they can clear the venue and turn it over to club nights. *157 Charing Cross Rd., WC2, tel. 020/7434–0403. Tube: Tottenham Court Rd.*

Blackheath Halls. This sizable mixed arts venue, way out beyond Greenwich, manages to attract a mostly rootsy bunch of big-name touring acts, who play here in addition to (or, sometimes instead of) a central London show. *23 Lee Rd., SE3, tel. 020/8463–0100. Rail: Blackheath.*

Brixton Academy. This Brixton institution is one of the bigger venues for hip indie and established acts. Despite a capacity of 4,000 people, the Academy's atmosphere seems more clublike than crowded, with interesting decor (look up at the ceiling), plenty of bars, and upstairs seating. The sloping floor can be a bit scary, especially when slicked up by a night full of beer, but it provides good views of the stage. Late shows are becoming a more regular occurrence on Saturday. *211 Stockwell Rd., SW9, tel. 020/7924–9999. Tube: Brixton. Walk north on Brixton Rd., turn left on Stockwell Rd.*

Electric Ballroom. The smallest of the main venues (it holds around a thousand), the Electric has a certain dated charm, but both sound and vision lines are usually good. The bands run the entire range of rock but tend to be fairly cutting edge; cover charges are decent. *Camden High St., NW1, tel. 020/7485–9006. Tube: Camden Town. Turn right out of the tube station and right again.*

Forum. This popular venue is similar to, although about half as large as, the Brixton Academy. The PA is usually good and everyone has a great view. Top bands take the stage through the week, clubs take over on weekends. Check out the rooms where you can watch a cult movie or play board games. "House of Fun" on Saturday sees new wave and club classics plus circus acts and trendies galore. *9–17 Highgate Rd., NW5, tel. 020/7284–2200. Tube: Kentish Town. Walk north on Kentish Town Rd., veer left on Highgate Rd.*

London Apollo Hammersmith. Formerly called the Hammersmith Apollo, it's still one of London's most famous mainstream venues—so mainstream that it's often used for touring theater productions. *Queen Caroline St., W6, tel. 020/7416–6080. Tube: Hammersmith. Follow signs from the station.*

Shepherds Bush Empire. This busy, award-winning venue in a former BBC-TV theater lines up an interesting roster of hot new bands and old favorites. The downstairs area has three bars to quench your thirst. Don't sit on the upper two levels if you have vertigo. *Shepherds Bush Green, W12, tel. 020/8740–7474. Tube: Shepherds Bush.*

CLUBS

ROCK AND REGGAE

In addition to having a variety of live acts, many of these clubs host one-nighters to fill their calendars. Always check current listings before heading out unless you want to be surprised by disco denizens when you were expecting a punk band. Camden Town is the traditional heart of the live music scene, with half a dozen small venues putting on fresh new bands each night of the week. October sees the annual **Camden Festival** with big names dropping into these sweaty clubs. The fest culminates in the excellent **Camdemonium** evening when one ticket allows you to bar crawl around five venues and see around 15 breaking bands.

Borderline. When record companies want to try out new bands, they send 'em to this subterranean Tex-Mex theme Soho establishment. Who knows, maybe you'll see the next big thing—or, better yet, *the* big thing playing under an assumed name. After the bands, there are indie and alternative-rock club nights with a small cover of £3–£5. *Orange Yard, off Manette St., W1, tel. 020/7734–2095. Tube: Tottenham Court Rd. Walk south on Charing Cross Rd., turn right on Manette St. Cover: £5–£10.*

Barfly Club. Barfly may be the finest and most eclectic small club in the capital. The trouble is that sometimes the little square back room gets crammed with people eager to see the next flash-in-the-pantheon. There are three bands seven nights a week with events regularly sponsored by the *NME, Melody Maker,* and *Kerrang!* publications. *The Falcon Pub, 234 Royal College St., NW1, tel. 020/7482–4884. Tube: Camden Town. Cover £4–£5.*

Bull & Gate. A little off the beaten Camden Town path, this shabby pub hosts a monthly night by Fierce Panda records, the rabidly independent label that first brought the likes of Placebo and Elastica to record decks. *389 Kentish Town Rd., NW5, tel. 020/7485–5358. Cover: £3–£5.*

Dingwalls. After spending several years as an exclusively comedy venue, Dingwalls is now back to what it was meant to do—hosting a variety of established and breaking rock acts several nights a week. It's in the cutesy Camden Lock warehouses. *Middle Yard, Camden Lock, off Camden High St., NW1, tel. 020/7267–1577. Tube: Camden Town. Cover: £5–£12.*

Dublin Castle. A great mix of lesser-knowns plays nightly at this noisy Camden Town pub. The crowd tends to be enthusiastic—perhaps because of the pub prices for beer. *94 Parkway, NW1, tel. 020/7485–1773. Tube: Camden Town. Walk southwest on Parkway. Cover: £4–£5.*

Garage. Clear views of the stage and a killer sound system make this a good place to see live rock and indie acts. It has a reputation for presenting London debuts of soon-to-be-mega U.S. bands. The appropriately named **Upstairs at the Garage** shares the building and telephone but hosts different acts—mostly lo-fi, acoustic, and spoken word—for a separate cover every night. Both places get pretty busy no matter what's offered. Be sure to join the correct line. *20–22 Highbury Corner, N5, tel. 020/7607–1818. Tube: Highbury and Islington. Cover: £4–£9.*

Half Moon Putney. Come linger in this solid suburban pub venue that specializes in bluesy-rock with some famous names from eras of Britrock past dropping in occasionally. *93 Lower Richmond Rd., SW15, tel. 020/8780–9383. Rail: Putney Bridge. Cover £3–£6.*

Hope & Anchor. A famous rock pub in the '70s, the Hope & Anchor has recently begun to put on bands and solo artists in its cramped little basement room beneath the pub. *207 Upper St., N1, tel. 020/7354–1312. Tube: Highbury and Islington. Turn left out of tube station and walk down Upper St.; the pub is on the left. Cover £3–£5.*

Mean Fiddler. The original piece of the ever-growing Mean Fiddler empire, this Irish-flavor club features a diverse mix of roots rock, reggae, heroes of days gone by, and a few big surprises. The adjacent Acoustic Room hosts—you guessed it—acoustic acts. Note that it's in an out-of-reach part of the city a long walk from the station. *22–28A High St. Harlesden, NW10, tel. 020/8961–5490. Tube/Rail: Willesden Junction. Turn right out of the station, then right onto Tubbs Rd. and left onto High St. Harlesden; the venue is on the left. Cover: £3–£12.*

Monarch. This Barfly competitor vies stiffly for new up-and-coming acts; its less attractive first-floor room often gets very cramped. Music policy centers pretty firmly on indie and alternative rock. *49 Chalk Farm Rd., NW1, tel. 020/7916–1049. Tube: Chalk Farm. Cover: £5–£8.*

Red Eye. LOUD music alert. New punk/metal/hardcore bands perform most nights of the week in this likable new venue that provides good value for the money. *105 Copenhagen St., N1, tel. 020/7387–4422. Tube: King's Cross or Angel. From King's Cross exit onto Caledonian Rd. and walk ½ mi, turn right onto Copenhagen St. From Angel cross Upper St. and walk up Liverpool Rd., turn left onto Cloudesley Pl., and sharp right onto Copenhagen St. Cover: £3–£5.*

Rock Garden. Buy the T-shirt. Eat the food. Oh, and there's also music—by mostly unknown acts, although the location means that cover charges are no bargain. Guitar-heavy rock may still have a place here, but the Garden has changed its lineup to include a more diverse mix of live funk and indie bands, and DJs playing house, garage, soul, and swing. Come during happy hour (weekdays 5–8) for £1–£2 drinks and free snacks; you pay £2 to get in but can stay and see that night's show for free. *6–7 The Piazza, Covent Garden, WC2, tel. 020/7836–4052. Tube: Covent Garden. Cover: £5–£10.*

Sound Republic. Just on the edge of Leicester Square, this big money venue (which also includes a theme bar and restaurant) opened in late 1998, but it's still lingering on the launch pad, even though it's used to film MTV special events. Live music mostly takes place on Wednesday, Friday, and Saturday, and it's a mixed bag of new and fairly safe mid-size names. *10 Wardour St, W1, tel. 020/7287–1010. Tube: Leicester Sq. or Piccadilly Circus. Cover: £5–£10.*

ULU (University of London Union). The capital's most central student union building has been putting on more and more hot gigs in the past few years. The first-floor Manning Hall holds around 600 people and is a good space for mostly up-and-coming acts. You'll have no problem getting in if you have an advance ticket. *Malet St., WC1, tel. 020/7664–2030. Tube: Goodge St. Turn left from station, cross Tottenham Court Rd., turn right on Torrington Pl., right onto Malet St. Cover: £5–£9.*

Underworld. This sprawling nightclub is located under the equally huge World's End pub. The music leans heavily toward the industrial, hardcore, and indie side, but anything is possible. *174 Camden High St., NW1, tel. 020/7482–1932. Tube: Camden Town. Cover: £4–£10.*

Venue. Close to Goldsmiths' College, this time-warped space used to promote good alternative bands. More recently, the Venue has focused on tribute bands and retro nights. *2A Clifton Rise, SE14, tel. 020/8692–4077. Rail: New Cross Gate or New Cross. From New Cross Gate walk east along New Cross Rd.; from New Cross, walk west. Cover: £4–£6.*

Water Rats. The small stage in the cozy old back room hosts gigs most nights of the week. The usual fare is tipped new bands (plus generally unknown support acts) mentioned in *Melody Maker* and *NME* that tend to be a little more rootsy and less loud and in-yer-face than those in the small Camden venues. *328 Gray's Inn Rd., WC1, tel. 020/7837–7269. Tube: King's Cross. Walk northeast on Euston Rd., turn right on Gray's Inn Rd. Cover: £5–£6.*

BLUES, ROOTS, AND WORLDBEAT

Many of the rock and pop clubs above also have blues, roots, and worldly sounds on certain nights. **Camden's WKD** (*see* Chapter 5) also has a good range of soul and R&B.

Africa Centre. Visiting musicians from Africa and the Caribbean often play in this shabby old hall that conjures up an often wild atmosphere. On other nights, DJs mix it up for a fairly diverse dance crowd. *38 King St., WC2, tel. 020/7836–1973. Tube: Covent Garden. Turn right on James St., right on King St. Cover: £5–£9.*

Ain't Nothing But Blues Bar. The name says it all. Come in and chill out to the nightly live blues in a crowded atmosphere. Most nights there's no cover. *20 Kingly St., W1, tel. 020/7287–0514. Tube: Oxford Circus. Walk south on Regent St., turn left on Great Marlborough St., quick right on Kingly St. Cover: free–£8.*

Bunjie's. What a throwback to the '50s and '60s, when coffee bars were trendy in the capital. This tiny basement room (a café by day) offers a rather unique atmosphere and gets in all sorts of acoustic folkie performers (a.k.a. well-meaning hippies). *27 Litchfield St., WC1, tel. 020/7240–1796. Tube: Leicester Sq. Walk north on Charing Cross Rd., and turn right on Litchfield (before Shaftesbury Ave.). Cover £2–£5.*

Cecil Sharp House. Home of the English Folk Society, this massive house boasts a classy ground-floor ballroom with a sprung parquet floor. In addition to modern and trad English folk, there are also raucous Cajun evenings. *2 Regents Park Rd., NW1, tel. 020/7485–2206. Tube: Camden Town. Cover: free–£5.*

Station Tavern. This West London pub is known for excellent blues bands and mellow crowds that pack the place every night of the week. And you can't beat the price—it's free. *41 Bramley Rd., W10, tel. 020/7727–4053. Tube: Latimer Rd. No cover.*

Swan. This big raucous Irish bar near Brixton has music nightly, including trad sessions and cover bands. The weekends see popular Celtic rock outfits, and the prices rise to nightclub levels. *215 Clapham Rd., SW9, tel. 020/7978–9778). Tube: Stockwell. Directly opposite the tube station. Cover: free–£12.*

Weaver's Arms. Here's a friendly little pub, slightly off the beaten track, that manages to get in some of the best Celtic roots talent as well as leading Texan country and Cajun musicians. *98 Newington Green Rd., N1, tel. 020/7226–6911. Tube: Highbury and Islington. Walk around the rotary and head west on St. Paul's Rd. (5 min), then turn left on Newington Green Rd. Cover: £3–£6.*

JAZZ

Jazz is alive and well in London; more and more restaurants are bringing in jazz musicians to entertain their diners, although of course this often means rather dull trad stuff. The tasty **Pizza Express** chain features some very good—and "free to diners"—jazz in some of its locations; try the Hampstead (70 Heath St., NW3, tel. 020/7433–1600) or Finchley (820 High Rd., N1, tel. 020/8445–7714) branch. More central locations (*see below*) attract big names and charge accordingly. The city also boasts a growing number of jazz fests. Two of the more established ones are the **Soho Jazz Festival** (held every

October and concentrating on the conservative end of the genre) and November's exciting **London Jazz Festival,** which pits innovative and experimental jazz against an eclectic array of top worldbeat names on the South bank and other major venues throughout the capital.

Bull's Head Barnes. This is one of the best jazz pubs in town, even if it is far away in Hammersmith. The pleasant scene—right on the Thames—and big names who jam here regularly make it well worth the trip. Shows start nightly at 8:30. *Barnes Bridge, SW13, tel. 020/8876–5241. Tube: Hammersmith. From the station, take Bus 9 to Barnes Bridge. Cover: £3–£10.*

100 Club. This basement was the site of one of the Sex Pistols' first London gigs. Yet the 100 Club has always been a hip jazz and blues joint, and nowadays there's also the occasional pop or indie band tossed in for good measure. Fortunately, it's still a lurid-colored dive. *100 Oxford St, W1, tel. 020/7636–0933. Tube: Tottenham Court Rd. or Oxford Circus. From Tottenham Court Rd. walk west along Oxford St.; from Oxford Circus walk east. Cover: £5–£10.*

Jazz Café. Lines can be long and empty seats few and far between, but the JC is a great relaxed place to see big-name talents (Gil Scott-Heron, Abdullah Ibrahim) as well as some of the best new sounds from the club world (The Egg, Jimi Tenor). Admission and drink prices do lean toward the high end, though. *5 Parkway, NW1, tel. 020/7916–6060. Tube: Camden Town. Cover: £6–£20.*

Pizza Express Jazz Club. This Soho basement club under the pizzeria gets in big names from around the world (Mose Allison, Art Farmer, and the like) several nights a week—the cover can be £20. At other times they have a resident band when prices are much more acceptable, or even free. *10 Dean St., W1, tel. 020/7439–8722. Tube: Tottenham Court Rd. Walk west on Oxford St. and turn left onto Dean St. Cover £5–£25.*

Pizza On The Park. This joint offers a similar experience to the Pizza Express Jazz Club, but with less-sweaty surroundings. *11 Knightsbridge, Hyde Park Corner, SW1, tel. 020/7235–5273. Tube: Hyde Park Corner. Cover £5–£25.*

Ronnie Scott's. This legendary Soho club, opened in the early '60s, is the leading venue for jazz in London—if they're the best, they'll play here. Its status is, unfortunately, reflected in the prices, although students can often get considerable discounts (40%–50% off). Book in advance or get in line early. *47 Frith St., W1, tel. 020/7439–0747. Tube: Tottenham Court Rd. Walk west on Oxford St., turn left on Soho St., cross Soho Sq. to Frith St. Cover: £12–£20. Closed Sun.*

606 Club. Pro jazz musicians often come to—and sometimes play at—this basement club following a gig; inexperienced players are often encouraged to join in. It has a nice vibe, although you may have to wait hours for a table on weekends. Make reservations or prepare to stand inside by the bar. One minor drawback: alcohol can only be served with meals. *90 Lots Rd., SW10, tel. 020/7352–5953. Tube: Fulham Broadway. Walk east on Fulham Rd., turn right on Wandon Rd., left on King's Rd., right on Lots Rd. Cover: £4–£6.*

Vortex. A popular good-value café venue with all kinds of jazz, including many breaking acts during the week and big names on weekends. The Sunday lunchtime improv session is free. *139 Stoke Newington Church St., N16, tel. 020/7254–6516. BritRail: Stoke Newington Tube/Manor House and take Buses 141 or 147A south. Bus: 73 from Victoria and King's Cross. Cover: £4–£8.*

FILM

London is home to many small repertory cinemas that specialize in seminal, epochal, and downright appetite-whetting flicks. These repertories are much more interesting than the multiscreen complexes around Leicester Square, which screen big-budget–small-plot Hollywood flicks, and they're cheaper to boot. Even though some charge a nominal membership fee of around £1 per day or year, the tickets are reasonable, and many have the bonus of bars and lounges where you can sit and deconstruct the latest viewing. Many also have midnight shows on Friday and Saturday. One of London's loveliest cinemas, Notting Hill's **Electric Cinema** (191 Portobello Rd., W11), has closed again, although it's hoped that someone will take over the venue and reopen it in the near future; keep your eyes peeled.

If it's a Hollywood blockbuster you're looking for, head straight for **Leicester Square.** Tickets at the spiffy multiscreen venues here cost £7–£10, and student discounts are rare—save for Virgin cinemas, which offer students a 40% discount at most shows. There are, of course, cheap weekday matinees at most cinemas—but did you come to London to spend your days indoors watching American films? Also remember that although British films open fairly quickly in the States, American-made films are released in London long after their debut in the colonies. Almost every London newspaper lists movie schedules in its entertainment section. The detailed reviews in *Time Out* are most useful, but the times, prices, and availability of concessions detailed in the *Evening Standard* are more easy to understand.

Londoners aren't known for their love of foreign films, and you'll have to do some digging to find the latest from the Continent. Filling the gap are two highly respected venues: **Ciné Lumière** (at the Institut Français, 17 Queensberry Pl., tel. 020/7838–2144 or 020/7838–2146) and, in spring and fall only, the **Goethe Institut** (50 Prince's Gate, Exhibition Rd., tel. 020/7411–3400), both in South Kensington. Most shows cost £2–£4.50, with double bills at £7. Some films aren't subtitled, so call ahead if it really matters.

Barbican Cinema. Foreign and arty films are rapidly being supplanted by mainstream stuff in the two cinemas here, which is a real shame. Tickets are £6.50, £4.50 for student standbys (when available). Every Monday, movies cost a mere £3.80. *Silk St., EC2, tel. 020/7638–8891. Tube: Barbican or Moorgate.*

Everyman Cinema. Billing itself as "London's oldest repertory," this cozy if a little basic venue shows an excellent selection of classic, foreign, avant-garde, and almost-new Hollywood titles. Many shows are double (even triple) features at no extra cost: Tickets are £4.50–£5, £3.50 students, and membership costs 60p a year. *Holly Bush Vale, NW3, tel. 020/7435–1525. Tube: Hampstead. Walk south on Heath St., turn right on Holly Bush Vale.*

Gate Cinema. Plop into a seat at this distinguished-looking neighborhood one-screen cinema with a tendency to put on offbeat or revivals at the weekend. *87 Notting Hill Gate, W11, tel. 020/7727–4043. Tube: Notting Hill Gate.*

ICA Cinema. Housed within the Institute of Contemporary Arts, this cinema shows practically anything arty and/or esoteric. Tickets for the main screen cost £6.50, £5 on Monday and for students. A £1.50 day membership is part of the price and includes admission to exhibits. The frequently changing films (£5) at the small ICA Cinematheque make the selection on the big screen look downright mainstream. *Nash House, The Mall, SW1, tel. 020/7930–3647. Tube: Charing Cross Rd. or Piccadilly Circus. From Charing Cross, walk southwest on The Mall. From Piccadilly Circus station, walk south on Regent St., turn right on The Mall.*

The increasingly popular London Film Festival is held each November, and features hundreds of flicks from Europe, India, and Australia. Screenings—which tend to sell out fast—take place in various cinemas, but most of the action is centered on the National Film Theatre; See *Festivals* in *Chapter 1 for more info.*

Lux Cinema. This recently opened movie house in the emerging Hoxton Square district is noted for its trendy club-bars and galleries, where you can catch a wild mix of movies (including foreign titles), music features, and the usual arts stuff. *2–4 Hoxton Sq., N1, tel. 020/7684–0201. Tube: Old St. Walk east on Old St., ½ mi. Hoxton Sq. is on the left.*

Metro. No need to fear the Hollywood slush. You can see the best American independents and some world cinema at this two-screen Soho establishment. *11 Rupert St., W1, tel. 020/7437–0757. Tube: Piccadilly Circus or Leicester Sq.*

Minema. This small venue is a film freak's dream. It seats 68 lucky people in broad, comfy chairs with plenty of legroom and prides itself on showing "only the best" international cinema. There's even a chic little café attached. Tickets are £7.50, £5.50 for students and matinees. *45 Knightsbridge, SW1, tel. 020/7369–1723. Tube: Hyde Park Corner.*

National Film Theatre. The NFT is one of London's best repertory cinemas. Its three cinemas screen more than 2,000 titles each year, including foreign films, documentaries, Hollywood features, and animation. Tickets are £6, £4.50 students. Members (£12/£8 per year) get priority on bookings (useful when guest speakers draw in crowds) and £1 off each screening. *South Bank Centre, SE1, tel. 020/7928–3232. Tube: Waterloo.*

Phoenix. Grand but out-of-the-way in East Finchley, the Phoenix has a reputation for good double bills and seat prices at a fiver or less. *52 High Rd., tel. 020/8883–2233. Rail: East Finchley.*

Prince Charles. Come for reasonably recent flicks, as well as artier and cult ones, at rock-bottom prices. Tickets are a real bargain for the West End: £2.50, £2 for weekday matinees. *7 Leicester Pl., WC2, tel. 020/7437–8181. Tube: Leicester Sq. Walk west on Cranbourn St., turn right on Leicester Pl.*

Renoir. Along with the Metro, Renoir stands out from the other commercial central London cinemas due to its choice of foreign and independent films. *Brunswick Sq., W1, tel. 020/7837–8402. Tube: Russell Sq.*

Rio. This great old Art Deco cinema squats in a shabby neighborhood. It was extensively refurbished in 1999 and now has a bar and continues its good mixed programming with arty double bills and matinees for kids. *107 Kingsland High St., E8, tel. 020/7254–6677. Rail: Dalston Kingsland. Turn left out of the station and stay on the same side of road.*

Riverside Studios. The rep program at this converted movie studio changes almost daily and seats are just £5, £4 students. *Crisp Rd., W6, tel. 020/8741–2255. Tube: Hammersmith.*

Ritzy. This cinema in the heart of bustling Brixton shows small arthouse flicks in addition to big mainstream films on its five screens. The groovy café serves excellent food, and there's also a busy bar. Tickets are £6; £4 students, Monday, and Tuesday–Friday before 6 PM. *Brixton Oval, Coldharbour La., SW2, tel. 020/7737–2121. Tube: Brixton. Turn left out of the tube station and cross Coldharbour La.*

Screen on the Green. With just under 300 seats, this venerable movie house in trendy Islington shows the artier new releases and also has late shows on weekends. *83 Upper St. at Islington Green, N1, tel. 020/7226–3520. Tube: Angel.*

Screen on the Hill. Similar in style to Screen on the Green, this cinema serves the well-heeled denizens of Belsize Park and Hampstead. *230 Haverstock Hill, NW3, tel. 020/7435–3366. Tube: Belsize Park.*

7 SHOPPING

UPDATED BY DAVID CLEE

If shopping in London conjures up for you an image of triple-digit pound signs and endless credit-card slips, read on; we may be able to change your mind. Yes, of course, you can have a perfectly fine time maxing out your platinum credit card at Vivienne Westwood, Britain's finest couturier—her Pompadour-punk smoking jackets and stunning Lady Hamilton frock coats can be yours for £2,000 a pop. And, yes, we have to warn those with high blood pressure and anyone who is prone to dizzy spells to stay away from oh-so-expensive Bond Street—unless you're looking for the sort of thing you would find in every Rockefeller's Christmas stocking. But London has so much more to offer. Take, for instance, London's amazing street markets, where you'll find everything from stuffed parrots and antique Toby jugs to the John Gallianos of tomorrow selling cutting-edge frocks from their stalls. The language of some of the hucksters in these markets is even more colorful than their wares, with a line of friendly banter that will make you long for your tape recorder. That's one free show; another awaits at Harrods' fabled Food Court. Case the joint, then head upstairs to find a special gift for your mother back home—perhaps a pair of specially monogrammed slippers? Gifts are what you make them, and London will come up with everything from plastic salt and pepper shakers shaped like Big Ben to a £3,000 antique print of St. Paul's. Between these two extremes, you'll find that London—and our list below—has it all: funky street markets, swank department stores, music stores for the most discriminating ears, shoe stores for the least discriminating feet. London may not trumpet its fashion sensibility the way New York or Paris does, but there's no disputing that those with a passion for fashion worldwide look to this city for the latest trends.

Be warned: competition doesn't do much to keep prices low, and you can easily empty your wallet before blinking. (Truth is, there's a good deal of stuff you can buy in London that you can find back home for half the price, so just go hunting for things that say London all over them.) For what it's worth, the weekly *Time Out* (£1.80) regularly lists bargains in its "Sell Out" section, and many of London's stores have huge, gala sales in January and July. But you might as well forget Harrods' post-Christmas sales: the sidewalks get so crowded you have to walk on the streets, and if the cars or buses don't run you over, shoppers in search of their blue-light specials will.

DEPARTMENT STORES

In 1870, William Whiteley started a revolution in London shopping by housing different departments—including men's and women's clothing, housewares, books, and even a funeral department—under one roof. Thus, London's first "department store" was born. His 1911 custom-built store, **Whiteleys** (Queensway, W2, tel. 020/7229–8844), has since mutated into an upscale shopping mall, but if you're in Bayswater, stop by to see the building and poke around the sale racks. Whiteley's road to becoming what he called "the Universal Provider" was no smooth one. As soon as he launched a meat department, local butchers took to the streets brandishing bones and cleavers, and the store was attacked by arsonists on several occasions. The shopping pioneer didn't even meet his maker in peace; Whiteley was shot by a man claiming to be his illegitimate son. Although Whiteleys does resemble a shopping mall more than a department store, it retains its original spirit of offering a great variety of products. If you insist on browsing through the high-priced selections at **Harrods** (*see* Kensington and Knightsbridge *in* Chapter 2), get an early start—crowds can be maddening by midday. For a glimpse at how the other half shops, head for **Fortnum & Mason** (*see* Markets and Specialty Stores *in* Chapter 4), where you can dreamily contemplate the old-fashioned opulence of its designer salons. At the other end of the price scale is **John Lewis** (278–306 Oxford St., W1, tel. 020/7629–7711), with its "never knowingly undersold" policy.

Harvey Nichols. Whether you worship at the shrine of Calvin, Ralph, or Versace, "Harvey Nicks"—the home-away-from-home for *Ab Fab*'s Patsy and Edina—should be your first shopping stop in London. More than 200 designers hang their labels here (often at astronomical prices). The selection of British designers is especially good, and the new "Swim and Gym" department provides spandex for all. A sumptuous food hall, a decently priced café, and a chic restaurant with nosebleed prices are on the fifth floor. Don't forget to pause and admire the witty, award-winning window displays. *109–125 Knightsbridge, SW1, tel. 020/7235–5000. Tube: Knightsbridge. Open weekdays 10–7 (Wed. until 8), Sat. 10–7, Sun. noon–6.*

Liberty. Arthur Lazenby Liberty opened this shop in 1875 to sell material from the Orient. Soon members of the Aesthetic Movement—including William Morris, Edward Burne-Jones, and John Ruskin—were clamoring for its trademark blue-and-white porcelain and brightly colored textiles. To this day, Liberty's atmosphere remains a cross between an Eastern bazaar and a rich aunt's living room: to experience it fully, climb to the top floor and peer down the central stairwell at the treasure trove of Oriental carpets, Liberty textiles, and international arts and crafts. Although prices are high, the sale at the end of June is a must-do. *214–220 Regent St., W1, tel. 020/7734–1234. Tube: Oxford Circus. Open Mon.–Sat. 10–6:30 (Thurs. until 7:30).*

Marks & Spencer. This store offers a good range of basics and some of the best bargains on fashionable new clothes in London. Not surprisingly, Prime Minister Tony Blair (as well as a ton of other people who'd look more at home in Harrods) shops for undies here. Princess Diana, too, was a regular at the Marble Arch branch. Like other big-name celebrities, she was given a clear run to peruse the shop outside normal opening hours. In the last year, M&S, for so long the giant of British high-street retailing, has seen its sheen dim and is now frantically trying to shake off a dull image. For the scoop on Marks & Spencer's vast array of edibles, *see* Chapter 4. *458 Oxford St., W1, tel. 020/7935–7954. Tube: Marble Arch. Open weekdays 9–8, Sat. 9–7, Sun noon–6. Other locations: 113 Kensington High St., W8, tel. 020/7938–3711; 85 Kings Rd., SW3, tel. 020/7376–5634; Queensway, W2, tel. 020/7229–9515.*

Peter Jones. The first shop collapsed, killing an apprentice, but Jones built again and by 1907 had a huge five-story shopping temple to his name. It was one of the first big department stores to replace gaslights—hated by shop workers for the headaches they induced—with electricity. Nowadays Peter Jones is able to pull off the neat trick of retaining enough prestige to attract high-falutin' local Chelsea residents while luring ordinary shoppers with a welcome lack of the snob factor. *Sloane Sq., SW1, tel.020/7730–3434. Tube: Sloan Sq. Open Mon.–Sat. 9:30–6 (Thurs. until 7).*

Selfridges. Founded by American businessman Gordon Selfridge in 1909, Selfridges didn't rise from humble beginnings like many other London shops—it *started* big. Godlike, Selfridge proclaimed, "I want my customers to enjoy the warmth and light, the colors and styles, the feel of fine fabrics." And so it was. Now, nearly a century later, the store has undergone a £50 million renovation and opened what's touted as the "largest cosmetics and beauty hall in the world." Other bonuses include a splendid food hall, fashionable clothing, friendly staff, and stunning Art Nouveau architecture. Prices are ever so slightly lower than those at Harrods and Harvey Nichols. Look for its spin-off Miss Selfridge boutiques if you're a chick on the hunt for low-price fashions. *400 Oxford St., W1, tel. 020/7629–1234. Tube: Bond St. Open Mon.–*

Wed. 10–7, Thurs., Fri. 10–8, Sat. 9:30–7, Sun. noon–6. Miss Selfridge: 40 Duke St., W1, tel. 020/7318–3833. Open Mon.–Wed. 10–6:30, Thurs., Fri., Sat. 10–7:30, Sun. noon–6. Other Miss Selfridge locations: 75 Brompton Rd., SW3, tel. 020/7584–7814; 42 Kensington High St., W8, tel. 020/7938–4182; 221–223 Oxford St., W1, tel. 020/7434–3541. All locations open Mon.–Sat. 9:30–7 (Thurs. until 8).

SPECIALTY STORES

CLOTHING

"Let's have a shop!" is a familiar rejoinder in a city whose most illustrious native designers have recently taken the reins at some of Paris's biggest fashion houses. Fear not, if you can't afford Galliano or McQueen originals, you can keep pace with the trends they dictate by exploring the shops and street markets listed below, all of which offer many affordable finds.

DESIGNER

London, particularly in swanky areas like Bond Street, Knightsbridge, and Covent Garden, is stuffed full of funky fashion outlets, with new ones opening all the time. Big names from overseas often have flagship stores here, too. But instead of focusing on the likes of Calvin Klein (New Bond Street) and Donna Karan (New Bond Street), which are available the world over, below we'll list a selection of some of the most interesting designers based in this fair and fashion-conscious city. Not all of them charge superstar prices, either, and all have regular sales.

Alexander McQueen. The media can't keep away from McQueen's bolshy antics, just the kind of attention Givenchy execs were presumably after when they brought in the Cockney couturier. But it's not just punked-up PR; the man with the magic scissors can cut it. Indeed, his tongue-in-cheek take on high fashion has outlasted many a skeptic's dim forecast and given fading couture itself a new lease on life. *Givenchy found at Harvey Nicholls and Selfridges; Alexander McQueen found at A La Mode, Browns, Harrods, Harvey Nicholls, Jones, Joseph, Liberty, and The Library.*

Amanda Wakeley. Wakeley's lovingly tailored gear is defined by elegant, simple lines for a predominantly Sloane Ranger–type clientele. These classic English clothes have hung on plenty of famous bodies, none more so than Princess Diana's. *80 Fulham Rd., SW3, tel. 020/7584–4009. Tube: South Kensington. Open Mon.–Sat. 10–6 (Wed. until 7).*

Betty Jackson. Go with the flow is the Jackson thing—not so much the flow of fashion's fickle ways, but the flow of the body, a canvas she adorns with sensual, often loose-fitting designs that have long attracted a loyal band of followers. *311 Brompton Rd., SW3, tel. 020/7589–7884. Tube: South Kensington. Open weekdays 10–6:30, Sat. 10–6.*

Browns. One of the real delights of the London fashion scene, Browns stocks a ridiculously wide range of designer clothes, from the biggest names around to students displaying their wares in public for the first time. *23–27 S. Molton St., W1, tel. 020/7491–7833. Tube: Bond St. Open Mon.–Sat. 10–6 (Thurs. until 7). Other locations: 38 S. Molton St., W1, tel. 020/7491–7833, 18 Molton St., W1, tel. 020/7491–7833.*

Burro. Bridging the gap between exorbitant and affordable, street-savvy designer lines, Burro exhibits its gear on the catwalk but doesn't forget the paying customer or wide-eyed tourist. You'll find a range of wearable, classy clothes to prove it. *19A Floral St., WC2, tel. 020/7240–5120. Tube: Covent Garden. Open Mon.–Sat. 10:30–6:30, (Thurs. 2–6, Sat. until 7).*

Caroline Charles. Princess Diana was a fan of this Charles, and it's at the landed classes that the designer's clothes have traditionally been aimed. That's not to say CC can't turn her hand to the more popular end of the market, just that her strength lies with Chelsea girls who have grown up a bit. *56–57 Beauchamp Pl., SW3, tel. 020/7589–5850. Tube: South Kensington or Knightsbridge. Open Mon.–Sat. 10–6 (Wed. until 6:30). Other locations: 9 St. John's Wood High St., NW6, tel. 020/7483–0080.*

Chloé. Stella McCartney—yes, darling daughter of Beatle Paul—has produced a series of well-received sets for French house Chloé. Her pretty detailings make exquisite play with the typical idea of feminine Paris fashion. In other words, she doesn't need her dad to hold her hand. *Found at A La Mode, Harrods, and Harvey Nicholls.*

Diesel. Kitsch kapital writ large—these innovative, witty interpretations of past fashion excesses have celebrities drooling at the mouth. Pulp's Jarvis Cocker (the man who raided the stage when Michael

QUEUE QUEST

Along with City gents in bowler hats, Big Ben, and the Spice Girls, the thing that most foreigners pick out as quintessentially British is the humble queue. Eastern European shoppers might stake a claim for commitment to the cause of standing in line but they do so out of sheer necessity rather than choice.

Standing in line is practiced here with a sense of almost patriotic duty, a solid conviction that appears to baffle the rest of the world, especially the rest of Europe, where even your grandmother would elbow you out of the way to claim service.

Indeed, Brits view with intense suspicion the foreigner's attempts to get served, so you'll find that in places most likely to receive visitors—such as banks, post offices, and tourist information centers—cunning ropes and fences are employed to ensure fair play. The classic urban myth is of the Englishman who, upon seeing a queue in a street, automatically attaches himself to its rear, without betraying a need to discover what is on offer up front.

The rules of engagement are simple: where there is a queue, join it; where there is no queue, grab someone else and form one of your own and on no account strike up a conversation of any kind. The only establishments exempted from these iron laws are pubs, where the promise of alcohol cuts through cultural boundaries and people spend years developing their aggressive bar-technique in order to speed delivery of that other quintessentially British invention, warm beer.

Jackson played at an award ceremony) is perhaps the shop's most public aficionado and its best poster boy. *43 Earlham St., WC2, tel. 020/7497–5543. Tube: Covent Garden. Open: Mon.–Sat. 10:30–7 (Thurs. until 8), Sun. noon–6.*

Jasper Conran. The son of furniture-meister Terence Conran has carved out a name for himself as a creator of classically styled clothes for the younger buyer. And he's not snobbish with it, as evidenced by prodigious work for the mid-price department store Debenhams and his own diffusion line, Jasper. *Found at Dickens and Jones, Harrods, Selfridges, and Debenhams.*

John Galliano. Johnny likes to juxtapose, whether it's in his outfits, which will one day undoubtedly mix chalk with cheese, or in his range of work, which includes stuff for Christian Dior, his own-name label, and couture fancies. Neck and neck with Alexander McQueen in the Brit Pack stakes. *Found at A La Mode, Harvey Nicholls, and Liberty.*

John Richmond. Some fashion gurus have had their knives out for Richmond recently, but he's ducked under the flak to produce some of the sassiest stuff to be found anywhere. *Found at Harrods, Jones, and Selfridges.*

Jones. Men flock to Jones for its incredibly wide variety of designer labels—everything from Alexander McQueen to Dries Van Noten and Helmut Lang. *13 Floral St., WC2, tel. 020/7240–8312. Tube: Covent Garden. Open Mon.–Sat. 10–6:30, Sun. 1–5.*

Katharine Hamnett. Hamnett has tried hard to move away from everyone's perception of her as the woman who annoyed Margaret Thatcher by designing startlingly sexy slogan T-shirts. As if to prove the past really is a foreign country, Hamnett now backs the Tories for their anti-European stance. *20 Sloane St., SW1, tel. 020/7823–1002. Tube: Knightsbridge. Open weekdays 10–6:30 (Wed. until 7), Sat. 10–6.*

Nicole Fahri. Modern classics made with great care and ambition distinguish Fahri as one for the fashion-conscious office habitué, girl or boy. Never afraid to add street touches to her standards, Fahri is likely to deliver the goods for her legion of fans for some years to come. *158 New Bond St., W1, tel. 020/7499–8368. Tube: Bond St. Open Mon.–Sat. 10–6 (Thurs. until 7). Other locations: 11 Floral St., WC2, tel. 020/7497–8713; 25–26 St. Christopher's Pl., W1, tel. 020/7486–3416; 27 Hampstead High St., NW3, tel. 020/7435–0866; 193 Sloane St., SW1, tel. 020/7235–0877. Men: 55–56 Long Acre, WC2, tel. 020/7240–5240.*

Paul Smith. Adored by anglophiles around the world for his clever takes on traditional English wear, Smith has achieved almost the status of a national institution. Now even kids can prance around in his well-tailored cuts and subdued colors, as long as their mummies and daddies don't mind splashing out a bit extra for a touch of latter-day class. *40–44 Floral St., WC2, tel. 020/7379–7133. Tube: Covent Garden. Open Mon.–Sat. 10–6:30 (Thurs. until 7).*

Rifat Ozbek. One of the big names of the Brit Pack is still cutting his cloth to suit a clientele—including the likes of Madonna—that demands near constant innovation. Like McQueen and Galliano, Ozbek shows few signs of running out of steam or ideas just yet. *Found at Browns.*

Vivienne Westwood. This is where it all began. The godmother of the whole Cool Britannia fashion generation continues to baffle and delight her (mostly) adoring public. With a new store in New York and a new house south of the Thames, Westwood is definitely not finished yet. *6 Davies St., W1, tel. 020/7629–3757. Tube: Bond St. Open Mon.–Sat. 10–6 (Thurs. until 7). Other locations: 44 Conduit St., W1, tel. 020/7439–1109; 430 King's Rd., SW3, tel. 020/7352–6551.*

Voyage. Hippyish, beautiful, demure, and effortlessly elegant clothes rendered with stunning attention to detail make this shop an essential voyage for every fashion tourist. You wish. Voyage operates the most stuck-up door policy imaginable—you have to be a member to get in, and you have to be wealthy or famous to become a member. Try impersonating sometime customer Kate Moss and you might stand a chance. *115 Fulham Rd., SW3, tel. 020/7823–9581. Tube: Sloane Sq. Open (if you're a chosen one) Mon.–Sat. 10:30–6:30 (Wed. until 7).*

MID-PRICE AND CHAIN STORES

Mid-range clothing boutiques of all shapes and sizes crowd the "Golden Mile" of **Oxford Street,** stretching east and west of the Oxford Circus tube station. You'll also find happy hunting around Covent Garden, Kensington High Street, King's Road in Chelsea, and South Molton Street in Mayfair. For cutting-edge fashion, head to **Petticoat Lane Market** (*see* Street Markets, *below*), where a number of aspiring designers have set up shop.

American Retro. Surprise: American Retro sells new, reasonably fashionable men's and women's gear—particularly accessories like belts, bags, and undies. The prices aren't exactly retro, but most things are cheaper than a single silk hanky at Harvey Nichols. *35 Old Compton St., W1, tel. 020/7734–3477. Tube: Leicester Sq. Open Mon.–Sat. 10:15–7.*

French Connection. Club fashion goes high-street in a shop that sometimes appears to try too hard. One recent ad featured the acronym FCUK, caused a storm of protest, and probably increased French Connection's street standing as well as, of course, its sales. *99–103 Long Acre, WC2, tel. 020/7379–6560. Tube: Covent Garden. Open Mon.–Sat. 10:30–7 (Thurs. until 8), Sun. noon–6. Branches located all over London.*

Hobbs. In trying to shake off its slightly staid image, Hobbs has come up with a selection of modern, classic *clobber* (clothes) without straying too near classic prices. *84–86 King's Rd., SW3, tel. 020/7581–2914. Tube: Sloane Sq. Open Mon.–Sat. 10–6:30 (Wed. until 7), Sun. noon–5. Branches located all over London.*

Hype D.F. This is the biggest new store for designer collections to open in London in years. It's a purpose-built miniature department store featuring the hottest, trendiest designers whose target is the 18–40 age group. Look around and you'll find some cool bargains. *48–52 Kensington High St., W8, tel. 020/7938–4343. Tube: High St. Kensington. Open Mon.–Sat. 10–6 (Thurs. until 8), Sun. noon–6.*

Jigsaw. One of the best of the chain stores, Jigsaw is more on the pulse than Next, less deliberately in-yer-face than French Connection. Although it was initially launched as a women's shop, its men's fashions knock the spots off most of its rivals. Branches can't compete with the concrete and frosted glass of the flagship Bond Street store. *126–127 New Bond St., W1, tel. 020/7491–4484. Tube: Bond St. Open Mon.–Sat. 10–6:30 (Thurs., until 7). Branches located all over London.*

VAT REFUNDS

Value Added Tax (VAT) is the European version of sales tax, although in this case it's an extortionate 17.5% of the net price. VAT is always included in the price, so half the time you don't even realize you're being taxed. Fortunately, foreigners are exempt from paying the VAT if any single purchase exceeds between £75 and £200; at some tourist-oriented shops, you can claim a refund on purchases of £20 or more. To collect a refund, ask the store for form VAT 407, which you'll submit to British customs when you leave the country. At the airport, look for the "VAT Refund" window either in the main concourse as you check in or in the departure lounge. For the complete scoop, see Taxes in Chapter 1.

Kensington Market. The indoor stalls here ply everything from silk scarves to studs to records to hair dye. Goths and grebos (motorcycle types) come here for denim and leather; club kids come for outrageous PVC and rubber gear. You'll find quite a few booths offering vintage clothing, shoes, and accessories from the '20s, '50s, and '70s, too. *49–53 Kensington High St., W8, tel. 020/7938–4343. Tube: High St. Kensington. Open Mon.–Sat. 10–6.*

Monsoon. Kinda groovy when hippy-chic made its comeback a decade ago, but now the style is almost exclusively associated with wishy-washy, flower designs. On the plus side, Monsoon's accessories are top-notch. *5 James St., WC2, tel. 020/7379–3623. Tube: Covent Garden. Open Mon.–Sat. 10–8, Sun. 11–6. Branches located all over London.*

Next. This British equivalent of The Gap offers a much wider range of styles, and the shops themselves are pretty classy, too. Men's and women's clothes are reasonably priced and fashionable. Next stores are found in all the major shopping districts. *327–329 Oxford St., W1, tel. 020/7409–2746. Tube: Bond St. Open Mon.–Wed. 10:30–7, Thurs. 10–8, Fri.–Sat. 10–7, Sun. noon–6. Branches located all over London.*

Oasis. Good interpretations of designer trends are the stock in trade here. Your friends back home probably won't even know the difference between Oasis and the real McCoy, so every pound spent here has the potential to reap hundreds in cred currency. *13 James St., WC2, tel. 020/7240–7445. Tube: Covent Garden. Open Mon.–Sat. 10–7 (Thurs. until 8), Sun. 11–6. Branches located all over London.*

Red or Dead. This cool seller of threads and shoes began as a stall in Camden Market. Now, people flock to the three stores for the reasonably priced stock of dresses, jeans, jackets, and accessories. Their line of big clunky shoes is a major draw. *33 Neal St., WC2, tel. 020/7379–7571. Tube: Covent Garden. Open weekdays 10:30–7, Sat. 10–6:30, Sun. noon–5:30. Other location: Hype D. F. 48–52 Kensington High St., W8, tel. 020/7937–2937.*

Shelly's Shoes. Shelly's sells outrageous, ultramodern shoes—some so cutting edge they look more like art than footwear. Leave those to RuPaul, and dive into the extensive selection of competitively priced Doc Martens and boots. Shelly's has branches all over the city. *159 Oxford St., W1, tel. 020/7437–5842. Tube: Oxford Circus. Open Mon.–Sat. 9:30–6:30 (Thurs. until 8), Sun. noon–6. Other locations: 40 Kensington High St., W8, tel. 020/7938–1082; 124B King's Rd., SW3, tel. 020/7581–5537; 266–270 Regent St., W1, tel. 020/7287–0939; 14–18 Neal St., WC2, tel. 020/7240–3726.*

Stock Market. You'll find T-shirts, flannel shirts, and other casual garb aplenty, but the large selection of Doc Martens (£40 and up) is the real reason to come. *245 Camden High St., NW1, tel. 020/7284–2174. Tube: Camden Town. Open weekdays 10–6:30, weekends 9:30–6:30.*

Top Shop/Top Man. Cheap is the word for this fashion megachain, with branches all over London. Smart shoppers avoid Top Shop's own label (the clothes are poorly made) and head for the faux-vintage "souled-out" section. The best selection and the loudest atmosphere are in the flagship store on Oxford

Street. *214 Oxford St., W1, tel. 020/7636–7700. Tube: Oxford Circus. Open Mon.–Sat. 9–8 (Thurs. until 9), Sun. noon–6.*

SECONDHAND CLOTHING

One of the best places to get used clothes in London is **Oxfam,** which runs 94 charity shops citywide. Each one offers the usual thrift-store finds: sturdy duds, household items, used books, and the like. Hipsters favor the shop near Oxford Circus, called **Oxfam Originals** (*see below*). Otherwise, try the Oxfam branches at 89 Camden High Street, NW1; 23 Drury Lane, WC2; and 202B Kensington High Street, W8.

If you'd rather browse for used clothes, head to **Camden Lock** in Camden Town or **King's Road** in Chelsea. Both avenues are lined with shops selling almost everything a bona fide clotheshorse could want. On weekends, Camden Lock is home to an excellent street market (*see below*). Finally, the indoor **Kensington Market** (*see above*) has a bunch of stalls devoted to clothing, shoes, and accessories of the '20s, '50s, and glorious '70s.

Blackout II. Attention, kitsch shoppers: Blackout stocks glam fashions from the 1920s to the 1970s, plus a wide selection of secondhand handbags and shoes. Look in the basement for real bargains (stuff that's out of season or needs repair). *51 Endell St., WC2, tel. 020/7240–5006. Tube: Covent Garden. Open weekdays 11–7, Sat. 11:30–6:30.*

Cornucopia. This is the place to find the vintage dress and accessories you've been searching for. The selection is varied, and prices range from bargain-basement to reasonable. *12 Upper Tachbrook St., SW1, tel. 020/7828–5752. Tube: Pimlico or Victoria. Open daily 11–6.*

Oxfam Originals. Of all the Oxfam shops in London, this is the best for funky castoffs. New stock arrives almost daily: As the sign proclaims, HUBBA HUBBA—WE'VE GOT SOME LOVELY NEW CLOTHES. *26 Ganton St., W1, tel. 020/7437–7338. Tube: Oxford Circus. Open Mon.–Sat. 11–6.*

Salvation Army Charity Shop/Cloud 9. Skip quickly past the ground-floor offerings (sportswear, kid's clothes, old books, etc.) and head upstairs to Cloud 9, where you'll find retro and groovy threads. Students get a 12% discount on all Cloud 9 purchases. *9 Princes St., W1, tel. 020/7495–3958. Tube: Oxford Circus. Open weekdays 10:30–6, Sat. 11–5:30.*

Yesterday's Bread. Take a step back in time and outfit yourself in retro gear. Yesterday's Bread specializes in never-before-worn garments from the '60s and '70s. *29–31 Foubert Pl., W1, tel. 020/7287–1929. Tube: Oxford Circus. Open weekdays 11:30–6:30, Sat. 11–6.*

BOOKSTORES

Generations of great authors have scribbled their lives away in London, from Henry Fielding, Charles Dickens, Oscar Wilde, and Virginia Woolf to current champs like Martin Amis, Kazuo Ishiguro, Doris Lessing, and Jeanette Winterson. And London has a plethora of bookstores to deal with its massive literary output. Note that many of these wonderful bastions of literacy hold free author signings, readings, workshops, and lectures weekly; check the "Books and Poetry" section of *Time Out* for more info.

GENERAL-INTEREST BOOKS

As far as chains go, one of the best is **Waterstone's,** whose main branch is at 121–129 Charing Cross Road (tel. 020/7434–4291). Nearby is **Books Etc.** (120–122 Charing Cross Rd., WC2, tel. 020/7379–6838), another major chain with a friendly and helpful staff, a basement full of bargains, and a logical layout. The award for largest and most chaotic bookstore goes to **Foyles** (119 Charing Cross Rd., WC2, tel. 020/7437–5660); if it's in print, they probably have it.

The **Dillons** chain has outlets all over London, including one dealing only in art books (*see below*). The best Dillons of all is the colossal, five-story behemoth in Bloomsbury at 82 Gower Street (tel. 020/7636–1577), which boasts 5 mi of shelving. At any given time it stocks 250,000–300,000 titles, guaranteed to stanch the reading frenzy of enrollees at the nearby University of London. Browsing at length is encouraged, and there's even a "CyberSt@tion" for net surfing.

SPECIALTY BOOKS

Compendium. With its potpourri of political tracts, new-age manifestos, and radical poetry, this alternative bookstore draws a devoted crowd. The store hosts frequent readings, and employees are extremely helpful and knowledgeable. *234 Camden High St., NW1, tel. 020/7485–8944. Tube: Camden Town. Open Mon.–Sat. 10–6, Sun. noon–6.*

SOUND SUPERMARKETS

These behemoths may be lacking in personality and service, but for one-stop shopping they can't be beat. Plus, they typically offer big discounts on CDs during the first week of release.

HMV. It's got branches everywhere, but make a special trip to the HMV flagship store for the widest selection. Check the listings in the windows for upcoming autograph sessions and free shows. 150 Oxford St., W1, tel. 020/7631–3423. Tube: Oxford Circus. Open Mon. 9–8, Tues.–Fri. 9:30–8, Sat. 9:30–7:30, Sun. noon–6.

TOWER RECORDS. Tower Records doesn't carry records—go figure. Overlook that and you'll find its specialty departments are some of the best in London. 1 Piccadilly Circus, W1, tel. 020/7439–2500. Tube: Piccadilly Circus. Open Mon.–Sat. 9 AM–midnight, Sun. noon–6.

VIRGIN MEGASTORE. Richard Branson's pride and joy is the second-largest entertainment store in the world, with 67,000 square ft of floor space (the Virgin Megastore in New York City is the largest). Come just to be seduced by the "shopping as entertainment" experience. 14–16 Oxford St., W1, tel. 020/7631–1234. Tube: Tottenham Court Rd. Open Mon. 9–9; Tues., Thurs.–Sat. 9:30–9; Wed. 10–9; Sun. noon–6.

Dillons Art Bookshop. This first-rate bookshop, part of the Dillons chain (*see above*), tempts academics, art students, and poets with a wide range of works on film, theater, fashion, art, and architecture. *8 Long Acre, WC2, tel. 020/7836–1359. Tube: Covent Garden or Leicester Sq. Open Mon.–Sat. 9:30 AM–10 PM (Tues. from 10), Sun. noon–6.*

Forbidden Planet. Horror, sci-fi, and fantasy fans will get sucked into this shop, never to return. The selection includes all those elusive anthologies you can't find elsewhere, trading cards, sci-fi videos, and a massive comics section. *71 New Oxford St., WC1, tel. 020/7836–4179. Tube: Tottenham Court Rd. Open Mon.–Sat. 10–6 (Thurs. and Fri. until 7).*

Gay's the Word. The name says it all. This Bloomsbury shop carries London's finest selection of gay and lesbian books (new and used), magazines, and videos. *66 Marchmont St., WC1, tel. 020/7278–7654. Tube: Russell Sq. Open Mon.–Sat. 10–6:30, Sun. 2–6.*

Murder One. Inside this dingy, unimposing shop lies an Aladdin's cave of British mysteries, true crime stories, and thrillers. If you're a fan of Hitchcock, Christie, and friends, don't miss it. Fantasy and science fiction junkies will get their fix, too. *71–73 Charing Cross Rd., WC2, tel. 020/7734–3485. Tube: Leicester Sq. Open Mon.–Wed. 10–7, Thurs.–Sat. 10–8.*

Silver Moon Women's Bookshop. This friendly, feminist bookshop is London's sisterhood central for literature by and about women. *64–68 Charing Cross Rd., WC2, tel. 020/7836–7906. Tube: Leicester Sq. Open Mon.–Sat. 10–6:30 (Thurs. until 8), Sun. noon–6.*

Soma Books. Soma specializes in black literature and in works on the history, art, politics, cuisine, folk traditions, women's studies, and landscapes of Asian, African, and Caribbean countries. Lose yourself in the latest Dominican fiction, or drool over cookbooks from South India. *38 Kensington La., SE11, tel. 020/7735–2101. Tube: Kensington. Open weekdays 9:30–5:30, Sat. 10–4.*

Sportspages. London's only comprehensive sports bookstore has a selection of football fanzines that's to die for (if that's your thing), plus books that will help you unlock the secrets of cricket or improve your performance at croquet. *Caxton Walk, 94–96 Charing Cross Rd., WC2, tel. 020/7240–9604. Tube: Leicester Sq. Open Mon.–Sat. 9:30–7.*

Stanfords. Stanfords's flagship store stocks more than 30,000 travel books that cover all sorts of exotic locales, and its selection of atlases, charts, and maps is simply astounding. If you need a map of your hometown or a topographical map of the moon, chances are you'll find it here. *12–14 Long Acre, WC2, tel. 020/7836–1321. Tube: Covent Garden. Open weekdays 9–7:30, Sat. 10–7. Other locations: 156 Regent St., W1, tel. 020/7434–4744; 52 Grosvenor Gardens, SW1, tel. 020/7730–1314.*

USED BOOKS

London's secondhand and antiquarian bookstores are excellent, though a bit chaotic—if you want that original edition of *Beowulf* pronto, expect to go dig it out yourself. Otherwise, you'll find the staff at most stores incredibly helpful and well informed. In Bloomsbury, you can make an entire day of wandering amid the dozens of secondhand bookstores on **Tottenham Court Road, Charing Cross Road,** and the adjacent **Cecil Court.**

Gloucester Road Bookshop. The fiction titles are especially well chosen in this cozy bookshop. *123 Gloucester Rd., SW7, tel. 020/7370–3503. Tube: Gloucester Rd. Open weekdays 8:30 AM–10:30 PM, weekends 10:30–6:30.*

Henry Pordes Books. The musty smell here cues visitors to the great selection of old books—some of the antiquarian variety and some just plain old. Fiction is one of the strongest sections. Prices for paperbacks start at 50p, not including a 10% student discount. *60 Charing Cross Rd., WC2, tel. 020/7836–9031. Tube: Leicester Sq. Open Mon.–Sat. 10–7.*

Pleasures of Past Times. Inside proprietor David Drummond's cozy little book kingdom you'll find a wealth of performing-arts books and related ephemera, as well as juvenilia. Titles range from the familiar to the obscure. *11 Cecil Ct., WC2, tel. 020/7836–1142. Tube: Leicester Sq. Open weekdays 11–2:30 and 3:30–5:45, generally on the first Sat. of each month, and other times by arrangement.*

Skoob. This is one of the best and most popular used-book stores in town, and the slightly higher prices reflect it. Most impressive are the humanities, foreign literature, and political science sections. Next door, **Skoob Two** (tel. 020/7404–3063) focuses on a more eclectic assortment of books about the occult, religion, anthropology, and so on. Students get a 10% discount at either store. *15–17 Sicilian Ave., at Southampton Row, WC1, tel. 020/7404–3063. Tube: Holborn. Open Mon.–Sat. 10:30–6:30.*

MUSIC

From postpunk and rockabilly to hip-hop and rave, London's music scene is first-rate, and plenty of record stores have sprouted up in recent years to meet the growing demand for both major label and indie music. Multinational chains like HMV and Virgin (*see box*) have megastores the size of small villages, and there are tons of tiny, funky, independent shops specializing in rare vinyl, bootleg recordings, dance 12"s, you name it. If you're in no hurry, you can spend an entire day cruising the music shops: try **Berwick Street** in Soho, **Camden High Street,** and **Hill Gate** at Ladbroke Grove.

Wherever you go, expect to pay £7–£12 for vinyl, £9–£16 for CDS, and around £2.50 for CD singles. Although prices aren't cheap, that same record or CD sells for at least $20 as an import the second it hits the shelves in the United States. (Of course, American collectors are known to travel to London to stock up on all those U.K.-*only* releases.) If you've brought your collection with you, know that London's smaller music stores pay top dollar for American CDS and indie records. For the latest buzz in town, check out mags like *Melody Maker, New Music Express, Q, Select,* and *Mixmag.* They are available at most music shops and newsstands.

Black Market. Twelve-inch import singles take up most of the ground floor, sharing some space with house music and listening turntables. Follow the booming music downstairs to the basement, which houses all music styles: drum 'n' bass varieties, techno, rap, and hip-hop. *25 D'Arblay St., W1, tel. 020/7437–0478. Tube: Oxford Circus. Open Mon.–Sat. 11–7.*

YE ODDE SHOPPES

ANYTHING LEFT-HANDED. Lefties of the world unite: buy yourself a left-handed can opener. 57 Brewer St., W1, tel. 020/7437–3910. Tube: Piccadilly Circus.

GALLERY OF ANTIQUE COSTUME AND TEXTILES. Although it's expensive, this is a great place to rummage through two floors of pre-1930 costumes, linens, drapes, and tapestries. 2 Church St., Marylebone, NW8, tel. 020/7723–9981. Tube: Marylebone.

*THE KITE STORE. Purchase a whimsical kite here and spend a sunny day flying it on Primrose Hill (*see *Camden Town in Chapter 2). 48 Neal St., WC2, tel. 020/7836–1666. Tube: Covent Garden.*

LUSH. The trendiest body-care shop in town sells delicious bath and shower potions, handmade every week. Its store in the city center has been so successful that Lush has now opened branches in other London locations. Don't leave town without a supply of Tisty Tosty Ballastics—heart-shape bath bombs. Way cool! 123 King's Rd., Chelsea, SW3, tel. 020/7376–8348. Tube: Sloane Sq. Other location: 7 and 11 The Piazza, Covent Garden, WC2, tel. 020/7240–4570. Tube: Covent Garden.

MYSTERIES. Here you'll find paraphernalia for the upcoming séance, including Ouija boards, magic oils, and how-to books. You can also make an appointment to have your palm read. 9 Monmouth St., WC2, tel. 020/7240–3688. Tube: Covent Garden.

THE ZIPPER STORE. For two decades, Zipper has kept fetishists well dressed in leather and PVC. 283 Camden High St., NW1, tel. 020/7284–0537. Tube: Camden Town.

Mister CD. There's something from every genre here: country, jazz, international, classical. You may have to sift through a lot of crazy stacks, but this is the cheapest place in town. *Berwick St., W1, no phone. Tube: Oxford Circus. Open daily 10–7.*

Music & Video Exchange. Those in the know give this London minichain top marks for prices (low), selection (enormous—the shop has expanded fourfold in recent years), and staff (friendly and helpful; never snarling, abrupt, or rude). The used CDS are tucked away in glass cases, and you have to crane your neck to read the titles, but the substantial markdowns are worth the trouble. *34–65 Notting Hill Gate, W11, tel. 020/7243–8573. Tube: Notting Hill Gate. Open daily 10–8. Other locations: 95 Berwick St., W1, tel. 020/7434–2939; 229 Camden High St., NW1, tel. 020/7267–1898; 480 Fulham Rd., SW6, tel. 020/7385–5350; 28 Pembridge Rd, W11, tel. 020/7221–1444.*

Rough Trade. The fine selection of indie music, lo-fi, and space rock imports on both vinyl and CD draws music fans from all over the world to this basement store below a skateboard shop, although the emphasis is shifting increasingly to dance music, and in particular drum 'n' bass. There are also frequent (free) performances by visiting bands. The original shop (130 Talbot Rd., London, W11, tel. 020/7229–8541) has a lot more punk memorabilia on the walls, but the selection is similar, with lots of techno and trance vinyl. *16 Neal's Yard, WC2, tel. 020/7240–0105. Tube: Covent Garden or Tottenham Court Rd. Open Mon.–Sat. 10–6:30, Sun. 1–5.*

GIFT IDEAS

Like any tourist mecca, London is stuffed full of tacky gift shops and souvenir stalls. Nothing wrong with that, of course; the capital would be a poorer place without fake police helmets, plastic Carnaby Street signs, and big-eared Prince Charles masks. But if you want to go that extra mile, impress the folks back home, and get your hands on a more lasting memento, it's worth checking out some specialist shops that offer perfect present material.

Asprey. English ladies and gentlemen plus their moneyed counterparts from the USA, Japan, and the new Russia can be spotted eyeing the delicious gifts on sale here. Stunningly intricate clocks vie for your money with diamond encrusted bags. If old, posh England is your thing, take a look. *165–169 New Bond St., W1, tel. 020/7493–6767. Tube: Bond St. Open weekdays 9:30–5:30, Sat. 10–5.*

Beatles for Sale. Okay, Liverpool might be the Fab Four's birthplace, but London was where they recorded the most memorable music of the pop age and here is where you can back up your own Beatles memories with an incredibly wide range of souvenirs and bric-a-brac. *8 Kingley St., W1, tel. 020/7434–0464. Tube: Oxford Circus. Open daily 10–7.*

The Christmas Shop. "I wish it could be Christmas every day" goes the song, and at this happily ridiculous shop, that wish has come true. Everything from trees and angels to tinsel and reindeer are on sale all year-round to allow would-be Santas the chance to bestow prezzies whenever they like. *Hay's Galleria, 55A Tooley St., SE1, tel. 020/7378–1998. Tube: London Bridge. Open weekdays 9:45–5:30, weekends noon–5.*

Crafts Council. Jewelry, glassware, and fine textiles make excellent gifts anywhere; here the extra bonus is knowing you are buying work made by the best of contemporary craftsmen and women. *44A Pentonville Rd., N1, tel. 020/7806–2559. Tube: Angel. Open Tues.–Sat. 11–5:45, Sun. 2–5:45. Other location: Victoria & Albert Museum, Cromwell Rd., SW7, tel. 020/7589–5070.*

Daisey and Toms. If you're buying for kids back home, this is the place to come for toys or clothes that are up-market of Hamley's. If you're with kids, this is the place to come to while away spare time—if it's raining, say—as the shop boasts a carousel, puppet shows, and soda bar. *181 King's Rd., SW3, tel. 020/7352–5000. Tube: Sloane Sq. Open weekdays 10–6 (Wed. until 7), Sat. 9:30–6:30, Sun. noon–6.*

Hamley's. The Harrods of the toy world draws tourists via its name alone, and the good news is the shop lives up to its hype. Seven floors of goodies keep kids and parents happy, and there are plenty of cheapo bargains to be had, despite some blatant overpricing. *188–196 Regent St., W1, tel. 020/7734–3161. Tube: Oxford Circus. Open Mon.–Wed. 10–7, Thurs.–Fri. 10–8, Sat. 9:30–7, Sun. noon–6.*

James Lock. If it's English clichés you're looking for, you'd better head for this ancient milliner's, established back in 1676. Bowler hats, top hats, and deerstalkers are all available from the place that counts Oscar Wilde among its previous customers. *6 St. James's St., SW1, tel. 020/7980–5849. Tube: Green Park. Open weekdays 9–5:30, Sat. 10–5:30.*

James Smith & Sons. To complete the English gent look, you'll need an umbrella, a piece of equipment that could come in handy on your stay in any case, given London's uncanny ability to attract the rain clouds. Here you'll find a breathtaking array of brollies in a setting straight out of the Victorian age. *53 New Oxford St., WC1, tel. 020/7836–4731. Tube: Tottenham Court Rd. Open weekdays 9:30–5:30, Sat. 10–5:30.*

Past Times. Tourists who demand a piece of old England to take home with them could do a lot worse than visit Past Times, where nostalgia is king. As a bonus, the price range is very wide, so you don't have to blow that last traveler's check on a cute little teapot. *146 Brompton Rd., SW3, tel. 020/7581–7616. Tube: Knightsbridge. Open Mon.–Sat. 9:30–6 (Wed. until 7), Sun. 11–5.*

R. Twining & Co. If tea is the English champagne, Twining is the Moët. This fascinating shop features a museum as well as a broad collection of superb teas, including fine versions of the all-time classics, English Breakfast and Earl Grey. *216 Strand, WC2, tel. 020/7353–3511. Tube: Charing Cross. Open weekdays 9:30–4:30.*

BY ROYAL APPOINTMENT

From soft drinks (Coca-Cola) and champagne (Moët & Chandon) to breakfast cereal (Weetabix) and household cleaning fluid (Jeyes), the Royal family chooses the products it likes and hands their makers a warrant, a kind of seal of satisfaction that confers much honor. Warrant holders can then adorn their packaging with a regal coat of arms, as well as the words "By Royal Appointment."

Only four Royals can dole out warrants: the Queen, the Duke of Edinburgh, Prince Charles, and the Queen Mother. Although, as far as can be told from their warrants, they all share a love of field sports, their individual tastes diverge in other areas. For one thing there's a generation gap. Prince Charles, for instance, is well-known as a fervent antismoker and has never given his stamp to a cigarette manufacturer. For years, the Queen's coat of arms could be found on packets of cigarettes made by Gallaher, but in 1999 HM pulled the plug on the nicotine kings. The Queen Mother, however, has few PC qualms, and her warrant is still to be found on John Player Specials. Specialist London establishments, particularly on the field sports front, are well represented in the list of appointees, so go net some royally approved fishing tackle at Farlow & Co. (5 Pall Mall, SW1, tel. 020/7839–2423) or lash out on whips used by the Queen at Swaine Adeney (10 Old Bond St., W1, tel. 020/7409–7277).

The Singing Tree. A fantastic display of classic English dollhouses and accessories makes this store the leader in its field. The houses themselves might not fit in your hand baggage, but you can still treat yourself to one or two of the exquisite extras. *69 New King's Rd., SW6, tel. 020/7736–4527. Tube: Fulham Broadway. Open Mon.–Sat. 10–5:30.*

World of Football. That's *soccer* to statesiders. English league football is revered around the world and you can get your hands on any replica kit you care to mention at this mammoth temple to the world's most popular sport. *119–121 Oxford St., W1, tel. 020/7439–0778. Tube: Oxford Circus. Open Mon.–Sat. 10–7 (Thurs. until 8), Sun. noon–6.*

HOUSEHOLD STUFF

Sure, London's department stores (*see above*) have just about all the furnishings and household items you need under one roof—but sometimes you feel you need a royal title and trust fund to afford them. If you want funky old stuff, spend your weekends scouring the street markets (*see below*). For cheap, functional, new furniture (the kind that's slapped together in the sweatshops of China or Eastern Europe), check out the shops lining **Holloway Road** or **Walworth Road.**

Cargo Home Store. This chain sells sturdy new furniture, rugs, and household items from around the world (Americans will be reminded of Pier One Imports). Prices are reasonable. *209 Tottenham Court Rd., W1, tel. 020/7580–2895. Tube: Goodge St. Open weekdays 9:30–6:30, Sat. 10–7, Sun. noon–6. Other location: 245–249 Brompton Rd., SW3, tel. 020/7584–7611. Tube: South Kensington.*

Conran Shop. If you're shopping with a rich aunt, or with someone else's credit card, this is the place to go. The stunning collection of household furnishings is presented like fine art. The store itself is located in the historic Michelin Building, which has been lovingly refurbished. *81 Fulham Rd., SW3, tel. 020/7589–7401. Tube: South Kensington. Open weekdays 10–6 (Wed. and Thurs. until 7), Sat. 10–6:30, Sun. noon–5:30.*

Habitat. All the cool furnishings, kitchen stuff, and linens here are by the store's own designers. Although most prices are decent, it would be a major investment to furnish your entire apartment here. *206 King's Rd., SW3, tel. 020/7631–3880. Tube: Sloane St. Other location: 196 Tottenham Court Rd., W1, tel. 020/7255–2545. Both stores open weekdays 10–6:30 (Wed. until 8), Sat. 9:30–6:30, Sun. noon–6.*

Inventory. Twenty-three thousand square feet filled with everything you could ever want for your home (except furniture) at affordable prices. Since it opened in late 1996, this store—whose motto is "a home store with ideas"—has revolutionized London's household goods market. *26 Kensington High St., W8, tel. 020/7937–2626. Tube: High St. Kensington. Open weekdays 10–7, Sat. 9–6, Sun. noon–6.*

OXO Tower. Set in the spectacularly renovated Art Deco landmark, this is a craft center with a difference. The craftspeople here have to pass rigorous selection procedures to set up in prime riverside workshops to make, display, and sell their work. Designs—from cushion covers to steel hoverbeds—are cutting edge. Nearby, and also in South Bank, is **Gabriel's Wharf,** at Upper Ground, another craft center. *Bargehouse St., tel. 020/7401–3610. Tube: Blackfriars or Waterloo. Design studios open Tues.–Sun. 11–6, bars and bistros open 11–late.*

Be wary of pickpockets while browsing the markets. Keep cash and other valuables close to your person, as London's Artful Dodgers can be very, very crafty.

STREET MARKETS

You'd be hard pressed to find a better way to shop than in London's street markets, where one person's junk routinely morphs into another person's treasure. And an ever-changing cast of characters—teenage hipsters, pram-pushing mums, Bedouin stall holders, and wide-eyed tourists—makes for excellent people-watching, even when you're down to your last pence. The biggest and best markets are in **Camden** and on **Portobello Road** (*see below*) and draw correspondingly huge crowds. Other, smaller markets are where Londoners have been going for centuries to stock the refrigerator (even before there was such a thing). Most markets even offer food stalls where you can get a cheap and tasty lunch.

Haggling is acceptable in most of the street markets—especially on items without a price tag—but more difficult if you're speaking in an obviously foreign accent. The smartest of hagglers do a little research (i.e., ask around at competing booths) to find out the relative worth of an item, and then bargain from there. One final note: although street markets are primarily a weekend pastime, some stalls and many shops remain open during the week—without the chatter, commotion, and congestion of claustrophobia-inducing crowds.

WEST AND CENTRAL LONDON

BERWICK STREET

Soho's once-thriving Berwick Street produce mart has shrunk recently, but it's still a great place to buy a cheap lunch of fruit, bread, and cheese. Stop by around 5 PM—when the merchants are desperate to get rid of their produce—and you'll walk away with incredible deals. Cheapie clothes, used CDS and records, and assorted trinketry can be found on Rupert Street. *Berwick and Rupert Sts., W1. Tube: Leicester Sq. or Piccadilly Circus. Open Mon.–Sat. 8–6.*

PORTOBELLO ROAD

The Portobello Road market is second only to the Camden markets (*see below*) for liveliness and funkiness. You can catch didgeridoo players, rasta cellists, and other performers at the small courtyard near the market's center. The southern end is the most touristy and has tons of Portobello's trademark item: antiques. At the northern end, locals shop for fruit, vegetables, flowers, and secondhand clothes. The whole affair lines Portobello Road for more than a mile and can take the entire day to conquer, but the best time to go is Saturday morning. *Portobello Rd., W10 and W11, tel. 020/7727–7684 or 020/7341–5277. Tube: Ladbroke Grove or Notting Hill Gate. Open Sat. 6–4; some clothing and produce stalls also open Mon.–Wed. 9–5, Thurs. 9–1, Fri. 7–6.*

ST. MARTIN-IN-THE-FIELDS

This small market is chiefly targeted at tourists. Even so, there are some surprisingly cool finds, including ethnic jewelry and art, and some decent clothing. The best stuff is hidden away near Adelaide Street. *St. Martin-in-the-Fields churchyard, off Trafalgar Sq., WC2, tel. 020/7930–7821. Tube: Charing Cross. Open Mon.–Sat. 11–5, Sun. noon–5.*

EAST END

BRICK LANE

You can find anything your heart desires at this East End institution, although it's primarily about tacky new clothes and cheap fruit. Best of all, it's rarely glutted with tourists. Listen and learn as the Cockney vegetable sellers twist the English language (and occasionally hurl handfuls of carrots) to hawk their wares. *Brick La. and surrounding streets, E1 and E2. Tube: Aldgate East and Shoreditch. Open Sun. 8–1.*

PETTICOAT LANE

Although not as hip as the Camden markets (*see below*), Petticoat Lane is almost as mammoth, swallowing Middlesex Street and a host of side streets. It's popular, so arrive early or prepare for heavy crowds. Goods for sale include cheap fashions, old watches, new and used shoes, luggage, household goods, and miscellaneous groovy bric-a-brac. Best time to go: 9 AM on Sunday. *Middlesex St., E1. Tube: Aldgate, Aldgate East, or Liverpool St. Open Sun. 9–2.*

SPITALFIELDS

Spitalfields Market is held inside a huge barnlike warehouse, featuring stalls selling antiques, crafts, and snacks. It's also one of the few markets selling organic meat, cheese, and produce (Friday and Sunday only). Performances of various sorts are held periodically on its small stage. *Commercial St. at Brushfield St., E1, tel: 020/7247–6590. Tube: Liverpool St. Open weekdays and Sun. 9–6.*

NORTH LONDON

CAMDEN MARKETS

Wait a few moments after stepping off the tube to orient yourself in the crushing mob; after all, Camden's markets are the best and busiest in London, unparalleled in atmosphere and selection. The sprawl actually includes five markets, of which **Camden Lock,** (Camden Lock Pl., near Chalk Farm Rd., tel. 020/7284–2084) is indisputably the best. Get your used clothes, bootlegs, incense, crystals, knickknacks, and smart drinks here. Lots of Londoners come just to hang out and breathe in the scenery. The lock itself—a pleasant waterway overlooked by cafés and more shops—is just north of the Camden Tube station.

Other Camden markets include **Camden Canal Market** (Chalk Farm Rd.), featuring everything from clothes to old toys; **Camden Market** (Camden High St. near Buck St., tel. 020/7938–4343), with stalls selling heaps of clothing and unique accessories; the indoor **Electric Ballroom,** tel. 020/7485–9006 (Camden High St. next to Camden Tube), best for clubbing garb and used clothes; and the **Stables** (Chalk Farm Rd., tel. 020/7485–5511), which has organic produce, some antiques, and lots of junk. *NW1. Tube: Camden Town. Camden Lock open weekends 10–6 (indoor stalls open Tues.–Sun. 10–6); Camden Canal Market open weekends 10–6; Camden Market open Thurs.–Sun. 10–6; Electric Ballroom open Sun. 10–5; Stables open weekends 9–6.*

CAMDEN PASSAGE

Not to be confused with the very cool Camden markets, Camden Passage is a narrow alley with antiques stores and a two-day-a-week street market. The shops are expensive, but you might find some bargains lurking in the market among the rugs, furniture, jewelry, prints, toys, and other small, oddly shaped items with ancient and obscure applications. *Camden Passage near Upper St., N1, tel. 020/7359–0190. Tube: Angel. Market open Wed. 7–2, Sat. 8–4; shops open Tues.–Sat. 10–5.*

CHAPEL

This is where locals from Islington and Pentonville have been coming to buy their fruit, flowers, household items, shampoo, clothing, and other essentials for more than a century. It's as untouristy as it gets in central London. Best times to go are the weekends. *Chapel Market, N1. Tube: Angel. Open Tues.–Sat. 9–3:30 (Thurs. until 1), Sun. 9–1.*

SOUTH OF THE THAMES

BERMONDSEY/NEW CALEDONIAN

Some loophole dating back to the 18th century makes it legal to sell furniture and antiques of questionable origin at this Bermondsey Square market. You certainly can't complain about the prices. *Bermondsey Sq., SE1, tel. 020/7351–5353. Tube: Borough or London Bridge. Open Fri. 5 AM–2 PM.*

BRIXTON

Rock down to vibrant Electric Avenue for this sprawling Latin- and Afro-Caribbean–flavored market. You'll find a scattering of used clothing, exotic produce, good deals on reggae tapes and records, and mounds of more mundane wares like soap, batteries, and shampoo. *Electric Ave., SW9, tel. 020/7926–2530. Tube: Brixton. Open Mon.–Sat. 8–6 (Wed. until 3).*

EAST STREET

This market has been popular with south London locals for more than 100 years. Crowds make it difficult to walk through, but that's part of East Street's appeal. The cocky shouts of vendors alert you to bargains on everyday items like film, batteries, and cosmetics, as well as cheap hi-fi items. A flower and plant market adds color on Sunday, which is the best time to go. *East St., SE17. Tube: Elephant and Castle. From the station walk ¾ mi south on Walworth Rd.; or take Bus 45, 68, or 171. Open Tues.–Sat. 8–5 (Thurs. until 2), Sun. 8–2.*

8 OUTDOOR ACTIVITIES

UPDATED BY TIM PERRY

The salaries of professional athletes in England may not be as preposterously huge as they are in the States, but don't believe for one second that the British aren't dead serious about sports. When things are going well for an English national team, especially in football, a definite "feel-good" factor envelopes the capital. If you feel like joining in as either a spectator or a participant, *Time Out* (£1.80) is a great resource: the "Sport" section lists upcoming events, classes, and sports clubs, along with times, dates, and prices. Also at your disposal is the London **Sportsline** (tel. 020/7222–8000, weekdays 10–6), with information on all participant sports throughout the region, for the price of a local call (be prepared to deal with a busy signal at most times). Headline events of all sorts take place at **Wembley Complex** (Empire Way, Wembley, Middlesex, tel. 020/8900–1234; Tube: Wembley Park), although the main **Wembley Stadium** is due to be pulled down in 2000 and turned into a new national stadium.

SPECTATOR SPORTS

ATHLETICS

Although the efforts of Linford Christie, Colin Jackson, Jonathan Edwards, and Euan Thomas in recent years have assured Britain a profile in the world of track and field, the country has few decent stadiums to accommodate the sport. The only one within the capital's environs is the **Crystal Palace National Sports Centre** (Ledrington Rd., off Anerley Hill, SE19, tel. 020/8778–0131; Rail: Crystal Palace, from Victoria), which stages most of the year's big meets. On such occasions the neighborhood's roads clog up, so it's best to make the 25-min train journey that drops you off right next to the stadium.

CRICKET

Like baseball, cricket—England's national summer game—is incomprehensible to most of the world outside the game's homeland. Residents in England's former colonies also usually know the difference between a batsman and a bowler, but those in the United States have never quite gotten on the ball, so to speak. Still, cricket and baseball are both derived from a sport now known as rounders, so these two sports are distant cousins. Very distant.

Cricket is an extremely complex sport: two batters, hundreds of runs, both teams (usually) wearing white, five-day matches, et cetera. Its beauty lies in its subtle developments and the intricacy of its tactical maneuvering. If you're confused, ask another spectator—he or she will probably enjoy sharing some knowledge. But the real fun of cricket lies in the relaxed pace, giving you the opportunity to sit outside and drink pints in the afternoon. If this sounds like your cup of tea, matches are held at **Lord's Cricket Ground** (St. John's Wood Rd., NW8, tel. 020/7432–1066; Tube: St. John's Wood) and **Foster's Oval** (Kennington Oval, SE11, tel. 020/7582–7764; Tube: Oval), the latter generally a friendlier and more laid-back place to witness the *thwack* of willow on leather. Tickets at both venues usually cost £6–£12 (with substantial discounts for students), although prices for the international test matches can go up to £40.

A recent development, following the 1996 Cricket World Cup, has been the adoption of brightly colored uniforms by the National League. Their Sunday matches, held between the different counties of England, have another strangely familiar feature to Americans: a white ball. Although some purists grumble about the "Americanization" of the sport, and wags see the shift to colored shirts as a marketing ploy to sell team jerseys, the matches are still pure cricket and it's refreshing to see student types and young kids—yes, often dressed in the jerseys—enjoying the matches alongside older viewers. Not so recent is the game of women's cricket, which has been played in England for years and is flourishing. The **Women's Cricket Association** (tel. 0121/440–0567) can clue you in to what's going on in the women's game.

A cricket ball is made of cork covered in red leather with a single seam running around the middle. If you see a bowler with red stains on his trousers, he's probably been trying to polish one side of the ball to increase its curve.

FOOTBALL/SOCCER

Of all sports, football (what Americans call soccer) is the one pursued most passionately by the Brits. It all started in Derby in AD 217 as part of a festival celebrating a victory over Roman troops. Although the country takes great pride in founding the professional sport, its attempts to win the FIFA World Cup have only come good once, and that was way back in 1966. In the grim days of the '70s and '80s, English soccer was perhaps best known overseas for the amount of hooliganism at games. Fortunately, the present-day soccer experience is a different matter; ticketed seating became the norm during the '90s, and facilities such as catering have been much improved. That doesn't mean that people don't get carried away with aggressive chants and shouts, especially if their team is getting goals thumped past them. A restructuring of the league has also brought more sponsorship and television rights, so that the top clubs can now afford some of the best stars around. Today, a typical Premiership fixture—far and away the elite of the four professional national leagues—offers the opportunity to see big names from around the world, such as the Italian pair of Gianfranco Zola and Roberto Di Matteo (of the Chelsea team) and the Dutch stars Denis Berkamp and Marc Overmars (of Arsenal), who play alongside such exciting French internationals as Nicholas Anelka, Emmanuel Petit, and Patrick Vieira. The best source of gossip and news is on the Internet; surf to the mega-size **Football 365 site** (www.Football365.co.uk) or the **Soccernet site** (www.soccernet.com), both of which include info on all the best clubs in the country, plus lists of all the big tournaments.

Two northern England teams—Liverpool and Manchester United—dominated the trophies during the '80s and '90s, respectively, but North London's Arsenal did the "double" in 1998, when they won the coveted Premiership League title and the hotly contested FA (Football Association) Cup Final, the sport's prestigious knockout competition. When it comes to local football, the most popular of London's eight major clubs are **Arsenal** (Arsenal Stadium, Avenell Rd., N5, tel. 020/7704–4000; Tube: Arsenal), followed by their long-time rivals, the **Tottenham Hotspur** (White Hart La., 748 High St., N17, tel. 020/8365–5050; Tube: Seven Sisters, then BritRail to White Hart La.). The Spurs, as they're often called, experienced a lean decade in the '90s but are currently rebuilding under the auspices of one George Graham, a controversial figure who had brought much success to Arsenal. The other big London team in the Premiership is **Chelsea** (Stamford Bridge, Fulham Rd., SW6, tel. 020/7385–5545; Tube: Fulham Broadway or Bus 221 from Waterloo), a fashionable club buoyed by recent big-money signings from Italy, France, Norway, and Uruguay. Other perennial Premiership teams from the capital are **West Ham United** (Boleyn Ground, Green St., E13, tel. 020/8548–2700; Tube: Upton Park), the representatives of the blue-collar East End and the polar opposite of West London's Chelsea. Then there's good old **Wimbledon;** as its name suggests, this team has its roots in southwest London. Since they lost the stadium a few years ago, they've been ground-sharing with Division 1's **Crystal Palace** at the opposite end of

FIGURE THIS: A BRIEF RUNDOWN OF CRICKET'S RULES

Cricket is played by two 11-member teams on a roughly circular pitch *about 90 yards in diameter, surrounded by a rope* boundary. *Most of the action, however, takes place on a central rectangle, 22 yards long. The batting team places two batters at opposite sides of the rectangle; a* wicket *(two* bails *balanced atop three* stumps *of wood) stands behind each batter. The object of the batter is twofold: to guard the wickets and to score runs. The fielding team's* bowler *(pitcher) at one end of the rectangle throws a ball to the batter at the opposite end, attempting to* bowl *the batter out by knocking the bails off the stumps. The ball is thrown overhand with a straight arm (bent elbows are penalized) and is usually bounced off the pitch, which has been hardened by rollers.*

The batter attempts to hit the ball far enough that he and his batting partner can exchange places and score runs. Unlike in baseball, there are no foul lines, so the ball may go in any direction. If the ball crosses the boundary on the ground, the batter scores four runs; if it crosses the boundary without touching the ground, six runs are scored. The batter's wicket is taken *(he's out) if the bails are knocked off the stumps, while the batsmen are changing places, or if his ball is caught on the fly. Once a player's wicket is taken, he is replaced by the next batsman.*

An over *(six throws) is bowled from one end of the rectangle; then another bowler takes over from the other end and the fielders rotate accordingly. The batting team remains at bat until 10 wickets have been taken (the end of an* inning*) or until they* declare *(decide to stop batting and take the field). A team will declare because to win, they must not only score the most runs but also take all of the opposing side's wickets by the scheduled end of the game.*

The length of a match varies widely: Limited over matches have a set number of overs and are usually one-day events, other county matches last four days, and international test matches last up to five days.

south London (Selhurst Park, Whitehorse La., SE25, tel. 020/8771–8841; BritRail to Selhurst). Despite their uprooting, Wimbledon players managed to stay afloat in the Premiership for a decade on shoestring resources. Another south London club that has managed to mix in with the Premiership big boys is **Charlton Athletic** (The Valley, Floyd Rd., SE7, tel. 020/8333–4010; Rail: Charlton, from Charing Cross). For years West London's **Fulham** (Craven Cottage, Stevenage Rd., SW6, tel. 020/7893–8383; Tube: Putney Bridge) poked around soccer's doldrums, but a massive cash injection by Mohammed Al-Fayed (owner of Harrods, the father of Princess Di's rumored fiancé, etc.), the recruitment of media darling Kevin Keegan as manager, and the purchase of some big-name players has meant that they are one of the hottest tickets around. Although Fulham is currently in the Nationwide Division 1 (the league below the Premiership), many expect the team to take off soon, leaving their inadequate little ground (stadium is too grand a word) behind.

The football season runs from mid-August to early May (when the FA Cup Final brings the full season to its traditional close), and most games are held at 3 PM on Saturday, although television contracts dictate that there is also usually one Premiership game on Sunday at 4 PM and another at 8 PM on Monday. There are also some games played on Tuesday and Wednesday, usually in the early or late part of the seasons to relieve fixture congestion. Tickets, available from each club's box office, run £15–£40, depending on the seats. Note, however, that most Arsenal, Tottenham, and Chelsea games are sold out well in advance. Important matches, like the FA Cup Final, are held at London's **Wembley Stadium** (*see above*). Wembley is also the home of the English national team, which has six to eight home fixtures per year.

MOTORSPORT

The world-famous **British Formula One Grand Prix** is held every July to sold-out crowds at **Silverstone Circuit** (Silverstone, Northants, tel. 01327/857271; Rail: Northampton). Tickets are hard to come by and expensive (£65 and up), so contact the box office as early as possible. During the off-season, Silverstone Circuit hosts local and qualifying races on an irregular basis; flip through *Time Out* for the latest. Another popular motorsports venue is **Brands Hatch** (Fawkham, Kent, tel. 01474/872331; Rail: Swanley from Charing Cross); it's closer to London but doesn't have the F1 appeal. Nevertheless, it stages top-flight races throughout the year in all other categories and also has several huge motorcycle meetings.

POLO

Depending on whom you talk to, polo either originated in Persia in the 6th century and was subsequently "discovered" by British army officers stationed in India, or the soldiers developed the sport themselves. In either case, polo rapidly gained ground with the upper classes and has remained the province of the rich, largely because polo requires a lot of horses. Players must be able to afford a "string" of steeds so they can switch mounts during each game as horse after horse tires of being slammed into other horses at high speeds.

The Guards Polo Club is the choicest of polo grounds, and it's the venue for the **Royal Windsor Cup** in early June. The Alfred Dunhill **Queen's Cup,** the traditional start of the London "season," is usually held in mid-June. The biggest event of the year is late July's **Cartier International,** which draws the best players from around the world; star-spotters can indulge themselves by watching for royals (the Queen usually presents the trophy herself), fading rock stars, and other notables. The club hosts matches most weekends, and quite often "picnic passes," costing £10 per carload of people, are available. Tickets for big matches start at £15. *Smith's Lawn, Windsor Great Park, tel. 01784/437797. BritRail: Windsor & Eton Central.*

RACING

GREYHOUND RACING

Many Londoners love to bet on what they affectionately call "the dogs." Greyhound racing is even shedding its unfashionable skin and becoming vaguely trendy. The top destination is the venerable **Walthamstow Stadium** (Chingford Rd., E4, tel. 020/8531–4255; Tues., Thurs., and Sat. at 7:30 PM; Rail: Highams Park from Liverpool St.), with its Art Deco trims, spacious bars, and surprisingly decent restaurants. Other tracks within relatively easy reach from central London are **Catford Stadium** (Ademore Rd., SE26, tel. 020/8690–8000; Thurs. and Sat. at 7:30 PM; Rail: Catford Bridge from Charing Cross), **Crayford Stadium** (Stadium Way, Crayford, tel. 01322/557836; Mon. and Sat. at 7:30 PM and also free on Sat. at 11 AM; Rail: Crayford from Charing Cross), **Romford Stadium** (London Rd., Romford, Essex, tel. 01708/762345; Mon. and Fri. at 7:35 PM, Sat. at 11 AM—free—and 7:35 PM; Rail: Romford from Liverpool St.), and **Wimbledon Stadium** (Plough La., SW17, tel. 020/8946–8000; Tues., Fri., and Sat. at 7:30 PM; Tube: Wimbledon Park). Races usually take place in the evening, and seat prices range from £2 to £5; check *Time Out* for schedules. And remember, no matter which dog you back, the rabbit always wins.

W. G. (DIS)GRACE(D)

W. G. Grace was the greatest cricket player of all time. He played first-class cricket for more than 40 years, scoring 54,986 runs, including more than 100 "centuries" (100 runs in one inning). England could use another like him today: although England invented cricket, its former colonies now excel at the game. A longstanding rivalry exists between England and Australia, culminating in the Test matches. The winner of this series is awarded the "Ashes," a tiny urn containing the remains of a ball symbolically burned to mourn the death of English cricket after a loss to Australia. In recent years the Aussies have usually trounced the Brits.

HORSE RACING

Although scruffy beer drinkers and quid bettors make up the daily crowd, you couldn't keep the Queen herself away from the pomp of the **Royal Meeting at Ascot,** Britain's most prestigious horse race. You'll need to book good seats far in advance for this event, held in mid-June every year, although some tickets—far away from the Royal Enclosure and winning post—can be bought on the day of the race for £6. There are also Ascot Heath tickets available for a mere £2, but these only admit you to a picnic area in the middle of the race course. You'll be able to see the horses, of course, but that's not why people come to Ascot. The real spectacle is the crowd itself: Enormous headgear is de rigueur on Ladies Day—usually the Thursday of the meet—and those who arrive inappropriately dressed (jeans, shorts, tank tops) will be turned away from their grandstand seats. For more info, contact the **Ascot Racecourse** (Ascot, Berkshire, tel. 01344/622211; Rail: Ascot from Waterloo). The racecourse is a 10-min walk from the station.

If you're lucky, you may spy members of the royal family watching from their private stand at the **Royal Windsor Racecourse** (Maidenhead Rd., Windsor, tel. 01753/865234), best accessed from BritRail's Windsor & Eton Riverside station from Waterloo. **Epsom Downs Racecourse** (Epsom, Surrey, tel. 01372/726311; BritRail: Epsom from Charing Cross, Victoria, or Waterloo stations) hosts relatively few races but is home to the highly prestigious **Derby** meeting held in the first full week of June. The Derby race is the first of the five "classics" in the flat racing calendar and is run over a testing and undulating 1½-mi course for three-year-olds. The other big race in that week is the **Oaks,** a similar event to the Derby but limited to three-year-old fillies. Other popular tracks just a short train ride from Waterloo station include **Kempton Park Racecourse** (Staines Rd. E, Sunbury-on-Thames, tel. 01932/782292; BritRail: Kempton Park from Waterloo), and the well-organized **Sandown Park** (Esher, Surrey, tel. 01372/463072; BritRail: Esher from Waterloo). Admission to the above courses runs £5–£15, though one notable exception to these prices is the Derby, where tickets start at £5 for distant enclosures and run up steeply to £90 for the "morning dress obligatory" Queen's Stand.

ROWING

The **Oxford and Cambridge Boat Race** (tel. 020/7379–3234) takes place on the Thames, southwest of central London between Putney and Mortlake. It begins at 4 PM (although tidal fluctuations can alter the time), usually on the last Saturday of March, when the weather can still be quite chirpy. Go early to secure yourself a spot in a pub along the river, or join the crowds on Chiswick or Putney Bridge. Rivalry is fierce between the universities, but most spectators don't really care whether Cambridge (light blue) or Oxford (dark blue) wins—it's just a nice way to spend a Saturday. During the **Henley Royal Regatta** (tel. 01491/572153), held June 28–July 2 in 2000, single sculls and two-, four-, and eight-person crews from all over the world race along the Thames. Although it's quite a trek from London to Henley-on-Thames, a day along the towpath watching the rowing—and the people—can be delightful. Take the train from Paddington Station toward Reading (£9.80 return), and change at Twyford to Henley-on-Thames.

RUGBY

Rugby has driven many a mother to an early grave because the players take as much body contact as American football players, but without the benefit of pads or helmets. Legend has it that the game was born in the Midlands, when a student of Rugby School picked up a soccer ball in his hands midmatch and ran from one end of the pitch to the other. The game concept hasn't changed much since then: players move the ball down the field and score goals through some combination of running, passing, and kicking. It's an old sport, steeped in tradition, and rugby's practitioners shun the modern arguments for protection against injury. Perhaps it's this attitude that makes the rowdy spectacle such a satisfying combination of mud, beer, and battle.

The home of the English national team and the Rugby Football Union governing body is at the stunningly redeveloped 75,000-seat **Twickenham Stadium** (Rugby Rd., Twickenham, TW1, tel. 020/8744–3111 for tickets; Rail: Twickenham from Waterloo). The two key international home tournaments take place each year in early spring in the Five Nations Tournament, with England fighting it out with France, Scotland, Ireland, and Wales, two of whom they play away from home. There are also a few friendlies against teams like Australia and Italy each year. Behind-the-scenes stadium tours are available, and there's also the **Museum of Rugby** for an affectionate and jocular look at a game that is currently enjoying its highest-ever profile. The tour and museum (tel. 020/8892–2000) each cost £2.50, with a combo ticket for £4. The hours of operation are Tuesday–Saturday 10:30–5 and Sunday 2–5.

It's possible to watch rugby year-round in Britain. The Rugby Union season runs September–May, with games held on Saturday afternoon. Tickets cost £10–£20, depending on the seat. London's principal teams (although some of them have moved out of the capital to better grounds) playing in the Allied Dunbar Premiership include the **Wasps** (Rangers Stadium, South Africa Rd., W12, tel. 020/8410–6004; Tube: White City); the **Harlequins** (Stoop Memorial Ground, Craneford Way, Twickenham, tel. 020/8410–6010; Rail: Twickenham from Waterloo); the **London Irish** (The Avenue, Sunbury-on-Thames, tel. 01932/783034; Rail: Sunbury from Waterloo); the **London Scottish** (Stoop Memorial Ground, Craneford Way, Twickenham, tel. 020/8410–6010; Rail: Twickenham from Waterloo); **Richmond** (Madejski Stadium, Junction 11, M4, Reading, tel. 0118/968–1000; Rail: Reading from Paddington); and Wasps' traditional rivals and current hotshots **Saracens** (Vicarage Rd. Stadium, Watford, tel. 01923/496200). Although the teams went professional in 1996, the atmosphere at the matches is still very friendly.

You'll find a unique vibe at a Rugby League match, where teams have 13 rather than 15 members. Whereas Union always saw itself as a gentlemen's sport, recruiting from private schools and fighting professionalization for years, the League code was founded in the north of England and drew its players from coal mines and factories. The new **Super League** is strongest in the north of England; it includes the **London Broncos** (Stoop Memorial Ground, Langhorn Dr., Twickenham, tel. 020/8410–5000; Rail: Twickenham from Waterloo) and a team from Paris. Tickets for League matches are usually £13, and the season runs March–'October.

TENNIS

The world's most prestigious and ballyhooed tennis event is the venerable **Wimbledon** fortnight (June 26–July 9 in 2000), held at the **All England Lawn Tennis & Croquet Club.** Never mind that a Brit hasn't won this Grand Slam tournament since anyone can remember—although Tim Henman did make it to the quarter-finals in 1996. Tennis enthusiasts around the world plan their trips to Wimbledon months in advance, so if you're reading this in June, you may be out of luck. Just 6,000 tickets are available each day at the gate, but to get one of the very limited Centre Court or No. 1 Court tickets you have to be willing to camp overnight or arrive very early (5 AM). The majority of tickets are Ground Passes (usually under a tenner, after 5 PM), which allow access to all courts except Centre and No. 1 courts, and will also get you into the Aorangi Park picnic terrace and the **Lawn Tennis Museum** (otherwise, daily 10–5; £4), which features a history of the game and is open year-round. If you're determined to get in but unwilling to camp, try showing up after 5 PM, when you can buy tickets returned by those who've left early—the money goes to charity. Play continues until dusk, so you will still be able to see a few hours of tennis, depending of course on the great British weather. Or plan ahead and get yourself in the public ticket ballot by writing to the All England Lawn Tennis & Croquet Club, Box 98, Church Road, Wimbledon SW19 5AE—the request should arrive before December 31. Good luck. *Church Rd., Wimbledon, SW19, tel. 020/8944–1066 or 020/8946–2244 for ticket info. Tube: Southfields or BritRail to Wimbledon.*

THE ENGLISH BETTING OBSESSION

*Horses, greyhounds, soccer, indeed every sport—and even stuff like who will be the next Prime Minister or whether it will snow on Christmas Day—are cause for a wager in virtually every high street in London. Every neighborhood has at least one betting shop—*Ladbroke *and* William Hill *are the biggest, near omnipresent chains. Formerly sleazy joints dedicated to horses and dogs, they now have live satellite link-ups for big events, so you place your bet and then see it go down the drain under one roof. The permutations allowed are virtually unlimited. For instance, in soccer (and, yes, they do American football as well) you can predict the scorer and time of the first goal or touchdown, and, if you want, double it with your prediction for which team is going to win the game.*

At racecourses these chains are also represented, but more colorful are the independent "bookies"; there's another option in the state-run Tote, *which operates on a different system (by pooling all the takings and then paying out accordingly).*

All bets are subject to a 9% tax, normally paid when the wager is placed; otherwise the state takes the tax out of your winnings, which can be a significant sum if you get lucky.

Another London landmark is the **Queen's Club,** which hosts major and minor competitive and exhibition matches throughout the year, such as the **Stella Artois Grass Court Championship** in early June. Tickets for nonmembers are sold exclusively by Ticketmaster (tel. 020/7413–1444) and are, don't you know it, subject to a booking fee. *Palliser Rd., W14, tel. 020/7385–3421. Tube: Barons Court.*

YANKEE SPORTS

BASEBALL

Baseball is cricket's distant cousin, but it has been played on an organized basis in Britain for nearly a century. Surprised? There's even a **British Baseball League,** and three Premier Division teams—the **Hounslow Blues,** the **Warriors,** and the **Wolves**—are based in London. These teams play during the summer at various fields around town. Check *Time Out* for current games and locations, or contact the **British Baseball Federation** (tel. 01482/643551).

BASKETBALL

The **Budweiser National Basketball League** (tel. 020/749–1355) oversees the nation's fledgling professional league. Premier-division teams around the capital include the **Greater London Leopards,** the 1997 champs (London Arena, E14, tel. 020/7538–1212; Tube: Crossharbour DLR); **London Towers** (Crystal Palace National Sports Centre, SE19, tel. 020/8776–7755; Rail: Crystal Palace); and **Thames Valley Tigers** (Bracknell Sports Centre, tel. 01344/454203; Rail: Bracknell from Waterloo). Attendance at games averages 2,000; the season runs September–May—check *Time Out* for current schedules. There's also a women's league, a semipro league, and various amateur divisions; call the English Basketball Association (tel. 0113/236–1166) for more info.

ICE HOCKEY

The beautiful game on ice has always had a hard-core and quite fanatical following in the United Kingdom, although it looks like it will never break into the mainstream. That said, the capital region does offer some of the thrills and spills of the sport through the **London Knights** (London Arena, Limeharbour, E14, tel. 020/7538–1212; Tube: Crossharbour DLR) and the out-of-town **Bracknell Bees** (John Nike Complex, John Nike Way, Amen Corner, Bracknell, tel. 01344/860033; Rail: Bracknell from Waterloo). Both play in the Sekonda Superleague.

PARTICIPANT SPORTS

NEIGHBORHOOD SPORTS CENTERS

Almost every neighborhood has at least one gym offering some combination of aerobics classes, weight rooms, trampolines, saunas, solariums, martial arts gyms, swimming pools, squash and badminton courts, and soccer fields. Charges and membership fees vary, although they tend to be reasonable. Some centers offer day memberships, and many offer discounts if you arrive with a member. Call in advance to see whether they admit nonmembers. To find the nearest center, look in the Yellow Pages under "Leisure Centres" or call the busy **Sportsline** (tel. 020/7222–8000). The following are some of London's most popular centers:

Jubilee Hall Leisure Centre. Day use of all facilities in this well-equipped gym is £6.50; exercise and dance classes cost £5.50. *30 The Piazza, WC2, tel. 020/7836–4835. Tube: Covent Garden. Open weekdays 7 AM–10 PM, weekends 10–5.*

London Central YMCA. Membership at this comfortable and popular gym is only available on a weekly (£35) basis or longer, but it gains you access to a pool, more than 100 fitness classes a week, and a full gym. *112 Great Russell St., WC1, tel. 020/7637–8131. Tube: Tottenham Court Rd. Open weekdays 7 AM–10 PM, weekends 10–9.*

Queen Mother Sports Centre. Fees for activities vary: Nonmembers pay £2.30 to swim, £4.35 for aerobics, and £4.95 to play squash for 30 minutes. *223 Vauxhall Bridge Rd., SW1, tel. 020/7630–5522. Tube: Victoria. Open weekdays 6:30 AM–10 PM, weekends 8–8. The pool closes at 7:30 PM on weekdays and at 5:30 PM on weekends.*

BOATING

If you're feeling inspired by the exertions of the crews at the Henley Royal Regatta or the Oxford and Cambridge Boat Race, you can try your hand at the oars in a few places in London. A vigorous afternoon can be had rowing about the large and scenic lake at Regent's Park: **Regent's Park Boating Lake** (tel. 020/7486–4759) rents rowboats that hold up to four adults for £6.50 per hour plus a £5 deposit. **Hyde Park** also offers pedalos (pedalboats), canoes, and rowboats for those wishing to splash along the Serpentine, for £6.50 per hour. Boats are available at both parks daily 9–6:30 or dusk, March through September, weather permitting.

BOWLING

Central London is a ten-pin desert, with most alleys way out in the 'burbs, although there are 12 lanes at the centrally located **Leisure Box** (formerly the Queens Ice Skating Club, 17 Queensway, W2, tel. 020/7229–0172; Tube: Queensway). It's open daily from 10 AM to 11 PM. A game costs just £3 before 6 PM and £4 after. Shoe rental is an extra quid.

BUNGEE JUMPING

The best alternative view of the capital's skyline is to get lifted 300 ft up into the air by a crane and then JUMP—plunging downward to the gray waters of the Thames. Sadly the land next to Chelsea Bridge on which the **UK Bungee Club** (020/7720–9496) had erected a crane was sold in spring 1999. They're looking for a new site but promise some weekend events around the capital. Ballpark prices are £15 for membership, plus £35 per jump.

PLAY BALL!

On any given summer evening you'll find baseball and softball games all over town, especially at Hampstead Heath (much to the chagrin of locals), Regent's Park, and Hyde Park. The British Baseball Federation (Box 45, Hessle, North Humberside, HU13 9JJ, tel. 01482/643551) can give you the current scoop; send a large, stamped envelope for their magazine or call to be pointed toward the nearest club. Local teams also ask for players through the sports pages of Time Out. The British Softball Federation's London Region contact, Bob Fromer (tel. 01886/884204), can put you in touch with local teams. Basketball courts are scarce in London, but there are a growing number in neighborhood sports centers (see below) like the London Central YMCA. Check with the English Basketball Association (tel. 0113/236–1166).

CYCLING

Lots of people bike in London, but frankly, the traffic-congested streets make for a perilous and carcinogenic ride. Hard-core bikers tie bandannas over their mouths to filter out the crud from passing traffic or invest in specially designed gas masks available at bike shops. Biking is great in London's parks, but those intending to brave the roads should invest in a good map that points out the less offensive routes through the city. **London Cycling Campaign** (228 Great Guildford Business Sq., 30 Great Guildford St., SE1 OHS, tel. 020/7928–7220) does its best to make London a more bike-friendly place. Send for a copy of their *Cyclists' Route Map* (£5.70 including postage), or look for it at bike shops. If you're planning to head out into the countryside, consider joining **Cyclists' Touring Club** (69 Meadrow, Godalming, Surrey GU7 3HS, tel. 01483/417217), the largest cycling organization in Britain. Annual membership is £25 (£15 for those under 26); in return they'll send you info on organized bike trips throughout the country.

Bikepark. It has everything a cyclist could need, including a repair and sale shop, bike storage (£1.50 for 12 hours, £5 a week), changing facilities, and bicycle rentals. Basic mountain bikes go for £10 for the first day, £5 the second day, and £3 each subsequent day, with a £200 deposit. Luckily, they accept credit cards. *11 Macklin St., WC2, tel. 020/7430–0083. Tube: Covent Garden. Open weekdays 8:30–7, Sat. 10–6.*

London Bicycle Tour Company. Weather permitting, this South Bank biking outfit offers three-hour bike tours of various London neighborhoods for £11.95 with bookings highly advisable. You can also go at it alone: traditional, mountain, or hybrid bikes cost £29.50 per week or £10 per day (£5 each subsequent day), including a helmet, maps, and route advice. A credit card deposit is required. Find out all the details on their new web site (www.londonbicycle.com). *1A Gabriel's Wharf, SE1, tel. 020/7928–6838. Tube: Blackfriars. Open Apr.–Oct., daily 10–6; Nov.–Mar. by appointment.*

Mountain Bike and Ski. Mountain bike rentals cost £7 per day or £13 for the whole weekend, not including insurance (£1 per day) and the refundable £50 deposit. This central London shop also has a good selection of bikes and bike-related accessories for sale. In-line skate rentals are also available at the same rates. *18 Gillingham St., SW1, tel. 020/7834–8933. Tube: Victoria.*

HORSEBACK RIDING

Hankering to stretch someone else's legs on a woodsy trek? Whether you're still learning how to stay upright in the saddle, or you want lessons in dressage and jumping, several stables can set you up with a steed and, if you're willing to pay, an instructor. You can rent a horse from **Belmont Riding Centre** (The Ridgeway, Mill Hill, NW7, tel. 020/8906–1255; Tube: Mill Hill East), open weekdays 9–6, weekends 9–

5, and ride through Totteridge Common's 150 acres in a group for £18 per hour, or £25 per hour for private lessons. The corresponding weekend rates are £20 and £30. **Wimbledon Village Stables** (24 High St., SW19, tel. 020/8946–8579; Tube: Wimbledon) charges £25 per hour during the week, £30 on weekends, for a chance to ride in a group across the scenic Wimbledon Common and Richmond Park. Private sessions cost an extra £5. The stables are open Tuesday–Sunday 9–5. **Hyde Park Stables** (63 Bathurst Mews, W2, tel. 020/7723–2813; Tube: Lancaster Gate), open Tuesday–Friday 10–4:30 and weekends 9–4:30, rents horses for £27 per hour if you join a group or are prepared to part with £50 for a private session. Either way, no galloping is allowed and if they catch you, there's a crisp £200 fine. Telephone reservations with a credit card are required. And, yes, you will find only English saddles here.

ICE-SKATING

Finding an ice rink in London isn't that easy. The most central is the **Leisure Box** (formerly the Queens Ice Skating Club, 17 Queensway, W2, tel. 020/7229–0172; Tube: Queensway). It's open daily from 10 AM to 11 PM, and skating costs £6.50 per session (times are 10 AM–noon, noon–2, 2–5, 5–7, and 8–10 or 8–11 on Friday and Saturday) including skate rental. The place attracts a mix of super-keen skate fanatics and London trendies. The United Kingdom's only outdoor skating rink is the circular **Broadgate Ice Rink** (Broadgate Arena, Eldon St., EC2, tel. 020/7505–4068; Tube: Liverpool St.). Available to skaters of all abilities, it's usually open between October and early April (Monday–Thursday noon–2:30 and 3:30–6; Friday noon–2:30, 3:30–6, and 7–10; weekends 11–1, 2–4, and 5–7 or 8:30 on Saturday) and also stages, on weekday evenings, broomball matches, a sport that entails trying to get a soccer ball into a net with . . . a broom. Phone for opening times and details of games. It costs £5 per session, and skate rental is an extra £2.

SWIMMING

Many of the city's neighborhood sports centers (*see above*) have indoor pools, so swimmers need not bend to the whims of London's weather. Many of these pools are open to the public regularly throughout the week. Remember that many pools require swimming caps and protective eyewear, and many do not provide towels. On the plus side, weight rooms, saunas, and whirlpools are often available for use by both guests and nonmembers.

It's £2.50 to swim at **University of London Union** (Malet St., WC1, tel. 020/7664–2000. Tube: Goodge St.), where students and nonstudents alike can swim weekdays 8:30–7 and Saturday 9–5. The most serious laps in town are swum in the Olympic-size pool at **Crystal Palace National Sports Centre** (Ledrington Rd., Upper Norwood, SW19, tel. 020/8778–0131; Rail: Crystal Palace from Victoria). It's the only place with high-diving boards in the capital. Opening times are generally 8 AM–5 PM and 8 PM–10 PM, but phone to check first as it does close to the public when swim meets are on. At the other extreme, some London pools feature fantabulous setups with slides, cascading waterfalls, wave-making machines, and bizarre floating art objects. A few of the coolest include **Britannia Leisure Centre** (40 Hyde Rd., N1, tel. 020/7729–4485; Tube: Old St.) and the **Elephant & Castle Leisure Centre** (22 Elephant & Castle, SE1, tel. 020/7582–5505; Tube: Elephant & Castle), which is in a daunting concrete maze that's confusing to get around, especially at night.

Brockwell Lido. This funky suntrap in Brockwell Park, just up the hill from Brixton, gets real crowded on hot days. There's also a café and barbecue restaurant in this '30s complex, which has been thoroughly modernized during the past few years. *Dulwich Rd. at Regent Rd., SE24, tel. 020/7274–3088. Rail: Herne Hill or Brixton and 10-min walk. Admission £2.50 (weekdays); £3 (weekends). Open late May–early Sept., Mon.–Thurs. 6:45–10 AM and noon–8, Fri.–Sun. 10–7.*

Hampstead Heath. Choose from three swimming ponds and an outdoor pool. The men-only **Highgate Pond** and the women-only **Kenwood Pond** are off Millfield Lane on the eastern edge of the heath, an uphill slog from the Gospel Oak railway station. If you prefer mixed bathing, try the **Parliament Hill Lido** (tel. 020/7485–3873), an outdoor pool just across the street from Gospel Oak, or the **Hampstead Mixed Bathing Pond** (East Heath Rd.), near the Hampstead tube station. You can get further information on bathing in the Heath from their information office, which is next to the Lido (tel. 020/7482–7073), open Wednesday–Friday 1–5, weekends 10 AM–12:30 PM and 1–5, and other erratic times. *Hampstead Heath. Admission to ponds free. Admission to Lido £2.80; free before 10 AM. Segregated ponds open daily 7 AM–1 hr before sunset. Mixed pond open summer, daily 7–7. Lido open summer, daily 7–9:30 and 10–7 (last admission at 6); winter, daily 7:30 AM–10 AM.*

WINDSURFING ON THE THAMES

With its miles of river frontage, the Docklands area is becoming a very popular place for all things aquatic. Pick up the free "Watersports in London Docklands" brochure at the London Docklands Visitor Centre for more info. One of the top water-sports centers is Docklands Watersports Club (Gate 14, King George V Dock, Woolwich Manor Way, E16, tel. 020/7511–7000), which specializes in jet skiing and rents jet skis and all the gear for £30 (for 30 min, or £55 per hour). Lea Valley Watersports Centre (Harbet Rd., E4, tel. 020/8531–1129), near Walthamstow on the end of the Victoria tube line, offers lessons in sailing, windsurfing, waterskiing, and canoeing. The Surrey Docks Watersport Centre (Rope St., Rotherhithe, SE16, tel. 020/7237–4009) does a similar job in the sailing, power boating, canoeing, and windsurfing disciplines.

The Oasis. A spot of water amid the parched concrete of central London, these indoor and outdoor pools get very crowded on hot days. *32 Endell St., WC2, tel. 020/7831–1804. Tube: Covent Garden or Holborn. Admission £2.50. Open weekdays 6:30 AM–9 PM, weekends 9:30–5.*

Serpentine Lido. This Hyde Park oasis is quite popular in summer, even if a couple of famous people have sunk to its murky depths and never come up again—Percy Bysshe Shelley's first wife, Harriet Westbrook, for one. Now, lifeguards prevent such mishaps from occurring. *Hyde Park, south side of the Serpentine, W2, tel. 020/7298–2100. Tube: Knightsbridge. Admission £3. Open July–Aug., daily 10–5.*

TENNIS

There are public tennis courts all over London, many administered by neighborhoods or boroughs. Ask at local council halls about ones nearby, as they're often located at neighborhood sports centers (*see above*). Policies and prices vary widely, although courts generally cost £4–£7 per hour. Sometimes reservations are accepted, sometimes they're required, and sometimes they're not accepted at all. Central London's larger parks, including Battersea Park, Holland Park, Clissold Park, and Hampstead Heath, also have courts. **Regent's Park Tennis Centre** (York Bridge, NW1, tel. 020/7486–4216) rents courts for £8 per hour for nonmembers (membership is £45 and the hourly rate goes down to £6.50). Racket rentals are £2 per hour plus a £10 deposit. A good resource is the **Lawn Tennis Association Trust** (Queen's Club, W14, tel. 020/7381–7111; *www.lta.org.uk)*, which can help with finding courts and clubs.

9 TRIPS FROM LONDON

UPDATED BY DAVID CLEE

At some point during your stay in London, the realization will hit you like a soggy sausage: as far as countries go, England is extremely compact, and absolutely nothing is very far from the Big City. Moreover, the train and bus networks—although uncomfortably expensive—are extensive, efficient, and easy to figure out. By train from London, it takes a mere 60 min to reach Oxford, 75 min to reach Bath, and 90 min to reach Cambridge. Only Stratford takes a bit of planning, as there is no direct daily train from London (there are, however, plenty of buses). Although you could tackle any one of the above on a frenzied day trip—heavy summer crowds make it difficult to cover the sights in a relaxed manner—consider staying for a day or two. You'd then have the time to explore a very different England, one blessed with quiet country pubs, fluffy sheep, and neatly trimmed farms. No matter where you go, lodging reservations are a good idea June—September, when foreigners (like us) saturate the English countryside.

OXFORD

Home of the world's first English-language university, Oxford today is bustling and crowded, a vast conurbation expanding ever-outward from the university at its center. Once upon a time, cattle herders led their flocks over this shallow junction of the Thames and Cherwell rivers; these days, the horde of buses and foot traffic in the city center are more comparable to those in Piccadilly Circus. Contrary to the way it looks in movies, Oxford is not nearly as small and idyllic as Cambridge, England's other ivory tower; blame the heavy industry on Oxford's outskirts, particularly the large Rover car factory. Even so, street performers and flying troops of bone-rattlers (those shaky bicycles associated with English academics) make Oxford an engaging city. You'll also find that the food and nightlife rank far above those of quiet Cambridge.

Oxford and Cambridge are the nation's most prestigious universities, and the rivalry between the two is intense. You can expect to hear an endless stream of comparisons while visiting Oxford's colleges and local pubs. To simplify outrageously, Oxford is better known for the arts, Cambridge for the sciences. Of course, the enormous number of graduates from both schools who occupy positions of power in Britain points out that what students actually study is largely irrelevant. Both Oxford and Cambridge are *names,*

OXFORD

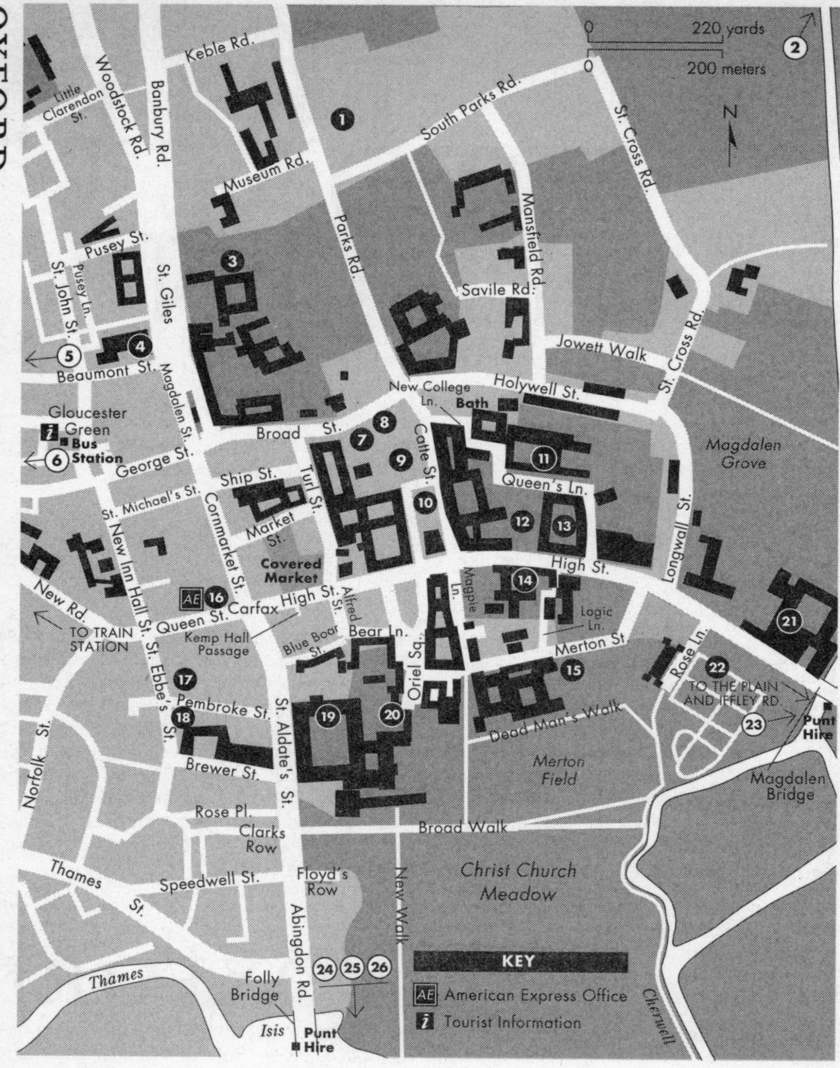

Sights ●

All Souls College, **12**

Ashmolean Museum, **4**

Bodleian Library, **9**

Botanic Garden, **22**

Carfax Tower, **16**

Christ Church College, **19**

Christ Church Picture Gallery, **20**

Magdalen College, **21**

Merton College, **15**

Museum of the History of Science, **7**

Museum of Modern Art, **17**

New College, **11**

Pembroke College, **18**

Queen's College, **13**

Radcliffe Camera, **10**

Sheldonian Theatre, **8**

St. John's College, **3**

University College, **14**

University Museum and Pitt Rivers Museum, **1**

Lodging ○

Brown's Guest House, **23**

Falcon Private Hotel, **24**

Mrs. O'Neil, **5**

Newton House, **25**

Oxford Backpackers Hostel, **6**

Oxford Camping International, **26**

Oxford YHA, **2**

and thanks to their legendary old-boy networks, a degree from either, in any field, can translate into a lucrative career. But, as in every other college town, Oxford student life is a perennial cycle of classes, drinking, more drinking, and frantic bouts of studying.

BASICS

AMERICAN EXPRESS

This office provides the usual services for cardholders. Noncardholders pay a £2 commission for currency exchange. *4 Queen St., OX1 1EJ, tel. 01865/792066. Open weekdays 9–5:30 (Wed. from 9:30), Sat. 9–5, Sun. (June–Sept.) 11–3.*

DISCOUNT TRAVEL AGENCIES

STA Travel (36 George St., tel. 01865/792800), the biggest of Oxford's budget-travel centers, sells ISIC cards, InterRail passes, and bargain airfares. When its office gets too busy, stop by **Campus Travel** (105 St. Aldate's, tel. 01865/242067) or **YHA Adventure Shop** (910 St. Clement's St., tel. 01865/247948), which offers cheaper transportation fares to those with a hostel card.

MAIL

The busy **main post office** (102104 St. Aldate's St., OX1 1ZZ, tel. 01865/779286) changes money for a 1% commission and handles poste restante. It's open until 12:30 on Saturday.

VISITOR INFORMATION

Oxford's **tourist office** seems more interested in selling merchandise than in offering helpful guidance. Nearly every map and leaflet costs something. Note: There is a very expeditious reservations desk on site, handy for those who arrive in town without overnight accommodations. *The Old School, Gloucester Green, tel. 01865/726871. Open Mon.–Sat. 9:30–5, Sun. in summer 10–3:30.*

COMING AND GOING

BY TRAIN

Thames Trains run frequent services from London's Paddington to **Oxford Station** (one hour, £14.20 day return, £18.20 five-day return). From the station, it's a steady 15-min walk to the town center. The train is convenient, but buses are cheaper. *Botley Rd., tel. 0345/484950.*

BY BUS

All long-distance buses stop at **Gloucester Green Station,** about an eight-block walk from the train depot. Bus company offices here have info and timetables. **National Express** (tel. 0990/808080) has direct service from Oxford to Birmingham, Bristol, Cambridge, and Nottingham. The 90-min journey from Oxford to London's Victoria Station costs £7.50 day return and £12 open return, the same prices as **Oxford Tube** (tel. 01865/772250), which runs buses to London every 12 min at peak time (and at least every hour through the night), and **Oxford City Link** (tel. 01865/785400), with a service every 20 min. Oxford Tube also operates express buses to Heathrow airport (£6 single).

GETTING AROUND

The town of Oxford and its 40 colleges are inextricably intertwined. The center of it all is **Carfax,** where Cornmarket, St. Aldate's, High, and Queen streets meet; people congregate; and baby strollers compete with buses for space. Beyond Carfax, streets can be hard to identify in the jumbled city center, even with a fairly detailed map; invest in an *Oxford A–Z* map (£1.75) if you want to avoid frustration. With so much to see and do, and so much of it spread over a large area, it's wise to make good use of buses; they're fast, frequent, and fairly cheap.

BY BICYCLE

Oxford's flat terrain and extensive network of cycle paths make for great cycling. The free *Cycling in Oxford: A Comprehensive Guide* includes detailed maps of all bicycle paths as well as info on local cycling organizations. Be extremely chary of leaving your expensive mountain bike locked in the town center—thousands are stolen each year, in broad daylight. If you haven't brought your own wheels, rent

WAR AND PEACE IN OXFORD

Throughout Oxford's history, tensions between the city and the university have often erupted into violence. The most famous and bloodiest event, the St. Scholastica's Day Riots, which took place in 1355, began with a tavern brawl between scholars and a local pub owner. During the next three days, colleges were sacked and six students were killed. In the end, the university gained the upper hand because it had royal backing. Despite several attempts on the part of townies to regain control, the university ran things around Oxford until the 19th century. Tension still exists today, but the sparring tends to be limited to the occasional sarcastic comment or verbal fisticuffs.

some from **Pennyfarthing** (5 George St., tel. 01865/249368) for £10 for the first day, £5 for each subsequent day, or £20 per week.

BY BUS

Two main companies, **Oxford Bus Co.** (tel. 01865/785400) and **Stagecoach** (tel. 01865/727000 or 01865/727002), vie for business on similar routes. The Oxford Bus Co. has come up with a handy free bus map of its sphere of influence, which you can grab from the tourist office. Oxford's red double-decker buses and green "Nipper" minibuses run about every seven min weekdays and summer Saturdays and at 30-min intervals at other times. Stagecoach's minibuses run less frequently but are about 5p–15p less expensive. Just about any bus marked CITY CENTRE will take you to within a ¼ mi of Carfax. Most buses to the suburbs also depart from within two blocks of there. Oxford Bus Co. offers various one-day passes for central zone (£1.80) and beyond, whereas Stagecoach offers a **City Hopper** pass good for one day of unlimited travel within Oxford for £1.80, or an **Explorer** pass (£4.90) for wider journeys, including Blenheim Palace. Free route maps are available at the bus station. Note that the numbers of bus routes change frequently.

WHERE TO SLEEP

Finding accommodations in Oxford isn't as easy as one would think. For such a sizable city, there are surprisingly few hotels and hostels to go around. With two hostels now open, prospects are improving; however, try to book ahead whenever possible. Peak season lasts from May to August, and arriving unprepared could lead to heartache and serious wallet damage. If you haven't booked in advance, your best bet is to head down Iffley Road, which is lined with small establishments. Iffley Road is to the east of the center. Follow High Street across Magdalen Bridge and your target is just beyond the roundabout. Abingdon Road, running due south from Carfax, also offers plenty of lodging opportunities.

Brown's Guest House. Brown's is heartily recommended by the hostel staff members, who often send overflow backpackers here for the comfortable beds, plush rooms, and yummy breakfasts. Try to get a room that doesn't face noisy Iffley Road. Singles are £25, doubles £44 (£50 with bath). There's a 5% surcharge on bills paid with credit cards. *281 Iffley Rd., OX4 4AQ, tel. and fax 01865/246822. From Carfax, take Oxford Bus 4 or Thames Transit Bus 3 toward Rose Hill and get off at Howard St. 9 rooms, 2 with bath.*

Falcon Private Hotel. This hotel really is a home away from home and definitely worth the splurge. The staff is friendly, and the attractive rooms have luxuries such as satellite TV and hair dryers. Singles are £35, doubles £56, triples £72. *8890 Abingdon Rd., OX1 4PX, tel. 01865/722995. From Carfax, walk south on Abingdon Rd. or take Bus X3, 16, 30, 31, 32, 32A, 33, or 35. 11 rooms, all with bath.*

Mrs. O'Neil. This is one of Oxford's true lodging bargains—and it's strictly cash only. The rooms are immaculate, but there are only two of 'em (one single, one double), so make reservations right now.

Bed-and-breakfast costs £12.50 per person, and you get a TV in your room. *15 Southmoor Rd., OX2 6RF, tel. 01865/511205. From Carfax, walk north on Cornmarket St., turn left on Beaumont St., right on Walton St., left on Southmoor Rd. 2 rooms, neither with bath. Cash only.*

Newton House. A number of bargain B&Bs lurk past Folly Bridge far from the city center, and Newton House is the best of them. Because of its larger size—15 spotless rooms with TVS and plenty of light—it's likely to have vacancies even in summer. Doubles cost £46 (£56 with bath), a bit less in winter. *8284 Abingdon Rd., OX1 4PL, tel. 01865/240561. From Carfax, walk south on Abingdon Rd. or take Bus X3, 16, 30, 31, 32, 32A, 33, or 35. 13 rooms, 5 with bath.*

HOSTELS

Oxford Backpackers Hostel. This recently opened hostel is the godsend that budget-minded visitors to Oxford have been waiting for. The central location, friendly staff, and 24-hour access make a perfect base for exploring the colleges, pubs, and nightlife (the hostel even organizes a pub crawl on Tuesday). A dorm bed costs £11, sheets included. *9A Hythe Bridge St., OX1 2EW, tel. 01865/721761. From bus station, turn left on Worcester St., right on Hythe Bridge St. 92 beds. Kitchen.*

Oxford YHA. Clean, comfortable, and expertly managed, Oxford's other hostel is a model of efficiency, with great kitchen facilities, a pool table, and lots of info. Beds fill quickly year-round in this brick Victorian about 1 mi outside the town center; reserve ahead and check in before 5 PM. Dorm beds cost £13.25. *32 Jack Straw's La., OX3 0DW, tel. 01865/762997, fax 01865/769402. From Carfax, take Bus 10, 13, or 14. 112 beds. Flexible midnight curfew.*

CAMPING

Oxford YHA (*see above*) has a few campsites available for £4.55 per person. At **Oxford Camping International** (426 Abingdon Rd., tel. 01865/246551) you'll be vying with motor homes, but hey, it's clean, green, cheap, and open year-round. Tent sites cost £5.70 for two people. To reach the campground, take the Park & Ride Bus; it stops at Carfax every 10 min or so.

Oxford University is where Lord Shelley was unceremoniously expelled only a few months after arriving, where swashbuckler T. E. Lawrence navigated treacherous underground canals, and where Hugh Grant perfected his "nervous Englishman" look.

FOOD

Oxford has great food, with all ethnicities and price ranges represented. If you're strapped, head to supermarkets like **J. Sainsbury** (Westgate Shopping Centre, tel. 01865/722179) and **Tesco** (159 Cowley Rd., tel. 01865/447600), both of which are open Sunday. At the **Covered Market,** on Market Street half a block east of Cornmarket Street, greengrocers, butchers, and bakers set up shop Monday–Saturday among the market's clothing and souvenir stands. For delicious hummus, breads, cheeses, and desserts visit **Gluttons Delicatessen** (110 Walton St., tel. 01865/553748). **Heroes** (8 Ship St., tel. 01865/723459) serves sandwiches on fresh-baked bread and Italian-style subs for £2–£3.

Café MOMA. This spacious joint is hidden beneath the Museum of Modern Art. By noon it's jumping with the local art crowd, but things quiet down around 3. Chow down on a large salad (£3.20), or try the vegan "Nutroast," a baked loaf of ground nuts and onions (£4.35). *30 Pembroke St., tel. 01865/722733. From Carfax, walk west on Queen St., turn left on St. Ebbe's St., left on Pembroke St. Cash only. Closed Mon.*

Chang Mai Kitchen. Oxford's best Thai food is served up in a ramshackle Tudor building less than a block from Carfax. Despite the classy wood-beam surroundings, most dishes cost only £7–£8. Splurges like the fish in coconut curry go for £8.70. *Kemp Hall Passage, 130A High St., tel. 01865/202233. From Carfax, walk east on High St., turn right on tiny Kemp Hall Passage.*

Cherwell Boathouse. About 1 mi north of town, this is a local landmark and an ideal spot for a meal in a riverside setting. The menus change weekly, but may include mussels in white wine and cream; loin of lamb with red wine, lime, and garlic; or hare with a vinegar and pepper sauce. Main courses run from £9 to £14, with a set lunch at £17 and dinner at £19. It's a very friendly spot so be prepared to linger. There is a good set menu available. *Bardwell Rd. off Banbury Rd., tel. 01865/552746. From Carfax, walk north up Cornmarket, which becomes St. Giles, bear right on Banbury Rd., walk ½ mi up, turn right on Bardwell Rd. Closed Mon. and Tues. No dinner Sun.*

Georgina's Coffee Shop. Toulouse-Lautrec posters line the walls in this hip café hidden within the hectic confines of the Covered Market. Strong coffee complements bagels, pastries, and lunch specials like mozzarella and tomato salad with ciabatta bread (£4.50). *Covered Market, above Beaton's Deli, tel. 01865/249527. Cash only. Closed Sun. No dinner.*

The Nosebag. This popular upstairs café has been around for more than 25 years. The ever-changing lunch menu features a soup du jour (£2. 30), stuffed baked potatoes (£3), a cold dish (£5.20), a vegetarian dish (£5.50), and a hot dish (£5.75). Dinners (heftier versions of lunch) cost about £8. Long lines form for both meals. *68 St. Michael's St., tel. 01865/721033. From Carfax, walk north on Cornmarket St., turn left on St. Michael's St. Cash only. No dinner Mon.*

Pizza Express. You'd never know you were in a chain restaurant from the looks of this place. The light, airy building dates back to the year 1200, when it opened as the Golden Cross Inn. Come for a basic pizza margherita (£4.40) or the fancier Cajun pizza (£7.75) topped with prawns, mozzarella, tomato, and Tabasco. Or you can enjoy a glass of wine (£2.75) at the downstairs bar. *Golden Cross, tel. 01865/790442. From Carfax, walk north on Cornmarket St., quick right on Golden Cross.*

The Trout. One of Lewis Carroll's favorite places to sup, this creeper-covered, historic, and still excellent Thame-side pub is located in Godstow, about 2 mi from the city center on the northern edge of Oxford. Its interior, fitted out with sporting prints by "Phiz" and engravings of Oxford by Turner, is remarkable in itself. The dinners are a good value—main courses run from £4.95 to £10. Trout, of course, is a specialty, and Beef Godstow—fillet cooked in bacon with a black-currant sauce—is a signature dish. Come in the evening for a meal or a drink, and watch its peacocks strutting back and forth beside the weir. *Godstow, tel. 01865/302071. Buses to Godstow from Oxford bus station.*

WORTH SEEING

Before publicly embarrassing yourself, you should know Oxford University isn't one big campus. The 29 undergraduate colleges, six graduate colleges, four permanent halls, and All Souls College (*see below*) collectively make up "the university." They're scattered all around town, each with its own dormitories and lecture halls. Many colleges charge a small admission fee to people who want to wander around or take a tour, but there's no harm in trying to pass yourself off as a student by walking determinedly into the colleges. Aside from what we list below, check out the beautiful gardens at **Merton College** (Merton St., tel. 01865/276310) and **St. John's College** (St. Giles, tel. 01865/277300). And definitely don't miss the **Bodleian Library,** Britain's second-largest, and the adjacent **Radcliffe Camera,** designed by James Gibbs (*see* Museums and Libraries, *below*). For a look at rare and historic keyboards, woodwind, brass, and percussion instruments, visit the **Bate Collection of Musical Instruments** (St. Aldates, tel. 01865/276139), free and open weekdays 2–5. Unless you're interested in a silly Disneyesque experience, skip **The Oxford Story** and save the steep admission price (£4.50).

BOTANIC GARDEN

In *Brideshead Revisited,* Sebastian Flyte tells Charles Ryder, "There's a beautiful arch there and more different kinds of ivy than I knew existed. I don't know where I should be without the Botanical Gardens." Few gardens are more beautiful or feature a greater diversity of plants than this 300-year-old complex of greenhouses (sometimes called "glasshouses" in England), the oldest in the whole country. On a cold day, saunter past the rows of rare tropical plants. *High St., across from Magdalen College, tel. 01865/276920. Admission £2 mid-Apr.–early Sept.; free early Sept.–mid-Apr. Gardens open daily 9–4:30 (until 5 in summer); greenhouses open daily 10–4.*

CARFAX TOWER

As the last remnant of St. Martin's Church (erected in 1032), Carfax Tower minds the corner all by itself now, marking the passage of time with little mechanical figures that dance every 15 min. After the 14th-century St. Scholastica's Day Riots, Edward III ordered the tower lowered to its current 74 ft to prevent townies from showering gownies with rocks, bottles, and flaming arrows. Climb up the tower via the dank stairwell for a good view of the town center. *Tel. 01865/726871. Admission £1.20. Open Apr.–Oct., daily 10–5:30; Nov.–Mar., daily 10–3:30.*

THE COLLEGES

Oxford University has been a major player in British history for the past 830 years. The establishment of several monasteries in the early 12th century attracted scholarly clerics, and before long, they organized themselves into a *studium generale,* offering a curriculum along the same lines as the University of Paris. The turning point for the university came in 1167 when the French expelled all English students from Paris following the assassination of Thomas à Becket, the Archbishop of Canterbury. Thereafter, Oxford multiplied its faculty and student body, gaining immense power and prestige along the way. Oxford University Press was born in 1477, and until 1948 the university had two representatives in Parliament (talk about privilege). Women, however, weren't granted full student status until 1959.

Most colleges will grudgingly allow visitors to snoop around on weekday afternoons between 2 and 5 (except during late-May to mid-June finals). Be sure to vacate the grounds by 9 PM: the gates shut at 9:05 on the dot, and some unfortunates have been known to get locked in. Student-run **Oxford Student Tours** arranges guided walks (about £5) on summer afternoons. To catch a tour, look for the guys in funny hats and bow ties hanging around the tourist office. **Oxford Walking Tours** (tel. 01865/726871) also run 90-min guided walks that leave three times a day from outside the tourist office (£4.50). If in doubt, look for the guides with blue badges.

ALL SOULS • Possibly the most beautiful college in Oxford, All Souls was founded in 1438 by the Archbishop of Canterbury for spiritual and legal studies. Until the 20th century, All Souls was the only college in Oxford dedicated exclusively to graduate research. The academic program is something of an enigma, but the fellows of All Souls are the best and the brightest; those invited are given academic carte blanche during their seven-year tenure. Today the North Quad is a whimsical 18th-century interpretation of Gothic spires and pinnacles, featuring Christopher Wren's sundial and John Hawksmoor's famous twin towers. Sadly, the college doesn't make itself very amenable to tourists; All Souls seems to close "for repairs" every time a light bulb blows out. *High St., tel. 01865/279379. Open weekdays 2–4 (until 4:30 in summer).*

Not all of Oxford's colleges are as well-off as they look. With ailing endowments and shrinking government funding, colleges like Pembroke, St. Edmund's, and St. Peter's can use every penny they get.

CHRIST CHURCH • Founded by Cardinal Wolsey in 1525, Christ Church is never referred to as "Christ Church College." Gracious, no—members call it "the House." In fact, everything seems to have a special name here at the House, which many regard as Oxford's snobbiest college. Professors, called "dons" elsewhere in Oxford, are referred to here as "students." The 6¼-ton bell in the clock tower over the entrance is named **Great Tom,** and the quad over which Great Tom presides is (big surprise) **Tom Quad.** Every night at 9:05, Great Tom rings 101 times, once for each of the original students (not professors); afterward, the college's gates are locked shut. Near the **Memorial Garden** is Christ Church's 800-year-old cathedral, one of the smallest and most ornate in the country. The cathedral's stained glass is exquisite: some pieces date back to the 14th century, whereas others are 19th-century work by Edward Burne-Jones and William Morris. Of the many famed authors who attended the college, the most beloved is Charles Dodgson, a.k.a. Lewis Carroll. If you want to "do" Carroll's Oxford, pick up the delightful "Alice's Adventures in Oxford" booklet (£2.99), with numerous pictures and text by Mavis Batey, available at the train station newsstand or tourist office. Science luminary Albert Einstein is one of many boffins who calls Christ Church his alma mater. Politicians, including 13 prime ministers, have learned their trade in the college's debating halls, most notably 19th-century PM William Gladstone.

If you have time, take a stroll through the quiet, tree-lined paths of **Christ Church Meadow** alongside the Thames. When school is in session, college "eights" practice their rowing on the Isis (what they call this section of the Thames). Early Italian paintings and drawings dominate the collection at the **Christ Church Picture Gallery** (admission £1). There are also several Dutch paintings and Inigo Jones drawings. The gallery is small, however, and the collection at the Ashmolean (*see below*) is better, larger, and free. *St. Aldate's St., tel. 01865/276150. Admission £3. Open Apr.–Sept., Mon.–Sat. 10:30–1 and 2–5:30, Sun. 2–5:30, Oct.–Mar., closes at 4:30.*

MAGDALEN COLLEGE • Magdalen (pronounced maudlin) opened its doors to undergrads in 1458 and boasts Oscar Wilde, C. S. Lewis, Peter Brook, and (best of all) Dudley Moore as alumni. Moore began his career in comedy here, in the talent hothouse known as the Fringe, where many of Britain's most famous acts have started out—including half of the Monty Python team. The quadrangle is a quiet area enclosed by ancient, vaulted cloisters covered with wisteria; beyond it lie a deer park, gardens, and the Cherwell River. At the foot of **Magdalen Bridge,** you can rent punts (*see* Outdoor Activities, *below*). **Magdalen Tower,** one of Oxford's most recognizable landmarks, presides over the college grounds. *High St., tel. 01865/276000. From Carfax, walk east on High St. Admission £2, free in winter. Open weekdays 2–6, weekends noon–6.*

THRILLS AND SPILLS

Perhaps to relieve the tension of impending finals, Oxford students get their blood pumping for four days every May during the Eights Week rowing competition. Boats containing eight rowers (plus coxswain) set off on the Thames in a single-file line with the aim of bumping a boat in front of their own without being bumped themselves. In short, it's bumper cars on water. Teams who "bump" on each of the four days win blades, which are oars inscribed with the names of their team members. Tradition also dictates that the first team of the first division—"the Head of the River"—burn one of their own boats in celebration. The feisty '95 winners, Pembroke College, created an even bigger spectacle by burning a defeated opponent's boat instead. Hey, this sounds rowdier than college football.

NEW COLLEGE • The first college built after the bloody St. Scholastica's Day Riot, New College (officially called St. Mary College of Winchester in Oxenford) incorporated a new design feature—the first enclosed quad—to protect students in the event of another town-versus-gown flare-up. The extra caution proved unnecessary, but founder William of Wykeham (Bishop of Winchester and a wealthy, wealthy man) probably didn't feel like taking chances on account of the shortage of well-educated people after the Black Death outbreak of 1349. Most of the college and its **chapel** were completed in 1386 with further major additions completed in the 17th century. In the ante chapel you'll find sculptor Jacob Epstein's stunning *Lazarus,* the one Soviet leader Nikita Khrushchev said kept him awake at night, such was its emotional impact (this from a man who lived through the Stalin purges). *Queen's La., tel. 01865/279555. From Carfax, walk north on Cornmarket St., turn right on Broad St., right on Catte St., left on New College La. Admission summer £1.50, winter free. Open daily summer 11–5, winter 2–4.*

UNIVERSITY COLLEGE • To its embarrassment, University (or *univ,* as it is known to the cognoscenti) is best remembered for expelling Percy Bysshe Shelley in 1811 because he wrote and distributed a little pamphlet called "The Necessity of Atheism." After he drowned in Italy, the college had second thoughts and erected a monument to him in the **Front Quad.** This is also where young Bill Clinton sat out the draft and networked like a whirling dervish—and where he inexplicably failed to inhale on a joint—while a Rhodes Scholar. But back to the college: the original foundation dates from 1249, the earliest extant evidence of any college in Oxford (although Merton claims to be 85 years older). University is not open to the public unless the students decide to organize tours; call for the latest word. *High St., tel. 01865/276602.*

QUEEN'S COLLEGE • Although it's closed to the public you can see a portion of Queen's straightforward beauty from the outside. If you join an arranged tour via the tourist office, you'll be able to see the chapel. St. Paul's of London architect Sir Christopher Wren was responsible for the chapel, whereas his protégé Nicholas Hawksmoor did the rest—and a mighty fine job he did, too.

MUSEUMS AND LIBRARIES

Not only do Oxford's museums house some tremendous collections, but almost all of them are free. The exceptions to the rule are the **Museum of Modern Art** (30 Pembroke St., tel. 01865/722733), which badly needs the £2.50 admission fee, and **Christ Church Picture Gallery** (Oriel Sq., tel. 01865/276172), which doesn't need the £1 fee but takes it anyway. MOMA does offer free admission Wednesday 11–1 and Thursday 6–9. All university libraries, with the exception of the Bodleian Library, are off-limits to the general public.

ASHMOLEAN MUSEUM OF ART AND ARCHAEOLOGY • The Ashmolean, opened in 1683 and recently extensively refurbished, is Britain's oldest public museum and boasts artifacts and masterworks ranging from drawings by Michelangelo and paintings by Pissarro to Bronze Age tools and weapons.

The Egyptian coffins, Byzantine frescoes, and Islamic pottery downstairs deserve a look, but don't miss the drawings and Rodin sculptures in the upstairs galleries. Then there's Powhatan's mantle, the somewhat obscure name given to a piece held to be the oldest example of Native American clothing anywhere in the world. The prize for Most Bizarre Objet d'Intérêt definitely goes to Oliver Cromwell's death mask. *Beaumont St. at St. Giles, tel. 01865/278000. From Carfax, walk north on Cornmarket St., turn left on Beaumont St. Admission free. Open Tues.–Sat. 10–4, Sun. 2–4.*

THE BODLEIAN LIBRARY • The Bodleian owns a copy of every book printed in Britain since printing began—about 5.5 million books, give or take a few. The Bodleian is notoriously stingy about who gets to look at the books, and it may take a full day to retrieve any requested title. Students can't get inside without a signed letter from their university specifically requesting library access, and even then one may have to haggle. A guided tour (£3.50) is your surest bet; they start at the Divinity School across the street, weekdays at 10:30, 11:30, 2, and 3, and Saturday at 10:30 and 11:30 (not weekday mornings in winter). The library's courtyard and the adjacent fan-vaulted divinity school lobby are always open and well worth a peek. Also take a look inside Duke Humfrey's library (1488), which is rather like a small church. *Catte St., tel. 01865/277180. From Carfax, walk east on High St., turn left on Catte St. Open weekdays 9–4:30, Sat. 9–12:30.*

MUSEUM OF THE HISTORY OF SCIENCE • Although it's hardly the Smithsonian, you get to see the blackboard Einstein once used and some impressive Islamic and European astrolabes. *Broad St., tel. 01865/277280. From Carfax, walk north on Cornmarket St., turn right on Broad St. Admission free. Open Tues.–Sat. noon–4.*

A handful of literary giants did time at Christ Church, including W. H. Auden, Jeremy Bentham, John Locke, and Charles Dodgson (Lewis Carroll).

PITT RIVERS MUSEUM • In the same building as the University Museum (*see below*), the Pitt harbors all sorts of things: masks, hanging sailboats, wooden clothing—fun for flea market enthusiasts or attic addicts. It also hosts special exhibitions of cultural significance. Parts of the huge collection—such as the array of weird and wonderful musical instruments and some archaeological artifacts—are housed at the Balfour Building (open the same hours at 60 Banbury Road, tel. 01865/274726). *Parks Rd., tel. 01865/270927 or 01865/270949. From Carfax, walk north on Cornmarket St., turn right on Broad St., left on Parks Rd. Admission free. Open Mon.–Sat. 1–4:30.*

RADCLIFFE CAMERA • "Camera" means room in Latin, and the Radcliffe is one heck of a reading room. Completed in 1749 by James Gibbs, the architect responsible for London's St. Martin-in-the-Fields, this huge Italianate rotunda keeps watch over the nearby Old Schools Quad. There is a snag, however; the tower is not open to the public. *Catte St. From Carfax, walk east on High St., turn left on Catte St.*

SHELDONIAN THEATRE • Christopher Wren's marble-covered Sheldonian Theatre, built in 1669, was intended as an appropriately sober venue to confer degrees upon graduates. With its painted ceiling, heavy columns, and enormous pipe organ, it does indeed feel like the sort of place everyone should pass through before graduating into "the real world." The cupola provides a decent view of central Oxford—it's definitely worth a visit. Greatest photo op: the gigantic and spectacular stone busts that adorn the front gates. The theater hosts concerts on Saturday evening. Visitors should call ahead, as the theater often closes for special events. *Broad St., tel. 01865/277299. Admission £1.50. Open Mon.–Sat. 10–12:30 and 2–4:30 (until 3:30 in winter).*

UNIVERSITY MUSEUM • One of the greatest natural history museums in the world sits just 20 min north of the town center in a massive Victorian Gothic building. There are hundreds of exhibits on just about every facet of nature, but the local dinosaur finds attract the most attention. The collection also includes the head and left foot of a dodo, a large, flightless bird that has been extinct since the mid-17th century. Lewis Carroll (Charles Dodgson) was familiar with the museum's display and cast himself in the role of the Dodo in *Alice's Adventures in Wonderland*. The building itself, designed by Benjamin Woodward, is also worth a gander. *Parks Rd., tel. 01865/272950. Admission free. Open Mon.–Sat. noon–5.*

AFTER DARK

Once the sun goes down, drinkers, clubbers, theatergoers, and lovers of classical music are set. Otherwise, the main after-dark pursuits are hanging out around Carfax near the kebab vans—pretty dismal. *Daily Information* is an invaluable guide to clubbing around town, while *This Month in Oxford* covers other events. Both are available free at the tourist office.

PUBS

Most pubs in Oxford stay open through the afternoon for posttutorial pints. All pubs listed below are open Monday–Saturday 11–11, Sunday noon–10:30.

The Head of the River. This is the biggest "activity" pub in Oxford, complete with barbecues, snooker playoffs, bucking bronco contests, and even bungee jumping on summer Saturday nights. The cement "beer garden" outside allows drinkers to hang by the riverside and get sloshed before taking out a rowboat. *Abingdon Rd. at Folly Bridge, tel. 01865/721600. From Carfax, walk south on St. Aldate's St. to Folly Bridge.*

The King's Arms. The good ales and cosmopolitan clientele make this one of the best traditional pubs in the center of town. Tweedy professor types mix with students, townies, tourists, straights, gays—what have you. The "K. A.," as the locals affectionately call it, also serves vegetarian dishes. *40 Holywell St., at Parks Rd., tel. 01865/242369. From Carfax, walk north on Cornmarket St., turn right on Broad St. (which becomes Holywell St.).*

The Philanderer and Firkin. This trendy but characterless pub offers student drink specials and live music with no cover charge. *56 Walton St., next to Phoenix Cinema, tel. 01865/554502.*

Turf Tavern. If you find this tiny 13th-century pub tucked away in a narrow alley, you may never want to leave (which would explain some of the ancient professors lurking in the dark corners). In warm weather, sit on the patio; in winter, try the mulled wine—cinnamon-spiced and guaranteed to lift even the most discouraged traveler's spirits. Its distinctive decor is featured in the *Inspector Morse* television series. *4 Bath Pl., tel. 01865/243235. From Carfax, walk north on Cornmarket St., turn right on Broad St., right on Catte St., left on New College La., walk under Hertford's Bridge of Sighs, and take the first quick left.*

CLUBS

Freud. Freud (or FREVD, as the sign says) is housed in a 19th-century church that retains its stained-glass windows. Don't ask what the holy builders would think of the enormous selection of cocktails. Live jazz or classical music starts at 11 most nights. *Walton St. at Great Clarendon St., tel. 01865/311171. Cover: £4 Fri. and Sat. after 10.*

Old Fire Station. This is the ultimate one-stop spot, with a restaurant, theater, bar, and art museum all under one roof. Come Friday or Saturday for live jazz and blues. *40 George St., tel. 01865/794490. Cover: £4–£6.*

Zodiac. Members of Britpop bands Radiohead, Supergrass, and Ride are among the shareholders of this hip music venue. Local and big-name bands are featured, along with DJs and club nights. *190 Cowley Rd., tel. 08165/420042. Cover: £3–£5.*

THEATER AND MUSIC

Home to the accomplished Oxford Stage Company, the **Oxford Playhouse** (Beaumont St., tel. 01865/798600) frequently hosts first-rate entertainment ranging from Shakespearean drama and Restoration comedy to contemporary dance and musicals. Tickets run £8–£22. **Apollo Theatre** (George St., tel. 01865/244544) has a varied program of plays, comedy, opera, ballet, and pop concerts. Tickets range £7–£45. In summer, plays are often performed in the gardens of some colleges; check with the tourist office for venues and ticket prices.

OUTDOOR ACTIVITIES

PUNTING AND ROWING

Punting, one of the great Oxford experiences, involves propelling a long, flat boat along the Thames River using a 15-ft pole to push off the riverbed; beginners will probably spin around in circles before getting the hang of it. If you find it easier to punt from the front, do so, even if, technically speaking, you're supposed to push from the rear. You can, of course, also get a normal rowboat for the same rate. The friendly **Magdalen Bridge Boathouse** (High St., tel. 01865/202643) rents punts and rowboats for £10 per hour with a £25 deposit. It also offers chauffeured punts if you're feeling lazy. Punts and rowboats cost £8 per hour with a £25 deposit at **Riverside Boating Co.** (beneath Folly Bridge), although the owner has been known to raise prices during high-demand periods. Both close for bad weather and boat races.

NEAR OXFORD

BLENHEIM PALACE

As a reward for his surprising victory over French forces in Blenheim, Germany, in 1704, John Churchill received the title Duke of Marlborough and a great plot of Oxfordshire land from Queen Anne and Parliament. As any good duke should, Churchill ordered a palace built on the grounds. The dizzying excess of John Vanbrugh's design makes Blenheim one of the greatest, most pleasure-bloated manor houses in England. The Baroque design—arches, columns, pediments, and classical statuary—is appropriately complemented by Capability Brown's landscaping, a whirlwind of manmade lakes, gardens, forest, and sculpted hedges. In fact, Blenheim claims to have the world's second-largest **hedge maze** (£1), but the hedges are only 4–6 ft high and all paths lead to the exit—Jack Nicholson would catch you for sure.

These days, the 11th Duke of Marlborough and his family hide in an inaccessible wing of the palace (even their "private parts," however, are open to tours some weeks of the year). Your appreciation of the interior is enhanced by the snappy, informative guided tour; note the family portraits by Joshua Reynolds and Van Dyck as you fly by. There's also a small exhibit on Winston Leonard Spencer Churchill—nephew to the eighth Duke of Marlborough—who was born at Blenheim six weeks prematurely in 1874. More intriguing is Winston's quiet grave, beside St. Martin's Church in the village of Bladon, a 1-mi walk from the palace. Another must-do lies just beyond the back gates (actually, the original old gates) of the palace: **Woodstock,** a quintessentially charming English village. In the postcard-pretty town square, you half expect to see Anthony Trollope taking his morning stroll among the historic inns (The Bear is where Richard Burton popped the question to Liz) and oh-so-chic shops. Have your camera ready to capture the quiet corners of this town—they are as picturesque as they come. From Oxford's Gloucester Green station, take Bus 20, 20A, 20B, or 20C straight to the palace (30 min, £2.80 return). *Woodstock, tel. 01993/811091. Admission £8.50; admission to grounds only, £2. Open mid-Mar.–Oct., daily 10:30–4:45.*

Wildness reigns on May Day, when Oxford celebrates the coming of warm weather. At 6 AM the little boys in the Magdalen College choir sing from Magdalen Tower, and the pubs open at 7 AM.

WHERE TO SLEEP

Blenheim Guest House and Tea Rooms. The Cinderella of all British hotels, this place sits in one of the most storybook corners in England—the quiet Woodstock cul-de-sac that leads to the back gates of imperial Blenheim Palace. It's a modest, small guest house, three stories tall, with its facade still bearing a Victorian-era painted banner that states "Views and Postcards of Blenheim," and a storefront tearoom. Guest rooms are unassuming and faux-traditional in furnishings, but the Marlborough room is unique—after all, its bathroom offers a view of Blenheim. Thanks to the cheery staff, breakfast is a delight. "And where are you off to today?" you're asked. "Oh, I'm going to visit the palace." The response, delivered with a big smile: "Sounds good to me!" Singles start at £40, doubles at £55. Stay here instead of Oxford and just take the frequent Woodstock–Oxford bus back and forth. *17 Park St., Woodstock, OX20 1SJ, tel. 01993/811467. Follow Park St.—the main artery of the village—till you nearly reach Blenheim's entrance. 6 rooms with shower.*

STRATFORD-UPON-AVON

To go, or not to go, that is the question. Whether 'tis nobler in the wallet to suffer the slings and arrows of outrageous prices, or to take arms against a sea of tourists and by opposing, end them. To die: of claustrophobia. No more; and by patience we say you'll end the headache and the thousand natural shocks that visitors are heir to: 'tis a resolution devoutly to be wished. To visit: to enjoy. To enjoy? Perhaps to go to the theater. Ay, there's the rub; for in that theater what plays may come, when we have shuffled off the mortifying crowds, must give us peace.

Stratford grew up in the 15th and 16th centuries as a stopover on the road to and from the capital; nowadays the former market hub plays the slightly modified role of prime day-trip center for Londoners. Indeed, Stratford is suffocatingly overcrowded—a veritable tourist trap—and its soul, some say, has been sucked dry by mercenary hucksters looking to make a few quid off Shakespeare's good name. If you're really that keen on saying you've "done" Stratford, you won't mind the crowds or the lack of cafés, movie theaters, and other forms of cultural life beyond the theater. And although the Royal Shakespeare Company (RSC) stages frequent productions in Stratford, equally prestigious productions run in London—minus the hype. That said, the RSC is the best thing going for Stratford, and we unabashedly recommend it.

Stratford is just fine during winter—the crowds thin out, the streets become walkable, and the RSC continues its first-rate program of drama. Even so, don't come expecting to find a sprawling Elizabethan town: Apart from a few heavily restored thatched cottages, the streets of modern-day Stratford are lined with high-fashion clothing stores and the ubiquitous McDonald's. The Shakespearean sights have a certain Old World appeal, but even these have been repeatedly reconstructed and restored. To make matters worse, there's no direct train service from London, which means you'll probably end up on one of three daily buses.

BASICS

AMERICAN EXPRESS

Located inside the tourist office, AmEx changes money, issues traveler's checks, and holds client mail. *Bridgefoot, CV37 6GW, tel. 01789/415856. Open Apr.–Oct., Mon.–Sat. 9–6, Sun. 11–5.; Nov.–Mar., Mon.–Sat. 9–5.*

VISITOR INFORMATION

The **tourist office**'s multilingual staff and piles of pamphlets can be very helpful—as is the office's hotel reservations service. *Bridgefoot, tel. 01789/293127. Open early Apr.–Oct., Mon.–Sat. 9–6, Sun. 11–5; Nov.–early Apr., Mon.–Sat. 9–6.*

Guide Friday (14 Rother St., tel. 01789/294466), a bus-tour company, also has tourist info and free flyers, and the lines are much shorter than at the tourist office. On the downside, they're also trying to sell something: a double-decker bus tour (£8) that stops at all five of Stratford's major sights. Since the price doesn't include admission to the sights and most are within walking distance, it's not really worth it unless you're lazy. Take the pamphlets and run.

COMING AND GOING

BY BUS

Buses stop on Bridge Street at Waterside, either directly in front of the McDonald's or across the street. **National Express** (tel. 0990/808080) sends buses from London three times a day (£14 return, £17 on Friday). Buy tickets at the National Express desk (tel. 01879/262718) inside Stratford's tourist office; it's closed Sunday. **Stagecoach** (tel. 01865/772250) runs a bus service to Oxford for £3.75 single, £6.50 return.

BY TRAIN

Although there are no direct trains from London, there is direct service from Birmingham (£3.40 single, £3.50 day return). Otherwise, from London's Paddington, take the train to Leamington Spa and change to the Stratford Line (2½–3 hours, £27 return). Stratford's **train station** (Alcester Rd., tel. 0345/484950) is closed on Sunday October–May, so you'll have to take the bus from London or Leamington.

GETTING AROUND

Stagecoach buses cover the main sights around Stratford: Bus X16 runs to Warwick (£2. 90 return) and Kenilworth, Bus X20 runs hourly to Birmingham, and Bus 18 runs to the YHA hostel. If you really want to go wild, rent a bike from the hostel and wheel around town; it's the best way to avoid the congested sidewalks, although the roads aren't much better.

WHERE TO SLEEP

Since nearly every tourist over the age of 40 is magnetically drawn to Stratford, there's no shortage of B&Bs. The hard part is finding a cheap one. No matter what, reserve space *at least* a few days in advance. Stratford has three concentrated pockets of B&Bs: on **Grove Road** near the train station; around **Evesham Road,** the southern extension of Grove Road; and on **Shipston Road,** across the River Avon from the center of town.

The Garth House. Unlike most B&B proprietors, Louise Thomas actually caters to backpackers. The double with bath is especially quiet. Doubles cost £32 (£35 en-suite). *9A Broad Walk, CV37 6HS, tel. 01789/298035. From the rail station, walk toward town, turn right on Grove Rd., which becomes Evesham Pl., left on Broad Walk. 3 rooms, 1 with bath. Cash only. Closed weekdays Oct.–Mar.*

Newlands. This unpretentious B&B is wonderfully quiet, and the rooms are surprisingly large. Proprietor Sue Boston is a sweetheart who loves to give advice on the best plays to see in Stratford. Rooms cost £20–£22 per person. *7 Broad Walk, CV37 6HS, tel. and fax 01789/298449. Follow directions to the Garth House (*see above*). 4 rooms, 3 with bath.*

Penshurst. If you searched the whole of Stratford, you wouldn't find a better place to stay than this pretty, centrally located B&B. The owner is an absolute treasure, and there are flexible breakfast hours to suit early birds and laggards alike. The rooms are named after Stratford's historic streets, and each contains a book on the history of the corresponding street. Singles start at £17, doubles run £16–£22 per person. *34 Evesham Pl., CV37 6HT, tel. 01789/205259, fax 01789/295322. From the rail station, walk toward town, turn right on Grove Rd., which becomes Evesham Pl. 8 rooms, 2 with bath. Cash only.*

Throw back a pint at the Dirty Duck (Waterside, tel. 01789/297312), Stratford's thespian hangout. Everybody from Olivier to Branagh has imbibed here, and nearly all have left signed photographs on the wall to prove it.

Victoria Spa Lodge. This upscale, no-smoking B&B lies just outside town, about a 20-min walk along the towpath. Draped with clematis, the building dates from 1837 and sports Queen Victoria's coat of arms in two of its gables. You'll enjoy your cornflakes in a grand lounge/breakfast room with tall windows, furnished with sofas and chairs for relaxing. Spacious rooms, some with fireplaces, go for £60. *Bishopton La., Bishopton, CV37 9QY, tel. 01789/267985, fax 01789/204728. From the rail station, walk toward town, turn left on Arden St., cross Birmingham Rd. to Clopton Rd., turn left on the towpath; you'll see the Lodge after about 10 min. 7 rooms with bath.*

HOSTEL

Stratford YHA. If you have the time, you should definitely walk the 2 mi to the village of Alveston, where this hostel is located—you'll pass some beautiful Tudor homes that aren't on the bus route. It's one of the few hostels in Britain with cafeteria-style meals for dinner, so if you only want a pot of tea, you can buy it separately without paying for a full meal. Clean rooms and helpful management make the price (beds £12.95), which includes breakfast, seem not so bad. Definitely reserve ahead. *Hemmingford House, Alveston, Warwickshire, CV37 7RG, tel. 01789/297093, fax 01789/205513. Take Bus 18 from Stratford (£1.50 return). 148 beds. Midnight curfew. Closed mid-Dec.–early Jan.*

CAMPING

Elms Camp. It's a great alternative to the local lodging scene and closer to Stratford than the hostel. The nearby village of Tiddington has a pub and market. Sites are £4 per person. As always in Stratford, reserve in advance. There's a shop on site. *Tiddington Rd., Tiddington, CV37 7AB, tel. 01789/292312. Take Bus 18 or X18 from Stratford to Tiddington, then follow signs. 50 sites. Check-in by 9 PM. Laundry, showers. Cash only. Closed Nov.–Mar.*

FOOD

Finding a reasonably priced, tasty meal in Stratford is nearly impossible. Pubs and greasy fast-food stands will cheaply plug the hole in your stomach, but if you want a full dinner, you'll be eating alongside other tourists and paying heavily inflated prices. Try your luck on **Sheep Street,** one block south of the train station. Nearby **Marco Italian Deli** (20 Church St., tel. 01789/292889) sells sandwiches for

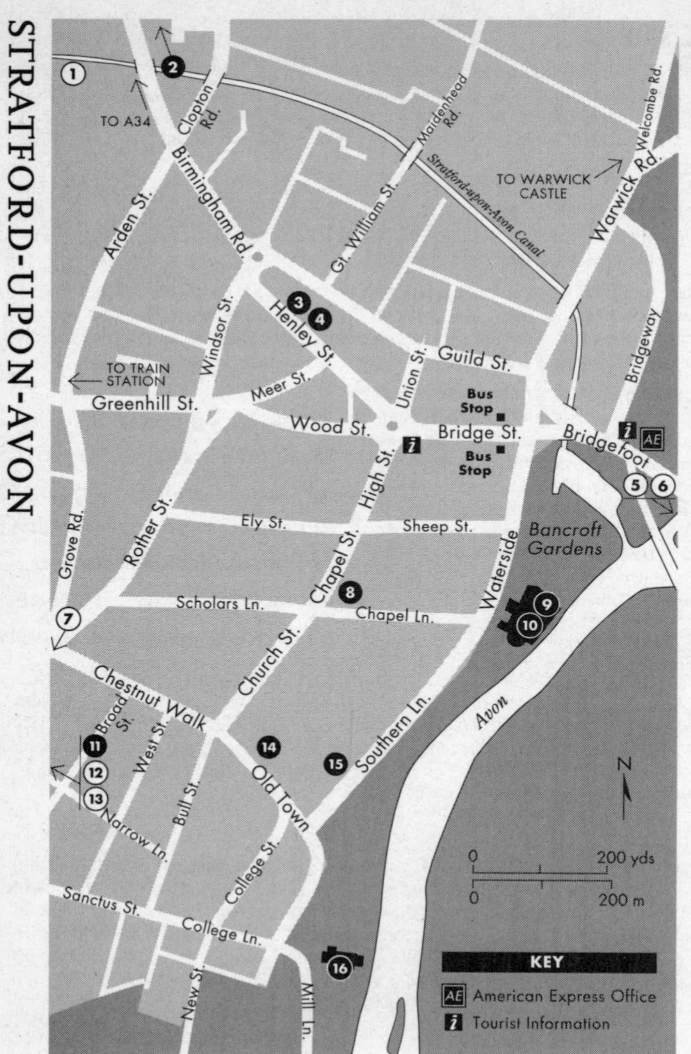

Sights ●

Anne Hathaway's Cottage, **11**

Hall's Croft, **14**

Holy Trinity Church, **16**

Mary Arden's House, **2**

New Place (Nash's House), **8**

The Other Place Theatre, **15**

Royal Shakespeare Theatre, **9**

Shakespeare Birthplace, **4**

Shakespeare Centre and Library, **3**

Swan Theatre, **10**

Lodging ○

Elms Camp, **6**

The Garth House, **13**

Newlands, **12**

Penhurst, **7**

Stratford YHA, **5**

Victoria Spa Lounge, **1**

less than £2 during the day. **Greenhill Street,** near the train station, is slightly removed from touristy ground zero and has some reasonable places.

The Garrick Inn. A "traditional" English establishment crammed with tourists, the Garrick Inn, built in 1595, still has the cramped feel of an Elizabethan pub. Surprisingly, the food isn't expensive: steak and ale pie (£5.95) and scampi with chips and peas (£5.75) are bargains by Stratford standards. There are good brews on tap, too. *25 High St., tel. 01789/292186. Cash only.*

River Terrace. At this informal cafeteria in the Royal Shakespeare Theatre, the meals and snacks are crowd pleasers. They include lasagna, shepherd's pie, salads, sandwiches, and cakes, with wine and beer available. *Royal Shakespeare Theatre, Waterside, tel. 01789/293226. Cash only. Closed when the theater is closed.*

The Slug and Lettuce. Don't let the name put you off—this pine-paneled pub serves excellent meals. Longstanding favorites are chicken breast baked in avocado and garlic, and poached cushion of salmon. *38 Guild St., tel. 01789/299700.*

Vintner Cafe and Wine Bar. An eclectic group of families, twentysomethings, and Europeans crowd one of Stratford's few cool places. Huge candles stuck in wine bottles dominate the small tables, leaving little room for the plates of fish pie (£8.75) or the vegetarian dish of the day (£6–£8). *5 Sheep St., tel. 01789/297259. Cash only.*

Wholefood Café. The antiseptic interior lacks character, but an encouraging mix of locals and visitors gives this vegetarian and whole-food restaurant some life. The soup (£2), quiche (£4.50), and stuffed potatoes (£2.75–£3) won't do you wrong. The adjacent **Stratford Health Foods** (tel. 01789/292353), open daily, sells bulk groceries and food to go. *Greenhill St., tel. 01789/415741. Cash only. Closed Sun. and evenings.*

WORTH SEEING

The Shakespeare Birthplace Trust (01789/204016) sells a convenient **all-inclusive ticket** (£11) to the five major sights listed below, not including **Holy Trinity Church.** If you want to skip Anne Hathaway's Cottage and Mary Arden's House, buy the **three-in-town** ticket (£7.50). For those actually interested in the work of the writer, the **Shakespeare Library** (Henley St., tel. 01789/204016; open weekdays 10–5, Sat. 9:30–12:30) has original Shakespeare folios and exhibits centered on the Bard's life. Surprisingly, admission to the library is free.

Shakespeare's birthday is traditionally assigned to April 23, 1564. More than 400 years later, it's one of the worst days to look for cheap lodging in Stratford.

ANNE HATHAWAY'S COTTAGE

Anne Hathaway lived in this thatched cottage—possibly the most picture-postcard perfect one in England—in nearby Shottery prior to her marriage to William Shakespeare on November 27, 1582. Be warned that your experience may be spoiled by the amount of merchandise forced down your throat. The Tudor furniture pales in comparison with the lovely apple orchard outside. From Stratford it's a 15-min walk west through open fields; follow the signs from Evesham Place or take a bus from the Bridge Street bus stop. *Admission £3.90. Open mid-Mar.–mid-Oct., Mon.–Sat. 9–5, Sun. 9:30–5; mid-Oct.–mid-Mar., Mon.–Sat. 9:30–4, Sun. 10–4.*

HALL'S CROFT

This sight has a tenuous connection at best to the Bard's dramatic life. It was the home of his daughter, Susanna, and her husband, Dr. John Hall. Of the 17th-century antiques on display, Dr. Hall's medical instruments are certainly the coolest. *Old Town. Admission £3.30. Open mid-Mar.–mid-Oct., Mon.–Sat. 9:30–5, Sun. 10–5; mid-Oct.–mid-Mar., Mon.–Sat. 10–4, Sun. 10:30–4.*

HOLY TRINITY CHURCH

The remains of Shakespeare lie buried underneath the altar of this traditional Gothic church—not in Westminster Abbey's Poets' Corner, as many think. Will's wife and family rest in peace next to him; above hovers a bust made immediately after his death in 1616 by Gheerart Jansen. It is believed to be one of only two likenesses created in Shakespeare's time. *Trinity St. at College La., tel. 01789/266316. Admission 60p donation. Open Mar.–Oct., Mon.–Sat. 8:30–6, Sun. 2–5; Nov.–Feb., Mon.–Sat. 9:30–4, Sun. 2–5.*

MARY ARDEN'S HOUSE

Mary Arden probably didn't live here, and the "home" of Shakespeare's mother is definitely on the boring side. This most undecorated of Tudor farmhouses has been expanded, however, to include the slightly more interesting **Glebe Farm,** where falconers display their art with live birds, all day, every day. To reach the house and farm, take the train from Stratford to Wilmcote (5 min, £1.30 return) and follow the signs from the station. *Wilmcote. Admission £4.40. Open mid-Mar.–mid-Oct., Mon.–Sat. 9:30–5, Sun. 10–5; mid-Oct.–mid-Mar., Mon.–Sat. 10–4, Sun. 10:30–4.*

NEW PLACE (NASH'S HOUSE)

Shakespeare bought the place in 1597 for £60 (big money at the time) and died here in 1616 at the age of 52. It's called Nash's House after the man who married Shakespeare's granddaughter. Inside, a small museum features artifacts from prehistoric Stratford; the attached garden is much more interesting.

SHAKESPEARE IN LOVE

What better way to relieve tourist-trap tension than to ponder Shakespeare's much talked-about love life? Rumors abound on this subject, a fact exploited to the full by one recent film we could mention. Because few proper historical records survive of Shakespeare's life, everyone is free to speculate.

No one's in any doubt that Anne Hathaway was the great writer's wife. But why did the pair get hitched in such a rush, especially when she was eight years (at 26) his senior, a rarity in those days? A big clue is to be found in the gap between two dates. The first, November 27, was the day Will and Anne tied the knot; the second, May 26, was the day they welcomed their first baby, Susanna, into the world.

Shotgun weddings were, and are, no rarity, but much more out of left field—certainly in those times—was Will's supposed relationship with Henry Wriothesley, Earl of Southampton. Many scholars believe it was the noble Earl's patronage that secured Shakespeare's position as the leading playwright in London, and some have it that Southampton was the "golden youth" referred to in the sonnets.

Then our bed-hopping hero is reckoned to have enjoyed sweet pleasures with Viola de Lesseps, the character made famous by Gwyneth Paltrow in Shakespeare in Love. *"I would not have thought it: there is something better than a play," Viola says of her entanglement with Will. Despite his amorous history, we don't think he would go that far.*

Chapel St., at Chapel La. Admission £3.30. Open mid-Mar.–mid-Oct., Mon.–Sat. 9:30–5, Sun. 10–5; mid-Oct.–mid-Mar., Mon.–Sat. 10–4, Sun. 10:30–4.

SHAKESPEARE'S BIRTHPLACE

The birthplace of the Bard has become an unhallowed shrine of vicious, camera-snapping tourists trying to elbow their way in to capture that precious Kodak moment. This small, heavily restored home is usually too crowded to allow for a casual stroll—which is frustrating since the biographical material is actually interesting. **Shakespeare Centre,** adjacent to the house, contains exhibits based on recent Stratford productions of Shakespeare plays. *Henley St. Admission £4.90. Open mid-Mar.–mid-Oct., Mon.–Sat. 9–5, Sun. 9:30–5; mid-Oct.–mid-Mar., Mon.–Sat. 9:30–4, Sun. 10–4.*

AFTER DARK

Stratford's nightlife *is* the Royal Shakespeare Company, which presents nightly performances on two main stages, the **Royal Shakespeare Theatre** (Waterside) and the **Swan Theatre** (Southern La.). In any given week there are five or six different plays, not all of them written by Shakespeare, especially during the company's annual hiatus (October–November), when visiting companies take the stage. Down the road, a third stage, **The Other Place** (Southern La.), runs smaller, more modern productions during high season. If you don't mind standing during a performance, you can buy tickets for as little as £4.50; balcony tickets start at £7. If the show hasn't sold out, students can buy discount tickets at 9:30 AM or 6:30

PM for about £11, £14 on Saturday. Outside the summer season, under-25s can also buy half-price tickets for Monday performances, although these should be booked in advance. Or, to be safe, you can get up early and catch one of the 20 or so tickets held for day-of-performance sales; be there when the box office opens at 9:30 AM.

The RSC conducts **backstage tours** (tel. 01789/412602) year-round; tickets cost £4. Try to book in advance, as groups fill the tours quickly. Otherwise, meet at the stage door following the evening's entertainment for a 30-min **postperformance tour** (£4). *Southern La., tel. 01789/269191 for recorded info or tel. 01789/295623 for box office. Performances usually are held Mon.–Sat. at 7:30; additional matinees Thurs. and Sat. at 1:30 or 2:30.*

BATH

Jane Austen's novel Persuasion, *much of which is set in Bath, is useful for an insight into the town's history and high-society past.*

Bath's history has been shaped by its hot springs, which pour out of the earth at a steady 116°F. In early times, the city's hot waters piqued the interest of Celts, who presumably assigned mystical powers to the springs. But the various pagan gods of the Celts had to bow to a greater authority when the Romans took center stage in the 1st century AD. These new invaders dedicated the township to the goddess Sulis Minerva, named it Aquae Sulis (Waters of Sulis), and constructed an intricate series of baths and pools around the hot springs. For hundreds of years after the Romans left town, the majestic bath houses fell into disuse; as with so much Roman culture and technology in Britain, they became a victim of the plunge into the messy barbarism of the Dark Ages. Saxon King Edgar made a good fist of bringing back the glory days and was crowned king of all England here. But it was centuries later that things really took off. Bath became synonymous with elegance, engendering a social scene second only to London's. The Royals have exhibited a conspicuous preference for the town: Queen Elizabeth I brought a certain prestige to the baths with her visit in 1574, and Queen Anne's visits to the waters in 1702 and 1703 established the "Bath season." In subsequent years, architect John Wood (1704–54) gave Bath its distinctive, harmonious look; using the yellowish "Bath stone" cut from nearby quarries, he created a city of crescents, terraces, and Palladian mansions that curve through the city like scalloped paper cutouts.

Sadly, you can no longer bathe in the springs, although you can drink the horrible-tasting water if you so desire. The museums, parks, and architecture make a visit worthwhile. Bath is on the itinerary of every scrambling tourist, from little old ladies to mangy backpackers. Remember that lodging is expensive and you'll hear lots of American accents.

BASICS

The very efficient **Tourist Information Centre** (Abbey Chambers, Abbey Churchyard, tel. 01225/477101), open Monday–Saturday 9:30–5 (May–September until 6), Sunday 10–4, gets miserably crowded in summer. Come early to book a room (£5 fee plus 10% deposit), as the bargains go fast. The tourist office also holds an **American Express** office (open during the same hours, tel. 01225/424416), which offers regular cardholder services and cashes all brands of traveler's checks free of charge (for cash transactions there's a £2 commission). There's also an AmEx branch at 5 Bridge Street (tel. 01225/444747). **Lockers** on Platform 1 of the train station are currently closed as an antibomb measure, but you might check anyway. If they're still not in use, leave your bags in the Badgerline office at the bus station, accessible 8:30–5:30, for £2 a day. The main **post office** (New Bond St., BA1 1AA, tel. 01225/445358) is open Monday–Saturday until 5:30.

COMING AND GOING

Great Western makes the 90-min trip from London's Paddington Station to **Bath Spa Station** for £30 return. Direct trains also run to Cardiff, Salisbury, and Southampton. The ticket office is open 5:30–8:30 (tel. 0345/484950). **National Express** (tel. 0990/808080) sends 10 coaches daily to and from London for £17.50 return. Buy National Express tickets at Bath's **bus station** (Manvers St., across from the train

BATH

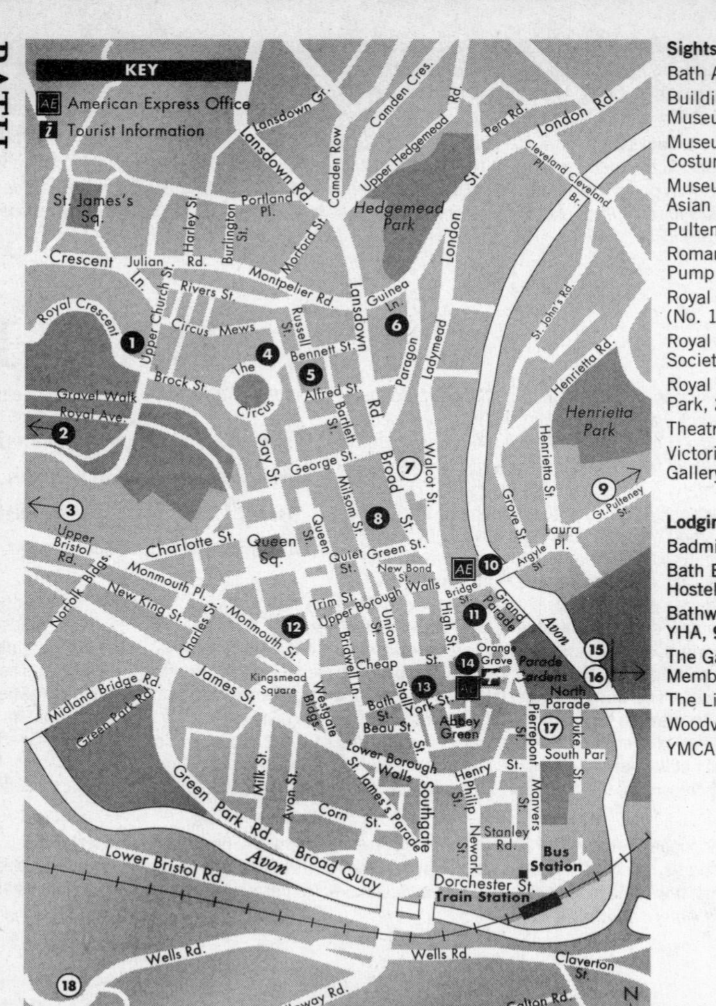

Sights ●

Bath Abbey, **14**

Building of Bath Museum, **6**

Museum of Costume, **5**

Museum of East Asian Art, **4**

Pulteny Bridge, **10**

Roman Baths and Pump Room, **13**

Royal Crescent (No. 1), **1**

Royal Photographic Society Gallery, **8**

Royal Victoria Park, **2**

Theatre Royal, **12**

Victoria Art Gallery, **11**

Lodging ○

Badminton Villa, **18**

Bath Backpackers Hostel, **17**

Bathwick Hill YHA, **9**

The Gardens and Membland, **16**

The Limes, **15**

Woodville House, **3**

YMCA, **7**

station, tel. 01225/464446). You can also get cheap service between London's Marble Arch and Bath from **Bakers Dolphin** (tel. 01934/616000): £9.50 for a single, £15.95 for open return. Tickets can be purchased by phone with a credit card at least a day in advance, or you can try getting a seat the same day, either by telephone or direct from the driver.

GETTING AROUND

The bus station, which is within striking distance of all Bath's attractions, also dispatches **Badgerline** buses to neighboring towns. If you plan to make day trips from Bath, purchase a **Day Rambler** pass (£5.10), good for unlimited travel on regional Badgerline buses. The blocks surrounding the depot contain bus stops for local routes that fan throughout the city and into the suburbs. Call the **Travel Information Line** (tel. 0117/9555111) for a listing of local bus times throughout the region.

WHERE TO SLEEP

Bath has some delightfully refined hotels. Seek, and ye shall also find, bargains here (so long as you don't mind a short bridge-crossing into town). Reasonably priced B&Bs are clustered along Pulteney Road in the east and along Charlotte Street and Upper Bristol Road in the west. The tourist office has a bulky accommodations brochure, but the hostel's list of cheap B&Bs is better. In summer it's wise to book at least two weeks in advance.

Badminton Villa. In one of Bath's sweeter neighborhoods—about a 10-min walk from the city center—this is a Victorian-period family house built in 1883 of honey-hue Bath stone. Located on a tree-lined road, the no-smoking hotel sits on a hillside offering lovely views over the Georgian city. Owners John and Sue Burton are eminently charming hosts, taking great pride in their recent refurbishments of the guest rooms, which run £45 for singles, £60 for doubles (breakfast included), and include color TV, clock radios, and hair dryers. *10 Upper Oldfield Park, BA2 3JZ, tel. 01225/426347, fax 01225/420393. From the station, head south ½ mi along Wells Rd., or take a taxi or Bus 14. 5 rooms with bath.*

The Gardens and Membland. Peter and Katey Moore, the young proprietors, make you feel like family in either of their two guest houses. Double rooms are £25 per head, although you can negotiate a 10% discount for longer stays. If you arrive in the evening, they may pick you up at the train station. Check in at The Gardens; they'll direct you to Membland. *7 Pulteney Gardens, BA2 4HG, tel. 01225/337642 or 01225/336712. From stations, walk up Manvers St., turn right on N. Parade, cross the bridge, turn right on Pulteney Rd., then second left. 9 rooms, all with shower. Cash only.*

The Limes. Mr. and Mrs. Ellis only let out two rooms because their kids and grandkids often come to stay. The guest rooms are large and decorated with white chenille bedspreads and some fine antiques. Pulteney Road is busy, but street noise is not a problem. Rooms cost £15 per person. *1 Pulteney Rd., BA2 4HF, tel. 01225/311044. Follow directions to The Gardens* (see above), *but entrance is first left on Pulteney Rd. 2 rooms, none with bath. Cash only.*

You can probably live quite happily without ever sampling the famous "Bath bun," a tea-time treat that's degenerated into a tourist attraction. If you do feel compelled to try one, Scoffs (20 Kingsmead Sq.) sells them for £1 in an unpretentious atmosphere.

Woodville House. Tom and Anne Toalster's classic Bath house is ideally positioned if you want to be near Victoria Park and the Royal Crescent. Basic rooms cost £36, even if you're alone, although they don't take in solo travelers during summer. The no-smoking rule is absolutely rigid. *4 Marlborough La., BA1 2NQ, tel. and fax 01225/319335. From the stations, walk to Bath Abbey, turn left on Cheap St., right on Monmouth St., which becomes Upper Bristol Rd., right on Marlborough La. 3 rooms, none with bath. TV lounge. Cash only.*

HOSTELS

Bath Backpackers Hostel. If you don't want to trek out to the official version (*see below*), this independent hostel offers cheap beds (£10 in dorms) right in the center of things. Double rooms start from just £25, and prices include breakfast. There's no curfew and no lockout, making for an amiable, relaxed atmosphere—indeed, there's a bar, pool room, and Jacuzzi on the premises. *13 Pierrepont St., BA1 1CA, tel. 01225/446787, fax 01225/446305. From the stations, walk up Manvers St., which becomes Pierrepont St. 50 beds. Kitchen. Cash only.*

Bathwick Hill YHA. This Italianate building has a mellow atmosphere, and the staff has lots of info on what's going on in Bath. The hostel is open year-round, and reservations are essential in summer. Beds are £10.50. You'll definitely want to take a bus up the steep hill. *Bathwick Hill, BA2 6JZ, tel. 01225/465674, fax 01225/482947. From the stations, take Badgerline Bus 18 or Streamline Bus 418 directly to the hostel. 121 beds. Reception open 7:15 AM–11 PM. Kitchen, laundry.*

YMCA. It's closer to the center of town than the YHA hostel, but the atmosphere is less lively. It's clean, but pretty spartan. A dorm bed costs £11, singles £15, doubles £28; all with breakfast. Credit-card payments are accepted. *Broad Street Pl., tel. 01225/460471. From the stations, walk up Manvers St. to Bath Abbey, walk north on High St., turn left on Broad St. (look for YMCA sign leading down the alley to the right). 180 beds in 73 rooms and 4 dorms. Laundry.*

THE SQUARE, THE CIRCLE, AND THE CRESCENT

Bath wouldn't be Bath without its distinctive 18th-century Georgian architecture, most of which was conceived of by John Wood the Elder, an architect obsessed. Wood saw Bath as a mythical city destined for greatness along the lines of Winchester and Glastonbury. He nurtured the myth that Bath was founded by Prince Bladud (ostensibly with the help of an errant pig rooting in the ground for acorns; Wood later used stone acorns as a motif). Wood sought an architectural style that would do justice to his great concept, and found it in the Palladian style, made popular in Britain by Inigo Jones.

Influenced by nearby ancient stone circles as well as round Roman temples, Wood broke loose from convention in his design for Bath's outstanding Circus, a full circle of houses broken only three times for intersecting streets. After the death of Wood the Elder, John Wood the Younger carried out his father's plans for the Royal Crescent, an obtuse crescent of 30 interconnected houses overlooking Victoria Park—the first row houses in Britain. Stop in at No. 1 Royal Crescent for a look at one of these Georgian homes decked out in period style. Tel. 01225/428126. Admission £4. Open mid-Feb.–Oct., Tues.–Sun. 10:30–5; Nov.–early Dec., Tues.–Sun. 10:30–4.

CAMPING

Newton Mill Touring Centre. This is the closest campground, 3 mi west of Bath. Sites cost £4.25 per person or £10.95 for two persons, tent, and car (a bit less in winter). Its facilities include a bar, a restaurant, and laundry. *Newton St., Loe, tel. 01225/333909. From the bus station, take Bus 5, alight at Twerton (ask driver), then walk through the playground and down the footpath. Showers.*

FOOD

You'll find plenty of burger stands and other cheap restaurants around the Theatre Royal, Sawclose, and Kingsmead Square. If you'd rather create your own gustatory masterpiece, there's a **Waitrose** supermarket in the Podium shopping center on High Street and a cheaper **Somerfield** market in the Southgate Shopping Centre behind the bus station. Enhance your meal with some fresh produce, meat, cheese, and pastries from the **Guildhall Market** on High Street.

Café Retro. The decor in this mellow and mirrored café-restaurant tends toward art nouveau but is pared down by simple tables and old wooden chairs. The food is good and reasonably priced, with main courses like "Smokie Fish Pie" and asparagus and smoked ham crepes for £5–£8. Bring your own alcoholic drink; the café offers free corkage. *18 York St., near tourist office, tel. 01225/339347.*

The Crystal Palace. This "very English" pub is a fine place to enjoy a large range of sandwiches, especially in its garden patio on a sunny day. Other dishes include a hot open-face prawn sandwich and six kinds of ploughman's lunches (£4–£6). *Abbey Green, tel. 01225/423944. From the entrance to the Roman Baths, turn left and walk less than 1 min. Cash only.*

Fodder's. Gourmet sandwiches, some for £1.95, are the specialty at this small takeout in the city center. Choose from prawns in garlic or mayo, pâté de campagne, vegetarian fillings, deli meats, and condiments like garlic olive pâté. *9 Cheap St., near High St., tel. 01225/462165. Cash only. Closed Sun. Sept.–May. No dinner.*

Tilley's Bistro. With the land of haute cuisine just across a narrow body of water, it's troubling that good French restaurants like Tilley's haven't infiltrated the English food scene. For £8–£9 you can order entrées such as sautéed medallions of pork in a brandy and Roquefort cream sauce, as well as vegetarian and vegan dishes. For lunch, try a set two- or three-course meal for £6.20 or £7.50, respectively. *3 N. Parade Passage, between Abbey Green and N. Parade Bridge, tel. 01225/484200. No lunch Sun.*

WORTH SEEING

Bath's city center is easily navigable by foot, and a free, comprehensive walking tour is a great way to learn about the city's highlights. Tours leave daily from the Roman Baths entrance (*see below*) in the Abbey Churchyard at 10:30 and 2 (Sunday at 2:30), and at 7 three times a week in summer; confirm times at the tourist office.

BATH ABBEY

For that picture-perfect moment, bring your camera to Pulteney Bridge, a spectacularly grand Palladian-style landmark, designed by Robert Adam in 1770 and lined with shops.

In one form or another, Bath Abbey has been around for 1,200 years; it evolved from a 7th-century Saxon structure to a Norman church, and eventually took shape as a 15th-century Gothic construction. Bishop Oliver King, who was charged with rebuilding the old Norman edifice, built the turret facades alongside the main window after he allegedly witnessed angels ascending a stairway to heaven. Maybe the man of the cloth had helped himself to the communion wine, or supped from the revolting Bath waters themselves. Under Henry VIII (1491–1547) Bath Abbey, like many churches in the country, was partly destroyed as the wayward king turned against all things Catholic. Luckily daughter Elizabeth I (1533–1603) restored the family reputation by initiating repairs. Stained-glass windows at the eastern end portray Christ's biography, although the abbey is better known for its spindly, fan-vaulted ceiling—don't forget to look up. If you don't mind the £2 admission, explore the subterranean **Heritage Vaults,** open Monday–Saturday 10–4, with some slightly cheesy exhibits on the abbey's history. In summer, also check for flyers advertising organ recitals in the abbey. *High St., tel. 01225/422462. Admission free, but £2 donation requested. Open Mon.–Sat. 9–6 (in winter until 4:30), Sun. 9–6, but not during services.*

BUILDING OF BATH MUSEUM

If "Norm" makes you think of *This Old House* instead of *Cheers,* you'll dig the architectural displays at the Building of Bath Museum. If not, the small print and paucity of big pictures make it a bit of a struggle. Check out the huge model of Bath. *The Countess of Huntingdon's Chapel, The Paragon, off Broad St., tel. 01225/333895. Admission £3.50. Open mid-Feb.–Nov., Tues.–Sun. 10:30–5.*

MUSEUM OF EAST ASIAN ART

Cultivated Bath makes the perfect setting for this amazing museum, which showcases a private collection of East Asian art spanning more than 7,000 years, from 5,000 BC to the 20th century. Since the museum is small, only one third of the more than 1,500 pieces of jade, gold, silver, wood, bronze, ceramics, and silk (many of which are quite rare) that compose the entire collection can be shown at once. The emphasis is on Chinese art, but works from Southeast Asia, Tibet, Japan, and Korea are also exhibited. *12 Bennett St., off The Circus, tel. 01225/464640. Admission £3.50. Open Mon.–Sat. 10–6 (Nov.–Mar. until 5), Sun. 10–5 (Nov.–Mar. from noon).*

ROMAN BATHS AND MUSEUM OF COSTUME

The Romans built their luxurious baths here between the 1st and 5th centuries AD, at a site where springs already bubbled from the earth. The bath network is well preserved, and the smell of sulfur, the looming Roman statuary, and the murky green pools make it easy to imagine what it was like being a Roman bather. Besides the impressive Great Bath, which features statues of famous Romans, there's also the Circular Bath, in which bathers cooled down, and the Norman King's Bath, a kind of watery throne. You can't swim here, but you can sample some vile-tasting mineral water at the overpriced

Pump Room restaurant, above the Roman Baths. Be forewarned: as one of those icons of Regency-era, Jane Austen–vintage England, this is one of the most popular attractions in England, and the large crowds can be a bit of a turnoff. The audio-guide handsets help to shut out some of the hubbub, however, and provide an informative commentary along the way. The man who, with John Wood, did the most to beautify Bath was Richard "Beau" Nash, who started out on his mission to impose the Regency style in 1704. Nash was a benevolent bully, banning smoking, swords, and gossip in the baths. His vision paid off when London society started to visit his creation in droves, much like the flocks of visitors do today.

If you have some extra time, buy a combined admission ticket and visit the **Museum of Costume** (Bennett St., tel. 01225/477785), one of the most prestigious and extensive collections of historical costumes in Britain; it covers more than 400 years of fashion, from the time of James I (1566–1625) to the present day. It's housed in the Assembly Rooms, a series of elegant chambers built in 1771. *Abbey Churchyard, tel. 01225/477000. Admission £6.70. Combined ticket with Museum of Costume £8.70. Open Apr.–Sept., daily 9–6 (Aug. until 9:30 PM); Oct.–Mar., Mon.–Sat. 9:30–5, Sun. 10:30–5.*

ROYAL PHOTOGRAPHIC SOCIETY GALLERY

This is one of the largest independent galleries devoted entirely to photography and home to the oldest photographic society in the world. The constantly rotating exhibits feature works by up-and-coming and renowned photographers as well as stock from the society's massive collection of everything from heliogravures to holograms. The society is particularly well endowed in its collection of 19th-century photographs from around the world—call it a perk of colonialism. *Octagon Galleries, Milsom St., tel. 01225/462841. Admission £2.50. Open daily 9:30–5:30 (last admission 4:45).*

ROYAL VICTORIA PARK

South of the Royal Crescent is one of Bath's best loved public spaces, the Royal Victoria Park, where visitors are well advised to rest their weary feet while enjoying an open air sandwich. As well as beautiful surroundings, the park features an aviary and botanical gardens.

AFTER DARK

Bath's nightlife is lively, if somewhat yupscale, which explains the £2–£6 cover many pubs charge for live music; for serious out-of-your-head clubbing, you may want to catch the next train to Bristol.

PUBS AND CLUBS

A handful of pubs and clubs have a more relaxed and down-to-earth feel, making them favorites of Bath University students. **The Bell** (103 Walcot St., tel. 01225/460426) is the most casual and progressive pub in town. It also has a peaceful back patio. **The Hush** (The Paragon, up from Broad St., tel. 01225/446288) and **The Loft** (off Queen Sq., next to Theatre Royal, tel. 01225/466467) are cool and casual places to hear live bands, with late-night drinking hours a plus. The **Garrick's Head** (St. John's Sq., next to Theatre Royal, tel. 01225/448819), which almost never charges a cover, has two bars: the Green Room (it's painted red) is Bath's gay bar, and the Nash Room next door is not. **Moles** (14 George St., tel. 01225/333423) is a private club that attracts good bands along with lots of unknowns and techno-playing DJs; either phone in advance to get on the guest list or chat up members in line so they'll let you in on their cards. For something sweaty, unglamorous, and raging, let it all hang out at the **Swamp** (89 North Parade, tel. 01225/420330).

THEATER

For highbrow theatrics, catch a show (or two) at the old and illustrious **Theatre Royal** (Sawclose, tel. 01225/448844), with comedy and plays starring renowned British actors like Derek Jacobi, Simon Callow, and Pauline Collins. Tickets range from £7 to £25, and the box office is open Monday–Saturday 10–8; standby tickets (£5) are available at noon on the day of the performance.

OUTDOOR ACTIVITIES

Although Bath feels like a minimetropolis, its surrounding area is green and lined with paths for walking and biking. Ask at the tourist office for pamphlets about the 80-mi **Avon Cycleway,** which takes you through a string of rural country villages, or the **Bristol and Bath Railway Path,** a 12-mi route along an old railway line, with great views and scenery. Mountain bikes can be rented at the **Avon Valley Cyclery**

(Arch 37, rear of the train station, tel. 01225/442442) for £9 per half day, £14 per day, £18 per 24 hours, £28 per weekend, £50 for a week. If you want to use your own two feet, pick up a copy of the pamphlet "Country Walks Within 5 Miles of Bath Abbey" from either the tourist office or the youth hostel to get *detailed* descriptions of the best local strolls. A great, easy day-hike is to follow the River Avon north from Cleveland Bridge and watch as the line between culture and countryside becomes progressively fuzzier. Rowboats and punts on the River Avon cost £4 per person for the first hour, £1.50 per person for every subsequent hour, and can be rented at the **Bath Boating Station** (Forester Rd., tel. 01225/466407); pick up a voucher at the tourist office to get a whole day's rental for just £5.

CAMBRIDGE

Even the most jaded dropout won't be able to resist the lure of Cambridge's stone walls, massive libraries, and robed fellows strutting about town. Cambridge is best known for producing some of the world's finest scientists (Stephen Hawking, author of *A Brief History of Time,* today occupies the faculty chair once held by Isaac Newton). The university's excellence in science has been tapped into by many high-tech companies that have set up shop in and around the town. Even Microsoft has unveiled plans to plow money into a research center here. But don't overlook Cambridge's exalted register of literary alumni—John Milton, E. M. Forster, Virginia Woolf, Vladimir Nabokov, and Ted Hughes, among others. Those numerous distinguished scholars might never have had the chance to nose their books in this pretty part of the world if a row hadn't broken out over at Oxford University in the early 13th century. By all accounts, Cambridge University was founded by a group of refugees from Oxford, scared off after hostile townsfolk lynched one poor academic.

Like many English universities, Cambridge is composed of a number of smaller colleges—35 of them. Some of the colleges date back to the 13th and 14th centuries, and nearly all of them have fine examples of architecture from every succeeding age. But for all the grandeur of ancient academia, Cambridge has plenty of life left: These days, you're just as likely to see death-rockers as gray-bearded deans putting down a pint or two in the town's pubs. Alcohol is no new arrival to Cambridge. From the late 17th century until the early 19th, the place was renowned for the bad behavior of its students; Romantic poet Byron, himself a student here, condemned Cambridge for its "drunkenness."

Since the student area is not concentrated on one campus, the center of town, Market Hill, also serves as the focal point for the university's social and cultural scene. Unfortunately, Cambridge isn't all open doors for tourists, even for visiting students. University students eat most meals in their respective colleges, and many activities, bars, and facilities are accessible only to them. For those expecting immediate acceptance into the Cambridge family, coming here cold may prove disappointing. If you happen to know any students at Cambridge, even barely, make an effort to contact them. Having a friend here will open all sorts of doors and improve your visit immeasurably. Even though reasonably collegiate-looking visitors can wander through the colleges without getting tossed, the budding Byrons and Newtons who call Cambridge home have to deal with hundreds of tourists on a daily basis and are understandably impatient.

Don't let this difficulty keep you from coming: Cambridge is beautiful. A narrow, shallow river flows through town, green lawns stretch to infinity, and it is relatively untouched by encroaching industry (unlike that plaguing Oxford). At the first promise of sunshine, many students head to the Botanic Gardens or the banks of the River Cam. Others cruise the streets of Cambridge on bikes, maneuvering between the tourists swarming the tea shops. Occasionally, just occasionally, some studying gets done.

BASICS

AMERICAN EXPRESS

The office offers the usual American Express services. *25 Sidney St., CB2 3HP, tel. 01223/461410. Open weekdays 9–5:30 (Wed. from 9:30), Sat. 9–5.*

DISCOUNT TRAVEL AGENCIES

STA books discount airfares and issues ISIC cards for £5, a photo, and proof of student status. Like hostels, STA offices are often good places to bump into fellow travelers who can be relied upon to proffer

CAMBRIDGE

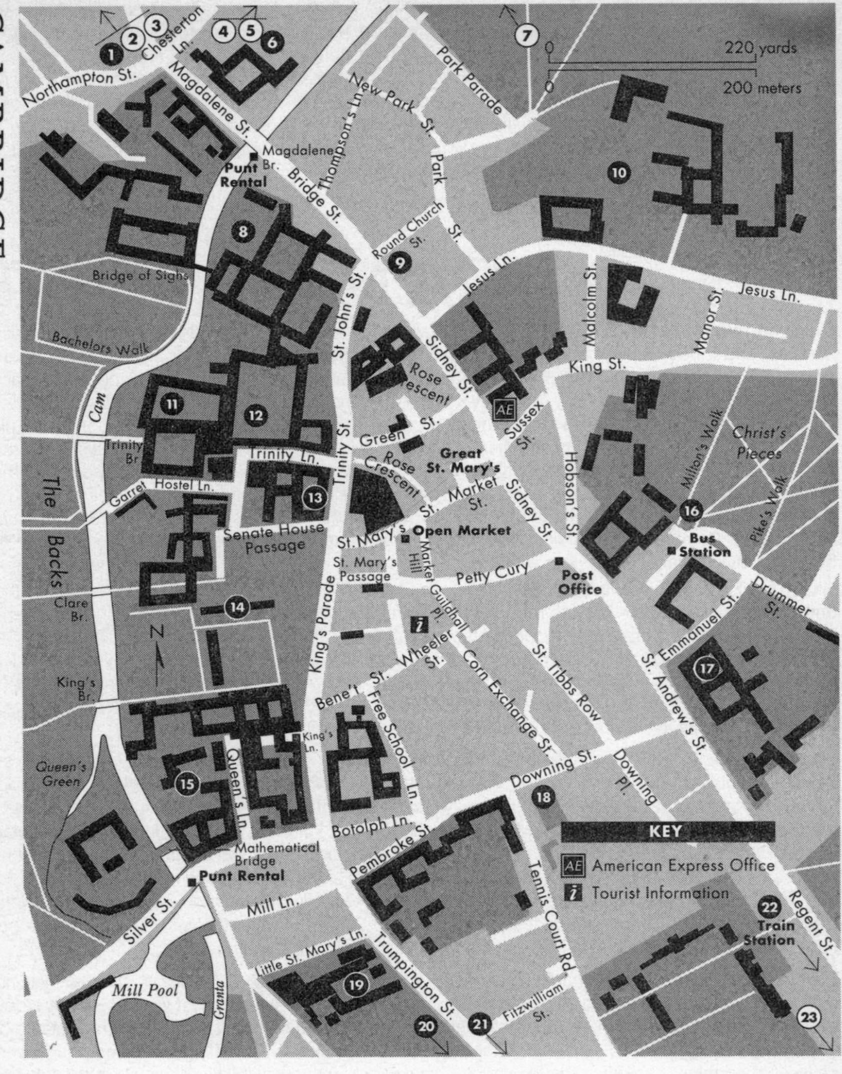

Sights ●
Christ's College, **16**
Downing College, **22**
Emmanuel College, **17**
Fitzwilliam Museum, **20**
Girton College, **1**
Gonville and Caius, **13**
Jesus College, **10**
King's College, **14**
Magdalene College, **6**
Peterhouse College, **19**
Queens' College, **15**
Round Church, **9**
St. John's College, **8**
Trinity College, **12**
University Botanic Garden, **21**
University Museum of Archaeology and Anthropology, **18**
Wren Library, **11**

Lodging ○
Aaron Guest House, **7**
Antoni's B&B, **2**
Arundel House Hotel, **5**
Belle Vue House, **4**
Benson House, **3**
Cambridge YHA, **23**

their own pearls of tourist wisdom. *38 Sidney St., tel. 01223/315185, fax 01223/221802. Open weekdays 9–5:30 (Thurs. from 10), Sat. 11–5.*

MAIL

The **main post office** cashes checks, processes film, and even has a photo booth. *911 St. Andrew's St., CD2 3HP, tel. 01223/323325. Open Mon.–Sat. 9–5:30.*

VISITOR INFORMATION

Cambridge Tourist Information Centre is cluttered with flyers, posters, and leaflets; you'll have to buy some of the more useful ones, including maps (20p) of town. Two-hour guided walking tours of the city and colleges leave the office daily. Although each tour is different, they are all highly informative if a bit pricey (£6). The staff will book lodgings (*see* Where to Sleep, *below*) for £3, plus a 10% deposit on your room bill. If you're strapped for cash on a Sunday, the office will give you change in pounds for a purchase made with a traveler's check. *Wheeler St., behind Guildhall, tel. 01223/322640. Open Apr.–Oct., weekdays 10–6 (Wed. from 9:30), Sat. 10–5, Sun. 11–4; Nov.–Mar., weekdays 10–5:30, Sat. 10–5.*

COMING AND GOING

Best photo-op in St. John's College: the Bridge of Sighs, spanning the Cam.

BY BUS

One advantage of taking the bus to Cambridge is the location of **Drummer Street Station,** near where St. Andrew's Street becomes Sidney Street. The cramped coach office is hectic, but it does have a good supply of timetables and a helpful staff. **National Express** (tel. 0990/808080) buses run to London (2 hours, £8 return) and other cities regularly. **Stagecoach Cambus** (tel. 01223/423554) services many East Anglian towns, as does **Cambridge Coach Services** (tel. 01223/423900), which also offers a service to Oxford (3 hours, £8 day return, £13 standard return). Buy tickets on board, as drivers often give special return fares the office doesn't offer. *End of Drummer St., tel. 01223/423554. Office open Mon.–Sat. 8:15–5:30.*

BY TRAIN

Two trains per hour leave for London King's Cross (1 hour, £16 day return, £18.40 standard return), and there's regular service to nearby towns like Ely (20 min, £4.50 day return) and King's Lynn (1 hour, £7.30 day return). There are a few **luggage lockers** (large £2.50, medium £1.50, small £1), but their availability depends on security measures. To reach town from the station, catch a Cityrail Link bus, or walk (25 min); head down Station Road, turn right on Hills Road (which keeps changing names), and continue straight ahead until you reach the city center. *Station St., tel. 0345/484950.*

GETTING AROUND

It's much easier to get around on foot than by car in Cambridge: much of the city center is off-limits to cars during the day, and traffic on those streets that are open is so bad the university forbids its students to drive cars within 12 mi of the town. Visitors will also get a better sense of the city by walking or cycling—or punting on the River Cam. The layout of the streets is a bit confusing; streets frequently change names and are diverted by the colleges. But thanks to the flat terrain and ubiquitous cycling lanes, two-wheelers are the most popular and efficient way of negotiating the city and its environs. **Geoff's Bike Hire** (65 Devonshire Rd., tel. 01223/365629) rents wobbly steeds for £6 a day (with a 10% discount if you're staying at the adjacent YHA hostel)—you'll have to leave a £25 deposit. **Mike's Bikes** (28 Mill Rd., tel. 01223/312591) also rents bikes for £5 per day, £8 per week. For a city overview, why not hop aboard one of **Guide Friday**'s open-top bus tours of Cambridge (tel. 01223/362444; early Apr.–Sept. every 12 min; Oct.–early Apr. every 30 min), which take in the Backs, the colleges, and the American war cemetery at Madingley. They're a bit (all right, a lot) touristy, but if you're short on time, it's a way to see everything quickly. Tours start from the Cambridge train station; tickets (£8) are bought from the driver, the Guide Friday office at the Cambridge train station, or the Cambridge Tourist Information Centre (*see above*). If you need to get to nearby **Stansted International Airport** (tel. 01279/680500), trains and Cambridge Coach Service's Bus 75 or 79 leave hourly and cost about £7 single.

PUNTING ON THE CAM

To punt means to maneuver a flat, wooden, gondolalike boat through the shallow River Cam, which flows along the "backs" of the colleges. (You get a better view of the ivy-covered walls from the water than from the front.) Mastery of this sport lies in one's ability to control a 15-ft pole, which you use to propel the punt. To avoid the humiliation and failure of losing your pole to the muddy river floor in full view of people watching from the banks, consider punting at night. The Granta Inn Punt Hire (Newnham Mill Pond, Newnham Rd., tel. 01223/301845) rents punts until 10 pm in high summer. Get a bottle of wine, some food, and a small group of people, and you'll find yourself saying things like, "It doesn't get any better than this." The lazier at heart may prefer chauffeured punting. Cambridge students wearing Venetian-type straw hats will punt you along the Cam and even give a fairly informative spiel on the colleges. Each chauffeur rents his or her punt independently so there's no organization to contact; just go down to the dock and wait for the first available boat. Prices are negotiable, although £5 a head is the usual rate. If you choose to get your own punt (which holds up to six people, price £12), hourly rentals are around; all companies require a deposit of £30 or some form of ID. One "dock" for rentals or tours is by the Anchor pub (see below), at the end of Mill Lane near the Silver Street Bridge; another is near the Magdalene Street Bridge.

WHERE TO SLEEP

Inexpensive, central lodging is hard to come by in Cambridge. You'd think the university dorms would throw their doors open to student visitors, but no, it doesn't work that way. Although the colleges' rental policies vary, generally those that *do* have rooms rent them only to large groups. The tourist office's "Where to Stay In and Around Cambridge" booklet (50p) may be worth studying. The office can also book lodgings for a 10% deposit and a £3 fee; it's as easy, and cheaper, to make your own calls. The closest budget accommodations to the colleges are the B&Bs on **Chesterton Road** or **Huntingdon Road.** Alternatively, the accommodations on **Tenison Road** and **Devonshire Road** are closer to the train station; walk down Station Road, hang the first right on Tenison Road, and walk a block or two. Another option is the **YMCA** (Gonville Pl., on Parker's Piece, tel. 01223/356998), which has single (£21.82) or shared (£17.69 per person) rooms available, breakfast included; no credit cards. There are about 200 bed spaces here, but availability varies dramatically, especially in summer, when language-school groups descend in droves.

Aaron Guest House. The views of the River Cam and Jesus Green give the Aaron the feel of an English country house that just happens to host a mix of international tourists and visiting professors. It's not the most cheerily run place in the world; singles are £27, doubles are £50, and the four-person family room is a good value at £70. *71 Chesterton Rd., tel. 01223/314723. Take Bus 3 or 5 from the train station or walk from the bus station across Jesus Green. 5 rooms, none with bath. Cash only.*

Antoni's Bed & Breakfast. This friendly B&B is so centrally located and such a bargain it seems too good to be true; fortunately, it's not. The proprietor is helpful, and the rooms are clean and comfortable—each shares a toilet down the hall. Singles range from £13 to £20, doubles from £26 to £40. *4 Huntingdon Rd., tel. 01223/357444. From the bus station, turn right on Emmanuel St., right on St. Andrew's St., which eventually becomes Huntingdon Rd. 12 rooms, 8 with shower. Cash only.*

Arundel House Hotel. This elegantly proportioned Victorian row hotel overlooks the River Cam, with Jesus Green in the background. The bedrooms are all furnished very comfortably with locally made mahogany furniture, and come equipped with TV and tea- and coffeemaking appliances; Continental breakfast is included in the room rate. A novel idea for first-time visitors to Cambridge is a videotape tour of the city, which can be viewed on the hotel's TV information channel. Ask about the hotel's special weekend rates, which are an excellent value. At the top of our price scale, doubles here run from £65 to £98, but you can take advantage of the nice restaurant and bar. *53 Chesterton Rd., CB4 3AN, tel. 01223/367701, fax 01223/367721. From the train and bus stations, head north through the city center and turn right on Chesterton La., which becomes Chesterton Rd. 105 rooms with bath or shower.*

Belle Vue House. Spacious rooms with color TVS and a good location make this simple B&B a sound deal. The single is £25 and two doubles go for £40 each. Call ahead to reserve a room. *33 Chesterton Rd., tel. 01223/351859. Follow directions to Aaron Guest House* (see above)*. 3 rooms, none with bath. Cash only.*

Benson House. Situated opposite Fitzwilliam and New Hall colleges, Benson House is a mere 10-min walk from the town center. With a cheery staff and tasteful decor, this has to be one of the best budget places to stay in Cambridge. Singles start at £15–£20, and a full range of doubles costs from £34 (standard) to £45 (full en-suite). *24 Huntingdon Rd., tel. 01223/311594. Follow directions to Antoni's B&B* (see above)*. 9 rooms with shower or bath. Cash only.*

The huge rivalry between Oxford and Cambridge comes to a head at two annual sporting events: the boat race, where their rowing eights race each other down the Thames near Putney; and the rugby match, played before an 80,000-strong sellout crowd at Twickenham in London.

HOSTELS

Cambridge YHA. The main hostel in Cambridge is a mere three blocks from the train station. Clean beds, powerful showers, an on-site cafeteria, and a mellow international crowd make up for the claustrophobia-inducing bedrooms, but *book ahead,* as this place fills early. At the very least, phone the moment you arrive; they'll hold a bed until 6 PM if you call in advance. Beds cost £11.15. *97 Tenison Rd., CB1 2DN, tel. 01223/354601, fax 01223/312780. From the train station, walk west on Station Rd., turn right on Tenison Rd. 102 beds. Reception open 24 hrs. Kitchen, laundry.*

Carpenter's Arms Backpackers' Accommodations. If cost is your number one concern, this hostel above a pub certainly fits the bill. You'll find a motley crew of characters staying here (some less savory than others), although the owners are quite friendly. Dorm beds in coed rooms are £8. *182186 Victoria Rd., tel. 01223/351814. From the bus station, walk down Drummer St., turn left on Emmanuel Rd., which becomes Short St. and Victoria Ave., left on Chesterton Rd., right on Albert St., left on Victoria Rd.*

CAMPING

Camping and Caravanning Club Ltd. Buses don't go often enough to this modern, sprawling campground, 3 mi south of Cambridge, to make it terribly convenient. Sites can be expensive if you turn up in a car or on a motorbike, since you pay per person and per site, but backpackers pay a special summer rate of £5.50 per person. Always book in advance. *Cabbage Moore, Cambridge Rd., Great Shelford, tel. 01223/841185. From Drummer St., take Bus 102 or 103 to Great Shelford. 120 sites. Laundry. Closed Nov.–late Mar.*

Toad Acre Caravan Park. This well-equipped campsite is frequented by mobile homes, but the grassy strip to the side is peaceful for tent campers, especially when the apple trees are in bloom. Sites are £4.75–£5.75 per person. *Mills La., Longstanton, tel. 01954/780939. From Drummer St., take Bus 155 or 157 to Longstanton. 48 sites. Laundry, showers.*

FOOD

Although the students generally eat within their colleges, there are plenty of cafés and restaurants vying to tempt your taste buds. Cambridge's many parks, gardens, and commons are also ideal spots for a

GRANTCHESTER: GETTING THERE IS ALL THE FUN

Need a challenge? Demonstrate your punting skill by boating 2 mi along the River Granta from Cambridge to Grantchester, a village favored by locals as a retreat from the academic maelstrom—and immortalized by Rupert Brooke, one of the generation of poets lost in World War I, who lodged here in the old vicarage as an undergraduate. You can reach Grantchester a number of ways: a 45-min walk, a 15-min bike ride, or the killer punt—not an easy task for beginners. It's hard to find the walking trail to begin the journey, but once you start along the River Granta just ask folks along the way. Keep in mind, though, that directions may be somewhat ambiguous (e.g., "turn left when you see the horses").

The town of Grantchester is only one "bend" long, and its three pubs are mainly frequented by punting heroes who've come up from Cambridge for the day. Mind you, if it's raining, don't bother: the thrill of visiting Grantchester lies in getting here and spending a lovely day outdoors.

picnic on a clear day. There are take-out sandwich joints all over the city, and in the center, **Market Hill** has an open market Monday–Saturday with a colorful selection of fruits and vegetables. **Cambridge Health Food** (5 Bridge St., tel. 01223/350433) is the best spot in town to pick up muesli and other whole-food supplies.

Brown's. This huge, airy, brasserie-diner is a classic—where students take their parents when they're in town. Call in for the daily pasta dishes (£6.95–£7.95), house hamburgers (£6.45–£7.55), or even breakfast (11–noon) or afternoon tea (3–5:30). It's very busy on weekends, when you may have to wait in line. *23 Trumpington St., opposite the Fitzwilliam Museum, tel. 01223/461655.*

Clown's. If you like smoky ambience, strong coffee, and an attractive, young clientele, you'll enjoy this coffee bar displaying clown memorabilia on the walls. Clown's serves sandwiches and quiches (£2.30, £3.50 with salad), too, but tends to run out of food around 9 PM. *52 King St., tel. 01223/355711. From the bus station, walk across Christ's Pieces to King St.*

Eraina. Crowded at the best of times, this cheap-and-cheerful taverna positively heaves on Saturday night (when no reservations are taken; wait in line with everyone else). It's not all Greek on the menu either—pizzas, salads, even curries, are served in monster portions for £5–£9. *2 Free School La., off Bene't St., tel. 01223/368786.*

Pizza Express. Scarf down gourmet pizzas (most less than £7) in the snazzy former dining room of one of Cambridge's most uptight eating clubs—still a popular place for college students to chat over a long meal. *7A Jesus La., tel. 01223/324033.*

Rainbow. This basement vegetarian and whole-food establishment feels like a friend's living room, with about 10 tables. All dishes are prepared fresh each day, and the restaurant specializes in vegan and gluten-free food. Breakfast costs £4.25, and the varied main dishes weigh in at less than £6.25. *9a King's Parade, across from King's College, tel. 01223/321551.*

WORTH SEEING

Because of the city's relatively compact size, Cambridge's main sights are all accessible by foot. For some striking architecture, saunter past the colleges clustered on the west bank of the River Cam, starting perhaps with King's College Chapel and Christopher Wren's library in Trinity College (*see below*). Other colleges worth seeing include **Christ's, Downing, Emmanuel, Jesus, Magdalene,** and **St. John's.** The list is hard to whittle down, but you'd be insane to attempt to see each of the 35 colleges that make up Cambridge University, especially if you've just come from, or are heading to, Oxford. When you've had your fill of academia, stop by the **Round Church** (St. John's and Bridge streets), built in the early 12th century. It is the oldest of the four remaining round churches in England and now houses the **Cambridge Brass Rubbing Centre,** where you can make rubbings of medieval church brasses in gold, silver, or bronze wax (tel. 01223/871621; £2–£15, depending on size). Also, don't miss the views from the tower of **Great St. Mary's**—known as the "university church"—opposite the Senate House on King's Parade. At 113 ft high, you get a superb view over the colleges and the marketplace (admission £1.75, open Monday–Saturday 10–5, Sunday after services until 4:15).

THE COLLEGES

Unlike most American universities, Cambridge University has no exact center but is spread over many residential colleges scattered around town. There are only a few large lecture classes, and students spend most of their scholastic careers attending weekly tutorials in the offices of "fellows," an upscale term for graduate students. And yes, students are required to wear black gowns when attending tutorials. The rest of their time is spent keeping up with the massive reading lists. Bear in mind many colleges close to visitors during final exams, from the fourth week of May until mid-June. The rest of the year, colleges often change their opening hours and close to the public unexpectedly, so call ahead.

The Eagle (Bene't St., tel. 01223/301286) is a traditional pub with a colorful past. It was frequented by scientists Watson and Crick, whose discovery of DNA was announced here. British and Allied airmen used the Eagle during World War II, and the ceiling still bears names and squadron numbers written in candle smoke.

The nonstudent residents of Cambridge don't always appreciate the way the town is considered synonymous with the university. This town-versus-gown rivalry is as old as the school itself, dating back more than 600 years to 1381, when the Peasants Revolt pitted ordinary folk against stuck-up academics. Another dollop of antipathy arrived with the English Civil War, when the university sided with the Royalists whereas the town's citizens were fiercely loyal to Cromwell (who, incidentally, attended Cambridge's Sidney Sussex College briefly in 1617). The university shares another endless antagonistic tradition with Oxford University: Both rank among the best universities in the world, with Cambridge leading the way in the sciences. Cambridge is also seen as the more traditional of the duo. It has a higher proportion of former public (i.e., private) school pupils than Oxford. Women, who were first admitted in the 1870s, were not awarded degrees until 1947, and some colleges didn't let women through their hallowed doors until the 1970s. To the outside world, the differences can seem quite cosmetic, and Brits not privileged enough to attend either often meld the two names to come up with "OxBridge," a useful adjective.

KING'S COLLEGE • King Henry VI founded King's College in 1441 and five years later began constructing its greatest monument, **King's College Chapel.** Calling it a chapel seems a bit reductive; it feels more like a cathedral. Completed in 1536, the 289-ft-long Gothic structure features the world's longest expanse of fan-vaulted ceiling (the spiderweb-style branches supporting the arches). Peter Paul Rubens's *Adoration of the Magi* hangs behind the altar. During the summer there are public recitals—look for a schedule inside—and on Christmas Eve a festival of carols is broadcast worldwide. *King's Parade: college tel. 01223/350411, chapel tel. 01223/331447, college tourist office tel. 01223/331212. Admission to chapel £3. Chapel open term-time weekdays 9:30–3:30, Sat. 9:30–3:15, Sun. 1:15–2:15; summer, Mon.–Sat. 9:30–4:30, Sun. 1:15–2:15 and 5–5:30.*

QUEENS' COLLEGE • Queens' College—founded in 1448 by Margaret of Anjou, wife of Henry VI, and later built up by Elizabeth of Woodville, wife of Edward IV —is a mess of architectural styles. The unspoiled Renaissance cloister court lies beside some ugly, recently constructed buildings funded by Sir John Cripps, owner of the worldwide patent for Velcro. Legend has it that the so-called **Mathematical Bridge** that crosses the Cam to connect both sides of the college was designed and built without screws or fastenings by Sir Isaac Newton. Not true. A local carpenter named James Essex designed the bridge in 1750, more than 20 years after Newton's death. The current bridge is a modern copy, supported by bolts and screws. The college allows visitors to stroll through quietly while term is in session, daily 10–12:45 and 1:45–4:30. *Queens' La., tel. 01223/335511. Admission £1.*

TRINITY COLLEGE • The largest and richest of Cambridge's colleges, Trinity counts among its graduates Lord Byron; Isaac Newton; William Thackeray; Prince Charles; and Pandit Nehru, one of the fathers of modern India. Trinity is also the third-largest landowner in Britain—after the Crown and Church, of course. It's literally possible to walk from Cambridge to Oxford and London to Dover entirely on Trinity-owned land. The college's impressive **Wren Library,** designed entirely by Christopher Wren down to the bookshelves and reading desks, contains an astonishing display of valuable books, including one of Shakespeare's first folios and Newton's pocket book. *St. John's St., tel. 01223/338400. Admission £1.75. Open daily 10–5; closed during exams. Wren Library, tel. 01223/338488. Open during the school year, weekdays noon–2, Sat. 10:30–12:30; during vacations, weekdays noon–2; closed during exams.*

MAGDALENE COLLEGE • Across Magdalene (pronounced maudlin) Bridge lies Magdalene College, the only one of the older colleges to be built across the river. Magdalene Street itself is narrow and traffic-heavy, but there's relative calm inside the pretty redbrick courts. It was a hostel for Benedictine monks for more than 100 years before the college was founded in 1542. In the second court, the college's Pepys Library—labeled *Bibliotecha Pepysiana*—contains the books and desk of the 17th-century diarist, Samuel Pepys. *Magdalene St., tel. 01223/332100. Admission to library free. Open Apr.–Sept., Mon.–Sat. 11:30–12:30 and 2:30–3:30; Oct.–Mar., Mon.–Sat. 2:30–3:30.*

OTHER COLLEGES • The granddaddy of them all, **Peterhouse College,** features structures dating from the 13th century, when a disgruntled monk from Oxford's Merton College decided to begin a little school of his own. **Emmanuel College,** known as Emma College by the faithful, has a beautiful layout—the chapel and colonnades are by Christopher Wren—and a magnificent duck pond. **St. John's College** (admission £1.50) features the famous Bridge of Sighs, spanning the Cam, built in 1831, and modeled on the original in Venice. **Christ's College,** which educated Milton and Darwin, houses some of Cambridge's best neoclassic architecture, as well as some of the worst architecture; in particular, a notoriously ugly, modern dorm dubbed "The Typewriter" because of its sloping, gridded design. The adventurous traveler may want to trek 2 mi north to **Girton College,** the first women's college in Cambridge. Set outside the city center to keep male and female students apart, Girton suffered much ridicule from the Cambridge community at first, before graduating enough distinguished alumna—Virginia Woolf, among them—to earn respect. Take the bus directly from Drummer Street or walk north up Sidney Street, which changes names several times, eventually becoming Huntingdon Road. **Gonville and Caius** (pronounced Keys), across Trinity Lane from Trinity College, has gates that outline the road to educational fulfillment. First up is the Gate of Humility as you enter the college, to be followed by the gates of virtue and honor. **Jesus** is the college with the most open spaces around it, creating an atmosphere of quiet contemplation befitting its former status as a monastery. Samuel Taylor Coleridge was given the boot from Jesus for running up debts.

MUSEUMS AND GARDENS

The Fitzwilliam Museum. The permanent collection of this first-rate museum features antiquities from ancient Greece and Egypt in the Lower Galleries as well as works by Picasso, Degas, Monet, Renoir, Cézanne, Seurat, Brueghel, Constable, Gainsborough, and more in the Upper Galleries. Temporary exhibits range from the fascinating to the truly snooze-worthy. *Trumpington St., tel. 01223/332900. Admission free, but £2 donation requested. Open Tues.–Sat. 10–5; Sun. 2:15–5; guided tours Sun. at 2:30.*

The University Botanic Garden. This is the perfect place to break the musty monotony of cobblestone or to kill time while waiting for a train. Among its many delights are a glass igloo, a limestone rock garden, and flowers, flowers, flowers. *Cory Lodge, Bateman St., tel. 01223/336265. From the train station, turn right on Hills Rd., left on Bateman St. Admission £2. Open daily Mar.–Oct. 10–6, Nov.–Feb. 10–5.*

The University Museum of Archaeology and Anthropology (UMAA). Cambridge University pioneered the study of social anthropology, and the UMAA traces conceptual progress in the field during the last 100 years. The Anthropology Gallery houses an interesting collection of totem poles, masks, costumes, and other culturally significant artifacts. This is one of Cambridge's most engrossing museums, and it's absolutely free. *Downing St. near Corn Exchange St., tel. 01223/333516. Open summer weekdays 10:30–5 (Anthropology Gallery closed 1–2), Sat. 10–12:30; call for winter hrs.*

AFTER DARK

Interested in what goes on behind the walls of the colleges late at night? You'll never know unless you make friends quickly. Still, there's plenty of culture happening outside the college gates: great rock bands come through Cambridge regularly, and classical concert dates are legion, so pick up a copy of *Varsity* (30p) at a newsstand for current listings. Art movies are cheap and abundant, and student theater is excellent. If you have a chance to see a student drama production at the ADC (*see below*), go. In the summer Cambridge gets festival fever: There's the **Cambridge Beer Festival** in May; the **Midsummer Fair** in June; and the **Film Festival, Fringe Festival,** and **Cambridge Folk Festival** in July. Plays are also staged in the gardens of some of the colleges during the month of June.

PUBS

The Anchor. Right along the Cam near the punt rental, this four-story, all-wood pub is filled with locals day and night. The outdoor deck is inviting if and when the sun comes out. *Silver St., tel. 01223/353554.*

Baron of Beef. This small, traditional pub enjoys a good mix of punters (no boating pun intended) and a cheery atmosphere. Real ale is served here along with a no-nonsense attitude toward drinking: do not, on a fate worse than death, ask for a piña colada! *19 Bridge St., tel. 01223/576720.*

The Free Press. Here is that rare beast, a no-smoking pub, and all the better for it, attracting a fresh-faced student rowing clientele. *Prospect Row, off Adam and Eve St. near Grafton Centre, tel. 01223/368337.*

The Maypole. The Maypole is *the* place in Cambridge to overhear pretentious conversation. Thespians hang out here when they're not working on the latest reinterpretation of a Beckett play. Don't leave without trying one of its award-winning cocktails. *Park St. near Jesus College, tel. 01223/352999.*

MUSIC

Look for flyers posted around town to determine what the big show is this week, or pick up a copy of the locally published *Varsity* to see who's playing. You'll find everything from jazz and classical to the *NME*'s flavor-of-the-month band playing at **The Corn Exchange** (Wheeler and Corn Exchange Sts., tel. 01223/357851). Tickets usually cost around £10. **The Junction** (Clifton Rd. near the train station, tel. 01223/511511) is home to local indie bands, hip-hop, house, jazz, and just about everything else six nights a week. Tickets range from £4 for small gigs to £15 for big-name bands. Cambridge supports its own symphony orchestra, and regular musical events are held in many of the colleges, especially those with large chapels (like St. John's and Trinity). Evensong at **King's College Chapel** is held Tuesday–Saturday at 5:30, Sunday at 3:30; call tel. 01223/350411 for information.

THEATER AND FILM

The **Amateur Dramatic Club (ADC)** (Park St. near Jesus La., tel. 01223/359547 or 01223/352001) presents two different student-produced plays per week, and late-night arty flicks. Ticket prices range from £3 to £8. The city's main repertory theater, the **Arts Theater** (6 St. Edward's Passage, tel. 01223/503333), built by economist John Maynard Keynes in 1936, sports a full program of theater, concerts, and events—Derek Jacobi, Ian McKellan, Jonathan Miller, Emma Thompson, John Cleese, Peter Cook, and others too numerous to squeeze onto one stage all began their careers here. Tickets for most productions run £5–£25. **Arts Cinema** (Market Passage, tel. 01223/504444), affiliated with the ADC, usually shows three different American and European art flicks a day; late-night shows are scheduled about four days a week. Seats are £4.50 from 5:30 to 11, £3.50 at all other times.

NEAR CAMBRIDGE

ELY

Global warming is a scary topic that exercises the best scientific minds of our day. But the classic combination of melting glaciers, rising sea levels, and falling land has already paid a visit to a strange part of the world known as The Fens or Fenland. Rising from these flat, former swamplands like a hazy desert mirage stands one of the most atmospheric of all English churches, **Ely Cathedral.** First built in 673 by Queen Etheldreda of Northumbria, the cathedral dominates the small town of Ely (pronounced EE-lee) and is visible from many miles away, across the severe, flat landscape.

Back in the 7th century, the Fens were a series of malarial swamps, punctuated by a few hills on which marginal people scratched a precarious living. The most hospitable of these hills became Ely (the name refers to the eels that were frequent visitors to the marsh lands), and the town grew in fame as a Fen stronghold, especially when Saxon leader Hereward the Wake holed up here in his forlorn battle against Norman invaders in 1070.

There must be something about the area that breeds stubborn leadership, as is evidenced by Ely-native Oliver Cromwell. The first proper attempt to drain the area around Ely was in 1630—the Romans had tried and failed years before—when Dutch engineer Cornelius Vermuyden dredged two rivers out of the mushy ground to create valuable peat farmland. Hundreds of small windmills, powering water pumps, were added to the landscape in a near replica of Vermuyden's native Holland, but the Fens were only really delivered from the threat of large-scale flooding with the advent of steam pumps in the 1820s.

COMING AND GOING

From Cambridge, Ely is only 20 min by train (£4.10 return). Direct trains also go from London King's Cross station (hourly in the daytime, £17.50 day return). From the **train station** (Station Rd., tel. 0345/484950), walk north on Station Road to get to the cathedral. Slow **Cambus** buses (tel. 01223/423554) from Cambridge and London arrive at Market Street near the Cathedral. The **tourist office** (29 St. Mary's St., tel. 01353/662062) is located in Oliver Cromwell's House (*see below*).

WORTH SEEING

ELY CATHEDRAL • The inside of Ely Cathedral makes a good stab at rivaling the outside for sheer spectacle, thanks in the main to its famous octagonal lantern, built in 1322 using eight of the strongest oak trees that could be found in the whole of the country. The lantern weighs in at more than 400 tons and is the only surviving example of its type in England. The ceiling is also noteworthy, having been painted by amateurs in the last century, and the presbytery, built in the 13th century to house Etheldreda's remains, attracts attention for largely historical reasons. Tours of the Cathedral are conducted for £3.50. Book your ticket at the entrance desk. *Tel. 01353/662432. Admission £3.50. Open June–Sept., daily 7–7, Oct.–May, daily 7:30–6 (Sun. until 5).*

In the north triforium of the cathedral, the **Stained Glass Museum** features an immense variety of stained glass fans dating from the 13th century right up to present times. *Tel. 01353/660347. Admission £2.50. Open Apr.–Sept., weekdays 10–5, Sat. 10:30–5:30, Sun. noon–6; Oct.–Mar., weekdays 11–4:30, Sat. 10:30–5:30, Sun. noon–4:15.*

ELY MUSEUM • Due to its longstanding geographical isolation, Ely boasts prime examples of medieval architecture, a sizable portion of which is used as a choir school—the kind of historical nugget to be gleaned at the Ely Museum. The museum traces the rest of Ely's history in entertaining detail, concentrating, to no great surprise, on the Cathedral and Fens. *Market St., tel. 01353/666655, Admission £1.80. Open Tues.–Sun 10:30–4.*

OLIVER CROMWELL'S HOUSE • Across the Palace Green from the Cathedral is the house in which Oliver Cromwell, Lord Protector of England after the English Civil War, spent 10 years as collector of taxes early on in his career. The timber-frame house has been cleverly restored to contain the tourist information desk and features oodles of material on the fascinating surrounding area. Cromwell is of prime importance to the history of the Fens as he brought Vermuyden back for a second and more successful go at draining the marshes. *29 St. Mary's St., tel. 01353/662062. Admission £2.75. Open Apr.–Sept., daily 10–6; Oct.–Mar., Mon.–Sat. 10–5.*

WHERE TO SLEEP AND EAT

Ely is tiny (population 10,000), so don't expect a wide choice of hotels. That said, waking up to look out the window in the shadow of the cathedral might be enough to tempt you into staying over, whatever the lack of sophisticated facilities. **The Black Hostelry** (Firmary La., tel. 01353/662612), a B&B that squats right in the intriguing medieval district, can serve as your portal to England's past. Double rooms cost £49. Tucked away behind the cathedral, the **Old Egremont House** (31 Egremont St., tel. 01353/663118) B&B is housed in a 17th-century oak-beam house with a private garden. Singles run £29, the double £44; ask for one of the two large rooms (of three) with a beautiful view of the cathedral.

There are plenty of fish and chip shops and tea rooms in Ely if you're just here for a quick visit. Otherwise head down to the waterside area and try the brasserie-style fare at the **Maltings Arts Centre** (tel. 01353/211498) or stay on the hill for a more expensive, gourmet-level feed-up at **Old Fire Engine** (25 St. Mary's St., tel. 01353/662582).

BRIGHTON

Brighton began its rapid rise to fame when the **Prince Regent** (later King George IV) first hit town in 1783 to sample the often chilly waters of the south coast. George truly set a trend; by the 20th century, Brighton had become *the* preeminent resort in the south of England. Along with most other English seaside retreats, Brighton was forced to compete with cheap foreign destinations after the 1960s; unlike the rest, Brighton has reemerged as one of the most dynamic resorts in the country. The resurgence can be partly attributed to successful conference centers and marina development, but the town's student, club, and gay scenes really deserve the credit for Brighton's renaissance as an ultrahip port of call. Not for nothing is it often known as London-by-Sea.

In a sense the new scene is a late 20th-century version of the Regency era, with a delicious hint of elegant decadence dominating certain parts of town. George IV would be pleased with the way things turned out, you suspect. The Regent's greatest bequest to the town, lurid atmosphere apart, was the **Royal Pavilion,** the beautiful mock-Eastern folly that is Brighton's signature building. Naturally you'll stumble upon masses of other Regency architecture throughout the town. Brighton's other great attraction is a series of curio shop–filled windy lanes and passages that have visitors flocking all year round. Oh, and there's a beach as well.

BASICS

The busy **tourist office** is well-run, offering info on all that's going down in Brighton. *10 Bartholomew Sq., tel. 01237/323755. Open June–Sept., weekdays 9–6:15, Sat. 10–5, Sun. 10–4; Oct.–May, Mon.–Sat. 9–5, Sun. 10–4.*

COMING AND GOING

Brighton is just an hour by train from London's Victoria Station; trains from London Bridge and King's Cross are less direct. Connex services run around the clock and cost £14 for a day return, £18.80 for a longer stay. Brighton's **train station** (Queen's Rd., tel. 0345/484950) is at the top of a hill, from which you can stroll all the way down to the seafront. **National Express** (tel. 0990/808080) buses connect London to Brighton every hour, arriving at the **bus station** (Pool Valley, tel. 01273/674881) between the Royal Pavilion and the sea. A day return costs £8 and takes roughly 1 hour 50 min.

WHERE TO SLEEP

There are loads of cheap and cheery B&Bs and small hotels all over town; you'll find the heaviest concentration in the blocks behind the sea front. Unfortunately Londoners' love affair with Brighton is reflected in mid-range hotel prices.

Ambassador. This hotel is conveniently located near both The Lanes and the shore. Single rooms go for £30, doubles for £50. *22 New Steine, BN2 1PD, tel. 01273/676869. Turn left onto Trafalgar St. from the train station, turn right at York Pl., walk along Victoria Gardens, past the Royal Pavilion, onto Old Steine St., then left onto New Steine St. 21 rooms.*

The Grand. Aaah, old English splendor by the sea. The Grand's the top hotel in Brighton and the place the IRA bombed, nearly killing former PM Margaret Thatcher. It's very expensive (doubles at £195)—but it could be worth an end-of-holiday splurge. Otherwise, try the afternoon tea. *King's Rd., BN1 2FW, tel. 01273/321188. From the train station go straight down Queen's Rd., turn right onto King's Rd. 200 rooms.*

Old Ship Hotel. You'll be right on the seafront and a 20-min walk to the center of town at this well-appointed hotel. Doubles cost between £40 and £60 and are en-suite with TVs. *31–38 King's Rd., Brighton, tel. 01273/329001. Head down Queen's Rd. out of the train station, turn right onto King's Rd. 152 rooms.*

Regency Hotel. This comfortable, well-run hotel sits opposite the defunct, haunting West Pier. Ask for sea views. Singles start at £35, doubles at £60. *28 Regency Sq., BN1 2FH, tel. 01273/202690. From train station, go straight down Queen's Rd., turn right on King's Rd.; walk to the West Pier. 13 rooms.*

HOSTELS

Brighton Backpackers. A congenial staff has given this well-liked independent hostel a good name. Top value includes access to a TV room, a bar, and luggage storage. At £9 for a dorm bed, £25 for a double room, you'll be hard-pressed to get a better deal. *75 Middle St., tel. 01273/777717. From Brighton station, walk straight down Queen's Rd. to the seafront, turn left, then left again on Middle St. 85 rooms. From the train station head down Queen's Rd., turn left at Duke St., then first right into Middle St. 150 beds. No credit cards.*

Baggies Backpackers. On the off-chance that Brighton's Backpackers is packed (or if you want to save £1), head to this clean and efficient hostel slightly out of the center (toward Hove). Dorm beds are £8. *33 Oriental Pl., tel. 01273/733740. From the train station walk down Queen's Rd. to King's Rd, then go west to just past the West Pier; Oriental Pl. is on the right. 50 beds. No credit cards.*

WORTH SEEING

Brighton's the kind of place people come to to lounge around and soak up the atmosphere. People-watching is at the top of many a visitor's agenda. But that doesn't mean it hasn't got several clear-cut tourist winners of a more permanent stamp.

THE LANES • A high concentration of antique, craft, and designer shops brings visitors flooding into this area, set between the sea and the Pavilion. But it's the lanes themselves that provide the bulk of the charm, as they wind their mazey ways up and down the gentle hill. The Lanes have been trendified a bit recently, but if you're after a more up-front look at bohemian Brighton, head for the **North Laine** area, which is just to the north of here.

ROYAL PAVILION • John Nash, one of London's key architectural figures, was the man responsible for this fascinating mixture of neo-Gothic and oriental styles, built for the Prince Regent from 1787 to 1815. Now restored to something like its former glory after many years of partial neglect—it was a radar station in the Second World War—the Pavilion's main features include a stunning Banqueting Room with huge chandeliers emerging from the mouth of a dragon. Next door, there's the **Dome,** a concert arena, and next to that is the **Brighton Museum and Art Gallery,** which is worth a quick look, mainly for Salvador Dalí's famous sofa in the shape of Mae West's lips. *Pavilion Parade, tel. 01273/290900. Admission £4.50 (includes Museum and Art Gallery). Open daily 10–6 (Oct.–May until 5).*

THE SEAFRONT • It's culture-clash time down by the sea as traditional English beach amusements (**Palace Pier,** ice cream, and chips) meet more arty attractions (henna tattoos, street musicians, and veggie food). The mix might be a strange one, but the Brighton experience is all the more entertaining for it. Other features include the **Volk's Electric Railway** (admission £1, Apr.–Sept.), which travels along the seafront, and the **Madeira Lift** (free, Apr.–Sept., 1:45–7:15), the summit of which offers fantastic views. Warning: don't bring your bucket and spade—Brighton's beach consists solely of pebbles.

CANTERBURY

Two million visitors a year make Canterbury England's second most popular tourist city, a status that goes back a long, long way to when Chaucer and thousands of other pilgrims traipsed down to Kent in homage to murdered Archbishop Thomas à Becket. It is admittedly touristy, but the mighty cathedral, medieval city walls, and Roman excavations will help you block out even the fiercest camera-wielders. If you've come to Britain for history, it would be little short of madness to miss out on this jewel.

Canterbury played a central role on the stage of history well before the cathedral was erected. The Romans first turned up in 55 and 54 BC under Julius Caesar; their settlement took shape under Claudius by AD 43. Next came the Angles, Saxons, and Jutes, who fought over the place but ended up destroying it. It was left overgrown for more than a century. But Canterbury's future was secured in AD 597, when Pope Gregory sent St. Augustine to England on a conversion mission—so began Canterbury's reign as the mother of British Christianity. Not so lucky on the conversion front was early Canterbury Puritan Robert Cushman, who was forced to flee the city in 1608. Twelve years later he organized the *Mayflower* voyage that would take the pilgrims to Cape Cod, United States.

BASICS

You might have to endure standing on line for a while at the city center **tourist office,** but the staff will provide you with free hiking, biking, and events pamphlets. For a fee of £1 per person (£2.50 for two or more), and a 10% deposit charged to your bill, they'll find you a place to stay. *34 St. Margaret's St., tel. 01227/766567. From Canterbury East, turn right and follow the city wall, turn left on Watling St., right on St. Margaret's St. Open Apr.–Sept., daily 9:30–5:30; Oct.–Mar., Mon.–Sat. 9:30–5.*

COMING AND GOING

BY BUS

National Express (tel. 0990/808080) buses have the slight advantage over trains in arriving at St. George's Lane, closer to the Cathedral than either train station. Buses leave every hour from London, take 1 hour 50 min, and cost £9 for a day return.

BY TRAIN

From London the quickest way (90 min) to Canterbury is by train via Victoria Station. A **Connex** day return (£14.80) and long-stay deal (£17.10) will whiz you from London's Victoria Station to **Canterbury East** station (Station Rd. E, off Castle St., tel. 0345/484950) in 90 min. Slower trains to Canterbury leave from Charing Cross and get in at **Canterbury West** station (Station Rd. W, off Dunstan St., tel. 08706/030405).

Chaucer's spirit shares Canterbury with the ghost of Joseph Conrad (buried in Canterbury Cemetery) and the head of Sir Thomas More (safeguarded in St. Dunstan's Church), author of Utopia.

WHERE TO SLEEP

A plethora of B&Bs lines New Dover, London, and Whitstable roads. During the summer, Canterbury is a popular destination and most B&Bs are tiny, so book ahead. Many B&Bs observe strict no-smoking policies, so smokers should inquire ahead. If you need to be in the Cathedral's very shadow, stay at the **Cathedral Gate Hotel** (36 Burgate, CT1 2HA, tel. 01227/464381), where a single will cost you £22 (and up), a double £40 (and up). Not far outside the city walls is the clean **Chaucer Lodge** (62 New Dover Rd., CT1 3DT, tel. 01227/459141), with an en-suite in every room. Singles start at £22, doubles at £38. Top of the line B&Bs include **Clare Ellen Guest House** (9 Victoria Rd., tel. 01227/760205), which charges £21–£25 per head, while **St. Stephen's Guest House** (100 St. Stephen's Rd., tel. 01227/767644) charges £18–£22.50 per head; both have rooms with private bath and are about a 10-min walk from town.

Courtney Guest House. This immaculate house has large, bright rooms and a sunny conservatory where you can catch up on your Chaucer. Doubles with bath cost £38 (the double without bath is £30), and the large room that sleeps up to five costs £15–£20 per person. *4 London Rd., CT2 8LR, tel. 01227/769668. From Canterbury West, turn right on St. Dunstan's St., left on London Rd. 5 rooms, 4 with bath.*

Dar-Anne. Theresa Morey loves students, and her place is always filled with young people. She is a vegan, so herbivores don't get that sidelong look when they pass up sausages at breakfast. The facilities are excellent (all rooms have TVs), and the house is only a short walk from the city center. Singles run £16, doubles £32. *65 London Rd., CT2 8JZ, tel. 01227/760907. From Canterbury West, turn right on St. Dunstan's St., left on London Rd. 3 rooms, none with bath. Cash only.*

Hampton House. The decor of this Victorian house is floral and romantic, and the beautiful garden features a pond. Double-glazed windows offer peace and quiet, while Frank and Coral, the owners, lend the place added character. Singles are £20, doubles £40, slightly less in winter. *40 New Dover Rd., CT1 3DT, tel. 01227/464912. From the bus station, turn right on St. George's Pl. and continue straight for ¾ mi. 4 rooms, all with bath. Cash only.*

Kingsbridge. For £16 per person you can't beat the incredibly central location of this large B&B. You can practically touch the Cathedral from most of its south-facing rooms. As a bonus, the downstairs breakfast room becomes a popular Italian restaurant by night. Unlike most Canterbury B&Bs, this one is a haven for smokers. *15 Best La., CT1 2JB, tel. 01227/766415. From the tourist office, turn left on High St., right on Best La. 12 rooms, 8 with bath. Cash only.*

HOSTEL

Canterbury YHA. Book well in advance if you want a bed (£10.15) at this hostel, just a 15-min stroll to the cathedral. If they're at capacity, the proprietors will gladly refer you to another cheap room. *54 New Dover Rd., 01227/462911, fax 01227/470572, e-mail canterbury£yha.org.uk. From the bus station, turn right on St. George's Pl. and continue straight for 1 mi. From Canterbury E. veer right on Rhodaus Town (which becomes Upper Bridge St.), then right on St. George's Pl. 91 beds. Laundry. Closed Jan.*

FOOD

One good method for finding a decent, affordable meal in Canterbury is to look for places filled with students. The cheaper restaurants are found mostly along the smaller lanes and alleys off High Street. Self-caterers can find a variety of ethnic and vegetarian foods near the North Gate at **Canterbury Wholefoods** (10 The Borough, tel. 01227/464625), which also sells scrumptious filled rolls.

UNDER £5 • August Moon. With its enormous menu and low prices, August Moon packs in the university crowd. For an even cheaper meal, request self service from the take-out counter, then bring your food to the seating area across from the bar. Dim sum, Kung Po Chili Chicken, or the Vegetarian Feast for two are just a few of the tantalizing options. *49A St. Peter's St., tel. 01227/786268. Cash only.*

Green Court Cafe. Slip into this side-street café for cheap sandwiches and jacket potatoes. It's low on atmosphere, but you can grab a window seat and watch the world go by. *17–18 The Borough, at Palace St., tel. 01227/458368. Closes at 7:30. Cash only.*

UNDER £10 • Beaus Creperie. This bright creperie serves a variety of crepes and interesting starters such as prawns with peaches and rye. Crepes range from the basic cheese to those loaded with goodies. Treat yourself to the specialty crepes such as Crepe Indonesia (chicken curry). *59 Palace St., tel. 01227/464285. Cash only.*

Fungus Mungus. With its psilocybin-inspired decor, this groovy eatery may make you think that your name is Alice and your best friend is a rabbit. The mushroom theme continues in dishes such as tasty garlic mushrooms on toast. Main dishes feature pastas, spinach and ricotta pancakes, and curries. *34 St. Peter's St., across from West Gate, tel. 01227/781922. Cash only.*

Simple Simon's. Housed in a 14th-century building, this restaurant faithfully maintains the atmosphere of a medieval hall—including an open fire. Although they serve a full range of game, poultry, steaks, and fish, they specialize in pies. The lamb and apricot pie and Chaucerberry pie are favored by the locals, while the vegetable pie is a hit with vegetarians. After finishing your meal, you can quaff a pint downstairs in their ever-popular ale house. The main restaurant serves dinner only, 7 PM–10 PM, but lunch is served in the downstairs bar from 11 to 3. *St. Radigund Hall, 3 Church La., off The Borough, tel. 01227/762355. Cash only.*

WORTH SEEING

CANTERBURY CATHEDRAL

Canterbury has practically become synonymous with the medieval cathedral that can trace its distinguished lineage of archbishops back to St. Augustine (597–603). The landmark towers over the city at an impressive height of 537 ft and also looms over the last millennium of England's past as the HQ of the English (Anglican) Church. Having entered the 7th century as the Saxon monastery of Christ Church, the structure succumbed to a Norman rebuilding program in 1070. During the centuries, a series of modifications further defined the cathedral we see today. The most notable addition is the 1505 **Bell Harry Tower,** which stands 235 ft tall. Before you set foot inside the Cathedral itself, take a look at the beautiful **Christ Church Gate,** added in the 16th century. Inside there's the shrine of Archbishop Thomas à Becket, who was assassinated in 1171 after King Henry II uttered the immortal, if ambiguous, words: "Who will rid me of this turbulent priest?" Henry later paid his penance by donning a hair shirt and getting himself whipped soundly by local monks. Elsewhere, there's a superbly atmospheric **crypt** and the 14th-century **Chapter House,** which contains the story of Thomas à Becket, stained-glass style. *Burgate, tel. 01227/762862. Admission £3. Open Mon.–Sat. 9–5, Sun. 12:30–2:30 and 4:30–5:30.*

CHAUCER'S CANTERBURY TALES

If your memory of Chaucer's masterpiece has dimmed (or if you slept through that lecture), you might appreciate this entertaining look at *The Canterbury Tales,* the woe of every student of English literature for its impenetrable language, but also the defining, seminal work of the whole subject. It's a bit pricey if you see it as a museum, but, with frolicking figures telling five of Chaucer's yarns, it's cheap for a show. Other famous literary figures associated with Canterbury include Christopher Marlowe, who wrote *Dr. Faustus* and Charles Dickens who set part of *David Copperfield* here. *St. Margaret's St., tel. 01227/454888. Admission £5.25. Open Nov.–Sept., daily 9:30–5:30.*

ROMAN MUSEUM

Before there were Christians, there were pagans. The polytheistic Romans left behind relics you can peruse in this entertaining museum, which features a computer-generated version of Durovernum Cantiacorum, Roman Canterbury. *Butchery La., tel. 01227/785575. Admission £2.30. Open weekdays 10–5 (June–Oct. also Sun. 1:30–5).*

ST. AUGUSTINE'S ABBEY

The ruins of this Norman abbey make for an evocative experience. But before you get too teary for the place, remember the Normans themselves destroyed the previous Saxon version, the one founded by English Christianity's founder, St. Augustine. Next door is **St. Martin's Church,** which occupies the site where Augustine baptized King Ethelbert in 597. *Monastery St., tel. 01227/767345. Admission £2.50. Open daily 10–6 (Nov.–Mar. until 4).*

For maximum enjoyment, travel from east to west on your hikes. The scenery keeps getting better in that direction.

AFTER DARK

According to the Church of England, gluttony is a deadly sin but beer drinking is not, and many pub owners have set up shop in the shadows of the cathedral. Most pubs in Canterbury are open Monday–Saturday 11–11, Sunday noon–10:30.

PUBS AND CLUBS

Modern, jazzy **Cubaa** (59 Northgate, tel. 01227/458857) attracts a diverse crowd for delectable fare (like orange and onion salad and lime chicken with rice) and happy hour (6–8). DJs get the place hopping with acid jazz, Latin funk, and the latest drum & bass Tuesday through Saturday nights. If you want to take a chill pill, escape to the back garden or do some net surfing in the budding Internet café upstairs. **Flying Horse** (1 Dover St., at Upper Bridge St., tel. 01227/463803), an updated, 16th-century pub, may be one of the friendliest places in town. The **New Penny Theatre** (30–31 Northgate, tel. 01227/470512) is highly regarded by hipsters as both a venue for live music and an after-hours club with an eclectic range of theme nights. The cover is £2–£5; it's open daily noon–midnight.

THEATER AND FILM

The **Marlowe Theatre** (The Friars, off St. Peter's St., tel. 01227/787787) stages first-rate London shows as well as punky pop bands and cheesy British slapstick plays. Before spending £4–£24 on a ticket, pick up a copy of their seasonal brochure to gauge what's on. Amateur drama and performance art get top billing at the University of Kent's **Gulbenkian Theatre** (University Rd., tel. 01227/769075), where tickets cost £3–£9. **Cinema 3,** which shares the same box office as the Gulbenkian, shows avant-garde oldies and some independent flicks for £3.50.

OUTDOOR ACTIVITIES

If you're interested in mountain biking, pick up an Ordnance Survey map of the area from the tourist office; it shows altitude contours in the **North Downs.** The **Canterbury Cycle Mart** (19 Lower Bridge St., tel. 01227/761488) rents mountain bikes for £6 per half day, £9 per day, and £30 per week. A credit-card number or £50 cash deposit is required.

About 3 mi northwest of Canterbury, the little-used **Forest of Blean** is the remnant of a much larger ancient forest of the same name. The hiking trails are quiet, and the forest is renowned for its bird life. The Ordnance Survey Map available at the tourist office gives details of various hikes. Many trails start at Rough Common, which can be reached by Bus 602 from Canterbury.

ALTHORP

Now hugely famous as the ancestral home of Diana, Princess of Wales, Althorp (pronounced Altrup) has been in the Spencer family since 1508. The town was previously used as a private residence, but Diana's death in August 1997 and subsequent burial here brought about some change: the doors of the grand old house and grounds are now thrown open to the public for part of the summer. Most visitors come to pay their respects to Diana, whose body lies on an island in the middle of a lake. The house itself is not without interest, however, as it contains a number of noteworthy works of art, such as paintings by Van Dyck and Rubens. You must purchase tickets (£9.50) in advance by calling 01604/592020. *Althorp House, tel. 01604/770107. Open July–Aug.*

COMING AND GOING

Hop on one of five daily **National Express** buses from London (two hours, £10 day return). You'll have to walk about 15 min from the bus station (Lady's La., tel. 0990/808080) to the train station, where you can pick up the Althorp bus. Northampton is the nearest train station, with trains arriving from London Euston (every 15 min, 1 hour 15 min, £13.90 day return). Althorp runs a bus service itself from the train station to Althorp House (tel. 0345/484950, £2).

STONEHENGE

One of the great sites and mysteries of the world, Stonehenge has spawned any number of theories as to its origins. The majority expert opinion is that the majestic ring of stones was used as a temple for grisly religious sacrifice. Indeed, modern-day druids try every year to access Stonehenge to act out bizarre rituals at solstice time. Others see the place as some kind of giant sundial, and a few crazies are convinced it was a handy staging post for ancient alien invasion. Whatever the truth of its function, there is little doubting the technical achievement involved. The story begins in 3000 BC, when the first ditches were dug; picks up pace in 2100 BC, when stones weighing anywhere up to 40 tons were dragged all the way from mid-Wales; and reaches a climax in 1500 BC, when extra stones were added, including the topping off boulders that give the site its trademark appearance. *Open daily 9:30–6 (Nov.–Feb. until 4). The Salisbury Tourist Office is on Fish Row, tel. 01722/744744. Open daily 9:30–5.*

COMING AND GOING

National Express (tel. 0990/808080) buses go to Amesbury, not far from Stonehenge. Tickets cost £15 for a day return. Pick up the No. 3 bus from there. Twice-hourly **trains** run out of London Waterloo to Salisbury (pronounced Sallsbury), the nearest sizable town to the stones; it takes 90 min to get there and costs £21.10 for a day return. The No. 3 bus from outside the station (S. Western Rd., tel. 0345/484950) reaches Stonehenge in 35 min.

INDEX

N

O

P

T

U

V

W

Y

Z

NOTES

NOTES

NOTES

NOTES